Samuel Beckett

a reference guide

A
Reference
Guide
to
Literature

Jackson Bryer
Editor

Samuel Beckett

a reference guide

CATHLEEN CULOTTA ANDONIAN

G.K.HALL&CO.

70 LINCOLN STREET, BOSTON, MASS.

Library of Congress Cataloging-in-Publication Data

Andonian, Cathleen Culotta.
    Samuel Beckett: a reference guide.

    (A Reference guide to literature)
    Includes index.
    1. Beckett, Samuel, 1906-   --Bibliography.
I. Title. II. Series.
Z8086.37.A5 1988 [PR6003.E282] 016.848'91409 88-24501
ISBN 0-8161-8570-0

This publication is printed on permanent/durable acid-free paper
MANUFACTURED IN THE UNITED STATES OF AMERICA

Contents

The Author

Cathleen Culotta Andonian received her doctorate in French and Italian Languages and Literatures from Wayne State University in 1979. Her doctoral thesis "After the Trilogy: A Study of Samuel Beckett's Novels and Short Stories from 1955 to the Present" includes an extended bibliography of the critical writings devoted to Samuel Beckett. She has published articles and reviews in Symposium, The Antigonish Review, The French Review, and L'Esprit Créateur, and has been a bibliographer for the MLA International Bibliography since 1982. Dr. Andonian is currently a lecturer at the University of Michigan-Dearborn.

Preface

The bibliography which follows includes critical articles and books on the life and works of Samuel Beckett through 1984. The entries for the year 1984 are limited, and are taken exclusively from the 1984 MLA International Bibliography and the 1984 French XX Bibliography. Due to the large number of works included, the annotations are in most cases brief and succinct. Whenever possible quotations have been included to give the reader an idea of the tone and style of the critical work, especially in the early reviews which are frequently more important because of their date of publication than for their content.

The bibliography is organized according to the following principles:

A. Works Included
   1. Critical books and articles on Samuel Beckett have been arranged chronologically by year, and alphabetically by author's name or title in the case of an anonymous article.
   2. Critical books and articles in French and English, which provide a contribution to Beckett scholarship are annotated.
   3. Reviews from prominent newspapers as well as reviews that contribute in a significant way to Beckett scholarship have been included.
   4. All works in French and English mentioned in any other bibliography on Beckett have been included either in the annotated section of the bibliography or in Appendix A or B.
   5. Items which could not be found due to a probable error in the bibliographical source

are listed with their source and labeled
"unverified."
6. Where it was necessary to add an entry, the
number for that entry is followed by a lower
case a. Thus 1956.27a is the entry that
follows 1956.27 and precedes 1956.28.
7. Ph.D. dissertations and M.A. theses have
been omitted.

B. Cross-Referencing
8. Reprints and revisions are annotated once
and cross-referenced accordingly. When the
original article was not available, the
annotation is based on an accessible reprint
and the location of the annotation is
indicated.
9. Articles included as part of a collection of
critical essays devoted to Beckett are
listed separately (under the author of the
article) and cross-referenced to the name of
the editor of the compilation.
10. Primary bibliographical sources devoted
solely to Beckett and all secondary bibliographical sources are annotated and listed
in the subject index under bibliography.

C. Appendixes and Indexes
11. Articles and books that briefly mention
Beckett or his works have been omitted from
the annotated section of the bibliography
due to lack of space, but have been included
in Appendix A or B.
12. A list of the location of periodicals and
newspapers in which articles on Beckett have
appeared is provided in Appendix C. Those
periodicals and newspapers which already
include the location of publication in their
titles have been omitted from this Appendix.
13. An author index lists the names of all
authors and editors of critical works
included in the annotated portion of the
bibliography and in Appendix A and B.
14. A subject index refers the reader to the
entries in the annotated section of the
bibliography or in Appendix A.

Acknowledgments

It gives me sincere pleasure to express my gratitude to a number of persons who have aided me in the preparation of this manuscript. I extend thanks to Professor John Fletcher for his expert advice and the use of his personal files, and to Professor Maria Rosaria Vitti-Alexander, Carol Shea, and Ingel Dickenson for their help in acquiring library materials. I am grateful for the encouragement of my editors Borgna Bruner, Ara Salibian, Meaghan Wander, and Jackson Bryer, and the cooperation of the libraries at Wayne State University, the University of Michigan, the University of Wisconsin, and the Library of Congress. I wish to acknowledge the skill and patience of Carla Pariseau, Julie Horn, and the staff of Cindy Hoops who have participated in the proof-reading and typing of the manuscript. Finally I wish to thank my husband, Jim, for his guidance and moral support throughout the project.

Introduction

Samuel Beckett was born in 1906 at his family home of Cooldrinagh in Foxrock, south of Dublin. He attended Earlsfort House School in Dublin (1911-1919), Portora Royal School in Enniskillin in Northern Ireland (1920-1923), and studied French and Italian at Trinity College, where he graduated first in his class in 1927.

From 1928 to 1930 Beckett was named lecturer at the Ecole Normale Supérieure in Paris, where he became close friends with Thomas McGreevy. Beckett's literary career began in this period from 1929 to 1930. Beckett wrote "Dante ... Bruno ... Vico ... Joyce" for <u>Our Exagimination Round his Factification for Incamination of Work in Progress</u>,[1] the volume of essays Joyce planned as a reply to the critics of <u>Work in Progress</u>. Joyce also asked Beckett to translate <u>Anna Livia Plurabelle</u> into French, which he did with the assistance of Alfred Péron. "Assumption" and "Che Schiagura" appeared in <u>Transition</u> in 1929; "Whoro-scope," Beckett's entry for the Hours Press poetry contest on the theme of time, won first place and was printed by Nancy Cunard at Hours Press in 1930. Beckett also received a commission from Chatto and Windus to write an essay on Proust for their Dolphin Series.

After completing his fellowship at the Ecole Normale Supérieure, Beckett returned to Trinity College to begin a three-year position as lecturer. During this time he continued writing poetry, published several of his works, and became close friends with Jack B. Yeats. "Hell Crane to Starling," "Casket of Pralinen for a Daughter of a Dissipated

Mandarin," "Text," and "Yoke of Liberty" appeared in
Samuel Putnam's The European Caravan; "Return to
Vestry"[2] and "Text"[3] were featured in the New Review;
and "Alba" was presented in the Dublin Magazine.[4]

Beckett abruptly resigned from his post in
December, 1931, and moved first to Germany, then to
Paris. At this time he published some of his short
works, such as "Sedendo and Quiescendo,"[5] "Text,"[6] and
"Dante and the Lobster."[7] He was also working on
Dream of Fair to Middling Women. Unable to support
himself in Europe, Beckett return to Foxrock, where he
wrote More Pricks than Kicks (1934). After his father
died of a heart attack, Beckett moved to London and
underwent psychoanalysis at the Tavistock Clinic. In
1935 he published Echo's Bones and began working on
Murphy, but he had great difficulty getting beyond the
initial stages of this novel.

In 1936 or 1937 Beckett decided to make Paris his
home. He re-established contact with his old friends,
including Joyce. Following an incident in which he
was attacked by an unknown assailant in a Paris
street, Beckett was visited in the hospital by Suzanne
Deschevaux-Dumesnil, who was to become his life-long
companion. They were married in 1961.

Murphy was finally published by Routledge in
1937, after being rejected by forty-two publishers. A
year or two later Beckett began working on the French
translation with the help of Alfred Péron. This was
the beginning of his dedication to the dual publication of all of his works in both English and French.

The Second World War brought Beckett into contact
with a broad spectrum of people. After working for a
Resistance network in Paris and nearly being captured
by the Nazis, he and Suzanne escaped to the South of
France in 1942 to Roussillon in the Vaucluse. Beckett
spent his time writing Watt and helping a local farmer
in his fields. In 1945 Beckett returned to Ireland to
visit his mother and brother. Anxious to re-enter
France, he joined an Irish Red Cross unit which was
leaving for Saint-Lô, Normandy. Working as a
storekeeper-interpreter from August until October,
1945, Beckett was finally allowed to return to Paris,

where he would be more useful to the Irish as an interpreter. He resigned from the assignment in January, 1946.

The years 1946 to 1949 represent the most intense period of creativity in Beckett's literary career. During these four years Beckett wrote four novels, four short stories and his first dramatic work: Mercier et Camier (1946), Premier Amour (1946), Nouvelles (1946-47), Molloy (1947), Malone meurt (1947), L'Innommable (1949), and En attendant Godot (1949). Waiting for Godot was written during a very short period of time between working on Malone Dies and The Unnamable. The manuscript is dated Oct. 9, 1948 to Jan. 29, 1949.

At the end of this productive stage, Beckett had great difficulty writing. Whenever he initiated a new work, he felt he was repeating what he had already written.[8] The Textes pour rien, which were probably written between 1950 and 1952, are the remnants of this literary impasse.

Beckett had learned a great deal about staging and technique from Roger Blin, who directed the first production of Waiting for Godot in 1952. From this experience, he developed his own style and technique which enabled him to create several innovative plays: Fin de partie (1954-56), Acte sans paroles I (1955), All That Fall (1956), Krapp's Last Tape (1958), and Embers (1959).

Beckett claims that he "turned to writing plays to relieve [himself] of the awful depression that prose led [him] into."[9] It appears that working with the dramatic medium altered Beckett's prose style. The structured format of the theater -- the confined space of the stage, the restricted movement and speech of the characters -- was to carry over into Beckett's prose works as well.

Beckett's first attempts to revert to the novel form led to frustrations similar to those he experienced after the completion of the trilogy. These fragments were later published as "From an Abandoned Work" (1955) and "Foirades" I-IV. In 1960 Beckett

began the composition of <u>Comment c'est</u>. This was the
last full length novel Beckett was to write. <u>How It
Is</u> was followed by the publication of a series of
short prose texts in French entitled <u>Têtes-mortes</u>
("D'un ouvrage abandonné," "Imagination morte im-
aginez," "Bing," "Assez," "Sans," 1955-1969).

It was during this decade that Beckett was
awarded an honorary doctorate from Trinity College, in
addition to receiving positive critical acclaim for
his literary achievements. In 1959 <u>Embers</u> won the
Prix Italia, and in 1961 he shared the Prix International des Editeurs with Jorge Louis Borges. In 1964
<u>Film</u>, directed by Alan Schneider and starring Buster
Keaton won the New York Film Festival Award, the
Diploma de Merito in Venice, and in 1965, the "Out-
standing Film" award at the London Film Festival. On
October 23, 1969, Beckett was awarded the Nobel Prize
for Literature, an event that would change his life
dramatically, expanding his reputation as a writer
known by a small circle of admirers to a world-
renowned author and director.

Beckett now spends most of his time in his home
in Ussy or his apartment in Paris, writing and
translating, or traveling in order to direct performances of his own works. He has since alternately
published numerous plays and prose pieces. He has
experimented with unusual staging techniques, abstract
or dehumanized dialogues, and vague fantasized images.
The prose works of this period include a short novel,
<u>Le Dépeupleur</u> (1966-1970) and a collection of short
prose works, <u>Pour finir encore et autres foirades</u>
(late fifties through 1975), a prose piece called "All
Strange Away" that appeared in the Summer 1978 <u>Journal
of Beckett Studies</u>, a short prose text "Crisscross to
Infinity" published in <u>College Literature</u> (1981), <u>Ill
Seen Ill Said</u> (1981), <u>Worstward Ho</u> (1983), and
<u>Disjecta</u> (1983).

The most recent plays Beckett has presented for
stage or television are <u>Actes sans paroles II</u> (1959),
<u>Happy Days</u> (1961), <u>Words and Music</u> (1962), <u>Play</u>
(1962), <u>Cascando</u> (1963), <u>Come and Go</u> (1965), <u>Eh Joe</u>
(1966). <u>Breath</u> (1966), <u>Not I</u> (1972), <u>Footfalls</u> (1976),
<u>That Time</u> (1976), <u>Ghost Trio</u> (1976), and "Roughs for

Theater and Radio," <u>... but the clouds ...</u> (1976), <u>A Piece of Monologue</u> (1979), <u>Rockaby</u> (1981), <u>Ohio Impromptu</u> (1981), <u>Quad</u> (1982), <u>Catastrophe</u> (1982), and <u>What Where</u> (1983).

* * *

   Beckett's works have been examined by numerous critics and writers. The variety of methodologies applied to his works include the more traditional, historical, philosophical, and thematic studies, as well as formalist, structuralist or psychological approaches to literature. Recently, a biography and several manuscript studies have also been published, which give insight into the genesis of Beckett's fiction.

   David Hesla[10] examines the novels and plays from the perspective of the history of ideas. Trying to relate Beckett to the Western intellectual tradition, Hesla discusses the structure of consciousness and its significance for the art of writing. Richard Coe[11] concentrates on the philosophical implications of Beckett's fiction. He analyzes the resemblances of certain Beckettian themes and the ideas expressed by Pascal, Proust, Descartes, Geulincx, Wittgenstein, the Greek Philosopher Zeno, and even Buddhism. In two more recent studies of Beckett as a philosophical writer, Eugene Kaelin[12] and Lance St. John Butler[13] examine the influence of Hegel, Heidegger, and Sartre on Beckett's works.

   The subject of Beckett's admiration for the writing of James Joyce and his influence on Beckett's fiction is widely discussed. While many authors briefly acknowledge the influence of Joyce, Barbara Reich Gluck provides insight into this topic in a more extended format in <u>Joyce and Beckett: Friendship and Fiction</u>.[14]

   John Fletcher and Hugh Kenner discuss the general evolution of Beckett's fiction, presenting textual commentaries that analyze the characters and the thematic orientation of his prose and dramatic works. In <u>The Novels of Samuel Beckett</u>[15] Fletcher provides a general introduction to each novel, and then turns to

the question of form in <u>Samuel Beckett's Art</u>.[16] This
second work examines several other aspects of
Beckett's career as a writer: Beckett as critic,
poet, dramatist, his sources and influences. Hugh
Kenner's <u>A Reader's Guide to Samuel Beckett</u>[17] offers a
textual explanation of the major plays, novels and
prose pieces, while his critical work <u>Samuel Beckett</u>[18]
emphasizes the coherence and unity of Beckett's
fiction through his repetition of similar themes.

A study of Beckett's "late" work is provided by
James Knowlson and John Pilling in their <u>Frescoes of
the Skull. The Later Prose and Drama of Samuel
Beckett</u>,[19] in which two unpublished works (<u>Dream of
Fair to Middling Women</u> and <u>Eleuthéria</u>), post-trilogy
prose, and drama after <u>Endgame</u> are analyzed, fulfill-
ing "the need for a coherent and integrated account of
what late Beckett is about, and where Beckett may be
adjudged to have been successful (or unsuccessful) in
emulating those works, like <u>Waiting for Godot</u> or
<u>Molloy</u>, that first established him as a writer of
stature and originality."

Since Beckett's works deemphasize the traditional
conceptions of time and place, it is interesting to
evaluate his portrayal of characters without memories,
whose recognition of the world in which they find
themselves is limited to the present moment and to a
confined environment. Charles Lyons' study of
Beckett's drama, <u>Samuel Beckett</u>,[20] and Brian Fitch's
analysis of the trilogy, <u>Dimensions, structures, et
textualité dans la trilogie romanesque de Beckett</u>[21]
present Beckett's unconventional use of the dimensions
of time and space.

In recent years the question of form and language
has preoccupied many critics. In <u>The Fiction of
Samuel Beckett</u>, H. Porter Abbott stresses Beckett's
importance as a "craftsman, disengaged from his
characters, seeking not to undertake but to present
their quest."[22] Hannah Case Copeland develops this
idea in her work <u>Art and the Artist in the Works of
Samuel Beckett</u>, in which she studies the theme of
self-consciousness in Beckett's art: "In each
successive work there are more and more direct
allusions to the work itself as novel or play; in each

one, fewer traditional devices veil its fabricated
nature. In the most recent works, in fact, fiction
and drama are stripped to the bare bones of work and
gesture."[23] Olga Bernal also focuses her attention on
the disintegration of language and form in Beckett's
novels. Once again the theories of Wittgenstein are
proposed to account for the character's inability to
use langauge in a meaningful way.

There is to date but one full-length biographical
study of Beckett's life, Deirdre Bair's <u>Samuel
Beckett: A Biography</u>, which has evoked numerous
critical responses. Despite the questions surrounding
the accuracy of some of the biographical statements
and the references to the autobiographical nature of
Beckett's works, there is a considerable amount of new
biographical material presented, especially from
Beckett's letters to his friend Thomas McGreevy.
Interviews with Beckett and reminiscences of friends
and fellow authors have also been published seperate-
ly.

The importance of Beckett's simplification of his
texts has become evident through studies of his
notebooks and official manuscripts. Three of the
recent works that document the evolution of his
creative works from the point of view of his
manuscripts are Richard Admussen's <u>The Samuel Beckett
Manuscripts: A Study</u>[24] and S.E. Gontarski's <u>The
Intent of Undoing in Samuel Beckett's Dramatic Texts</u>[25]
and <u>Beckett's "Happy Days": A Manuscript Study</u>.[26]

Dina Sherzer[27] analyzes the formal structure of
the novels of the trilogy, studying the role of the
narrator, his "style" and language. The use of
narrative, or the art of story telling continues to be
of utmost importance in Beckett's recent novels and is
commented on in numerous critical writings, in
particular Kristin Morrison's study <u>Centers and
Chronicles. The Use of Narrative in the Plays of
Samuel Beckett and Harold Pinter</u>.[28]

Since there are so many critical writings on
Samuel Beckett, the categories described above offer a
general outline of the critical response to Beckett's

fiction. Although very few works concentrate on his private life, there are numerous books and articles which discuss his fiction in detail.

NOTES

1. London: Faber and Faber, 1972.

2. Aug. Sept. Oct. 1931.

3. Winter 1931-32.

4. Sept. 1931.

5. <u>Transition</u>, 21 (Mar. 1932).

6. <u>New Review</u>, 2 (April 1932).

7. <u>This Quarter</u> (Dec. 1932).

8. Ronald Hayman, <u>Samuel Beckett</u> (London: Heinemann, 1968), pp. 5-6.

9. Deirdre Bair, <u>Samuel Beckett: A Biography</u> (New York and London: Harcourt Brace Jovanovich, 1978), p. 361.

10. Minneapolis: University of Minnesota Press, 1971.

11. <u>Beckett</u> (London: Oliver and Boyd, 1964).

12. <u>The Unhappy Consciousness. The Poetic Plight of Samuel Beckett. An Inquiry at the Intersection of Phenomenology and Literature</u>. (London: D. Reidel Publishing Co., 1981).

13. <u>Samuel Beckett and the Meaning of Being. A Study in Ontological Parable</u>. (London: Macmillan Press, 1984).

14. Lewisberg: Buchnell University Press, 1979.

15. London: Chatto and Windus, 1964.

16. London: Chatto and Windus, 1967.

17. New York: Farrar, Strauss and Giroux, 1973.

18. New York: Grove Press, 1983.

xxii

19. London: John Calder, 1979.

20. New York: Grove Press, 1983.

21. Paris: Lettres Modernes Minard, 1977.

22. Berkeley: University of California Press, 1973, p. 1.

23. The Hague and Paris: Mouton and Co., 1975, p. 11.

24. Boston: G.K. Hall & Co., 1979.

25. Bloomington: Indiana University Press, 1985.

26. Columbus: Ohio State University Libraries, 1977.

27. <u>Structures de la trologie de Beckett: "Molloy," "Malone meurt," "L'Innommable"</u>. Paris: Mouton, 1976.

28. Chicago: University of Chicago Press, 1983.

A Chronological List of Major Works by Samuel Beckett

1931   <u>Proust</u>. London: Chatto and Windus.

1934   <u>More Pricks than Kicks</u>. London: Chatto and Windus.

1938   <u>Murphy</u>. London: Routledge and Kegan Paul.

1951   <u>Malone meurt</u> (<u>Malone Dies</u>). Paris: Editions de Minuit.

           <u>Molloy</u>. Paris: Editions de Minuit.

1952   <u>En attendant Godot</u> (<u>Waiting for Godot</u>). Paris: Editions de Minuit.

1953   <u>L'Innommable</u> (<u>The Unnamable</u>). Paris: Editions de Minuit.

           <u>Watt</u>. Paris: Olympia Press.

1957   <u>Act sans paroles I</u> (<u>Act Without Words I</u>). Paris: Editions de Minuit.

           <u>Act sans paroles II</u> (<u>Act Without Words II</u>). Paris: Editions de Minuit.

           <u>All That Fall</u> (<u>Tous ceux qui tombent</u>). New York: Grove Press; London: Faber and Faber.

           <u>Fin de partie</u> (<u>Endgame</u>). Paris: Editions de Minuit.

*This is not a complete list of Beckett's works. The works are listed chronologically in the language in which they were originally written. The title of the translation is given in parenthesis when it differs from the original. The first publisher is given. If the work was published simultaneously by two publishers, both publishers are listed.

1958   Nouvelles et textes pour rien. Paris:
        Editions de Minuit.

1959   Krapp's Last Tape (La Dernière Bande).
        London: Faber and Faber.

1960   Embers (Cendres). London: Faber and Faber;
        New York: Grove Press.

1961   Comment c'est (How It Is). Paris: Editions
        de Minuit.

        Happy Days (Oh les beaux jours). New York:
        Grove Press.

        Poems in English. London: John Calder.

1964   Play (Comédie). London: Faber and Faber;
        Paris: Editions de Minuit.

1967   Come and Go (Va et vient). Paris: Editions
        de Minuit; London: Calder and Boyars.

        Eh Joe (Dis Joe). London: Faber and Faber.

        Film. London: Faber and Faber.

        Têtes-mortes. Paris: Editions de Minuit.

1968   Poèmes. Paris: Editions de Minuit.

1970   Le Dépeupleur (The Lost Ones). Paris:
        Editions de Minuit.

        Mercier et Camier (Mercier and Camier).
        Paris: Editions de Minuit.

        Premier Amour (First Love). Paris:
        Editions de Minuit.

1973   Not I (Pas moi). London: Faber and Faber.

1976   Ends and Odds: Eight New Dramatic Pieces.
        New York: Grove Press.

Footfalls (Pas). New York: Grove Press.
Pour finir encore et autres foirades
(Fizzles). Paris: Editions de Minuit.

That Time (Cette fois). London: Faber and
Faber.

1978   "All Strange Away." Journal of Beckett
Studies, no. 3 (Summer).

Poèmes suivi de mirlitonnades. Paris:
Editions de Minuit.

1980   Company (Compagnie). New York: Grove
Press; London: John Calder.

1981   Mal vu mal dit (Ill Seen Ill Said). Paris:
Editions de Minuit.

Rockaby and Other Short Pieces. New York:
Grove Press.

1982   A Piece of Monologue. London: Faber and
Faber.

Solo suivi de catastrophe. Paris: Editions
de Minuit.

1984   Quad. London: Faber and Faber.

What Where. London: Faber and Faber.

A List of Primary
Bibliographical Sources

Annual Bibliography of English Language and Literature. London: Cambridge University Press.

Bellingham, Susan, Anne Dennison, and Jacqueline
Tucker, eds. Samuel Beckett Collection in
McMaster University Library. Hamilton, Ont.:
University Library Press at McMaster University,
1973.

Bryer, J.R. "Critique de Samuel Beckett. Sélection
bibliographique." Revue des Lettres Modernes 100
(1964):169-84.

Bryer, J.R., R.J. Davis, M.J. Friedman and P.C. Hoy,
eds. Calepins de bibliographie (2): Samuel
Beckett. Paris: Lettres Modernes Minard,
unpaginated, 1972.

Book Review Digest. New York: H.W. Wilson.

Cabeen, David C. A Critical Bibliography of French
Literature. Twentieth Century. Syracuse:
Syracuse University Press, 1980.

Catholic Periodical and Literature Index. Haverford,
Pa.: Catholic Library Association.

Essay and General Literature Index. New York: H.W.
Wilson.

Federman, Raymond, and John Fletcher, eds. Samuel
Beckett: His Works and His Critics. Berkeley:
University of California Press, 1970.

French XX Bibliography: Critical and Biographical
References for the Study of French Literature
Since 1885.

Friedman, Melvin J. "Samuel Beckett (Summary
Bibliography)." In A Critical Bibliography of
French Literature: The Twentieth Century. Vol.
3. Edited by Douglas W. Alden and Richard A.
Brooks. Syracuse: Syracuse University Press,
1980.

xxviii

Index to Book Reviews in the Humanities. Williamston,
    Mich.: Phillip Thomson.

International Index to Periodicals. After 1964
    retitled Social Science and Humanities Index.
    New York: H.W. Wilson.

Journal of Beckett Studies. London: John Calder
    Publishers; New York: Riverrun Press.

MLA: International Bibliography of Books and Articles
    on the Modern Languages and Literatures. New
    York: MLA.

National Union Catalog, Author List. Washington,
    D.C.: Library of Congress.

New York Times Book Review Index, 1896-1970. New
    York: New York Times Co., 1976.

Rancoeur, René. Bibliographie de la littérature
    française du Moyen Age à nos jours. Paris:
    Armand Colin.

Reader's Guide to Periodical Literature. New York:
    H.W. Wilson.

Revue d'Histoire du Théâtre. Paris: Centre National
    de la Recherche Scientifique.

Subject Index to Periodicals. After 1960 retitled
    British Humanities Index. London: Library
    Association.

Tanner, James T.F., and J. Don Van. Samuel Beckett:
    A Checklist of Criticism. Kent, Ohio: Kent
    State University Press, 1969.

Times Literary Supplement, Yearly Index. London:
    Times Publishing Co.

Times Official Index. London: Times Publishing Co.
    Year's Work in English Studies. Oxford: Oxford
    University Press.

Year's Work in Modern Language Studies. Cambridge,
    England: Cambridge University Press.

Writings About Samuel Beckett

1931

1   DOBREE, BONAMY. "Symbolism To-day." Spectator,
    18 Apr., pp. 641-42.
        Although he feels that Proust is an
    "agreeable and stimulating pamphlet," Dobrée
    points out that "it is a good deal too
    'clever,' and disfigured with pseudo-scien-
    tific jargon and philosophic snippets."
    Reprinted 1979.22.2

2   F[LINT], F.S. "Proust by Samuel Beckett."
    Criterion 10 (10 July):792.
        Offers a very brief description of Proust.
    Reprinted: 1979.22.3.

3   *"Marcel Proust (Samuel Beckett)." Listener,
    25 Mar.

4   "Proust by Samuel Beckett." Times Literary
    Supplement (London), 2 Apr., p. 274.
        Briefly outlines the major points em-
    phasized in Proust: the nature and effect of
    time, with its attributes memory and habit.
    Reprinted 1979.22.1

5   *T., B. "Life Eternal." Time and Tide, 9 May.

1934

1   CALDER-MARSHALL, ARTHUR. "Dubliners."
    Spectator 152 (1 June):863.
        Reviews More Kicks than Pricks, charac-
    terizing Beckett as a humorist who delights

in words, "in grotesque, ludicrous and
obsolete words."

2   "More Pricks than Kicks." Times Literary
     Supplement (London), 26 July, p. 526.
          Comments on More Pricks than Kicks,
     calling attention to Beckett's humor: "An
     implicit effect of satire is obtained by
     embellishing the commonplace with a wealth of
     observation and sometimes erudition, alter-
     nated with sudden brusqueness. Belacqua is
     more of a theme than a character, an oppor-
     tunity for the exercise of a picturesque
     prose style." Reprinted: 1979.22.5.

3   MUIR, EDWIN. "New Short Stories." Listener 12
     (4 July):42.
          Reviews More Pricks than Kicks, emphasiz-
     ing Beckett's ability to reduce everything to
     intellectual fantasy, to "extremely good and
     calculated and quite impossible talk": "The
     point of the story is in the style of
     presentation, which is witty, extravagant and
     excessive." Reprinted: 1979.22.4.

4   QUENNELL, PETER. "New Novels." New Statesman
     and Nation 7, no. 170 (26 May):801-2.
          Briefly describes More Pricks than Kicks
     as an "annoying book" in which Beckett
     indirectly imitates Joyce's style and
     characters.

5   *SUNNE, RICHARD. "Men and Books." Time and
     Tide, 26 May.

6   WATSON, FRANCIS. "More Pricks than Kicks by
     Samuel Beckett." Bookman 86, no. 514
     (July):219-20.
          Offers a brief review of More Pricks than
     Kicks, pointing out the influence of Joyce,
     the major episodes of the stories, and
     Beckett's style.

1936

1   *"Echo's Bones. By Samuel Beckett."   Dublin
    Magazine 11, n.s., no. 2 (Apr.-June):78.
         Source: Bryer et al. 1972.7;unverified.

1938

1   "Murphy. By Samuel Beckett." Times Literary
    Supplement (London), 12 Mar., p. 172.
         Views Murphy as an elaborate, yet "oddly
    real" parody of the world that relies on
    verbal dexterity: "Erudition, violent wit
    and a large vocabulary are brought to his
    analysis of Murphy, and what his hero lacks
    in zest or liveliness is fully supplied by
    the manner in which his disposition is
    studied." Reprinted: 1979.22.6

2   O'BRIEN, KATE. "Fiction." Spectator, 25 Mar.,
    p. 546.
         Briefly reviews Murphy, recommending that
    the reader should "sweep along ... and taking
    the whole contentedly, as a great draught of
    brilliant, idiosyncratic commentary, a most
    witty, wild and individualistic refreshment."
    Reprinted: 1979.22.8.

3   POWELL, DILYS. "Flight from Reality." Sunday
    Times (London), 13 Mar., p. 8.
         Notes Murphy's withdrawal into the private
    world of his mind and the novel's "brutal
    hilarity in a peculiarly Irish Idiom."

4   THOMAS, DYLAN. "Recent Novels." New English
    Weekly 12, no. 23 (17 Mar.):454.
         Reprinted: 1971.97; 1979.22.7; see
    1971.97 for annotation.

1939

1   "Murphy. By Samuel Beckett." Dublin Magazine
        14, n.s., no. 2 (Apr.-June):98.
            Briefly reviews Murphy as a study "in
        words and phrases," not a novel -- "The whole
        thing is a bizarre fantasy, with a nasty
        twist about it that its self-evident clever-
        ness and scholarship cannot redeem."

1946

1   GUGGENHEIM, MARGUERITE. Out of This Century.
        The Informal Memoirs of Peggy Guggenheim.
        New York: Dial Press, pp. 194-200.
            Describes her love affair and friendship
        with Beckett, and mentions Maria Jolas'
        birthday dinner-party for Joyce. Reprinted
        in 1960.28.

1951

1   *ASTRE, GEORGES ALBERT. "L'Humanisme de la
        pourriture." Action (7-13 May).
        Reprinted: 1963.5.

2   BATAILLE, GEORGES. "Le Silence de Molloy."
        Critique 7 (15 May):387-96.
            Proposes that Molloy represents the most
        basic reality of "le fond de l'être" --
        silence. This is the first full-length
        review article on Beckett. Reprinted:
        1979.22.10.

3   BLANZAT, JEAN. "Les Romans de la semaine:
        Molloy de Samuel Beckett." Figaro Lit-
        téraire, 14 Apr., p. 9.
            Believes Molloy is a "livre-événement."
        The story depicts the destruction of man -- a
        two part adventure in which Molloy is the
        victim and Moran gradually approaches the
        same deprivation and nihilistic Odyssey.
        Reprinted in part: 1963.7.

4   *BRENNER, JACQUES. "Samuel Beckett: Molloy."
      Observateur, 28 June.

5   *FOUCHET, MAX-POL. "Molloy." Carrefour, 24
      Apr.

6   GADENNE, PAUL. "Faut-il 'savonner' l'humanité?"
      Cahiers du Sud, no. 307, pp. 511-18.
          Reprinted in part: 1963.29.

7   KANTERS, ROBERT. "Autant en emporte le vent."
      Age Nouveau 62 (June).
          Reprinted in part: 1963.40.

8   *NADEAU, MAURICE. "En avant vers nulle part."
      Combat, 12 Apr.
          Reprinted: 1963.57, 1979.22.9; see
      1963.57 for annotation.

9   _____. "Samuel Beckett: L'Humour et le néant."
      Mercure de France 312 (Aug.):693-97.
          Reprinted: 1952.1a, 1965.59; see 1965.59
      for annotation.

10 PICON, GAETAN. "L'Impossible néant." Samedi-
      Soir, 12 May.
          Reprinted in part: 1963.61.

11 PINGAUD, BERNARD. "Le Roman. Samuel Beckett:
      Molloy." Esprit 19, no. 182 (Sept.):423-25.
          Believes Molloy is presented as a mon-
      strous and disturbing myth. Pingaud suggests
      that Beckett appears to let himself be
      carried along by the language in the novel,
      much as Molloy is led on by "life," and
      remarks that Beckett has succeeded in saying
      "nothing," knowing full well that to say
      nothing allows one to infer his meaning.
      Reprinted: 1979.22.12.

12 POUILLON, JEAN. "Molloy." Temps Modernes 7
      (July):184-86.
          Believes Beckett does not distinguish the
      absurd from the norm in Molloy. Although the
      inconsistency of Molloy's projects and his

lack of determination may set him apart from us, it is merely a matter of degree. Reprinted: 1963.65; 1979.22.11.

1952

1   NADEAU, MAURICE. "Malone meurt par Samuel
    Beckett."   Mercure de France 314 (Mar.):503-
    4.
        Briefly reviews Malone Dies, emphasizing
    Beckett's attempt to portray an undefinable
    "inner being." Nadeau feels that Malone Dies
    "proclaims the nothingness of life, the
    nothingness of man, it moves in an absolute
    nihilism." Reprinted: 1979.22.15.

la   _____. "Samuel Beckett, l'humour et
    le néant." In Littérature présente. Paris:
    Corrêa, pp. 274-79.
        Reprint of 1951.9; reprinted and trans-
    lated: 1965.59; see 1965.59 for annotation.

2   _____. "Samuel Beckett ou le droit au silence."
    Temps Modernes 7, no. 75 (Jan.):1273-82.
        Analyzes "The Expelled" and the novels of
    the trilogy. Nadeau compares Beckett's
    fictional world to that of Artaud, Joyce, and
    Kafka.

3   SEAVER, RICHARD. "Samuel Beckett: An 1952
    Introduction." Merlin 1, no. 2 (Autumn):73-
    79.
        Offers a brief introduction to Beckett's
    work, and points out the change in emphasis
    that takes place in the novels from Murphy
    through Malone Dies -- the portrayal of the
    physical situation of the protagonist has
    been replaced by a representation of the
    character's mental state. Reprinted
    1979.22.16; see 1976.135.

1953

1   ANOUILH, JEAN. "Godot ou le sketch des <u>Pensées</u>
    de Pascal traité par les Fratellini." <u>Arts-</u>
    <u>Spectacles</u> 400 (27 Feb.-5 Mar.):1.
        Reviews the production of <u>Waiting for</u>
    <u>Godot</u> at the Théâtre de Babylone, stressing
    the importance of the event: "Je pense que
    la soirée du Babylone a l'importance du
    premier Pirandello monté à Paris par Pitoeff
    en 1923." Reprinted (in English): 1967.1,
    1979.22.19.

la AUDIBERTI, JACQUES, "Au Babylone et au Lancry,
    deux coups heureux sur le damier du théâtre."
    <u>Arts-Spectacles</u> 394 (16-22 Jan.):3.
        Briefly reviews <u>Waiting for Godot</u> at the
    Théâtre de Babylone: "... a perfect work
    which deserves a triumph." Reprinted in part
    1967.4.

2   BELMONT, GEORGES. "Un classicisme retrouvé."
    <u>Table Ronde</u> 62 (Feb.):171-74.
        Comments on Roger Blin's production of
    <u>Waiting for Godot</u> at the Théâtre de Babylone.
    Belmont sees the play as an example of the
    classic tradition: the unities of time,
    place, and action are, if not strictly
    observed, at least "present."

3   BLANCHOT, MAURICE. "Où maintenant? Qui
    maintenant?" <u>Nouvelle Revue Française</u> 2, no.
    10 (Oct.):678-86.
        Examines the identity of the narrator in
    <u>The Unnamable</u> and the experience of creating
    a fictional work. Reprinted: 1959.5;
    reprinted and translated: 1959.6,
    1979.22.26.

4   BLIN, ROGER. "Une solidarité entre maigres."
    <u>Arts-Spectacles</u> 418 (3-9 July):5.
        Briefly summarizes his first encounters
    with Beckett.

5   *BROUSSE, JACQUES. "Theater in Paris."
      European (Dec.), pp. 39-43.

6   *CHONEZ, CLAUDINE. "En attendant Godot de
      Samuel Beckett." Observateur, 8 Jan.

7   GENET. "Letter from Paris." New Yorker 29, no.
      5 (21 Mar.):84-88. Beckett: pp. 87-88.
          Praises Waiting for Godot, which she feels
      is written with "an extraordinary sense of
      theatre, by which a drama with nearly no
      action and presented on an impoverished small
      stage maintains acute interest in mere talk
      between people who do nothing but hope and
      get defrauded."

8   *GRENIER, JEAN. "En attendant Godot." Disque
      Vert 1 (July-Aug.):81-86.

9   HARTLEY, ANTHONY. "Samuel Beckett." Spectator,
      23 Oct., pp. 458-59.
          Summarizes Murphy, Watt, and the trilogy
      and analyzes their common features: physical
      abjection, and mental disintegration.
      Beckett's characters create and are created:
      "Just as the author imposes a pattern on them
      by means of his imagination, so they impose a
      pattern on the world by means of theirs.
      Reprinted: 1979.22.28.

10 JOSBIN, RAOUL. "Chronique du théâtre." Etudes,
      no. 150 (July-Aug.), pp. 77-83.
          Reprinted: 1956.24.

11 LEMARCHAND, JACQUES. "En attendant Godot de
      Samuel Beckett, au Théâtre de Babylone."
      Figaro Littéraire, 17 Jan., p. 10.
          Admires the simplicity and expressiveness
      of Waiting for Godot but is at a loss of
      words to describe the emotion he experienced.
      Reprinted: 1979.22.18.

12 LEVENTHAL, A.J. "Nought into Zero." Irish
      Times, 24 Dec., p. 6.
          Reviews Watt and the trilogy: Beckett's

"world is an uncertain one full of negation,
barren of hope....It is not just Unamuno's
tragic sense of life, which the existentialists share, but a superhuman (often
subhuman) tragic indifference to a state of
quasi-existence."

13 POLAC, M. "Controverse autour de Godot." Arts-
    Spectacles 400 (27 Feb.-5 Mar.):3.
         Characterizes the emotion surrounding the
    first production of Godot by printing letters
    criticizing the play.

14 ROBBE-GRILLET, ALAIN. "Samuel Beckett, auteur
    dramatique." Critique 9 (Feb.):108-14.
         Introduces the characters, situation,
    dialogue and dramatic gestures in Waiting for
    Godot. This article was slightly expanded to
    include an analysis of Endgame and a brief
    introduction to Beckett's novels, see
    1963.69, 1965.63, 1967.89.

15 *RYAN, SEBASTIAN. "Samuel Beckett." Icarus 3
    (Nov.):79-86.

16 SIMON, ALFRED. "Samuel Beckett et les rendez-
    vous manqués." Esprit 21, no. 201
    (Apr.):595-98.
         Feels that Beckett's Waiting for Godot
    contributes to the installation of the
    "théâtre de demain": faithful to man in his
    pessimism, he replaced the impossible victory
    of contemporary literature with its impos-
    sible failure and the man who cannot live
    with the man who cannot die.

17 THOMAS, JEAN. "Lecteur à l'Ecole Normale."
    Arts-Spectacles 418 (3-9 July):5.
         Presents memories of Beckett written by a
    former student at the Ecole Normale.

18 *ZEGEL, SYLVAIN. "Au Théâtre de Babylone: En
    attendant Godot de Samuel Beckett." La
    Libération, 7 Jan.
         In the first review of Waiting for Godot,
    Zegel identifies Beckett as "one of today's

best playwrights":   "... an author who can
give his dialogue true poetic force, who can
animate his characters so vividly that the
audience identifies with them, suffering and
laughing with them ...; who deserves comparison with the greatest." Reprinted in
part 1967.109, 1979.22.17.

1954

1   *DELFOSSE, G. "Aspects du théâtre d'aujour-
     d'hui: L'Impasse de l'hermétisme." Aspects
     1 (Dec.):45-48.

2   HOGAN, THOMAS. "The Reversed Metamorphosis:
     The World of Samuel Beckett." Irish Writing
     26, no. 26 (Mar.):54-62.
          Discusses several elements in Beckett's
     major works, Murphy, Watt, the trilogy, and
     Waiting for Godot: isolation, disintegra-
     tion, will, the importance of waiting, the
     body-soul relationship, and the influence of
     Geulincx and Vico.

3   LEVENTHAL, A.J. "Mr. Beckett's En attendant
     Godot." Dublin Magazine 29 (Apr.-June):11-
     16.
          Outlines and comments on Waiting for
     Godot: "Mr. Beckett is at one with Pascal
     who declares that misery comes to those who
     are thrown on themselves, who cannot bear
     solitude. Thus, Estragon and Vladimir make
     numerous efforts to leave each other but they
     always come back."

4   MONTGOMERY, NIALL. "No Symbols Where None
     Intended." New World Writing 5 (Apr.):324-
     37.
          Amusingly depicts Beckett's life and
     works: "The writing is respectfully examined
     here first in the light of nationality-
     religion, second in the light of personality,
     third in terms of supposed mythical obses-
     sions. Polite reference will be made to

Beckett's independence of certain literary
influences proposed for him. Finally, and
with deference, attention will be directed to
the general and specific qualities of his
language, his feeling for fun, hats, sex,
etc."

5   ONIMUS, JEAN. "L'Homme égaré: Notes sur le
     sentiment d'égarement dans la littérature
     actuelle." Etudes 283 (Oct.-Dec.):320-29.
        Reprinted: 1962.59.

1954-55

1   KERN, EDITH. "Drama Stripped for Inaction:
     Beckett's Godot." Yale French Studies, no.
     14 (Winter), pp. 41-47.
        Comments on the absence of traditional
     dramatic action, situation, and character
     development in Waiting for Godot.

1955

1   A[RON], S[UZANNE]. "Balzac a-t-il inspiré En
     attendant Godot?" Figaro Littéraire, 17
     Sept., p. 12.
        Compares the situation in Beckett's Godot
     to that of Balzac's Le Faiseur in which the
     characters await the arrival of Godeau.

2   CHAUCER, DANIEL. "Waiting for Godot by Samuel
     Beckett." Shenandoah 6, no. 2 (Spring):80-
     82.
        Summarizes the plot of Waiting for Godot,
     speculates on the identity of Godot, and
     briefly compares Beckett's fiction to that of
     Joyce.

3   HARTLEY, ANTHONY. "Theatre." Spectator, 12
     Aug., p. 222.
        Reviews Peter Hall's production of Waiting
     for Godot at the Arts in London: "What this
     new school of dramatists is telling us is

that all the subjects which have traditional-
ly engaged the attention of practitioners of
the art ... are superficialities, and that
the real subject for the playwright is the
basic minimum of human life."

4   HOPE-WALLACE, PHILIP. "Theatre." Time and Tide
     36 (13 Aug.):1045.
     Examines the production of Waiting for
     Godot at the Arts Theatre in London:
     "Exasperating though the pointlessness of
     such an exercise is, it finally distills a
     pungent sense of the loneliness, insecurity
     and folly of human life, so long, so short a
     space and with such dusty answers even for
     the faithful."

4a   LALOU, RENEE. "Le Livre de la semaine:
     Nouvelles et textes pour rien." Nouvelles
     Littéraires, 22 Dec., p. 3.
     Believes Stories and Texts for Nothing
     provide a key to a better understanding of
     the trilogy since they were written prior to
     his major prose works yet in the Stories and
     Texts for Nothing "we already find
     [Beckett's] constant use of monologue as an
     artistic technique, his implacably pessimis-
     tic vision and his insistence on the degrad-
     ing functions of the human body." Reprinted:
     1979.22.31.

5   MERCIER, VIVIAN. "A Pyrrhonian Eclogue."
     Hudson Review 7, no. 4 (Winter):620-24.
     Reviews Waiting for Godot as a play that
     "radiates the same kind of patient Pyrrhonism
     as Finnegans Wake." Mercier examines
     Beckett's use of satirical methods typical of
     Irish literature.

6   _____. "Beckett and the Search for Self." New
     Republic 133 (19 Sept):20-21.
     Proposes that the search for identity in
     Beckett's novels is synonymous with the
     Anglo-Irish tradition. Mercier suggests that
     the novels of the trilogy correspond

respectively with the three zones of Murphy's
mind.

7   RATTIGAN, TERENCE. "Aunt Edna Waits for Godot."
     New Statesman and Nation 50, no. 1,284 (15
     Oct.):468-70.
          "Aunt Edna" compares Waiting for Godot to
     Expressionist drama, "a movement that led
     absolutely nowhere."

8   ROUSSEAUX, ANDRE. "L'Homme désintégré de Samuel
     Beckett." In Littérature du vingtième
     siècle, vol 5. Paris: Albin-Michel, pp.
     105-13.
          Presents a general discussion of man's
     dehumanization and disintegration in Molloy
     and Malone Dies.

9   TYNAN, KENNETH. "New Writing." Observer, 7
     Aug., p.11.
          Reviews Waiting for Godot, discussing
     dramatic form, situation, characterization,
     and use of vaudeville double-talk.
     Reprinted: 1979.22.21.

                          1956

1   *ANOUILH, JEAN. "Du chapitre des chaises."
     Figaro Littéraire, 23 Apr., p. 1.
          Source: Federman and Fletcher,
     1970.39;unverified.

2   BAGBY, PHILIP H. "Waiting for Godot." Times
     Literary Supplement (London), 23 Mar., p.
     181.
          In a letter to the editor, responds to the
     article by G.S. Fraser: "They also serve."
     Bagby believes there can be no clear message
     deduced from Godot -- rather, the play's
     strength lies in its uncertainties and am-
     biguities. See 1956.13.

3   BARRETT, WILLIAM. "Real Love Abides." New York
     Times Book Review, 16 Sept., p. 5.

stylistic innovations with those of other
abstract artists -- he removes recognizable
points of reference from the novel (plot,
situation, characters), yet manages to
maintain the reader's interest.

4   *BECKETT, JEREMY. "Waiting for Godot."
     Meanjin, no. 65, 15, no. 2:216-18.

5   BENTLEY, ERIC. "The Talent of Samuel Beckett."
     New Republic 134 (14 May):20-21.
          In his review of the New York production
     of Waiting for Godot, Bentley rebuffs the
     anti-intellectual criticism of the play. He
     feels that Godot is "highly theatrical" and
     clearly defines an "existentialist" point of
     view. Reprinted with postscript: 1967.9,
     1979.22.23.

6   _____. "Undramatic Theatricality." In What Is
     Theatre? A Query in Chronicle Form. New
     York: Horizon Press, pp. 148-58.
          Defends Waiting for Godot in response to
     the anti-intellectualism of the Broadway
     critics; discusses the undramatic but highly
     theatrical aspect of the play, Beckett's
     definition of the existentialist point of
     view, and the triumphs and shortcomings of
     the New York production.

7   BONNEFOI, GENEVIEVE. "Textes pour rien?"
     Lettres Nouvelles 36 (Mar.):424-30.
          Demonstrates the evolution of Beckett's
     works and the basic themes they present
     through a textual study of the Nouvelles et
     textes pour rien. Reprinted: 1979.22.32.

8   CARR, BILL. "Samuel Beckett." Delta 9
     (Summer):17-20.
          Supports the theory that Beckett's work is
     influenced by the philosopher Bishop Berke-
     ley. Since Beckett's world is no longer
     comprehended in the mind of God, it does not
     exist outside of the character's momentary
     perception of it.

9   CLURMAN, HAROLD. "Theatre." <u>Nation</u> 182 (5
        May):387-90.
            Reviews <u>Waiting for Godot</u>, pointing out
        that the images of waiting and the pain and
        emptiness of existence are "almost childlike
        images of the contemporary European --
        particularly French -- mood of despair, a
        distorted mirror reflection of the impasse
        and disarray of Europe's present politics,
        ethic, and common way of life ..."

10 DAVIN, DAN. "Mr. Beckett's Everymen." <u>Irish
        Writing</u> 34 (Spring):36-39.
            Considers <u>Molloy</u> as a "special kind of
        tragic-comic lyric in prose. It is his own
        feelings, his own life, he is directly
        expressing and not the lives of characters
        with whom we can be expected to identify
        ourselves."

11 DOBREE, BONAMY. "Drama in England." <u>Sewanee
        Review</u> 64, no. 3 (July-Sept.):470-84.
        Beckett: pp. 478-82.
            Categorizes <u>Waiting for Godot</u> as a contem-
        porary morality play. Dobrée defines the
        characters, situation and themes of the play.
        A "realistic" fantasy, <u>Godot</u> presents
        universal characters and issues. In techni-
        que, it combines neo-classical unities with
        the freakishness of the music-hall.

12 EMPSON, WILLIAM. "<u>Waiting for Godot</u>." <u>Times
        Literary Supplement</u> (London), 30 Mar., p.
        195.
            Elaborates on Philip Bagby's comment on
        the ambiguity of <u>Waiting for Godot</u>. See
        1956.2, 1956.13.

13 [FRASER, G.S.] "They Also Serve." <u>Times
        Literary Supplement</u> (London), 10 Feb., p. 84.
            Contrasts <u>Waiting for Godot</u> with Beckett's
        prose works to date. Unlike the blank
        despair of the novels, <u>Waiting for Godot</u>
        offers a new light or consolation to the
        audience. Fraser goes on to categorize

Beckett's drama as a modern morality play
based on permanent Christian themes.
Reprinted: 1956.13, 1958.12, 1967.43,
1979.22.22.

14   GASSNER, JOHN. "They Also Serve." <u>Times
      Literary Supplement</u> (London), 10 Feb., p. 84.
          Reprinted: 1965.40.

15   GIBBS, WOLCOTT. "Enough is Enough is Enough."
      <u>New Yorker</u> 32 (5 May):89.
          Summarizes and briefly interprets <u>Waiting
      for Godot</u> as Gogo and Didi's Wait for God.
      Pozzo and Lucky represent wealth and the
      artist who has been bought and destroyed by
      it.

16   GOLD, HERBERT. "Beckett: Style and Desire."
      <u>Nation</u> 183 (10 Nov.):397-99.
          Examines <u>Waiting for Godot</u>, <u>Molloy</u>, and
      <u>Malone Dies</u>. Although Gold finds Beckett
      odd, even mad, his fantasies are controlled:
      Beckett "gropes for fictional adequacy in
      dramatizing scenes which are scatological,
      morbid, perverse, pathological - and yet the
      wit and the powerful will to communicate
      change the tone for anyone attuned to the
      play of a lively imagination."

17   GREGORY, HORACE. "Beckett's Dying Gladiators."
      <u>Commonweal</u> 65, no. 4 (26 Oct.):88-92.
          Points out the poetic, comic, heretical
      aspects of Beckett's prose, concentrating on
      <u>More Pricks than Kicks</u>, <u>Waiting for Godot</u>,
      <u>Molloy</u>, and <u>Malone Dies</u>. Reprinted in part:
      1959.19; reprinted: 1961.32, 1973.37.

18   *HARTLEY, ANTHONY. "<u>Molloy</u>." <u>Spectator</u>, 4
      May.
          Source: Bryer et al. 1972.7;unverified.

19   HAYES, RICHARD. "The Stage: Nothing." <u>Common-
      weal</u> 64 (25 May):203.
          Reviews <u>Waiting for Godot</u>, praising
      Beckett's "poetry of desolation" and

criticizes the lack of a sustaining sense of
life in the play.

19a HEWES, HENRY. "Mankind in the Merdecluse."
     Saturday Review 39, no. 18 (5 May):32.
          Reviews Herbert Berghof's production of
     Waiting for Godot, pointing out that the play
     is "primarily concerned with the basic human
     problem of dualism, whether it be psychic,
     religious, social, or economic. The last
     fifty years widespread acceptance of the
     ideas of Freud and Marx has decreased man's
     individuality and dignity and tended to make
     him the pawn of paired opposing opposite
     forces without and within." Reprinted:
     1967.53.

20   HOBSON, HAROLD. "Samuel Beckett. Dramatist of
     the Year." International Theatre Annual, no.
     1, pp. 153-55.
          Quotes Beckett's remarks on the two
     thieves in reference to Waiting for Godot,
     pointing out the importance of the shape and
     cadence of phrases, and the symmetry,
     balance, and shape of the work.

21   HUTCHINSON, MARY. "Samuel Beckett." New
     Statesman and Nation 51 (21 Jan.):75.
          In a letter to the editor, suggests that
     the order of the two parts of Molloy should
     be reversed, and that Moran and Molloy are
     actually the same character.

22   *INGLIS, BRIAN. "Waiting for Godot." Spec-
     tator, 4 May.
          Source: Bryer et al. 1972.7;unverified.

23   JOHNSTON, DENIS. "Waiting with Beckett." Irish
     Writing 34 (Spring):23-28.
          Claims that Beckett is not imitating Joyce
     in Waiting for Godot, on the contrary, they
     both utilize Vico's repetitive conception of
     life. Johnston also discusses the universal
     application of the play and the differences
     in the French, English, and American

versions. Reprinted: 1967.61.

24 JOSBIN, RAOUL. "<u>Waiting for Godot</u>." <u>Cross</u>
    <u>Currents</u> 6, no. 3 (Summer):204-7.
        In his review of <u>Waiting for Godot</u>, Josbin
    suggests religious implications of the play
    but emphasizes its universal significance.
    Reprint of 1953.10.

25 LEVY, ALAN. "The Long Wait for Godot." <u>Theatre</u>
    <u>Arts</u> 40 (Aug.):33-35, 96.
        Reviews the British and American produc-
    tions of <u>Waiting for Godot</u>, their producers
    and critics. Reprinted in part: 1967.65.

26 LUMLEY, FREDERICK. "The Case Against Beckett."
    In <u>Trends in Twentieth Century Drama</u>.
    London: Rockliff, pp. 139-51.
        Views <u>Waiting for Godot</u> and <u>Endgame</u> as the
    logical conclusion of the school of pes-
    simism. Reprinted in part: 1967.66.

27 MAGNY, OLIVIER DE. "Samuel Beckett ou Job
    abandonné." <u>Monde Nouveau/Paru</u> 11, no. 97
    (Feb.):92-99.
        Describes Beckett's trilogy as literature
    that is drawn to silence as to an impossible
    and unattainable end.

27a *MAILER, NORMAN. "Reflections on <u>Waiting for</u>
    <u>Godot</u>." <u>Village Voice</u>, 2-7 May.
    Reprinted: 1962.54; see 1959.28.

28 MAURIAC, CLAUDE. "Samuel Beckett." <u>Figaro</u>
    <u>Littéraire</u>, 11 Aug., pp. 1-2.
        Sees Beckett's world as one of interroga-
    tion: uncertainty of time, place and
    identity are coupled with a disintegration of
    language.

29 _____. "Samuel Beckett." <u>Preuves</u> 61
    (Mar.):71-76. (French)
        Feels that Beckett's works have arrived at
    a point of perfection -- absolute silence.
    Beckett systematically strips life of

everything that makes it liveable. Beckett
describes absolute Man confronted with the
double mystery of life and death. A slightly
different version was reprinted in 1958.24,
1959.30.

30   MERCIER, VIVIAN. "The Uneventful Event." Irish
        Times, 18 Feb., p. 6.
           Reviews Waiting for Godot pointing out
        that of Beckett's work to date only Godot
        "reads like the work of a man who has
        actually suffered." Mercier finds that
        making fun of despair is proof of Beckett's
        Irishness and indicates several differences
        between the English, Irish, and French
        versions of the play.

31   PAULDING, GOUVERNEUR. "Samuel Beckett's New
        Tale." New York Herald Tribune Book Review,
        16 Sept., p. 5.
           A novel of affliction and suffering,
        Malone Dies is written in a style that is
        "crystal clear," although it introduces many
        unanswerable questions. Paulding summarizes
        Malone's situation and the stories he tells.

32   "Puzzling About Godot." Times Literary Supple-
        ment (London), 13 Apr., p. 221.
           Reviews the varied correspondence received
        in response to Fraser's article "They Also
        Serve," pointing out that despite the
        numerous expressions of opinion stated the
        evaluation of Beckett's Waiting for Godot
        still remains an open question. See 1956.13.

33   REXROTH, KENNETH. "The Point is Irrelevance."
        Nation 182, no. 15 (14 Apr.):326-28.
           Summarizes Beckett's work to date, Murphy,
        Watt, the trilogy, and Waiting for Godot,
        concluding with what he believes to be
        Beckett's "message": "The World is blind and
        random. If we persist in judging it in human
        terms it is malignant and frivolous."
        Reprinted: 1959.40, 1964.84.

34   SHENKER, ISRAEL. "Moody Man of Letters." New
      York Times, 6 May, sec. 2, pp. 1-3.
          Presents a portrait of Beckett, quoting
      the author's comments on his background,
      Joyce, the trilogy, Texts for Nothing, and
      Waiting for Godot. Reprinted: 1979.22.33.

35   SOUTHERN, HUGH. "Waiting for Godot: Arts."
      Cambridge Review 77, no. 1,887 (2 June):651.
          Briefly reviews the Cambridge production
      of Waiting for Godot, noting the lack of
      internal poetic structure in Beckett's play
      as well as its extraordinary theatrical
      qualities.

36   TOMPKINS, J.M.S. "Waiting for Godot." Times
      Literary Supplement (London), 24 Feb., p.
      117.
          In response to G.S. Fraser's article "They
      Also Serve," considers the importance of the
      image of the two thieves at the beginning of
      the play and the dual nature of the human
      being as represented by each couple. See
      1956.13.

37   *VIVIER, M. DE. "A Propos de Beckett." Thyrse,
      no. 9 (1 Sept.), pp. 359-60.

38   WALSH, J.S. "Waiting for Godot." Times
      Literary Supplement (London), 9 Mar., p. 149.
          In a letter to the editor, states that
      Waiting for Godot is neither an existen-
      tialist play nor a Christian allegory. Walsh
      believes that Vladimir alone waits for Godot,
      revealing the simple truth "that in a world
      of materialism, brutality, ignorance and
      despair the only hope of survival lies in the
      spiritual awareness of the few." See
      1956.13, 1956.39.

39   WILSON, KATHERINE M. "Waiting for Godot."
      Times Literary Supplement (London), 2 Mar.,
      p. 133.
          In a letter to the editor, refutes G.S.
      Fraser's interpretation of Waiting for Godot

as a Christian allegory, stating that it is a
perfect example of an existentialist play.
See 1956.13.

1957

1   "A Successor to <u>Waiting for Godot</u>." <u>Times</u>
(London), 14 Jan., p. 4.
    The radio drama, <u>All That Fall</u>, portrays
an allegory of the human pilgrimage, using
rational matter-of-fact language and dry
humor to convey the progress of the nightmare.

2   BARRETT, WILLIAM. "Samuel Beckett's World in
Waiting: II. The Works of Beckett Hold
Clues to an Intriguing Riddle." <u>Saturday
Review of Literature</u> 40 (8 June):15-16.
    Presents an introduction to Beckett's
novels, plays, and critical essay <u>Proust</u>,
commenting on the theme of self-identifica-
tion, Beckett's pessimism and the audience's
reaction to his works.

2a   BERNARD, MARC. "<u>Fin de Partie</u>." <u>Nouvelles
Littéraires</u>, 9 May, p. 10.
    Believes <u>Endgame</u> resembles a parody or a
medieval fatrasie: "Surrounding these four
characters who symbolize, in an abridged
fashion ..., all mankind, the universe of
course continues to turn, aimless, gloomy,
absurd, desolate.... All that is left is the
intellectual with his ridiculous crown and
the childish game of his own creation."
Reprinted 1979.22.38.

3   CHAPSAL, MADELEINE. "Un célèbre inconnu:
Samuel Beckett." <u>Express</u>, 8 Feb., pp. 1,
26-27.
    Traces Beckett's background and literary
career. Chapsal calls attention to his then
current production of <u>Endgame</u>: Beckett's
characters demonstrate the agony of existence
as they wait for the last moment.

4 COLE, CONNOLLY. "A Note on <u>Waiting for Godot</u>." <u>Icarus</u> 7 (Jan.):25-27.
Describes Beckett's vision of despair: "Beckett's characters have no religion, no politics, no hope, no conscience, no ethics, no convictions of any sort." References are made to <u>Hamlet</u> and Chekhov.

5 *DORT, BERNARD. "Sur une avant-garde: Adamov et quelques autres." <u>Théâtre d'aujourd'hui</u>, no. 3 (Sept.-Oct.), pp. 13-16.

6 DREYFUS, DINA. "Vraies et fausses énigmes." <u>Mercure de France</u> 331 (Oct.):268-85.
Beckett: pp. 276-83.
Rather than strictly considering Beckett's work as symbolic, proposes that his prose asks the questions: What is a novel? What is a novelist? What is the situation of the novelist with respect to the novel? What are the ontological conditions of the novel?

7 FIEDLER, LESLIE A. "Search for Peace in a World Lost." <u>New York Times Book Review</u>, 14 Apr., p. 27.
Reviews <u>Murphy</u> in retrospect -- although the novel seems to contain too much of the "merely mannered," too many asides, and cryptic remarks, Beckett's humor is already present, as well as his mathematic calculations.

8 GONNET, HUBERT. "Fin de Beckett." <u>Lettres Françaises</u> (9-15 May), p. 5.
Studies <u>Endgame</u> and the mini-drama <u>Act Without Words</u> at the Studio des Champs-Elysées, discussing the characters, themes and the use of language. Gonnet feels that <u>Endgame</u> presents an intensely dramatic situation and some humor, but on the whole is long and almost boring.

9 GRAY, RONALD. "<u>Waiting for Godot</u>." <u>Listener</u> 57 (7 Feb.):235.
Defends his right to stress the positive,

Christian interpretation of <u>Waiting for
Godot</u>, even though Beckett does not impose an
answer. See 1957.14.

10   _____. "<u>Waiting for Godot</u>: A Christian
Interpretation." <u>Listener</u> 57 (24 Jan.):160-
61.
Views <u>Waiting for Godot</u> as a Christian
play in which Pozzo symbolizes the authority
of Christ: "so the promise made by Godot was
kept.... It is true that he will not come
this evening. He has already been in the
shape of Pozzo (and Lucky) at the time
appointed." This article gave rise to a
number of letters to the editor. See 1957.9,
1957.14, 1957.49.

11   HAWTREY, FREDA. "<u>All That Fall</u>." <u>Listener</u> 57
(31 Jan.):197.
Differs with the interpretation of Roy
Walker; Hawtrey finds that <u>All That Fall</u>
moves toward a crisis rather than remaining
at a standstill. See 1957.50.

12   HOBSON, HAROLD. "Samuel Beckett's New Play."
<u>Sunday Times</u> (London), 7 Apr., p. 23.
Reviews <u>Endgame</u> at the Royal Court
Theatre, focusing on the recurrent theme of
death or the end of the world, specifically
Hamm's fear that when the world comes to an
end its meaning will be revealed. Reprinted:
1979.22.36.

13   *HODGART, MATTHEW. "Black Humor." <u>Granta</u> 62,
no. 1,176 (Nov.):23-25.

14   HOUFE, E.A.S. "<u>Waiting for Godot</u>." <u>Listener</u> 57
(31 Jan.):197.
In a letter to the editor, refutes Ronald
Gray's interpretation of <u>Waiting for Godot</u> as
a Christian play: "It is the portrayal of
the hopeless condition of a Godless world
without the Christian solution." See 1957.9.

15   HUGHSON, KENNETH. "Another Puzzle Play."
          Socialist Leader 49 (26 Jan.):7.
              Summarizes All That Fall and criticizes
          Beckett's inability to communicate his ideas.

16   "Hurry, Godot, Hurry." Time, 18 Mar., p. 108.
              Underlines Beckett's inability to break
          out of his circle of despair, as exemplified
          by his novel Murphy. Murphy cannot bridge
          the gap between his own hopeless world and
          that of the insane who do not really need
          him.

17   *JESSUP, BERTRAM. "About Beckett, Godot and
          Others." Northwest Review 1 (Spring):25-30.

17a   JOYCE, JAMES. Vols. I, III. London: Faber and
          Faber, 1957.
              Briefly mentions biographical details, his
          friendship with Beckett, and Beckett's
          translations.

18   KEENAN, GERARD. "Beckett Country." Letter to
          Spectator, 27 Sept., p. 398.
              In a brief letter to the editor, suggests
          that All That Fall resembles material
          discarded from Watt.

19   LANZMANN, JACQUES. "Fin de Beckett."
          Lettres Françaises, 9-15 May, p. 5.
              Compares Endgame to Waiting for Godot and
          examines the subject and the portrayal of
          characters in the play.

20   LEE, WARREN. "The Bitter Pill of Samuel
          Beckett." Chicago Review 10, no. 4
          (Winter):77-87.
              Since so many critics were "baffled" and
          "offended" by Beckett's work, undertakes a
          discussion of Waiting for Godot and Molloy.
          Lee criticizes previous reviewers and the
          available American editions of Beckett's
          works.

21 LEHARDOUIN, MARIA. "L'Anti-Héros, ou 'Richard
    n'aime plus Richard.'" Synthèses, no. 139
    (Dec.), pp. 398-405.
         Analyzes the protagonist's ability to
    dissociate himself from his own consciousness
    in Endgame, comparing a similar "impasse"
    demonstrated by the writers Sartre, Malraux,
    and Camus.

22 LEMARCHAND, JACQUES. "Fin de partie." Nouvelle
    Revue Française 5, no. 54 (1 June):1085-89.
         Discusses the use of farce and parody in
    Endgame, the "artistic" endeavors of the four
    characters, and the overall absence of
    "lyrisme" in the play.

23 _____. "Fin de partie de Samuel Beckett, au
    Studio des Champs-Elysées." Figaro Lit-
    téraire, 11 May, p. 14.
         Describes the frightening reality of the
    situation portrayed in Endgame, leaving each
    spectator to interpret the metaphysical con-
    clusions implied by the play. Reprinted:
    1979.22.39.

24 LEVENTHAL, A.J. "Close of Play: Reflections on
    Samuel Beckett's New Work for the French
    Theatre." Dublin Magazine 32, no. 2 (Apr.-
    June):18-22.
         Describes the situation and characters in
    Endgame, comparing the play to Waiting for
    Godot.

25 _____. "Reflections on Samuel Beckett's New
    Work for the French Theatre." Dublin
    Magazine 32 (Apr.-June):18-22.
         Reviews Endgame, which had not yet been
    produced due to commercial considerations:
    "... we are in a hell à la Beckett....
    Creatures suffering from physical disabili-
    ties, cripples whose locomotion is either
    unbelievably difficult or nonexistent, whose
    life is limited to involuntary as well as
    voluntary memory, or a frantic ratiocination
    as the impulse to live or not to live burns

into thought in a wretched remnant of a
brain."

26   _____. "Samuel Beckett: Poet and Pessimist."
          Listener 57 (9 May):746-47.
                 Believes Beckett is "in sympathy with the
          ironic reaction of the dadaists and the early
          surrealists, for Beckett too shares the
          notion of the futility of the arts, the
          futility of any statement...."

27   LOGUE, CHRISTOPHER. "For Those Still Stand-
          ing." New Statesman 54 (14 Sept.):325.
                 Finds All That Fall typical of Beckett's
          work: "One character is blind, another
          raddled, the third a fool. They fulfill
          their wishes. But they get nowhere."

28   *MCWHINNIE, DONALD. "All That Fall." Radio
          Times, 11 Jan., p. 4a.

29   *_____. "Writing for Radio (I)." Ariel 2, no.
          7 (July):b.
                 Source: Zilliacus, 1975.105;unverified.

30   MARCEL, GABRIEL. "Atomisation du théâtre."
          Nouvelles Littéraires, 20 June, p. 10.
                 Reviews Endgame, explaining his personal
          response to the play (boredom) and charac-
          terizing the work as a demonstration of the
          destruction of theater and of man himself.

31   MAULNIER, THIERRY. "De Beckett à Bernanos."
          Revue de Paris 64 (June):139-42. Beckett:
          pp. 139-40.
                 Questions the theatricality of Endgame, a
          play without development or movement, which
          closes all doors.

32   MAYOUX, JEAN-JACQUES. "Le Théâtre de Samuel
          Beckett." Etudes Anglaises 10, no. 4 (Oct.-
          Dec.):350-66.
                 Discusses the subject, language, charac-
          ters, and theatrical reality of Waiting for
          Godot, Endgame and All That Fall. Beckett's

theater does not mimic reality, it is its own
reality.

33   MERCIER, VIVIAN. "Savage Humor." Commonweal
        66, no. 7 (17 May):188, 190.
        Comments on Murphy, Proust, and the first
     issue of the Evergreen Review in which "Dante
     and the Lobster" and most of the poems in
     Echo's Bones are reprinted. Mercier
     criticizes the poems as "fashionable but
     bad," and the style of the critical work as
     "jargon-ridden, allusive, spawning mixed
     metaphors." He feels that Murphy, on the
     other hand, is a "remarkable" novel.

34   NADEAU, MAURICE. "Beckett: La Tragédie
        transposée en farce." Avant-Scène Fémina-
        Théâtre 156:4-6.
        Points out the transposition of tragedy
     into farce. Endgame deals with death and
     suffering, yet on stage the audience observes
     the garish make-up of the actors, and bitter
     jokes, and their music-hall clowning.

35   NORES, DOMINIQUE. "La Condition humaine selon
        Beckett." Théâtre d'Aujourd'hui 3 (Sept.-
        Oct.):9-12.
        Examines the imperative of the universal
     characters in Beckett's dramas: the obliga-
     tion to speak and the hesitation to die.

36   PAUL, ROBERT. "What Way Am I Facing? All That
        Fall by Samuel Beckett." Northwest Review 1,
        no. 2 (Fall):59-61.
        Describes the play thematically, as a
     journey, the senseless journey of Mrs.
     Rooney, and reveals "the paradox that art
     needs movement for its expression, while the
     artist's need is for stasis, for point of
     view."

37   PRONKO, LEONARD C. "Beckett, Ionesco, Schehadé:
        The Avant-Garde Theatre." Modern Language
        Forum 42, no. 2 (Dec.):118-23.
        Notes Beckett's pessimism and his

theatrical effectiveness or ineffectiveness.
In <u>Waiting for Godot</u>: "Beckett's genius has
been to make such a play palatable....
Beckett has saved his play by the introduction of an element of clownish humor. The
comedy affords relief from the depressing
atmosphere, and at the same time it heightens
the tragic effect." On the contrary, Pronko
feels that <u>Endgame</u> possesses minimal action
and dramatic interest.

38   ROBINSON, ROBERT. "Adio: Samuel Beckett."
     <u>Sunday Times</u> (London), 20 Jan., p. 12.
         Assesses the BBC production of <u>All That</u>
     <u>Fall</u> briefly analyzing the characters'
     actions. Robinson finds that the play has a
     strong vivid dialogue while the only weakness
     is that Beckett has "dwelt first and longest
     upon the universal significance he is
     concerned with, and only secondarily upon the
     creatures who are to express it."

39   ROUSSELOT, JEAN. "Deux nouvelles oeuvres de
     Beckett." <u>France-Asie</u> 131 (Apr.):67-60.
         Briefly reviews <u>Endgame</u> and <u>Act Without</u>
     <u>Words</u> at the Studio des Champs Elysées,
     pointing out Beckett's pessimism and obses-
     sion with myths.

40   SELZ, JEAN. L'Homme finissant de Samuel
     Beckett." <u>Lettres Nouvelles</u> 5, no. 51 (July-
     Aug.):120-23.
         Believes there is no longer an individual
     rapport between man and death -- man has
     become an object and dies the death of an
     object. In his works Beckett focuses on
     man's death and his inability to free himself
     from his identification with the objective
     world.

41   SIMON, ALFRED. "<u>Fin de partie</u>." <u>Esprit</u> 25, no.
     252 (July-Aug.):108-12.
         Describes his deception and disappointment
     with <u>Endgame</u> after the brilliance of
     Beckett's first play, <u>Waiting for Godot</u>.

42   STRACHEY, JULIA. "Beckett Country."
          Spectator, 20 Sept., p. 373.
              Stresses the similarity of all of Bec-
          kett's heroes and their dual nature (de-
          spairing and hopeful) in a brief review of
          All That Fall.

42a   *TALLMER, JERRY. "Godot: Still Waiting."
          Village Voice, 30 Jan.
          Reprinted: 1962.74.

43   "Le Théâtre: Fin de partie." Nouvelles
          Littéraires, 9 May, p. 10.
              Feels that Endgame does not have the rich-
          ness or the effectiveness of Godot, and
          appears to resemble the structure of a play
          from the Middle Ages. Act Without Words is
          also briefly described.

44   TRACY, HONOUR. "Where the Voices Rattle On."
          New Republic, 6 May, p. 19.
              Believes Murphy fails as a novel for two
          reasons: 1) Beckett cannot create a hero of
          flesh and blood, and 2) Murphy himself is
          portrayed as mean and trivial.

45   "The Train Stops." Times Literary Supplement
          (London), 6 Sept., p. 528.
              Praises the use of language, setting, and
          melancholic humor in All That Fall. Sum-
          marizes the play and analyzes the shock of
          the last page, the death of the child who
          fell from the carriage. Reprinted:
          1979.22.34.

46   TYNAN, KENNETH. "Theatre -- A Philosophy of
          Despair." Observer, 7 Apr.:15.
              Reviews and interprets the French produc-
          tions of Endgame and Act Without Words at the
          Royal Court Theatre, emphasizing Beckett's
          pessimism: Beckett's latest play, Endgame,
          "... makes it clear that his purpose is
          neither to move nor to help us. For him, man
          is a pygmy who connives at his own inevitable

degradation." Reprinted: 1961.57,
1979.22.37.

47   VAHANIAN, GABRIEL. "The Empty Cradle."
     <u>Theology Today</u> 13, no. 4 (Jan.):521-26.
          Feels Beckett's <u>Waiting for Godot</u> depicts
     the emptiness man experiences when confronted
     with the irrelevance of Christianity.

48   VANNIER, JEAN. "<u>Fin de partie</u> de Samuel Beckett
     ... <u>Actes sans paroles</u>, pantomime, du même
     auteur ..." <u>Théâtre Populaire</u> 25 (July):68-
     72.
          Points out the similarities between
     <u>Endgame</u> and Beckett's other works, especially
     <u>Waiting for Godot</u>. Vannier feels Beckett has
     committed a technical error in <u>Endgame</u> due to
     his use of immobile characters and the
     "death" of the outside world.

49   WACE, MICHAEL. "<u>All That Fall</u>." <u>Listener</u> 57
     (14 Feb.):275.
          In a letter to the editor, speculates on
     the motives for the actions of Dan in <u>All
     That Fall</u>, citing the possibility that Dan
     and Maddy also had a child who was killed by
     a train. See 1957.11.

50   WALKER, ROY. "It's Tragic, Mysterious and
     Wildly Funny: That's What You Get When the
     B.B.C. Asks Samuel Beckett to Write a Play."
     <u>Tribune</u> (London), 18 Jan., p. 8.
          Recommends Beckett's <u>All That Fall</u> as the
     "most important and irresistible new play for
     radio," in which Beckett again portrays man's
     journey through life. See 1957.11.

51   _____. "Shagreen Shamrock." <u>Listener</u> 57 (24
     Jan.):167-68.
          Believes Beckett's <u>All That Fall</u> defies
     attempts at critical interpretation: "Its
     subject is the thing itself, unaccommodated
     man. Man stumbling around in the waste land
     of immediate experience...." Reprinted:
     1964.103.

52   *Y., K. "Subtle Play of Moods." Daily
       Telegraph (London), 14 Jan.
             Source: Zilliacus, 1975.105;unverified.

                           1958

1   ALLSOP, KENNETH. The Angry Decade: A Survey of
       the Cultural Revolt of the Nineteen-Fifties.
       London: Peter Owen, pp. 37-42 and passim.
             Feels that although Beckett's point of
       view is severe -- it is a "surprisingly
       orthodox" one in the environment of the
       fifties. Allsop describes Beckett's
       portrayal of despair: "Beckett is uncon-
       cerned with writing requiems for humanity,
       for he sees life as polluted and pointless:
       he merely scrawls its obituary, without
       bitterness or compassion because he cannot
       really believe it worth the words he is
       wasting."

1a   ATKINSON, BROOKS. "The Theatre: Beckett's
       Endgame." New York Times, 29 Jan., p. 32.
             Reviews Alan Schneider's production of
       Endgame, at the Cherry Lane Theater, "a
       portrait of desolation, lovelessness,
       boredom, ruthlessness, sorrow, nothingness."
       Reprinted: 1972.22.40.

2   *BARNETT, CORRELLI. "Faces to the Wall." New
       Chapter 1, no. 3 (Sept.):23.

3   BLOOMFIELD, ANTHONY. "Enjoyable Experiment."
       Books and Bookmen 3, no. 11 (Aug.):27.
             Criticizes Murphy (which he finds easier
       to read and more straightforward than the
       trilogy): "nevertheless, among much bril-
       liance some of the humor seems almost
       undergraduate, and this novel of Dubliners in
       the dingier districts of London lacks the
       sense of necessity, the sombre passion of Mr.
       Beckett's later work."

4   BOWLES, PATRICK. "How Samuel Beckett Sees the
       Universe." Listener 59 (19 June):1011-12.

Points out the resemblances between Molloy
and Moran: their solitary journeys, their
deterioration of mind and body, and their
choice of language.

5   BRIEN, ALAN. "Waiting for Beckett." Spectator
     201 (7 Nov.):609.
        Describes the productions of Krapp's Last
     Tape and Endgame at the Royal Court Theatre
     as exercises in despair. Not only do the
     plays make the spectator conscious of his own
     mortality, they also convey Beckett's refusal
     of immortality as a dramatist: "Art is the
     last illusion and Beckett seeks to destroy
     even that by creating deliberately inartistic
     works of art."

6   BROOKE-ROSE, CHRISTINE. "Samuel Beckett and the
     Anti-Novel." London Magazine 5, no. 12
     (Dec.):38-46.
        Finds that Beckett reduces great passions
     and ideas to a level of insignificance that
     suits his self-mocking form.

7   *CAVANAGH, MAURA. "Waiting for God. Parody."
     Audience 5 (Summer):94-114.

8   CURTIS, ANTHONY. "Mood of the Month -- IV."
     London Magazine 5 (May):60-65.
        Analyzes Beckett's "world picture of
     decaying man," examining each novel and play
     individually.

9   DAVIE, DONALD. "Kinds of Comedy." Spectrum 2,
     no. 1 (Winter):25-31.
        Notes Beckett's use of humor in All That
     Fall, his application of Joycean perceptions
     of parody to a different dimension of
     language and his return to an earlier point
     in his development, prior to his movement
     towards abstraction and generalization.
     Reprinted: 1979.22.35.

10   DOBREE, BONAMY. "The London Theater, 1957: The
     Melting Pot." Sewanee Review 66, no. 1

(Winter):146-60.
Questions how Beckett's <u>Endgame</u> changes
one's notion of what a play is when it is not
even an imitation of life: "Nothing is given
us; nothing is added to our sense of life.
We do not even enjoy vicarious living for an
hour or two. The piece being deliberately
stripped of any human quality lacks either
delight or any sense of glory."

11   DRIVER, TOM F. "Out in Left Field." <u>Christian
     Century</u> 75 (5 Mar.):282-83.
     Reviews the Cherry Lane Theater's produc-
     tion of <u>Endgame</u>. He expresses his disap-
     pointment that <u>Endgame</u> is not as good as
     <u>Waiting for Godot</u>. He was later to change
     his opinion of the play. See 1961.19.

12   FRASER, G.S. "<u>Waiting for Godot</u>." In <u>English
     Critical Essays: Twentieth Century</u>. Edited
     by Derek Hudson. London: Oxford University
     Press, pp. 324-32.
     Reprint of 1956.13.

13   *"'From an Abandoned Work.'" <u>Times Literary
     Supplement</u> (London), 26 Dec.
     Source: Bryer et al., 1972.7;unverified.

14   "Godot Gets Around." <u>Theater Arts</u> 42, no. 7
     (July):73-74.
     Discusses the production of <u>Waiting for
     Godot</u> at the state penitentiary in San
     Quentin -- the selection of the play and its
     success in a prison setting.

15   *GOODER, RICHARD D. "Samuel Beckett." <u>Granta</u>
     63, no. 1,185 (8 Nov.):27-30.

16   GRANSDEN, K.W. "The Dustman Cometh." <u>Encounter</u>
     11 (July):84-86.
     Reviews <u>Watt</u>, <u>Malone Dies</u>, and <u>Endgame</u>
     from the point of view of the incarcerated
     but innocent hero: "Man is in the condemned
     cell, but whereas for other writers he is
     guilty and deserves to be there for Beckett

he is absolutely and wretchedly innocent.
And all concepts outside this world are
unimaginable; all concepts inside it are
undistinguishable."

17   GROSSVOGEL, DAVID. "Ionesco, Adamov, Beckett."
      In The Self-Conscious Stage in Modern French
      Drama. New York: Columbia University Press,
      pp. 324-34.
          Reprinted: 1961.34.

18   HICKS, GRANVILLE. "Beckett's World." Saturday
      Review of Literature 41 (4 Oct.):14.
          Offers a general introduction to the
      trilogy, focusing on the character's physical
      attributes, their individual situations, the
      images of decay, and the pessimism of the
      novels.

19   *HOBSON, HAROLD. "Beckett Finds Champion in
      BBC's Third Program." Christian Science
      Monitor, 24 June.
          Source: Zilliacus, 1975.105;unverified.

20   KENNER, HUGH. "The Beckett Landscape."
      Spectrum 2, no. 1 (Winter):8-24.
          Examines the narrators, objects,
      memories,inventions and language used to
      portray the mental landscapes of Beckett's
      novels and plays.

21   _____. "Samuel Beckett vs. Fiction." National
      Review 6, no. 10 (11 Oct.):248-49.
          Demonstrates how Beckett has built his
      trilogy around his perception of what a novel
      is: "A Novel ... is a piece of writing
      performed with considerable endurance by a
      solitary man who sits in a room, collecting
      what congruent memories he can of things he
      experienced before his siege in the room
      commenced."

22   MCCOY, CHARLES S. "Waiting for Godot: A
      Biblical Appraisal." Florida Review 2

(Spring):63-72.
   Reprinted: 1959.26.

23   MAGNY, OLIVIER DE. "Panorama d'une nouvelle
     littérature romanesque." <u>Esprit</u> 7-8, nos.
     263-64 (July-Aug.):3-53. Beckett: pp. 36-
     39.
        Presents the new field of experiences
     introduced by Proust, Joyce, Kafka, and
     Faulkner which permanently altered the form
     of the novel. Ten authors are discussed
     individually.

24   MAURIAC, CLAUDE. "Samuel Beckett." In <u>L'Alit-
     térature Contemporaine</u>. Paris: Albin-
     Michel, 77-92.
        Reprinted from 1956.29; translated:
     1959.30.

25   "Messenger of Gloom." <u>Observer</u>, 9 Nov., p. 13.
        Discusses Beckett's direction of <u>Endgame</u>
     and <u>Krapp's Last Tape</u> at the Royal Court
     Theatre. Beckett's life, career and motives
     for his selection of subject matter in his
     works are summarized.

26   "Paradise of Indignity." <u>Times Literary</u>
     <u>Supplement</u> (London), 28 Mar., p. 168.
        Believes the principles of selection used
     in Beckett's narratives are based more on
     poetry than on the novel: "As in the poem,
     the interest is in a state of mind, the
     impact of experience, the inevitability of
     which we accept, on the consciousness." The
     author also discusses the mordant humor of
     the prose works.

27   PEARSON, GABRIEL. "The Monologue of Samuel
     Beckett." <u>Spectator</u> 200 (11 Apr.):466.
        Criticizes the tediousness and the lack of
     "meaning" in Beckett's works. Although
     Beckett is a "born writer" his style seems to
     exist independently of what is being said:
     "Some internal consistency there is, but a
     world whose only connection with the society

we know is based on the lowest common
denominator of physical degradation soon
ceases to affect us below the level of
shock."

28   PINETTE, G.   "Samuel Beckett: Fin de partie
      suivi de Actes sans paroles."   Books Abroad
      32, no. 1 (Winter):21.
           Briefly reviews Endgame, comparing
      Beckett's work to Sartre's No Exit.

29   SCHNEIDER, ALAN.   "Beckett's Letters on Endgame.
      Extracts from His Correspondence with
      Director Alan Schneider."   Village Voice, 19
      Mar., pp. 8, 15.
           Prints passages from Beckett's letters to
      Schneider which provide a chronicle of the
      development of Endgame.

30   _____.   "Waiting for Beckett: A Personal
      Chronicle."   Chelsea Review 2 (Autumn):3-20.
           Reprinted in part: 1967.7, 1967.95;
      reprinted 1969.104, 1979.22.41.

31   SCHUMACH, MURRAY.   "Why They Wait for Godot."
      New York Times Magazine, 21 Sept., pp. 36-
      41.
           Summarizes various interpretations of
      Waiting for Godot, quoting Beckett, actors,
      directors, and writers, and then comments on
      different audiences' responses to the play.

32   SCOTT, NATHAN A., JR.   Modern Literature and the
      Religious Frontier.   New York: Harper &
      Brothers, pp. 84-90.
           Describes the period through which we are
      now living as an "age of vigil," effectively
      dramatized in Beckett's Waiting for Godot.

33   *SLATER, BARRY.   "Bald Prima Donnas."   Granta
      62, no. 1,182 (10 May):3-5.

34   SPENDER, STEPHEN.   "Lifelong Suffocation."   New
      York Times Book Review, 12 Oct., p. 5.
           Reviews The Unnamable, defines his view of

un-self-knowing, death-sentenced, muting body
and mind." Spender compares Beckett to
Wyndham, Lewis, Kafka and Joyce among others.

35   STONIER, G.W. "Waiting for What-Not." New
      Statesman 55, no. 1,409 (15 Mar.):342-43.
          Reviews Watt and Malone Dies, focusing on
      the comic elements in Watt and the tedious
      portrayal of "life and death" in Malone Dies.

36   TINDALL, WILLIAM YORK. "Beckett's Bums."
      Critique: Studies in Modern Fiction 12, no.
      1 (Spring-Summer):3-15.
          Examines the major protagonists in Murphy,
      Watt and the trilogy as aspects of the same
      person or variations on a single obsessive
      theme.

37   *WALKER, ROY. "Love, Chess, and Death."
      Twentieth Century 164 (Dec.):532-40.
          Reprinted: 1980.111.

38   WORSLEY, T.C. "Private Worlds and Public." New
      Statesman 56 (8 Nov.):630.
          Compares Endgame with Waiting for Godot,
      and finds that in Endgame Beckett has
      concentrated on more private images revealing
      his solitary despairs. Worsley also very
      briefly reviews Krapp's Last Tape.

                            1959

1   ABBEY, EDWARD. "Watt." New Mexico Quarterly
      29, no. 3 (Autumn):381-83.
          Compares Watt to Beckett's other novels
      and plays, and points out that the novel is
      concerned with the "comic and horrible"
      aspects of human existence: "Watt, like his
      counterparts in the later novels, is a shabby
      and derelict figure, a passive non-resister,
      who shambles through the same abstract and
      malevolent landscape toward the same obscure
      extinction."

2   ABEL, LIONEL. "Joyce the Father, Beckett the
        Son." New Leader 42 (14 Dec.):26-27.
            Believes that Endgame is about the
        relationship of Joyce and Beckett. Not only
        does Endgame clarify many of the questions
        the reader may have had about Waiting for
        Godot, in many respects it is superior to
        Waiting for Godot, "it is purer in form,
        denser in meaning, a deeper expression of
        Samuel Beckett's ultimate purposes."
        Reprinted: 1963.1.

3   "The Anti-Novel in France." Times Literary
        Supplement (London), 13 Feb., p. 82
            Presents the subject of a debate on the
        New French Novel at the Institute of Contem-
        porary Arts. Although the fiction of each
        novelist is different, they all attempt to
        eliminate the faults of modern classical
        fiction. A general survey of the opinions
        and techniques of the novelists is offered.

4   BARRETT, WILLIAM. "How I Understand Less and
        Less Every Year ..." Columbia University
        Forum 2 (Winter):44-48.
            Views The Unnamable as a "general indict-
        ment of language" comparable to what Barrett
        was personally experiencing at the time.

5   BLANCHOT, MAURICE. "Où maintenant? Qui
        maintenant?" In Le Livre à venir. Paris:
        Gallimard, pp. 256-64.
            Reprint of 1953.3; reprinted and trans-
        lated: 1959.6.

6   _____. "Where Now? Who Now?" Evergreen Review
        2 (Winter):222-29.
            Reprint and translation of 1953.3, 1959.5.

7   BRICK, ALLAN. "The Madman in his Cell: Joyce,
        Beckett, Nabokov, and the Stereotypes."
        Massachusetts Review 1, no. 1 (Oct.):40-55.
            Describes the efforts of twentieth century
        writers to make their work inaccessible to
        the general public.

8   BULL, PETER. "Peter Bull as Pozzo." In <u>I Know</u>
      <u>the Face But</u>. London: Peter Davies, Ltd.
      Reprinted: 1967.17.

9   COHN, RUBY. "A Checklist of Beckett Criticism."
      <u>Perspective</u> 11, no. 3 (Autumn):193-96.
            Presents the first bibliography of
      critical works devoted to Beckett.

10   _____. "The Comedy of Samuel Beckett: 'Someth-
      ing old, something new ...!'" <u>Yale French</u>
      <u>Studies</u>, no. 23, pp. 11-17.
            Reveals Beckett's use of comedy of
      situation, language, and character, incor-
      porating two critical views of comedy: "1)
      that laughter arises from a malicious feeling
      of superiority over a victim, or 2) that it
      is a tool of instruction by negative
      example."

11   _____. "Preliminary Observations." <u>Perspective</u>
      11, no. 3 (Autumn):119-31.
            As editor of this special issue, reviews
      Beckett's life and works from 1929 to the
      fifties underlining the "reduction of plot,
      personality and linguistic richness that has
      taken place in the prose and drama."

12   _____. "Still Novel." <u>Yale French Studies</u>, no.
      24 (Fall), pp. 48-53.
            Interprets the quest motif in the trilogy
      as the need of the individual to discover his
      "idiosyncratic self" and the writer to find
      his fiction.

13   EASTMAN, RICHARD M. "The Strategy of Samuel
      Beckett's <u>Endgame</u>." <u>Modern Drama</u> 2, no. 1
      (May):36-44.
            Attempts a reading of <u>Endgame</u> "first by
      assessing the frames of fantasy in which the
      action takes place; then by examining the
      characters; and finally by tracing the tragic
      action and its implicit effect upon the
      audience."

14   *"Embers: Award." Times (London), 15 Sept., p.
      5.
            Source: Tanner, 1969.113;unverified.

15   FERRIS, PAUL. "Radio Notes." Observer, 25
      Jan., p. 16.
            Describes the effect of Patrick Magee's
      reading from The Unnamable as "punishment for
      the nerves and a strange blankness of spirit,
      as if a dog or a cat had learned to communi-
      cate the futility of being animals.

16   FOWLIE, WALLACE. "The New French Theater:
      Artaud, Beckett, Genet, Ionesco." Sewanee
      Review 67, no. 4 (Autumn):643-57. Beckett:
      pp. 648-51.
            Views the "little theater" movement as a
      means of reaching a simplicity which would
      "give to the work of art, to the play its
      maximum human quality, its power of pathos
      and poetry." Fowlie briefly analyzes the
      characters and action in Waiting for Godot
      and Endgame. Reprinted in part: 1960.18.

17   FRIEDMAN, MELVIN J. "The Achievement of Samuel
      Beckett." Books Abroad 33, no. 3 (Sum-
      mer):278-81.
            Summarizes Beckett's literary career, his
      sudden rise to prominence, and his creation
      of a new literary type, "Beckett's 'M' man."

18   GIRAUD, RAYMOND. "Unrevolt Among the Unwriters
      in France Today." Yale French Studies, no.
      24 (Fall), pp. 11-17.
            Comments on the gulf that separates the
      "existentialists" (Malraux, Sartre, Camus)
      and the anti-writers of the fifties (Beckett,
      Adamov, Ionesco, Sarraute, Robbe-Grillet,
      Butor, Simon).

19   GREGORY, HORACE. "Prose and Poetry of Samuel
      Beckett." Commonweal 71, no. 5 (30
      Oct.):162-63.
            Reprinted from 1956.17.

20   HAMILTON, KENNETH. "Boon or Thorn? Joyce Cary
      and Samuel Beckett on Human Life." Dalhousie
      Review 38, no. 4 (Winter):433-42.
          Contrasts Joyce Cary's optimism in his
      trilogy, Herself Surprised, To Be A Pilgrim,
      and The Horse's Mouth with Beckett's pes-
      simism in his trilogy. Cary's Gully Jimson,
      like Beckett's Molloy, finds the universe as
      a whole meaningless, but unlike Molloy, Gully
      believes there is meaning in human existence
      and can thus experience joy and love.

21   HOEFER, JACQUELINE. "Watt." Perspective 11,
      no. 3 (Autumn):166-82.
          Feels that Watt is an exploration of the
      nihilistic theory of art advanced in the
      Beckett-Duthuit dialogues. The meaning of
      Watt's quest is examined in terms of his
      interest in language and logic. Reprinted:
      1965.46.

22   KENNER, HUGH. "The Cartesian Centaur."
      Perspective 11, no. 3 (Autumn):132-41.
          Reprinted: 1961.40, 1965.50, 1968.37.

23   KERN, EDITH. "Moran-Molloy: The Hero as
      Author." Perspective 11, no. 3 (Autumn):183-
      93.
          Points out the oneness of Moran and
      Molloy, comparing the symbolic significance
      of Molloy's journey with Moran's artistic
      quest. Kern sees the Moran-Molloy journey
      against the background of Nietzschean
      esthetics, a departure from the Apollonian
      and an arrival at the Dionysian element in
      art: "Moran's escape from time, habit, and
      intelligence and his surrender to the
      Molloyan, the Dionysian element within him
      are to a certain degree paralleled in
      Beckett's own artistic development. Beckett
      has found artistic fulfillment in the
      creation of a world without causality and
      will, the new-old world myth and the subcon-
      scious." Reprinted: 1970.78.

24 _____. "Samuel Beckett -- Dionysian Poet."
Descant 3 (Winter):33-36.
Analyzes Beckett's use of two myths in
Molloy, the myth of the "hero in two aspects"
and the myth of the hero in search of the
mother-bride. The representation of
Dionysian and Apollonian elements is also
presented.

25 LAMONT, ROSETTE. "The Metaphysical Farce:
Beckett and Ionesco." French Review 32, no.
4 (Feb.):319-28.
Compares Beckett's Endgame and Ionesco's
The Chairs as two examples of "metaphysical
farce," a new genre created by both authors,
which is "philosophical in essence" while
"its intellectual concern is couched in the
rough and tumble language of the most
primitive type comedy." Reprinted, revised,
and translated: 1964.61.

26 McCOY, CHARLES S. "Waiting for Godot: A
Biblical Appraisal." Religion in Life 28
(Fall):595-603.
Presents evidence to support the conten-
tion that Waiting for Godot portrays a
biblical interpretation of the human situation. McCoy examines: 1) biblical allusions
in the text, 2) crucial points of kinship
with the Christian existentialists, and 3)
Beckett's quotation from the Old Testament
Book of Proverbs. Reprint of 1958.22.

27 McDONNELL, THOMAS. "The Unnamable." Critic 17
(Apr.-May):49-50.
Finds The Unnamable "all but completely
unreadable," since the novel is a subjective
recording of the narrator's state of mind and
emotions, rather than an objective attempt in
communication: "... Beckett has become so
obsessed with the human predicament that he
has interpreted it in sub-human terms; and he
has become so obsessed with extending,
perhaps demolishing, the limits of art that
his creation must necessarily result in the

destruction of form itself."

28   MAILER, NORMAN.   "A Public Notice on <u>Waiting for</u>
     <u>Godot</u>."   In <u>Advertisements for Myself</u>.   New
     York: G.P. Putnam's Sons, pp. 320-25.
         Attempts to soften his previously harsh
     review of <u>Waiting for Godot</u> by offering a
     clearer presentation of Beckett's portrayal
     of impotence, despair, sex, and God.
     Reprinted: 1967.67; see 1962.54.

29   MARCABRU, PIERRE.   "Le Théâtre étranger de
     langue française: Ionesco, Beckett, Adamov,
     Schehadé."   <u>Signes du Temps</u> 8-9 (Aug.-
     Sept.):32-33.
         Traces the influences undergone by these
     four authors who escaped from their cultural
     and hereditary roots and choose to write in a
     foreign language.

30   MAURIAC, CLAUDE.   "Samuel Beckett."   In <u>The New</u>
     <u>Literature</u>.   Translated by Samuel I. Stone.
     New York: George Braziller, pp. 75-90.
         Reprinted and translated from: 1956.29,
     1958.24; reprinted: 1969.104.

31   MAYOUX, JEAN-JACQUES.   "The Theatre of Samuel
     Beckett."   <u>Perspective</u> 11, no. 3
     (Autumn):142-55.
         Focusing on two of Beckett's plays,
     <u>Waiting for Godot</u> and <u>Endgame</u>, analyzes the
     subject of Beckett's theater (man and man's
     fate), examines his methods of conveying
     ideas and feelings (music-hall tradition,
     parody, human relationships), and discusses
     the question of theatrical reality.

32   MERCIER, VIVIAN.   "The Arrival of the Anti-
     Novel."   <u>Commonweal</u> 70, no. 6 (8 May):149-51.
         Discusses the new novelists' works in
     terms of Claude de Magny's categories: 1)
     "the novel's search for itself," 2) "the
     novel's negation of itself," and 3) "novels
     not without a search but without questions,
     without dispute, without ambiguity."   Mercier

briefly describes Beckett's trilogy as an
example of the second category.

33   _____. "How to Read <u>Endgame</u>." <u>Griffin</u> 8
          (June):10-14.
          Recommends listening to <u>Endgame</u> before
     reading the text in order to "experience" the
     play before interpreting it. Mercier points
     out the major themes and classifies <u>Endgame</u>
     as a "tragicomedy," more tragic than comic.
     See 1960.23.

34   _____. "The Mathematical Limit." <u>Nation</u> 188,
          no. 7 (14 Feb.):144-45.
          Examines the "finite and calculable"
     variety of choices available to the Becket-
     tian hero -- Beckett appears to be searching
     for the limit of the novel and that of
     existence itself.

35   "The Mexican Tradition." <u>Times Literary</u>
          <u>Supplement</u> (London), 6 Feb., p. 72.
          Points out the strengths and weakness of
     Beckett's translation of the <u>Anthology of</u>
     <u>Mexican Poetry</u>.

36   MILLER, KARL. "Beckett's Voices." <u>Encounter</u>
          13, no. 3 (Sept.):59-61.
          Reviews Beckett's radio plays <u>All That</u>
     <u>Fall</u> and <u>Embers</u>: "In each play the theme is
     the anguish and boredom of an old couple, and
     through it there seems to run even more than
     ever the sense that we are confined for life
     in a set of ruinously selfish dreams and
     aggressions."

37   MILLS, RALPH J., JR.   "Samuel Beckett's Man."
          <u>Christian Century</u> 76 (30 Dec.):1524-25.
          Comments on Beckett's break with the
     traditional novelistic forms and considers
     the occurrences and characters in the three
     volumes of the trilogy: "Because the stories
     themselves are interrupted, doubted, ter-
     minated without actual conclusions, and
     finally denied altogether, we are forced to

realize that the concept of fiction as an art
is called into question. And this inquiry is
closely linked to the themes of the trilogy."

38   MINTZ, SAMUEL I.   "Beckett's <u>Murphy</u>: A
     'Cartesian' Novel." <u>Perspective</u> 11, no. 3
     (Autumn):156-65.
          Believes Beckett used Cartesianism to give
     his novel structure, action, and meaning.
     Mintz examines the implications of the sixth
     part of the book in which Murphy's mind is
     metaphorically divided into three zones.

39   POLITZER, HEINZ. "The Egghead Waits for Godot."
     <u>Christian Scholar</u> 42, no. 1 (Mar.):46-50.
          Describes <u>Waiting for Godot</u> as a parable
     "deprived of any clear-cut didactic message
     .... instead of persuading everyman to
     contemplate a betterment of his destiny they
     shock him into the awareness of this des-
     tiny's absurdity."

40   REXROTH, KENNETH. "Samuel Beckett and the
     Importance of Waiting." In <u>Bird in the Bush:</u>
     <u>Obvious Essays</u>. New York: New Directions,
     pp. 75-85.
          Reprint of 1956.33.

41   RODGER, IAN. "Perishing on the Shore."
     <u>Listener</u> 62 (2 July):35-36.
          Suggests that Beckett's message in <u>Embers</u>
     is "that there is nothing we can do, that the
     sin of our incapacity is limitless and that,
     at the last, there is only remorse and regret
     and no forgiveness." Rodger regrets
     Beckett's use of "ostentatious mystique" to
     convey his message.

42   "Samuel Beckett's New Play." <u>Times</u> (London), 25
     June, p. 5.
          Reviews Beckett's radio drama <u>Embers</u>,
     focusing on the central figure, Henry, his
     feelings and his relationships with his
     father and his wife.

43   STRAUSS, WALTER. Dante's Belaqua and Beckett's
        Tramps." <u>Comparative Literature</u> 11 (Sum-
        mer):250-61.
            Reprinted in part (in French): 1976.143;
        see 1960.6.

44   UNTERECKER, JOHN. "Samuel Beckett's No-Man's-
        Land." <u>New Leader</u> 42 (18 May):24-25.
            Presents Beckett's "framing plan" for the
        trilogy, which he compares to that of <u>Waiting
        for Godot</u>. Unterecker briefly analyzes the
        characters, their stories and their changing
        identities: "Mere meaningless being is man's
        lot, a lot made almost but not quite unen-
        durable by man's anguished necessity to
        define himself. As the Unnamable at the end
        of his book faces the door that will give him
        identity as a 'character,' he struggles
        against the inevitable lie which that
        identity will be ..."

45   WILSON, COLIN. "Existential Criticism."
        <u>Chicago Review</u> 13, no. 2 (Summer):152-81.
            Believes existential criticism can
        facilitate an assessment of Beckett's
        fiction, since his works are concerned with
        absolute despair, while "the sloth and
        stagnant misery of Beckett's characters is
        the basic experience of existentialism."

                            <u>1960</u>

 1   BLAU, HERBERT. "'Meanwhile Follow the Bright
        Angels.'" <u>Tulane Drama Review</u> 5 (Sept.):89-
        101. Beckett: pp. 90-101.
            In a letter written to the members of the
        Actor's Workshop in San Francisco, Blau re-
        evaluates his theater's standards in light of
        his recent experiences studying the major
        theatre companies in Europe. Blau describes
        meeting Beckett and Roger Blin.

 2   BRUSTEIN, ROBERT. "Krapp and a Little
        Claptrap." <u>New Republic</u> 142 (22 Feb.):21-22.

Praises Krapp's Last Tape as "possibly Beckett's best dramatic poem about the "old age of the world": "Still obsessed with the alienation, vacuity and decay of life upon a planet devoid of God and hope, Beckett is finally able to sound those chords of compassion which have always vibrated quietly in his other work. Yet, what really strikes me as new is the extraordinary economy of the writing, the absolute flawlessness of the form." Reprinted: 1979.22.43.

3   CHADWICK, C. "Waiting for Godot: A Logical Approach." Symposium 14, no. 4 (Winter):252-57.

Investigates Waiting for Godot as an allegory whose characters have a hidden significance. Vladimir and Estragon symbolize mankind, Pozzo may be Godot and Lucky may represent the misery of "God's servants." Chadwick defines Godot as an anti-Christian play telling "the story of mankind eternally waiting for a merciful God to bring salvation, but waiting in vain since God is a malevolent and jesting tyrant who is callously indifferent to the fate of his creatures."

4   CLURMAN, HAROLD. "Theatre." Nation 190 (13 Feb.):153-54.

Discusses Beckett's Krapp's Last Tape and Edward Albee's The Zoo Story, as studies in loneliness.

5   CMARADA, GERALDINE. "Malone Dies: A Round of Consciousness." Symposium 14, no. 3 (Fall): 199-212.

Feels that Malone Dies is a "testament to the existential vision of man" which utilizes the doctrine of absurdity to present despair and satire.

6   COHN, RUBY. "A Note on Beckett, Dante, and Geulincx." Comparative Literature 12, no. 1(Winter):93-94.

Re-examines the subject of a study by
Walter Strauss. See 1959.43.

7   _____. "Endgame: The Gospel According to Sad
       Sam Beckett." Accent 20, no. 4 (Autumn):223-
       34.
           Summarizes the dramatic action in Endgame
       as the death of a world.

8   _____. "Waiting is All." Modern Drama 3, no. 2
       (Sept.):162-67.
           Believes Beckett creates tension between
       surface stagnancy and dramatic development in
       Waiting for Godot: "the drama of the waiting
       is a tightly structured art-work, where
       developments are played against repetitions
       and equilibria, so that the seeming stasis
       finds its meaning only in terms of dramatic
       action, Godot in terms of waiting."

9   COLEMAN, JOHN. "Under the Jar." Spectator 204
       (8 Apr.):516.
           Points out the comic and poetic elements
       in the trilogy. Coleman denies the univer-
       sality of the characters since they "fuse
       into a collective mash for something un-
       pleasantly private, because shrill and
       deformed."

10   DELYE, HUGUETTE. Samuel Beckett ou la
       philosophie de l'absurde. Aix-en-Provence:
       La Pensée Univ., 135 pp.
           After examining biographical sources and
       influences, analyzes "the Beckettian message"
       as it concerns Beckett's view of the human
       condition (sin, powerlessness, time, suffer-
       ing) or an evasion of the human condition
       (God, science, society, death, and resigna-
       tion to life). Delye then turns to a study
       of "the Beckettian aesthetic" (absurd
       creation, humor, style, symbolism, dramatic
       art and the novel). A Selected Bibliography
       is included.

11   *DILLON, JOHN. "'The New Writing': Stein,

Joyce, Beckett." <u>Isis</u>, no. 1,362 (10 Feb.),
pp. 20-21.

12   DRIVER, TOM F. "Rebuke to Nihilism." <u>Christian
     Century</u> 77 (2 Mar.):256-57.
          Reviews <u>Krapp's Last Tape</u> at the Provin-
     cetown Playhouse, New York: "Man's attempts
     to control his destiny have brought him to
     the point where he seems to have no destiny
     ... how shall man recover himself? ... by
     looking for a quality of life rather than by
     seeking for an elusive pattern or meaning in
     the whole."

13   "The Dying of the Light." <u>Times Literary
     Supplement</u> (London), 8 Jan., p. 20.
          Qualifies <u>Krapp's Last Tape</u> and <u>Embers</u> as
     realistic and psychological rather than
     allegorical and philosophical as are some of
     Beckett's other plays. The plays are similar
     because they each portray an image of
     individual misery and loneliness, and the
     major characters of the plays are both
     creators who have squandered their creative
     gift, Krapp in a series of monologues on
     tape, and Henry in a long story, he repeats
     to himself.

14   ESSLIN, MARTIN. "The Absurdity of the Absurd."
     <u>Kenyon Review</u> 22, no. 4 (Autumn):670-73.
          Responds to an article by Ward Hooker,
     pointing out that the terms "irony" and
     "absurdity" are used incorrectly in his
     article -- Hooker follows common usage rather
     than the meaning given to these terms by the
     French avant-garde dramatists, Ionesco and
     Beckett, among others. See 1960.32.

15   *FAGIN, BRYLLION. "New Books in Review: A
     Pessimist's Plays." <u>Baltimore Evening Sun</u>,
     27 May.

16   *FERRIS, PAUL. "Beckett Embalmed." <u>Observer</u>,
     1 May, p. 22.
          Source: Zilliacus, 1975.105;unverified.

17   FITZGERALD, T.M. "Beckett's Charades." <u>Nation</u>
      (Sydney), no. 42 (23 Apr.), pp. 23-24.
           Presents religious imagery in <u>Waiting for</u>
      <u>Godot</u> and <u>Endgame</u> and then briefly reviews
      <u>Krapp's Last Tape</u>, Beckett's most stageworthy
      "charade" since <u>Waiting for Godot</u>.

18   FOWLIE, WALLACE. "Beckett." In <u>Dionysus in</u>
      <u>Paris: A Guide to Contemporary French</u>
      <u>Theater</u>. New York: Meridian Books, pp. 210-
      17 and passim.
           Briefly discusses <u>Waiting for Godot</u> and
      <u>Endgame</u> describing the decor, situation,
      action, and characters. Reprinted from
      1959.16.

19   FRIEDMAN, MELVIN J. "The Creative Writer as
      Polyglot: Valéry Larbaud and Samuel
      Beckett." <u>Wisconsin Academy of Science, Arts</u>
      <u>and Letters</u> 49:229-36.
           Valéry Larbaud and Samuel Beckett
      represent two types of polyglot. Larbaud's
      knowledge of numerous languages and his
      translations of other writers have served to
      enrich his own work. Beckett, on the other
      hand, translates his own works, thereby
      creating "original" versions in two lan-
      guages.

20   _____. "The Novels of Samuel Beckett: An
      Amalgam of Joyce and Proust." <u>Comparative</u>
      <u>Literature</u> 12, no. 1 (Winter):47-58.
           Claims that Beckett's indebted to Proust
      for his narrative point of view and temporal
      awareness, and to Joyce for his concentration
      on "things" and spatial awareness.

21   _____. "Samuel Beckett and the 'Nouveau
      Roman.'" <u>Wisconsin Studies in Contemporary</u>
      <u>Literature</u> 1, no. 2 (Spring-Summer):22-36.
           In agreement with the opinions stated by
      Claude Mauriac in <u>The New Literature</u>,
      Friedman believes that Beckett fits into an
      "experimentalist" tradition in novel writing.

Beckett's works have much in common with
those of other writers of his generation:
Alain Robbe-Grillet, Nathalie Sarraute,
Michel Butor, Claude Simon, Claude Ollier and
Marguerite Duras. Reprinted: 1964.33,
1970.47.

22 FRYE, NORTHROP. "The Nightmare Life in Death."
Hudson Review 13, no. 3 (Autumn):442-49.
Reviews the trilogy from the point of view
of Beckett's earlier works and the works of
Proust and Joyce. Reprinted: 1970.47,
1978.26, 1979.22.46.

23 GASSNER, JOHN. "Beckett's Endgame and Sym-
bolism." In Theatre at the Crossroads. Plays
and Playwrights of the Mid-Century American
Stage. New York: Holt, Rinehart and
Winston, pp. 256-61.
Interprets Endgame, summarizing Vivian
Mercier's article "How to Read Endgame,"
adding his own comments. See 1959.33.

24 _____. "Beckett: Waiting for Godot." In
Theatre at the Crossroads. Plays and
Playwrights of the Mid-Century American
Stage. New York: Holt, Rinehart and
Winston, pp. 252-56.
Explains how Michael Myerberg's Manhattan
production of Waiting for Godot combined
meaningful drama with showmanship to create a
version of the play that is more affirmative
than negative.

25 GERARD, MARTIN. "Molloy becomes Unnamable." X:
A Quarterly Review 1, no. 4 (Oct.):314-19.
Believes that the trilogy has "a form, and
an over-all anagogical meaning." Gerard
defends the asceticism of Beckett's prose and
the mockery of traditional stylistic devices
which reveals the falsity of literary
experience.

26 *GERRARD, DAVID. "Beckett: Dead or Alive?"
Isis, no. 1,361 (3 Feb.), pp. 29, 31.

27   *_____. "The Latest Beckett." <u>Isis</u>, no. 1,359
      (20 Jan.), p. 35.

28   GUGGENHEIM, PEGGY. <u>Out of This Century:</u>
      <u>Confessions of an Art Addict</u>. London: André
      Deutsch, p. 49.
           Describes her relationship with Beckett,
      whom she called Oblomov from the book by
      Goncharov.

29   HARVEY, LAWRENCE E. "Art and the Existential in
      <u>En attendant Godot</u>." <u>PMLA</u> 75, no. 1
      (Mar.):137-46.
           Reprinted: 1967.50.

30   HATCH, ROBERT. "Laughter at Your Own Risk."
      <u>Horizon</u> 3 (Sept.):112-16.
           Reviews <u>Krapp's Last Tape</u> at the Province-
      town Playhouse in New York. Hatch portrays
      Krapp as a kind of artist, a man "overwhelmed
      by language: the sound of words, their power
      to make experience real, their power in the
      end, to supplant experience ... For Krapp,
      reality became not the punt and the girl and
      the sun and the flags -- but the tape that
      records those things."

31   *HEPPENSTALL, R. Review of <u>Molloy</u>, <u>Malone Dies</u>,
      <u>The Unnamable</u>. <u>Observer</u>, 10 Mar.
           Source: Webb, 1966.72;unverified.

32   HOOKER, WARD. "Irony and Absurdity in the
      Avant-Garde Theater." <u>Kenyon Review</u> 22, no.
      3 (Summer):436-54.
           Studies examples of dramatic irony in the
      plays of Marivaux, Anouilh, and Ionesco in
      order to shed light on Beckett's <u>Waiting for
      Godot</u>. Hooker examines the function of irony
      in the plot, characterization, and themes of
      Beckett's play, and concludes that the
      dramatic irony of "waiting" is never
      resolved. See 1960.14.

33   HOROVITZ, MICHAEL. "Notes on 3 Novels by Samuel

Beckett." Tomorrow 4:57-59.
    Comments on the act of writing in the
trilogy: The disintegration of subject and
form, the futility of all statement, and the
weakness of the first-person narrator.

34 KENNER, HUGH. "Beckett: The Rational Domain."
    Forum 3, no. 4. (Summer):39-47.
        Examines Beckett's style: the rhythm,
    symmetry and impact of his phrases, the
    subtle differences in the French and English
    texts, and his use of the processes of
    mathematics.

35 KERMODE, FRANK. "Beckett, Snow, and Pure
    Poverty." Encounter 15, no. 1 (July):73-77.
        Discusses Proust as a general introduction
    to Waiting for Godot and the trilogy.
    Reprinted: 1962.47, 1979.22.45.

36 LEMARCHAND, JACQUES. "La Dernière Bande de
    Samuel Beckett au T.N.P. -- Récamier."
    Figaro Littéraire, 2 Apr., p. 16.
        Describes the confrontation that takes
    place in Krapp's Last Tape: the youth who
    describes his dreams of intellectual purity,
    of comprehension of self and the meaning of
    existence who contrasts with the being who
    can no longer understand his former self.

37 LUCCIONI, GENNIE. "Samuel Beckett: La Dernière
    Bande, suivi de Cendres." Esprit 29, no. 284
    (May):913-15.
        Believes silence is the dénouement in
    modern drama just as death was in classical
    tragedy. The characters in Krapp's Last Tape
    and Embers are portrayed at the moment when
    the monologue approaches madness, just before
    silence or the "degrée zéro" of art.

38 LUCHS, FRED E. "Waiting for Godot." Chris-
    tianity Today, 6 June, pp. 6-8.
        Offers several interpretations for Waiting
    for Godot, finally deciding that "Samuel
    Beckett is telling us that man is waiting for

a God who isn't there ..." Luchs compares
Beckett's play with philosophies from the
Bible and points out that the trouble with
Beckett's play is that it does not realize
that Christ was born.

39   MAYOUX, JEAN-JACQUES. "Samuel Beckett et
       l'univers parodique." Lettres Nouvelles.
       Vivants Pilliers: Le Roman anglo-saxon et
       les symboles, no. 6 (Sept.), pp. 271-91.
       Reprinted and translated: 1965.55.

40   METMAN, EVA. "Reflections on Samuel Beckett's
       Plays." Journal of Analytical Psychology 5,
       no. 1 (Jan.):41-63.
           Emphasizes the Jungian and existentialist
       approaches to modern man's dilemma of "self-
       estrangement." In order to force the
       audience to experience something itself, "be
       it a reawakening of the awareness of arche-
       typal powers or a reorientation of the ego,
       or both," Beckett utilizes a new development
       in drama, the "alienation effect" (Brecht's
       term): "Instead of merely showing human
       existence in its unadorned nakedness, he
       strips his figures so thoroughly of all those
       qualities in which the audience might
       recognize itself that, to start with, an
       'alienation effect' is created that leaves
       the audience mystified." A detailed analysis
       of Waiting for Godot and Endgame is given.

41   MOORE, JOHN R. "A Farewell to Something."
       Tulane Drama Review 5, no. 1 (Sept.):49-60.
           Presents the originality of the avant-
       garde play, Waiting for Godot: "On the
       surface it seemed simple almost to the point
       of idiocy, yet it implied all the complica-
       tions that human intelligence has been able
       to create for itself." The cyclical nature
       of the play is inevitable, Didi and Gogo
       exist in a single place, a single moment.

42   MORSE, J. MITCHELL. "The Uses of Obscurity."
       New World Writing 17:246-56. Beckett: pp.

249-50.
Introduces numerous possibilities for
Godot and equates <u>Waiting for Godot</u> with the
quest for meaning in modern literature.

43   NORES, DOMINIQUE. "Un théâtre de la mémoire et
     de l'oubli." <u>Lettres Nouvelles</u> 8, no. 2
     (June):146-48.
         Reviews Robert Pinget's <u>Lettre Morte</u> and
     Beckett's <u>Krapp's Last Tape</u> as the progres-
     sion of solitude from a state in which it is
     open to dreams to a state in which it is
     closed in on itself.

44   PRITCHETT, VICTOR SAWDON. "An Irish Oblomov."
     <u>New Statesman</u> 59 (2 Apr.):489.
         Discusses Beckett major themes in the
     trilogy (flight, old age, personal identity),
     Beckett's comic gift, and Beckett's use of
     stream of consciousness. Reprinted:
     1964.79, 1979.22.44.

45   *REID, ALEC. "'All I Can Manage, More than I
     Could' -- Beckett to the American Producer
     Alan Schneider." <u>Guardian</u>, 15 Apr.

46   THIBAUDEAU, JEAN. "Un théâtre de romanciers."
     <u>Critique</u>, nos. 159-160 (Aug.-Sept.), pp. 696-
     92. Beckett: pp. 690-92.
         Notes Beckett's (<u>Krapp's Last Tape</u>,
     <u>Embers</u>, <u>All That Fall</u>) and Robert Pinget's
     interest in writing plays. Thibaudeau
     stresses the differences in emphasis on
     syntax and "spectacle" in Beckett's prose and
     drama.

47   THOORENS, L. "Deux pièces de Beckett." <u>Revue
     Générale Belge</u> 96 (Apr.):152-54.
         Comments on <u>Krapp's Last Tape</u> and <u>Embers</u>,
     remarking that Beckett's theater from <u>Waiting
     for Godot</u> to <u>Embers</u> has undergone an evolu-
     tion in which the essential values, word and
     silence, have become more and more indepen-
     dent to the point where they could do without
     the rest and become radio plays.

48   *TOUCHARD, PIERRE-AIME. "Le Jeune Théâtre
      contemporain." Confluent, no. 7 (May), pp.
      274-90.

49   *WHITEHEAD, FRANK. "Postscript: The Nineteen-
      Fifties." In English Literature of the
      Twentieth Century. Edited by A.S. Collins.
      London: University Tutorial Press, pp. 378-
      80.

50   *WHITTICK, ARNOLD. Symbols, Signs and Their
      Meaning. London: Leonard Hill, pp. 327-74.

                            1961

1   ADAM, GEORGES. "A formentor: Débats fiévreux
      au Prix International des Editeurs." Figaro
      Littéraire, 13 May, pp. 1-3.
            Describes the circumstances surrounding
      the decision to award the Prix International
      des Editeurs to both Beckett and Luis Borgès.

2   ALVAREZ, A. "Poet Waiting for Pegasus."
      Observer Weekend Review (31 Dec.), p. 21.
            In a review of Poems in English, points
      out that Beckett's poetry, with the exception
      of a few short lyrics, is conventional and
      lacks originality.

3   AUBAREDE, GABRIEL d'. "En attendant ...
      Beckett." Nouvelles Littéraires, 16 Feb.,
      pp. 1, 7.
            Short interview in which Beckett describes
      his "enthusiasm" in writing the trilogy and
      the following impasse, and denies any
      relationship to existentialists. Reprinted
      and translated: 1961.4, 1979.22.47.

4   _____. "Waiting for Beckett." Trace, no. 42
      (Summer), pp. 156-58.
            In this interview, Beckett claims his
      works are not philosophical treatises and
      denies a direct debt to the existentialists.

Reprint and translation of 1961.3.

5   BELMONT, GEORGES. "Samuel Beckett -- L'honneur
    d'être homme." Arts 82 (10-16 May):14.
        Speaks of his thirty year acquaintance
    with Beckett, Beckett's kindness, his love of
    life, and his dislike of interviews.

6   *BIALOS, ANNE. "Samuel Beckett." Studies in
    Literature 1 (Spring):unpaginated.

7   BLANZAT, JEAN. "Les Romans de Samuel Beckett."
    Figaro Littéraire, 13 May, p. 2.
        Emphasizes the importance of Molloy,
    Malone Dies, The Unnamable, and How It Is to
    an understanding of Beckett's work as a
    whole. Blanzat briefly comments on the
    characters and situations of the novels.

8   BOURDET, DENISE. "Marcel Mihalovici: 'Beckett
    a colloboré à la musique de Krapp, l'opéra
    que j'ai tiré de sa pièce.'" Figaro Lit-
    téraire, 1 July, pp. 14, 16.
        Mihalovici explains how he came to compose
    his opera based on Krapp's Last Tape and
    discusses Beckett's collaboration on the
    work.

9   BOYLE, KEVIN. "Molloy: Icon of the Negative."
    Westwind 5 (Fall):unpaginated.
        Views Molloy as a literary satire, which
    provides a negative reversal of the most
    stereotyped characteristics of conventional
    fiction.

10 BRICK, ALLAN. "A Note on Perception and
    Communication in Beckett's Endgame." Modern
    Drama 4 (May):20-22.
        Defines Beckett's portrayal of the self in
    Endgame through the characters' attempts at
    perception and communication.

11 BRUSTEIN, ROBERT. "An Evening of 'Déjà-vu.'"
    New Republic 45 (2 Oct.):45-46.
        Criticizes Happy Days as being "too

predictable": "The language ... is flat and prosaic; the symbols are almost nude in their ambiguousness; and those repetitions of which Beckett is so fond ... have finally become rather boring." Reprinted: 1965.11, 1979.22.55.

12   BUTLER, MICHAEL. "Anatomy of Despair." <u>Encore</u> 8, no. 3 (May-June):17-24.
      Discusses the theme of the impossibility of communication in <u>Waiting for Godot</u>: "The failure in communication is worked out on several levels: as between equals -- Vladimir and Estragon; in terms of power -- the tramps and Pozzo; in terms of human misery -- the tramps and Lucky; as between master and servant -- Pozzo and Lucky; and finally in terms of religion and man -- Boy and the tramps.

13   CAMPROUX, CHARLES. "La Langue et le style des écrivains. Samuel Beckett: <u>Comment c'est</u>." <u>Lettres Françaises</u>, 11-17 May, p. 5.
      Analyzes the language and style of <u>How It Is</u> from several points of view: precision of details, refrains, use of present tense, punctuation, meaning of the words, syntax, structure.

14   CLURMAN, HAROLD. "Theatre." <u>Nation</u> 193 (7 Oct.):234-35.
      Reviews <u>Happy Days</u> at the Cherry Lane Theatre, "a poem of despair and forbearance ... to be seen and suffered." Clurman finds that the portrayal of pity and tenderness weakens the play.

15   COHN, RUBY. "Samuel Beckett Self-Translator." <u>PMLA</u> 76, no. 5 (Dec.):613-21.
      Examines the fundamental differences between the French and English versions of <u>Murphy</u>, <u>Waiting for Godot</u>, <u>Endgame</u>, and the trilogy.

16   _____. "<u>Watt</u> in the Light of <u>The Castle</u>."

Comparative Literature 13, no. 2 (Spring):
154-66.
Compares and contrasts Watt and The
Castle, two works in which the "authors have
given contemporary relevance to the myth of
the questing hero." Reprinted: 1976.33.

17   CORRIGAN, ROBERT W. "The Theatre in Search of a
Fix." Tulane Drama Review 5, no. 4 (June):
21-35.
Believes that the playwrights Beckett,
Ionesco, Adamov, Genet, and Ghelderode
attempted to revitalize contemporary theater,
to search for new techniques which would
express their vision of the world. Corrigan
points out the similar convictions of the
dramatists of the "Theatre of the Absurd":
the irrationality of all human actions, the
sense of man's isolation, and the impossibility of communication.

18   DRIVER, TOM F. "Beckett by the Madeleine."
Columbia University Forum 4, no. 3 (Summer):2155.
In this often quoted interview with
Beckett, Driver notes Beckett's feelings
about "the tension in art between the mess
and form," the battle between life and death
in his plays, religion, and the subject of
distress in his writings. Driver emphasizes
Beckett's personal qualities of sympathy and
friendliness and postulates his "love for
human beings" in his works: "The plays are
themselves evidence of a human capacity to
see one's situation and by that very fact to
transcend it." Reprinted: 1964.25,
1979.22.48; reprinted in part: 1968.48.

19   _____. "Unsweet Song." Christian Century 78
(11 Oct.):1208-9.
Since he feels he had underestimated
Endgame (1958.11) in a previous review,
Driver wonders whether he will also change
his mind about this review of Happy Days. He
believes Happy Days lacks "the poetic

incantations one is used to finding in
Beckett" and the "second level of import that
belongs to non-realistic theater."

20   *[Endgame: Plans.] Times (London), 18 Sept.,
      p. 14.
           Source: Tanner, 1969.113;unverified.

21   ESSLIN, MARTIN. "Samuel Beckett: The Search
      for the Self." In The Theatre of the Absurd.
      Garden City, N.Y.
           Reprinted: 1963.24, 1968.24, 1969.38; see
      1968.24 for annotation.

22   ESTANG, LUC. "Comment c'est." Figaro Lit-
      téraire, 18 Feb., p. 15.
           Reprinted: 1961.23.

23   _____. "Comment c'est: Samuel Beckett." Atlas
      1, no. 2 (Apr.):76-77.
           Describes the language, form, and situa-
      tion in How It Is, defining the novel as
      "Aliterature": "The rather visceral expres-
      sion of a man, of his obsessions, of his
      revolt and of his own derision, and also an
      example of the disorder of the contemporary
      spirit." Reprint of 1961.22.

24   *FABRE, PIERRE. "Beckett et Borgès -- Le Prix
      International des Editeurs revient à des
      auteurs difficiles." Carrefour, no. 870 (17
      May), p. 25.

25   FITCH, BRIAN. "Narrateur et narration dans la
      trilogie romanesque de Samuel Beckett:
      Molloy, Malone meurt, L'Innommable."
      Bulletin des Jeunes Romanistes 3 (May):13-20.
           Examines the distance between the narrator
      and his narration in the novels of the
      trilogy: the uncertainty of the world
      described, the reduction of words to meaning-
      less sounds, and the unnatural and complex
      character of the rapport between narrator and
      narration.

26   FLETCHER, JOHN. "Actualités: Comment c'est,
       par Samuel Beckett." Lettres Nouvelles, 9,
       no. 13 (Apr.):169-71.
          Believes Beckett pursues a double "quest"
       in How It Is: 1) that of a completely
       renewed literary genre, in which poetry and
       novel blend, and 2) that of a syntax and
       language suited to the portrayal of a hero
       who inhabits a world totally different than
       our everyday world.

27   No entry.

28   FLOOD, ETHELBERT. "A Reading of Beckett's
       Godot." Culture 22 (Sept.):257-62.
          Analyzes the characters, their "human"
       actions, and emotions in Waiting for Godot.

29   FOURNIER, EDITH. "Pour que la boue me soit
       contée ..." Critique 17, no. 168 (May):412-
       18.
          Underlines the major themes and the poetic
       structure of How It Is. Fournier sees this
       work as an exploration of self, an attempt to
       communicate with one's inner being, and a
       quest of the other.

30   *GALEY, MATTHIEU. "Comment c'est." Arts, 25
       Jan.
          Source: Bryer et al, 1972.7;unverified.

31   GILMAN, RICHARD. "The Stage: Beckett's Happy
       Days." Commonweal 75, no. 3 (13 Oct.):69-70.
          Assesses Happy Days as less successful
       than Beckett's previous plays but also
       demonstrates its undeniable effectiveness:
       "The miracle lies in the fact that here every
       element that has been thought to be necessary
       to the theater's conquest of life ... has
       dwindled to a set of notations and gestures
       ... and yet life continues to rise from
       Beckett's stage as it does from few others."

32   GREGORY, HORACE. "The Dying Gladiators of
       Samuel Beckett." In The Dying Gladiators and

Other Essays. London: Evergreen Books; New
York: Grove Press, pp. 165-76.
    Reprint of: 1956.17; reprinted: 1973.37.

33   GRESSET, MICHEL. "Le 'Parce que' chez Faulkner
      et le 'donc' chez Beckett." Lettres Nouvel-
      les 9, no. 19 (Nov.):124-38.
          Evaluates the use of the words "because"
      and "therefore" or "then" in the works of
      Faulkner and Beckett respectively. He
      analyzes these expressions as "signs" which
      designate the author's philosophy or lan-
      guage: whereas Faulkner strove to renew the
      complex structural elements of the novel,
      Beckett chose to severely limit his prose
      works to reflect the inability to communi-
      cate.

34   GROSSVOGEL, DAVID. "Ionesco, Adamov, Beckett."
      In Twentieth Century French Drama. New York:
      Colombia University Press, pp. 313-34.
      Beckett: pp. 324-34.
          Analyzes Waiting for Godot and Endgame.
      Grossvogel finds that Endgame is a more
      temporal, superficial play: "Because these
      people [Hamm and Clov] are making metaphysi-
      cal statements at a time when they should be
      enacting a genuine drama, the lament of a
      terrible waiting fails to awaken in the
      spectator an awareness of his own being and
      of man's fate. The promise of Godot has not
      been fulfilled." Followed by a general
      bibliography. Reprint of 1958.17.

35   *"Happy Days." Times (London), 17 Nov., p. 21.
          Source: Tanner, 1969.113;unverified.

36   HEPPENSTALL, RAYNER. The Fourfold Tradition:
      Notes on the French and English Literatures
      with Some Ethnological and Historical Asides.
      London: Barrie and Rockcliff; Norfolk: New
      Directions, pp. 254-65.
          Reviews the major stages of Beckett's life
      and literary career and examines his bilin-
      gualism, his characters, his use of interior
      monologue.

37   JUIN, HUBERT. "Le Premier Prix International
        des Editeurs: Samuel Beckett et Jorge Luis
        Borges." Lettres Françaises, 11-17 May, pp.
        1-4.
           Announces the award of the Prix Interna-
        tional des Editeurs to Beckett and Borges and
        briefly describes Beckett's career and the
        subject of his works.

38   KANTERS, ROBERT. "En attendant Godot." Express
        11 May, p. 49.
           Reviews Waiting for Godot as it returns to
        Paris after being performed around the world,
        describing the play as a theater of amnesia
        and the "a-humain" condition."

39   KARL, FREDERICK R. "Waiting for Beckett: Quest
        and Re-Quest." Sewanee Review 69, no. 4
        (Oct.-Dec.):661-76.
           Examines the quest for identity in Murphy,
        Watt, and the trilogy: "For Beckett,
        moreover, the quest is not melodramatic or
        tragic, but comic, the quest for a self that
        even the protagonist knows cannot be
        recovered." Reprinted: 1962.45, 1963.41.

40   KENNER, HUGH. Samuel Beckett: A Critical
        Study. New York: Grove Press, 208 pp.
           Reprinted in part 1959.22, 1967.62;
        reprinted in a revised edition 1968.37; see
        1968.37 for annotation.

41   _____. "Voices in the Night." Spectrum 5, no.
        1 (Spring):3-20.
           Focuses on two aspects of Beckett's works;
        the voice of the Beckett personage and the
        Beckett plot, which Kenner feels is simply an
        encounter between persons. Kenner examines
        the "strangest, most abstract, and most
        hauntingly intimate development" of these
        themes in How It Is. References are made to
        Wordsworth, Descartes, and Newton. Reprinted
        from 1961.40; reprinted 1979.22.52.

42   LENNON, PETER. "Samuel Beckett's Month."

Manchester Guardian Weekly, 8 June, p. 14.
Reviews Waiting for Godot at the Théâtre
de France in Paris. Since Roger Blin had to
leave Paris in the early stages of rehearsal,
Beckett remained to supervise the production,
which turned out to be lacking in comical
touches.

43   "The Long Wait." Times Literary Supplement
(London), 5 May, p. 277.
Discusses a feature on the Third Programme
"Waiting for What?" in which Peter Bull,
Pozzo in the 1955 production of Waiting for
Godot and Peter Hall, the producer, presented
their memories and experiences with the play.

44   MAYOUX, JEAN-JACQUES. "Comment c'est."
Mercure de France 342 (June):293-97.
Feels that Melville's "Mardi" portrays the
first "Beckettian" character, resembling
Murphy, Molloy and Malone. This type of
personage is contrasted with the narrators of
The Unnamable and How It Is. Specifically
How It Is, which resumes the vision and
themes of The Unnamable, presents a more
austere and inflexible portrait of this
dissociated voice, an "author who, having
become his own copyist, records with some
kind of indifference the first motion of
spontaneous creation coming out of himself."
Reprinted: 1979.22.51.

45   MELESE, PIERRE. "Avant-Garde Theatre in
France." Theatre Annual 18:1-16. Beckett:
pp. 6-8.
Describes two trends in the avant-garde
theater, works brought about by poetic
imagination and those dependent on concrete
realism. In this context, Mélèse briefly
portrays Beckett's theater as a parody of
human behavior in which life represents only
negation and suffering.

46   MERCIER, VIVIAN. "Samuel Beckett and the
Sheela-na-gig." Kenyon Review 23, no. 2

(Spring):299-324. Beckett: pp. 322-24.
Discusses the Irish propensity for the grotesque and macabre descending from pre-history and continuing in the works of the moderns. Beckett's use of the grotesque and macabre is presented through examples from Waiting for Godot, Watt, Endgame and Malone Dies. Mercier concludes that Beckett's relationship to traditional Irish humor is tangential: "Beckett might be described as in the Gaelic tradition but not of it."

47   MITGANG, HERBERT. "Waiting for Beckett -- And His Happy Days Premiere." New York Times, 17 Sept., sec. 2, pp. 1-3.
Discusses the world premiere of Happy Days which was to take place at the Cherry Lane Theatre, focusing on director Alan Schneider's relationship with Beckett and his productions of Beckett's plays.

48   MONNIER, ADRIENNE. Dernières gazettes et écrits divers. Paris: Mercure de France, pp. 15-20.
Gives her impressions of Roger Blin's production of Waiting for Godot and Beckett's translation of Anna Livia Plurabelle.

49   NADEAU, MAURICE. "Comment c'est par Samuel Beckett." Express, 26 Jan., pp. 25-26.
In this review of How It Is, provides a description of the situation of the narrator and his cyclical journey, and points out the disappearance of the bitter humor of Beckett's previous novels and plays. Reprinted: 1972.22.49.

50   *PARIS, JEAN. "L'Engagement d'aujourd'hui." Liberté 3 (Nov.):683-90.

51   *PINGET, ROBERT. "Old Tune: Translated by Samuel Beckett." New Yorker 37 (1 Apr.): 100.
Source: Tanner, 1969.113;unverified.

52   PORTAL, GEORGES. "Pour l'amour de Dieu."
      Ecrits de Paris (July-Aug.), pp. 139-46.
            Reviews the revival of Waiting for Godot
      ten years later, emphasizing the play's ever
      present value of surprise and novelty.
      Portal feels that Beckett's work is a
      "Pascalian" force that questions man, his
      destiny, his end, and his relationship with
      God.

53   SMITH, MICHAEL. "Theater: Cafe Round-Up."
      Village Voice, 23 Feb., p. 10.
            Describes a reading of Beckett's All That
      Fall at the Figaro. Smith suggests that
      Beckett combines the approaches of Synge and
      Joyce with his own point of view.

54   TALLMER, JERRY. "The Magic Box." Evergreen
      Review 5 (July-Aug.):117-22.
            Criticizes Alan Scheider's television
      production of Waiting for Godot with Burgess
      Meredith and Zero Mostel as a failure due to
      the nature of the television medium, which is
      inadequate to reproduce dramatic works with
      integrity.

55   THIBAUDEAU, JEAN. "Comment c'est." Temps
      Modernes 16, no. 180 (Apr.):1384-92.
            After briefly discussing Beckett's work
      from The Unnamable through Krapp's Last Tape,
      Thibaudeau analyzes the situation, narrator,
      and form of How It Is.

56   TOUCHARD, PIERRE-AIME. "Le Théâtre de Samuel
      Beckett." Revue de Paris 68 (Feb.):73-87.
            Interprets Beckett's tragic vision of the
      world through an analysis of his plays
      Waiting for Godot, Endgame, Act Without
      Words, and Krapp's Last Tape.

57   TYNAN, KENNETH. "Fin de partie and Acte sans
      Paroles (1957)." In Curtains. Selections
      from the Criticism and Related Writings. New
      York: Atheneum, pp. 401-3.
            Reprint of 1957.46.

58 _____. "Waiting for Godot (1955)." In Curtains. Selections from the Criticism and
   Related Writings. New York: Atheneum, pp.
   101-3.
      Believes Waiting for Godot appeals to a
   more fundamental definition of drama than had
   previously existed and serves as a metaphor
   of life: "Passing the time in the dark,
   [Beckett] suggests, is not only what drama is
   about but also what life is about. Existence
   depends on those metaphysical micawbers who
   will go on waiting, against all rational
   argument, for something which may one day
   turn up to explain the purpose of living."

59 *"[U.S. Performance of Happy Days.]" Times
   (London), 19 Sept., p. 14.
      Source: Tanner, 1969.113;unverified.

60 WELLWORTH, G.E. "Life in the Void: Samuel
   Beckett." University of Kansas City Review
   28, no. 1 (Oct.):25-33.
      Describes Beckett's pessimism, the
   uselessness of thought and the pointlessness
   of all human action. Reprinted: 1964.106.

61 WILLIAMS, RAYMOND. "Hope Deferred." New
   Statesman 61 (19 May):802.
      Reviews Waiting for Godot at the Theatre
   Royal Stratford. Williams describes Godot as
   a morality play of uncertainty in which the
   basic themes have Christian origins. The
   opposition of good and evil and the interaction of the two contrasting pairs of characters are introduced.

62 YERLES, PIERRE. "Le Théâtre de Samuel Beckett."
   Revue Nouvelle 33, no. 4 (15 Apr.):401-7.
      Examines different aspects of Beckett's
   theater: the absence of action, the disappearance of nature, the absence of time, and
   the condition of his characters.

1961-1962

1   LEES, F.N. "Samuel Beckett." <u>Manchester
     Literary and Philosophical Society. Memoirs
     and Proceedings</u> 104:33-46.
          Offers a general description of Beckett's
     ideas and an introduction to his major works:
     <u>Watt</u>, <u>Waiting for Godot</u>, <u>Endgame</u>, the
     trilogy, and <u>How It Is</u>.

1962

1   ALBERES, RENE MARILL. <u>Histoire du roman
     moderne</u>. Paris: Albin-Michel, pp. 372-74.
          Believes Beckett's novels <u>Molloy</u>, <u>Malone
     Dies</u>, and <u>How It Is</u>, lack a definite form,
     and present a pessimistic image of the human
     condition. In <u>How It Is</u>, Beckett goes so
     far as to choose a symbol for mankind from
     the "sub-human."

2   ASHMORE, JEROME. "Philosophical Aspects of
     <u>Godot</u>." <u>Symposium</u> 16, no. 4 (Winter):296-
     306.
          Views <u>Waiting for Godot</u> as an exposure of
     man's limitations and the futility of
     existence: "<u>Waiting for Godot</u> is a great
     parody of man's notions of divinity, of
     progress, of comfort, and of intersubjec-
     tivity. It is a delineation of the triumph
     of the void and a vast panorama of the
     collapse of man's claims to value and to
     knowledge."

3   ASHWORTH, ARTHUR. "New Theater: Ionesco,
     Beckett, Pinter." <u>Southerly</u> 22, no. 3:145-
     54.
          Describes the revolt against realism in
     the New Theater. In Beckett's dramas
     character, action, and dialogue are reduced
     to a minimum.

4   *BARTHOLOMEW, RATI. "Theatre: Three One-Act
     Plays." <u>Thought</u> 14 (10 Feb.):18.

5   BECKETT, SAMUEL. "Beckett's Letters on Endgame:
     Extracts from His Correspondence with
     Director Alan Schneider." In The Village
     Voice Reader: A Mixed Bag from the Greenwich
     Village Newspaper. Edited by Daniel Wolf and
     Edwin Francher. Garden City, New York:
     Doubleday, 1962; Reprinted by Grove Press,
     New York, 1963, pp. 182-86.
         Reprints excerpts from Beckett's letters
     to Alan Schneider, dated Dec. 1955-Mar. 1958,
     regarding the development of Endgame.

6   "Beckett's Play for B.B.C." Times (London), 1
     Nov., p. 8.
         Briefly comments on Words and Music,
     remarking that the play is a new working of a
     theme common to Beckett's fiction -- "the
     master and the servant and the power of each
     over the other."

7   BERGHOF, HERBERT. "Letters to the Editor." In
     The Village Voice Reader: A Mixed Bag from
     the Greenwich Village Newspaper. Edited by
     Daniel Wolf and Edwin Fancher. Garden City,
     New York: Doubleday, 1962. Reprinted by
     Grove Press, New York, 1963, pp. 72-73.
         Attacks Jerry Tallmer's review of Waiting
     for Godot. As director of the play, Berghof
     feels that his production is faithful to
     Beckett's work and that "no concession was
     made in the Broadway production." See
     1962.65, 1962.74.

8   BLAU, HERBERT. "Windlasses and Assays of Bias."
     Encore 9, no. 5 (Sept.-Oct.):24-40. Beckett:
     pp. 26-30.
         As co-director of the Actors' Workshop in
     San Francisco, Blau reminisces about his
     productions of Waiting for Godot and Endgame.

9   BLOCK, HASKELL M., and ROBERT G. SHEDD.
     "Samuel Beckett." In Masters of Modern
     Drama. New York: Random House, pp. 1102-3.
         This introductory essay to Endgame offers
     biographical information, possible

influences, and interpretations of Beckett's major prose and dramatic works. Block feels that all of Beckett's plays are based on a system of antitheses.

10   BOISDEFFRE, PIERRE DE. "Samuel Beckett et la fin de la littérature." In <u>Où va le roman</u>? Paris: Del Duca, pp. 269-80.
      Quoting extensively from the trilogy, offers a general description of the Beckettian narrator, as the voice of a poet announcing his own death. Uncertain of his identity or destiny, the voice can only be sure of his own suffering.

11   BRAY, J.J. "<u>The Ham Funeral</u>." <u>Meanjin Quarterly</u> 21 (Mar.):32-34.
      Produced at the Union Theatre, Adelaide in November, 1961, Patrick White's <u>The Ham Funeral</u> anticipates the techniques used by Fry, Dylan Thomas, Beckett, Ionesco, and Pinter.

12   BROOK, PETER. "<u>Happy Days</u> and Marienbad." <u>Encore: The Voice of Vital Theatre</u> 9 (Jan.- Feb.):34-38.
      Compares Beckett's <u>Happy Days</u> with Robbe-Grillet's <u>Last Year at Marienbad</u>: "I feel that the world of <u>Marienbad</u> ... is an intellectual illustration using visual material that we've grown used to over the years in the ballet, in Cocteau's films and so on. This is a very different cup of tea to the haunting, worrying, challenging images struck by Beckett." Reprinted: 1965.9.

13   BUTLER, HARRY L. "Balzac and Godeau, Beckett and Godot: A Curious Parallel." <u>Romance Notes</u> 3, no. 2 (Spring):13-17.
      In his comparison of <u>Waiting for Godot</u> and Balzac's <u>Mercadet</u>, discovers similarities between the characters Godot and Godeau which suggest a common role in the two plays and differences which reveal "the wide divergences of perspective and preoccupation of their

authors": "Whereas Balzac was concerned with
man's struggle in society, whose values were
simply stated as rules of the game, not
questioned, Beckett writing with an existentialist orientation, is concerned with the
problem of man's existence in a world that is
absurd and in which there are no values
external to man himself, in which life has no
essential meaning."

14   CHAMBERS, ROSS. "The Other." Nation (Sydney),
     no. 103 (22 Sept.), pp. 22-23.
         Reviews Happy Days focusing on the role of
     Willie, "the Other who gives us the only
     existence we have while depriving us of the
     only existence we would like to have ..."

15   _____. "Samuel Beckett and the Padded Cell."
     Meanjin 21, no. 4:451-62.
         Uses Murphy, "one of the embryonic forms
     of Beckett's later works," to shed light on
     the structure of the trilogy. Chambers
     examines Beckett's portrayal of a conscious-
     ness which exists outside of space and time
     but cannot conceive of itself except in space
     and time.

16   *CHANAN, GABBY. "Incantations." Isis, no.
     1,407 (24 Jan.), p. 23.

17   CLURMAN, HAROLD. "Introduction." In Seven
     Plays of the Modern Theatre. New York:
     Grove Press, pp. vii-xii.
         Introduces Waiting for Godot as the
     "seminal play" of the modern theater.
     Clurman briefly describes the situation of
     the characters and praises the terseness of
     eloquence in the drama.

18   COFFEY, BRIAN. "Memory's Murphy Maker: Some
     Notes on Samuel Beckett." Threshold 17:28-
     36.
         Presents memories of Beckett and a brief
     commentary of his work.

19   COHN, RUBY. "Comment c'est de quoi rire."
        French Review 35, no. 6 (May):563-69.
            Examines the unidentifiable characters in
        How It Is, their actions, and their posses-
        sions.

20   _____. "Play and Player in the Plays of Samuel
        Beckett." Yale French Studies, no. 29
        (Spring-Summer), pp. 43-48.
            Feels that Beckett enacts a new variation
        on the metaphor of "theatrum mundi": "Man,
        the actor, no longer believes in the play;
        only a spectator can force the show to dodder
        on. And to this end, says Beckett, the actor
        may have to invent his audience."

21   _____. Samuel Beckett: The Comic Gamut. New
        Brunswick, New Jersey: Rutgers University
        Press, 340 pp.
            Uses Bergson's catalog of comic techniques
        as a spring-board for this study of the comic
        elements in Beckett's prose and drama.
        Demonstrating almost the entire comic range,
        Beckett gives "new depth ... to old tradi-
        tions," as well as illuminating the recent
        study of irony as a comic mode (Northrop
        Frye). Followed by a "Checklist of Beckett
        Criticism." Reprinted in part: 1963.17,
        1969.27.

22   "The Core of the Onion." Times Literary
        Supplement (London), 21 Dec., p. 988.
            Calls attention to the concepts of meaning
        and self-exploration in Beckett's work, as
        well as Beckett's discarding of the normal
        properties of the novel and play.

23   DONOGHUE, DENIS. "The Play of Words." Listener
        68, no. 1,737 (12 July):55-57.
            Claims that dialogue has degenerated into
        a "sequence of purely verbal events" in the
        works of Beckett and Pinter, and has nothing
        to do with the theatre of cruelty created by
        Artaud.

24   DUKORE, BERNARD F. "Gogo, Didi and the Absent
         Godot." Drama Survey 1 (Winter):301-7.
         Interprets the names of the characters in
         Waiting for Godot, underscoring the possible
         religious and existential interpretations of
         the play. See 1963.20, 1963.51, 1966.33.

25   ESSLIN, MARTIN. "Forget the Dustbins." Plays
         and Players 10, no. 2 (Nov.):32-33.
         Refutes the "misconceived" notion that
         Beckett's works are uniformly depressing.
         Esslin feels that Beckett can make us see the
         world with serenity and cheerfulness: "Once
         we have accepted the basic precariousness of
         our situation ... we can laugh about most of
         the things we are apt to take too seriously."

26   _____. "Samuel Beckett." In The Novelist as
         Philosopher. Studies in French Fiction,
         1935-1960. Edited by John Cruickshank.
         London: Oxford University Press, pp. 128-46.
         Introduces Beckett's novels (from More
         Pricks than Kicks through How It Is) as a
         progressive exploration of the self.
         Reprinted: 1980.29.

27   *FLETCHER, D. "Molloy for Prime Minister."
         Left Wing, (Nov.), pp. 22-24.

28   FLETCHER, JOHN. "Samuel Beckett et Jonathan
         Swift: Vers une étude comparée." Littéra-
         tures, X: Annales publiées par la Faculté
         des Lettres de Toulouse 11, no. 1:81-117.
         Reviews the life, character, and literary
         evolution of Swift and Beckett, then examines
         the "myths and obsessions" that appear in
         both their works, and finally studies the
         literary methods they have in common.

29   FRIEDMAN, MELVIN J. "The Neglect of Time:
         France's Novel of the Fifties." Books Abroad
         36 (Spring):125-30.
         Comments on representatives of the New
         Novel movement: Robbe-Grillet, Sarraute,
         Butor, Simon, Mauriac, and Beckett.

30   GASCOIGNE, BAMBER. "Dying of the Light."
      Spectator 209 (19 Nov.):715-17.
           Suggests a continuity between Krapp's Last
      Tape and Happy Days: whereas Krapp's
      reaction to death was a defiant one, Winnie
      consoles herself and is no longer fearful of
      death.

31   *"Gaudy and Inane ...?" Times Literary
      Supplement (London), 25 May.
           Source: Bryer et al., 1972.7;unverified.

32   GELLERT, ROGER. "Long Pause for Gallantry."
      New Statesman 64 (9 Nov.):679.
           In this review of Happy Days at the Royal
      Court Theatre, questions whether "the
      experience that Beckett communicates to us
      can any longer be called dramatic, or moving,
      or poetic, -- or in a word -- valid."
      Gellert analyzes the scene and characters, in
      particular Winnie's "happiness."

33   GLICKSBERG, CHARLES. "The Lost Self in Modern
      Literature." Personalist 43, no. 4
      (Autumn):527-38. Beckett: pp. 535-37.
           In the twentieth century certain writers
      have struggled to reveal imaginatively the
      breakdown of the ego. Glicksburg believes
      Beckett has carried this theory of fiction to
      its conclusion: "His 'dramatis personae' are
      picaresque ghosts in a nameless region,
      wandering lost in a fugue of wretched and
      invariably futile self-awareness, seeking an
      identity or an illumination of meaning that
      forever eludes them."

34   _____. "Samuel Beckett's World of Fiction."
      Arizona Quarterly 18, no. 1 (Spring):32-47.
           Discusses Beckett's "exploration of the
      chaos of the human mind" in Murphy and the
      trilogy: "Beckett's fiction draws the
      portrait of the modern nihilistic hero,
      alienated, solipsistically inarticulate,
      drowned in existential confusion and despair,
      full of fear and trembling but without faith,

entirely lost."

35   GROSSVOGEL, DAVID I.   "Samuel Beckett: The
        Difficulty of Dying."   In <u>Four Playwrights
        and a Postscript: Brecht, Ionesco, Beckett,
        Genet</u>.   Ithaca, New York: Cornell University
        Press, pp. 85-131.
            Identifies the anger these playwrights all
        experienced: they "were outraged by life as
        their society accepted it; and eventually,
        they were outraged by the human condition
        itself ... When they turned to the theater.
        it was not only in order to find a platform
        from which to speak the words of their
        revolt, but to find an expression whose very
        form might be that of their subverting
        anger."   Grossvogel focuses on Beckett's
        major theatrical achievements: <u>Waiting for
        Godot</u>, <u>Endgame</u>, <u>All That Fall</u>, <u>Embers</u>,
        <u>Krapp's Last Tape</u>, <u>Happy Days</u>.   Reissued
        under new title, see 1965.43.

36   GUICHARNAUD, JACQUES.   "The 'R' Effect."   <u>Esprit
        Créateur</u> 2 (Winter):159-65.
            Discusses the adverse criticism of the
        "new theatre" in France, and then underlines
        the major elements of the theatrical works of
        Beckett, Ionesco, Genet, Adamov, and Shehadé.
        The 'R' effect refers to the extra r in the
        word "merdre" spoken at the beginning of <u>Ubu
        roi</u>, and in this article it is used to
        designate "the systematic distortion of all
        the dark aspects of man's condition; the
        transposition, into free, whimsical, and even
        childish symbols, of stupidity, violence, and
        the fundamental injustice of the world of
        things."

37   HAMILTON, CAROL.   "Portrait in Old Age: The
        Image of Man in Beckett's Trilogy."   <u>Western
        Humanities Review</u> 16, no. 2 (Spring):157-65.
            Believes Beckett's characters are on the
        last lap of their metaphoric journeys: "...
        Beckett has created an image of man in his
        decline, that we recognize as our own.   His

personality like his clothes is tattered. He is alone; he is irrational; he is without hope or future. But he is alive to this world in which we also live, and which we know so little."

38   HAMILTON, KENNETH. "Negative Salvation in Samuel Beckett." <u>Queen's Quarterly</u> 69, no. 1 (Spring):102-11.
        Examines the concept of salvation in Beckett's plays and novels. While there is only one positive element in Beckett's understanding of salvation, man's freedom of choice, Beckett does not totally eradicate man's hope in the most futile of circumstances: "From the standpoint of Christian belief his vision must simultaneously attract and repel; for here is a powerful expression of the longing of man for a salvation which will transform him at the heart of his being, coupled with a Manichean repudiation of the goodness of creation."

39   HAYMAN, DAVID. "Quest for Meaninglessness: The Boundless Poverty of Molloy." In <u>Six Contemporary Novels: Six Introductory Essays in Modern Fiction</u>. Edited by William O.S. Sutherland. Austin, Texas: Humanities Research Center, University of Texas Department of English, pp. 90-112.
        Reprinted in a slightly different version: 1964.47, 1970.59.

40   HOFFMAN, FREDERICK. <u>Samuel Beckett: The Language of Self</u>. Carbondale: Southern Illinois University Press, 177 pp.
        Defines the two major metaphors of twentieth-century self-analysis: 1) metaphysical and moral, and 2) rationalist. The first part of the discussion follows a line of descent from Dostoevsky to Kafka, while the second part shows a line of inquiry leading from Descartes to Beckett.

41   HUBERT, RENEE RIESE. "The Couple and the

Performance in Samuel Beckett's Plays."
<u>Esprit Créateur</u> 2 (Winter):175-80.
Documents the relationship of the couple
in <u>Waiting for Godot</u>, <u>Endgame</u>, <u>Krapp's Last
Tape</u>, and <u>Happy Days</u>.

42   HUGHES, CATHERINE. "Beckett and the Game of
Life." <u>Catholic World</u> 195 (June):163-68.
Sees Beckett as "at best, the echo of an
almost pre-Christian tradition, at worst, the
banal repetition ... of Sartre, Camus, and a
host of others." Hughes examines Beckett's
view of God and the human condition in
<u>Waiting for Godot</u>, <u>Endgame</u>, and <u>Happy Days</u>.

43   _____. "Beckett's World: Wherein God Is
Continually Silent." <u>Critic</u> 20, no. 5 (Apr.-
May):40-42.
Discusses the theological implications of
<u>Waiting for Godot</u>, <u>Endgame</u>, and <u>Happy Days</u>,
man's "consciousness of his own lack of
permanence, his own need of a reason for
being, and an explanation."

44   JOHNSON, BRYAN S. "Saying is Inventing."
<u>Spectator</u>, 20 July, p. 92.
Believes <u>Happy Days</u> occupies a place in
Beckett's dramatic works similar to that of
<u>The Unnamable</u> in his novels -- it is a
statement on the writer's condition.

45   KARL, FREDERICK R. "Waiting for Beckett: Quest
and Request." In <u>The Contemporary English
Novel</u>. New York: Farrar, Straus, and
Cudahy, pp. 19-39 and passim.
Reprinted: 1961.39, 1963.41.

46   KENNER, HUGH. <u>Flaubert, Joyce and Beckett: The
Stoic Comedians</u>. Boston: Beacon Press;
London: W.H. Allen, 107 pp.
Defines the stoic as one who perceives the
field of possibilities available to him as
closed. Beckett as the heir to Joyce,
attempts to deal with the problem of the
impasse: "... plucking the fruits of

incompetence -- plays that seem unable to get
the title character onto the stage, novels
that issue merely in the fact that someone is
sitting in bed writing a novel, or that
founder amid logical perplexities of their
own propounding -- he evolves meanwhile, ...
a yet more comprehensive theory of what the
writer is doing with himself, and a yet more
general set of rules for the game he plays."
Reprinted and revised from 1962.46.

47   KERMODE, FRANK. "Beckett, Snow, and Pure
     Poverty." In <u>Puzzles and Epiphanies: Essays
     and Review, 1958-1961</u>. New York: Chilmark
     Press; London: Routeledge and Kegan Paul,
     pp. 155-63.
          Reprint of 1960.35.

48   KERN, EDITH. "Beckett's Knight of Infinite
     Resignation." <u>Yale French Studies</u>, no. 29,
     (Spring-Summer), pp. 49-56.
          Believes that Winnie in <u>Happy Days</u> comes
     to resemble Kierkegaard's "Knight of Infinite
     Resignation" who "convinced there is no
     happiness and knowing the absurdity of
     existence, shares the humdrum life of his
     fellow citizens."

49   KOTT, JAN. "<u>Le Roi Lear</u>, autrement dit <u>Fin de
     partie</u>." In <u>Shakespeare notre contemporain</u>.
     Translated by Anna Posner. Paris: Julliard,
     pp. 115-58.
          Reprint of 1962.50; reprinted: 1964.59,
     1964.60; see 1964.60 for annotation.

50   _____. "<u>Le Roi Lear</u> autrement dit <u>Fin de
     Partie</u>." <u>Temps Modernes</u> 18, no. 194
     (July):48-77.
          Reprinted: 1962.49, 1964.59, 1964.60; see
     1964.60 for annotation.

51   LE CLEC'H, GUY. "Sur une scène de Londres,
     Beckett crée sa 'première' femme et l'enterre
     aussitôt." <u>Figaro Littéraire</u>, 17 Nov., p.
     21.
          In <u>Happy Days</u> Beckett creates his first

female character. Le Clec'h points out that
since there is little movement on stage the
play is dependent on language to convey the
pathetic situation of our times.

52   LEWIS, ALLAN. "The Theater of the 'Absurd' --
     Beckett, Ionesco, Genet." In The Contem-
     porary Theatre: The Significant Playwrights
     of Our Time. New York: Crown, 259-81.
          Discusses Waiting for Godot as a "morality
     play in which not faith but doubt binds man
     to God," and evaluates the significance of
     the characters' names and the conflict set up
     between the two couples.

53   MAGUIRE, BRIAN PAUL. "L'Anti-Théâtre: Le
     Langage." Zagadnienia Rodzajów Literackich
     5, no. 9:43-65. Beckett: pp. 57-63.
          Characterizes "anti-théâtre" as theatre in
     which situations of language replace dramatic
     situations. Maguire discusses the works of
     Ionesco, Adamov and Beckett (Waiting for
     Godot, Endgame) in this context.

54   MAILER, NORMAN. "The Hip and the Square." In
     The Village Voice Reader: A Mixed Bag from
     the Greenwich Village Newspaper. Edited by
     Daniel Wolf and Edwin Fancher. Garden City,
     New York: Doubleday, 1962, pp. 76-77.
          Hypothesizes some alternate meanings for
     the title of Waiting for Godot and the
     importance of the theme of impotence in the
     play. Reprint of 1956.27a; see 1959.28.

55   MAROWITZ, CHARLES. "Paris Log." Encore: The
     Voice of Vital Theatre 36 (Mar.-Apr.):37-46.
     Beckett: pp. 43-45.
          Describes his meeting with Beckett to
     discuss Act Without Words II which Marowitz
     was to be staging, and comments on the New
     York production of Godot with Bert Lahr.

56   MERCIER, VIVIAN. "Samuel Beckett: In the
     Tradition though Not of It." In The Irish
     Comic Tradition. London: Oxford University

Press, pp. 74-77.
Explores the relationship between
sexuality and grotesque and macabre humor in
Beckett's works.

57   OATES, J.C. "The Trilogy of Samuel Beckett."
      Renascence 14, no. 3 (Spring):160-65.
      Compares the condition of Beckett's world
to the world suggested by David Hume in his
Treatise on Human Nature and his Inquiry
Concerning Human Understanding.

58   "One Sided Dialogue by Half-Buried Wife." Times
      (London), 2 Nov., p. 6.
      Believes the text of Happy Days conveys
the heart of the play: "the text is an
elaborate structure of internal harmonies,
with recurring clichés twisted into bitter
truths, and key phrases chiming ironically
through the development as in a passacaglia."

59   ONIMUS, JEAN. "L'Homme égaré: Notes sur le
      sentiment d'égarement dans la littérature
      actuel." In Face au monde actuel. Paris:
      Desclée de Brouwer, pp. 77-86.
      Reprint of 1954.5.

60   PRONKO, LEONARD C. "Samuel Beckett." In Avant-
      Garde: The Experimental Theater in France.
      Berkeley: University of California Press,
      pp. 22-58.
      Evaluates Beckett's major plays: action,
characters, themes, structure, grim humor,
dialogue, interpretation, Beckett's view of
life, poetic language, and stylistic devices.

61   _____. "Theater and Anti-Theater." In Avant-
      Garde: The Experimental Theater in France.
      Berkeley: University of California Press,
      pp. 112-53.
      Investigates two fundamental definitions
of anti-theater which relate to the works of
Beckett and Ionesco: 1) that the new drama
is fundamentally different from other
theaters we know and 2) that anti-drama

suggests an attempt to return to the roots of
drama, freeing theater from superfluous and
unauthentic elements.

62   RADKE, JUDITH. "The Theater of Samuel Beckett:
      Une durée à animer." Yale French Studies no.
      29 (Spring-Summer), pp. 57-64.
      Demonstrates how the same problem faces
      Beckett and his characters Vladimir and
      Estragon: Beckett must provide his charac-
      ters with verbal and physical actions to
      perform throughout the play, while the
      characters must animate the duration of their
      lifetime.

63   REID, ALEC. "Beckett and the Drama of Unknow-
      ing." Drama Survey 2, no. 2 (Fall):130-38.
      Demonstrates the way Beckett deals with
      the emotion of non-knowing in his dramas for
      radio and stage. Reid points out that the
      viewer should not seek to interpret Beckett's
      plays through "allegory and symbol": "In his
      avoidance of material detail, in his use of
      evocation, in his rejection of naturalistic
      theatrical convention, he is trying to get to
      the general avoiding the particular. Hence
      content and form alike must avoid definition
      ..."

64   RICKELS, MILTON. "Existential Themes in
      Beckett's Unnamable." Criticism 4, no. 2
      (Spring):134-47.
      Examines the experience of existence in
      The Unnamable: the uncertainty, anxiety,
      suffering, solitude, and meaninglessness of
      existence as well as the concept of God and
      the "other." Rickels briefly refers to
      Sartre's Being and Nothingness.

65   ROSSET, BARNEY. "A Note." In The Village Voice
      Reader: A Mixed Bag from the Greenwich
      Village Newspaper. Edited by Daniel Wolf and
      Edwin Fancher. Garden City, New York:
      Doubleday, 1962. Reprinted by Grove Press,
      New York, 1963, p. 73.

Mentions that he and Beckett appreciated
Jerry Tallmer's review of <u>Waiting for Godot</u>.
See 1962.74.

66   *"Samuel Beckett malade mental ou visionnaire."
      <u>Courrier Dramatique de l'Ouest</u>, no. 47.

67   SCOTT, NATHAN A.   "The Recent Journey into the
      Zone of Zero: The Example of Beckett and His
      Despair of Literature."   <u>Centennial Review</u> 6,
      no. 2 (Spring):144-81. Beckett: pp. 160-81.
           Outlines the main sources of modern French
      literature: Baudelaire, Lautréamont,
      Rimbaud, Mallarmé, Valéry, Pierre Reverdy,
      and the Surrealists.   Presenting Beckett as
      the most impressive representative of the
      French contemporary tradition, Scott analyzes
      the characters of Beckett's major novels and
      plays: "... they are bereft of every
      imaginable security, and, in their cheerless,
      hopeless world of zero, they have only enough
      vitality remaining to summon a dry and feeble
      gesture of irony, the suggestion that maimed
      though they are, they can still perhaps exult
      in nothingness."

68   SHAW, IAIN. "But What Does It Mean?"   <u>Tribune</u>
      (London), 16 Nov., p. 11.
           Reviews <u>Happy Days</u>, finding the play
      boring and Beckett's talent diminishing.

69   *SIGAL, CLANCY AND GRAHAME WALLACE.   "Leave
      Yahooism to Your Enemies."   <u>Tribune</u> (London),
      23 Nov., p. 8.

70   SIMPSON, ALAN.   <u>Beckett and Behan and a Theater
      in Dublin</u>. London: Routeledge, 193 pp.
      Beckett: pp. 62-137 and passim.
           Describes his association with Beckett and
      Brendan Behan and his productions of Behan's
      <u>The Quare Fellow</u> in 1954 and Beckett's
      <u>Waiting for Godot</u> in 1955 at the Pike Theatre
      in Dublin. Simpson portrays the two play-
      wrights, Ireland, and the theater of the
      fifties in general. His memories of the

difficulties, objectives, and practical
considerations of his productions are
presented informally. Reprinted in part:
1967.98.

71   SMITH, H.A. "Dipsychus Among the Shadows." In
     Contemporary Theatre. Edited by John Russell
     Brown and Bernard Harris. London: Edward
     Arnold, pp. 139-64. Beckett: pp. 155-63.
          Describes the "two fundamental states of
     consciousness Beckett presents in Waiting for
     Godot: Pozzo/Lucky belong to the world of
     time, Estragon/Vladimir to the timeless."

72   STYAN, J.L. "Beckett, Ionesco and Others." In
     The Dark Comedy. The Development of Modern
     Comic Tragedy. London: Cambridge University
     Press, pp. 226-38.
          Offers a brief description of the humor,
     manner of presentation, and the human
     allegory depicted in Waiting for Godot, All
     That Fall, and Endgame.

73   SYPHER, WYLIE. "The Anonymous Self: A Defen-
     sive Humanism." In Loss of the Self in
     Modern Literature and Art. New York: Random
     House, pp. 147-58.
          Notes Beckett's desire to eliminate the
     "self" in his novels, particularly The
     Unnamable.

74   TALLMER, JERRY. "Godot: Still Waiting." In
     The Village Voice Reader: A Mixed Bag from
     the Greenwich Village Newspaper. Edited by
     Daniel Wolf and Edwin Fancher. Garden City,
     New York: Doubleday, 1962. Reprinted by
     Grove Press, New York, 1963, pp. 73-76.
          Refutes point by point, statements made by
     Brooks Atkinson in his review of Waiting for
     Godot. Reprint of 1957.42a.

75   TAYLOR, JOHN RUSSELL. "Do-It-Yourself." Plays
     and Players 10, no. 3 (Dec.):54-55.
          Reviews Happy Days at the Royal Court
     Theatre, pointing out the variety of

interpretations and responses provoked by
this "hermetically sealed off" play.

76   TYNAN, KENNETH. "Intimations of Mortality."
        Observer, 4 Nov., p. 29.
        Briefly comments on Happy Days which he
        feels is too long and too full of pauses, a
        feminine counterpart of Krapp's Last Tape:
        "It is a dramatic metaphor extended beyond
        its capacities."

77   VIA, DAN O., JR. "Waiting for Godot and Man's
        Search for Community." Journal of Bible and
        Religion, n.v. (Jan.):32-37.
        Suggest an alternative interpretation for
        Waiting for Godot -- "The theme of the play
        appears to be the unfulfilled search for
        community, for I-Thou relationships in
        contrast to I-It relationships." Via feels
        that Vladimir and Estragon represent hope
        before the Incarnation, thus men estranged
        from others, lacking a true community.

78   WEALES, GERALD. "The Language of Endgame."
        Tulane Drama Review 6, no. 4 (June):107-17.
        Reviews Endgame, stressing the in-
        dividuality of the characters, and the way
        Beckett uses langauge (contrasts, verbal
        play, repetitions, sound of words, verbal
        simplicity, etc.).

79   WILSON, COLIN. "Samuel Beckett." In The
        Strength to Dream: Literature and the
        Imagination. Boston: Houghton Mifflin, pp.
        86-91.
        Examines the implications of pessimism in
        Beckett's works, comparing him to Leonid
        Andeyev, Chekhov, Kafka and Eliot. Wilson
        feels Beckett's work is unoriginal and
        objects to his refusal to alter his nihilis-
        tic stance: "Beckett accidentally brought
        off the right combination in Godot. But
        apparently he decided he was betraying his
        own pessimism by sugaring the pill. His

later works make one think of a man trying to
write a symphony using only one note."

1962-1963

1   MORSE, J. MITCHELL. "The Contemplative Life
      According to Samuel Beckett." <u>Hudson Review</u>
      15, no. 4 (Winter):512-24.
         Describes the protagonists of Beckett's
      novels -- how they "suffer from ... the
      intensity of life with which they live in
      their own minds." Morse believes Beckett has
      reconciled the atheist and antitheist
      positions: "... in the novels God becomes
      man repeatedly, incarnating himself in a
      series of weary neurotics who he delights in
      frustrating, tormenting, mutilating and
      driving mad."

1963

1   ABEL, LIONEL. "Beckett and James Joyce in
      Endgame." In <u>Metatheater: A New View of
      Dramatic Form</u>. New York: Hill and Wang, pp.
      134-40.
         Reprint of 1959.2

2   _____. "Beckett and Metatheater." In <u>Meta-
      theater: A New View of Dramatic Form</u>. New
      York: Hill and Wang, pp. 83-85.
         Beckett's plays suggest that some decisive
      action has gone on before the curtain rises:
      the characters "show us the results of drama-
      tic action, but not that action itself.
      Their drama consists in having been capable
      of drama at some time, and in their remem-
      brance of that time."

3   ALLEY, J.N. "Proust and Art: The Anglo-
      American Critical View." <u>Revue de Littéra-
      ture Comparée</u> 37 (July-Sept.):410-30.
         Beckett: p. 411.
         Quotes Beckett's interpretation of the

significance of music in Proust's A la
recherche du temps perdu.

4   ANGUS, WILLIAM. "Modern Theatre Reflects the
    Times." Queen's Quarterly 70, no. 2 (Sum-
    mer):255-63. Beckett: pp. 259-60.
        Examines Beckett's protrayal of death in
    life -- human decay and futility -- in
    Krapp's Last Tape.

5   ASTRE, GEORGES ALBERT. "L'Humanisme de la
    pourriture." Molloy. Paris: Union Générale
    d'Editions, pp. 279-81.
        Criticizes Molloy as a laborious exercise;
    feels that Beckett's ideal is the acceptance
    of a "decaying" existence, a passive wait for
    death. Reprinted from 1951.1.

6   "Beckett and the Theatre of the Concrete." Time
    81 (28 June):48-50.
        Presents the audience's reaction to
    Beckett's Play produced in Ulm, West Germany.
    Their disappointment stems from their
    preference for the more modern "Theatre of
    the Concrete."

7   BLANZAT, JEAN. "Un livre-événement." In
    Molloy. Paris: Union Générale d'Editions,
    pp. 264-65.
        Reprinted from 1951.3.

8   *BOLL, DAVID. "Questing for Godot." Books and
    Bookmen 8 (May):45-46.

9   BRAY, BARBARA. "The New Beckett." Observer,
    16 June, p. 29.
        Reviews the premiere performance of Play
    and the production of two mimes Act Without
    Words I and II in Ulm, West Germany.
    Although the story of Play is banal, the
    inventiveness and the theatrical and poetic
    power are so intense that "these three
    suffering heads conjure up not only three
    whole lives, but also awaken the
    reverberations that transform them from the

trivial to the universal."

10   BREE, GERMAINE. "Beckett's Abstractors of
         Quintessence." <u>French Review</u> 36, no. 6
         (May):567-76.
            Compares and contrasts the satirical
         techniques used in Beckett's <u>Watt</u> and
         Rabelais' works: "Beckett sardonically
         undermines that 'good giant' Pantagruel and
         the reassuring vision of the world on which
         we rely. Instead we have the mismatched
         shoes, the tentative gait, the unstable image
         of Mr. Watt ... no abstractor of quintessence
         as he would like to be, but rather an odd
         creature in an incongruous world."
         Reprinted: 1976.13.

11   BROWN, JOHN RUSSELL. "Mr. Beckett's Shake-
         speare." <u>Critical Quarterly</u> 5, no. 4
         (Winter):310-26.
            Juxtaposes new dramatists and
         Shakespearean critics: using <u>Waiting for
         Godot</u> as an example, Brown discusses the
         ambiguity of the symbols in the play and its
         unity.

12   _____. "Mr. Pinter's Shakespeare." <u>Critical
         Quarterly</u> 5, no. 3 (Autumn):251-65.
            Redefines the format of traditional drama
         to more accurately analyze the works of
         Pinter, Ionesco, and Beckett. Shakespeare's
         plays are also viewed from this new perspec-
         tive. Reprinted: 1964.11.

13   No Entry.

14   CHAMBERS, ROSS. "Beckett, homme des situations
         limites." <u>Cahiers Renaud-Barrault</u> 44
         (Oct.):37-62.
            Reprint of 1963.15.

15   _____. "Beckett's Brinkmanship." <u>AUMLA</u> 19
         (May):57-75.
            Compares and contrasts Beckett's ex-
         perience of time in the trilogy, <u>Waiting for</u>

<u>Godot</u>, and <u>Endgame</u> with that experienced by
Proust in <u>A la Recherche du temps perdu</u>.
Although Proust's recognition of the existence within us of "some timeless essential
being" is subscribed to "emotionally if not
intellectually" by Beckett, Proust believed
that the emancipation from time is possible,
being brought about by memory or artistic
creation, while Beckett finds it is
impossible: "Beckett's characters are ... on
the endless, uncrossable brink of entry into
a kind of paradise (the paradise of eternal
self-possession), so that for them, existence
is a purgatory-on-earth, a purgatory of
exclusion and waiting. They are in a kind of
no-man's-land, lying somewhere, somehow,
between their existence in time and their
life in eternity, neither the one nor the
other, but with characteristics of both."
Reprinted: 1963.14.

16   COE, RICHARD N.   "Le Dieu de Samuel Beckett."
      <u>Cahiers Renaud-Barrault</u> 44 (Oct.):6-36.
          Describes the existence/non-existence of
      God, His attributes, judgments, and relation-
      ship to man. Reprinted in original English
      version: 1965.16.

17   COHN, RUBY.   "Bibliographie des études critiques
      sur l'oeuvre de Samuel Beckett." <u>Cahiers
      Renaud-Barrault</u> 44 (Oct.):73-77.
          Presents a list of critical works in
      French and English. Reprinted from 1962.21.

18   CORVIN, MICHEL.   <u>Le Théâtre nouveau en France</u>.
      Paris: Presses Universitaires de France, pp.
      67-72.
          Claims that Beckett transforms theater
      into a circus and his actors into clowns.
      Corvin introduces the characters' tragic
      inability to divert themselves (in the
      Pascalian sense) or to really know each
      other. Beckett portrays an empty, absurd
      existence in which language is the sole
      character.

18a DENNIS, NIGEL. "Burying Beckett Alive." Show
     3, no. 11 (Nov.):46, 54-55.
        Distinguishes those who see Beckett as a
     philosopher from those who see him as a
     dramatist. Nigel points out that those who
     see Beckett's characters as they are on stage
     without being burdened by the numerous
     critical interpretations that surround them,
     tend to be most interested in the form
     Beckett uses to represent the same ideas:
     "Lightness, flexibility, a never-failing
     readiness to laugh, and a plain eye for the
     text -- these are the only means by which
     Beckett's mordant vitality can be preserved."

19   DORT, BERNARD. "Oh! les beaux jours." Théâtre
     populaire, no. 52 (4th trimester), pp. 107-
     11.
        Reviews the production of Happy Days
     directed by Roger Blin at the Odéon Théâtre
     de France, recognizing Beckett's fidelity to
     the same obsessive themes. However Happy
     Days is a completely closed work, unlike
     Godot, where anything could happen.

20   DUKORE, BERNARD F. "Controversy: A Non-
     Interpretation of Godot." Drama Survey 3
     (May):117-19.
        Defends his original position in a reply
     to Thomas B. Markus's criticism of an earlier
     article. See 1962.24, 1963.51, 1966.33.

21   DUPREY, RICHARD A. "The Battle for the American
     Stage." Catholic World 197 (July):246-51.
        Believes that two different trends are
     competing to influence the American stage:
     the "epic" theater of Brecht and the avant-
     garde theater of Ionesco, Beckett, and Genet.

22   *[Endgame.] Times (London), 7 Nov., p. 16.
        Source: Tanner, 1969.113;unverified.

23   ESSLIN, MARTIN. "Godot and his Children. The
     Theatre of Samuel Beckett and Harold Pinter."
     In Experimental Drama. Edited by William A.
     Armstrong. London: G. Bell and Sons, pp.

128-46.
Reprinted: 1968.23.

24   _____. "Samuel Beckett: The Search for Self."
In Le Thèâtre de l'absurde. Paris: Buchet-
Chastel.
Reprint of 1961.21; reprinted: 1968.24,
1969.38; see 1968.24 for annotation.

25   *FLETCHER, D. "The Language of Godot." Sixty-
One, n.v., (May).

26   FLETCHER, JOHN. "Balzac and Beckett Revisited."
French Review 37 (Oct.):78-80.
Responds to an article by S.A. Rhodes,
pointing out that the parallel between
Balzac's play and Beckett's Waiting for Godot
was first discovered by the author of the
article "Balzac a-t-il inspiré En attendant
Godot?" in the September 1955 issue of the
Figaro Littérature. Fletcher believes the
possibility of influence should be considered
and that Beckett has in fact "absorbed Le
Faiseur and re-written it in accordance with
his own feelings and with the spirit of the
age." See 1955.1, 1963.68.

27   *FRENCH, JUDITH A. "The Destruction of Action."
Kerygma 3 (Spring):9-12.
Source: Federman, 1970.39;unverified.

28   FRISCH, JACK E. "Endgame: A Play as Poem."
Drama Survey 3 (Oct.):257-63.
Considers Beckett's Endgame as a poem to
be performed in the theater: "By virtue of a
proposed correspondence between a poem and a
play, the way in which a play works is
virtually involved with the use of story,
language, silence, and poetic techniques in
Endgame.

29   GADENNE, PAUL. "Genêt [sic] dépassé." In
Molloy. Paris: Union Générale d'Editions,
pp. 271-74.
Finds that this novel cannot really be

compared in a satisfying way to Jean Genet
because one cannot pose the same questions
that Sartre examines with respect to Genet.
To speak of humility in Molloy makes no sense
because there is no "subject" in this novel.
Reprinted from 1951.6.

30   GLICKSBURG, CHARLES.   "Waiting for Godot and
      Endgame: The Lost Self in Beckett's Fic-
      tion." In The Self in Modern Literature.
      University Park, Pa.: Pennsylvania State
      University Press, pp. 117-33.
          Focuses on the introspective aspects of
      modern fiction: the problems of identity,
      perception, language, personality, reason,
      reality, etc. Glicksburg utilizes examples
      from Endgame, Waiting for Godot, Murphy, and
      the trilogy. Reprinted from 1962.34.

31   GOLDBERG, GERALD JAY.   "The Search for the
      Artist in Some Recent British Fiction."
      South Atlantic Quarterly 62, no. 3 (Sum-
      mer):387-401. Beckett: pp. 396-401.
          Focuses on the "search for the man through
      the art" in the fiction of Lawrence Durrell,
      William Golding, Iris Murdoch, and Beckett.
      Whereas Durrell, Golding and Murdoch deal
      with the sensitive individual's attempts to
      find his identity, Beckett concentrates on
      the subject of art itself.

32   GOUHIER, HENRI.   "Le Théâtre a horreur du vide."
      Table Ronde, no. 182 (Mar.), pp. 120-24.
          Presents ideas of Charles Apothéloz, the
      director of the Swiss company, Les Faux Nez,
      on the concept of nothingness in Endgame.

33   GRESSET, MICHEL.   "Création et cruauté chez
      Beckett." Tel Quel 15 (Autumn):58-65.
          Comments on the cruelty and sadism
      demonstrated by the Beckettian couples in
      Waiting for Godot, Act Without Words,
      Endgame, the trilogy, and How It Is comparing
      their relationships to those between parents
      and children, friends, master and slave, God

and man, or Creator and created being.

34   HAHN, PIERRE. "Roger Blin: 'J'ai dû attendre
      trois ans pour monter En attendant Godot
      ...'" Paris-Théâtre 16, no. 201:22.
          Describes his first meeting with Beckett
      and his preliminary impressions of Waiting
      for Godot.

35   HANOTEAU, GUILLAUME. "Samuel Beckett: Ecrivain
      génial ou maître de l'ennui?" Paris-Match,
      no. 762 (16 Nov.), pp. 111-14, 121, 126, 131,
      137-38.
          Describes the triumphs of Madeleine Renaud
      in Happy Days at the Théâtre de France.
      Hanoteau provides numerous biographical
      details prior to the first production of
      Waiting for Godot in France.

36   HESLA, DAVID H. "The Shape of Chaos: A Reading
      of Beckett's Watt." Critique: Studies in
      Modern Fiction 6, no. 1 (Spring):85-105.
          Discusses Beckett's desire "to find a form
      that accommodates the mess." Hesla examines
      the way in which the formal structure of Watt
      has been altered to convey ambiguity in the
      interpretation of the incidents in the novel,
      the narrative voice, and the identity of the
      characters. Reprinted in part 1971.46.

37   JACOBSEN, JOSEPHINE and WILLIAM R. MUELLER.
      "Beckett as Poet." Prairie Schooner 37
      (Fall):196-216.
          Study three types of poetic qualities in
      Beckett's works: the poetry of intensifica-
      tion, the poetry of disparity, and the poetry
      of intimation.

38   JOHNSON, B.S. "A Master Stylist." Spectator,
      13 Dec., p. 800.
          Reviews Murphy and Watt. While Murphy is
      a humorous novel that offers the best
      introduction to Beckett's work, it is in Watt
      that an individual style evolved.

39   KANTERS, ROBERT. "La Reine grise, les deux
     pieds dans la tombe ... et le reste."
     Express, 7 Nov., pp. 34-35.
          Reviews Madeleine Renaud's performance of
     Happy Days, seeing the play as an example of
     symbolism comparable to the theater of
     Maurice Maeterlinck.

40   _____. "Un chef-d'oeuvre préfabriqué." Molloy.
     Paris: Union Générale d'Editions, pp. 275-
     77.
          Feels that the first part of Molloy
     imitates the works of Joyce while the second
     part is influenced by the works of Kafka:
     the only originality Beckett demonstrates is
     in his vision of the world and the strength
     of his obsessions. Reprinted from 1951.7.

41   KARL, FREDERICK R. "Waiting for Beckett: Quest
     and Request." In A Reader's Guide to the
     Contemporary English Novel. London: Thames
     and Hudson, 304 pp.
          Reprint of 1961.39, 1962.45.

42   KILLINGER, JOHN. The Failure of Theology in
     Modern Literature. New York: Abingdon
     Press, pp. 215-17.
          Points out that although Waiting for Godot
     poses a spiritual problem, it is not a
     Christian play: "It belongs to the documen-
     tation of the absence of God, not of the
     presence of God. And therefore we can hardly
     credit it with being more than sub-Chris-
     tian."

43   LITTLEJOHN, DAVID. "The Anti-Realists."
     Daedalus 92, no. 2 (Spring):250-64. Beckett:
     pp. 251-53.
          Defines Beckett as a third generation
     anti-realist, whose novels share certain
     traits with other writers of this genre,
     namely "a radical and willful distortion of
     the nature of real experience, a distortion
     commonly made in the manner of dreams or
     other manifestations of subconscious

experience." In this context, Littlejohn
briefly describes <u>Molloy</u>, <u>Watt</u>, and the
novels of the trilogy.

44   MAGNAN, JEAN-MARIE. "Jalons. I. -Samuel
      Beckett ou les chaînes et relais du néant;
      II. -Alain Robbe-Grillet ou le labyrinthe du
      voyeur." <u>Cahiers du Sud</u> 50, no. 371:73-80.
      Beckett: pp. 73-76.
          Believes <u>The Unnamable</u> represents the
      refusal or the impossibility to accept our
      pitiful condition, in a language that has
      been reduced to an elementary if not primor-
      dial level.

45   MAGNY, OLIVIER de. "Ecriture de l'impossible."
      <u>Lettres Nouvelles</u> 32, no. 13 (Feb.):125-38.
      Beckett: pp. 135-36.
          Using <u>The Unnamable</u> as an example, points
      out that today's writers frequently make the
      "impossibility of writing" the subject of
      their works.

46   _____. "Samuel Beckett et la farce métaphysi-
      que." <u>Cahiers Renaud-Barrault</u> 44 (Oct.):67-
      72.
          Feels that Beckett's metaphysical drama is
      based on a radical negation of the fundamen-
      tal theatrical elements of person, place, and
      action that constitute our idea of theater.

47   MARINELLO, LEONE J. "Samuel Beckett's <u>Waiting
      for Godot</u>. A Modern Classic Affirming Man's
      Dignity and Nobility and Ultimate Salvation."
      <u>Drama Critique</u> 6, no. 1 (Spring):75-81.
          Juxtaposes the two couples in <u>Waiting for
      Godot</u>: the cruelty, despair and damnation of
      Pozzo and Lucky counter balances the love,
      faith, hope, and salvation of Vladimir and
      Estragon. Both sides of man's nature are
      portrayed -- giving the characters the option
      lost or saved.

48   MARISSEL, ANDRE. "Molloy, Macmann, Malone et
      tant d'autres." <u>Marginales</u> 18, no. 93

(Dec.):16-24.
Analyzes Beckett's characters, their
physical and psychological weaknesses, their
confrontation with death and evil, their
suffering and incompetence.

49   _____. Samuel Beckett. Paris: Editions
Universitaires, 126 pp.
Offers an introduction to Beckett's prose
and dramatic works, focusing on fundamental
questions: the anti-novel, the decomposition
of his characters, their Freudian complexes,
the absence of God, and Beckettian humor.
The text is followed by a select bibliography.

50   _____. "L'Univers de Samuel Beckett; un noeud
de complexes." Esprit 31, no. 320
(Sept.):240-55.
In his discussion of the novels and short
stories through Texts for Nothing, focuses on
the characters' need of love, their inability
to be "born into life" and their regret at
being ejected from the womb.

51   MARKUS, THOMAS B. "Bernard Dukore and Waiting
for Godot." Drama Survey 2, no. 3
(Feb.):360-63.
Refutes Bernard Dukore's 1962 article on
Waiting for Godot, and seeks Beckett's
meaning in the changes undergone by the
characters from Act I to Act II. See
1962.24, 1963.20.

52   *MAROWITZ, CHARLES. "A View from the Gods."
Encore 10 (Jan.-Feb.):6-7.

53   MAULNIER, THIERRY. "Claudel et Beckett." Revue
de Paris 70, no. 12 (Dec.):124-27. Beckett:
pp. 126-27.
Briefly reviews Happy Days with Madeleine
Renaud, summarizing Winnie's actions and
sentiments.

54   MORSE, DAVID. "He Who Gets Slapped." <u>Cambridge</u>
      <u>Review</u> 84 (4 May):413-14.
          Reviews the production of <u>Waiting for</u>
      <u>Godot</u> at the Arts Theatre in which the
      director changed many of Beckett's stage
      directions. Morse feels that the production
      is reduced to a "clown show," destroying both
      the seriousness and humor of the play.

55   MORSE, J. MITCHELL. "The Choreography of 'The
      New Novel.'" <u>Hudson Review</u> 16, no. 3
      (Autumn):396-419. Beckett: pp. 414-17.
          Presents the difficulties of understanding
      France's New Novel. Beckett's writings seem
      to follow the Talmudic tradition, where the
      image of God varies between that of a kind
      father and incomprehensible and capricious
      being.

56   NADEAU, MAURICE. "Le Chemin de la parole au
      silence." <u>Cahiers Renaud-Barrault</u> 44
      (Oct.):63-66.
          Summarizes <u>Murphy</u>, <u>Molloy</u>, <u>Malone meurt</u>,
      <u>The Unnamable</u>, and <u>How It Is</u>. These works
      trace a movement from word to silence, from
      life to death. Nadeau feels that Beckett has
      reached the limit -- it is impossible to go
      further in the search of silence. Reprinted:
      1963.58.

57   _____. "En avant vers nulle part." In <u>Molloy</u>.
      Paris: Union Générale d'Editions, pp. 257-
      63.
          Using "L'Expulsé" as an introduction to
      Beckett's works, explores the quests,
      objectives and tone of Beckett's narrator-
      authors, Murphy, Moran and Molloy. Reprint
      of 1951.8; reprinted 1979.22.9.

58   _____. "Samuel Beckett." In <u>Le Roman Français</u>
      <u>depuis la guerre</u>. Paris: Gallimard, pp.
      155-59.
          Reprint of 1963.56.

59   No entry.

60   NORTH, ROBERT JOSEPH. <u>Myth in the Modern French
     Theatre</u>. Keele: Keele University Press, pp.
     14-16.
          Believes Beckett has created a new myth in
     his portrayal of man's futility and loneli-
     ness and his demonstration of the insig-
     nificance of language.

61   PICON, GAETON. "L'Impossible néant." <u>Molloy</u>.
     Paris: Union Générale d'Editions,
     pp. 266-70.
          Contrasts the styles of Joyce and Beckett
     and expounds on Beckett's use of infirmity as
     symbolic of existence: Molloy wants to leave
     life behind to reduce it to nothingness, but
     his goal is impossible -- there is always
     something new to say or something that has
     been omitted. Reprinted from 1951.10.

62   PINGAUD, BERNARD. "Beckett le précurseur." In
     <u>Molloy</u>. Paris: Union Générale d'Editions,
     pp. 287-311.
          Reprinted: 1963.63.

63   _____. "<u>Molloy</u> douze ans après." <u>Temps
     Modernes</u> 18, no. 200 (Jan.):1283-1300.
          Discusses the literary and historical
     importance of <u>Molloy</u>, the major theme of
     decomposition and various interpretations of
     the novel. Reprint of 1963.62.

64   *"Plans to Write Film Episode." <u>Times</u> (London),
     13 Nov., p. 5.
          Source: Tanner, 1969.113;unverified.

65   POUILLON, JEAN. "Une morale de la conscience
     absolue." In <u>Molloy</u>. Paris: Union Générale
     d'Editions, pp. 283-86.
          Reprint of 1951.12.

66   *"Problems that Confront the New Abbey Theatre."
     <u>Irish Digest</u>, (Oct.), pp. 79-82.

67 PRONKO, LEONARD CABELL. "Samuel Beckett." In
    Théâtre d'avant-garde. Beckett, Ionesco, et
    le théâtre expérimental en France. Paris:
    Denoel, pp. 36-80.
       Examines Waiting for Godot (structure,
    language, humor, situation, characters,
    subject, Christian interpretations, and
    meaning of Godot) and Endgame (poetic
    elements, names and significance of charac-
    ters and somber humor) and Beckett's short
    plays (as technical innovations).

68 RHODES, S.A. "From Godeau to Godot." French
    Review 36, no. 3 (Jan.):260-65.
       Points out a coincidental analogy in the
    theme of "waiting" in Beckett's Waiting for
    Godot and Balzac's Mercadet "between ... an
    essentially metaphysical tragicomedy with a
    Judaeo-Christian background in one case, and
    a social satire with a realistic structure in
    the other."

69 ROBBE-GRILLET, ALAIN. "Samuel Beckett ou la
    présence sur la scène." In Pour un nouveau
    roman. Paris: Editions de Minuit, pp. 95-
    107.
       Reprinted from 1953.14; reprinted:
    1965.63, 1965.64, 1967.89.

70 SAUREL, RENEE. "Dieux contumax, le vicaire
    complice." Temps Modernes 19, no. 211
    (Dec.):1137-44. Beckett: pp. 1137-40.
       Reviews Happy Days at the Odéon-Théâtre,
    demonstrating that the themes of the agony of
    existence, aging, the impotence of language,
    the silence of God, among others, are unified
    in this play through an economy of means.

71 SICLIER, JACQUES. "Tous ceux qui tombent de
    Samuel Beckett." Monde, 26 Jan., p. 17.
       Discusses the adaptation of All That Fall
    for television, and introduces Beckett and
    his drama to an audience that may not be
    familiar with avant-garde theater.

72   SIMON, ALFRED. "Le Degré zéro du tragique."
         Esprit 31, no. 323 (Dec.):905-9.
              Views Beckett's characters as "larvaires
         et clownesques" having nothing to do with
         psychological or social reality. In a world
         in which God has killed himself out of spite,
         Simon proposes that they represent humanity
         returned to infancy and primordial terrors,
         maintaining only that portion of adult
         consciousness that provides irony and
         sarcasm. Reprinted 1979.22.57.

73   *SWANSON, ROY ARTHUR. "Samuel Beckett: Waiting
         for Godot." In Heart of Reason: Introduc-
         tory Essays in Modern-World Humanities.
         Minneapolis: T.S. Denison, pp. 187-207.

74   TILLIER, MAURICE. "Mais qui est donc l'étrange,
         l'envoûtant Monsieur Beckett?" Figaro
         Littéraire, 14-20 Nov., p. 21.
              Interviews Madeleine Renaud and Roger Blin
         on the subject of Beckett and the presenta-
         tion of his new play, Happy Days.

75   *TOYNBEE, PHILIP. "Art and Catastrophe."
         Observer, 19 May, p. 23.

76   WARHAFT, SIDNEY. "Threne and Theme in Watt."
         Wisconsin Studies in Contemporary Literature
         4, no. 3 (Autumn):261-78.
              Gives a detailed description of a quartet
         of voices heard by Watt from the ditch to
         demonstrate the centrality of the interlude
         to the whole novel and to clarify the
         "development of Watt toward his fate": "The
         content of both stanzas ... forms a kind of
         fragmented summary of, and commentary upon,
         the human condition moving through the full
         term of life in a cold and meaningless
         universe."

1964

1   ABIRACHED, ROBERT. "La Voix tragique de Samuel
     Beckett." Etudes 320 (Jan.):85-88.
          Analyzes the Beckettian themes of im-
     mobility and reduction in Happy Days.

2   "An Early Failure is Now Almost a Riot." Times
     (London), 10 July, p. 7.
          Reviews a revival of Endgame at the
     Aldwych Theatre. Compared with the austerity
     of Beckett's more recent works Endgame seems
     "almost a riot": "Beckett is dealing with
     last things -- with a world stripped of the
     illusions of appetite, affection, and
     ambition, and where there is nothing but
     meaningless, habit-ridden routine ..."

3   ARNOLD, BRUCE. "Samuel Beckett." Dubliner 3,
     no. 2 (Summer):6-16.
          Presents a general study of the novels and
     plays, focusing on the theme of friendship
     and the fragmentation of time, character, and
     action. Beckett's early years are also
     discussed: Beckett as a cricketer, Beckett
     as a witness in the case against Oliver St.
     John Gogarty in 1937, and Beckett as a writer
     in one of his earliest literary efforts, a
     paper given to the Dublin University Modern
     Languages Society entitled "le convergism
     ..."

4   BARO, GENE. "Where is the Where, Why is Why."
     New York Times Book Review, 22 Mar., p. 5.
          Reviews How It Is, describing the situa-
     tion of the novel and the direction of
     Beckett's works to date. Baro feels that
     Beckett's imagery has become increasingly
     pessimistic, while the sphere of activity he
     portrays is more confined.

5   "Beckett." New Yorker 40 (8 Aug.):22-23.
          Describes the making of Film, and
     Beckett's working relationship with Alan

Schneider and the technicians.

6   BLANCHOT, MAURICE. "Where Now? Who Now?" In
      On Contemporary Literature: An Anthology of
      Critical Essays on the Major Movements and
      Writers of Contemporary Literature. Edited
      by Richard Kostelanetz. New York: Avon
      Books, pp. 249-54.
           Reprinted from 1953.3, 1959.5, 1959.6.

7   BLAU, HERBERT. "Counterforce II: Notes from
      the Underground." In The Impossible Theater:
      A Manifesto. New York: Macmillan; London:
      Collier-Macmillan, pp. 228-51.
           Comments on the possible "meaning" of
      Beckett's plays Waiting for Godot and
      Endgame, examining style, atmosphere, action,
      characters, visual aspects and silence in
      Beckett's drama.

8   *BONCZEK, JANE C. "Being and Waiting: A Sign
      of Our Times." Lit, no. 5, pp. 6-10.

9   *BOURNE, RICHARD. "Happy Days and Bedlam Galore
      at Manchester." Guardian, 4 June.
           Source: Bryer et al., 1972.7;unverified.

10   BREE, GERMAINE. "L'Etrange monde des 'Grands
      Articulés.'" Revue des Lettres Modernes.
      Samuel Beckett: Configuration Critique 100,
      no. 8:83-97.
           Traces some of the possible influences for
      Beckett's works, in particular, Descartes,
      Geulincx, Schopenhauer, Dante, Milton, Joyce,
      Proust. Different aspects of Beckett's prose
      works are introduced: the characters,
      geography, language, and drama of literary
      creation. Reprinted (in English): 1970.12.

11   BROWN, JOHN RUSSELL. "Mr. Pinter's Shake-
      speare." In Essays in the Modern Drama.
      Edited by Morris Freedman. Boston: D.C.
      Heath, pp. 352-66.
           Reprint of 1963.12.

12   BROWN, ROBERT McAFEE. "The Theme of Waiting in
        Modern Literature." Ramparts 3, no. 1 (Sum-
        mer):68-75. Beckett: pp. 69-70.
           Demonstrates how the attitude of "waiting-
        for-we-know-not-what" is mirrored in Waiting
        for Godot. Brown introduces some of the
        Christian imagery in the play, and suggests
        that Gogo and Didi represent modern man: "We
        too must relieve the boredom of waiting ...
        and surely we too find our only refuge and
        solace in the fact that we wait together."

12a   BRUSTEIN, ROBERT. "Med-Season Gleanings." New
        Republic 150 (1 Feb.):28, 30.
           Reviews Alan Schneider's production of
        Play at the Cherry Lane Theatre, focusing on
        the role of the light: "Unguided by a
        malicious unseen will, this diabolical beam
        sets the rhythm and the tone of their
        damnation - regular and irregular, swift and
        lazy, stern and humorous." Reprinted:
        1979.22.59.

13   BRYDEN, RONALD. "Absurds." New Statesman, 17
        Apr., p. 616.
           Believes Beckett is indebted to Sartre
        (Huis Clos) and Giraudoux (Sodom and Gomor-
        rah) for his stage imagery in Play. Bryden
        finds the play to be unoriginal and tedious.

14   BRYER, J.R. "Critique de Samuel Beckett.
        Sélection bibliographique." Revue des
        Lettres Modernes. Samuel Beckett: Con-
        figuration Critique 100, no. 8:169-84.
           Supplements the bibliography provided by
        Ruby Cohn in Samuel Beckett: The Comic Gamut
        (See 1962.21); includes books and articles in
        English, French, German, and Italian, as well
        as a few important works in other languages.
        Reprinted: 1970.15; see 1971.10, 1972.7.

15   *CAIN, ALEX M. "Oldies." Tablet, 18 July.
        Source: Bryer et al., 1972.7;unverified.

16   CHAMPIGNY, ROBERT. "Les Aventures de la
        première personne." Revue des Lettres
        Modernes. Samuel Beckett: Configuration
        Critique 100, no. 8:117-30.
            Attempts to discern the semantic condi-
        tions of the monologuist in The Unnamable,
        considering the historical, novelistic, or
        dramatic frameworks. The narrator is
        generally defined as a "totality" (as opposed
        to an individual or a class of individuals),
        while that which the pronoun represents
        remains indecisive, unnamable. Reprinted:
        1970.20.

17   *C[HAVARDES], M[AURICE]. "La Littérature pour
        quoi faire." Signes du Temps 5 (Feb.):38.
            Source: Bryer et al., 1972.7;unverified.

18   COE, RICHARD. Samuel Beckett. New York: Grove
        Press, 118 pp.
            Concentrates on the philosophical implica-
        tions of Beckett's fiction. Coe analyzes the
        resemblance of certain Beckettian themes and
        the ideas expressed by Pascal, Proust,
        Descartes, Geulincx, Wittgenstein, the Greek
        philosopher Zeno, and Buddhism.

19   COHEN, ROBERT S. "Parallels and the Possibility
        of Influence between Simon Weil's Waiting for
        God and Samuel Beckett's Waiting for Godot."
        Modern Drama 6, no. 4 (Feb.):425-36.
            Postulates a Christian interpretation of
        Waiting for Godot based on a comparison of
        Beckett's play with the religious essays of
        the French theologian Simon Weil: "If
        Beckett took from Weil the situation, the
        characters, and the symbolism, he did not
        take her ultimate faith. His vision is of
        man suffering through the bleakness of
        affliction and enduring it with humor and
        pathos, always relieved and affrighted with
        the hope of ultimate salvation."

20   COHN, RUBY. "Philosophical Fragments in the
        Works of Samuel Beckett." Criticism 6, no. 1

(Winter):33-43.
   Although Beckett denies any interest in
philosophizing, believes his characters
continue to examine the age-old philosophical
questions about the nature of the Self, the
World, and God. Cohn demonstrates the
influence of the ideas of Descartes,
Geulincx, Wittgenstein, and Heidegger on
Beckett's works.

21   CUNARD, NANCY. "The Hours Press: Retrospect --
     Catalogue -- Commentary." <u>Book Collector</u> 13
     (Winter):488-96.
        Records memories of her printing -
     publishing venture from 1928 to 1931 and
     catalogues the productions of the Hours Press
     with commentaries. Beckett's "Whoroscope,"
     pp. 494-95.

22   CURTIS, JEAN-LOUIS. "La Voix qui babille dans
     le désert." <u>Cahiers des Saisons</u> 36 (Winter):
     105-6.
        Reviews the production of <u>Happy Days</u> at
     the Théâtre de France as a drama without
     action or characters, an "allegory of our
     mortal condition."

23   *DeSTEFFANO, Sister MARY VENISE. "Man's Search
     for Meaning in Modern French Drama."
     <u>Renascence</u> (Winter), pp. 81-91.
        Source: Tanner, 1969.113;unverified.

24   DONOGHUE, DENIS. "And Me If It's Me."
     <u>Manchester Guardian</u>, 1 May, p. 11.
        Outlines suppositions under which <u>How It
     Is</u> proceeds: 1) being is described as a
     "linguistic event" and a man's life "the sum
     of the images he receives or invents," 2) the
     narrator is quoting another and is released
     from responsibility, 3) the few details the
     narrator can conjure up are useful for making
     images. Donoghue also questions the effec-
     tiveness of Beckett's experimental techniques
     in this novel.

25   *DRIVER, TOM F. "Beckett by the Madeleine." In
     Drama in the Modern World: Plays and Essays.
     Edited by Samuel I. Weiss. Boston: D.C.
     Heath, pp. 505-8.
          Reprint of 1961.18.

26   EASTMAN, RICHARD M. "Samuel Beckett and Happy
     Days." Modern Drama 6, no. 4 (Feb.):417-24.
          Analyzes Happy Days as part of the
     recurrent dramatic pattern of Beckett's
     previous plays, "the Beckett myth," and looks
     for signs of growth or newness of this myth.

27   *ESSLIN, MARTIN. "A New Work by Samuel
     Beckett." Radio Times, 1 Oct., p. 35.

28   FEDERMAN, RAYMOND. "Beckett and the Fiction of
     Mud." In On Contemporary Literature: An
     Anthology of Critical Essays on the Major
     Movements and Writers of Contemporary
     Literature. Edited by R. Kostelanetz. New
     York: Avon Books, pp. 255-61.
          Revised version reprinted: 1965.24.

29   _____. "Beckett's Belacqua and the Inferno of
     Society." Arizona Quarterly 20 (Summer):
     231-41.
          Describes the themes in More Pricks than
     Kicks that are found in Beckett's later
     fiction, such as Belacqua's physical defects
     and mental idiosyncrasies.

30   FLETCHER, JOHN. "Beckett et Proust." Caliban:
     Annales Publiées par la Faculté des Lettres
     de Toulouse, no. 1 (Jan.), pp. 89-100.
          Examines the value, importance, and
     originality of Beckett's Proust as a critical
     study. Similarities between A la recherche
     du temps perdu and Beckett's novels are
     pointed out.

31   _____. "Beckett's Verse: Influences and
     Parallels." French Review 37 (Jan.):320-31.
          Suggests probable influences and a "few
     striking affinities" for Beckett's verse

(Rimbaud, Apollinaire, Pierre Jean Jouve,
Aragon, Tristan Tzara, Eliot) and examines
the principal stages in the development of
his poetry.

32   FRIEDMAN, MELVIN J. "Préface." Revue des
     Lettres Modernes. Samuel Beckett: Con-
     figuration Critique 100, no. 8:9-21.
          As editor of the special issue of the
     Revue des Lettres Modernes devoted to
     Beckett, Friedman reviews many of the
     previous critical essays on Beckett and gives
     a general overview of the articles presented
     in this issue. Reprinted: 1970.46.

33   _____. "Les Romans de Samuel Beckett et la
     tradition du grotesque." In Un nouveau
     roman? Edited by J.H. Matthews. Paris:
     M.J. Minard, pp. 31-50.
          Describes the similarities between
     Beckett's creatures and Sherwood Anderson's
     "grotesque" -- however Beckett's characters
     are not only psychologically "dispropor-
     tionate," they are also physically inept. In
     the second part of this essay, Friedman
     compares Beckett's use of the grotesque and
     the parody of the quest to the writers from
     the American South (Carson McCullers, William
     Styron, Flannery O'Conner, Eudora Welty,
     Truman Capote). Reprinted from 1960.21;
     reprinted: 1964.34.

34   _____. "Les Romans de Samuel Beckett et la
     tradition du grotesque." Revue des Lettres
     Modernes 94-99:31-50.
          Reprinted from 1960.21; reprinted:
     1964.33.

35   FROIS, ETIENNE. "Oh! Les Beaux Jours."
     Français dans le Monde 3, no. 24 (Apr.-
     May):25.
          Reviews Happy Days, pointing out that the
     play seems to illustrate the Pascalian themes
     of destitution and man's blindness.

36   FURBANK, P.N. "A New Work by Samuel Beckett."
      Listener 72 (15 Oct.):604.
           Compares Cascando to Beckett's other works
      -- like all of Beckett's fiction Cascando is
      about the impossibility of not writing, of
      not telling oneself stories.

37   _____. "Beckett's Purgatory." Encounter 22
      (June):69-72.
           Discusses Beckett's literary "ancestors"
      (Joyce, Valéry, Maeterlinck, Dante) and his
      personal style as it appears in the trilogy
      and How It Is.

38   *GASCOIGNE, BAMBER. "Five Brief Encounters in
      W.C. 2." Observer, 5 July, p. 24.

39   _____. "How Far Can Beckett Go?" Observer, 12
      Apr., p. 24.
           Reviews Beckett's production of Play at
      the Old Vic Theatre, describing the "plot,"
      the vividness of the writing, the precision
      of the spotlight, the effect of the rapid
      dialogue. Gascoigne speculates on the future
      possibilities of Beckett's drama.

40   GLAUBER, ROBERT H. "Minority Report: How It
      Is, by Samuel Beckett." Christian Century 81
      (8 Apr.):461.
           Criticizes Beckett's work because it
      portrays a vision of life that is "unchris-
      tian."

41   GOUHIER, HENRI. "Boulevard et avant-garde."
      Table Ronde 192 (Jan.):122-28.
           Reviews André Roussin's La Voyante,
      Beckett's Happy Days, and Maurice Béjart's La
      Reine verte. Gouhier finds Beckett's play to
      be remarkable, but unsettling.

42   GROSS, JOHN. "Amazing Reductions." Encounter
      23 (Sept.):50-52.
           Gives a brief account of the Royal
      Shakespeare Company's production of Endgame
      at Aldwich: "What does indubitably lie at

the heart of Endgame is an image of warring
brothers, all-too inseparable companions, men
chained to each other, however reluctantly,
by mutual need."

43   GRUEN, JOHN. "Beckett: Rare Playwright, Rare
      Interview." New York Herald Tribune, 19
      July, p. 31.
         Quotes a few of Beckett's remarks from a
      short interview during Beckett's visit to New
      York to direct Film: "Writing becomes not
      easier, but more difficult for me. Every
      word is like an unnecessary stain on silence
      and nothingness."

44   GUICHARNAUD, JACQUES. "Existence on Stage." In
      On Contemporary Literature: An Anthology of
      Critical Essays on the Major Movements and
      Writers of Contemporary Literature. Edited
      by R. Kostelanetz. New York: Avon Books,
      pp. 262-85.
         Reprinted: 1967.48.

45   HAINSWORTH, J.D. "Shakespeare, Son of Beckett?"
      Modern Language Quarterly 25, no. 3
      (Sept.):346-55.
         Reviews Jan Kott's Shakespeare notre
      contemporain in which King Lear is compared
      to Endgame. Hainsworth disagrees with Kott's
      perspective because the points of view of the
      two authors are as different as their place
      in history: "The basis of Beckett's gro-
      tesqueness is that the world is without point
      or purpose ... For Shakespeare a transcendent
      reality exists."

46   HARVEY, LAWRENCE E. "Samuel Beckett: Initia-
      tion du poète." Revue des Lettres Modernes.
      Samuel Beckett: Configuration Critique 100,
      no. 8:153-67.
         Tries to establish the relationship
      between Beckett's origins and his first work
      of poetry Echo's Bones and Other Precipi-
      tates. Reprinted: 1970.56.

47   HAYMAN, DAVID. "Molloy à la recherche de
      l'absurde." <u>Revue des Lettres Modernes.</u>
      <u>Samuel Beckett: Configuration Critique</u> 100,
      no. 8:131-51.
         Sees <u>Molloy</u> as a unique novel, in which
      the two parts complement one another to
      provide a portrait of universal man and a
      satire of his aspirations and realizations.
      Reprint of 1962.39; reprinted: 1970.59.

48   HOFFMAN, FREDERICK. "L'Insaisissable moi: Les
      'M' de Beckett." <u>Revue des Lettres Modernes.</u>
      <u>Samuel Beckett: Configuration Critique</u> 100,
      no. 8:23-53.
         Examines specific issues in <u>Murphy</u>, <u>Watt</u>,
      and the trilogy: the problem of identity,
      creation, the separation of mind and body,
      and language. Reprinted: 1970.61.

49   *HOLMSTROM, JOHN. "Come On!" <u>New Statesman</u>, 10
      Oct.
         Source: Bryer et al., 1972.7;unverified.

50   HOOKER, WARD. "Irony and Absurdity in the
      Avant-Garde Theatre." In <u>Essays in the</u>
      <u>Modern Drama</u>. Edited by Morris Freedman.
      Boston: D.C. Heath, pp. 335-48.
         Reprint of 1960.32.

51   HOY, CYRUS HENRY. <u>The Hyacinth Room. An</u>
      <u>Investigation Into the Nature of Comedy,</u>
      <u>Tragedy, and Tragicomedy</u>. New York: Alfred
      A. Knopf, pp. 254-64.
         Studies the confrontation in Beckett's
      plays (especially <u>Waiting for Godot</u>, <u>Endgame</u>,
      and <u>Happy Days</u>) of the will to be and the
      ultimate reality of death: "Recognizing
      which, one sustains oneself as one can: with
      visions of evanescence, with memories of
      happy days, with the ever-deferred hope that
      is both the blessing and the curse of
      waiting."

52   HUDSON, ROGER. "Play Without Theatricality."
      <u>Prompt</u>, no. 5, p. 50.

Briefly reviews the production of <u>Play</u>
presented at the National Theatre in which
Beckett tackles the problem of the audience's
subjective reactions: "Beckett has succeeded
in objectifying his picture of the banality
of human existence in a medium which normally
relies on some sort of empathy between
audience and characters."

53   JACOBSEN, JOSEPHINE and WILLIAM MUELLER. <u>The</u>
      <u>Testament of Samuel Beckett</u>. New York: Hill
      & Wang, 199 pp.
            Examines Beckett's technique as a vehicle
      for his vision, or "testament." The first
      section of this work is devoted to certain
      aspects of Beckett's fictional technique:
      his poetic mode, his statement on the
      relationship between the human consciousness
      and the world of space and time, and his
      comic approach to mankind. The presentation
      of Beckett's vision, or his reflection on the
      human condition, constitutes the second
      section of the study.

54   JONES, MERVYN. "Sophocles and Beckett."
      <u>Tribune</u> (London), 17 Apr., p. 14.
            Reviews the production of <u>Play</u> at the
      National Theatre, stressing the importance of
      the words since all other dramatic resources
      have been relinquished. Jones finds however
      that the words are "depressingly commonplace,
      flat, and devoid of resonance or implica-
      tion."

55   KAUFFMAN, STANLEY. "MacGowran in Beckett." In
      <u>Persons of the Drama. Theater and Criticism</u>
      <u>and Comment</u>. New York: Harper & Row, pp.
      211-13.
            Reprinted: 1970.74.

56   No Entry.

57   KERMODE, FRANK. "Beckett Country: <u>How It Is</u> by
      Samuel Beckett." <u>New York Review of Books</u> 2
      (19 Mar.):9-11.

Discusses the difficult language used in
How It Is, the situation described in the
novel, comparing the protagonist of this
novel with the heros of Beckett's previous
fiction.

58   KERN, EDITH. "Samuel Beckett et les poches de
      Lemuel Gulliver." Revue des Lettres Moder-
      nes. Samuel Beckett: Configuration Critique
      100, no. 8:69-81.
          Compares the objects that emerge from the
      pockets of Swift's character, Lemuel Gul-
      liver, which represent the rational, ordered
      world of the seventeenth and eighteenth
      centuries, with the contents of the pockets
      of several of Beckett's characters in Watt,
      Molloy, Happy Days, and How It Is. Re-
      printed: 1970.77.

59   KOTT, JAN. "King Lear or Endgame." Evergreen
      Review 33 (Aug.-Sept.):53-65.
          Reprint of 1962.49, 1962.50; reprinted:
      1964.60; see 1964.60 for annotation.

60   _____. "King Lear or Endgame." In
      Shakespeare Our Contemporary. Translated by
      Boleslaw Taborski. New York: Doubleday and
      Co., Inc., pp. 87-124.
          Points out that the use of grotesque in
      the new theater parallels that of tragedy in
      the Shakespearean theater: "In the final
      instance, tragedy is an appraisal of human
      fate, a measure of the absolute. The
      grotesque is a criticism of the absolute in
      the name of frail human experience. That is
      why tragedy brings catharsis, while grotesque
      offers no consolation whatsoever." In the
      new theater tragic situations become gro-
      tesque and fate, gods, and nature have been
      replaced by history. Kott compares the
      pantomime of Gloucester's suicide to Act
      Without Words and then contrasts the charac-
      ters and situations in King Lear with those
      of Endgame and Waiting for Godot. Reprint of
      1962.49, 1962.50, 1964.59.

61   LAMONT, ROSETTE. "La Farce métaphysique de
         Samuel Beckett." <u>Revue des Lettres Modernes.</u>
         <u>Samuel Beckett: Configuration Critique</u> 100,
         no. 8:99-116.
               Reprint of 1959.25; reprinted: 1970.83.

62   LEVENTHAL, A.J. "Le Héros de Beckett." <u>Lettres</u>
         <u>Nouvelles</u>, (June-July-Aug.), pp. 32-52.
               Reprinted: 1964-1965.1, 1965.53.

63   LEWIS, JOHN. "Samuel Beckett and the Decline of
         Western Civilization." <u>Marxism Today</u> 8, no.
         12 (Dec.):381-84.
               Examines Beckett's vision of "anguish and
         despair" as it is presented in <u>Waiting for</u>
         <u>Godot</u>, <u>Endgame</u>, <u>Happy Days</u>, <u>Play</u>, and the
         novels, especially <u>How It Is</u>.

64   LYONS, CHARLES R. "Beckett's <u>Endgame</u>: An Anti-
         Myth of Creation." <u>Modern Drama</u> 7, no. 2
         (Sept.):204-9.
               Believes that the playwright manipulates
         the spectator's sense of reality. In <u>Endgame</u>
         there is no reality beyond Beckett's abstrac-
         tion of character, action and setting:
         "<u>Endgame</u> projects the reduced human condition
         through the decreasing sense perception, the
         decreasing availability of pleasure-giving
         stimuli and a decreasing ability to respond
         to them, the elimination of any desire to
         make an ethical commitment, the decreasing
         sense of continuity between the present and
         the remembered past, and a decreasing ability
         and desire to relate the individual con-
         sciousness to any other being or object.

65   MacGOWRAN, JACK. "Working with Samuel Beckett."
         <u>Gambit</u> 2, no. 8:140-41.
               Reprinted: 1967.7.

66   MARCEL, GABRIEL. "Le Théâtre: <u>Comédie</u>."
         <u>Nouvelles Littéraires</u>, 9 July, p. 12.
               Briefly reviews <u>Play</u>. Marcel finds that
         the story disintegrates, revealing that
         language itself is "unnatural and humbled."

67   *MARISSEL, ANDRE. "Samuel Beckett et l'Ire-
         lande." Iô, no. 3 (July), pp. 27-33.

68   MAROWITZ, CHARLES. "Play & ..." Encore 11
         (May-June):48-52.
               Criticizes George Devine for discouraging
         the spectator from seeking the "meaning" of
         Beckett's play. Marowitz believes Beckett's
         Play could benefit from slower rhythm when
         the text is repeated: "Would greater
         comprehensibility have made for greater
         richness without sacrificing the style? If
         not, there is something wrong with the play."

69   *MERCIER, MAURICE. "Chronique parisienne."
         Entretiens sur les Lettres et les Arts, no.
         23 (Feb.), p. 58.

70   MIGNON, PAUL LOUIS. "Le Théâtre de A jusqu'à Z:
         Samuel Beckett." Avant-Scène, no. 313 (15
         June), p. 8.
               Summarizes Beckett's life and career
         through 1959, quoting from the author.

71   MORRISSETTE, BRUCE. "Les Idées de Robbe-Grillet
         sur Beckett." Revue des Lettres Modernes.
         Samuel Beckett: Configuration Critique 100,
         no. 8:55-67.
               Analyzes the evolution of Robbe-Grillet's
         ideas on Beckett's theater and his use of
         illustrations from Beckett to support his own
         literary theories in his articles "Samuel
         Beckett, auteur dramatique" (1953.14) and
         "Samuel Beckett ou la présence sur la scéne"
         (1963.69). Reprinted: 1970.92.

72   MORSE, J. MITCHELL. "The Ideal Core of the
         Onion: Samuel Beckett's Criticism." French
         Review 38, no. 1 (Oct.):23-29.
               Feels that Beckett's criticism acts as a
         form of self expression, revealing the ideas
         that underlie his novels and plays: "It is
         not only an exposition of his intellectual
         conception, but an intellectualization of his
         passions. It is poetry. To trace the

development of its principal themes is to
gain some insight into the evolution of
conception and style in Beckett's novels and
plays."

73   NORES, DOMINIQUE. "Une nouvelle voix dans le
théâtre de Beckett." Lettres Nouvelles 11
(Feb.-Mar.):165-71.
       Reviews Happy Days and analyzes the
character of Winnie as tender and optimistic.

74   "Oh les beaux jours." Avant-Scène, no. 313 (15
June), pp. 1-7.
       Presents photos of Happy Days with
Madeleine Renaud.

75   PEAKE, CHARLES. "Waiting for Godot and the
Conventions of the Drama." Prompt, no. 4,
pp. 19-23.
       Examines Beckett's rejection of the
traditional dramatic conventions of plot,
character, time, and space in Waiting for
Godot.

76   PIERRET, MARC. "Du théâtre anti-roman." France
Observateur, 18 June, p. 17.
       Reviews the production of Play at the
Pavillon de Marsan, pointing out that the
spectator experiences a more profound
comprehension of the play during the moments
of silence that separate the characters'
monologues, than during their anguished
speeches.

77   "Pinget Adapted by Beckett." Times (London), 24
Nov., p. 15.
       Reviews the production of a dialogue by
Roger Pinget, adapted for the stage by
Beckett, and entitled The Old Tume. These
overheard reminiscences of two Old Irishmen
presents a "pleasant exercise in nostalgia."

78   PORTAL, GEORGES. "Les Gens à talent." Ecrits
de Paris, (Jan.), pp. 89-94.
       Reviews Happy Days which Portal found to

be insupportably boring -- in contrast to
Godot there was "no music, no style, no
breath."

79   *PRITCHETT, VICTOR SAWDON.   "An Irish Oblomov."
     In The Living Novel and Later Appreciations.
     New York: Random House, pp. 315-320.
        Reprint of 1960.44.

80   _____.   "No Quaqua."   New Statesman 67, no.
     1,729 (1 May):683.
        Reviews How It Is, stressing the form and
     subject of the novel and the influence of
     Irish farce.

81   PRONKO, LEONARD C.   "Modes and Means of the
     Avant-garde Theatre."   Buchnell Review 12,
     no. 2 (May):46-56.
        Compares the purposes and techniques of
     the dramas of Beckett and Ionesco: meta-
     physical preoccupations, language, meaning,
     and the relationship between object and
     viewer.

82   RECHTIEN, JOHN, Brother, S.M.   "Time and
     Eternity Meet in the Present."   Texas Studies
     in Literature and Language 6, no. 1
     (Spring):5-21.
        Stresses the tension between the scien-
     tific and religious "myths" in Waiting for
     Godot, the audience's experience of cathar-
     sis, the dramatization of the play element,
     and the timeless waiting of mankind for
     salvation.

83   REID, ALEC.   "Beckett's Krapp's Last Tape."   In
     European Patterns. Contemporary Patterns in
     European Writing.   Edited by T.B. Harward.
     Dublin: Dolmer Press, pp. 38-43.
        Considers Beckett's attitudes toward life,
     literature and being and doing as it is
     expressed in Krapp's Last Tape.

84   REXROTH, KENNETH.   "The Point is Irrelevance."
     In On Contemporary Literature: An Anthology

<u>of Critical Essays the Major Movements and
Writers of Contemporary Literature</u>. Edited
by Richard Kostelanetz. New York: Avon
Books, pp. 244-48.
Reprinted from 1956.33.

85   RICKS, CHRISTOPHER. "Beckett and the Lobster."
     <u>New Statesman</u> 67, no. 1,718 (14 Feb.):254-55.
         Stresses Beckett's attempt to "rewrite"
     Dante's <u>Inferno</u> and Swift's <u>Struldbrugs</u>, "two
     unforgettable evocations of the human longing
     for extinction."

86   _____. "The Roots of Samuel Beckett." <u>Listener</u>
     72 (17 Dec.):963-64, 980.
         Examines the influence of Beckett prede-
     cessors: Swift and Dante (man's longing for
     extinction), Bunyan (<u>Pilgrim's Progress</u>),
     Defoe (style and the subject of man's
     solitude), Sterne (ridicule of the conven-
     tions of the novel and of pedantry), Milton
     (the desire of oblivion), Dickens (<u>Little
     Dorrit</u>, <u>Great Expectations</u>), and Shakespeare
     (<u>King Lear</u>).

87   ROY, CLAUDE. "Samuel Beckett." <u>Nouvelle Revue
     Française</u> 12, no. 143 (Nov.):885-90.
         Discusses Roger Blin's production of <u>Happy
     Days</u> at the Odéon Theatre with Madeleine
     Renaud. Roy feels that Beckett's works bring
     us back to the origins of the theater and
     poetry. Reprinted: 1965.66.

88   SELZ, JEAN. "L'Homme finissant de Samuel
     Beckett." In <u>Le Dire et le faire ou les
     chemins de la création</u>. Paris: Mercure de
     France, pp. 134-37.
         Explores the theme of man and his end,
     pointing out that a man's reflections at the
     end of his life are different in Beckett's
     works because man has become an object called
     to die the death of objects.

89   SENNEFF, SUSAN F. "Song and Music in Samuel
     Beckett's <u>Watt</u>." <u>Modern Fiction Studies</u> 10,

no. 2 (Summer):137-49.
Examines the consistency of the Ditch,
Frog and Descant songs, as well as minor
musical references, noises and incidents
about music.

90   SIGAL, CLANCY. "Is This the Person to Murder
      Me?" Sunday Times Colour Magazine (London),
      1 Mar., pp. 17-22.
          Gives a day-by-day account of the rehear-
      sals for Endgame in London.

91   SIMON, JOHN. "Unteaching Us, from Z to A."
      Book Week, 8 Mar., pp. 5, 10.
          Feels that the reader cannot empathize
      with the undefined voice in How It Is, and
      can therefore neither believe nor disbelieve
      it: "... when things become so exclusively
      universal, they lose that individuality which
      remains the starting point of art."

92   SURER, PAUL. "Samuel Beckett." In Le Théâtre
      français contemporain. Paris: Société
      d'Edition d'Enseignement Supérieur, pp. 435-
      49.
          Offers an introduction to Beckett's
      theater: his major plays, settings, charac-
      ters, symbols, language, comedy, and origi-
      nality.

93   SUTHERLAND, D. "Man on a High Wire." New
      Leader, 11 May, pp. 12-14.
          Reviews the new English translation of How
      It Is, criticizing Beckett's "little scenes"
      in which he "lets loose his Irish sentimen-
      tality on dying, women, flowers, and the
      like," images out of the past of Proust and
      Joyce. Yet Sutherland feels that How It Is
      resolves a problem of expression in contem-
      porary writing, that is "the coalescence of
      lyric and narrative."

94   TAYLOR, JOHN RUSSELL. "At the Aldwych." Plays
      and Players 11, no. 12 (Sept.):29.
          Reviews Endgame at the Aldwych Theatre.

> Taylor feels that the play is "haunting" but boring.

95 TINDALL, WILLIAM YORK. <u>Samuel Beckett</u>. New York and London: Columbia University Press, 48 pp.
    Provides a general description of Beckett's works: characterization, thematic elements, style, influences. Passages from Beckett's letters to Jacob Schwartz and Tindall are quoted. Followed by a selected bibliography.

96 TRUSSLER, SIMON. "<u>Happy Days</u> - Two Productions and a Text." <u>Prompt</u>, no. 4, pp. 23-25.
    Reviews two productions of <u>Happy Days</u>: Brenda Bruce at the Royal Court Theatre, and Marie Kean at the Stratford East Theatre. Trussler also analyzes the relationship of Winnie and Willy.

97 "Two Voices in New Beckett Play." <u>Times</u> (London), 7 Oct., p. 8.
    Presents the problems of form in Beckett's radio drama <u>Cascando</u> through a discussion of the three dimensions or levels of meaning of the play.

98 TYNAN, KENNETH. "<u>Fin de partie</u> and <u>Acte sans paroles</u>." <u>Tynan on Theatre</u>. Harmondsworth: Penguin Books.
    Reprint of 1961.57.

99 UPDIKE, JOHN. "How <u>How It Is</u> Was." <u>New Yorker</u> 40 (19 Dec.):165-66.
    Offers a parody review of <u>How It Is</u>, which "... is written how it is I quote unqote in works like this unpunctuated clumps of words with spaces white between the I guess you'd call them paragraphs I write it as I read it." Reprinted: 1965.76, 1979.22.54.

100 VERDOT, GUY. "Recherche de Beckett chez ceux qui l'ont découvert les premiers." <u>Paris-Théâtre</u> 16, no. 206:24-27.

Directors, writers, and colleagues (Roger
Blin, Jérôme Lindon, Maurice Nadeau, Ionesco)
recount their experiences working with
Beckett and their impressions of him.

101   "Waiting for the Dark." Times Literary Supplement (London), 9 Apr., p. 292.
Feels Beckett may be committed to a course
of diminishing returns in his new works,
Play, Words and Music and Cascando: "Play is
a moving invention but it is too close to
Happy Days to make a full and fresh impact.
Compared to Waiting for Godot it seems a
purer, more precise image, but lacking in
richness and complexity, closer to mere
statement."

102   WALKER, ROY. "Beckett's Play." Times Literary
Supplement (London), 16 Apr., p. 311.
In a letter to the editor, points out that
the directions for the repetition of Play are
ten lines from the end of the published text,
"so that the repetition is followed by a
slightly variant version of what could
otherwise be the beginning of another
repetition."

103   *_____. "Shagreen Shamrock." In Drama in the
Modern World: Plays and Essays. Edited by
Samuel I. Weiss. Boston: D.C. Heath, pp.
503-4.
Reprint of 1957.51.

104   WEIGHTMAN, JOHN. "Talking Heads." Observer
Weekend Review, 3 May, p. 27.
In a review of How It Is and Play demonstrates how language is vital in Beckett's
works, while the physical processes of life
no longer function properly. Weightman links
Beckett's writing to that of Sartre.

105   *WEISS, SAMUEL I., ed. Introductory note to All
That Fall. In Drama in the Modern World:
Plays and Essays. Boston: D.C. Heath, pp.
487-502.

106   WELLWORTH, GEORGE E.   "Samuel Beckett: Life in
      the Void."   In The Theater of Protest and
      Paradox.   Developments in the Avant-Garde
      Drama.   New York: New York University Press,
      pp. 41-56.
            Reprint of 1961.60.

107   WENDLER, HERBERT W.   "Graveyard Humanism."
      Southwest Review 49, no. 1 (Winter):44-52.
            Points out several general interpretations
      of Beckett's works and comments on the
      cynicism, the despair, the boredom, and the
      apathy of Beckett's characters, his unconven-
      tional modes of expression, and his portrayal
      of the absurdity of the human condition.

108   WILSON, ROBERT N.   "Samuel Beckett: The Social
      Psychology of Emptiness."   Journal of Social
      Issues 20, no. 1 (Jan.):62-70.
            Analyzes several prominent themes in
      Waiting for Godot and Endgame: deprivation,
      hostility, anarchy, enervation, sexlessness,
      hopelessness, and meaninglessness. Reprinted:
      1979.59.

109   ZERAFFA, MICHEL.   "Aspects structuraux de
      l'absurde dans la littérature contemporaine."
      Journal de Psychologie Normale et Pathologi-
      que 61, no. 4 (Oct.-Dec.):437-56.   Beckett:
      pp. 452-56.
            After a lengthy discussion of the works of
      Kafka, Faulkner, Camus and Sartre, introduces
      the theme of the absurd in Molloy from the
      point of view of language.

                              1964-1965

  1   LEVENTHAL, A.J.   "The Beckett Hero."   Critique:
      Studies in Modern Fiction 7, no. 2
      (Winter):18-35.
            Reprint of 1964.62; reprinted: 1965.53.

1965

1   *"An Epoch-Making Play." Times (London), 1 Jan.
       Source: Bryer et al. 1972.7;unverified.

2   ANDERS, GUNTHER. "Being without Time: On
       Beckett's Play Waiting for Godot." In Samuel
       Beckett: A Collection of Critical Essays.
       Edited by Martin Esslin. Englewood Cliffs,
       N.J.: Prentice-Hall, Inc., pp. 140-51.
       Discusses several aspects of Beckett's
       Waiting for Godot: the play as a negative
       parable, the characters' inability to
       recognize the senselessness of their posi-
       tion, ways in which the play differs from
       nihilism, the absurdity of the conviction of
       God's existence "ex absentia," the nonexis-
       tence of time and memory, and the image of
       master and servant. Anders refers to Rilke,
       Kafka, Hegel, Marx, and Sartre.

3   ANSORGE, PETER. "Theater of Silence: In Search
       of Contemporary Drama." Circuit, no. 1
       (Summer), pp.23-26.
       Comments on the audience response to a
       contemporary production of King Lear.
       Ansorge supports Jan Kott's position in his
       Shakespeare Our Contemporary. See 1962.49,
       1962.50, 1964.59, 1964.60.

4   BALL, PATRICIA M. "Browning's Godot." Vic-
       torian Poetry 3, no. 3 (Summer):245-53
       Believes Browning's poems postulate the
       world of Beckett's Estragon and Vladimir.

5   BARJON, LOUIS. "Le Dieu de Beckett." Etudes
       323 (Dec.):650-62.
       Focuses on the problem of God in Beckett's
       theater: Beckett's obsession with the idea
       of God, his evocation of an "absurd" world,
       his portrayal of two themes -- the useless-
       ness of life and the tragic solitude of man.

6   "Beckett and Ionesco in Prague." Times (Lon-
       don), 30 Mar., p. 8.

Reviews <u>Waiting for Godot</u>, <u>The Bald Prima
Donna</u>, and <u>The Lesson</u> at the Theatre on the
Balustrade in Prague. These productions
stress the metaphysical aspects of our
estrangement from life; they are highly
stylized and intellectually defined.

7   "Beckett Play Acted by French Company." <u>Times</u>
     (London), 5 Apr., p. 6.
         Points out that Roger Blin's French
     production of <u>Happy Days</u> at the Aldwych
     Theatre moves between comic irony and
     outright passion avoiding any tendency to
     easy pathos.

8   BROOK, PETER. "<u>Endgame</u> as <u>King Lear</u> or How
     to Stop Worrying and Love Beckett." <u>Encore</u>
     12 (Jan.-Feb.):8-12.
         Defends Beckett's works, in particular
     <u>Endgame</u>, as positive: "... Beckett's wish to
     tell the truth is a positive wish, this wish
     is an emotion of incandescent power, this
     intense charge results in a moment of
     creation ... and thus is positively assertive
     and assertively positive."

9   _____. "<u>Happy Days</u> and Marienbad." In <u>The
     Encore Reader: A Chronicle of the New Drama</u>.
     Edited by Charles Marowitz, Tom Milne, and
     Owen Hall. London: Methuen and Co. Ltd.,
     pp.164-69.
         Reprint of 1962.12

10   "Les Bruits de la ville." <u>Nouvel Observateur</u>,
     13-19 Oct., p. 24.
         Briefly describes <u>Film</u> and presents Buster
     Keaton's thoughts on his inability to
     comprehend the film or its appeal.

11   BRUSTEIN, ROBERT. "Déjà vu." In <u>Seasons of
     Discontent. Dramatic Opinions 1959-1965</u>.
     New York: Simon and Schuster, pp. 53-56.
         Reprint of 1961.11

12   _____. "Listening to the Past: <u>Krapp's Last</u>

Tape by Samuel Beckett and The Zoo Story by
Edward Albee." In Seasons of Discontent.
Dramatic Opinions 1959-1965. New York:
Simon and Schuster, pp. 26-29.
Feels that the economy of writing and
flawlessness of the form in Krapp's Last Tape
best portray the Beckettian themes of
"alienation, vacuity, and decay of life."

13   *BRYDEN, RONALD. "Second Not-Coming." New
Statesman, 8 June.
Source: Bryer et al. 1972.7;unverified.

14   CHIARI, JOSEPH. Landmarks of Contemporary
Drama. London: Herbert Jenkins, pp. 68-80
and passim.
Claims that Waiting for Godot is "the most
original play of the post-war years" -- the
language of the play is poetic, while the
world Beckett represents is symbolic. Chiari
demonstrates how many of Beckett's other
plays repeat certain aspects of Godot.

15   CLURMAN, HAROLD. "Theatre: Happy Days."
Nation 201 (18 Oct.):258-59.
Discusses the alternate performances of
Happy Days at the Cherry Lane Theatre,
performed by Madeleine Renaud (in French) and
Ruth White (in English). Clurman notes the
differences in approach to the role of
Winnie, which he feels is linked "to national
character ..."

16   COE, RICHARD N. "God and Samuel Beckett."
Meanjin 24:66-85.
Reprint of 1963.16 (French Version).

17   COHN, RUBY. "The Absurdly Absurd: Avatars of
Godot." Comparative Literature Studies 2,
no. 3:233-40.
Redefines the absurd, and claims that
Waiting for Godot is the first absurdist
drama. Two plays which Cohn believes reflect
the basic pattern of Godot are discussed:
Pinter's Dumb Waiter and Bromberg's Defense

of Taipei.

18   _____. "The Plays of Yeats Through Beckett
        Coloured-Glasses." Threshold 19 (Autumn):41-
        47.
            Compares the plays of Beckett and Yeats,
        pointing out references to Yeats in Beckett's
        plays, their common rejection of conventional
        plot and character and, their similarity in
        attitude toward a purgatorial view of earthly
        life.

19   _____. "Tempest in an Endgame."   Symposium
        19, no. 4 (Winter):328-34.
            Focuses on those aspects of Shakespeare's
        Tempest which illuminate Beckett's play:
        "Beckett's Endgame mockingly reflects on
        Shakespeare's Tempest -- its richness and
        resonance, its morality and humanity - 'old
        endgame lost of old.'"

20   DAVISON, PETER. "Contemporary Drama and
        Popular Dramatic Forms." In Aspects of Drama
        and the Theatre. Five Kathleen Robinson
        Lectures Delivered in the University of
        Sydney 1961-63. Sydney: Sydney University
        Press, pp. 145-97.
            Examines the relationship between legiti-
        mate and popular drama, specifically devoting
        his attention to the music hall monologue and
        the cross-talk act -- relating them to the
        plays of Beckett, Pinter, and Osborne.

21   *DONOGHUE, DENIS. "The Human Image in
        Modern Drama." Lugano Review 1, nos. 3-4
        (Summer):155-68.

22   DUKORE, BERNARD F. "Beckett's Play, Play."
        Educational Theater Journal 17 (Mar.):19-23.
            Discusses several aspects of the dramatic
        content and the theatrical techniques in
        Play: the anti-Aristotelian aesthetic, the
        comic effect of linguistic juxtaposition, the
        probing light vs. the paradoxical peace and
        isolation of the darkness, the tension

created between the memories of past external
action and present interior action, and the
toneless, rapid tempo of the monologues.

23   ESSLIN, MARTIN, ed. "Introduction." In <u>Samuel
     Beckett: A Collection of Critical Essays</u>.
     Englewood Cliffs, N.J.: Prentice-Hall, pp.
     1-15.
          In his introduction to this series of
     essays, examines the recurring themes in
     Beckett's fiction, his statements about the
     work of creative artists, the links between
     Beckett and Kierkegaard, and Beckett and the
     French Surrealists, and the task of the
     critic analyzing Beckett's works.
     Reprinted: 1980.29.

24   FEDERMAN, RAYMOND. "'How It Is' with Beckett's
     Fiction." <u>French Review</u> 38, no. 4
     (Feb.):459-68.
          Views <u>How It Is</u> as the final step in a
     chronological progression toward fictional
     absurdity and disorder: "The deterioration
     of man, of form, and of language follows an
     irrevocable course which produces in <u>How It
     Is</u> the image of a reptilian creature mutter-
     ing disconnected sounds as it crawls in the
     mud of a fantastically unreal landscape."

25   _____. <u>Journey to Chaos: Samuel Beckett's
     Early Fiction</u>. Berkeley and Los Angeles:
     University of California Press, 243 pp.
          Demonstrates the gradual disintegration of
     form and content in Beckett's work and its
     development into an aesthetic system in the
     novels of the trilogy and <u>How It Is</u>.
     Concentrating on the early fiction, with
     references to the later works, Federman
     divides his study into two parts: 1) the
     gradual alienation of the characters from
     social reality, and 2) the dehumanization of
     the early French heroes. Summaries are given
     for the following works: <u>More Pricks than
     Kicks</u>, "Dream of Fair to Middling Women,"
     <u>Mercier and Camier</u>, "Premier Amour," and

"Eleuthéria." A Chronology of Beckett's
works and a selected bibliography of Beckett
criticism are included.

26   FINCH, ROY. "The Reality of the Nothing: The
      Importance of Samuel Beckett." Lugano Review
      1, nos. 3-4 (Summer):211-22.
          Describes Beckett's concept of "nothing"
      as a beginning again after everything has
      been swept away. Finch points out that the
      reader of Beckett's fiction witnesses the
      disintegration of the world, the protago-
      nists, space and time, and language.

27   FLANNER, JANET. Paris Journal 1944-1965.
      Edited by William Shawn. New York: Athe-
      neum, pp. 197-98.
          Highlights the significance of the first
      performances of Waiting for Godot at the
      Théatre de Babylone in Paris.

28   FLETCHER, JOHN. "Beckett and the Fictional
      Tradition." Caliban: Annales Publiées par
      la Faculté des Lettres et Sciences Humaines
      de Toulouse, no. 1:147-58.
          Believes that Beckett's novels belong to
      the tradition of the anti-novel in European
      literature, which "refuses to take either the
      world or itself seriously, and usually,
      though not always, sets out to burlesque and
      debunk some contemporary or near contemporary
      form that does." Fletcher traces the
      similarity and differences between Beckett's
      novels and those of Cervantes, Swift,
      Fielding, Diderot, Voltaire, and Sterne.

29   _____. "Beckett's Debt to Dante." Nottingham
      French Studies 4, no. 1 (May):41-52.
          Examines Dantean allusions in Beckett's
      fiction.

30   _____. "Only New Understanding." Journal of
      General Education 17 (Oct.):246-48.
          Although Beckett is never mentioned in
      Leon Ebel's critical work, The Modern

Psychological Novel, Fletcher feels that this
work helps to explain Beckett's fiction.

31 _____. "The Private Pain and the Whey of Words:
A Survey of Beckett's Verse." In Samuel
Beckett: A Collection of Critical Essays.
Edited by Martin Esslin. Englewood Cliffs,
N.J.: Prentice-Hall, Inc., pp. 23-32.
Traces the stages of Beckett's "increas-
ingly poetic maturity" (1929-1949) which
Fletcher believes shows the influence of
surrealist techniques: "Over the years,
however, he has moved from an erudite but
superficial manner and from sporting his
influences brazenly to a more genuinely
personal poetry in which the influences are
harmoniously absorbed."

32 _____. "Samuel Beckett and the Philosophers."
Comparative Literature 17, no. 1 (Winter):43-
56.
Considers the philosophers who have
influenced Beckett: the Presocratics, St.
Augustine, Bruno, Vico, Faulhaber, Gassendi,
Descartes, Geulincx, Spinoza, Malebranche,
Leibniz, Locke, and Berkeley, among others.

33 _____. "Samuel Beckett as Critic." Listener
74 (25 Nov.):862-63.
Feels that Beckett's critical writings
shed light on Beckett's view of his craft and
the artistic vocation in general. Fletcher
defines the themes in the critical writings
as "the difficulty and sacredness of the
artist's calling, the emphasis on a necessary
modernity within a respect for tradition ...
and finally the importance of a genuine,
clear-sighted and unsentimental humanism on
the part of the artist."

34 _____. "Samuel Beckett or the Morbid Dread of
Sphinxes." New Durham, (June), pp. 5-9.
Reprinted as Chapter 8 in 1967.42.

35 _____. "Sur un roman inédit de Samuel Beckett."

Littératures XII: Annales publiées par la
Faculté des Lettres et Sciences Humaines de
Toulouse, n.s. 1, no. 3 (Nov.):139-52.
     Describes the characters and action in
Mercier and Camier, comparing the novel to
Waiting for Godot. Fletcher points out that
the theme of the "voyage inutile" is a
constant in Beckett's works, and comments on
the return of characters described in
previous novels.

36   *FORD, PETER. "Waiting for Godot." Guardian,
     5 June.
          Source: Bryer et al. 1972.7;unverified.

37   FOTHERGILL, ROBERT. "The Novels of Samuel
     Beckett. The Search for Identity. The
     Galley-Slave." Peace News, 10 Dec., pp. 5,
     10.
          Examines the theme of self-consciousness
     and the search for identity in the trilogy
     and the image of the galley-slave (Arnold
     Geulincx -- Man is free only in the mind) in
     the trilogy and How It Is.

38   FRANCIS, RICHARD LEE. "Beckett's Metaphysical
     Tragicomedy." Modern Drama 8, no. 3 (Dec.):
     259-67.
          Views Godot as a "repetitive ritual drama
     of words": "Beckett invites us to encompass
     the full nature of human experience as it has
     dramatically evolved in the mixed mode of
     tragicomedy from its origins in ancient
     religious rites.

39   *GARLAND, PATRICK. "Beckett in Monitor."
     Radio Times, 18 Feb., p. 32.

40   GASSNER, JOHN. "They Also Serve." In Direc-
     tions in Modern Theatre and Drama: An
     Expanded Edition of Form and Idea in Modern
     Theatre. New York: Holt, Rinehart and
     Winston, Inc., pp. 318-25.
          Reviews Waiting for Godot, describing the
     play as a modern morality play, based on

Christian themes: "Questioning and expecta-
tion do give life dignity, even though
expectations are never satisfied ..."
Reprint of 1956.14.

41   *GILLET, JOHN. "Battles of Venice." Sunday
       Telegraph (London), 12 Sept.

42   *GILLIATT, PENELOPE. "Growing up with
       Godot." Observer, 3 Jan.

43   GROSSVOGEL, DAVID. "Samuel Beckett: The
       Difficulty of Dying." In The Blasphemers:
       The Theater of Brecht, Ionesco, Beckett,
       Genet. New York: Cornell University Press,
       227 pp.
         Reprint of 1962.35.

44   HARVEY, LAWRENCE E. "Samuel Beckett on Life,
       Art, and Criticism." Modern Language Notes
       80:545-62.
         Outlines Beckett's view of life, art, and
       criticism as it is represented in "Three Dia-
       logues," Beckett's essays on the Van Velde
       brothers, "La Peinture des Van Velde ou le
       monde et le pantalon," "Peintres de l'em-
       pêchement," and the epigraph to the 1962 Le
       Prat edition of Bram van Velde's painting, an
       unpublished manuscript entitled "Les Deux
       Besoins."

45   HAYTER, AUGY. "Paris." Plays and Players 12,
       no. 4 (Jan.):19.
         Finds Beckett's Play moving and powerful,
       not depressing, and believes that a critical
       commentary of Beckett's work seems a vain
       activity: "Because Beckett himself sees with
       such complete clarity what is important and
       what is superficial in our lives, it makes
       idle speculation seem kind of ridiculous."

46   HOEFER, JACQUELINE. "Watt." In Samuel Beckett:
       A Collection of Critical Essays. Edited by
       Martin Esslin. Englewood Cliffs, N.J.:
       Prentice-Hall, Inc., pp. 62-76.
         Surveys the failure of Watt's quest from

a philosophic point of view. Like the
logical positivists, Watt has an obsessive
interest in language and holds that the only
kind of empirical knowledge is scientific.
Hoefer analyses Wittegenstein's ladder of
logic to clarify Arsen's monologue. Reprint
of 1959.21.

47   *HOPE-WALLACE, PHILIP. "Oh! les beaux jours."
      Guardian, 5 Apr.
          Source: Bryer et al. 1972.7;unverified.

48   HURLEY, PAUL J. "France and America: Versions
      of the Absurd." College English 26:634-40.
          Distinguishes current avant-garde theater
      in France and America: French "absurd" drama
      avoids precise symbolism and refuses to
      sermonize while the American theater preaches
      moral and social issues. Examples are taken
      from the plays of Ionesco, Albee, Kopit,
      Beckett, and Gelber.

49   JACOBSEN, JOSEPHINE and WILLIAM R. MUELLER.
      "Samuel Beckett's Long Saturday: To Wait or
      Not to Wait." In Man in the Modern Theatre.
      Edited by Nathan A. Scott. Richmond, Virgin-
      ia: John Knox Press, pp. 76-97.
          Defines Beckett's style as impressionis-
      tic, "He records not with a camera's eye, but
      with some more intuitive sense of the nature
      of that which he describes. He is interested
      not in exterior detail, but in what he
      conceives to be the inner life of his charac-
      ters." In their discussion of Waiting for
      Godot, Endgame, Krapp's Last Tape, and Happy
      Days, Jacobsen and Mueller introduce Bec-
      kett's use of Christian myth, Biblical
      references, the themes of despair and hope,
      the determination of the characters to "keep
      going," the couple, and waiting.

50   KENNER, HUGH. "The Cartesian Centaur." In
      Samuel Beckett: A Collection of Critical
      Essays. Edited by Martin Esslin. Englewood
      Cliffs, N.J.: Prentice-Hall, Inc., pp. 52-
      61.

Discusses the "problem of bodies in motion" in <u>Mercier and Camier</u> and the trilogy with examples from the other works. Kenner views the cyclist in Beckett's fiction as "a glorified body ... the supreme Cartesian achievement, a product of the pure intelligence, which has preceded it in time and dominates it in function." Reprint of 1959.22.

51   *LAING, LLOYD. "'All Life Long the Same Inanities.'" <u>Gambit</u> (Edinburgh), (Autumn), pp. 28-30.

52   LAMONT, ROSETTE. "Death and Tragi-Comedy: Three Plays of the New Theatre." <u>Massachusetts Review</u> 6, no. 2 (Winter-Spring):381-402.
            Classifies <u>Happy Days</u> as "a comedy about the tragedy of the marriage relationship, and the inescapable catastrophe of final dissolution."

53   LEVENTHAL, A. J. "The Beckett Hero." In <u>Samuel Beckett: A Collection of Critical Essays</u>. Edited By Martin Esslin. Engelwood Cliffs, N.J.: Prentice-Hall, Inc., pp. 37-51.
            Originally a lecture delivered at Trinity College, Dublin in June 1963, shows that the "germ" of Beckett's character lies in Dante's <u>Divine Comedy</u> and traces the metaphysical background of Beckett's works to a Sicilian rhetorician and sophist, Gorgias of Lentini. Leventhal also evaluates the names of Beckett's characters and discusses the question of reality and unreality. Reprint of 1964.62.

54   McGRATH, TOM. "In Defence of Beckett." <u>Tribune</u> (London), 15 Jan., p. 14.
            Criticizes Iain Shaw as presenting an incomplete portrait of Beckett's work. McGrath points out that Beckett also presents the message of hope in <u>Waiting for Godot</u>, he praises Beckett's insight into the most

painful aspects of the human predicament, his
humor, and his use of language. See 1965.73.

55   MAYOUX, JEAN-JACQUES. "Samuel Beckett and
     Universal Parody." In Samuel Beckett: A
     Collection of Critical Essays. Edited by
     Martin Esslin. Englewood Cliffs, N.J.:
     Prentice-Hall, Inc., pp. 77-91.
        Illustrates Beckett's use of his "most
     obsessive and involuntary" symbols in Stories
     and Texts for Nothing and the trilogy:
     guilt, cruelty, unreality of reality,
     solitude, sin and punishment, expiation and
     penitence, artistic creation, habit and
     suffering. Reprint of 1960.39 (in French).

56   MONTAGUE, JOHN. "The Trinity Scholard."
     Manchester Guardian, 26 Nov., p. 17.
        Reviews Proust and Three Dialogues, noting
     that these essays provide the best possible
     introduction to Beckett's later work.

57   *MORSE, J. MITCHELL. "The Ideal Core of the
     Onion: Samuel Beckett's Criticism." In
     Literary History and Literary Criticism.
     Edited by Leon Edel. New York: New York
     University Press, p.227.

58   MUELLER, WILLIAM R. and JOSEPHINE JACOBSEN.
     "Samuel Beckett's Long Saturday: To Wait or
     Not to Wait?" In Man in the Modern Theatre.
     T.S. Eliot/Eugene O'Neill. Bertolt Brecht/
     Samuel Beckett. Edited by Nathan Scott.
     Richmond, Virginia: John Knox Press, pp. 76-
     97.
        Examine Beckett's dramatic canon pointing
     out variations on the theme of Easter
     Saturday, "... a day which beckons to
     despair ... a day which calls for rebellion
     ... a day which calls for faith and hope ..."
     The authors present Beckett's image of the
     human condition and the actions of Beckett's
     characters waiting, reminiscing, clinging to
     a partner.

59   NADEAU, MAURICE. "Samuel Beckett: Humor and
          the Void." In <u>Samuel Beckett: A Collection
          of Critical Essays</u>. Edited by Martin Esslin.
          Englewood Cliffs, N. J.: Prentice-Hall, Inc.,
          pp. 33-36.
              Believes the key to <u>Molloy</u> is to be found
          in the three zones of Murphy's mind, pointing
          out that Beckett tries to convey an idea of
          the third and last zone in the world of
          Molloy and Moran: "Every novel is in a way
          the story of a disintegration -- either of
          the hero, or of time, or of life. Here
          disintegration precedes all story -- hero,
          time, and world appear in it but as waves on
          the surface of the sea. No one has ever
          ventured so far in search of an absolute that
          is a minus quality." Reprint of 1951.9,
          1952.1a

60   No entry.

61   NANDAKUMAR, PREMA. "Samuel Beckett." In <u>The
          Glory and the Good. Essays on Literature</u>.
          Bombay, N.Y.: Asia Publishing House, pp.
          146-57.
              Describes Beckett's drama as an "epic
          stalemate" and Beckett as a "cynical opti-
          mist"; Nandakumar considers cynicism,
          pessimism, hope, and redemption as they are
          presented in <u>Godot</u>, <u>Endgame</u>, and <u>Happy Days</u>.

62   RATCLIFFE, MICHAEL. "Beckett in North Ken."
          <u>Sunday Times</u> (London), 28 Feb.
              Calls attention to Beckett's collaboration
          with Jack MacGowran in "Beginning to End," a
          monologue based on Beckett's less familiar
          prose works.

63   ROBBE-GRILLET, ALAIN. "Samuel Beckett or
          'Presence' on the Stage." In <u>For a New
          Novel: Essays on Fiction</u>. New York: Grove
          Press, pp. 111-25.
              Translation of "Samuel Beckett sur la
          scène." Reprinted from 1953.14, 1963.69,

1967.89; see 1965.64 for annotation.

64   _____. "Samuel Beckett or 'Presence' in the
        Theater." In <u>Samuel Beckett: A Collection
        of Critical Essays</u>. Edited by Martin Esslin.
        Englewood Cliffs, N.J. : Prentice Hall,
        Inc., pp. 108-116.
            Compares the plays <u>Waiting for Godot</u> and
        <u>Endgame</u> with Beckett's novels. Robbe-Grillet
        demonstrates that the prose narrators, like
        the characters of the plays, are inventors of
        fiction: "After imagining for a moment that
        we had at last found man himself we are
        forced to admit our mistake. Didi was only
        an illusion ... He too was no more than a
        lie, a provisional being, who soon sank back
        again into the world of dream, the world of
        fiction." Reprinted from 1953.14, 1963.69;
        reprint of 1965.63, reprinted 1967.89.

65   *ROSBO, PATRICK de. "Le Théâtre et la mort."
        <u>Cahiers du Théâtre</u> 2, no. 3:26-35.

66   ROY, CLAUDE. "Sur Samuel Beckett." In <u>Descrip-
        tions Critiques, Vol. 6. L'Amour du théâtre</u>.
        Paris: Gallimard, pp. 158-65.
            Simulates the audience response to <u>Happy
        Days</u>, discussing the play as an example of
        Beckett's interest in presenting eternal
        truths in his works. Roy views Beckett's
        works as parables, or "apologues philoso-
        phiques." Reprint of 1964.87.

67   RUTHERFORD, MALCOLM. "Camp Tramps." <u>Spectator</u>
        214 (8 Jan.):42.
            Stresses the comic elements in the
        production of <u>Waiting for Godot</u> at the Royal
        Court Theatre. Rutherford believes <u>Godot</u> is
        a better play than Beckett's other dramas,
        because the characters are not confined.

68   SAINT-PHALLE, THERESE de. "La Littérature
        envahit le cinéma." <u>Figaro Littéraire</u>, 16-
        22 Sept., p. 3.

Offers a general discussion of the film
scenarios written by Beckett, Ionesco,
Marguerite Duras, Robbe-Grillet, and Harold
Pinter.

69   *SARTRE, JEAN PAUL. <u>Politics and Literature</u>.
Translated by J.A. Underwood and John Calder.
London: Calder and Boyars.

70   SCHNEIDER, ALAN. "Reality is Not Enough."
<u>Tulane Drama Review</u> 9, no. 3 (Spring):118-52.
Beckett: pp. 129-43.
Interviewed by Richard Schechner, Alan
Schneider discusses his strict adherence to
Beckett's intentions, comments on the various
Beckett works he has directed (<u>Play</u>, <u>Happy
Days</u>, <u>Endgame</u>, <u>Film</u>, <u>Godot</u>), and discusses
Beckett's development and theatricalism.

71   SCOTT, NATHAN. <u>Samuel Beckett</u>. London: Bowes
and Bowes; New York: Hillary House; Toronto:
Queenswood, 141 pp.
Places Beckett in the French literary
tradition introduced by Baudelaire, Rimbaud,
and Lautréamont, extended by Mallarmé,
Valéry, and the Surrealists, and continued by
the novelists of the post World War II era.
Referring to Beckett's world as the "Zone of
Zero," Scott hails Beckett as the most
considerable figure of the generation of
Robbe-Grillet and Butor "because the progress
that is marked by his fiction has the effect
of disclosing the motive that is at work in
all the new 'alittérature' -- which is a
profound mistrust of the possibility of any
real adequation between the world and the
human actuality." Scott discusses the plays,
novels, and stories, and explains how
Heidegger's essay "What is Metaphysics?" can
help to clarify the meaning of Beckett's
work. The text is followed by a biographical
note and a selected bibliography. Portions
of this essay appeared in 1962.67.

72   SEAVER, RICHARD. "Samuel Beckett." In <u>The</u>
     <u>Olympia Reader. Selections from the Travel-</u>
     <u>ler's Companion Series</u>. Edited by Maurice
     Girodias. New York: Grove Press, pp. 220-
     25.
        Sketches the background concerning the
     literary quarterly <u>Merlin</u> and the publication
     of Samuel Beckett's <u>Watt</u>.

73   SHAW, IAIN. "Philosophy of Nihilism." <u>Tribune</u>
     (London), 8 Jan., p. 14.
        Reviews <u>Waiting for Godot</u> at the Royal
     Court Theatre: criticizes Beckett's play as
     boring, his viewpoint as nihilistic, and his
     comic genius as overrated.

74   *SHEARER, ANN. "The Art of Samuel Beckett."
     <u>Guardian</u>, 3 Sept.
        Source: Bryer et al. 1972.7;unverified.

75   SIMPSON, ALAN. "<u>Waiting for Godot</u>." <u>Plays and</u>
     <u>Players</u> 12, no. 5 (Feb.):45, 50.
        Reviews <u>Waiting for Godot</u> at the Royal
     Court Theatre (revival in 1964) -- stating
     that the play can now be viewed in perspec-
     tive, with its potential "as a star vehicle
     for the actor playing Vladimir."

76   UPDIKE, JOHN. "How <u>How It Is</u> Was." In <u>Assorted</u>
     <u>Prose</u>. New York: Alfred A. Knopf; London:
     André Deutsch, pp. 214-18.
        Reprint of 1964.99.

77   *"<u>Waiting for Godot</u>." <u>Times</u> (London), 16 Jan.,
     p. 5.
        Source: Tanner, 1969.113;unverified.

78   WELLERSHOFF, DIETER. "Failure of an Attempt at
     De-mythologization: Samuel Beckett's
     Novels." In <u>Samuel Beckett: A Collection of</u>
     <u>Critical Essays</u>. Edited by Martin Esslin.
     Englewood Cliffs, N.J.: Prentice-Hall, Inc.,
     pp. 92-107.
        Demonstrates the gradual dissolution of

subject (trilogy) and language (<u>Texts for Nothing</u>) and the continual failure in the quest for truth (<u>How It Is</u>) in Beckett's prose works.

79 *WORDEN, BLAIR. "Is Godot a Bicycle?" <u>Isis</u>, 27 Oct.

80 *"Why Actors are Fascinated by Beckett's Theatre." <u>Times</u> (London), 27 Feb., p. 14.
      Source: Tanner, 1969.113;unverified.

81 *YOUNG, NICK. "<u>Waiting for Godot</u>." <u>Isis</u>, 27 Oct., p. 20.

<u>1966</u>

1 ABIRACHED, ROBERT. "Beckett Romancier." <u>Nouvelles Littéraires</u>, 24 Feb., p. 6.
      Comments on the gradual changes that take place in Beckett's novels (<u>Murphy</u>, the trilogy, <u>How It Is</u>), the deprivation of the characters, disintegration of language and the corresponding spontaneity and ingenuity of the novels.

2 _____. Images d'enfer." <u>Nouvel Observateur</u>, 16-22 Feb.
      Source: Bryer et al. 1972.7;unverified.

3 ADAMS, VAL. "WDNT Will Present Beckett and Ionesco Plays." <u>New York Times</u>, 11 Apr.
      Source: Zilliacus, 1975.105;unverified.

4 ALPAUGH, DAVID J. "Negative Definition in Samuel Beckett's <u>Happy Days</u>." <u>Twentieth Century Literature</u> 11, no. 4 (Jan.):202-10.
      Believes Beckett presents his vision of modernity by negative definition is achieved through references to an ideal past ("the old style"): "Beckett focuses on the Victorian period as a means of negatively defining modernity because the Victorians were the

last to rationalize the disparity between
scientific discoveries and spiritual beliefs
and obtain some degree of universal credence
for their rationalizations.

5   _____. "The Symbolic Structure of Samuel
       Beckett's All That Fall." Modern Drama 9,
       no. 3 (Dec.):324-32.
            Concentrates on the symbolic implications
       of Beckett's treatment of language, Christi-
       anity, movement, and death in All That Fall.

6   ATKINS, ANSELM. "A Note on the Structure of
       Lucky's Speech." Modern Drama 9, no. 3
       (Dec.):309.
            Briefly comments on the tripart division
       of Lucky's speech, classifying the parts as
       an unfinished protasis of a theological or
       philosophical argument and two incomplete
       objections to a rational argument.

7   *A[UDOUARD], Y[VAN]. "Pieces détachés."
       Canard Enchaîné, 16 Mar.

8   *BANERJEE, C. "Theatre. Endgame, by Samuel
       Beckett." Thought 18, no. 17 (23 Apr.):20-
       21.

9   *"Belgrade Theatre Casts Its Net Wide." Times
       (London), 6 Sept.
            Source: Bryer et al. 1972.7;unverified.

10   BERNARD, MARC. "Un raz de marée: Spectacle
       Beckett -- Pinget -- Ionesco." Nouvelles
       Littéraires, 17 Mar., p. 13.
            Analyzes the visual impact of Play, the
       question of religion in the works of Beckett
       and Joyce, and briefly comments on Come and
       Go.

11   BERSANI, LEO. "No Exit for Beckett." Partisan
       Review 33, no. 2 (Spring):261-67.
            Evaluates Beckett's intention to fail
       as it is expressed in his fiction. In a
       struggle against content, Bersani remarks

that "the process rather than the achievement
becomes the subject of Beckett's work."

12   *BISHOP, MORRIS. "Drama Mid-Decade." Times
     Literary Supplement (London), 16 June.
          Source: Bryer et al. 1972.7;unverified.

13   *"Bleak Genius is Honoured." Times (London), 13
     Jan.
          Source: Bryer et al. 1972.7;unverified.

14   *BREE, GERMAINE. "Journey to Chaos: Samuel
     Beckett's Early Fiction." Modern Language
     Quarterly 28, no. 2 (June):235-37.
          Source: Bryer et al. 1972.7;unverified.

15   BROOKS, CURTIS M. "The Mythic Pattern in
     Waiting for Godot." Modern Drama 9, no. 3
     (Dec.):292-99.
          Suggests that Waiting for Godot reflects a
     seasonal mythic pattern and resembles a
     ritual drama. His discussion centers around
     references to Frye, Frazer and Cassirer.

16   "Les Bruits de la ville." Nouvel Observateur,
     19-25 Jan., pp. 32-33.
          Briefly describes the making of the film
     version of Beckett's Play under the direction
     of Jean-Marie Serreau, Jean Ravel and Marin
     Karmitz, with Beckett's supervision.

17   BURGESS, ANTHONY. "Enduring Saturday." Spec-
     tator 216 (29 Apr.):532-33.
          Considers Beckett a dramatist of the
     absurd, using Camus' definition of absurdity
     from The Myth of Sisyphus. Burgess points
     out that unlike Camus' heroes, Beckett's
     characters do not act, they only wait, and
     whereas "in Camus we catch echoes of the
     stoicism of Seneca, in Beckett we smell the
     leavings of Christian hope."

18   CHAMBERS, ROSS. "A Theatre of Dilemma and
     Myth." Meanjin Quarterly 25, no. 3 (Spring):
     306-17. Beckett: pp. 314-16.

Feels that a sense of disharmony or
dilemma has become the thematic material of
many plays grouped under the heading "theater
of the absurd." Thus in Waiting for Godot
the spectator experiences the "ambiguous
time-world of Beckett's purgatory" which
words are powerless to convey.

19   CHAPSAL, MADELEINE. "Samuel Beckett suit son
      cours." Express, 21-27 Nov., p. 35.
          Points out that Beckett's recent short
      prose pieces "Imagination Dead Imagine" and
      "Ping" continue the same "adventure" that
      Beckett has been recounting from the begin-
      ning -- that of a being cast into the world
      in spite of his own wishes.

20   CHASE, N.C. "Images of Man: Le Malentendu and
      En attendant Godot." Wisconsin Studies in
      Contemporary Literature 7, no. 3 (Autumn):
      295-302.
          Studies the dramatists' divergent images
      of man which are determined in this case by
      the difference in the audience's response to
      comic technique in Beckett's Waiting for
      Godot and dramatic irony in Camus' Le
      Malentendu.

21   CLURMAN, HAROLD. "Happy Days." In The Naked
      Image. Observations on the Modern Theatre.
      New York: Macmillan Co., pp. 40-42.
          Discusses Winnie's irrepressible optimism
      and the portrayal of pity and repressed
      tenderness behind the irony in the play.

22   ____. "The Lover and Beckett's Play." In The
      Naked Image. Observations on the Modern
      Theatre. New York: Macmillan, pp. 112-14.
          Reviews the double bill of one-act plays
      by Harold Pinter and Beckett. Clurman
      briefly describes the stage situation,
      subject, and his personal reaction to
      Beckett's drama.

23   COHN, RUBY. "The Beginning of Endgame." Modern
     Drama 9, no. 3 (Dec.):319-23.
     Traces Beckett's revisions of his first
     two act version of Endgame.

24   ____. "Joyce and Beckett, Irish Cosmopolitans."
     In Proceedings of the Fourth Congress of the
     International Comparative Literature Associa-
     tion. Edited by François Jost. The Hague:
     Mouton, pp. 109-113.
     Compares and contrasts the backgrounds,
     influences, and writing of Beckett and Joyce:
     "Beckett himself emphasizes the difference
     between these Irish Cosmopolitans -- Joyce
     attempting to embrace all knowledge, all
     experience, all language; Beckett doubting
     all knowledge, all experience, all language,
     and doubting even his cartesian heritage of
     doubt." Reprinted: 1971.17

25   COURNOT, MICHEL. "Les Malles d'Albertine."
     Nouvel Observateur, 9-15 Feb., p. 40.
     Writes a tribute to Buster Keaton after
     his death, recalling the last time he saw
     Keaton at a Press Conference in Venice
     following the showing of Film. Cournot sees
     an image of death in general and the death of
     Keaton in Beckett's film.

26   CRONIN, ANTHONY. "Molloy Becomes Unnamable."
     In A Question of Modernity. London: Secker
     and Warburg, pp. 97-110.
     Comments on the cumulative effect of the
     trilogy and the over-all form of Beckett's
     work through the circumstances, characters,
     and vision of life and art portrayed in
     Beckett's prose.

27   *DEGUY, MICHEL. "De Rimbaud à Beckett." Quin-
     zaine Littéraire, no. 15 (1-15 Nov.), p. 14.
     Source: Bryer et al. 1972.7;unverified.

28   DUBOIS, JACQUES. "Beckett and Ionesco: The
     Tragic Awareness of Pascal and the Ironic
     Awareness of Flaubert." Modern Drama 9,

no. 3 (Dec.):283-91.
Demonstrates the structural similarity of
Beckett's Waiting for Godot and Ionesco's The
Chairs and points out the basis for the
differences in their sociological vision.

29 DUCKWORTH, COLIN. "The Making of Godot."
Theatre Research 7, no. 3:123-45.
Studies the genesis of Waiting for Godot,
comparing this play to Mercier and Camier
written four years prior. Duckworth limits
his comparison to specific points of reference: the setting of the play, the origins
and meaning of the tree, Godot, the rendezvous and the theme of waiting, the creation
of the characters and the relationships
between them, the perfection of the dialogue
and the suppression of certain precise
details to be found in the manuscript.

30 ELLIOT, ROGER. "Prize Winning Student Directors
Speak Their Minds." Illustrated London News,
15 Jan., pp. 18-19.
Two of the student directors explain what
Beckett's theater meant to them and how they
went about producing Act Without Words and
Endgame.

31 FLETCHER, JOHN. "Action and Play in Beckett's
Theater." Modern Drama 9, no. 3 (Dec.):242-
50.
Introduces Beckett's use of the three
basic forms of action in his theater:
clownery, music hall crosstalk, and mime.

32 _____.   "Roger Blin at Work." Modern Drama 8,
no. 4 (Feb.):403-8.
Traces the evolution of Blin's production
of Godot in Toulouse with the company Le
Grenier de Toulouse. Each time Blin stages
the play "he approaches the text afresh,
because ... he must inevitably adjust that
idea in accordance with differing circum-
stances and different personalities in his
actors."

33   FRIEDMAN, MELVIN J.   "Crritic!" [sic] <u>Modern
      Drama</u> 9 (Dec.):300-308.
           Enumerates the articles which present
      contradictory interpretations of <u>Waiting for
      Godot</u>. Reprinted: 1967.41.

34   GARELLI, JACQUES.   "De l'absurdité au non-sens
      ontologique: Molloy ou la passion de
      l'être." In <u>La Gravitation Poétique</u>. Paris:
      Mercure de France, pp. 63-71.
           Remarks that Molloy, by his acceptance of
      the nonsense of questions and answers, his
      renouncement of desire and his social and
      psychological identity, is closer to
      oriental philosophers than he is to the
      despair of Kierkegaardien existentialism.

35   GLICKSBERG, CHARLES I.   "The Flight from Self in
      the World of Samuel Beckett." In <u>Modern
      Literature and the Death of God</u>. The Hague:
      Martinus Nijhoff, pp. 33-35.
           Analyzes the nihilistic disintegration of
      the Beckett hero, the desperate flight from
      self, and the hopelessness of the mythic
      quest.

36   *GOULD, JACK.   "TV: Dramas by Ionesco and
      Beckett." <u>New York Times</u>, 19 Apr.
           Source: Zilliacus, 1975.105;unverified.

37   GREENBERG, ALVIN.   "The Death of the Psyche: A
      Way to the Self in the Contemporary Novel."
      <u>Criticism</u> 8, no. 1 (Winter):1-18.
           Emphasizes the significance of a pheno-
      menological approach to the modern novel,
      utilizing <u>Watt</u> as an example.

38   HATZFELD, HELMUT A.   <u>Trends and Styles in Twen-
      tieth Century French Literature</u>. Washington
      D.C.: Catholic University of America Press,
      1952; Revised and enlarged edition, 1966.
      Beckett: 176-77, 266-68.
           Focuses on Beckett's nihilism in <u>Molloy</u>
      and <u>How It Is</u> and his "metaphysical" farces,

<u>Waiting for Godot</u>, <u>Endgame</u>, and <u>Krapp's Last
Tape</u>.

39   HUBERT, RENEE RIESE. "Beckett's <u>Play</u> Between
     Poetry and Performance." <u>Modern Drama</u> 9,
     no. 3 (Dec.):339-46.
          Compares and contrasts Beckett's <u>Play</u> and
     Sartre's <u>No Exit</u>. The poetic qualities of
     Beckett's language are also discussed with
     special reference to Apollinaire, Reverdy,
     Michaux, and Desnos.

40   ISER, WOLFGANG. "Samuel Beckett's Dramatic
     Language." <u>Modern Drama</u> 9, no. 3 (Dec.):
     251-59.
          Claims that language has lost its dramatic
     character in Beckett's plays.

41   JANVIER, LUDOVIC. <u>Pour Samuel Beckett</u>. Paris:
     Editions de Minuit, 285 pp.
          Comments on the development of character,
     theme, and language and the function of humor
     in Beckett's drama and prose. Three final
     chapters describe more specific topics: 1) a
     comparison of quotations from Pascal,
     Rimbaud, and Artaud with those from Beckett's
     works, 2) the letter M, 3) hat, father, and
     the inner core of being. Reprinted in part:
     1970.67, 1970.68.

42   _____. "Réduire à la parole." <u>Cahiers
     Renaud-Barrault</u> 53 (Feb.):42-48.
          Underlines the interrelation of incarcera-
     tion and discourse to Beckett's art, noting
     that the character's reduction in movement
     is compensated for by his verbosity.
     Examples are taken from the novels and plays,
     with special emphasis on <u>Play</u>.

43   JHA, A. "Notes on the Nature of Comic Laugh-
     ter." <u>Calcutta Review</u> 180, no. 1
     (July):63-69.
          Considers the contemporary dramas of
     Giraudoux, Anouilh, Ionesco, Fry, Beckett,
     and Pinter which suggest "a unique comic

vision and [provoke] a kind of laughter which
does not ignore the tragic."

44   JOUFFROY, ALAIN.   "Un cri dans la nuit."
     Express, no. 766 (21-27 Feb.), pp. 70-71.
         Portraying Beckett as a "visionary of lan-
     guage," underlines the apparent paradoxes in
     Beckett's works, with specific reference to
     Molloy, Play and Ludovic Janvier's Pour
     Samuel Beckett.

45   KERMODE, FRANK.   "The New Apocalyptists."
     Partisan Review 33, no. 3 (Summer):339-61.
     Beckett: pp. 354-55.
         Categorizes Beckett's work as a link
     between two stages in the modernist movement.

46   KERN, EDITH.   "Beckett and the Spirit of the
     Commedia dell'Arte."   Modern Drama 9, no. 3
     (Dec.):260-67.
         Despite the fact that Beckett's plays
     utilize none of the obvious features of the
     Commedia dell'Arte, Kern feels that they
     still embody the spirit of Commedia dell'Arte
     tradition: its lazzi, its attitude toward
     language, and its grotesque stylization.

47   KOTT, JAN.   "A Note on Beckett's Realism."
     Tulane Drama Review 10, no. 3 (Spring):156-
     59.
         Examines the realism of Happy Days,
     suggesting possible comparisons between
     Winnie's world and life in a hospital or
     nursing home.

48   LENNON, PETER.   "Beckett on Buster."   Manchester
     Guardian, 19 Feb., p. 6.
         Beckett describes Buster Keaton and his
     experience working with him on Film.

49   *MARRIGAN, NICK.   "The Grotesque in Modern Art
     and Literature."   Circuit, no. 3 (Winter),
     pp. 45-48.

50   MAYOUX, JEAN-JACQUES. "Beckett and Expression-
      ism." Translated by Ruby Cohn. <u>Modern Drama</u>
      9, no. 3 (Dec.):238-41.
          Believes that Beckett's theater is
      expressionist and parodic -- he holds up a
      "horrible distorting" mirror for the average
      man to recognize his condition.
          Excerpted and translated from a longer
      study "Beckett and the Paths of Expression-
      ism" written in French but published only in
      German. Reprinted: 1967.73.

51   ____. "Beckett et l'humour." <u>Cahiers Renaud-
      Barrault</u> 53 (Feb.):33-41.
          Regards humor as "essential" to Beckett's
      works. Mayoux traces Beckettian humor to its
      beginnings in <u>More Pricks than Kicks</u> and
      examines several possible influences: Swift,
      Stern, Rabelais, Joyce, Jarry, and the music-
      hall tradition.

52   *MAZARS, PIERRE. "Grâce à Beckett et Agnès
      Varda Venise 66 sera une bonne année."
      <u>Figaro Littéraire</u>, 1 Sept.
          Source: Bryer et al. 1972.7;unverified.

53   MELESE, PIERRE. <u>Samuel Beckett</u>. Paris: Pierre
      Seghers, 192 pp.
          Briefly introduces Beckett's prose and
      poetry and gives a detailed account of each
      play with excerpts from the works. Comments
      on Beckett's works by numerous critics and
      writers are included, as well as a table
      comparing major historical events with
      Beckett's life and works and a select
      bibliography.

54   MIHALYI, GABOR. "Beckett's <u>Godot</u> and the Myth
      of Alienation." <u>Modern Drama</u> 9, no. 3
      (Dec.):277-82.
          Exposes Beckett's repudiation of the myths
      of redemption, enlightenment, progress,
      nature, and love. Mihalyi feels that Beckett
      implements Brecht's theory of alienation
      through his use of farce.

55   MOORE, HARRY T.   "The Mud and Ashcan World of
      Samuel Beckett."   In <u>Twentieth Century French
      Literature Since World War II</u>.   Carbondale:
      Southern Illinois University Press, pp. 165-
      76.
          Describes Beckett's literary career and
      his contribution to the literature of the
      absurd.

56   *NIGHTINGALE, BENEDICT.   "Endgame at Liverpool."
      <u>Guardian</u>, 19 Jan.
          Source: Bryer et al. 1972.7;unverified.

57   OBERG, ARTHUR.   "<u>Krapp's Last Tape</u> and the
      Proustian Vision."   <u>Modern Drama</u> 9, no. 3
      (Dec.):333-38.
          Claims that <u>Krapp's Last Tape</u> dramatizes
      the parodic nature of memory processes.
      Reprinted: 1980.85.

58   PARKER, R.B.   "The Theory and Theatre of the
      Absurd."   <u>Queen's Quarterly</u> 73, no. 3
      (Autumn):421-41.
          Discusses the theory of absurdity as it is
      presented by Albert Camus in his <u>Myth of
      Sisyphus</u>.   Parker applies Camus' analysis to
      aspects of the work of Beckett, Ionesco,
      Genet, Pinter, and Albee.   Following the same
      format as <u>The Myth of Sisyphus</u> his study is
      divided into 3 parts: 1) the anxiety before
      the "otherness" of existence, 2) the problem
      of consciousness especially as it applies to
      art, and 3) a consideration of the "posi-
      tives" with which the absurdists conclude.

59   PARSONS, MICHAEL.   "Samuel Beckett: <u>Imagination
      Dead Imagine</u>."   <u>New Left Review</u>, no. 38
      (July-Aug.), pp. 91-92.
          Reviews "Imagination Dead Imagine"
      emphasizing the increasing anonymity and
      disembodiment of the Beckettian subject.
      Parsons remarks that the later work provides
      a logical continuation of Beckett's earlier
      novels: the "loss of individual identity is

shown to be an ultimate derivation from loss
of social identity."

60   POIROT-DELPECH, BERTRAND. "Beckett dramaturge."
      Nouvelles Littéraires, 24 Feb., p. 7.
          Presents a general analysis of Beckett's
      theatre, Beckett's vision of man and the
      world, the physical situation or location of
      the characters, his portrayal of human
      relations and his choice of language.

61   "Quand Beckett tourne Comédie." Arts 17 (19-25
      Jan.):29.
          Provides photos of the filming of Play and
      very briefly describes the use of a machine
      to speed up the voices.

62   RENAUD, MADELEINE. "Beckett le magnifique."
      Nouvelles Littéraires, 24 Feb., p. 7.
          Describes her experiences acting in Happy
      Days, her admiration for Beckett, and their
      friendship.

63   RICKS, CHRISTOPHER. "Beckett's Bizarre Text:
      'Imagination Dead Imagine.'" Sunday Times
      (London), 20 Feb., p. 31.
          Questions the "greatness" of Beckett's
      latest short prose pieces, comparing Bec-
      kett's vision of hell in "Imagination Dead
      Imagine" to that of Blake, Dante, and Milton.

64   SCHECHNER, RICHARD. "There's Lots of Time in
      Godot." Modern Drama 9, no. 3 (Dec.):268-
      76.
          Sees Waiting for Godot as a confrontation
      between place and time, "coordinates of the
      same function," which form the center of the
      action in this play. Reprinted: 1967.94.

65   SERREAU, GENEVIEVE. "Samuel Beckett." In
      Histoire du nouveau théâtre. Paris:
      Gallimard, pp. 83-116.
          After a brief introduction to Beckett's
      literary career, analyzes Waiting for Godot,
      Endgame, Krapps's Last Tape, All That Fall,

Happy Days, and Play. Serreau underlines the
gradual reduction that has taken place in
Beckett's plays and the emphasis placed on
self-knowledge. Reprinted in part: 1967.96.

66   SHEEDY, JOHN J. "The Comic Apocalypse of King
        Hamm." Modern Drama 9, no. 3 (Dec.):310-18.
        Views Endgame as "an oracle of man's
     doom." Yet the comic and the apocalyptic
     have been fused and Hamm becomes the figura-
     tive as well as the literal center of the
     play: "Endgame depicts Hamm not only as son,
     father, master, King, and Jesus, but also as
     God become Jesus, King, master, father, and
     son -- at once the writer, director, and star
     actor sufferer in the only show on earth."

67   *"10's for the Film Rights." Times (London), 26
        Apr.
        Source: Bryer et al. 1972.7;unverified.

68   *"10's for the Film Rights of Act Without
        Words." Times (London), 25 Apr., p. 16.
        Source: Tanner, 1969.113;unverified.

69   TOYNBEE, PHILIP. "Order Out of Chaos."
        Observer, 2 Jan., p. 24.
        Criticizes the portrayal of chaos and
     despair in the works of William Burroughs who
     reproduces chaos in the form of "wild
     sadistic fantasy" and Beckett who has
     "reduced his human protagonists to situations
     of increasing impotence, mutilation, and
     ridicule."

70   WALCUTT, CHARLES CHILD. "Coda: Beckett or Man
        as Nothing." In Man's Changing Mask: Modes
        and Methods of Characterization in Fiction.
        Minneapolis: University of Minnesota Press,
        pp. 339-46.
        Feels that Malone Dies expresses a
     sequence of trivial associations, making a
     virtue of disorder, while the sentences are
     little more than automatic writing. Walcutt
     believes that Beckett has expanded a descrip-

tion of "the twilit, wandering mind, groping
spinning free, lingering, repeating, striving
feebly for order" -- into 120 full pages.

71   WARDLE, IRVING. "Arts in Society: Drama inside
      the Head." New Society 7, no. 180 (10 Mar.):
      23.
          Describes the impact of hearing a Beckett
      reading at the Traverse Theatre in Edinburgh,
      comparing the experience to the medium of
      radio.

72   WEBB, EUGENE. "Critical Writings on Samuel
      Beckett: A Bibliography." West Coast Review
      1, no. 1 (Spring):56-70.
          Lists the crtical material that has
      appeared on Beckett from 1938 to the first
      months of 1966. The entries consist mainly
      of English language criticism and include
      most of the French language material as well
      as selected works in other European lan-
      guages.

73   *"When Joe Has a Voice." Times (London), 6
      July.
          Source: Bryer et al. 1972.7;unverified.

74   WILLIAMS, VIVIAN CRADDOCK. "Samuel Beckett's
      'Birthday Book.'" Weekend Telegraph (Lon-
      don), no. 81 (Friday 15 Apr.), p. 15.
          Previews a "birthday book" of tributes
      from actors, writers, and critics to be
      published by John Calder.

75   WORTH, KATHARINE J. "Yeats and the French
      Drama." Modern Drama 8, no. 4 (Feb.):382-
      91.
          Believes Yeats anticipates some of
      Beckett's central themes, stage settings, and
      dramatic techniques.

76   *"Yugoslav Play Starts from Beckett." Times
      (London), 3 June.
          Source: Bryer et al. 1972.7;unverified.

1966-1967

1   FEDERMAN, RAYMOND. "Film." Film Quarterly, 20
     no. 2 (Winter):46-51.
        Stresses that Film "represents an attempt
     to expose one of the cinema's most flagrant
     failings today: the exploitation of sound,
     action, plot, and message to the detriment of
     the visual image." Reprinted: 1979.22.60.

2   *MERRIGAN, NICK. "The Grotesque in Modern Art
     and Literature." Circuit, no. 3 (Winter):
     45-48.

3   ONIMUS, JEAN. "Samuel Beckett devant Dieu."
     Annales du Centre Universitaire Méditerranéen
     20, pp. 145-54.
        Summarizes Beckett's origins and the
     influences he's undergone, and comments on
     Beckett's portrayal of a hidden, tyrannical
     God.

1967

1   ANOUILH, JEAN. "Godot or the Music-Hall Sketch
     of Pascal's Pensées as Played by the
     Fratellini Clowns." In Casebook on "Waiting
     for Godot." Edited by Ruby Cohn. New York:
     Grove Press, pp. 12-13.
        Reprint of 1953.1 (in French); see
     1967.24.

2   ATKINS, ANSELM. "Lucky's Speech in Beckett's
     Waiting for Godot: A Punctuated Sense-Line
     Arrangement." Educational Theater Journal 19
     (Dec.):426-32.
        Gives a detailed analysis of Lucky's
     speech in Act I. By dividing the monologue
     into three parts, Atkins shows how the
     individual sections project a slightly
     different style and meaning.

3   ATTOUN, LUCIEN. "Qui est Godot? Au Festival de
     Liège." Nouvelles Littéraires, 19 Oct., p. 14.

Describes a production of <u>Waiting for Godot</u> and the sequel written by the Yugoslav Miodrag Bulatovic in which Godot arrives and Lucky obtains his freedom.

4   AUDIBERTI, JACQUES. "At the Babylone: A Fortunate Move on the Theater Checkerboard." In <u>Casebook on "Waiting for Godot."</u> Edited by Ruby Cohn. New York: Grove Press, pp. 13-14.
Translation of an excerpt of a 1953 review of <u>Waiting for Godot</u>. Reprinted from 1953.1a; see 1967.24.

5   BABY, YVONNE. "Courts -- Métrages à la Pagode." <u>Monde</u>, 28 Feb., p. 14.
Includes brief reviews of the film version of <u>Play</u>, which she finds uninspiring, and <u>Film</u>, "the true film of despair and absolute solitude: in which Buster Keaton represents his own death and a disappearing era."

6   BALLARDINI, VITTORIO. "Beckett -- Ecrivain irlandais." <u>Langues Modernes</u> 61, no. 2 (Mar.-Apr.):218-24.
Examines Beckett's Irish background, his use of the French language, his originality, and the differences between Beckett's fiction and that of his Irish predessors.

7   <u>Beckett at 60: A Festschrift</u>. London: Calder and Boyars, 99 pp.
Presents a series of reminiscences, critical examinations, and tributes written by friends, fellow writers and critics to commemorate Beckett's sixtieth birthday. Contributors to the <u>Festschrift</u> include: A.J. Leventhal, Maria Jolas, Jerôme Lindon, Marcel Mihalovici, Jack MacGowran, Harold Hobson, John Fletcher, Alan Schneider, Martin Esslin ("Samuel Beckett's Poem," reprinted: 1980.29), Hugh Kenner, Madeleine Renaud, Robert Pinget, Harold Pinter, Charles Monteith, Fernando Arrabal, Philippe Staib, Aidan Higgins, Mary Hutchinson, Alan Simpson, Jocelyn Herbert and George Devine.

8   *BENMUSSA, SIMONE. "Samuel Beckett." <u>Biblio</u>
     35, no. 1 (Jan.):2-3.

9   BENTLEY, ERIC. "The Talent of Samuel Beckett."
     In <u>Casebook on "Waiting for Godot."</u> Edited
     by Ruby Cohn. New York: Grove Press, pp.
     59-66.
          Reprint of 1956.5, with a Postscript from
     1967. Bently records his first impressions
     of <u>Godot</u> and then acknowledges the sufficien-
     cy of his first comments; see 1967.24.

10   BERLIN, NORMAND. "Beckett and Shakespeare,"
     <u>French Review</u> 40, no. 3 (Apr.):647-51.
          Disagrees with the premise of Jan Kott's
     <u>Shakespeare, Our Contemporary</u>. Berlin
     believes that the works of Beckett and
     Shakespeare both deal with the human condi-
     tion and man's nature, but that is where the
     similarities end. In Shakespeare we encoun-
     ter movement, the progression of time, and
     the communication of meaning through
     language. Beckett, on the other hand,
     presents static situations and uses language
     to show that there is no meaning to be
     communicated.

11   BESSE, JEAN. "Au 'Drapiers' de Strasbourg: <u>Fin
     de partie</u> de Beckett." <u>Lettres Françaises</u>,
     16-24 May, p. 20.
          Reviews a "humanized" production of
     <u>Endgame</u>, set in an eerie cave. Besse
     emphasizes the comic aspects of the play.

12   BLAU, HERBERT. "Notes from the Underground."
     In <u>Casebook on "Waiting for Godot."</u> Edited
     by Ruby Cohn. New York: Grove Press, pp.
     113-21.
          Speaking from experience, describes the
     "net of inexhaustibility" in <u>Godot</u> which
     tested the very limits of style and stage:
     "the effort was to extend the natural into
     the unnatural, to create the reality of
     illusion and the illusion of reality, to make

the theatrical real and the real theatrical
..." See 1967.24.

13   ____. "Politics and the Theater." <u>Wascana
        Review</u> 2, no. 2:5-23.
            Analyzes <u>Waiting for Godot</u>, the lack of
        action and plot, the characters' lack of
        memory, and the lack of a solution to the
        human condition on the social level: "<u>Godot</u>
        describes the political condition of men who
        created a world in which powerlessness seems
        our common plight." Blau points out that
        both <u>Waiting for Godot</u> and <u>Endgame</u> are
        concerned with the conquest of Self, the loss
        of Self, and the consequent problem of
        identity.

14   BORRELI, GUY. "Samuel Beckett et le sentiment
        de la déréliction." In <u>Le Théâtre moderne,
        II: Depuis la deuxième guère mondiale</u>.
        Edited by Jean Jacquot. Paris: Editions du
        Centre National da la Recherche Scientifique,
        pp. 45-55.
            Stresses the solitude of Beckett's
        dramatic figures. Beckett portrays the
        distress of mankind: resigning themselves to
        their uselessness, "forgotten" by nature,
        physically immobile or blind, separated from
        others, their projects and their dreams,
        Beckett's characters bitterly accept their
        aloneness.

15   BORY, JEAN-LOUIS. "Effarouchables s'abstenir
        ...!" <u>Nouvel Observateur</u>, 22-28 Feb., pp.
        54-55.
            Briefly describes the themes and the
        dramatic and cinematographic techniques used
        in <u>Film</u> and the film version of <u>Play</u>.

16   "Les Bruits de la ville." <u>Nouvel Observateur</u>,
        15-21 Feb., p. 32.
            Argues that the film version of <u>Play</u>
        betrayed Beckett's drama; briefly comments on
        <u>Film</u>.

17   BULL, PETER. "Peter Bull as Pozzo." In
      Casebook on "Waiting for Godot." Edited by
      Ruby Cohn. New York: Grove Press, pp. 39-43.
         Reprint of 1959.8; see 1967.24.

18   CALDER, JOHN, ed. A Samuel Beckett Reader.
      London: Calder and Boyars, 192 pp.
         Offers selections and quotations from the
      novels, plays, poetry and critical writing
      with a general introduction to Beckett's
      background and works. Followed by a short
      selected bibliography.

19   CASE, SUE-ELLEN. "Image and Godot." In
      Casebook on "Waiting for Godot." Edited by
      Ruby Cohn. New York: Grove Press, pp. 155-
      59.
         Identifies the structure of Godot as the
      relationship between image and action. Image
      conveys the play's content in two ways,
      "abstractly, through the use of allusion ...
      and sensually, through the evocation of
      emotion." The action of the play is
      described as the inverse of traditional
      dramatic progression, a backing away. See
      1967.24.

20   CHAMBERS, ROSS. "Vers une interprétation de Fin
      de partie." Studi Francesi 31 (Jan.-Apr.):
      90-96.
         Analyzes the dramatic elements of time and
      space in Endgame. Reprinted: 1969.19.

21   CHAMPIGNY, ROBERT. "Waiting for Godot: Myth,
      Words, Wait." In Casebook on "Waiting for
      Godot." Edited by Ruby Cohn. New York:
      Grove Press, pp. 137-44.
         Translated and revised from A52; see
      1967.24.

22   CODD, ALAN. "Nothing To Do, Nowhere To Go."
      Cambridge Review, 18 Nov., pp. 119-21.
         Believes Beckett's achievement is to have
      destroyed the distant idea of "art" and to
      have demonstrated to the audience or reader

an experience in which everyone is creatively
involved.

23   *COHEN, RICHARD. "Waiting for Godot." Granta,
      24 Feb., pp. 23-24.

24   COHN, RUBY, ed. Casebook on "Waiting for
      Godot." New York: Grove Press, 192 pp.
         Presents a series of reviews and interpre-
      tations of Waiting for Godot. Followed by a
      select bibliography of works in English. See
      1967.1, 1967.4, 1967.9, 1967.12, 1967.17,
      1967.19, 1967.21, 1967.29, 1967.33, 1967.37,
      1967.41, 1967.43, 1967.50, 1967.53, 1967.54,
      1967.59, 1967.61, 1967.62, 1967.65, 1967.67,
      1967.69, 1967.89, 1967.92, 1967.93, 1967.94,
      1967.95, 1967.96, 1967.97, 1967.98, 1967.102,
      1967.109.

25   *____. "Dialogues of Cruelty." Southern
      Review 19, no. 2 (Spring):2-23.

26   ____. "'Theatrum Mundi' and Contemporary
      Theatre." Comparative Drama 1, no. 1
      (Spring):28-35. Beckett: pp. 30-31.
         Examines variations upon the 'theatrum
      mundi' topos in the works of Bertolt Brecht,
      Samuel Beckett, Jean Genet, and Peter Weiss.
      In addition to manipulating world-stage and
      man-actor imagery Beckett also calls atten-
      tion to the stage, and the play as play.

27   *"College Theatre Named After Irish Playwright."
      Oxford Times, 20 Oct.

28   COOK, ALBERT S. Prisms: Studies in Modern
      Literature. Bloomington and London: Indiana
      University Press, pp. 100-110, 140-147 and
      passim.
         Explores the functions of allegory and
      action in Endgame and Waiting for Godot.

29   "Dialogue: The Free Southern Theatre." In
      Casebook on "Waiting for Godot." Edited by
      Ruby Cohn. New York: Grove Press, pp. 79-82.

Reprinted from B495; see 1967.24.

30 *DOBREE, BONAMY. "Waiting for Beckett."
   Yorkshire Post, 13 July.

31 DOMENACH, JEAN-MARIE. "L'Infra-tragédie." In
   Le Retour du tragique: Essai. Paris:
   Editions du Seuil, pp. 258-82.
       Believes the modern tragedy of Beckett and
   Ionesco finds its origins in comedy, specifically, farce and parody. Domenach focuses on
   specific elements of Beckett's theater:
   fatality, man's freedom to act, to speak and
   to move, language, and the agony of being.

32 _____. "La Tragédie ne revient pas du coté où
   on l'attendait." Quinzaine Littéraire, no.
   23 (1 Mar.), pp. 8-10.
       Claims that contemporary tragedy has a new
   origin in metaphysical farce and parody in
   the works of Jarry, Ionesco and Beckett.
   This new "anti-tragedy" finds its source in
   the failure of that which gave tragedy it
   consistency: character transcendance and
   affirmation.

33 DUCKWORTH, COLIN. "The Making of Godot." In
   Casebook on "Waiting for Godot." Edited by
   Ruby Cohn. New York: Grove Press, pp. 89-
   100.
       Studies the genesis of Waiting for Godot,
   comparing Godot to Murphy and Mercier and
   Camier. Excerpted and reprinted from an
   edition of Waiting for Godot, edited with an
   introduction by Duckworth (London: George G.
   Harrap, 1966). See 1967.24.

34 *DUVIGNEAU, MICHEL. "Quatre courts métrages."
   Témoignage Chrétien, 2 Mar.

35 *EDDELMAN, W.S. "Design Notes for All That
   Fall." Drama at Calgary 2, no. 1 (Nov.):47.

36 ERICKSON, JOHN D. "Objects and Systems in the

Novels of Samuel Beckett." <u>Esprit Créateur</u>
7, no. 2 (Summer):113-22.
   Explores the narrators' dual relationship
towards objects, as it is reflected in the
"symbol" of calculus: one attitude considers
objects as the sum of abstract units, the
other attitude views objects as unique
entities.

37   ESSLIN, MARTIN. "Godot at San Quentin." In
      <u>Casebook on "Waiting for Godot."</u> Edited by
      Ruby Cohn. New York: Grove Press, pp. 83-
      85.
         Reprinted from 1961.21; see 1967.24.

38   _____. "Is it All Gloom and Doom?" <u>New York</u>
      <u>Times</u>, 24 Sept., sec. 2, pp. 1-3.
         Comments on the impact of Beckett's plays,
      Beckett as a comic writer, and the reasons
      for Beckett's portrayal of characters on the
      "edge" of existence: Beckett "does this not
      because he delights in gloom for its own sake
      but because characters reduced to the
      essentials and put into extreme situations
      will tell us the most about our own lives."

39   FEDERMAN, RAYMOND. "Le Bonheur chez Samuel
      Beckett." <u>Esprit</u> 362 (July-Aug.):90-96.
         Examines the question of whether there can
      be happiness in a world characterized by the
      disintegration of self and the absence of a
      rapport with reality. Modified version of
      1967.40.

40   _____. "Samuel Beckett ou le bonheur en
      enfer." <u>Symposium</u> 21, no. 1 (Spring):14-21.
         Modified version of 1967.39.

41   FLETCHER, JOHN. "Roger Blin at Work." In
      <u>Casebook on "Waiting for Godot."</u> Edited by
      Ruby Cohn. New York: Grove Press, pp. 21-
      26.
         Characterizes Blin's manner of directing
      and his views on Beckett and his works.
      Reprinted and modified from 1966.33; see

1967.24.

42   _____. <u>Samuel Beckett's Art</u>. London: Chatto
        and Windus, 154 pp.
             Provides a general introduction to several
        aspects of Beckett's career as a writer:
        Beckett as critic, poet, dramatist, his
        sources, influences, and bilingual ability.
        A Chronology of Beckett's works (1929-1966)
        is included.

43   FRASER, G.S. "Waiting for Godot." In <u>Casebook
        on "Waiting for Godot."</u> Edited by Ruby Cohn.
        New York: Grove Press, pp. 133-37.
             Reprint of 1956.13; see 1967.24.

44   FRIEDMAN, MAURICE. <u>To Deny Our Nothingness:
        Contemporary Images of Man</u>. New York Dela-
        corte Press, 385 pp.
             Includes Beckett in his section on the
        Absurd Man, the "most decidedly modern and
        problematic type of contemporary image of
        man." Friedman portrays Beckett's world
        through the "absurdity of personal experience
        of the dialogue between man and man, and of
        the search for beauty and order in the world
        ..." in <u>Waiting for Godot</u>, <u>Endgame</u>, and the
        trilogy.

45   FRIEDMAN, MELVIN J. "Molloy's 'Sacred' Stones."
        <u>Romance Notes</u> 9, no. 1 (Autumn):8-11.
             Believes Beckett's <u>Molloy</u> is very close
        in spirit to Lawrence Sterne's <u>Tristram
        Shandy</u>. Friedman points out that Beckett may
        have borrowed his metaphor of stones from
        Mircea Eliade's <u>The Sacred and the Profane</u>.

46   GADDIS, MARILYN. "The Purgatory Metaphor of
        Yeats and Beckett." <u>London Magazine</u> 7, no. 5
        (Aug.):33-46.
             Notes that both Yeats and Beckett present
        man's fate as a round in Purgatory: "Yeats
        and Beckett confront us with two views of
        human experience that are distinct -- yet
        kindred ... The plays of Yeats with their

dancers and musicians create a concise,
insistent metaphor of men, doomed and
solitary, living a death even when working
together. Beckett, beginning where Yeats
ends, in effect expands this metaphor grimly
and comically."

47   *GROSVENOR MYER, VALERIE. "A Lovely War and
         Godot at Cambridge." Guardian, 18 Feb.
         Source: Bryer et al. 1972.7;unverified.

48   GUICHARNAUD, JACQUES. "Existence Onstage:
         Samuel Beckett." In Modern French Theatre
         from Giraudoux to Beckett. New Haven and
         London: Yale University Press, 1961, new
         expanded edition, 1967, pp. 230-58.
            Provides an indepth analysis of Beckett's
         "basic play," Waiting for Godot, as a new
         form of static drama in which three levels
         are juxtaposed: "the words and actions
         (poetry, clownish tricks, embryonic scenes),
         the direct significance of those words and
         actions (love, misery, hunger, the role of
         the intellectual, the dialectic of master and
         slave, the dimness and confusion of memories,
         fear, bad faith, even a certain 'miserabil-
         ism'), and the waiting which levels every-
         thing off." Guicharnaud discusses some of
         Beckett's other plays which he feels develop
         a particular aspect already present in
         Waiting for Godot: Endgame, Krapp's Last
         Tape, Happy Days, Eh Joe, Acts Without Words,
         Play, All That Fall, Embers, Cascando, and
         Words and Music. Followed by a list of first
         performances and revivals and a selected
         bibliography. Reprint of 1964.44.

49   *HAMPTON, CHARLES. "Staging All That Fall."
         Drama at Calgary 2, no. 1 (Nov.):48-52.

50   HARVEY, LAWRENCE. "Art and the Existential in
         Waiting for Godot." In Casebook on "Waiting
         for Godot." Edited by Ruby Cohn. New York:
         Grove Press, pp. 144-54.
            Reprinted from 1960.29; see 1967.24.

51   HASSAN, IHAB. The Literature of Silence: Henry
      Miller and Samuel Beckett. New York: Alfred
      A. Knopf, 225 pp. Beckett: pp. 113-200.
          Dividing his discussion into two parts,
      "Henry Miller, Prophecy and Obscenity," and
      "Samuel Beckett: Reduction and Apocalypse,"
      argues that literature has adopted a new
      attitude toward itself, with silence as its
      metaphor. Followed by a selected biblio-
      graphy.

52   _____. "The Literature of Silence: From Henry
      Miller to Beckett and Burroughs." Encounter
      28, no. 1 (Jan.):74-82.
          Describes the new literature of outrage
      and apocalypse in which "... Miller and
      Beckett reflect inverse worlds. For Beckett
      leaves us with a world so depleted of life
      ... And presents us with a chaotic world
      constantly on the verge of transformation ...
      What both worlds share is the decree of
      silence. For the human tongue is speechless
      in fright and ecstasy." Hassan outlines the
      ways in which literature strives for silence:
      absurd creation, literature as game and
      action, literary obscenity, concreteness,
      irony, and change and improvisation.

53   HEWES, HENRY. "Mankind in the Merdecluse." In
      Casebook on "Waiting for Godot." Edited by
      Ruby Cohn. New York: Grove Press, pp. 67-
      69.
          Reprint of 1956.19a; see 1967.24.

54   HOBSON, HAROLD. "Tomorrow." In Casebook on
      "Waiting for Godot." Edited by Ruby Cohn.
      New York: Grove Press, pp. 27-29.
          Reprint of A150; see 1967.24.

55   HODGART, MATTHEW. "Saint Beckett." New York
      Review of Books 9 (7 Dec.):3-4.
          Reviews Stories and Texts for Nothing,
      defining the Texts as meditations on nothing-
      ness, and comparing Beckett's repeated
      variations on the same themes to twentieth

century art.

56   HUGHES, D.A. "The Work of Samuel Beckett."
      Humanist 82, no. 9 (Sept.):271-75.
           Offers a general introduction to Beckett's
      work, emphasizing his drama and stage techni-
      ques, and concludes with an analysis of
      Waiting for Godot.

57   *"ICA Notes. Beckett at the ICA." ICA Bulle-
      tin, no. 175-6 (Nov.-Dec.), p. 4.

58   *JANVIER, LUDOVIC. "Beckett et ses fables."
      Biblio 35, no. 1 (Jan.):4-13.

59   _____. "Cyclical Dramaturgy." In Casebook on
      "Waiting for Godot." Edited by Ruby Cohn.
      New York: Grove Press, pp. 166-71.
           Reprinted from 1966.41 (in French); see
      1967.24.

60   _____. "Le Lieu du retrait de la blancheur de
      l'écho." Critique 237 (Feb.):215-38.
           Focuses on "From an Abandoned Work,"
      "Enough," "Imagination Dead Imagine," and
      "Ping." Janvier presents many of the charac-
      teristic thematic elements of these "oeuvres
      de la mutation" -- the breakdown of language,
      the relativity of point of view, the immen-
      sity of time and space, the incarceration of
      the imagination, the repetition of meaning-
      less words, and the whiteness and emptiness.

61   JOHNSTON, DENIS. "Waiting with Beckett." In
      Casebook on "Waiting for Godot." Edited by
      Ruby Cohn. New York: Grove Press, pp. 31-
      38.
           Reprint of 1956.23; see 1967.24.

62   KENNER, HUGH. "Life in the Box." In Casebook
      on "Waiting for Godot." Edited by Ruby Cohn.
      New York: Grove Press, pp. 107-13.
           Reprinted from 1961.40; see 1967.24.

63   KERN, EDITH. "L'Infirme divinisé: Apollinaire
      and Beckett." Kentucky Romance Quarterly 14,
      no. 1, pp. 149-56.
         Compares Beckett's heroes to the crippled
      poet-protagonist of Apollinaire's story
      "L'Infirme divinisé," suggesting that
      Beckett's work may also be seen as part of
      the tradition of the grotesque.

64   KOLVE, V.A. "Religious Language in Waiting for
      Godot." Centennial Review 9, no. 1 (Winter):
      102-27.
         Explores Beckett's use of religious
      language in Waiting for Godot in terms of
      four categories of dramatic language: the
      language of setting, stage-action, character-
      relationships and enunciated speech.

65   LEVY, ALAN. "The Long Wait for Godot." In
      Casebook on "Waiting for Godot." Edited by
      Ruby Cohn. New York: Grove Press, pp. 74-
      78.
         Reprinted from 1956.25; see 1967.24.

66   LUMLEY, FREDERICK. "The Case Against Beckett."
      In New Trends in Twentieth Century Drama. A
      Survey Since Ibsen and Shaw. New York:
      Oxford University Press, p. 202-8.
         Reprinted in a slightly modified form from
      1956.26. The chapter has been updated by a
      brief discussion of Happy Days.

67   MAILER, NORMAN. "A Public Notice on Waiting for
      Godot." In Casebook on "Waiting for Godot."
      New York: Grove Press, pp. 69-74.
         Reprint of 1959.28; see 1967.24.

68   MALOFF, SAUL. "The Last Frontier." Newsweek 70
      (4 Sept.):76.
         Stories and Texts for Nothing provide
      variations on Beckett's theme of radical
      estrangement and survival in the world's
      "farthest frontier" where pathos and comedy
      merge.

69   MANNERS, MARYA. "Two Tramps." In <u>Casebook on</u>
     <u>"Waiting for Godot."</u> Edited by Ruby Cohn.
     New York: Grove Press, pp. 30-31.
          Reprint of A213; see 1967.24.

70   *MARGUET, ARTHUR. "<u>All That Fall</u> fell."
     <u>Albertan</u>, 29 Sept., p. 15.

71   MATTHEWS, HONOR. "Samuel Beckett and Franz
     Kafka: The Ambiguous Directive." In <u>The</u>
     <u>Primal Curse. The Myth of Cain and Abel in</u>
     <u>the Theatre</u>. London: Chatto and Windus, pp.
     152-68.
          Compares the presentation of the myth of
     the two brothers in the works of Beckett and
     Kafka, and points out Kierkegaard's influence
     on Beckett's imagination. Beckett's por-
     trayal of the brothers' relationship may
     either appear in the conflicts of the divided
     personality or the process of mutual destruc-
     tion exhibited by many of the couples.

72   *[May Produce the First Play at Oxford Theatre
     in Memory.] <u>Times</u> (London), 15 Nov., p. 10.
          Source: Tanner 1969.113;unverified.

73   MAYOUX, JEAN-JACQUES. "Beckett et les chemins
     de l'expressionisme." <u>Langues Modernes</u> 61,
     no. 2 (Mar.-Apr.):225-38.
          Traces Beckett's Irish predecessors, the
     influence of Joyce, Proust, and Kafka and
     examines the expressionist "vision" in the
     plays <u>Happy Days</u> and <u>Play</u>. Reprint of
     1966.50.

74   *_____. "Samuel Beckett, homme de théâtre."
     <u>Biblio</u> 35, no. 1 (Jan.):14-21.

75   *MAZARS, PIERRE and MARCEL LASSEAUX. "A propos
     de <u>Comédie</u>." <u>Biblio</u> 35, no. 1 (Jan.):22-23.

76   MENACHEM, EPHRAT BEN. "<u>Waiting for Godot</u> and
     the Form of Tragedy." In <u>Studies in the</u>
     <u>Drama</u>. Edited by Arieh Sachs. Jerusalem:
     Hebrew University, pp. 89-99.

Interprets <u>Waiting for Godot</u> and shows
that its dramatic movement is essentially
tragic with comic elements functioning within
the mechanism of tragedy: "The whole tragic
dialectic of the waiting inheres in its being
comically pulled down to the abdurately
physical, the trivial, the limited, and the
alien."

77   *MONTALBETTI, JEAN. "15 ans de nouveau roman --
       enquête." <u>Magazine Littéraire</u>, no. 6 (Apr.),
       pp. 4-9.

78   MOORE, J.R. "Some Night Thoughts on Beckett."
       <u>Massachusetts Review</u> 8, no. 3 (Summer):529-
       39.
          Discusses the couples in Beckett's plays,
       "teller and listener, executioner and victim,
       ego and alter ego." Through his characters
       Beckett is able to portray extremes of gaiety
       and anguish, aggressiveness and passivity,
       order and chaos.

79   MUELLER, WILLIAM R. and JOSEPHINE JACOBSEN.
       "The Absurd Quest." <u>Kenyon Review</u> 29, no. 2
       (Mar.), 223-45.
          Define and analyze the theatre of the
       absurd, in particular the plays of Beckett,
       Eugene Ionesco and Jean Genet, comparing
       their plays, techniques, and goals: "Among
       the influences, then, on the drama of
       Beckett, Ionesco, and Genet are man's sense
       of his mortality, alienation, and inhumanity;
       the proclaimed death or silence of God; and
       the loss of communicability through words or
       feelings."

80   O'BRIEN, JUSTIN. "Samuel Beckett and André
       Gide: An Hypothesis." <u>French Review</u> 40, no.
       4 (Feb.):485-86.
          Suggests that Beckett's drama <u>All That
       Fall</u> may have been influenced by Gide's <u>Les
       Caves du Vatican</u>. Reprinted: 1971.73.

81   *"Oeuvres de Samuel Beckett: Essai de biblio-
         graphie." <u>Biblio</u> 35, no. 1 (Jan.):25-28.

82   O'HARA, J.D. "Deathbed and Bored." <u>Carleton
         Miscellany</u> 8, no. 1 (Winter):108-18.
              Surveys Beckett's fiction as a preamble to
         a discussion of his latest work "Imagination
         Dead Imagine," in which Beckett makes a clean
         break with his earlier writings: "The
         imagined world we all know is destroyed, and
         the voice of IDI, untrammeled by that world,
         by a past, by any feelings of guilt, sin or
         expiation, by any personality at all, is free
         -- as no earlier voice has been -- to start
         from scratch and do things right this time."

83   *OLIVER, CORDELIA. "<u>Waiting for Godot</u> at the
         Traverse Theatre, Edinburgh." <u>Guardian</u>, 27
         Dec.
              Source: Bryer et al. 1972.7;unverified.

84   O'NEILL, JOSEPH P. "The Absurd in Samuel
         Beckett." <u>Personalist</u> 48, no. 1 (Jan.):56-
         76.
              Attempts to define the expression of the
         absurd in Beckett's works: "The surface
         absurdities of action, situation, and
         language point to the profound, essential ir-
         rationalities at the root of the human condi-
         tion."

85   *"Par Express." <u>Express</u>, 17-23 July.
              Source: Bryer et al. 1972.7;unverified.

86   PIATIER, JACQUELINE. "Le Nouveau Roman."
         <u>Tendances</u>, no. 48, fasc. 3 (Aug.), pp. 1-23.
         Beckett: pp. 7-8.
              Introduces the "theoreticians" of the New
         Novel, and examines the major authors con-
         sidered to be part of this group. Beckett's
         metaphysical dimension is emphasized in
         Piatier's brief analysis of <u>How It Is</u>.

87   *POORE, CHARLES. <u>New York Times</u>, 20 (July),
         p. 39.

Source: Index to Book Reviews in the
Humanities, 1967;unverified.

88   PORTMAN, JAMIE.   "University of Calgary Drama
     Gains New Lustre."   Calgary Herald, 29 Sept.,
     p. 19.
          Reviews the opening of the world premiere
     stage performance of All That Fall at the
     University of Calgary's new Studio Theatre
     describing the difficulties in transferring
     this radio play to the live stage and the
     successful use of optical and sound effects.

89   ROBBE-GRILLET, ALAIN.   "Samuel Beckett or
     Presence on the Stage."   In Casebook on
     "Waiting for Godot."   Edited by Ruby Cohn.
     New York: Grove Press, pp. 15-21.
          Reprinted from 1953.14, reprint of
     1963.69, 1965.63, 1965.64; see 1967.24;
     see 1965.64 for annotation.

90   ROBINSON, ANDREW.   "Murphy's Mind."   Tracks 1
     (Summer):13-15.
          Analyzes Beckett's characterization of
     Murphy, the possibility that he is schizo-
     phrenic, the restatement of the Cartesian
     mind/body duality, Murphy's "mind pictures,"
     and the three zones of Murphy's mind.

91   ROSE, MARILYN.   "Ifor's Ladder."   Approach
     Magazine, no. 1 (June), pp. 36-43.
          Believes Beckett is attempting to make the
     novel a vehicle for philosophical thought.
     To prove her point Rose links Ifor's ladder
     to some representative European philosophical
     novels (François Mauriac's The Desert of
     Love, Julien Green's Each in His Darkness,
     Roger Ikor's If Time ..., Cesare Pavese's
     Among Women Only, and Nathalie Sarraute's
     Portrait of a Man Unknown) and then to Watt.

92   SALACROU, ARMAND.   "It Is Not an Accident but a
     Triumph."   In Casebook on "Waiting for Godot."
     Edited by Ruby Cohn. New York: Grove Press,
     pp. 14-15.

Reprint and translation of A279; see
1967.24.

93   SASTRE, ALFONSO. "Seven Notes on <u>Waiting for</u>
      <u>Godot</u>." In <u>Casebook on "Waiting for Godot."</u>
      Edited by Ruby Cohn. New York: Grove Press,
      pp. 101-7.
           Addresses seven points of interest: "Of
      Realism and Its Forms," "The Great Circus of
      the World," "At Last," "A Tragicomedy," "A
      Death Certificate for Hope," "Being Rent
      Asunder," "Toward a Metaphysics of Boredom,"
      "A Drama in Which Absolutely Nothing Hap-
      pens." See 1967.24.

94   SCHECHNER, RICHARD. "There's Lots of Time in
      <u>Godot</u>." In <u>Casebook on "Waiting for Godot."</u>
      Edited by Ruby Cohn. New York: Grove Press,
      pp. 175-87.
           Time, habit, memory and games are analyzed
      as they form the basic rhythm of the play and
      provide its theatrical interest. Reprint of
      1966.64; see 1967.24.

95   SCHNEIDER, ALAN. "Waiting for Beckett: A
      Personal Chronicle." In <u>Casebook on "Waiting</u>
      <u>for Godot."</u> Edited by Ruby Cohn. New York:
      Grove Press, pp. 51-52.
           Chronicles his first introduction to
      <u>Waiting for Godot</u>, and the set of circumstan-
      ces that led to his directing the Miami
      production of the play. Reprinted from
      1958.30; see 1967.7.

96   SERREAU, GENEVIEVE. "Beckett's Clowns." In
      <u>Casebook on "Waiting for Godot."</u> Edited by
      Ruby Cohn. New York: Grove Press, pp. 171-
      75.
           Suggests Vladimir and Estragon's resem-
      blance to clowns, "second-degree characters
      who have a precise stage function, resembling
      that of the Shakespearean fool." Reprinted
      from 1966.65 (in French); see 1967.24.

97   SHEEDY, JOHN J.   "The Net."   In <u>Casebook on
      "Waiting for Godot."</u>   Edited by Ruby Cohn.
      New York: Grove Press, pp. 159-66.
          Emphasizes the traditional theatrical
      elements of <u>Godot</u> and its formal plot.   The
      image of the entangling net is examined:
      "When a play makes a point of the reality of
      its artifice, illusion dissolves; audience
      and players are linked in whatever dilemma
      they can imaginably share."   See 1967.24.

98   SIMPSON, ALAN.   "Producing Godot in Dublin."   In
      <u>Casebook on "Waiting for Godot."</u>   Edited by
      Ruby Cohn.   New York: Grove Press, pp. 45-
      49.
          Reprinted from 1962.69; see 1967.24.

99   SOLOMON, PHILIP H.   "Samuel Beckett's <u>Molloy</u>:   A
      Dog's Life."   <u>French Review</u> 41, no. 1
      (Oct.):84-91.
          Comments on dog imagery in <u>Molloy</u> in order
      to evaluate Beckett's view of human existence
      and to give insight into Beckett's artistic
      procedures.

100   SPRAGUE, CLAIRE.   "The Pain of Being."   <u>New York
      Times Book Review</u>, 12 Nov., p. 67.
          Reviews <u>Stories and Texts for Nothing</u>,
      summarizing the Beckettian narrator, his
      experiences and his speech.

101   STAMIROWSKA, KRYSTYNA.   "The Conception of a
      Character in the Works of Joyce and Beckett."
      <u>Kwartalnik Neofilologiczny</u> 14, no. 4:443-47.
          Compares methods of presenting a character
      in the works of Joyce and Beckett.
      Stamirowska points out the process of
      alienation from physical and social back-
      ground undergone by Beckett's characters and
      the degradation suffered by his "unheroic"
      heroes.

102   SUVIN, DARKO.   "Preparing for Godot -- or the
      Purgatory of Individualism."   In <u>Casebook on
      "Waiting for Godot."</u>   Edited by Ruby Cohn.

New York: Grove Press, pp. 121-32.
   Believes Beckett is faced with a paradox
that is insoluble from within the Individualist frame: "the self, final atom of
the Individualist world, has been broken up,
leaving a void, yet the Individualist
tradition of self-questioning goes on
undaunted, dryly enclosing the void." See
1967.24.

103   THEOBALD, DAVID W. "The Imagination and What
      Philosophers Have to Say." <u>Diogenes</u>, no. 57
      (Spring), pp. 47-63. Beckett: pp. 59-63.
         Presents the reaction of literary artists
      to the ways in which language is used by
      philosophers, illustrating his remarks with
      examples from the works of Lawrence Sterne,
      Beckett, and Maurice Blanchot.

104   THIEL, ANDRE. "La Condition tragique chez
      Samuel Beckett." <u>Revue Nouvelle</u> 45 (15
      May):449-63.
         Claims Beckett's characters resemble the
      mythic dimensions of Greek theater -- in this
      case however, the tragic hero is a clown
      rather than a king. Thiel notes that all of
      Beckett's characters face the same meaning-
      less existence made up of suffering, insig-
      nificance, isolation, and physical mutila-
      tion.

105   *"To Stage Own Play at W. Berlin Arts Festival."
      <u>Times</u> (London), 17 Aug., p. 6.
         Source: Tanner, 1969.113;unverified.

106   TODD, ROBERT E. "Proust and Remption in <u>Waiting</u>
      <u>for Godot</u>." <u>Modern Drama</u> 10, no. 2
      (Sept.):175-81.
         Examines <u>Waiting for Godot</u> in light of
      Beckett's essay on Proust, focusing on
      possible religious interpretations of the
      play.

107   TORRANCE, ROBERT M. "Modes of Being and Time in
      the World of <u>Godot</u>." <u>Modern Language</u>

<u>Quarterly</u> 28, no. 1:77-97.
With reference to Beckett's essay on
Proust, studies the two contrasting conditions of human life, suffering and boredom,
and their interrelations with time. The
possibility of significant change in the two
character groups in <u>Waiting for Godot</u>, (Didi-
Gogo and Pozzo-Lucky), from Act I to Act II
is considered.

108   WILSON, ANGUS. "The Humanism of Beckett"
      <u>Observer Review</u>, 16 July, p. 20.
      Denies that Beckett rejects the body
totally, on the contrary, Wilson feels that
Beckett emphasizes the physical characteristics in his novels through the trilogy and
later in his plays: "To force us to accept
this open statement of our secret physical
life is one of Beckett's greatest contribu-
tions to the slow, painful rebuilding of man
from the ruins of the old humanism."

109   ZEGEL, SYLVAIN. "At the Théâtre de Babylone:
      <u>Waiting for Godot</u> by Samuel Beckett." In
      <u>Casebook on "Waiting for Godot."</u> Edited by
      Ruby Cohn. New York: Grove Press, pp. 11-
      12.
      Reprinted from 1953.18; see 1967.24.

110   ZELTNER, [-NEUKOMM] GERDA. "Le Lyrisme
      burlesque (Samuel Beckett)." In <u>La Grande
      Aventure du roman français au XX<u>e</u> Siècle</u>.
      Paris: Editions Gonthier, pp. 181-97.
      Demonstrates how Beckett's works mark a
turning point for the new novel: renouncing
psychology and philosophy, Beckett preoc-
cupies himself with symbols and myths.
Zeltner describes the progression in
Beckett's novels towards silence and a preoccupation with the inner self in <u>Molloy</u>, <u>The
Unnamable</u>, as well as the role of language
and the novel itself as an adventure rather
than a representation of human experiences.

1967-1968

1   LYONS, CHARLES R. "Some Analogies Between the
    Epic Brecht and the Absurdist Beckett."
    Comparative Drama 1, no. 4 (Winter 1967-
    68):297-304.
        Points out some similarities between the
    epic theater of Brecht and the "absurd"
    theater of Beckett: 1) the disintegration of
    the conventional sense of dramatic time, 2)
    the denial of the conventional pretense that
    the play's action is real, 3) the presenta-
    tion of " ... a self-directed isolation in
    the image of an energetic woman ..."
    (Brecht's Mutter Courage and Beckett's Happy
    Days).

1968

1   ASTIER, PIERRE A.G. La Crise du roman français
    et le nouveau réalisme. Paris: Nouvelles
    Editions Debresse, 349 pp.
        Studies the material and techniques of the
    new novelists Samuel Beckett, Michel Butor,
    Marguerite Duras, Claude Mauriac, Robert
    Pinget, Alain Robbe-Grillet, and Claude
    Simon. These writers represent a movement
    away from the contemporary writers whose
    works reflect the realism imposed by the
    great writers of the last century.

2   *BANERJI, N.N. "The Theater of the Absurd."
    Modern Review 123, no. 4 (Apr.):269-75.

3   "Beckett Manuscripts at Washington University."
    French Review 41, no. 4 (Feb.):551-52.
        Lists the autographed manuscripts and
    revised typescripts added to the Special
    Collection of Modern Literature at Washington
    University, St. Louis.

4   "Beckett up the Pole." Times Literary Supple-
    ment (London), 16 May, p. 504.

In this review of Eh Joe, Act Without
Words II, and Come and Go, notes that
although Beckett may have discarded many of
the traditional trappings of the novelist or
dramatist, the last two works are little more
than illustrations due to their lack of
words: "A wordless existence is meaningless
except in a context of verbal existences and
can be expressed only by verbal negations of
verbal terms."

5   *BERGONZI, BERNARD, ed. Innovations: Essays on
     Art and Ideas. London: Macmillan, 252 pp.

6   BERNAL, OLGA. "Glissement hors du langage."
     Cahiers du Chemin 4 (Oct.):121-33.
          Proposes that Watt provides the real
     beginning of Beckett's prose style since it
     is in this novel, not Murphy that the
     disintegration of language is evident. In
     order to understand how the literary form of
     How It Is came to be, it is necessary to
     examine Watt with Beckett's most recent
     novels in mind.

7   _____. "L'Oubli des noms." Monde [des livres],
     17 Jan., p. 5.
          Suggests that the anonymity of Beckett's
     characters signals not only a lack of
     identify but also the breakdown of language,
     time and space.

8   *BLAKEY, J. Notes on "Waiting for Godot."
     Toronto: Forum House Publishing Co., 60 pp.

9   BREE, GERMAINE. "The Ambiguous Voyage: Mode or
     Genre." Genre 1, no. 2 (Apr.):87-96.
          Briefly examines three voyage narratives,
     Beckett's Molloy, Céline's Voyage au bout de
     la nuit, and Patrick White's Voss, and
     compares them with Butor's La Modification.

10   BRERETON, GEOFFREY. "Beckett: Waiting for
     Godot." In Principles of Tragedy: A
     Rational Examination of the Tragic Concept in

Life and Literature. Coral Gables, Florida:
University of Miami Press, pp. 224-65.
    Confronts several of the key issues
introduced in Waiting for Godot: God,
society, existence, nothingness, time,
tragedy, and comedy.

11   *CHANAN, GABRIEL. "Modern Fiction: The Plight
      of the Novelist." Cambridge Review 89a, no.
      2,170 (26 Apr.):399-401.

12   CHRIST, YVAN. "La Revue théâtrale." Revue des
      Deux Mondes 14 (15 July):273-77. Beckett:
      pp. 273-75.
          Reviews Endgame, comparing Beckett's use
      of interior monologue to that of Edouard
      Dujardin, author of Les Lauriers sont coupés.

13   CLEVELAND, LOUISE O. "Trials in the Soundscape:
      The Radio Plays of Samuel Beckett." Modern
      Drama 11, no. 3 (Dec.):267-82.
          Demonstrates the importance of Beckett's
      radio dramas as experiments in sound:
      "Beckett's choice of the radio medium ...
      [indicated] an acute awareness of the
      conditions which underlie our perception of
      organized sound, and ... he has manipulated
      such elements as plot and character to
      maximize the dramatic tension which can be
      wrought from our struggle to perceive."

14   COE, RICHARD N. "Les Anarchistes de droite:
      Ionesco-Beckett-Genet-Arrabal." Cahiers
      Renaud-Barrault 67 (Sept.), pp. 99-125.
      Beckett: pp. 112-14.
          Presents Beckett's arguments in favor of
      "non-engagement": 1) Beckett does not view
      an individual as distinct from "society," 2)
      language forms an insurmountable barrier to
      the knowledge of self and 3) all language is
      the language of "others," therefore invalid
      and inauthentic.

15   CURNOW, D.H. "Language and Theater in Beckett's
      'English' Plays." Mosaic 2, no. 1 (Fall):54-65.

Remarks the disappointment the admirers of
Beckett's early work experienced when
confronted with Happy Days, Play, and Come
and Go. Curnow notes that there appears to
be a disharmony between language and theater
in Beckett's English plays. In the plays
since Endgame, Beckett treats recurrent
themes in theatrical rather than literary
terms: "... the basic elements of drama are
being emphasized ... separately in Beckett's
recent work: mime in the mime plays and the
Buster Keaton movie, theatrical effect in the
stage plays, sound in the radio plays, and
language -- most creatively -- in the
novels."

16   *DOMMERGUES, PIERRE. "Etude: Samuel Beckett --
     la voix de mon silence." Monde [des Livres],
     17 Jan., p. 4.

17   DOUGLAS, DENNIS. "The Drama of Evasion in
     Waiting for Godot." Komos: A Quarterly of
     Drama and Arts of the Theater 1, no. 4
     (Jan.):140-46.
        Points out numerous inconsistencies,
     contradictions, and ambiguities in Waiting
     for Godot which reinforce the central theme
     of the play, the drama of evasion.

18   DUKORE, BERNARD F. "The Other Pair in Waiting
     for Godot." Drama Survey 7 (Winter):133-37.
        Studies the similarities and differences
     between the two couples, Estragon-Vladimir
     and Pozzo-Lucky in Waiting for Godot.

19   D[UMUR], G[UY]. "L'antichambre du néant: Fin
     de partie de Samuel Beckett." Nouvel
     Observateur, no. 183 (15-21 May), p. 59.
        Reviews Endgame, praising the theatrical
     language, and the finesse of Roger Blin's
     production.

20   EASTHOPE, ANTHONY. "Hamm, Clov, and Dramatic
     Method in Endgame." Modern Drama 10, no. 4
     (Feb.):424-33.

Analyzes Hamm's character, the relationship between Hamm and Clov, and the tension
created by a juxtaposition of a formal
conversational surface with serious, often
terrifying depths in Endgame. Reprinted:
1969.35.

21   *"Edition: De Beckett à Evtouchenko." Express,
     8-14 (Nov.).
     Source: Bryer et al. 1972.7;unverified.

22   ELSEN, CLAUDE. "Une Soirée inoubliable." La
     Revue de Paris 75, no. 4 (Apr.):138-40.
     Briefly describes the television produc-
     tion of Film and Eh Joe as the creative
     portrayal of two "solitaires," summarizing
     their behavior and actions.

23   ESSLIN, MARTIN. "Godot and His Children: The
     Theatre of Samuel Beckett and Harold Pinter."
     In Modern British Dramatists. Edited by John
     Russell Brown. Englewood Cliffs, N.J.:
     Prentice-Hall, pp. 58-70.
     Unlike the conventional well-made drama,
     Esslin believes that Beckett's Waiting for
     Godot is a complex poetic image. Esslin
     examines the effect of this kind of play on
     its audience and Beckett's influence on
     contemporary literature, specifically on the
     drama of Harold Pinter. Reprint of 1963.23.

24   _____. "Samuel Beckett: The Search for the
     Self." In The Theatre of The Absurd. Garden
     City, N.Y.: Doubleday, pp. 11-65. Revised
     and expanded edition.
     Traces the early stages of Beckett's
     literary career and then analyzes Waiting for
     Godot, Endgame, Act Without Words, I, All
     That Fall, Krapp's Last Tape, Happy Days,
     Come and Go, En Joe, with special emphasis on
     his interpretation of Waiting for Godot.
     Esslin views Beckett's entire work as "a
     search for the reality that lies behind mere
     reasoning in conceptual terms." Esslin
     believes that Beckett devalues language as a

mode of communication creating a new consciousness which like an abstract painting
bypasses the stage of conceptual thinking.
Reprint of 1961.21, 1963.24, 1967.37;
reprinted: 1969.38.

25   EVERS, FRANCIS. "Samuel Beckett: The Incurious
       Seeker." Dublin Magazine 7, no. 1
       (Spring):84-88.
         Examines Beckett's works utilizing the
       "three ideal elements of critical discourse:
       evaluation, the communication of insights,
       and the rhetorical study of the language of
       the imaginative work in question."

26   FREEMAN, ELSIE T. "Beckett on the Mississippi."
       Manuscripts 20, no. 1 (Winter):48-50.
         Points out an addition of a major collec-
       tion of the author's autograph manuscripts,
       revised typescripts and editorial matter to
       the collection of modern literature at
       Washington College, St. Louis.

27   FRUTKIN, REN. "A Theater of Final Games."
       Yale/Theatre, no. 1 (Spring), pp. 88-92.
         In response to André Gregory's production
       of Endgame at Yale, Frutkin examines the
       concept of games which he believes relates to
       the major dramatic elements of character,
       action, and imagery in the play.

28   GASSNER, JOHN. "Foray Into the Absurd." In
       Dramatic Soundings, Evaluations and Retrac-
       tions Culled from 30 Years of Dramatic
       Criticism. New York: Crown Publishers, pp.
       503-7.
         Presents two examples of the Theatre of
       the Absurd from the sixties: Beckett's Happy
       Days and Harold Pinter's The Caretaker.
       Gassner finds that Beckett's drama becomes an
       "overextended metaphor" for the human
       condition and as a work written for the
       stage, it seems unduly prolonged.

29   GILBERT, SANDRA M. "All the Dead Voices: A
      Study of <u>Krapp's Last Tape</u>." <u>Drama Survey</u> 6,
      no. 3 (Spring):244-57.
          Views this work as Beckett's "finest short
      play." Gilbert studies the themes of aging,
      relinquishing memory, and art.

30   GREENBERG, ALVIN. "Breakable Beginnings: The
      Fall into Reality in the Modern Novel."
      <u>Texas Studies in Language and Literature</u> 10,
      no. 1 (Spring):133-42.
          Comments on the fragility or precarious-
      ness of the imperfect relationship between an
      individual and his world as it is portrayed
      in the modern novel, citing examples from
      many of Beckett's works.

31   *HAMPTON, CHARLES CHRISTY. "<u>All That Fall</u>:
      Productions II and III; Final Report." <u>Drama
      at Calgary</u> 2, no. 4 (May):37-41.

32   _____. "Samuel Beckett's <u>Film</u>." <u>Modern Drama</u>
      11, no. 3 (Dec.):299-305.
          Explores Beckett's use of dramatic action
      and his emphasis on visual perception in
      <u>Film</u>.

33   HARRISON, ROBERT. <u>Samuel Beckett's Murphy: A
      Critical Excursion</u>. Athens: University of
      Georgia Monographs, 99 pp.
          Utilizes a diagrammatic approach to
      analyze four aspects of Beckett's <u>Murphy</u>:
      form, character, symbol/motif, and style.

34   HAYMAN, RONALD. "Landscape Without Pictures:
      Pinter, Beckett and Radio." <u>London Magazine</u>
      8, no. 4 (July):72-77.
          Feels that Beckett was more relaxed with
      the radio medium than with either theatre,
      film or television, since it offered nothing
      but a confined space for voices and sound.
      Hayman points out that Beckett's four plays

for radio, <u>All That Fall</u>, <u>Embers</u>, <u>Words and Music</u> and <u>Cascando</u> present more characters and exploit a wide range of sound effects.

35   JACOBSEN, JOSEPHINE and WILLIAM R. MUELLER. <u>Ionesco and Genet, Playwrights of Silence</u>. New York: Hill and Wang, pp. 224-31.
        Notes many similarities with the works of Ionesco and Genet: "the mélange of the grandiose and the sordid, the protagonist as outcast from an order he never established, the belief in the virtues of pantomime and in the resources of burlesque and farce," the theme of Good Things Past, circular progress of the plays, the consideration that "predicament has overwhelmed identity," and nostalgia for the human community, etc. They also point out how Beckett, Ionesco, and Genet convey a feeling of absurdity representative of life in our times in their dramas.

36   *JANVIER, LUDOVIC. "La Plaie ... et le couteau." <u>Monde [des Livres]</u>, 17 Jan., p. 4.

37   KENNER, HUGH. <u>Samuel Beckett: A Critical Study</u>. Berkeley: University of California Press, 226 pp.
        Analyzes the formal elements, methods, situations, and philosophical and mathematical domains of Beckett's works. Kenner discusses the importance of Cartesianism, the disintegration of character and the reduction of bodily movement: "The Cartesian Centaur was a seventeenth-century dream, the fatal dream of being, knowing and moving like a god. In the twentieth century he and his machine are gone, and only a desperate élan remains ..." An additional chapter added to the 1968 edition brings the work up-to-date by including a study of the short dramatic works for radio, television, film, and stage. Reprint of 1961.40, with a supplementary chapter. Chapter 3 is a reprint of 1959.22 and 1965.50.

38   KORG, JACOB. "The Literary Esthetics of Dada."
      <u>Works</u> 1, no. 3 (Spring):43-54.
         Argues the importance of Dada experimental
      techniques as new expressive resources,
      especially in literature, where automatism,
      chance, and the subversion of conventional
      grammatical forms were assimilated. Korg
      calls attention to the "Dada spirit" in the
      observations about language in Beckett's
      <u>Unnamable</u> and in Lucky's speech in <u>Waiting
      for Godot</u>, as well as in much of the dialogue
      of Ionesco's plays.

39   KOTT, JAN. "A Note on Beckett's Realism." In
      <u>Theatre Notebook, 1947-1967</u>. Trans. from the
      Polish by Boleslaw Taborski. Garden City,
      New York: Doubleday & Co., Inc., pp. 241-45.
         Points out the realistic details in <u>Happy
      Days</u>, comparing the play to the actual
      setting and routine in a nursing home or
      hospital.

40   LEMARCHARD, JACQUES. "<u>Fin de partie</u> de Samuel
      Beckett." <u>Figaro Littéraire</u>, 13-19 May, pp.
      35-36.
         Beckett's <u>Endgame</u> dramatizes the terror of
      "emptiness, absence and the end," rephrasing
      the messages of Bossuet and Montaigne in a
      more sober fashion.

41   LODGE, DAVID. "Some Ping Understood." <u>En-
      counter</u> 30, no. 2 (Feb.):85-89.
         Suggests that "Ping" is "about something":
      "'Ping' is the rendering of the consciousness
      of a person confined in a small, bare, white
      room, a person who is evidently under extreme
      duress, and probably at the last gasp of
      life." Lodge discusses Beckett's use of
      language, and the possible significance of
      numerous words or phrases to the text as a
      whole. Reprinted: 1971.63, 1979.22.63.

42   LOMBARDI, THOMAS W. "Who Tells Who <u>Watt</u>?"
      <u>Chelsea</u>, nos 22/23 (June), pp. 170-79.
         Analyzes the transmission of Watt's tale

in order to demonstrate how "the form of the
narrative becomes itself an ironic symbol of
the impossibility of communicating in a
contingent world."

43 MAMBRINO, JEAN. "Carnet de Théâtre: Fin de
    partie de Samuel Beckett au Théâtre Alpha
    347." Etudes 329 (Dec.):737-39.
       Believes that Endgame (modern, but already
    classic), expresses in a universal language
    the profound question of man before the
    silence of his death, a story of damnation
    and pity.

44 MATTHEWS, HONOR. "Samuel Beckett: The Am-
    biguous Journey." In The Hard Journey. The
    Myth of Man's Rebirth. London: Chatto &
    Windus, pp. 139-68.
       Focuses on the ambiguous journeys of
    Beckett's characters: their movement, their
    self-images, their illusions, their situa-
    tions, their goals, their refusal to move in
    some instances (waiting), Beckett's mythology
    (Greek and Christian), their environments.
    Matthews offers various interpretations of
    Molloy's "Hard Journey."

45 MORSE, J. MITCHELL. "The Case of Irrelevance."
    College English 30, no. 3 (Dec.):201-11.
       Stresses the importance of literary values
    in a pragmatic world. Morse briefly discus-
    ses Beckett's use of language, his preference
    for "the vocabulary of simple concreteness,"
    using a passage from Watt as an example.

46 NURIDSANY, MICHEL. "Soirée Samuel Beckett: Il
    a rendu impossible une certaine forme de
    théâtre." Figaro, 2 Feb., p. 23.
       Notes Beckett's uncanny ability to adapt
    to the various technical media: film, radio,
    television.

47 O'NAN, MARTHA. Samuel Beckett's Lucky: Damned.
    Athens: Ohio University's Modern Language

Department, 9 pp.
Reprinted: 1969.80.

48 ONIMUS, JEAN. Beckett. Paris-Bruges: Desclée
de Brouwer, 190 pp.
Following a general introduction to
Beckett's life and works, studies the inner
self or "conscience" of the Beckettian hero,
analyzes the question of the presence or
absence of God in Beckett's works, and
briefly exposes the alienation of Beckett's
characters. The study is followed by
excerpts from the trilogy, Waiting for Godot,
How It Is, and an interview with Tom Driver.
Reprinted in part from 1961.18.

49 _____. "Samuel Beckett, le clochard et
l'asile." Revue Générale Belge, no. 2
(Feb.), pp. 5-17.
Finds the Beckettian tramp and the asylum-
refuge a double symbol for the same experience: transcendency and imprisonment.

50 PIVOT, BERNARD. "Samuel Beckett." In Les
Critiques Littéraires. Paris: Flammarion,
pp. 200-205.
Presents excerpts from critical reviews of
Molloy.

51 PIOROT-DELPECH, B. "Fin de partie de Samuel
Beckett." Monde, 5-6 May, p. 17.
Reviews Roger Blin's revival of Endgame,
pointing out that the passage of time has
removed some of the shocked response by the
audience, so that the true value of the black
humor and tenderness of the dialogue can be
appreciated.

52 REID, ALEC. All I Can Manage, More than I
Could; An Approach to the Plays of Samuel
Beckett. Dublin: Dolmen Press, 94 pp.
Confining himself to Beckett's plays with
special emphasis on the impact they produce
on an audience in a theater, Reid seeks to
establish two basic premises, that Beckett

has created a new kind of play and that in so
doing he has greatly enlarged the scope of
the theater. He offers information about the
publication and performance of each play, as
well as a synopsis or description of the
situation presented. He considers the plays
Waiting for Godot through Come and Go.

53 SARRAUTE, CLAUDE. "Quand Patate joue Beckett
    avec la Comédie de Limoges." Monde, 7 Feb.,
    p. 15.
        Describes Pierre Dux's role as Hamm in the
    Comédie de Limoges' production of Endgame.

54 SCHOELL, KONRAD. "The Chain and the Circle: A
    Structural Comparison of Waiting for Godot
    and Endgame." Modern Drama 11, no. 1
    (May):48-53.
        Contrasts the form of Waiting for Godot
    with that of Endgame, demonstrating that his
    first two plays represent two different
    principles of construction -- a straight line
    and a circle.

55 SCOTT, NATHAN A. "Beckett's Journey into the
    Zone of Zero." In Craters of the Spirit,
    Studies in the Modern Novel. Washington
    D.C.: Corpus Books, pp. 157-200. Beckett:
    pp. 176-200.
        Examines the tradition that extends from
    the poètes-maudits of the mid-nineteenth
    century through the surrealists and the
    writers of the nouveau roman. Beckett's
    major works are commented on individually.

56 STEINER, GEORGE. "Books of Nuance and Scruple."
    New Yorker 44 (27 Apr.):164, 167-70,
    173-74.
        Claims that Beckett, as a writer, seems
    "to embody the dignity and solitude of the
    entire profession." Steiner reviews the
    major publications, stressing the sparsity,
    solitude, grim hilarity of the works and the
    bilingual prowess of the author.

57   SZANTO, GEORGE H. "Beckett's Quest." Catholic
      World 208, no. 1,243 (Oct.):46-48.
          Reviews Stories and Texts for Nothing,
      stating that Beckett's genius rests in his
      ability to form a quest out of the explora-
      tion of impotence.

58   _____. "The Phenomenological Novel: A Third
      Way in Modern Fiction." Texas Quarterly 11,
      no. 4 (Winter):119-26.
          Comments on the observations of Kafka,
      Beckett and Robbe-Grillet -- that the
      writer's domain is no longer the impossible
      environment, it is rather the knowledge man
      attains through his perceptions: "A man is
      defined by the aspects of the world he
      chooses to know and the manner in which he
      sees them; his descriptions rarely begin to
      clarify the nature of the world."

59   TROUSDALE, MARION. "Dramatic Form: The Example
      of Godot." Modern Drama 11, no. 1 (May):1-9.
          Believes Waiting for Godot is unique
      because it demonstrates how the mechanics of
      a play can become the essential mode of
      statement. In Godot, something more than
      traditionally sound dramatic technique is
      involved; individual actions and characters
      are metaphoric, as in the play as a whole.

60   TYNAN, KENNETH. "Shouts and Murmurs."
      Observer, 2 June, p. 24.
          Reports Beckett's refusal to allow
      Lawrence Olivier to produce All That Fall on
      stage.

61   *"Une sélection bibliographique." Monde [des
      livres], 17 Jan., p. 5.

62   VIA, DAN. Samuel Beckett's "Waiting for Godot."
      New York: Seaburg, 28 pp.
          Briefly introduces the play and playwright
      and discusses a few of the important themes
      in the play: the emptiness of life, the
      search for community, the absence of time,

the failure of language.

63   VOS, NELVIN L. "The Act of Waiting in Contem-
      porary Drama." In Muhlenberg Essays. In
      Honor of The College Centennial. Edited by
      Katherine S. Van Eerde and Nelvin L. Vos.
      Allentown, Pa.: Muhlenberg College, pp. 230-
      50.
          Examines the art of waiting as it is found
      in recent plays. Voss studies a panoramic
      view of contemporary theatre to reveal the
      types of waiting portrayed and then analyzes
      Waiting for Godot, the pivotal play on
      waiting: "The artistry of the play lies
      precisely in the way Beckett has perfectly
      balanced the hope with the hopelessness, the
      Biblical allusions with his ironic use of
      them, the tragedy with the comedy, ...
      Beckett's characters are ... in Purgatorio,
      for what is central to the play is the
      perfect balance between salvation and
      damnation."

64   WEBNER, HELENE L. "Waiting for Godot and the
      New Theology." Renascence 21, no. 1
      (Autumn):3-9,31.
          Observes that the tree in Waiting for
      Godot has connotations of divinity and
      redemption and that Beckett's questioning
      points in the same direction as the theolo-
      gian Dietrich Bonhoeffer.

65   WERNICK, ROBERT. "The Three Kings of Bedlam."
      Life, 2 Feb., pp. 60-69. Beckett:
      pp. 62A-B.
          Describes the theater of the three
      "revolutionaries" -- Beckett, Ionesco, and
      Genet and their attempt to "[sink] the
      audience in a total dramatic situation where
      its own fears, hopes, shames, obsessions are
      acted out in an atmosphere as inescapable and
      as absorbing as a nightmare, or a religious
      ceremony, or a circus." Discusses Godot and
      presents a brief biographical sketch.

66   YUNGBLUT, JUNE J.   "Beckett: Art as Impasse."
      Monks Pond, no. 3 (Fall), pp. 10-16.
          Considers Beckett's aesthetic of failure:
      his comments in the Duthuit dialogues on his
      view of the creative process, his statements
      on the effect of time in his essay on Proust,
      the problem of the relationship between the
      interior and the exterior for the artist, the
      question of the impasse and the characters
      inability to escape from it.

67   Z[and], N[icole].   "Roger Blin reprend Fin de
      partie onze ans après sa création."   Monde, 4
      May, p. 15.
          Focuses on the changes that have taken
      place in Roger Blin's new production of
      Endgame (11 years later).

                          1969

1   ADAMS, ROBERT M.   "Ssh."   New York Review of
      Books 8, no. 5 (25 Sept.):30-32.
          Reviews Cascando and Other Short Dramatic
      Pieces.   Adams notes that the majority of the
      texts are variants of the theme of despairing
      old age, while the characters are manipulated
      like marionettes.

2   ADORNO, THEODOR W.   "Towards an Understanding of
      Endgame."   In Twentieth Century Interpreta-
      tions of "Endgame":   A Collection of Critical
      Essays.   Edited by Bell Gale Chevigny.
      Englewood Cliffs, New Jersey: Prentice-Hall,
      pp. 82-114.
          Discusses several aspects of Endgame:
      setting, dramatic personae, time, history,
      situation, identity, humor, form, language,
      plot, themes, with references to Sartre,
      Joyce, Kafka, Eliot, Mann, Husserl, Kierke-
      gaard, Lukács, Brecht, Heidegger, Ibsen and
      Proust.   See 1969.23.

1969

1   ADAMS, ROBERT M. "Ssh." New York Review of
     Books 8, no. 5 (25 Sept.):30-32.
     Reviews Cascando and Other Short Dramatic
     Pieces. Adams notes that the majority of the
     texts are variants of the theme of despairing
     old age, while the characters are manipulated
     like marionettes.

2   ADORNO, THEODOR W. "Towards an Understanding of
     Endgame." In Twentieth Century Interpreta-
     tions of "Endgame": A Collection of Critical
     Essays. Edited by Bell Gale Chevigny.
     Englewood Cliffs, New Jersey: Prentice-Hall,
     pp. 82-114.
     Discusses several aspects of Endgame:
     setting, dramatic personae, time, history,
     situation, identity, humor, form, language,
     plot, themes, with references to Sartre,
     Joyce, Kafka, Eliot, Mann, Husserl, Kierke-
     gaard, Lukács, Brecht, Heidegger, Ibsen and
     Proust. See 1969.23.

3   ARAGON, LOUIS. "J'avais voté Samuel Beckett."
     Lettres Françaises, 29 Oct.-4 Nov., pp. 3-4.
     Reveals his personal reactions to
     Beckett's works quoting long passages from
     The Unnamable.

4   "Au fil des lettres: A la recherche de Samuel
     Beckett." Figaro, 25-26 Oct., p. 9.
     Presents comments made by Beckett's
     publisher Jérôme Lindon on the author's
     desire for privacy and his dislike of the
     notoriety brought on by the Nobel Prize.

5   BAJOMEE, DANIELLE. "Lumière, ténèbres at chaos
     dans L'Innommable de Samuel Beckett."
     Lettres Romanes 23, no. 2 (May):139-58.
     Assesses the narrator of The Unnamable
     from both a psychological and psychoanalytic
     point of view. He compares The Unnamable to
     M.A. Sechehaye's Journal d'une schizophrène,
     the book of Job, Kierkegaard's Le Concept

d'angoisse and Dante's Divine Comedy.

6   BEAR NICOL, BERNARD de, ed. "The 'Absurd'
    Dramatists -- Beckett and Ionesco: Waiting
    for Godot; The Bald Prima Donna; The Lesson;
    The Chairs; Amédée; The Killer; Rhinoceros;
    Exit the King." In Varieties of Dramatic
    Experience: Discussions on Dramatic Form and
    Themes Between Stanley Evernden, Roger
    Hubank, Thora Burnley Jones and Bernard de
    Bear Nicole. London: University of London
    Press Ltd., pp. 249-73.
        Discusses the form and themes of Waiting
    for Godot: the wretched condition of man,
    the need for companionship, the inability to
    communicate, the commitment to wait, the
    parody of the relations of men in society,
    the awareness of the absurd, the meaning of
    Godot, the analogy of a musical composition,
    the dramatic impact of the play.

7   "Beckett mondain." Figaro, 10 Nov., p. 17.
        Announces the reception given in Beckett's
    honor by the governor of Nabeul, Tunisia.

8   "Beckett to accept Prize." Times (London), 27
    Oct., p. 4.
        Remarks that after three days of avoiding
    reporters, Beckett posed for photographs
    though he refused to comment on the award of
    the Nobel Prize.

9   "Beckett vu par Marcel Achard, Roger Blin, Jean-
    Pierre Faye, Ionesco, Claude Mauriac, Alain
    Robbe-Grillet, Claude Simon." Magazine
    Littéraire, no. 35 (Dec.), pp. 19-21.
        Presents collected impressions of Beckett
    from his associates at the time of his
    receipt of the Nobel Prize.

10 *"Beckett's Waiting World." International
    Herald Tribune, 25-26 Oct., p. 8.

11 BENSKY, ROGER. "La Symbolique du mime dans le
    théâtre de Beckett." Lettres Nouvelles,

Sept.-Oct., 157-63.
Explains the function of mime in Beckett's
theater as an expression of the failure of
thoughts and words, the awareness of the
"néant ultime," and the absence of reality.

12   BERNAL, OLGA. <u>Samuel Beckett: Langage et
fiction dans le roman de Beckett</u>. Paris:
Gallimard, 234 pp.
Focuses on the disintegration of language
and form in Beckett's novels. Language can
only create "fiction" since words are
incapable of realistically portraying the
exterior world or an individual's inner
consciousness. According to Fernand de
Saussure the acquisition and utilization of
langauge are subjective activities abstractly
uniting mental and linguistic images. It is
this relationship between the theme or
subject of the fiction and its expression
from the narrator's subjective point of view
that provides the basis for Beckett's art.

13   BISHOP, TOM. "Samuel Beckett." <u>Saturday
Review</u> 52, no. 46 (15 Nov.):26-27, 59.
In honor of his winning the Nobel Prize,
summarizes Beckett's life and career, his
artistic vision, his use of language, and the
quality of his writings.

14   *BLANCHOT, MAURICE. <u>L'Entretien infini</u>. Paris:
Gallimard, 640 pp.

15   BODART, ROGER. <u>"En attendant Godot."</u> <u>Bulletin
de l'Académie Royale de Langue et de Littéra-
ture Françaises</u> 47, nos. 3-4; 209-27.
Analyzes <u>Waiting for Godot</u>, emphasizing
the question of waiting, the universality of
man, the identity of Godot, the humanness of
the characters and their roles in the play,
the lack of action, and biographical details
that have some barring on the play.

16   BRUNS, GERALD L. "The Storyteller and the
Problem of Language in Samuel Beckett's

Fiction." Modern Language Quarterly 30, no.
2 (June):265-81.
   Evaluates the paradox of Beckett's art,
"that there is nothing to express ...
together with the obligation to express." In
the novels after Murphy, which center around
a storyteller, Beckett's fiction not only
grows out of this paradox, but directs itself
toward it, as though to make it a central
theme. Bruns analyzes the narrative form of
Watt, the trilogy, and How It Is.

17   CAVELL, STANLEY. "Ending the Waiting Game, A
     Reading of Beckett's Endgame." In Must We
     Mean What We Say? New York: Charles
     Scribner's Sons, pp. 115-62.
        Presents a detailed interpretation of
     Endgame, focusing on the ordinariness of the
     play's events, the literatization of lan-
     guage, the form of the dialogue, the situa-
     tion of the characters, Christian references,
     waiting vs. ending, and the effect of theater
     (actors and the audience).

18   No entry.

19   CHAMBERS, ROSS. "An Approach to Endgame." In
     Twentieth Century Interpretations of "End-
     game": A Collection of Critical Essays.
     Edited by Bell Gale Chevigny. Englewood
     CLiffs, New Jersey: Prentice-Hall, pp. 71-
     81.
        Reprint, translation, and revision of
     1967.20; see 1969.23.

20   CHAPSAL, MADELEINE. "Le Nobel à l'écrivain du
     silence." Express, 28 Oct.-2 Nov., pp. 115-
     16.
        Reviews Beckett's literary career,
     examining his style, his use of language and
     silence, and his portrayal of characters
     reduced to the words they speak.

21   _____. "Samuel Beckett: On n'en sort pas."
     Express, 3-19 Jan., p. 57.

Believes language has become the "tyrant" of the body in Beckett's works -- the only way to escape the body is to talk, nothing else is left, not even love.

22   CHEVIGNY, BELL GALE, ed. "Introduction." In _Twentieth Century Interpretations of "End-game": A Collection of Critical Essays._ Englewood Cliffs, New Jersey: Prentice-Hall, pp. 1-13.
Briefly introduces Beckett's life and works as a background for the creation of _Endgame_ "which was at once a way out of the impasse and an expression of it and more than _Godot_ a dramatization of the thwarted and unchartable findings of the fictions." Describing Beckett's obsession with the illusion of life and the elusiveness of being his works are compared to those of Ionesco, Pirandello, and Genet. The early draft of _Fin de partie_ is also contrasted with the finished French version and Beckett's English translation. See 1969.23.

23   _____. _Twentieth Century Interpretations of "Endgame": A Collection of Critical Essays._ Englewood Cliffs, New Jersey: Prentice-Hall, 120 pp.
The essays that make up this volume present specific aspects of _Endgame_: character analysis, thematic material, formal structural elements, philosophical and literary comparisons. A chronology of important dates and a select bibliography are included. See 1969.2, 1969.19, 1969.22, 1969.35, 1969.38, 1969.44, 1969.60, 1969.104.

24   CIXOUS, HELENE. "Le Prix Nobel décerné à Samuel Beckett: Le Maître du texte pour rien." _Monde_, (hebdomadaire) 23-29 Oct., p. 13; _Monde_, 24 Oct., pp. 1, 10.
Defines Beckett's ideology, summarizes the major themes of his works, and reviews the stages of his career.

25   COHN, RUBY. "Beckett's Recent Residua."
     Southern Review 5, no. 4 (Autumn):1045-54.
        Claims that "From an Abandoned Work" is
     the key to understanding "Imagination Dead
     Imagine," "Ping," and "Enough."

26   _____. Currents in Contemporary Drama.
     Bloomington and London: Indiana University
     Press, 276 pp.
        In her examination of trends in Con-
     temporary English, French, and German
     language theater, considers Beckett's works
     from several different perspectives: the
     questions of absurdity, cruelty, tragicomedy,
     roles vs. reality, and the play as a play.
     Play, Godot, and Endgame are discussed
     individually and Beckett's works are compared
     with those of Genet.

27   _____. "Endgame." In Twentieth Century
     Interpretations of "Endgame": A Collection
     of Critical Essays. Edited by Bell Gale
     Chevigny. Englewood Cliffs, New Jersey:
     Prentice-Hall, pp. 40-52.
        Discusses the plot, themes, the ambiguous
     relationships of the characters, and the
     complex interpretations of Endgame. Re-
     printed from 1962.21; see 1969.23.

28   CRONKHITE, GARY. "Samuel Beckett: En attendant
     fin de l'univers." Quarterly Journal of
     Speech 55:45-53.
        Attempts to clarify the philosophy of
     existence expressed in two of Beckett's
     plays: Waiting for Godot and Endgame.
     Cronkhite believes the two plays taken
     together portray a universe operating in
     accordance with the three laws of ther-
     modynamics.

29   CUNARD, NANCY. "Samuel Beckett. 'Whoroscope.'"
     Those Were the Hours. Memories of My Hours
     Press Réanville and Paris, 1928-1931. Edited
     by Hugh Ford. Carbondale and Edwardsville,

Southern Illinois University Press, pp. 109-
22.
Documents Beckett's entry in the poetry
contest sponsored by Hours Press, her meeting
with the author, and her impressions of
Beckett.

30   "De Dublin à Paris." Figaro, 24 Oct., p. 15.
Traces Beckett's personal and professional
life from 1928 to 1969.

31   DOUTRELIGNE, MICHEL. "Ebauche d'exégèse de Oh!
les beaux jours de Samuel Beckett." Marginales 24, no. 124 (Feb.):67-71.
Offers a textual analysis of Happy Days,
focusing on the subject, themes, and characters of the play.

32   DUBOIS, JACQUES. "Deux représentations de la
société dans le nouveau théâtre." Revue
d'Histoire du Théâtre 21, no. 2:151-61.
Feels that Waiting for Godot and Ionesco's
The Chairs resemble one another in the
following ways: the structure of the initial
situation, the same narrative direction, and
the same dramatic symbolism. Although the
authors express a "négation fataliste," they
represent different points of view. Dubois
points out that they both reveal their
dissatisfaction with society, but Ionesco
conforms to the system whereas Beckett
resists.

33   *DUMAS, ANDRE. "Quand la personne échappe: Le
Romanesque de notre demi-siècle." Réforme,
20 Sept.

34   DUMUR, GUY. "Prix Nobel: Beckett le grand
anonyme." Nouvel Observateur, 27 Oct.-2
Nov., p. 39.
Briefly summarizes Beckett's career, his
choice of the French language, his Irish
heritage, and the anonymity of his fiction.

35   EASTHOPE, ANTHONY. "Hamm, Clov, and Dramatic
        Method in <u>Endgame</u>." In <u>Twentieth Century</u>
        <u>Interpretations of "Endgame": A Collection</u>
        <u>of Critical Essays</u>. Edited by Bell Gale
        Chevigny. Englewood Cliffs, New Jersey:
        Prentice-Hall, pp. 61-70.
            Considers the relationship between Hamm
        and Clov, King and servant, master and dog,
        and the relationship between surface and
        depth. Reprint of 1968.20; see 1969.23.

36   EHLER, SIDNEY A. "Beckett: Irlandais
        déraciné." <u>Nouvelles Littéraires</u>, 11 Dec.,
        p. 5.
            Summarizes Beckett's life up to his
        receipt of the Nobel Prize, and his detach-
        ment from his Irish heritage, briefly
        comparing and contrasting Beckett with Joyce.

37   "En recherchant Beckett." <u>Figaro</u>, 24 Oct., p.
        15.
            Describes the search for Beckett after his
        award of the Nobel Prize for Literature was
        announced.

38   ESSLIN, MARTIN. "Samuel Beckett: The Search
        for the Self." In <u>Twentieth Century Inter-</u>
        <u>pretations of "Endgame": A Collection of</u>
        <u>Critical Essays</u>. Edited by Bell Gale
        Chevigny. Englewood Cliffs, New Jersey:
        Prentice-Hall, pp. 22-32.
            Reprint of 1961.21, 1963.24, 1967.37,
        1968.24; see 1969.23; see 1968.24 for
        annotation.

39   FINDLAY, ROBERT R. "Confrontation in Waiting:
        <u>Godot</u> and the Wakefield Play." <u>Renascence</u>
        21, no. 3 (Spring):195-202.
            Compares the anonymous, fifteenth-century
        Wakefield mystery play <u>The Shepherds</u> with
        Beckett's <u>Godot</u>: "Each treats the archetypal
        myth of man's struggle for meaning and
        purpose ... The essential difference lies in
        the medieval dramatist's desire to show
        purpose in man's struggle and resolution to

his anguish, while Beckett in the twentieth
century permits man's struggle and agony to
persist into infinity."

40   FISCHER, ERNST. "Samuel Beckett: Play & Film."
      Mosaic 2, no. 2 (Winter):96-116.
           Analyzes specific themes in Play (the
      spotlight, reduction, parody, power of music,
      concept of play, and laughter) and Film (the
      world after the collapse, eye and object,
      self-knower -- self-executioner, the two
      fools, identity and responsibility, reality
      as mathematics, the clown and the "Conditio
      Humana").

41   FLETCHER, JOHN. "The Arrival of Godot." Modern
      Language Review 64, no. 1 (Jan.):34-38.
           Reviews recent contributions to Beckett
      studies, including criticism, critical
      editions, and possibilities for future
      scholarly studies.

42   FRENCH, PHILIP. "Krone for Sam." New Statesman
      78 (31 Oct.):619.
           Recognizes Beckett's importance to modern
      literature, but has difficulty appreciating
      his later fiction. French criticizes
      Beckett's recent work as a move into an
      "abstract world of unchallengeable asser-
      tion."

43   GLICKSBERG, CHARLES I. "Beckett's Vision of the
      Absurd." In The Ironic Vision in Modern
      Literature. The Hague: Martinus Nijhoff,
      pp. 236-41.
           Devotes his discussion to an analysis of
      the ironic devices Beckett uses in Watt: the
      use of blasphemous parody, the problem of
      identity and language (the difficulty of
      making any affirmation at all), the meta-
      physical irony of Beckett's one theme -- the
      obsessive but hopeless quest for meaning.

44   GOLDMAN, RICHARD M. "Endgame and its Score-
      keepers." In Twentieth Century

Interpretations of "Endgame": A Collection
of Critical Essays. Edited by Bell Gale
Chevigny. Englewood Cliffs, New Jersey:
Prentice-Hall, pp. 33-39.
Describes the many attempts at criticism
of Beckett's Endgame as "beautiful failures
... For we need to determine what kind of art
Beckett is practicing rather than translating
his works into a set of meanings or placing
them along the continuum of literary history." See 1969.23.

45   GREENBERG, ALVIN. "The Revolt of Objects: The
Opposing World in the Modern Novel." Centennial Review 13, no. 4 (Fall):366-88.
Discusses the presentation of the hostility of the physical world in the modern
novel, using Watt as an example: "... the
possibility for a genuine formulation of the
self seems damned by the self's inability to
accept its immersion in the world of things
... Watt, no longer knowing things as what
they were and not seeing them as they are, is
left unable to meet them on their own ..."

46   GRUEN, JOHN. "Samuel Beckett Talks About Samuel
Beckett." Vogue 154, no. 10 (Dec.):210.
Interviews Beckett, recording Beckett's
impressions on writing, James Joyce, and his
visit to New York. Beckett comments on his
writing: "... I am constantly working in the
dark. It would be like an insect leaving his
cocoon. I can only estimate my work from
within. If my work has any meaning at all,
it is due more to ignorance, inability, and
an intuitive despair than to any individual
strength."

47   GUTH, PAUL. "Paul Guth vous explique qui est
Samuel Beckett, Prix Nobel." Elle, 24 Nov.,
pp. 142-46.
Outlines Beckett's literary career and
presents some of the major themes in his
works and his characters with references to
Pascal and Descartes.

48   HAMILTON, IAIN. "Godot Arrives." <u>Illustrated</u>
      <u>London News</u>, 1 Nov., p. 9.
           Examines the significance of the awarding
      of the Nobel Prize to Beckett.

49   *HANRAHAN, JOHN. "The Agony of Waiting."
      <u>Annals</u> 80 (Feb.):28-31.

50   *HAYMAN, RONALD. "The Most Courageous Writer
      Going." <u>Observer</u>, 26 Oct., p.6.

51   HINCHLIFFE, ARNOLD P. <u>The Absurd</u>. London:
      Methuen & Co. Ltd., pp. 63-72.
           Discusses several aspects of Beckett's
      fiction: the lack of plot and conventional
      characters, the limitations of language, and
      the difficulty of finding meaning in a world
      subject to change. Hinchliffe mentions
      Beckett's major novels and plays as examples,
      with special emphasis on <u>Waiting for Godot</u>
      and <u>Endgame</u>.

52   HOBSON, HAROLD. "Samuel Beckett: An Un-
      published Text, 'Imagination Dead Imagine.'"
      <u>Sunday Times</u> (London), 26 Oct., p. 53.
           Congratulates Beckett as the new Nobel
      Prizewinner and ennumerates his achievements.

53   *HOFFMAN, FREDERICK J. <u>Samuel Beckett: The Man</u>
      <u>and his Works</u>. Toronto and London: Forum
      House Publishing Co.

54   HUBERT, RENEE RIESE. "The Paradox of Silence:
      Samuel Beckett's Plays." <u>Mundus Artium</u> 2
      (Summer):82-90.
           Examines the interplay of silence and the
      human voice in the earlier plays, the
      mechanical or artificial voice of the later
      works, the absence of memories which creates
      "an empty solitary present," and the trans-
      formation in Beckett's plays of the relation
      of silence to speech. Examples are taken
      from <u>Waiting for Godot</u>, <u>Endgame</u>, <u>Krapp's Last</u>
      <u>Tape</u>, <u>Play</u>, and <u>Happy Days</u>.

55 JANVIER, LUDOVIC. "Au travail avec Beckett."
    <u>Quinzaine Littéraire</u>, no. 67 (16-28 Feb.),
    pp. 6-7.
        Discusses the difficulties of translating
    <u>Watt</u> from English into French.

56 _____. <u>Beckett par lui-même</u>. Paris: Editions
    du Seuil, 189 pp.
        Following a detailed chronology of
    Beckett's life and works, organizes his
    commentary by selected themes and key words
    from Beckett's fiction. Each of the 59
    entries includes comments by Janvier and
    quotations from Beckett's works. Followed by
    a selected bibliography.

57 _____. "Les Difficultés d'un séjour." <u>Critique</u>
    25 (Apr.):312-23.
        Reviews <u>Watt</u>, focusing on the insecurity
    of language and of Watt himself, the break-
    down of logic, the instability of a shelter
    or resting place, and the "other".

58 JEAN, RAYMOND. "Ancien et nouveau Beckett: Un
    personnage nommé Watt." <u>Monde [des Livres]</u>,
    1 Feb., pp. 1-2.
        Summarizes <u>Watt</u>: characters, situations,
    language. Reprinted: 1979.22.29.

59 JOUFFROY, ALAIN. "Hommage à Samuel Beckett:
    Silence s'il vous plaît." <u>Lettres Fran-</u>
    <u>çaises</u>, 22-28 Jan., pp. 3-5.
        Offers his personal reactions, impres-
    sions, and interpretations of <u>Watt</u>.

60 KENNER, HUGH. "Life in the Box." In <u>Twentieth</u>
    <u>Century Interpretations of "Endgame": A</u>
    <u>Collection of Critical Essays</u>. Edited by
    Bell Gale Chevigny. Englewood Cliffs, New
    Jersey: Prentice-Hall, pp. 53-60.
        Comments on the symbolic actions and
    structure of <u>Endgame</u>: "theater reduced to
    its elements in order that theatricalism may
    explore without mediation its own boundaries
    ..." See 1969.23.

61   LAHR, JOHN, "The Fall and Rise of Beckett's Bum:
        Bert Lahr in <u>Godot</u>." <u>Evergreen Review</u>, no.
        70 (Sept.), pp. 29-32.
            The actor's son describes the rehearsals
        and performances of <u>Waiting for Godot</u> in
        Miami and New York.

62   LASSON, ROBERT. "Book Buzz: Beckett." <u>Chicago</u>
        <u>Tribune Book World</u>, 28 Dec., p.2.
            Praises selection of Beckett as Nobel
        Prize laureate.

63   LEMARCHAND, JACQUES. "Un dramatuge vision-
        naire." <u>Figaro Littéraire</u>, 27 Oct.-2 Nov.,
        p.7.
            Examines in retrospect the impact of
        <u>Waiting for Godot</u> on the first parisien
        critics in Jan. 1953.

64   *[MACGOWRAN, JACK]. "Jack MacGowran talks to
        Michael Foley." <u>Honest Ulsterman</u>, no. 9
        (Jan.). pp. 9-11.

65   *MARCUS, FRANK. "I Wait, Therefore I Am."
        <u>Sunday Telegraph</u>, (London), 26 Oct., p. 16.

66   MARISSEL, ANDRE. "Beckett, Prix Nobel de
        Littérature: L'Eternelle désintégration."
        <u>Nouvelles Littéraires</u>, 30 Oct., pp. 3, 12.
            Offers a general discussion of Beckett's
        vision of man and the world as it is por-
        trayed in his works at the time he was
        awarded the Nobel Prize. Reprinted:
        1979.22.65.

67   *_____. "Samuel Beckett, Prix Nobel de Littéra-
        ture: L'Homme est-il 'mort,' la vie sera-t-
        elle reinventée?" <u>Réforme</u>, 1 Nov.

68   MATHER, IAN. "Now the World is Waiting for
        Beckett." <u>Daily Mail</u> (London), 24 Oct.,
        p.10.
            Describes Beckett's private life and
        career opportunities at the time he won the

Nobel Prize. Many of the stated "facts" are
erroneous.

69 MAURIAC, CLAUDE. "Samuel Beckett, Prix Nobel:
    Les Enlisés de Beckett." Figaro Littéraire,
    27 Oct.-2 Nov., p. 6.
        Believes Beckett's works though "cruel"
    are not hopeless. Mauriac claims that like
    the works of Pascal and Nietszche Beckett's
    fiction attests to the greatness of man.

70 _____. "Un même cri dans la même nuit,"
    Figaro, 24 Oct., p. 15.
        Reviews Beckett's literary career,
    demonstrating his unified vision, or the
    similarity of his message in each of the
    genres he used to express himself.

71 *MAYS, J.C.C. "Beckett and the Irish."
    Hibernia 33, no. 21 (7 Nov.):14.

72 MONTAGUE, JOHN. "Beckett, inconnue, et
    inconnaissable." Magazine Littéraire 35
    (Dec.):9-12.
        Offers a retrospective of Beckett's
    literary career and background, indicating
    the major themes of his works.

73 Murch, Anne C. "Les Indications scéniques dans
    le Nouveau Théâtre: Fin de partie, de Samuel
    Beckett." Australian Journal of French
    Studies 6, no. 1:55-64.
        Studies the implications of Beckett's
    stage directions in Endgame, underlining the
    importance of the decor, the distribution of
    the roles, the action, and the tone of the
    discourse.

74 Murray, Patrick. "Samuel Beckett and Tradi-
    tion." Studies 58, no. 230 (Summer): 166-78.
        Focuses on Beckett's debt to literary
    tradition through his use of grotesque humour
    which could be influenced by the Irish
    writers Swift, Joyce, Yeats, Synge, Fielding,
    and Sterne, Shakespeare's King Lear, and the

Absurdists and Existentialists, Ionesco,
Adamov, Pinter, Genet, Sartre and Camus.
Murray discusses <u>Godot</u>, <u>Endgame</u>, and <u>Happy
Days</u> as examples.

75   *"Nobel Prize for Dublin-born Samuel Beckett."
      <u>Oxford Mail</u>, 23 Oct., p. 1.

76   "Nobel Prize: Kyrie Eleison Without God." <u>Time</u>
      94 (31 Oct.):55.
          Points out that when Beckett was awarded
      the Nobel Prize, the judges were acknowledg-
      ing the fact that Beckett had become the
      representative of an age "that feels suffo-
      cated by its sense of nothingness."

77   *"Novels of 1964: Samuel Beckett." <u>Times
      Literary Supplement</u> (London) 3, pp. 45-47.
          Source: Tanner, 1969.113;unverified.

78   "Oeuvres de Samuel Beckett." <u>Lettres Fran-
      çaises</u>, 29 Oct.-4 Nov., p. 4.
          Provides a list of Beckett's works and
      first representations of his plays through
      1966.

79   *OHMANN, R.M. "Speech, Action, and Style." In
      <u>International Symposium on Literary Style,
      Bellagio, 1969</u>, pp. 241-54.

80   O'Nan, Martha. "Samuel Beckett's Lucky:
      Damned." In <u>The Role of Mind in Hugo,
      Faulkner, Beckett and Grass</u>. New York:
      Philosophical Library, pp. 23-25.
          Examines the significance of Pozzo and
      Lucky's roles in <u>Waiting for Godot</u> and the
      impact of habit on Lucky's "thinking."
      Reprint of 1968.47.

81   OSTER, ROSE-MARIE G. "Hamm and Hummel --
      Beckett and Strindberg on the Human Condi-
      tion." <u>Scandinavian Studies</u> 41, no. 4
      (Nov.):330-45.
          Compares and contrasts the works of
      Beckett and Strindberg: their visions of the

world, their protagonists and the writer's
role in clarifying the relation between man
and his world.

82   *"People: Nobel Pursuits and Vice Versa."
       <u>International Herald Tribune</u>, 25-26 Oct.,
       p. 8.

83   PERCHE, LOUIS. <u>Beckett: L'Enfer à notre portée</u>.
       Paris: Le Centurion/Sciences Humaines, 194
       pp.
            Part of a series of books devoted to the
       "works and ideas" of modern writers, this
       study offers a general introduction to the
       thematic development of Beckett's prose and
       drama. Perche defines the scope of Beckett's
       works as an exploration of a grey zone in
       which the characters know the limits of their
       condition. The "I" is defined as powerless,
       as the symbol of man's "enfer," but the
       author is still tempted to see occasional
       signs of hope in the desolation Beckett
       depicts.

84   PINGAUD, BERNARD. "'Dire, c'est inventer.'"
       <u>Quinzaine Littéraire</u>, no. 67 (16-28 Feb.),
       pp. 5-6.
            Reviews the French translation of <u>Watt</u>.
       Pinguad examines the use of language in <u>Watt</u>
       from the point of view of Ludovic Janvier's
       analysis of three "moments" in Beckett's
       narratives: 1) that in which the narrator
       views the story from a distance (<u>Murphy</u>,
       <u>Watt</u>), 2) that in which the character and the
       narrator coincide (trilogy), and 3) that in
       which the narrator is the interpreter of a
       voice that comes from somewhere else (<u>How It
       Is</u>). Reprinted: 1979.22.30.

85   POIROT-DELPECH, BERTRAND. <u>En attendant Godot</u> de
       Samuel Beckett." In <u>Au soir le soir:
       Théâtre 1960-1970</u>. Paris: Mercure de
       France, pp. 61-63.
            Reexamines <u>Waiting for Godot</u> nearly a
       decade after its first performance and feels

this delay is useful to an appreciation of
the play.

86   _____. "Madeleine Renaud dans <u>Oh! les beaux</u>
        <u>jours</u> de Beckett." In <u>Au soir le soir:</u>
        <u>Théâtre 1960-1970</u>. Paris: Mercure de
        France, pp. 113-16.
            Describes the setting, themes, force of
        language and brilliance of Madeleine Renaud's
        performance in <u>Happy Days</u> at the Odéon
        Théâtre de France.

87   PORTER, THOMAS E., S.J. "Samuel Beckett:
        Dramatic Tradition and the <u>Ausländer</u>." <u>Eire-</u>
        <u>Ireland</u> 4, no. 1:62-75.
            Views Beckett as the Ausländer, "the alien
        who has dissociated himself from his own
        heritage without adopting any other." Porter
        examines the cultural features of mise en
        scène, dramatis personae and especially the
        dramatic structure of <u>Waiting for Godot</u> and
        <u>Endgame</u> in light of Western dramatic tradi-
        tion.

88   *POULET, ROBERT. "Samuel Beckett: l'étrange
        Prix Nobel de Littérature." <u>Spectacle du</u>
        <u>Monde</u>, no. 93 (Dec.), pp. 128-32.

89   PRASTEAU, JEAN. "Chronique d'une ascension"
        <u>Figaro Littéraire</u>, 27 Oct.-2 Nov., p. 8.
            Follows Beckett's rise in popularity
        through quotations from articles published in
        the <u>Figaro Littéraire</u>.

90   READ, HERBERT. "The Limits of Permissiveness in
        Art." <u>Malahat Review</u> 9 (Jan.):37-50.
        Beckett: pp. 44-46.
            Deals with developments in modern art
        which he considers excessive, such as
        Beckett's "permissive logorrhea that compels
        the reader to plunge into a sea of words with
        so little aesthetic reward."

91   REYNOLDS, STANLEY. "Television: TV Philis-
        tinism." <u>Manchester Guardian</u>, 27 Oct., p. 8.

Reviews television coverage of the award
of the Nobel Prize to Beckett.

92   ROSE, MARILYN GADDIS. "Solitary Companions in
     Beckett and Jack B. Yeats." Eire-Ireland 4,
     no. 2:66-80.
        Traces the friendship of Beckett and Jack
     B. Yeats, their similarities and differences,
     and their representation of human relation-
     ships in their works.

93   ROUDAUT, JEAN. "Introduction à une lecture
     (partielle) de Samuel Beckett." Français
     dans le monde 63 (Mar.):12-17.
        Offers a general introduction to Beckett's
     works: themes, characters, their possessions,
     and the passage of time.

94   _____. "La Parole de Beckett." Magazine
     Littéraire, no. 35 (Dec.), pp. 13-14.
        Depicts Beckett's "chronicle of deper-
     sonalization": the impersonal voice, the
     reduction of physical action, and the futile
     creation of stories.

95   _____. "Samuel Beckett: Pages Commentées."
     Français dans le monde 63 (Mar.):28-31.
        Presents a textual explanation of two
     passages from Molloy.

96   ROY, CLAUDE. "La Non-passion du non-homme."
     Nouvel Observateur, no. 222 (10-16 Feb.), pp.
     32-34.
        Reviews both Watt and Poems in English as
     "poetic" works.

97   _____. "Un drole de rire pas drôle." Nouvel
     Observateur, 3 Nov., pp. 38-40.
        Argues that Beckett should have received
     the Nobel Prize for Peace -- Beckett gives
     "peace" to those that live with him, listen
     to him, or follow him. Roy discusses the
     effect of Beckett's works on his readers and
     the effect of Beckett's success on Roger
     Blin.

98   "Samuel Beckett Goes into Hiding." Times
      (London), 25 Oct., p. 3.
          States the distress caused by the
      announcement that Beckett had won the
      Nobel Prize and his attempts to avoid any
      publicity brought on by the award.
      Reprinted: 1979.22.64b.

99   "Samuel Beckett Wins Nobel Prize." Daily
      Telegraph, (London), 24 Oct., p. 15.
          Summarizes Beckett's life and literary
      works.

99a   "Samuel Beckett Wins Nobel Prize." Times
      (London), 24 Oct., p. 1.
          Announces Beckett's winning of the Nobel
      Prize, identifying the current themes of his
      works as human degradation, loneliness, and
      despair. Reprinted: 1979.22.64a.

100   SANDIER, GILLES. "Un Eschyle de notre temps."
      Magazine Littéraire, no. 35 (Dec.), pp. 15-
      18.
          Gives an account of Beckett's theatrical
      achievements with special attention given to
      Madeleine Renaud's performance of Happy Days.
      Sandier compares Beckett's play with
      Claudel's Le Soulier de Satin and The Book of
      Job.

101   SARRIS, ANDREW. "Buster Keaton and Samuel
      Beckett." Columbia Forum 12, no. 4 (Winter):
      42-43.
          Contrasts Beckett's stark literary style
      with Keaton's elaborate comic spectacles.
      Because of these differences, Sarris feels
      that Keaton does not belong in Beckett's
      Film, that Keaton would not have participated
      in an "overtly symbolic enterprise" if he
      hadn't needed the money.

102   *SAUREL, RENEE, BERTRAND POIROT-DELPECH, GEORGES
      LERMINIER, GILLES SANDIER and ANDRE ALTER.
      "Comme il vous plaira, Madeleine Renaud: Un
      portrait en cinq critiques." Cahiers

<u>Littéraires de l'O.R.T.F.</u>, no. 13 (30 Mar.-
26 Apr.), pp. 25-28.

103   SCHNEIDER, ALAN. "On Directing <u>Film</u>." In <u>Film</u>.
      New York: Grove Press, pp. 63-94.
         Offers a detailed description with
      numerous photos of the preparation, and
      directing of <u>Film</u>, his interactions with
      Beckett and Buster Keaton, and public
      reaction to the film at the New York Film
      Festival of 1965.

104   _____. "Waiting for Beckett: A Personal
      Chronicle." In <u>Twentieth Century Interpre-</u>
      <u>tations of "Endgame": A Collection of</u>
      <u>Critical Essays</u>. Edited by Bell Gale
      Chevigny. Englewood Cliffs, New Jersey:
      Prentice-Hall, pp. 14-21.
         Describes his preparations for his off-
      Broadway production of <u>Endgame</u>, his impres-
      sions, observations of the French production,
      meetings with Beckett, and rehearsals.
      Reprint of 1958.30; see 1969.23.

105   *SHANDOIAN, JACK. "Samuel Beckett's Poetry."
      <u>Research Studies of Washington State Univer-</u>
      <u>sity</u> 37:259-73.
         Source: <u>Annual Bibliography of English</u>
      <u>Language and Literature</u>, 1969;unverified.

106   SHAPIRO, BARBARA. "Toward a Psychoanalytic
      Reading of Beckett's <u>Molloy</u>, I." <u>Literature</u>
      <u>and Psychology</u> 19, no. 2 (1969):71-86.
         Part one of an article devoted to a
      psychoanalytic approach to Beckett's <u>Molloy</u>.
      Through close textual analysis of individual
      images and fantasies, Shapiro develops the
      following themes: Molloy's ambivalent
      attachment to his mother; Moran and Molloy as
      two sides of the same fictional personality;
      Moran's metamorphosis (a process which brings
      to consciousness hitherto unconscious
      elements of his experience of himself); and
      the psychology of anality. See 1969.107.

107   _____. "Toward a Psychoanalytic Reading of
       Beckett's Molloy, II." Literature and
       Psychology 19, no. 3-4:15-30.
            Continuation of an article devoted to a
       psychoanalytic approach to Molloy. See
       1969.106.

108   SHERREL, RICHARD. "Samuel Beckett." In The
       Human Image: Avant-Garde and Christian.
       Richmond, Virginia: John Knox Press, pp. 45-
       64.
            Focuses on certain aspects of the English
       version of Waiting for Godot: Individual
       identity, the relationship of the characters,
       time, theatrical imagery, language and the
       inability to communicate, and theological
       imagery.

109   SOLOMON, PHILIP HOWARD. "Lousse and Molloy:
       Beckett's Bower of Bliss." Australian
       Journal of French Studies 6, no. 1:65-81.
            Analyzes Molloy's sojourn with Lousse,
       attempting to interpret the significance of
       this episode. Parallels between the Lousse
       episode and the closely related enchanted
       garden scenes of Homer's Odyssey, Ariosto's
       Orlando Furioso, Tasso's Jerusalem Delivered,
       and Spenser's The Faerie Queene are pointed
       out.

110   Stein, Walter. Criticism as Dialog. Cambridge:
       Cambridge University Press, 75-85, 116-23.
            Compares and contrasts Waiting for Godot
       with works by Lawrence and Shakespeare.

111   STROMBERG, KJELL. "Un Irlandais de langue
       française." Figaro, 24 Oct., p. 15.
            Announces Beckett's winning of the Nobel
       Prize, pointing out the major themes of
       Beckett's works and the authors that may have
       influenced him.

112   SURER, PAUL. "Samuel Beckett." In Cinquante Ans
       de théâtre. Paris: Société d'Edition
       d'Enseignement Supérieur, pp. 348-60, and

<u>passim</u>.
     Offers a general introduction to Beckett's
life and dramatic works (<u>Waiting for Godot</u>
through <u>Play</u>). Surer discusses some of the
major elements of the plays: the characters,
their situations, Beckett's tragic vision of
the world, the religious context of the
dramas, the basic themes, the decor, the
symbols, the language, comedy, and Beckett's
originality.

113   TANNER, JAMES T.F. AND J. DON VANN. <u>Samuel</u>
       <u>Beckett: A Checklist of Criticism</u>. Kent,
       Ohio: Kent State University Press, 85 pp.
            Briefly lists Beckett's major books in
       chronological order and provides a checklist
       of criticism about Samuel Beckett. Separate
       sections are devoted to bibliographies, books
       about Beckett, chapters about Beckett in
       books, articles about Beckett, and reviews of
       Beckett's books.

114   TAYLOR, ANDREW. "The Minimal Affirmation of
       <u>Godot</u>." <u>Critical Review</u>, no. 12, pp. 3-14.
            Attempts to prove that Beckett's vision of
       life is not totally negative as it is
       expressed in <u>Waiting for Godot</u>: "The
       integrity with which [Beckett] holds to his
       vision, exemplified by his refusal to take
       the easy way out and succumb either to the
       intoxicant of hope or the narcotic of
       despair, gives authority and importance to
       Godot's affirmation that although man has no
       value to the world, he nonetheless has value
       to man."

115   THOMAS, KEITH. "Godot's Return." <u>Nation</u>
       (Sydney), no. 263 (8 Mar.), pp. 18-19.
            Reviews the production of <u>Waiting for</u>
       <u>Godot</u> at the Independent in North Sydney in
       which the director Peter O'Shaughnessy has
       muted the play's use of mime and clowning and
       makes the characters more realistic and less
       like "circus props."

116   *"Une vie, une oeuvre." Nouvelles Littéraires,
         30 Oct.
            Source: Bryer et al., 1972.7;unverified.

117   "Waiting for Nobel." Guardian, 24 Oct., p. 1.
            Announces that Beckett has been awarded
         the Nobel Prize for Literature and very
         briefly summarizes the most important stages
         of his career.

118   WEBB, EUGENE. "Samuel Beckett, Stories and
         Tests for Nothing [...] Tetes-mortes [...]
         No's Knife: Collected Shorter Prose [...]
         Cascando and Other Shrot Dramatic Pieces
         [...]." West Coast Review 4, no. 2
         (Fall):63-66.
            Establishes the general tone and interest
         of the works, as well as their importance to
         Beckett's continuing literary development.

119   WEBB, W.L. "Beckett's Words and Silence."
         Guardian, 24 Oct., pp. 1, 11.
            Assesses Beckett's career, the subject
         matter of his fiction, and his winning of the
         Nobel Prize.

120   WET, BETTY de. "Waiting for Godot by Samuel
         Beckett." Unisa English Studies, no. 2
         (May), pp. 19-28.
            Interprets Waiting for Godot in a reli-
         gious context, examining specific Christian
         references, the identity of Godot, the
         questions of faith and salvation, and the
         roles of the characters in the drama.

121   WILLIAMS, RAYMOND. "Waiting for Godot: Samuel
         Beckett." In Drama from Ibsen to Brecht.
         New York: Oxford University Press, pp. 299-
         305.
            Emphasizes the dramatic form of Waiting
         for Godot. Williams demonstrates that the
         play is an example of an expressionist method
         in which a private feeling (uncertain
         waiting) is dramatized by its projection into

contrasting characters who also represent
contrasting modes of action.

122   *YSMAL, PIERRE. "Dans l'édition." Témoignage
       Chrétien, 20 Mar.

123   ZEGEL, SYLVAIN. "Une retraite pour un vain-
       queur." Figaro Littéraire, 27 Oct.-2 Nov.,
       p. 8.
            Jérome Lindon reminisces about his initial
       contact with Beckett and describes the
       confusion that took place after the official
       announcement of Beckett's winning of the
       Nobel Prize.

124   ZERAFFA, MICHEL. Personne et Personnage: Le
       Romanesque des années vingt aux années
       cinquante. Paris: Editions Klincksieck, pp.
       397-400.
            Using Molloy as an example, demonstrates
       that Beckett refuses to make the absurd into
       a code of ethics, because he feels that the
       absurdity of existence is organic.

                          1970

  1   ABBOTT, H. PORTER. "Farewell to Incompetence:
       Beckett's How It Is and 'Imagination Dead
       Imagine.'" Contemporary Literature 11, no. 1
       (Winter):36-47.
            Hopes to demonstrate that How It Is and
       "Imagination Dead Imagine" show a significant
       change in Beckett's approach to fiction.
       Abbott discusses specific innovations in
       these works: the ordered structure of the
       work, the irrelevancy of the narrator's
       identity, the compatibility of extremes, and
       the rejection of incompetence as an artistic
       device.

  2   ALBERES, R.M. "Voix inimitables." Nouvelles
       Littéraires, 18 June, p. 5.
            Discusses Beckett's first two works in
       French, First Love and Mercier and Camier, in

which man is represented by a voice.

3   *ALTER, ANDRE. "En deça ou au delà du temps."
     Cahiers Littéraires 8, no. 8 (1-14 Feb.):20-
     22.

4   ATTOUN, LUCIEN. "Beckett, clown génial."
     Nouvelles Littéraires, 1 Jan., p. 13.
          Analyzes Beckett's characters who are
     neither dehumanized victims nor stereotypes
     of human decadence, they simply "continue."

5   BAKEWELL, MICHAEL. "Working with Beckett."
     Adam: International Review, nos. 337-339,
     pp. 72-73.
          Describes working with Beckett on the
     radio version of the first French production
     of Endgame and the television production of
     Eh Joe?

6   BARNARD, GUY CHRISTIAN. Samuel Beckett: A New
     Approach. A Study of the Novels and Plays.
     London: J.M. Dent & Sons; New York: Dodd,
     Mead, 144 pp.
          Deals with the psychological and human
     aspects of the plays and novels available in
     English. Barnard sees Beckett's characters
     as a series of schizophrenic tramps who have
     lost their sense of identity and reality.
     The works are summarized and the basic themes
     and stylistic devices, as well as certain
     similarities between the works are examined.

7   BASTIDE, FRANÇOIS, REGIS. "En attendant Godot
     de Samuel Beckett." Nouvelles Littéraires, 2
     Apr., p. 13.
          Underscores the difficulties experienced
     during the production of Waiting for Godot at
     the Théâtre Récamier, the structure of the
     play, and the audience's problems understand-
     ing the work. Reprinted 1972.3.

8   BEDIENT, CALVIN. "Beckett and the Drama of
     Gravity." Sewanee Review 78, no. 1 (Jan.-
     Mar.):143-55.

Believes Beckett's tragicomedies belong to the realm of "dramatic gravity": "the irremediable lowness of human life, the obscenity of time's continual defecation, the nothingness corroding the heart of everything -- this is the theme of Beckett's plays, and it is boldly, almost laughably, unrelieved."

9   BERSANI, JACQUES; MICHEL AUTRAND; JACQUES LECARME; and BRUNO VERCIER, eds. La Littérature en France depuis 1945. Paris; Montréal, Bruxelles, Lausanne, London: Bordas, Asedi Specs, George G. Harrop & Co. Ltd., pp. 474-93.
     Offers a survey of Beckett's literary career highlighting analyzed excerpts from his major works.

10   BERZANI, LEO. "Beckett and the End of Literature." In Balzac to Beckett: Center and Circumference in French Fiction. New York: Oxford University Press, pp. 300-28.
     Contemplates Beckett's advocacy of failure in the novels of the trilogy. Although the Beckettian motifs of imprisonment, impoverishment, and meaninglessness give the trilogy its unity, they are countered by a richness of the imagination and a stylistic virtuosity.

11   BLOT, JEAN. "Samuel Beckett et l'antiroman." Nouvelle Revue Française 18 (Apr.):592-97.
     Claims that Beckett has pushed the "tradition" of anti-novel to its ultimate limit, since it is not only the rules of composition, and the conception of character and plot that have been put in question, but the fabric of the novel itself, and the words and language. In opposition to Olga Bernal's identification of a true language crisis in Watt, Blot feels that Beckett is demonstrating the inexpressiveness of everyday language and utilizing this form of the anti-novel to present his antihumanism.

12   BREE, GERMAINE.   "The Strange World of Beckett's
      'grands articulés.'"   In <u>Samuel Beckett Now:
      Critical Approaches to his Novels, Poetry,
      and Plays</u>. Edited by Melvin J. Friedman.
      Chicago and London: University of Chicago
      Press, p. 73-87.
         Reprint and translation of 1964.10; see
      1970.46.

13   BRUNEL, PIERRE.   "Autour de Samuel Beckett --
      Devanciers, épigones et hérétiques."   In <u>La
      Mort de Godot: Attente et évanescence au
      théâtre: Albee, Beckett, Betti, Duras,
      Hazaz, Lorca, Tchékhov</u>.   Paris: Minard, pp.
      11-39.
         Believes modern theater is born of the
      confrontation of an author with his world.
      Brunel examines the question of time (dis-
      location of time, degradation, death) in
      <u>Waiting for Godot</u>, as well as general
      dramatic concerns (time, language, gestures,
      plot).

14   BRUNS, GERALD L.   "Silent Orpheus: Annihilating
      Words and Literary Language."   <u>College
      English</u> 31, no. 8 (May):821-27.   Beckett:
      pp. 825-26.
         Discusses the theme of annihilation or
      negativity and the language of literature.
      Bruns compares the Beckettian character's
      compulsion to speak coupled with the impos-
      sibility of expression with a similar paradox
      in the works of Maurice Blanchot, reflecting
      the Hegelian idea of speech.

15   BRYER, JACKSON R.   "Samuel Beckett: A Checklist
      of Criticism."   In <u>Samuel Beckett Now:
      Critical Approaches to his Novels, Poetry,
      and Plays</u>.   Edited by Melvin J. Friedman.
      Chicago and London: University of Chicago
      Press, pp. 219-59.
         Brings earlier listings up to date (see
      1964.14) and offers a different arrangement
      of the material.   The checklist is divided
      into two parts: Part I is made up of general

studies on Samuel Beckett as "author and
man," and Part II consists of studies of
individual Beckett works. See 1970.46.

16 CAINE, CINDY S.A.M. "Structure in the One-Act
    Play." <u>Modern Drama</u> 12, no. 4 (Feb.):390-98.
       Demonstrates how the structure of modern
    one-act plays can be traced to classical
    form. Classical form is divided into two
    major components, the tension line and
    individual sections, as illustrated by
    Pinter's <u>The Dumb Waiter</u> and Beckett's
    <u>Krapp's Last Tape</u>.

17 CALDER, JOHN. "Beckett -- Man and Artist."
    <u>Adam: International Review</u> 35, nos. 337-339,
    pp. 70-71.
       Describes Beckett's personality, his
    literary success, and his ardent desire to
    keep his personal life separate from his
    artistic work.

18 CASANOVA, ALAIN. "Beckett ou l'honneur de
    l'homme." <u>Tendances</u>, no. 66, fasc. 11
    (Aug.), pp. 1-16.
       Offers an introduction to Beckett and his
    works, analyzing the characters, the major
    themes, the simplification of language, the
    apocalypse, the tenderness between charac-
    ters, humor, despair, and the representation
    of time.

19 CHAITANYA. "Dramatic Language in Samuel
    Beckett." <u>Calcutta Review</u> n.s. 2, no. 1
    (July-Sept.):73-83.
       Explores the functions of language in
    Samuel Beckett's dramas as they are distin-
    guished by Roman Ingarden (<u>Das literarische
    Kunstwerk</u>): statement, expression, com-
    munications, and influence of one character
    upon another.

20 CHAMPIGNY, ROBERT. "Adventures of the First
    Person." In <u>Samuel Beckett Now: Critical
    Approaches to his Novels, Poetry, and Plays</u>.

Edited by Melvin J. Friedman. Chicago and
London: University of Chicago Press, pp.
119-28.
      Reprint of 1964.16; see 1970.46.

21   CIORAN, E.-M. "L'Horreur d'être né." <u>Monde</u>
     <u>[des Livres]</u>, 13 June, pp. 1-2.
      Declares that Beckett's people can all be
characterized by their regret of being born.
Incapable of "gestes" Beckett's characters
cannot commit suicide, their only hope of
freedom comes from living as though they were
never born.

22   COE, RICHARD. "God and Samuel Beckett." In
     <u>Twentieth Century Interpretations of "Mol-</u>
     <u>loy," "Malone Dies," "The Unnamable": A</u>
     <u>Collection of Critical Essays</u>. Edited by
     J.D. O'Hara. Englewood Cliffs, N.J.:
     Prentice-Hall, Inc., pp. 91-113.
      Defines the nature, attributes, and
imagery of "Beckett's God" as he can be
deduced from the characters in the novels and
plays, and his relationship to their concept
of self and "void."

23   COETZEE, J. M. "The Comedy of Point of View in
     Beckett's <u>Murphy</u>." <u>Critique: Studies in</u>
     <u>Modern Fiction</u> 12, no. 2:19-27.
      Catalogues types of sentences which
manipulate the code of point of view,
alternately attributing the authorial role to
author, narrator, or character: "The play on
the conventions of point of view which we
find in <u>Murphy</u> and to a lesser extent in <u>Watt</u>
is the residue of an attitude of reserve
toward the novel, ... it is neither peri-
pheral or transitory: it grows, and by the
time of <u>L'Innommable</u> (1953) has become, in a
fundamental sense, the subject of Beckett's
work."

24   COHN, RUBY. "The Laughter of Sad Sam Beckett."
     In <u>Samuel Beckett Now: Critical Approaches</u>
     <u>to his Novels, Poetry, and Plays</u>. Edited by

Melvin J. Friedman. Chicago and London:
University of Chicago Press, pp. 185-97.
    Basing her discussion on Arsene's defini-
tion of the three types of laughter in <u>Watt</u>,
Cohn analyzes the moments when laughter
occurs in the plays: "Beckett's dramas do
not abound in laughter, but most of the
extant laughter is attracted by these
magnetic poles, cruelty and suffering, which
inspire, respectively, the ethical and the
dianoltic laugh." See 1970.46.

25   COURNOT, MICHEL. "Du bon emploi des restes."
      <u>Nouvel Observateur</u>, 6 July, pp. 27-28.
          Using <u>First Love</u> as a point of reference,
      discusses the differences between the spoken
      and written word, the speech of clowns and
      "parleurs solitaires" as they apply to
      Beckett's stylistic techniques.

26   CRONK, GEORGE FRANCIS. "Vicissitudes." <u>Kinesis</u>
      2, no. 2 (Spring):106-24.
          Examines the treatment of the problem of
      change in three novels: Beckett's <u>Murphy</u>,
      Hermann Hesse's <u>Siddhartha</u> and the Marquis de
      Sade's <u>Justine</u>. Cronk describes Beckett's
      temporalism which defines the world as
      meaningless change and elicits Murphy's
      futilitarianism.

27   DUKORE, BERNARD. "Theatre in Review: <u>Waiting</u>
      <u>for Godot</u>. By Samuel Beckett. Abbey
      Theatre, Dublin. December, 1969." <u>Educa-</u>
      <u>tional Theatre Journal</u> 22, no. 1 (Mar.):91-
      92.
          Suggests that the subtitle of the play,
      "Tragicomedy," describes this production's
      vision and method: "Among the merits of the
      Abbey's <u>Godot</u> was director Sean Cotter's
      realization that it is through comedy, often
      low comedy, that Beckett reveals the abyss."

28   DURBACH, ERROL. "The Formal Pattern of <u>Waiting</u>
      <u>for Godot</u>." <u>English Studies in Africa</u> 13,
      no. 2 (Sept.):379-89.

> Reveals the structural shape of <u>Waiting
> for Godot</u>: "its symmetry of form, its
> careful balance of contrasts and comparisons,
> its technique of juxtaposition and parallel,
> of similarity within apparent dissimilarity
> ..." The skeletal structure of the play is
> defined by three units: the Second Coming
> and the crucifiction of Christ; Didi-Gogo or
> a metaphor for another means of existence in
> the Waste Land; and Pozzo-Lucky, representing
> the subjection of man's intellectual nature
> to material conquest by a suppression of his
> humanity.

29 *"Echos et nouvelles." <u>Monde [des Livres]</u>, 20
       June.

30 *"Echos et nouvelles." <u>Monde [des Livres]</u>, 11
       Dec.

31 *"Echos et nouvelles: Une conférence sur Samuel
       Beckett." <u>Monde [des Livres]</u>, 21 Feb.
          Source: Bryer et al., 1972.7;unverified.

32 ELLMANN, RICHARD. "Down and Going Under is his
       Favorite Orientation." <u>New York Times Book
       Review</u>, 27 Dec., pp. 1-2, 14.
          Follows Beckett's life and literary
       career, pointing out characteristics of his
       works: Beckett's subject -- morbundity, his
       characters -- old men, his favorite orienta-
       tion -- the underside of experience.

33 *Esslin, Martin. <u>Brief Chronicles. Essays on
       Modern Theatre</u>. London: Temple Smith, 303
       pp.

34 ESTANG, LUC. "Une ballade irlandaise." <u>Figaro
       Littéraire</u> 10-16 Aug., pp. 18-19.
          Reviews <u>Mercier and Camier</u>, noting that
       these two characters prefigure the dramatic
       persona Estragon and Vladimir: their voyage
       conveys a similar sense of waiting and their
       conversations resemble theatrical dialogues.

35   F., S. "Beckett au Festival de Royan."
      Quinzaine Littéraire, no. 93 (16-30 Apr.) p.
      27.
          Discusses the composition of Arié Dzier-
      latka's Words and Music, based on the text by
      Beckett, commenting on Dxierlatka's faithful-
      ness to Beckett's work and the audience
      response.

36   FABRE-LUCE, ANNE. "Les Sentinelles du néant."
      Quinzaine Litteraire, no. 99 (16-31 July),
      p. 3.
          Analyzes First Love and Mercier and
      Camier, examining the relationships between
      the characters, in the first case love, in
      the second, friendship. Fabre-Luce feels
      that these two works are important because
      they mark the first stages of the progressive
      reduction that Beckett continues to develop
      in his writing.

37   FANIZZA, FRANCO. "The Word and Silence in
      Samuel Beckett's The Unnamable." In Twen-
      tieth Century Interpretations of "Molloy,"
      "Malone Dies," "The Unnamable": A Collection
      of Critical Essays. Edited by J.D. O'Hara.
      Englewood Cliffs, N.J.: Prentice-Hall, Inc.,
      pp. 71-81.
          Points out the renunciation of cultural
      patterns and the problem of the foundation of
      an aesthetic in Beckett's works.

38   FEDERMAN, RAYMOND. "Beckettian Paradox: Who is
      Telling the Truth?" In Samuel Beckett Now:
      Critical Approaches to his Novels, Poetry,
      and Plays. Edited by Melvin J. Friedman.
      Chicago and London: University of Chicago
      Press, pp. 103-17.
          Notes the "confusion that exists between
      actuality (the present) and the pseudo-
      reality (the past) created by the "conscious
      writer" in Molloy. The invented statements
      of the narrator-hero do not necessarily
      relate to the reality of the writer before a
      blank sheet of paper. Starting with Malone

Dies, however, pseudo-reality and sub-fiction
are unified as author, narrator, and nar-
rator-hero are identified with one voice.
Reprinted in part 1976.50; see 1970.46.

39   FEDERMAN, RAYMOND and JOHN FLETCHER. Samuel
Beckett: His Works and his Critics.
Berkeley: University of California Press,
383 pp.
Offers an extensive annotated bibliography
of Beckett's works (in French and English)
and the critical response to his fiction
(primarily from Europe and America): reviews,
dissertations, articles, and special issues
of journals, and books through 1966. The
sections on Beckett's works and books devoted
entirely to his work were updated to include
entries through 1968.

40   FLETCHER, JOHN. "Interpreting Molloy." In
Samuel Beckett Now: Critical Approaches to
his Novels, Poetry, and Plays. Edited by
Melvin J. Friedman. Chicago and London:
University of Chicago Press, pp. 157-70.
Reveals the attitudes of the narrator-
heroes to maternal and paternal figures and
the psychological tensions resolved in the
novel -- "the work as a whole is a profound
study of the sado-masochistic syndrome which
is so firmly rooted in our psyche." See
1970.46.

41   _____. "Malone 'Given Birth to Into Death.'"
In Twentieth Century Interpretations of
"Molloy," "Malone Dies," "The Unnamable": A
Collection of Critical Essays. Edited by
J.D. O'Hara. Englewood Cliffs, N.J.:
Prentice-Hall, Inc., pp. 58-61.
Studies the notion of death in Malone
Dies.

42   _____. The Novels of Samuel Beckett. London:
Chatto and Windus, 256 pp.
Attempts to trace the evolution of the
hero in Beckett's novels and the development

of his style in English and French from
"Dream of Fair to Middling Women" to How It
Is. The novels are examined chronologically
as a progressive evolution in which phases of
the development of the hero are analyzed: 1)
"the hero as citizen" (Belacqua, Murphy), 2)
"the hero as outcast" (Watt, the hero of the
Nouvelles, Mercier and Camier, Molloy and
Moran, Malone), 3) "the hero as voice" (the
Unnamable, the heroes of Texts for Nothing
and How It Is). A bibliography of Beckett's
writing and a selective list of criticism
follow the text.

43   FOUCRE, MICHELE. Le geste et la parole dans le
     théâtre de Samuel Beckett. Paris: A.-G.
     Niget, 156 pp.
          Examines three aspects of visual and oral
     presentation in Beckett's drama, linking his
     creation of dramatic fiction with the
     disintegration of language and action in his
     novels: 1) stage presence and dramatic
     action, 2) laughter, diversion, and derision,
     3) the characters' feelings of mutilation and
     incompleteness and the lack of interaction
     between characters. Followed by a select
     bibliography.

44   FOURNIER, EDITH. "'Sans': Cantate et fugue
     pour un refuge." Lettres Nouvelles, Sept.-
     Oct., pp. 149-60.
          Treats the six "families" of ten phrases
     each that make up the text of "Lessness,"
     pointing out the motifs or themes presented
     in each family and the musical qualities of
     the repetitions and variances within the
     phrases and paragraphs.

45   FOWLIE, WALLACE. "A Stocktaking: French
     Literature in the 1960's." Contemporary
     Literature 11, no. 2 (Spring):137-54.
          Emphasizes the immediacy Waiting for Godot
     imposed on the public of the fifties and
     sixties -- the audience recognized itself.
     With this play, Beckett altered the theater

and today <u>Godot</u> has become part of our mythology.

46   FRIEDMAN, MELVIN J., ed. "Introduction." In <u>Samuel Beckett Now: Critical Approaches to His Novels, Poetry, and Plays</u>. Chicago and London: University of Chicago Press, pp. 3-30.
An earlier version of this work appeared in French as <u>Configuration Critique de Samuel Beckett</u> (<u>Revue des Lettres Modernes</u>, 1964). The collection contains three previously unpublished essays by Raymond Federman, John Fletcher, and Ruby Cohn. Slight changes have been made in the reprinted essays in the course of preparing the present English edition. The essays represent a variety of approaches and subject matter, with emphasis on the novel. Reprint of 1964.32; see 1970.12, 1970.15, 1970.20, 1970.24, 1970.38, 1970.40, 1970.56, 1970.59, 1970.61, 1970.77, 1970.83, 1970.92.

47   FRYE, NORTHROP. "The Nightmare Life in Death." In <u>Twentieth Century Interpretations of "Molloy," "Malone Dies," "The Unnamable": A Collection of Critical Essays</u>. Edited by J.D. O'Hara. Englewood Cliffs, N.J.: Prentice-Hall, Inc., pp. 26-34.
Discusses the theory of personality in Beckett's works in which the "ego is stripped of all individuality and is seen merely as a representative of all of its kind." Reprint of 1960.21.

48   G., C. "Avant-Première: Cycle Beckett au Théâtre Récamier." <u>Monde</u>, 10 Feb., p. 17.
Announces Jean-Louis Barrault's and Roger Blin's preparation of a Beckett "cycle" at the Théâtre Récamier, including <u>Happy Days</u> and <u>Waiting for Godot</u>.

49   *GAUTHIER, YVON. "Le Langage absolu et le mythe de la parole chez Samuel Beckett." <u>Revue de</u>

l'Université Laurentienne 2, no. 3 (Feb.):17-
26.

50   GLICKSBERG, CHARLES I. "The Literature of
      Silence." Centennial Review 14, no. 2
      (Spring):166-76.
         Analyzes the major themes and stylistic
      elements of The Unnamable. In The Unnamable
      Beckett substitutes a monologue that ques-
      tions everything for traditional plot,
      characters, and action. Beckett portrays the
      spiritual lostness of the modern anti-hero
      and stresses the impossibility of the
      situation the artist finds himself in.

51   GODARD, COLETTE. "Sail-sous-couzan: Fin de
      partie, de Bechett." Monde, 29 July, p. 12.
         Describes an open air production of
      Endgame in the ruins of a chateau in a small
      town made up of factory employees. Godard
      considers the play's appeal to this type of
      audience and the effect of the setting on the
      play.

52   GOLDSMITH, HELEN H. "Waiting for Godeau."
      Forum 8, no. 1:15-18.
         Studies the similarities and structural
      differences in the original version of
      Balzac's play Le Faiseur, Dennéry's version,
      Mercadet, and Beckett's Waiting for Godot.

53   GOODRICH, NORMA LORRE. "Molloy's Musa Mater."
      In Proceedings of the Comparative Literature
      Symposium Vol. III. From Surrealism to the
      Absurd. Edited by Wolodymyr T. Zyla.
      Lubbock, Texas: Interdepartmental Committee
      on Comparative Literature, Texas Tech.
      University, pp. 31-53.
         Considers artistic creation as the central
      theme in the novel Molloy "in which the
      author as hero undergoes a quest for the
      fountain of wisdom. His journey is a
      betwitched sojourn in the Kingdoms of the
      dead, an admission of failure in one of his
      lives as Molloy, but an eventual triumph in

the abode of his Muse," Molloy's mother.

54   GUPTA, G.S. BALARAMA. "Samuel Beckett."
      Thought (Delhi) 22, no. 50 (12 Dec.):14-15.
          Stresses the importance of Beckett's drama
      over his prose work and defines Beckett's
      role as one of the founding fathers of the
      theater of the absurd. Gupta briefly
      describes some of Beckett's plays, categoriz-
      ing them by theme: 1) most popular (Godot),
      2) alienation (Krapp's Last Tape), Embers,
      Happy Days), 3) despair (All That Fall,
      Endgame).

55   GUSSOW, MEL. "Theatre: The Quintessence of
      Beckett." New York Times, 20 Nov., p. 32.
          Reviews Jack MacGowran's reading of
      Beckett's work at the New York Festival's
      Newman Theater: "MacGowran is the Beckett
      man -- aware of the meaninglessness of
      existence and the necessity to exist, despe-
      rately longing for death but unable to die,
      facing again and again the inevitability that
      life is merely a stop -- a long seemingly
      endless stop -- between birth and death.

56   HARVEY, LAWRENCE E. "A Poet's Initiation." In
      Samuel Beckett Now: Critical Approaches to
      His Novels, Poetry, and Plays. Edited by
      Melvin J. Friedman. Chicago and London:
      University of Chicago Press, pp. 171-84.
          Reprint of 1964.46; see 1970.46.

57   _____. Samuel Beckett, Poet and Critic.
      Princeton: Princeton University Press, 451
      pp.
          Studies Beckett's literary beginnings, his
      republished poetry (poems analyzed in-
      dividually), the early prose (through Watt),
      and the criticism and aesthetics of Beckett
      (his criticism of Joyce and Proust). Harvey
      expanded the original scope of the book which
      was to deal strictly with Beckett's poetry
      because he "discovered that the early prose,
      the 'jettisoned' poems, and Watt contain

elaborations, variations, and extensions of
attitudes and aesthetic materials utilized in
the collected poetry."

58   HASSAN, IHAB. "Joyce-Beckett: A Scenario in
     Eight Scenes and a Voice." Journal of Modern
     Literature 1, no. 1:7-18.
          Opening talk given at the Second Interna-
     tional James Joyce Symposium held in Dublin
     in 1969. Alternately mimicking the fiction
     of Joyce and Beckett, Hassan remarks on the
     authors' lives, works, and critics.

59   HAYMAN, DAVID. "Molloy or the Quest for
     Meaninglessness: A Global Interpretation."
     In Samuel Beckett Now: Critical Approaches
     to His Novels, Poetry, and Plays. Edited by
     Melvin J. Friedman. Chicago and London:
     University of Chicago Press, pp. 129-56.
          Reprint of 1962.39, 1964.47; see 1970.46.

60   HAYMAN, RONALD. "Martin Held Talks to Ronald
     Hayman." Times Saturday Review (London), 25
     Apr., I.
          Martin Held, acting in Krapp's Last Tape,
     discusses working with Beckett and the
     relationship between Beckett and his charac-
     ters.

61   HOFFMAN, FRIEDERICK J. "The Elusive Ego:
     Beckett's M's." In Samuel Beckett Now:
     Critical Approaches to his Novels, Poetry,
     and Plays. Edited by Melvin J. Friedman
     Chicago and London: University of Chicago
     Press, pp. 31-58.
          Reprint of 1964.48; see 1962.40, 1970.46.

62   *HOPE-WALLACE, PHILIP. "Beckett." Guardian, 1
     Apr., p. 8.
          Source: Bryer, et al. 1972.7;unverified.

63   HUBBARD, GRAHAM E. "Beckett's 'Lessness.'" New
     Statesman 79 (29 May):771.
          In response to a letter by Brian Finney,
     suggests that Beckett's "Lessness:" is about

inability and desirability. See B102.

64   HUGHES, CATHARINE. "The paradox of Samuel
     Beckett." Catholic World 211, no. 1
     (Apr.):26-28.
        Examines the ambiguity and inconclu-
     siveness of Beckett's plays.

65   HUNTER, G.K. "English Drama 1900-1960." In
     The Twentieth Century. Edited by Bernard
     Bergonzi. London: Barrie & Jenkins, pp.
     310-35.
        Briefly comments on Joyce's influence on
     Beckett and Beckett's contributions to the
     revolution of English drama.

66   "In Pursuit of Failure." Times Literary
     Supplement, (London), 11 Dec,. p.1442.
        Compares and contrasts three of Beckett's
     earlier works that were just recently
     published or reissued (Mercier and Camier,
     Premier Amour, More Picks Than Kicks) with
     his latest fragment ("Lessness"): "The mind,
     like nature, abhors a vacuum, and as, in
     these last fragments, the image is purified
     to the point of sterility, stillness,
     lifelessness, it begins to seem clinical,
     aseptic, anaesthetized; instead of suggesting
     the emptiness at the center of existence, it
     begins to smell of the operating theater, of
     a willed and contrived sterility."

67   JANVIER, LUDOVIC. "Molloy." In Twentieth
     Century Interpretations of "Molloy," "Malone
     Dies," "The Unnamable": A Collection of
     Critical Essays. Edited by J.D. O'Hara.
     Englewood Cliffs, N.J.: Prentice-Hall, Inc.,
     pp. 46-57.
        Considers the symbolic journeys of Molloy
     and Moran, their actions and the structure of
     their tales: "Molloy is a metaphor of the
     journey toward the self. Soon, immobile and
     straining itself to hear, being will turn
     towards its immediate future: words."
     Reprinted from 1966.41.

68   _____. "Style in the Trilogy." In <u>Twentieth
      Century Interpretations of "Molloy," "Malone
      Dies," "The Unnamable": A Collection of
      Critical Essays</u>. Edited by J.D. O'Hara.
      Englewood Cliffs, N.J.: Prentice-Hall, Inc.,
      pp. 82-90.
            Stresses that <u>Molloy</u> is characterized by
      hesitant speech, an oral style of exclama-
      tions and interrogations which interrupt
      narration, as "two writers at grips with
      words." The following two works demonstrate
      "a kind of mutation of speech or pulverizing
      of superfluous syntactic elements" underlin-
      ing an "oral substance whose richness raises
      <u>Malone Dies</u> and especially <u>The Unnamable</u>
      perhaps to the summit of discursive achieve-
      ment ..." Reprinted from 1966.41.

69   *JARRETT-KERR, MARTIN, C.R. "Christian Values
      in Modern Literature (the Dissolution of the
      Self)." <u>New Fire</u> 1, no. 4 (Autumn):31-36.

70   JOHN, S.B. "A Theater of Victims: The Contem-
      porary French Avant-Garde." In <u>French
      Literature and Its Background, 6: The
      Twentieth Century</u>. Edited by John Cruick-
      shank. London: Oxford University Press, pp.
      266-83. Beckett: pp. 270-75.
            Describes the portrayal of man as "a
      victim in an ambiguous world of acceptable
      systems of value and belief" in the dramas of
      Beckett, Ionesco, Adamov and Arrabal among
      others.

71   JOHNSON, RAYMOND. "Waiting for Beckett." <u>Adam:
      International Review</u> 35, nos. 337-339:74-76.
            Comments on Beckett's refusal to accept
      the Nobel Prize in person.

72   JORDAN, CLIVE. "Newsletter: Beckett at
      Oxford." <u>Observer</u>, 15 Mar., p. 36.
            Gives an account of the English premiere
      of <u>Breath</u> and a reading of extracts from
      Beckett for a fund-raiser at Oxford for the
      Samuel Beckett Memorial Theatre.

73   *KASTOR, FRANK S.   "Pinter and Modern
      Tragicomedy." <u>Wichita State University
      Bulletin University Studies</u> 46, no. 3
      (Aug.):3-15.

74   KAUFFMAN, STANLEY. "MacGowran in Beckett." <u>New
      Republic</u> 163, no. 24 (12 Dec.):20.
          Reviews MacGowran's one-man show of
      readings from Beckett's novels, poems, and
      plays. Reprint of 1964.55.

75   KENNER, HUGH. "Beckett Translating Beckett:
      <u>Comment c'est</u>." <u>Delos</u> 5:194-211.
          Demonstrates how Beckett's English
      version of <u>Comment c'est</u> is more a re-
      experiencing of the text in English than a
      translation. Kenner offers examples from
      Beckett's corrections of Kenner's translation
      of <u>How It Is</u> for the manuscript of <u>Samuel
      Beckett</u>.

76   KERN, EDITH. "Beckett." In <u>Existential Thought
      and Fictional Technique: Kierkegaard,
      Sartre, Beckett</u>. New Haven and London: Yale
      University Press, pp. 167-240.
          Scrutinizing form and technique in
      Beckett's prose works through <u>How It Is</u>,
      hopes her study will lead "to new insights
      into ... the 'unnamableness' of the Becket-
      tian world, and the tendency of existential
      writers to present their heroes as authors
      who disclose themselves as they disclose
      Being, of which they are a part, in language
      ..." Followed by a selected bibliography.

77   _____. "Black Humor: The Pockets of Lemuel
      Gulliver and Samuel Beckett." In <u>Samuel
      Beckett Now: Critical Approaches to His
      Novels, Poetry, and Plays</u>. Edited by Melvin
      J. Friedman. Chicago and London: University
      of Chicago Press, pp. 89-102.
          Reprint of 1964.58; see 1970.46.

78   _____. "Moran-Molloy: The Hero as Author." In
      <u>Twentieth Century Interpretations of "Mol-</u>

loy," "Malone Dies," "The Unnamable": A
Collection of Critical Essays. Edited by
J.D. O'Hara. Englewood Cliffs, N.J.:
Prentice-Hall, Inc., pp. 35-45.
   Compares the inseparable events of
Molloy's symbolic journey and Moran's
artistic quest to the conceptions of the
world of art in the works of Nietzsche and
Proust. Reprint of 1959.23.

79   KRAMER, HILTON. "The Anguish and the Comedy of
     Samuel Beckett." Saturday Review 53 (3
     Oct.):27-30,43.
        Offers a general introduction to Beckett's
     prose and dramatic works. Although Beckett's
     style has changed drastically over the years
     his essential focus has remained the same:
     in Beckett's world, time "is always a form of
     tyranny, pushing the mind back into the much
     of its own experience, frustrating all action
     and aspiration for the future."

80   KRAUSE, DAVID. "The Principle of Comic
     Disintegration." James Joyce Quarterly 8,
     no. 1 (Fall):3-12.
        In a review of Windfalls, Beckett
     describes O'Casey's comedy as his discernment
     of "the principle of disintegration." Krause
     applies this insight to the comic genius of
     Beckett and Joyce.

81   KROLL, JACK. "Sam's First Tape. More Picks
     than Kicks by Samuel Beckett." Newsweek 76,
     no. 14 (5 Oct.):104.
        Studies the character of Belacqua Shuah in
     Beckett's first published work of fiction.

82   LALANDE, BERNARD. Beckett: "En Attendant
     Godot." Analyse Critique. Paris: Hatier,
     64 pp.
        As part of the series "Profil d'une
     oeuvre," summarizes Waiting for Godot, offers
     pertinent historical data, and discusses the
     characters, language, and the theme of
     waiting. The text is followed by a brief

bibliography and an index of principal
themes.

83   LAMONT, ROSETTE. "Beckett's Metaphysics of
     Choiceless Awareness." In <u>Samuel Beckett
     Now: Critical Approaches to His Novels,
     Poetry, and Plays</u>. Edited by Melvin J.
     Friedman. Chicago and London: University of
     Chicago Press, pp. 199-217.
          Reprint of 1959.25, 1964.61; see 1970.46.

84   LEMARCHAND, JACQUES. "D'un pleutre at de
     Plaute." <u>Figaro Littéraire</u>, 11-17 May, pp.
     33-34.
          Reviews two Beckett productions at the
     Théâtre Récamier, <u>Krapp's Last Tape</u> and <u>Act
     Without Words (I and II)</u>, focusing on the
     actions of the characters.

85   _____. "En retrouvant Godot." <u>Figaro
     Littéraire</u>, 6-12 Apr., p. 37.
          Assesses the production of <u>Waiting for
     Godot</u> at the Theatre Récamier, comparing it
     with the original 1953 production.

86   LORICH, BRUCE. "The Accommodating Form of
     Samuel Beckett." <u>Southwest Review</u> 55:354-
     69.
          Evaluates Beckett's prose style in <u>Watt</u>,
     <u>Murphy</u>, and the trilogy, analyzing the
     evolution of style in these works: "<u>Watt</u> is
     a transitional novel between the not unusual
     fictional structure of <u>Murphy</u>, and the
     incessant communication between narration ...
     and reader to be found in <u>Molloy</u>."

87   *MAHON, DEREK. <u>Ecclesiastes</u>. Didsbury;
     Manchester: Phoenix Pamphlet Poets.

88   MARRISSEL, ANDRE. "Samuel Beckett: <u>Premier
     Amour</u> et <u>Mercier et Camier</u>." <u>Esprit</u>, no. 394
     (July-Aug.), pp. 301-3.
          Emphasizes the elements of despair and
     absurdity in <u>First Love</u> and <u>Mercier and
     Camier</u>. Beckett considers life impossible

and therefore places his characters in
unlivable situations.

89   MIHALOVICI, MARCEL.   "Ma collaboration avec
     Samuel Beckett."   Adam: International Review
     35, nos. 337-339:65-67.
         Mentions three collaborations with
     Beckett: the opera Krapp, the radio play
     Cascando, and the first and third movements
     of Mihalovici's Fifth Symphony, in which one
     of Beckett's poems is used for the vocal
     part.   Mihalovici discusses the difficulties
     he encountered writing the musical score for
     Krapp's Last Tape.

90   MOOD, JOHN J.   "'Silence Within':   A Study of
     the Residua of Samuel Beckett."   Studies in
     Short Fiction 7, no. 3 (Summer):385-401.
         Offers a textual study of three of
     Beckett's short prose pieces: "Imagination
     Dead Imagine,"   "Assez," and "Ping."   Mood
     discusses the structure and form of the works
     and the development of the language and
     images.

91   MOROT-SIR, EDOUARD.   "Apparition de l'humour
     dans la littérature française au XXe siècle."
     Bulletin de la Société des Professeurs
     Français en Amerique, pp. 35-52.
         Attempts to show humor in French litera-
     ture from the end of the 19th century through
     the 20th century with Alfred Jarry and his
     creation of Ubu, the Surrealists, André
     Breton's Anthologie de l'humour noir and
     finally Samuel Beckett whose Irish humor
     pervades the French language and gives it new
     forms of expression and thought.

92   MORRISSETTE, BRUCE.   "Robbe-Grillet as a Critic
     of Samuel Beckett."   In Samuel Beckett Now:
     Critical Approaches to his Novels, Poetry,
     and Plays.   Edited by Melvin J. Friedman.
     Chicago and London: University of Chicago
     Press, pp. 59-71.
         Reprint of 1964.71; see 1970.46.

93   MURRAY, PATRICK. <u>The Tragic Comedian: A Study</u>
     <u>of Samuel Beckett</u>. Cork: Mercier Press, 131
     pp.
          In a general introduction to Beckett's
     novels and plays, discusses various influen-
     ces on Beckett's fiction, Christian symbo-
     lism, Beckett as a dramatist and novelist,
     and Beckett's importance and achievements.
     Followed by a selected critical bibliography.

94   O'HARA, J. D. ed. "About Structure in <u>Malone</u>
     <u>Dies</u>." In <u>Twentieth Century Interpretations</u>
     <u>of "Molloy," "Malone Dies," "The Un-</u>
     <u>namable": A Collection of Critical Essays</u>.
     Englewood Cliffs, N.J.: Prentice-Hall, Inc.,
     pp. 62-70.
          Presents duality (the split between Malone
     and Sapo) and disintegration (heaps of
     millet) as both a theme and a structural
     device in <u>Malone Dies</u>.

95   _____. "Introduction." In <u>Twentieth Century</u>
     <u>Interpretations of "Molloy," "Malone Dies,"</u>
     <u>"The Unnamable": A Collection of Critical</u>
     <u>Essays</u>. Englewood Cliffs, N.J.: Prentice-
     Hall, Inc., pp. 1-25.
          Examines Beckett's earlier works as
     preparation for the trilogy. O'Hara discus-
     ses the philosophic ideas in his work,
     referring to Descartes, Geulincx, Berkeley,
     Husserl, Schopenhauer, Hume, Heidegger,
     Sartre, Stevens, and the similarities and
     differences in his use of systems of thought
     and that of Conrad, Hardy, Stevens, Joyce,
     and Yeats. Also includes a brief analysis of
     form in the trilogy.

96   _____. "Watt, Krapp & Co." <u>Chicago Tribune</u>
     <u>Book World</u>, 14 Nov., p. 12.
          Reviews <u>The Collected Works of Samuel</u>
     <u>Beckett</u> (Grove Press) pointing out the
     evolution of Beckett's literary style and his
     obsessive topic, the "attempts of sensitive
     men to do what they should do, to discard the
     illusions of happiness, success, knowledge,

friendship, and love, and to go on existing
in the reality of nothing ..."

97   PARKIN, ANDREW. "'... scraps of an ancient
      voice in me not mine ...': Similarities in
      the Plays of Yeats and Beckett." Ariel: A
      Review of International English Literature 1,
      no. 3 (July):49-58.
         Emphasizes Beckett's position as inheritor
      of the Anglo-Irish dramatic legacy of Yeats:
      discusses direct allusions to Yeats' work,
      adaptations of Yeats' ideas, the structure of
      memory patterns, the reduction of dramatic
      situations to essentials, and experimentation
      with words and music.

98   PEARCE, RICHARD. "The Limits of Realism."
      College English 31, no. 4 (Jan.):335-43.
         Searches for a definition of "realistic":
      structure by comparing Ibsen's Doll's House
      with Beckett's Waiting for Godot. Pearce
      demonstrates that Godot is not designed to
      imitate experience but to present it -- that
      in fact reality of experience cannot be
      imitated.

99   _____. "Which Way Is Up? Ralph Ellison's
      Invisible Man, Günther Grass's Tin Drum, and
      Samuel Beckett's Trilogy." In Stages of the
      Clown. Perspectives on Modern Fiction from
      Dostoyevsky to Beckett. Carbondale, Ill.:
      Southern Illinois University Press, pp. 117-
      135. Beckett: pp. 128-35.
         Points out that Beckett like Ellison and
      Grass utilizes the split perspective as the
      subject of his novels. The reader is denied
      a stable and objective observer, the narrator
      (or narrators) is unreliable, without
      identity or history: "When we finish his
      trilogy, we come to understand that identity
      requires definition, requires that one
      discover the differentia between himself and
      the rest of the world and in a truly absurd
      world, ... finding the differentia is

impossible -- hence the comedy and hence the terror."

100   POIROT-DELPECH, BERTRAND. "Actes, sans paroles et La Dernière Bande de Samuel Beckett." Monde, 3-4 May, p. 15.
      Feels that although Act Without Words and Krapp's Last Tape may be works of secondary importance when compared to Waiting for Godot and Happy Days (the other works presented in the "Beckett cycle" at the Théâtre Récamier) they both illustrate the themes of isolation and human silence.

101   _____. "En attendant Godot de Samuel Beckett." Monde, 19 Mar., p. 19.
      Compares the differences in the audience response to Waiting for Godot in Roger Blin's original production and the production at the Théâtre Récamier 17 years later. Poirot-Delpech claims that the major theme of the play is time rather than waiting.

102   _____. "Oh les beaux jours de Samuel Beckett." Monde, 19 Feb., p. 19.
      Reviews Happy Days at the Théâtre Récamier with Madeleine Renaud and Jean-Louis Barrault, briefly analyzing the major character, Winnie, and contrasting the effect this play had on the audience in 1970 and in 1963.

103   PORTAL, GEORGES. "D'un Irlandais à l'autre." Ecrits de Paris, (June), pp. 122-28.
      Comments on Acts Without Words and Waiting for Godot at the Théâtre Récamier discussing the use of mime and circus routines as well as audience response.

104   *QUEANT, GILLES. "De Godot à Orden." Plaisir de France, no. 378 (May), p. 60.
      Source: French XX Bibliography, 1971; unverified.

105   *RACHETT, SAMUEL. "Much of a Moreness." New Statesman, 8 May.

Source: Bryer, et al. 1972.7;
unverified.

106   *"La Rentrée littéraire: D'André Dhôtel à
Samuel Beckett, du merveilleux à l'absurde
..." Figaro, 30 Sept.

107   *Retour de Beckett Rive Gauche." Figaro
Littéraire, 2-8 Feb.
Source: Bryer, et al. 1972.7;unverified.

108   RIVA, RAYMOND T. "Beckett and Freud." Criticism 12, no. 2 (Spring):120-32.
Claims that like Freud, Beckett concentrates on the subconscious and the
language of our repressed selves: "...
Beckett's cracked and broken creations may be
considered in the same way, somewhat as
mental patients, for their reality -- being
internal and unusual -- forces us to realize
often unpleasant things about our own
external realities."

109   *ROBB, PETER. "Criticizing Modern Drama:
Beckett's Godot." Words 3:11-20.

110   ROBINSON, MICHAEL. The Long Sonata of the Dead:
A Study of Samuel Beckett. New York: Grove
Press, 318 pp.
Following a thorough introduction to
Beckett's fiction, critical writings, and
philosophical and literary ideas as they are
presented in his works, Robinson continues to
discuss each work individually, describing
the characters, situations, themes, style,
and language. A select bibliography follows.

111   "Samuel Beckett in Books Abroad: 1955-1970."
Books Abroad 44, no. 2 (Spring):250.
Provides a short bibliography of articles
and reviews from Books Abroad.

112   SANDIER, GILLES. "Beckett." In Théâtre et
Combat: Regards sur le théâtre actuel.
Paris: Editions Stock, pp. 45-52.

Believes Beckett's theatre resembles that
of antiquity in which drama was created
through the use of the basic elements of
time, space, and the word. Sandier views
Beckett's vision as essentially religious and
briefly juxtaposes Happy Days with Claudel's
Le Soulier de Satin.

113   SELLIN, ERIC. "Samuel Beckett" The Apotheosis
       of Impotence." Books Abroad 44, no. 2
       (Spring):244-50.
            Evaluates the importance of Beckett's
       plays to man's contemporary view of the human
       condition and the reasons why Beckett's work
       would meet the prerequisite of "idealism":
       set by the Swedish Academy in order to be
       awarded the Nobel Prize.

114   SEN, SUPTI. Samuel Beckett: His Mind and His
       Art. Calcutta: Firma K. L. Mukhopadhyay,
       214 pp.
            Expresses a critical appreciation of
       Beckett's thought and technique as found in
       his novels, dramas, and poetry. Sen em-
       phasizes Beckett's exploration of the human
       soul, his conception of an Absolute Reality,
       the influences of the philosophical doctrines
       of Positivism, Existentialism, and Absurdity,
       Beckett as a Symbolist novelist, and his
       departure toward a more original development.
       A selected bibliography is included.

115   SENART, PHILIPPE. "La Revue Théâtrale: Samuel
       Beckett." Revue des Deux Mondes, no. 8
       (Aug.), pp. 441-44.
            Feels Beckett's plays extend hope --
       presented through "austerity, contemplation,
       prayer."

116   SHADOIAN, JACK. "The Achievement of Comment
       c'est." Critique: Studies in Modern Fiction
       12, no. 2:5-18.
            Compares How It Is with Beckett's previous
       works. He considers the content and struc-
       tural "triumph" of this "unquestionable

masterpiece" as "perhaps the most imaginative distillation of spiritual nausea to date in human history."

117 SIMON, JOHN. "Theatre." New York 3, no. 25 (22 June):57.
Criticizes Roberta Sklor's use of comic effects in her production of Endgame and the poor performances of the actors.

118 *SIMON, K. "The Interstices of Silence: Modern Dialogue as a Genre in Itself." South Central Bulletin 30, no. 3 (Oct.):134.

119 SMITH, MICHAEL AND TREVOR JOYCE. "Editorial." Lace Curtain, no. 2 (Spring), p. 2.
Deny Dublin's importance as a literary centre and feel that Beckett should have refused the Nobel Prize.

120 SUEUR, GEORGES. "A Lille: En attendant Godot de Beckett." Monde, 14 Apr., p. 17.
Describes the audience reaction to Waiting for Godot in Lille -- surprisingly enough the audience was not bored and appeared to understand and appreciate the play.

121 TRIVISSONNO, ANN M. "Meaning and Function of the Quest in Beckett's Watt." Critique: Studies in Modern Fiction 12, no. 2:28-38.
Proposes the philosophical, epistemological, and aesthetic implications of the metaphor of Watt's journey to the house of Mr. Knott.

122 *"Un Irlandais en ballade." Figaro Littériare, 29 June - 5 July.
Source: Bryer, et al., 1972.7; unverified.

123 *Van DER STARRE, E. "La Pensée du Knouk." Franse Boek (Apr.), pp. 125-32.

124 VILLELAUR, ANNE. "L'Amour de rien." Lettres Françaises, 29 July - 4 Aug., p. 6.

Reviews <u>First Love</u> and <u>Mercier and Camier</u>,
remarking that <u>First Love</u> represents a direct
attack against the couple, while <u>Mercier and
Camier</u> explores the question of human
relationships.

125   WALL, STEPHEN. "Aspects of the Novel 1930-
       1960." In <u>The Twentieth Century</u>. Edited by
       Bernard Bergonzi. London: Barrie & Jenkins,
       pp. 222-76. Beckett: pp. 224-28.
            Surveys Beckett's prose works through <u>How
       It Is</u>, pointing out the struggle between the
       beauty and power of his work and his attempts
       to present "nothing."

126   WEBB, EUGENE. <u>Samuel Beckett: A Study of His
       Novels</u>. London: Peter Owen, 1970; Seattle:
       University of Washington Press, 1972, 192 pp.
            Concentrates on the development of
       Beckett's themes and his artistic presenta-
       tion of them in his novels. Webb believes
       that the subject of Beckett's works has
       remained constant from his earliest to his
       later works, "the difficulties of twentieth-
       century man in his efforts to understand his
       place in the universe."

127   WEISS, JONATHAN M. "The Dialectic of Movement
       in Beckett's <u>Happy Days</u>." <u>Adam: Internation-
       al Review</u> 35, nos. 337-339:67-69.
            Due to the physical immobility of the
       characters, <u>Happy Days</u> is a static play:
       "... the basically extroverted action of the
       'I' in attempting to possess, to identify, is
       thwarted by the very inability of the 'I' to
       create existence in a void."

128   WHITE, PATRICIA O. "Existential Man in
       Beckett's Fiction." <u>Critique: Studies in
       Modern Fiction</u> 12, no. 2:39-49.
            Notes that Beckett incorporates many of
       the tenets of French existentialism in his
       fiction: "Beckett does not reject the
       existential 'faith' that man is possibility,
       that man is always becoming. Yet he also

accepts the existentialist realization that
since all men die, human existence is rooted
in nothingness."

129   WRIGHT, D. "A Short Guide to Samuel Beckett
        Studies." Critical Survey 4, no. 4 (Sum-
        mer):213-16.
             Describes ten major critical studies and
        several key articles devoted to Beckett.

130   ZILLIACUS, CLAS. "Samuel Beckett's Embers: 'A
        Matter of Fundamental Sounds.'" Modern Drama
        13, no. 2 (Sept.):216-25.
             Approaches Embers as a "guiding descrip-
        tion of a radio production," not as a work
        that can be analyzed in purely literary
        terms.

131   _____. "Three Times Godot: Beckett, Brecht,
        Bulatovic." Comparative Drama 4, no. 1
        (Spring):3-17.
             Juxtaposes Beckett's Waiting for Godot,
        Brecht's "Gegenentwurf," and Miodrage
        Bulatovic's work Godo je dosao (Godot est
        arrivé).

                         1971

1   "A Landscape of Desolation." Radio Times, 18
        Feb., p. 12.
             Describes the making of the radio produc-
        tion of "Lessness." Six voices, each
        assigned a group of sentences in which one
        particular image prevails, were recorded
        separately and then the tapes were inter-
        woven. The voices "do not represent charac-
        ters but merely indicate strands of connected
        images in a complex structure of thought and
        sound."

2   ALVAREZ, A. " The Savage God." Listener, 9
        Sept., pp. 329-32. Beckett: p. 330.
             Comments on the two ways in which modern

artists have evolved a "language of mourn-
ing": the first is "totalitarian art" which
directly confronts a historical situation in
order to create a human perspective, and the
second is "extremist art" in which the
destruction is turned inwards and the artist
explores himself. Alvarez describes
Beckett's fictional world as "the totalitari-
anism of the inner world" or the place where
totalitarian and extremist art meet.

3   BAJOMEE, DANIELLE. "Beckett devant Dieu."
     Lettres Romanes 25, no.4 (Nov.):350-57
          Addresses the problems of religious themes
     in Beckett's works. See 1968.48.

4   BARBER, JOHN. "About the Theatre: Apotheosis of
     a Pessimist." Daily Telegraph (London), 17
     May, p.10.
          Gives an account of the evolution of
     Beckett's artistic development, and the
     exhibition devoted to his work at the
     University of Reading assembled by James
     Knowlson and his staff. See 1971.61

5   *[BARRAULT, JEAN-LOUIS]. "'Do What You Will, for
     Man Is Free': Jean-Louis Barrault Inter-
     viewed by Melinda Benedek." Isis, 25 Apr.,
     pp. 22-23.

6   BEAUSANG, MICHAEL. "Myth and Tragi-Comedy in
     Beckett's Happy Days. Mosaic 5 (Fall):59-
     77.
          Compares individuals depicted in specific
     myths (Ishtar and Tammuz) and tragedies
     (Racine's Phèdre and Euripides' Hippolytus)
     to the characters in Beckett's Happy Days.
     The relationship between tragi-comedy and
     mythic tradition is examined.

7   BONNEROT, SYLVANIE. "Beckett." In Visages du
     théâtre contemporain. Paris: Masson et
     Cie., pp. 31-52.
          Feels that Beckett's drama touches its
     audience because the spectators sense a

reflection of our human condition --
Beckett's characters win us over by their
truth and their presence on stage. Bonnerot
comments on excerpts from Waiting for Godot,
Endgame, and Happy Days.

8   BRINK, A.W. "University in Samuel Beckett's
     Endgame." Queen's Quarterly 78, no. 2 (Sum-
     mer):191-207.
         Demonstrates Beckett's accomplishment of
     an "illusion" of university in Endgame and
     compares Beckett's play to King Lear.

9   BRUNS, GERALD L. "Samuel Beckett's How It Is."
     James Joyce Quarterly 8, no. 4 (Summer):318-
     31.
         Studies the implications of the structure-
     less present in How It Is: the attenuation of
     syntax, the narrator's memory and imagination,
     the roles of the travellers, and the narrator
     as storyteller.

10   No Entry.

11   *BURNS,JIM. "That Time, Samuel Beckett."
     Ambit, no. 70, pp.90-91.

12   CAUVIN, JEAN-PIERRE. "Samuel Beckett: Le
     Dépeupleur." French Review 45, no. 2
     (Dec.):461-62.
         Summarizes The Lost Ones and briefly
     compares Beckett's work to Dante's Inferno and
     Jérôme Bosch's Ascension vers l'Empyrée.

13   CAWS, MARY ANN. "A Rereading of the Traces,"
     Esprit Créateur 11, no.3 (Fall):14-20.
         Discusses three intersecting "traces" in
     the Nouvelles et textes pour rien: the
     reductive lines of consciousness, the ex-
     hausted writing hand, and the incessant will
     to write.

14   CHAMBERS, ROSS. "The Artist as Performing Dog."
     Comparative Literature 23, no. 4 (Fall):312-
     24.

Contrasts Beckett's works, in particular
Molloy, with Cervantes' tale of a dog's life,
El Coloquio de los perros, and Hoffman's
imitation of the Cervantes' text in Nachricht
von den neuesten Schicksalen des Hundes
Berganza.

15   CISMARU, ALFRED.   "Beckett's 'Le Calmant':
        Attempt at Elucidation."   Forum 9, no. 2
        (Summer):29-32.
             Analyzes Beckett's short text "Le Calmant"
        on the 25th anniversary of its appearance.
        Cismaru notes that the text contains most of
        the author's major themes and preoccupations
        as they appear in his other works.

16   CLURMAN, HAROLD.   "Theatre."   Nation, 212 (22
        Feb.):253-54.
             Considers Waiting for Godot as a turning
        point in theatre history of our time.   The
        play is an abstract comedy, a "parable of
        total disenchantment."   Clurman believes that
        the return performance in New York, directed
        by Alan Schneider, is too loud in tone and
        too violent with activity.

17   COHN, RUBY.   "Joyce and Beckett, Irish Cos-
        mopolitans."   James Joyce Quarterly 8, no. 4
        (Summer):385-91.
             Highlights Irish names, settings, and
        memories found in the works of Joyce and
        Beckett.   Reprint of 1966.24.

18   COOVER, ROBERT.   "The Last Quixote: Marginal
        Notes on the Gospel According to Samuel
        Beckett."   In New American Review, no. 11.
        New York: Simon and Schuster.   (Touchstone
        Book), pp. 132-43.
             Presents his impressions of Beckett's
        works, from a personal point of view, conjec-
        turing that Beckett's trilogy might be "a
        gloss on Quixote's first sally."

19   CORMIER, RAMONA, and JANIS PALLISTER.   "En
        attendant Godot: Tragedy or Comedy?"   Esprit

Créateur 11, no. 3 (Fall):44-45.
Feels that En attendant Godot is neither a comedy nor a tragedy, but a subtle fusion of the two modes. In this play Beckett has altered the stylistic devices and the conventional concepts of character and action found in traditional drama.

20   CROUSSY, GUY. Beckett. Paris: Hachett, 233
     pp.
          Following an analysis of the Irish writer in exile, considers two aspects of Beckett's fiction: the conquest of form demonstrated by the works written before Waiting for Godot (the period of words without acts), and the period of reduction characterized by the creation of the works Waiting for Godot through The Lost Ones (the period of acts without words).

21   DAVIS, WILLIAM V. "The Waiting in Waiting for
     Godot." Cresset 34, no. 4:10-11.
          Quoting Paul Tillich (The Shaking of the Foundations, 1948), concludes that Beckett's theme of waiting is not necessarily a pessimistic one: "... Waiting for Godot can be seen not as a negative commentary on contemporary existence, but as a realistic portrayal of the dilemma of modern man -- a dilemma which incorporates the possibility of hope even in the midst of despair."

22   DEJEAN, JEAN-LUC. "Samuel Beckett fidèle à
     soi." In Le Théâtre français d'aujourd'hui.
     Paris: Nathan-Alliance Française, pp.100-
     104.
          Believes Beckett has maintained a uniform conception of man and the world in his fiction from Waiting for Godot to Play. Dejean reviews Beckett's image of the human condition, as it is reflected in the actions and speech of his characters and briefly mentions the influence of Kafka and Dante on Beckett's work.

23   DENNIS, NIGEL. "Original Sin and Dog Biscuits."
      New York Review of Books 16 (8 Apr.):21-23.
      Discusses the tragicomic method in
      Beckett's plays, comparing his works to those
      of Chekhov.

24   DOHERTY, FRANCIS. Samuel Beckett. London:
      Hutchinson, 156 pp.
      Individually studies the prose and drama
      works in order to define Beckett's gradual
      progression toward reduction and silence.

25   DOUTRELIGNE, MICHEL. "Le Thème de la 'berne'
      existentielle: d'Amphitryon à En attendant
      Godot." Revue de l'Université de Bruxelles,
      nos. 2-3. pp. 182-91.
      Compares Plato's Amphitryon with Waiting
      for Godot and examines the consequences of
      their similarities: 1) the two plays were
      written at a moment of a crisis in religious
      faith, 2) both plays utilize the form of
      tragi-comedy, and 3) the couple is presented
      as the motivating force behind the dramas.

26   DUCKWORTH, COLIN. "Beckett's Dramatic Inten-
      sity." New Theatre Magazin 11, no. 3:20-25.
      Reports how spectators react to Beckett's
      plays, and documents the intensity of their
      reactions or experiences. Duckworth focuses
      on the creation of tension and the archetypal
      qualities of the plays and offers some of the
      results of a survey of audience reactions to
      Waiting for Godot and Endgame.

27   EMERSON, SALLY. "Borges and Beckett: Beckett
      on Show." Books and Bookman 16, no. 10
      (July):36.
      Briefly summarizes the exhibition documen-
      ting the life and work of Beckett on display
      at Reading University.

28   ESSLIN, MARTIN. "A Landscape of Desolation.
      'Lessness': Thursday 10.5 Radio 3." Radio
      Times, 20-26 Feb., p. 12.
      Describes the taping procedure used to

prepare "Lessness" for radio broadcast, and attempts to clarify the subject of the text.

29 FABRE-LUCE, ANNE. "Rites crépusculaires." <u>Quinzaine Littéraire</u>, no. 113 (1-15 Mar.), p. 5.

Believes <u>The Lost Ones</u> represents the last possible stages of "humanity" before a return to the inorganic. Fabre-Luce admires the alliance of the individual and the general -- in this world no one is alone, yet each is solitary. Reprinted: 1979.22.69.

30 _____. "Tant de choses en si peu de mots." In <u>Etranges Etrangers</u>. Paris: <u>Le Nouvel Obser-</u> <u>vateur</u>, pp. 17-18.

Focuses on the minimalism of Beckett's art, and categorizes the few elements that remain: the physical presence of the characters, the relationship of the couple, the objects the characters retain, and the wait for death.

31 FEDERMAN, RAYMOND. "The Impossibility of Saying the Same Old Thing the Same Old Way -- Samuel Beckett's Fiction Since <u>Comment</u> <u>c'est</u>." <u>Esprit Créateur</u> 11, no. 3 (Fall):21-43.

Discusses the devalorization of language, the reduction of all emotive qualities, and the time/space dimension in the later fiction.

32 _____. "Samuel Beckett's Film on the Agony of Perceivedness." <u>James Joyce Quarterly</u> 8, no. 4 (Summer):363-71.

Views Beckett's first cinematic venture as an attempt to renew art through a return to the primary sources of the artistic medium. Federman discusses Beckett's use of the eye as the symbol of perception: exposing the limitations of the artistic medium and the human limitations of external and internal vision.

33   *FERGUSON, T.S.   "What's Happening: Drama on
       Three."   Sunday Telegraph (London), 28 Feb.,
       p. 13.

34   FINNEY, BRIAN.   "A Reading of Beckett's 'Im-
       agination Dead Imgine.'"   Twentieth Century
       Literature 17 (Jan.-Oct.):65-71.
           Examines the obscurity, inconsistencies,
       and pseudo scientific observations in the ab-
       breviated work "Imagination Dead Imagine."

35   FORTIER, PAUL.   "Beckett émule de Gide."   Esprit
       Créateur 11, no. 3 (Fall):55-56.
           Evaluates Waiting for Godot in light of a
       remark made by André Gide in the preface to
       his work L'Immoraliste, in which Gide
       explained that he intended to prove nothing
       by his literature, but only to portray and
       clarify his artistic creations.

36   FREUSTIE, JEAN.   "Le Dépeupleur par Samuel
       Beckett."   Nouvel Observateur, no. 336 (19-25
       Apr.), p. 56.
           Feels Beckett attempts to define the human
       condition in terms of a single image in The
       Lost Ones.   Freustie describes the physical
       situation of the characters and the rules of
       their confining environment.

37   *GARDINER, ALAN.   "The Human Couple and the
       Theme of Decay in Beckett's Work."   Studies
       in English and American Philology 1:270-94.

38   GILMAN, RICHARD.   "Beckett's Happy Days."   In
       Common and Uncommon Masks, Writings on
       Theatre, 1961-1970.   New York: Random House,
       pp. 90-92.
           Underlines the effectiveness of Beckett's
       theater in his review of Happy Days.

39   GODWIN, GAIL.   "For Samuel Beckett: More."
       James Joyce Quarterly 8, no. 4 (Summer):332-
       35.
           Dedicates this short creative work to
       Beckett.

40   *GOSSEN, EMMETT. "Circularities." <u>Diacritics</u>
        1, no. 1 (Fall):19-26.

40a   GRANT, JOHN E. "Imagination Dead?" <u>James Joyce</u>
        <u>Quarterly</u> 8, no. 4 (Summer):336-62.
             Offers a detailed description and analysis
        of "Imagination Dead Imagine," discussing the
        narrative voice, characters, language,
        content, sources, and influences. Grant ends
        his article with a study of the interrelation
        of "Ping," "Enough," and "Imagination Dead
        Imagine."

40b   GRAY, STANLEY E. "Beckett and Queneau as
        Formalists." <u>James Joyce Quarterly</u> 8, no. 4
        (Summer):392-404.
             Believes Beckett and Raymond Queneau are
        the first to see Descartes' <u>Discours de la</u>
        <u>Methode</u> as a work of fiction, and although
        they differ in many ways, they share similar
        views on the role of form in the literary
        message. Gray compares three categories from
        their prose récits or novels: "The first
        consists of devices which call unexpected
        attention to the fact that a language is
        being used; the second assembles various
        means used to expose the arbitrariness of
        literary structures and criticize their
        mimetic pretensions; the third describes
        forms which, liberated from mimetic func-
        tions, are free to generate some other
        meaning."

41   GREEN, NAOMI. "Creation and the Self: Artaud,
        Beckett, Michaux." <u>Criticism</u> 13, no. 3 (Sum-
        mer):265-78.
             Considers a fundamental complaint of
        Beckett, Artaud, and Michaux, that they are
        forced to use a language which is not their
        own: "In their effort to discover the self
        through the creative process these writers
        are led to use an objective language which
        imprisons them in an impersonal realm from
        which all individual language, and indeed
        existence, is banished."

42   HASSAN, IHAB. "Beckett: Imagination Ending."
     In <u>Dismemberment of Orpheus: Toward a Post-
     modern Literature</u>. New York: Oxford Univer-
     sity Press, pp. 210-46.
          Believes that Beckett is one of four major
     figures (with Hemingway, Kafka, Genet) who
     exemplifies the "sovereignty of the void."
     Hassan reviews Beckett's life and literary
     career and then traces the evolution of
     Beckett's prose and drama towards silence,
     emphasizing the dislocation and devaluation
     of language, the characters, the categories
     of time and space, the hero as absurd
     narrator, the contradictions, reductions, and
     comic devices.

43   HAYMAN, DAVID. "A Meeting in the Park and a
     Meeting on the Bridge: Joyce and Beckett."
     <u>James Joyce Quarterly</u> 8, no. 4 (Summer):372-
     84.
          Suggests that Joyce's influence on Beckett
     evolved from conscious imitation to pastiches
     and parodies.

44   _____. "A Prefactory Note." <u>James Joyce
     Quarterly</u> 8, no. 4 (Summer):275-77.
          As guest editor, briefly introduces the
     special issue of the journal and explains the
     inclusion of a Beckett issue in the <u>James
     Joyce Quarterly</u>. Hayman discusses Beckett's
     relationship to Joyce, their interactions,
     resemblances and differences.

45   HAYWARD, SUSAN. "Quelques considérations sur
     les dernières oeuvres romanesques de Samuel
     Beckett." <u>Language and Style</u> 4, no. 3 (Sum-
     mer):229-36.
          Feels that "From an Abandoned Work,"
     which was written at the same time as
     Beckett's first dramatic works, marks an
     important turning point in Beckett's fiction.
     Hayward studies the influence of the theater
     on the prose works which followed through
     Beckett's use of leitmotif and rhythm.

46   HESLA, DAVID. <u>The Shape of Chaos: An Inter-
      pretation of the Art of Samuel Beckett</u>. Min-
      neapolis: University of Minnesota Press, 248
      pp.
           Presents the novels and plays from the
      perspective of the history of ideas. Through
      an examination of the problems Beckett faces
      as a writer, most importantly, the structure
      of consciousness and its significance for the
      art of writing, Hesla attempts to relate
      Beckett to the Western intellectual tradi-
      tion. He believes that Beckett has been in-
      fluenced by the ideas of the pre-Socratics,
      the rationalists of the seventeenth and
      eighteenth centuries, Schopenhauer, Bergson,
      Hegel, Kierkegaard, Heidegger, Sartre, and
      Husserl, among others.

47   *HOBSON, HAROLD. "Judgement Day." <u>Sunday Times</u>
      (London), 31 Jan., p. 29.

48   HOKENSON, JAN. "A Stuttering Logos: Biblical
      Paradigms in Beckett's Trilogy." <u>James Joyce
      Quarterly</u> 8, no. 4 (Summer):293-310.
           Believes Beckett uses Biblical allusions
      in the triology to build a parodic dialectic
      between <u>Genesis</u> and <u>Revelation</u>, sardonically
      reversed in Beckett's work.

49   HUBERT, RENEE RIESE. "A la trace de Bing."
      <u>Sub-Stance</u> 1 (Fall):21-27.
           Analyzes the "mechanical order" of "Ping,"
      the limitations of the situation, character,
      movement, and language.

50   HUNT, ALBERT. "Arts in Society: Playing with
      the Elements," <u>New Society</u> 17 (11 Feb.):239.
           Discusses gags and games in Beckett's
      fiction -- the sucking stones in <u>Molloy</u> and
      the music-hall antics in <u>Waiting for Godot</u>.

51   JAMET, DOMINIQUE. "Beckett fait les beaux jours
      de Reading." <u>Figaro Littéraire</u>, 28 May, p. 5.
           Describes an exposition devoted to Beckett

at Reading University, emphasizing the
universality of Beckett's work.

52 JANVIER, LUDOVIC. "Peupler dépeupler c'est
      écrire." Critique 27, no. 288 (May):432-45.
      Focuses on the situation, characters,
      environment and text of The Lost Ones.

53 *JONGH, NICHOLAS de. "Young Vic: Endgame."
      Guardian, 2 Feb., p. 8.
          Source: French XX Bibliography, no. 24
      (1972); unverified.

54 KAY, WALLACE G. "Blake, Baudelaire, Beckett:
      The Romantics of Nihilism." Southern
      Quarterly 9, no. 3 (Apr.):253-59.
          Links the nihilistic characteristics of
      these three writers: "I propose to take each
      of these forms, show how the works of Blake,
      Baudelaire, and Beckett evolve some of these
      nihilistic situations, discuss the responses
      of characters and narrators in their works to
      these situations, and show how these respon-
      ses are nearly all familiar romantic poses."

55 KENNEDY, SIGHLE. Murphy's Bed: A Study of Real
      Sources and Sur-Real Associations in Samuel
      Beckett's First Novel. Lewisburg, Pa.:
      Bucknell University Press, 325 pp.
          Examines Murphy from the point of view of
      "real" and "sur-real" sources. His "real"
      sources are identified as: Giordano Bruno's
      theory of identified contraries, the related
      concept of a spherical purgatory, Giambattis-
      ta Vico's theories concerning the cycle
      through which human language and history
      develop, the literary achievements of Dante
      and Joyce, Homeric and Hesiodic animisms for
      sun, moon and stars, and the Greek myth of
      Endymion. The "sur-real" sources include
      surrealism and verticalism.

56 KERN, EDITH. "Ironic Structure in Beckett's
      Fiction." Esprit Créateur 11 no. 3 (Fall):3-
      13.

Attempts to elucidate the ironic structure
of Beckett's prose works by juxtaposing his
fictional technique with that of Kierkegaard.

57   *_____.   "Reflections on The Castle and Mr.
Knott's House: Kafka and Beckett." In
Proceedings of the Comparative Literature
Symposium. Vol. 4. Franz Kafka: His Place
in World Literature. Edited by Wolodymyr T.
Zyla, Wendell M. Aycock and Pat Ingle Gillis.
Lubbock: Texas Tech. University, pp. 97-111.

58   _____. "Samuel Beckett: Premier Amour."
French Review 45, no. 2 (Dec.):462-64.
Reviews First Love and Mercier and Camier,
assessing these prose works as the missing
link between Murphy and the trilogy.

59   _____. "Structure in Beckett's Theater." Yale
French Studies, no. 46, pp. 17-27.
Calls attention to the structure underly-
ing Beckett's drama, the archetypal couple,
representing in some cases two aspects of the
same individual.

60   KNOWLSON, JAMES. "Beckett in Black and White:
The Reading Exhibition." New Theatre
Magazine 11, no. 3:4-7.
Highlights the preparation, the process of
selection, and the problems of presentation
for the Reading Exhibition. See 1971.61.

61   _____, ed. Samuel Beckett: An Exhibition.
London: Turret Books, 123 pp.
Describes the exhibition held at Reading
University Library, May to July 1971.
References to photos, texts, and manuscripts
are arranged chronologically. See 1971.4,
1971.60

62   KUHN, REINHARD. "The Knife and the Wound:
From Baudelaire to Beckett." James Joyce
Quarterly 8, no. 4 (Summer):405-12.
Identifies the twentieth century theme of
self-inflicted torment in the works of

Baudelaire, Musset, Valéry, Kafka, Gide, Sartre, and Beckett.

63 LODGE, DAVID. "Samuel Beckett: Some Ping Understood." In <u>The Novelist at the Cross-roads and Other Essays on Fiction and Criticism</u>. Ithaca, N.Y.: Cornell University Press, pp. 172-83.
Reprint of 1968.41.

64 McLELLAN, JOHN. "Samuel Beckett and the Novel of 'Philosophic Monologue.'" <u>Fu Jen Studies</u> 4:79-95.
Offers a general discussion of Beckett's novels and plays, emphasizing Beckett's interest in the inner workings of the mind, his use of "abstract description," his resolution of difficult technical problems, and the influence of Descartes, Geulincx, Joyce, and Proust.

65 MAYOUX, JEAN-JACQUES. "Samuel Beckett and the Mass Media." In <u>English Association Essays and Studies, 1971</u>. Edited by Bernard Harris. London: John Murray, pp. 83-100.
Analyzes Beckett's use of various mass media: radio, television, cinema, and the contribution of their techniques, instruments, sounds, lights, and images to his near-solipsist vision.

66 MAYS, JAMES. "Samuel Beckett's 'Lessness' [...]. Eugene Webb, <u>Samuel Beckett: A Critical Study of His Novels</u> [...]. Melvin J. Friedman, editor, <u>Samuel Beckett Now: Critical Approaches to His Novels, Poetry and Plays</u>." <u>Irish University Review</u> 1, no. 2 (Spring):266-76. Beckett: pp. 266-73.
Outlines the basic situation presented in "Lessness," the reader's experience, the rhythm, and the progression or the degree of movement the piece achieves. Two critical works are also reviewed.

67   MERCIER, VIVIAN. "Beckett's Anglo-Irish Stage
      Dialects." James Joyce Quarterly 8, no. 4
      (Summer):311-17.
         Discusses Beckett's use of Irish English
      in his dramatic works written for stage,
      radio, and television. Because Beckett's
      dramatic works are universal, frequently
      formal in tone, his dialogue is rarely
      colloquial. Mercier found that Beckett used
      more Dublin dialect in translating Pinget's
      radio play La Manivelle than he did for his
      own plays.

68   METWALLY, ABDALLA A. "Beckett's Waiting for
      Godot and the Theater of the Absurd." In
      Studies in Modern Drama, II. Beirut: Beirut
      Arab University, pp. 97-131.
         Examines Waiting for Godot as a model for
      the Theater of the Absurd, from the point of
      view of the characters, the act of Waiting,
      the precariousness of time, farcical effects,
      and language.

69   MOOD, JOHN J. "'The Personal System' -- Samuel
      Beckett's Watt." PMLA 86, no. 2 (Mar.):255-
      65.
         Focuses on the plot, portrayal of rationa-
      lity, the comedy of exhaustive enumeration in
      Watt, and the formal element of credibility
      in the novel in general.

70   MURCH, ANNE C. "Encore un pas." Critique
      Française, no. 284, pp. 45-57.
         Follows the stages of the Beckettian hero
      enclosed in a defined space, refuge, prison,
      or personal inferno in "Imagination Dead
      Imagine," "Ping," and "Lessness."

71   MURRAY, PATRICK. "The Shandean Mode: Beckett
      and Sterne Compared." Studies 60 (Spring):
      55-67.
         Notes that Beckett and Sterne belong to
      the same literary tradition: parallels in
      literary techniques, use of similar material,
      their attitudes toward the art of the novel,

their treatment of character, the satire of
form, content, and the conventional novel,
and their Rabelaisian delight in the parody
of pedantry and learned jargon.

72   NORES, DOMINIQUE, ed. Les Critiques de notre
      temps et Beckett. Paris: Garnier Frères,
      191 pp.
         Provides numerous extracts from commen-
      taries on Beckett's life and works. Followed
      by a chronology and a select bibliography

73   O'BRIEN, JUSTIN. "Samuel Beckett and André
      Gide: An Hypothesis." In Contemporary
      French Literature. New Brunswick, New
      Jersey: Rutgers University Press, pp. 5-6.
      Reprint of 1967.80.

74   O'MALLEY, KEVIN, ed. "Beckett Symposium." New
      Theatre Magazine 11, no. 3:8-19.
         Martin Esslin (Chairman), A.J. Leventhal,
      Colin Duckworth, Raymond Federman and John
      Calder participated in this Symposium on
      Beckett and discussed several topics: the
      Irishness of Beckett's humor, the evolution
      (or regression) in the structure of his
      works, aliterature, the mixture of tragedy
      and comedy, Beckett as poet, Beckett's
      imagery (Irish and Christian), the future of
      Beckett, the original text of Godot, "audi-
      ence participation," the mood of the plays,
      and agnosticism vs. Christianity.

75   *PIATIER, JACQUELINE. "Une inhumaine comédie:
      Le Dépeupleur, de Samuel Beckett." Monde
      [des Livres], 12 Feb., p. 13.

76   PINTER, HAROLD. "Pinter on Beckett." New
      Theatre Magazine" 11, no. 3:3.
         Presents the text of Pinter's brief
      opening speech for the Samuel Beckett
      Exhibition at the University of Reading.

77   ROBINSON, C.J. BRADBURY. "A Way With Words:
      Paradox, Silence, and Samuel Beckett."

<u>Cambridge Quarterly</u> 5, no. 3 (Spring):249-64.
Poses two questions: whether Beckett's
work is philosophically sound, and if it
matters. In this pursuit, Robinson examines
the paradox of expression, the futility of
existence, and the regression of Beckett's
works.

78   ROSE, MARILYN G. "The Irish Memories of
Beckett's Voice." <u>Journal of Modern Litera-
ture</u> 2, no. 1 (Sept.):127-32.
Clarifies specific Irish images in
Beckett's novels and plays, comparing certain
portraits with paintings by Jack B. Yeats.

79   _____. "The Lyrical Structure of Beckett's
<u>Texts for Nothing</u>." <u>Novel</u> 4, no. 3
(Spring):223-30.
Examines the lyricism of Beckett's <u>Texts
for Nothing</u> in which the voice expresses
itself rhythmically and imaginatively: "We
begin in Text I with the outer scene,
established then obliterated by the eye,
partially re-established by the ear. Texts
II, III, and IV take up the inner scene, the
conjuring brain and its fictions. Text V
establishes the solipsism of the inquiry ...
Texts VI, VII, and VIII move to the word ...
Texts IX, X, XI, and XII record abortive
attempts of the voice to free itself from
speech by speech. Text XIII is the reconci-
liation reached through reasoned, and hence
verbalized desperation."

80   ROUD, RICHARD. "Mouth Piece: Richard Roud, in
New York, on Beckett's Latest and Most
Original Play." <u>Guardian</u>, 24 Nov., p. 12.
Reviews the world premiere of <u>Not I</u> at the
Forum Theatre of Lincoln Center. Roud notes
the surprising visual and hypnotic effect of
the play.

81   RUNDALL, JEREMY. "Sounds of Silence." <u>Sunday
Times</u> (London), 28 Feb. p. 28.
Describes Martin Esslin's radio production

of <u>Lessness</u> in which six voices "orchestrate"
Beckett's own translation and arrangement.

82   SCARRY, E.M. "Six Ways to Kill a Blackbird or
      Any Other Intentional Object: Samuel
      Beckett's Method of Meaning." <u>James Joyce
      Quarterly</u> 8, no. 4 (Summer):278-89.
         Concentrates on <u>No's Knife</u>, examining the
      nature of the story's setting and landscapes,
      and Beckett's methods of minimizing the
      significance of objects and specific details.

83   *SCHULT-ULRIKSEN, SOLVEIG. "Samuel Beckett."
      <u>Minerva's Kvartalsskrift</u> 15:332-38.

84   *SEBBA, G. "Time and the Modern Self: Descar-
      tes, Rousseau, Beckett." <u>Stadium Generale</u>
      24, no. 3 (24 Mar.):308-25.

85   SEN, A.C. "Beckett's <u>Waiting for Godot</u>."
      <u>Calcutta Review</u> 2, no. 4 (Apr.-June):435-42.
         Believes that although <u>Waiting for Godot</u>
      has been associated with the myth of Sisy-
      phus, the presence of biblical imagery in the
      play overshadows the "absurd" elements and
      provides a sense of meaning and respon-
      sibility.

86   SIMON, JOHN. "The Sorcerer and His Appren-
      tices." <u>New York</u> 4, no. 9 (1 Mar.):58.
         Reviews <u>Waiting for Godot</u> and Pinter's <u>The
      Birthday Party</u>, contrasting the two authors
      and briefly pointing out why he considers
      "Beckett the greatest living playwright and
      Pinter one of the biggest impostors in the
      history of theater ..."

87   SOLOMON, PHILIP. "A Ladder Image in <u>Watt</u>:
      Samuel Beckett and Fritz Mauthner." <u>Papers
      on Language & Literature</u> 7, no. 4 (Fall):422-
      27.
         With the composition of <u>Watt</u>, Solomon
      feels that Beckett became interested in
      problems analogous to those treated in Fritz
      Mauthner's <u>Beitrage zu Einer Kritik der</u>

Sprache. Mauthner's work examines the
relationship between language and our
knowledge of reality and introduces ladder
images.

88   _____. "Samuel Beckett's L'Innommable: The
        Space of Fiction." Forum for Modern Language
        Studies 7, no. 1:83-91.
            Points out that Beckett's narrators have
        all sought to free themselves from "space-
        bound reality" in the hope of finding an
        inner self or consciousness. In relation to
        the Unnamable's search for self, Solomon
        discusses the problems of language, physical
        space, and fictional representation.

89   *SPURLING, JOHN. "The Geography of a Cul-de-
        sac." Europa Magazine 1, no. 3 (May):45.

90   STAMIROWSKA, KRYSTYNA. "Some Remarks on Lucky's
        Monologue in Waiting for Godot by Samuel
        Beckett." Kwartalnik Neofilogiczny 18, no.
        4:427-31.
            Believes Beckett's view of the chaos in
        the world and the decay of humanity, as it is
        presented in Waiting for Godot, becomes clear
        through Lucky's monologue. The form of the
        monologue is significant because it resembles
        the process of thinking in its prearticulated
        stage.

91   STAPLES, HUGH. "Beckett in the Wake." James
        Joyce Quarterly 8, no. 4 (Summer):421-24.
            Rebuffs criticism of Nathan Halper
        concerning the quotation of a story Richard
        Ellmann heard from Beckett in which Beckett
        included the phrase "Come in" in a dictation
        of Finnegans Wake.

92   STEFAN, JUDE. "Samuel Beckett: Le Dépeupleur."
        Cahiers du Chemin 12 (15 Apr.):96-99.
            Briefly reviews The Lost Ones, comparing
        the description of the characters in the
        cylinder to the experiences of the reader,

with brief references to Dante, Piranese and
Kafka.

93   STEIN, KAREN F.   "Metaphysical Silence in Absurd
     Drama." <u>Modern Drama</u> 13, no. 4 (Feb.):423-
     31.
           States that in modern literature silence
     represents lack of meaning, the void. Stein
     remarks that Beckett's use of silence and
     dialogue manifests this new attitude of
     metaphorical silence: "Yearning for silence
     the characters are compelled to talk; seeking
     obliteration, they are condemned to reitera-
     tion.

94   STEINER, GEORGE. "Of Nuance and Scruple." In
     <u>Extraterritorial: Papers on Literature and
     the Language Revolution</u>. New York: Atheneum,
     pp. 12-21.
           Contrasts the works and visions of two
     "Masters," Henry James and Beckett. Steiner
     briefly comments on Beckett's bilingualism,
     the Beckettian landscape, and essential
     motifs.

95   SWANSON, ELEANOR. "Samuel Beckett's <u>Watt</u>: A
     Coming and a Going." <u>Modern Fiction Studies</u>
     17, no. 2 (Summer):264-68.
           Views Beckett's concern with time in <u>Watt</u>
     as "an absurd system that makes any knowledge
     of objective reality impossible for man."

96   SWERLING, ANTHONY. "Beckett's <u>En attendant
     Godot</u> and <u>Fin de partie</u>." In <u>Strindberg's
     Impact in France 1920-1960</u>. Cambridge:
     Trinity Lane Press, pp. 111-35.
           Explores the influence of Strindberg'a
     theater on Beckett. Swerling finds that the
     genesis and significance of <u>Waiting for Godot</u>
     is to be found in <u>To Damascus, A Dream Play</u>,
     and <u>The Great Highway</u>, while <u>Endgame</u> is a
     metamorphosis of <u>The Dance of Death</u>.

97   THOMAS, DYLAN. "Documents: Recent Novels."
      <u>James Joyce Quarterly</u> 8, no. 4 (Summer):290-
      92.
          Reviews <u>Murphy</u> and William Carlos
      Williams'collection of stories <u>Life Along the
      Passaic River</u>. Thomas stresses <u>Murphy</u>'s
      qualities of "energy, hilarity, irony, and
      comic invention," and defines the work as
      "difficult, serious, and wrong." He feels
      that it fails to clearly portray the conflict
      of man's inner and outer worlds because the
      minds and bodies of the character are not
      related to one another. Reprint of 1938.4;
      Reprinted: 1979.22.7.

98   *TISDALL, CAROLINE. "Reading Samuel Beckett."
      <u>Guardian</u>, 24 May, p. 8.
          Source: <u>French XX Bibliography</u>, no. 24
      (1972); unverified.

99   *Van ITALLIE, CLAUDE. "Alan Schneider." In
      <u>Behind the Scenes: Theater and Film Inter-
      views from the Transatlantic Review</u>. New
      York: Holt, Rinehart, and Winston. p. 279-
      92.

100   Van VACTOR, ANITA. "Predicaments." <u>Listener</u> 85
      (25 Feb.):250.
          Presents the futility of Beckett's attempt
      to reduce the value or expressiveness of his
      text "Lessness": "in spite of its entranced,
      runic quality, in spite of its diminishing
      returns, 'Lessness' is trope not entropy, and
      therefore dramatic expression.

101   VERCIER, BRUNO. "Samuel Beckett: <u>Le Dépeu-
      pleur</u>." <u>Nouvelle Revue Française</u>, no. 221
      (May), pp. 107-10.
          Summarizes <u>The Lost Ones</u> and analyzes its
      place in Beckett's creative fiction.

102   WADE, DAVID. "'Lessness I': Radio 3." <u>Times</u>
      (London), 25 Feb., p. 13.
          Describes the radio version of "Lessness"
      repeating many of Martin Esslin's

introductory remarks to the presentation of
the prose text.

103   WARDLE, IRVING. "Endgame: Young Vic." Times
       (London), 2 Feb., p. 12.
            Points out that Peter James' production of
       Endgame places the play under a harsh white
       light, suggesting "a well equipped modern
       torture chamber."

104   _____. "Krapp's Last Tape/Endgame: Aldwych."
       Times (London), 30 Apr., p. 10.
            Feels that Krapp's Last Tape provides a
       better performance than Endgame: "Rarely
       have the eccentricities of solitary behavior
       been more ruthlessly exposed in public ..."

105   _____. "Reverence for Beckett Text: Waiting
       for Godot, Nottingham Palace." Times
       (London), 27 Jan., p. 8.
            Believes Frederich Monnoyer's production
       of Waiting for Godot shows too much reverence
       for the text: "We are never allowed to
       forget that the piece is a statement on the
       human condition. Its vaudeville element is
       held severely in check; every little canter
       between Didi and Gogo is followed by an
       appropriate silence for the dark chasm to
       reopen under their feet."

106   WARNER, FRANCIS. "The Absence of Nationalism in
       the Work of Samuel Beckett." In Theater and
       Nationalism in Twentieth Century Ireland.
       Edited by Robert O'Driscoll. Toronto:
       University of Toronto Press, pp. 179-204.
            Emphasizes that Beckett is still Irish,
       not French, and examines his place in Irish
       literary tradition, considering the influence
       of James Joyce, Oscar Wilde, and the Irish
       Comic Theatre, as well as the importance of
       the visual arts (Jack Yeats, Kandinsky, Klee,
       Braque, and Picasso).

107   *YOUNG, B.A. "Beckett Double Bill." Financial
       Times, 30 Apr., p. 3.

108   _____. "Young Vic. Endgame." Financial Times,
       2 Feb., p. 3.
          Reviews Endgame, which he would have
       preferred to have seen played with a little
       more humor. Young acknowledges, however,
       that "a director can't do much with Endgame
       except ensure that it is played according to
       the author's specification."

                        1971-1972

1   LYONS, CHARLES R. "Beckett's Major Plays and
       the Trilogy." Comparative Drama 5, no. 4
       (Winter):254-68.
          Explores the central experience depicted
       in the trilogy and the plays published around
       the same time: "The protagonist is engaged
       in a strange journey, quest, or course of
       action which involves the gradual releasing
       or denying of commitments to phenomenal
       experience ... Simultaneously, he finds
       satisfaction in the repetition of a formal
       exercise ... with some understanding that
       this exercise is a created thing, an invented
       object or behavior."

                          1972

1   *ANDREACH, ROBERT J. "Henry James' The Sacred
       Fount: The Existential Predicament." Nine-
       teenth Century Fiction 17, no. 3 (Dec.):197-
       216.
          Source: French XX Bibliography, no. 27
       (1975); unverified.

2   BAQUE, FRANÇOISE. "La Destruction. Robert
       Pinget, Samuel Beckett." In Le Nouveau
       Roman. Paris: Bordas, pp. 14-29.
          Demonstrates that beginning with the

stories of 1946, "L'Expulsé," "La Fin," and
"Le Calmant," Beckett develops the major
themes that are to be repeated in all of his
works. Beckett's novels appear as a progression in which character and story are
gradually suppressed.

3   BASTIDE, FRANÇOISE-REGIS. "En attendant Godot
de Samuel Beckett." In Au théâtre certains
soirs, chroniques. Paris: Editions du
Seuil, pp. 131-35.
Reprint of 1970.2.

4   BORIE, MONIQUE. "Structures du temps théâtral
dans le théâtre de Beckett." Revue des
Sciences Humaines, n.s., no. 147 (July-
Sept.), pp. 415-26.
Analyzes the structure of time in
Beckett's plays, pointing out that Beckett
uses the most ancient or traditional theatrical structures but in a different way so as
to change their significance. In many cases
outside stimulations define time in the
plays: the role of a light, a regard, a
camera, the sound of knocking, repetitions of
gestures or words. In a final analysis,
Borie demonstrates how it is the absence of
time that best defines Beckett's theater.

5   BRADBROOK, MURIEL CLARA. "En attendant Godot."
In Literature in Action: Studies in Con-
tinental and Commonwealth Society. London:
Chatto and Windus; New York: Barnes and
Noble, pp. 13-33, and passim.
Examines (in English) the French version
of Waiting for Godot which the author
believes is closer to tragedy while the
Anglo-Irish version is nearer to comedy.
Bradbrook studies aspects of Beckett's life,
as they pertain to the play, the structure of
Godot, or the conventional repertoire of
stage clowns. Reprinted: 1983.8.

6   BROOKS, MARY ELLEN. "The British Theatre of
Metaphysical Despair." Literature and

<u>Ideology</u> 12:49-58.
　　Considers Beckett's <u>Waiting for Godot</u> and
Pinter's <u>Birthday Party</u> as examples of the
theater of metaphysical despair that emerged
in England after WWII.

7　　BRYER, J.R., R.J. DAVIS, M.J. FRIEDMAN, AND P.C.
　　HOY, eds. <u>Calepins de bibliographie (2):
　　Samuel Beckett</u>. Paris: Lettres Modernes
　　Minard, unpaginated.
　　　　Presents a bibliography in three parts:　a
　　listing of Beckett's works (1929-1966), a
　　compilation of critical reviews, articles,
　　theses and books in French and English
　　devoted to Beckett or his works (1931-1966
　　and then expanded to include 1929-1970), and
　　a brief bibliographical sketch of studies in
　　other languages (1953-1970). Reprinted from
　　1971.10.

8　　BUSI, FREDERICK. "The Transfigurations of
　　Godot." <u>Research Studies</u> 40:290-96.
　　　　Evaluates <u>Waiting for Godot</u> from the
　　perspective of two related literary techni-
　　ques, the psychological double and the play
　　within the play.

9　　"Can't Stop Climbing." <u>Times Literary Supple-
　　ment</u> (London), 11 Aug., p. 935.
　　　　Interprets the symbol of the ladder in <u>The
　　Lost Ones</u>, referring to its appearance in
　　Beckett's previous works. Reprinted
　　1979.22.71.

10　　CARTER, A. "Towards a Third World of Meaning."
　　<u>Linguistica Antverpiensia</u> 6:21-25.
　　　　Establishes Beckett and Pinter's response
　　to the limitations of language both as a
　　means of communication and as a method to
　　express thought and emotion.

11　　*CHAPLIN, SID. "Newcastle-on-Tyne: <u>Godot</u>."
　　<u>Guardian</u>, 21 Mar.
　　　　Source: <u>French XX Bibliography</u>, no. 25
　　(1973); unverified.

12   CLURMAN, HAROLD. "Theatre." Nation 215 (11
          Dec):596-98.
             Reviews Not I, Happy Days and Krapp's Last
          Tape at the Forum of the Repertory Theatre of
          the Lincoln Center, briefly describing the
          situations of the 3 major protagonists of the
          plays.

13   COETZEE, JOHN M. "The Manuscript Revisions of
          Beckett's Watt." Journal of Modern Litera-
          ture 2, no. 4 (Nov.):472-80.
             Describes the Watt papers at the Univer-
          sity of Texas from two points of view: 1) a
          compositional biography, and 2) the stylistic
          revisions controlled by the principle of
          symmetry.

14   COHN, RUBY. "Beckett and Shakespeare." Modern
          Drama 15, no. 3 (Dec.) 223-30.
             Finds that both Beckett and Shakespeare
          are possessed by "Nothing." References to
          Shakespeare in Beckett's drama are most
          pronounced in Endgame and Happy Days.

15   COMBS, EUGENE. "Impotency and Ignorance: A
          Parody of Prerogatives in Samuel Beckett."
          Studies in Religion: A Canadian Journal 2,
          no. 2, pp. 114-30.
             Attempts to show that the trilogy is a
          caricature which exaggerates certain features
          of modernity (the loss of restraints, the
          creation of truth, mathematical truth) and
          that Waiting for Godot is a dramatic recol-
          lection of the classical, philosophical, and
          biblical assumption that man is subject to a
          higher eternal order. Then Combs demon-
          strates how Beckett develops various states
          of deprivation to sustain this caricature and
          recollection.

16   CONELY, JAMES. "Arcana, Molloy, Malone Dies,
          The Unnamable: A Brief Comparison of Forms."
          Hartford Studies in Literature 4, no. 3:187-
          96.
             Compares the basic form of Edgar Varese's

Arcana with that of Beckett's trilogy in
order to give "insight into the purposes and
techniques of these two artists."

17   *CRAFT, ROBERT. "Stravinsky: The Banquet
      Years." Observer, 16 July, p. 23.

18   *DALMAS, ANDRE. "Beckett et son étrange
      démarche." Monde [des Livres], 31 Mar.,
      p. 13.

19   DOHERTY, FRANCIS. "Samuel Beckett's All That
      Fall or 'All the Oppressions.'" Recherches
      Anglaises et Américaines no. 5, pp. 80-84.
          Demonstrates Beckett's incorporation of
      Biblical allusions, specifically from
      Ecclesiastes, in All That Fall. Doherty
      feels that this play is unique because it was
      written in English, and "it returns to an
      Irish landscape and Irish voices, and
      especially, to Irish Protestantism."

20   DUCKWORTH, COLIN. Angels of Darkness: Dramatic
      Effect in Samuel Beckett with Special
      Reference to Eugéne Ionesco. London: George
      Allen and Unwin Ltd., 153 pp.
          Studies Beckett's plays and attempts to
      explain their effectiveness. Duckworth
      compares Beckett's plays to those of Ionesco
      because they frequently elicit similar kinds
      of response from empathic spectators. The
      author tries to discover and describe the
      function and effect of the dramatic struc-
      tures of these two dramatists as a form of
      inner exploration leading to deeper self-
      knowledge. The problems of dramatic impact
      and intensity are examined to find out how
      and why people react to performances, and to
      account for the degree and kind of tension
      created by plays written with a minimum of
      conscious control. Duckworth illustrates his
      theories through the results of a survey of
      audience reaction to performances of Waiting
      for Godot and Endgame that he compiled in
      1971.

21   DUROZI, GERARD. <u>Beckett</u>. Paris-Monréal:
     Bordas, 242 pp.
          Summarizes Beckett's background, describes
     each of his works, and offers commentaries on
     language, style, themes, movement in space,
     and sources and influences. Followed by a
     selected bibliography.

22   DUTTON, K.R. "The Pre-Theology of Samuel
     Beckett." <u>Colloquium</u>, Oct., pp. 17-33.
          Discusses the theological dimensions of
     two of Beckett's dramas, <u>Waiting for Godot</u>
     and <u>Endgame</u>, referring to the critical
     interpretations of Frederick Lumley, George
     Wellwarth, Gunther Anders, and Eva Metman.

23   *Entertainment in New York." <u>International</u>
     <u>Herald Tribune</u>, 24 Nov., p. 8.

24   ESSEN, MARTINA VON. "Samuel Beckett, traducteur
     de lui-meme." <u>Neuphilologische Mitteilungen</u>
     73, no. 4:866-92.
          Evaluates Beckett's method of translation,
     from three points of view: syntactic,
     semantic, and stylistic.

25   FINNEY, BRIAN. <u>Since "How It Is": A Study of</u>
     <u>Samuel Beckett's Later Fiction</u>. London:
     Covent Garden Press, 45 pp.
          Studies the short prose texts written
     since <u>How It Is</u> ("Imagination Dead Imagine,"
     "Enough," <u>The Lost Ones</u>, "Ping," and "Less-
     ness") concentrating on specific aspects of
     these works: order and chaos, light and
     darkness, space and time, the perceiver and
     the perceived, artistic failure, and form and
     content.

26   FLETCHER, JOHN and JOHN SPURLING. <u>Beckett: A</u>
     <u>Study of His Plays</u>. London: Eyre Methuen;
     New York: Hill & Wang, 222 pp.
          An introduction to Beckett's novels and
     plays, their characters, pictorial elements,
     language, and a discussion of the general
     evolution of Beckett's fiction precedes an

analysis of the following theatrical works:
"Eleuthéria," Waiting for Godot, Endgame, All
That Fall, Krapp's Last Tape, Embers, Eh Joe,
Words and Music, Cascando, Happy Days, Play,
Acts Without Words, Come and Go, and Breath.
In a final chapter numerous performances of
Beckett's plays and the critical response to
those performances are presented. A chrono-
logy of Beckett's life and works and a brief
bibliography are also included.

27   GARZILLI, ENRICO. "Man alone: ... Murphy and
His Successors -- Samuel Beckett"; "The Other
and Identity: The Couples of Samuel Beckett"
and "Myth and Self: The Unnamable -- Samuel
Beckett ..." In Circles Without Center:
Paths to the Discovery and Creation of Self
in Modern Literature. Cambridge, Mass.:
Harvard University Press, pp. 18-38, 47-52.
Poses the question of the loss of identity
of modern man and deals with the "fragments
of self" portrayed in modern prose fiction:
the journey inward, the need for other
people, myth and language, public masks, and
the labyrinth and the self. Garzilli
discusses the changes in literary form as a
reflection of man's evolution. Murphy, the
trilogy, Waiting for Godot, Endgame, "Cascando," Happpy Days, and How It Is are discussed
in this context.

28   *GAZKELL, RONALD. "Beckett: Endgame." In
Drama and Reality: The European Theatre
Since Ibsen. London and Boston: Routledge &
Kegan Paul, 182 pp.

29   GILLARD, DAVID. "'You Can't Fool About with
This Play.'" Radio Times, 1 June, p. 10.
Discusses the effect of All That Fall on
the lives of J.G. Devlin, Donald McWhinnie
and Desmond Brisoe who reproduced a new
version of the radio play.

30   GILMAN, RICHARD. "Beckett." In The Making of
Modern Drama. A Study of Büchner, Ibsen,

<u>Strindberg, Chekhov, Pirandello, Brecht,</u>
<u>Beckett, Handke</u>. New York: Farrar, Straus
and Giroux, pp. 234-66.
Considers Beckett's decision to turn to
the theater and the close relationship of the
plays to the fiction. Gilman analyzes
<u>Waiting for Godot</u> and <u>Endgame</u> and then
discusses the elimination of extraneous
details in Beckett's later plays -- in
<u>Krapp's Last Tape</u> and <u>Play</u> experience is
abstracted to the irreducible human response
to being alive.

31   GLICKSBERG, CHARLES I. "Beckett's Universe of
      the Absurd." In <u>Literature and Society</u>. The
      Hague: Martinus Nijhoff, pp. 39-42.
      Describes Beckett's "asocial aesthetic":
      aging, infirmity, impotence, futility, and
      the disintegration of the novel as a tradi-
      tional form.

32   GULLETTE, DAVID. "Mon jour chez Sam: A Visit
      with Beckett." <u>Ploughshares</u> 1, no. 2:65-69.
      Recalls an informal meeting with Beckett.
      Gullette repeats several of Beckett's
      comments on his work and the works of
      Johnson, Joyce, Melville, and Camus.

33   HAGBERG, PER OLOF. <u>The Dramatic Works of Samuel</u>
      <u>Beckett and Harold Pinter: A Comparative</u>
      <u>Analysis of Main Themes and Dramatic Techni-</u>
      <u>que</u>. Göteborg: University of Gothenburg,
      Dept. of English, 162 pp.
      Considers Beckett's influence on Pinter,
      stressing the similarity of the major themes
      in the dramatic works of the two authors and
      the questions of identity and communication.
      Hapberg shows how these themes find expres-
      sion in their plays and compares their
      dramatic techniques.

34   HALLORAN, STEPHEN M. "The Anti-Aesthetics of
      <u>Waiting for Godot</u>." <u>Centennial Review</u> 16
      (Winter):69-81.
      Examines <u>Waiting for Godot</u> from the point

of view of traditional aesthetics. Beckett's
theater opposes dramatic "reality," and
Kant's theory of aesthetic or psychical
distance: Vladimir and Estragon "are not
symbols; they do not mean anything. They are
no less than they are, and they could not
possibly be more. They are men, and we come
to the play to sit and look, to really see
men."

35   HANNA, BLAKE T. "Samuel Beckett: Traducteur de
     lui-meme." <u>Meta: Journal des Traducteurs</u>
     17:220-24.
        Discusses Guy Simpson's analysis of
     Beckett's bilingualism in his doctoral thesis
     "Le Bilinguisme de Samuel Beckett d'après ses
     traductions du français à l'anglais et vice
     versa." Simpson presents Beckett's methods
     of translation and stylistic differences in
     the English and French texts. He also
     contrasts Beckett's methods of translation
     with those of Vladimir Nabokov.

36   HASSAN, IHAB. "Joyce -- Beckett: A Scenario in
     Eight Scenes and a Voice." In <u>New Light on
     Joyce from the Dublin Symposium</u>. Edited by
     Fritz Senn. Bloomington: Indiana University
     Press, 219 pp.
        Reprint of 1970.58; Reprinted 1975.46

37   HEDBERG, JOHANNES. <u>Samuel Beckett's 'Whoro-
     scope': A Linguistic-Literary Interpreta-
     tion</u>. Stockholm: Moderna Spräk Monographs,
     43 pp.
        Presents the poem, photographs of the
     original cover of "Whoroscope," the Hals
     painting of Descartes, and a detailed
     commentary.

38   HEWES, HENRY. "Heaven is Murky." <u>Saturday
     Review</u> 55 (19 Aug.):68.
        Reviews the stage adaptation of <u>The
     Unnamable</u> by the Performance Research Unit of
     the American Contemporary Theatre, Inc. in
     Buffalo, N.Y. The speaker sits in a huge

black drum with a window which rotates on the
stage, while the characters from the novel
move counter to the rotation of the drum,
illuminated by small flash lights.

39　HIBON, BERNARD.　"Samuel Beckett:　Irish
Tradition and Irish Creation."　In Aspects of
the Irish Theater.　Edited by Patrick
Rafroidi, et al.　Paris:　Editions Universitaires, Publications de l'Université de
Lille, pp. 225-41.
　　Considers the "Irishness" of Beckett's
characters, the Irish world they inhabit, and
the influence of Irish writers and traditions
on Beckett's fiction (Joyce, Swift, Berkeley,
John Millington Synge).

40　INGLIS, RUTH,　"Why Beckett's Boxes Became
Tins."　Radio Times, 25 Nov.-1 Dec., pp. 13,
15.
　　Explains why Beckett changed cardboard
boxes to biscuit tins in the radio production
of Krapp's Last Tape.　Inglis presents
impressions of Beckett and his works by
Patrick Magee and Tim Aspinall.

41　JACQUART, EMMANUEL C.　"Beckett, Ionesco,
Adamov:　Le Théâtre de dérision vingt ans
après."　Bonnes Feuilles 1, no. 2:3-13.
　　Characterizes the theater of "dérision,"
explains why these three authors are grouped
together under this heading, and summarizes
the critical writings on the topic.

42　JONES, ANTHONY.　"Samuel Beckett Is Only Human."
American Society of Legion of Honor Magazine
43, no. 2:73-88.
　　Analyzes the self-conscious aspects of the
trilogy and How It Is.　Jones focuses on the
preoccupations of the narrator, from the
auto-criticism and self-interrogation to pure
fantasy:　"... Beckett's prose ... is among
the most self-conscious that man has ever
composed ... It constantly comments on
itself, examines itself, analyses its own

genesis and motivation, its aims and intentions: it is a prose which talks about
itself ..."

43   KALEM, T.E. "In the Minds I." <u>Time</u> 100 (11
      Dec.):122.
           Criticizes the absence of traditional
      dramatic elements of plot, characters and
      action in Beckett's theater: "One may only
      speculate that a despairing age simply
      mistakes his statements of paralysis,
      alienation and isolation for some sort of
      apocalyptic wisdom."

44   KAUFFMANN, STANLEY. "On Theater." <u>New Republic</u>
      167, no. 23 (16 Dec.):24.
           Reviews <u>Not I</u>, pointing out Beckett's
      ability to visualize theatrically the
      intangible: "From the verbal torrent, though
      perfectly lucid phrase by phrase, comes not
      content but pattern -- of rhythm and repeti-
      tion, like themes in music."

45   KAWIN, BRUCE F. "Stein and Beckett: Beginning
      Again." In <u>Telling It Again and Again.</u>
      <u>Repetition in Literature and Film</u>. Ithaca,
      N.Y.: Cornell University Press, 131-53.
           Compares repetition in the works of
      Beckett and Gertrude Stein -- whereas
      "Beckett exhausts nonintuitive language in
      frustration at unsayable reality," Stein's
      process depends on the accumulation of
      described "instants" for its sense of life.

46   KENNEDY, SIGHLE. "'The Devil and Holy Water'
      -- Samuel Beckett's <u>Murphy</u> and Flan O'Brien's
      <u>At Swim-Two-Birds</u>." In <u>Modern Irish Litera-</u>
      <u>ture. Essays in Honor of William York</u>
      <u>Tindall</u>. Edited by Raymond Porter and James
      D. Brophy. New York: Iona College Press and
      Twayne Publishers, pp. 251-60.
           Compares and contrasts Beckett's <u>Murphy</u>
      with Flan O'Brien's <u>At Swim-Two-Birds</u>: both
      writers present critical guidelines for the
      novel in their narratives, both works

introduce "puppets" as characters, both
writers stray from realistic fiction, indulge
in digressions, are concerned with the
problems of madness, weave chess games into
their narratives, and portray young men who
are interested in retiring to the privacy of
their own mental spheres. Whereas O'Brien
creates a "crystal-clear fictional entity,"
Kennedy views Beckett's <u>Murphy</u> as a "murkier
brand of distillation."

47   KNOWLSON, JAMES. <u>Light and Darkness in the</u>
     <u>Theater of Samuel Beckett</u>. London: Turret
     Books, 41 pp.
          Presents the text of a public lecture
     delivered at Trinity College, Dublin in 1972,
     in which he examines the structural and
     thematic roles of the imagery of light and
     darkness in Beckett's fiction.

48   *LAVIELLE, EMILE. <u>"En attendant Godot" de</u>
     <u>Beckett</u>. Paris: Classiques Hachette, 91 pp.

49   LAW, RICHARD A. "Mock Evangelism in Beckett's
     <u>Watt</u>." <u>Modern Language Studies</u> 2, no. 2:68-
     82.
          Studies references to <u>Ecclesiastes</u> and the
     narrative about Christ and the disciples
     given in Saint John's writings and <u>Acts of</u>
     <u>the Apostles</u>. These references call atten-
     tion to incompatible ideas in the Old and New
     Testaments which implies some doubt about
     relying on sacred documents.

50   LEVENTHAL, A.J. "Samuel Beckett: About Him and
     About." <u>Hermathena</u> 114 (Winter):5-22.
          In the text of a lecture delivered on Feb.
     22, 1972 at Trinity College on the occasion
     of an exhibition of Beckett's works, Leven-
     thal examines several of Beckett's plays and
     prose works: <u>Waiting for Godot</u>, <u>Endgame</u>,
     "Imagination Dead Imagine," "Enough," "Ping,"
     "Lessness," and <u>The Lost Ones</u>.

51   LE VOT, ANDRE. "Vladimir Nabokov: <u>Roi, dame,</u>
     <u>valet</u>. Samuel Beckett: <u>Paroles et musique</u>,
     <u>Comédie</u>, <u>Dis Joe</u>." <u>Esprit</u>, no. 414 (June),
     pp. 1089-92.
          Remarks that while Nabokov found his
     creativity enriched by writing in an acquired
     language, Beckett found constraints.

52   McELROY, JOSEPH. "Dreams of a Way Out in a
     Closed World." <u>New York Times Book Review</u>,
     29 Oct., pp. 4, 20.
          Reviews <u>The Lost Ones</u>, analyzing the
     situation, characters and images in the
     novel. McElroy sees the cylinder as not only
     the human condition, but also the human mind.

53   MARTEL, FRANÇOIS. "Jeux formels dans <u>Watt</u>."
     <u>Poétique: Revue de Théorie et d'Analyse</u>
     <u>Littéraires</u> 10:153-75.
          Analyzes the mathematical enumerations in
     <u>Watt</u> in three categories, indicating a
     progressive diminuation in the constraint
     applied to their construction: 1) numerical
     games, 2) exhaustive enumerations, 3)
     enumerations utilizing various degrees of
     freedom.

54   *MAYOUX, JEAN-JACQUES. <u>Samuel Beckett bilangue</u>.
     Paris: Flammarion, 251 pp.

55   MAYS, JAMES. "Samuel Beckett Bibliography:
     Comments and Corrections." <u>Irish University</u>
     <u>Review</u> 2, no. 2 (Autumn):189-208.
          Comments on the Federman and Fletcher
     bibliography <u>Samuel Beckett: His Works and</u>
     <u>His Critics</u>, providing corrections, comments
     and additions.

56   *MURRAY, EDWARD. "The Theater of the Absurd and
     Film: Eugene Ionesco and Samuel Beckett."
     In <u>The Cinematic Imagination: Writers and</u>
     <u>the Motion Pictures</u>. New York: Ungar, pp.
     86-99. Beckett: pp. 91-94.

56a   OLIVER, EDITH.   "Off Broadway.   Beckett Back to
        Back."   New Yorker, 2 Dec.:123-26.
        Reviews Jules Irving's productions of
        Happy Days, Act Without Words, I, Krapp's
        Last Tape, and Not I at the Forum in Lincoln
        Center, describing the actors' performances,
        the staging, and the characters' actions or
        words.   Reprinted: 1979.22.73.

57   PICKAR, GERTRUDE B.   "Goll, Beckett and Walser
        -- Three Variations on a Theme," Language
        Quarterly 11, nos. 1-2 (Fall-Winter):11-17.
        Compares Martin Walser's Überlebensgrosz
        Herr Krott to Beckett's Endgame and Iwan
        Goll's Methusalem Oder der Ewige Bürger.
        Pickar feels these three plays are similar in
        basic philosophy and intent, are "united by
        central figures of apparent immortality, as
        well as by aspects of theme, language and
        mood."

58   POPOVICH, HELEN H.   "Hamm: Beckett's God in
        Nagg's Image."   South Atlantic Bulletin 37,
        no. 1 (Jan.):35-38.
        Analyzes the possible symbolism of the
        characters in Endgame: Hamm is pictured as
        god the father, Clov as god the son, and Nagg
        represents man.

59   RABINOVITZ, RUBIN.   "Watt from Descartes to
        Schopenhauer."   In Modern Irish Literature:
        Essays in Honor of William York Tindall.
        Edited by Raymond J. Porter and James D.
        Brophy.   New York: Iona College Press and
        Twayne Publishers, Inc. pp. 261-87.
        Outlines the influence of Descartes and
        Schopenhauer on the creation of Watt: Watt
        as a parody of Descartes' Rules, Watt as a
        modern Cartesian, Watt's inability to resolve
        metaphysical questions without being faced
        with innumerable paradoxes, man's tragically
        insatiable need for knowledge, Schopenhauer's
        division of the mind into subject and object,
        the futility of epistemological quests, etc.

60   *RAIDY, WILLIAM A.   "Season Looks Good for the
      White Way." Shreveport Journal 78 (19
      Sept.):18A.

61   REID, ALEC.   "Comedy in Synge and Beckett."
      Yeats Studies 2:80-90.
           Points out the common backgrounds of John
      Millington Synge and Beckett and the inherent
      sensitivity, humor, and verbal wit of the
      Anglo-Irishman which links these two drama-
      tists.

62   REITER, SEYMOUR.   "The Structure of Waiting for
      Godot." Costerus 3:181-95.
           Undertakes a structural analysis of
      Waiting for Godot, emphasizing the issue of
      hope as central to the plot and structure of
      the play.

63   RICKS, CHRISTOPHER.   "Beckett First and Last."
      New York Review of Books 19 (14 Dec.):42-44.
           Reviews The Lost Ones and More Pricks than
      Kicks, describing the comedy of More Pricks,
      the "tonelessness" of the two works, and
      pointing out allusions to Shakespeare,
      Milton, T.S. Eliot, Dante, and Swift.

64   ROSE, MARILYN GADDIS.   "The Sterne Ways of
      Beckett and Jack B. Yeats." Irish University
      Review 2, no. 2 (Autumn):164-71.
           Examines Tristram Shandy, The Unnamable,
      and The Charmed Life, demonstrating Sterne's
      influence on Beckett and Yeats: "The three
      writers treat mankind ... humbly making
      themselves part of the species, as a subject
      for comedy, more deserving of sympathy than
      scorn, and direct their genial attacks on
      monuments of human arrogance, man-made
      systems like logic, rhetoric, fashion, and on
      the human limiters themselves: sex, disease,
      decrepitude, death.

65   ROUDIEZ, LEON S.   "Samuel Beckett." In French
      Fiction Today. A New Direction. New

Brunswick, N.J. Rutgers University Press, pp.
81-103.
   Discusses Murphy and the trilogy, relating
the three zones of Murphy's mind to Molloy,
Malone Dies and The Unnamable, with special
emphasis on humor and language.

66   SHERZER, DINA. "Quelques manifestations du
     narrateur-créateur dans Molloy de Samuel
     Beckett." Language and Style 5, no. 2
     (Spring):115-22.
        Defines "narrateur-créateur" and examines
     how the presentation of Molloy is affected by
     the presence of the narrator, types of
     intervention, manipulation of language and
     differences between the two parts of the
     novel.

67   SIMON, JOHN. "Ablative Absolute." New York 5,
     no. 50 (11 Dec.):76,78.
        Reviews the productions of Krapp's Last
     Tape, Happy Days, Act Without Words I and Not
     I at the Forum Theater in Lincoln Center.
     Simon compares the monologues of Krapp and
     Winnie: both plays are concerned with the
     ebbing away of life, both present isolated
     protagonists, both end in silence.

68   STARNES, PATRICK. "Samuel Beckett: An Inter-
     view." Antigonish Review 10:49-53.
        Describes his impressions of Beckett
     during an interview he had with him.

69   STEINBERG, S.C. "The External and Internal in
     Murphy." Twentieth Century Literature 18
     (Jan.-Oct.):93-110.
        Notes the distinction between the external
     and the internal in Murphy which is created
     through the use of motifs, word patterns, and
     structural incidents.

70   SZANTO, GEORGE. Narrative Consciousness:
     Structure and Perception in the Fiction of
     Kafka, Beckett, and Robbe-Grillet. Austin:
     University of Texas Press, pp. 71-120.

Analyzes narrative point of view in the
writings of these three authors who "conclude
by the example of their fictions that the
writer's province is no longer the impossible
environment, but is instead the only knowledge any one man can have, the knowledge he
attains through his perceptions." Szanto
believes that Kafka was the first to recognize the possibilities of narrative consciousness. Like Kafka, Beckett experimented
with narrative consciousness in his fiction,
but for Beckett the problems of memory and
projection become much more important than
they were for Kafka (demonstrating the
influence of Proust and Joyce): "Although
his narratives are presented in the past
tense, the senses of perception are constantly at work, as if the narrative were being
lived at the moment."

71   THOMPSON, PHILIP. The Grotesque. London:
      Methuen & Co. Ltd.
          Bases his definition of the grotesque on a
      passage from Watt describing the Lynch family
      in which the reader is confronted with
      incompatible reactions -- laughter and
      horror.

72   TONELLI, FRANCO. "Samuel Beckett: Godot ou le
      temps de la cruauté." In L'Esthétique de la
      cruauté. Paris: Nizet, pp. 109-25.
          Finds that Waiting for Godot is structured
      on the dichotomy existing between time seen
      as exterior to man in which the scene evolves
      according to a systemized causal pattern, and
      time which is regulated by man's inner self
      transcending social considerations and
      representative of the Theater of Cruelty.

73   TREWIN, J.C. "Going to Extremes." Illustrated
      London News 261 (Mar.):57.
          Briefly reviews Krapp's Last Tape and Not
      I at the Royal Court Theatre. Trewin points
      out that both characters respond to the
      unseen presence of death.

74   *VON ESSEN, MARTINA. "Samuel Beckett, traduc-
     teur de lui-même." <u>Neuphilologische Mit-
     teilungen</u> 73:866-92.

75   WEBB, EUGENE. <u>The Plays of Samuel Beckett</u>.
     Seattle: University of Washington Press, 160
     pp.
          After a general introduction to Beckett's
     works and the philosophical tradition of the
     absurd, Webb examines chronologically the
     dramatic works for the stage, radio, tele-
     vision, and cinema. He presents the at-
     titudes, problems, visions, and relationships
     of the characters and the imagery, underlying
     patterns, and approaches to the plays. The
     plays reach out in two principal directions:
     "One of these is ... the exploitation of form
     more or less for its own sake. The other is
     that of continued exploration, the attempt to
     diagnose more adequately the causes of our
     failure and to find a way beyond it."

76   *"The Week's T.V. Briefing." <u>Observer</u>, 26 Nov.,
     p. 48.

77   WILSON, EDWIN. "The Uncluttered Style of Samuel
     Beckett." <u>Wall Street Journal</u>, 28 Nov., p.
     26.
          Demonstrates how Beckett's dramas il-
     lustrate the theory "less is more," using
     Alan Schneider's production of <u>Not I</u> as an
     example: "When we add the verbal images of
     the woman's monologue, which throw off a
     thousand sparks in the mind, to the stark
     visual image of the mouth and the auditor in
     the theater, the effect is overwhelming."

<u>1973</u>

1   ABBOTT, H. PORTER. <u>The Fiction of Samuel</u> _
     <u>Beckett: Form and Effect</u>. Berkeley, Los
     Angeles, and London: University of
     California Press, 175 pp.
          Describes three major stages of Beckett's

approach to form in fiction: 1) two preliminary fictional experiments (<u>More Pricks than
Kicks</u>, <u>Murphy</u>), 2) the exploration of
imitative form from 1940 to 1959 (<u>Watt</u> to
<u>Texts for Nothing</u>), and 3) the rejection of
imitative form and restoration of a sense of
order in the recent prose works (<u>How It Is</u>,
<u>The Lost Ones</u>).

2   ADMUSSEN, RICHARD. "A New Dimension in Beckett
    Studies: The Manuscripts." In <u>Proceedings:
    Pacific Northwest Conference on Foreign Lan-
    guages</u>. Edited by Walter C. Kraft. Corval-
    lis: Oregon State University, pp. 178-81.
        Believes much of Beckett criticism is
    repetitive and urges scholars to concentrate
    on manuscript studies. To demonstrate the
    wealth of unexplored material in this area,
    Admussen describes two manuscript runs --
    that of <u>Play</u> and <u>Le Dépeupleur</u>.

3   _____. "The Manuscripts of Beckett's <u>Play</u>."
    <u>Modern Drama</u> 16, no. 1 (June):23-27.
        Examines the French and English drafts of
    Beckett's <u>Play</u>, noting the attention given to
    the setting, stage directions, form, and
    language. The precision of Beckett's art and
    the harmony of form and content are demon-
    strated.

4   ALPAUGH, DAVID. "<u>Embers</u> and the Sea: Becket-
    tian Intimations of Mortality." <u>Modern Drama</u>
    16, nos. 3 & 4 (Dec.):317-28.
        Compares the key images of the embers and
    the sea in Beckett's radio play <u>Embers</u> and
    Wordsworth's '<u>Immortality Ode</u>': "Because
    Wordsworth responds so differently to the
    same stimuli, the <u>Ode</u> offers a convenient
    reference point for a study of Beckett's
    anti-romantic symbolism and its relation to
    Henri's personality."

5   ALVAREZ, A. <u>Beckett</u>. London: Fontana-
    Collins; N.Y.: Viking Press, 148 pp.
        Presents a general overview of Beckett's

life and works for the "ordinary reader."
Alvarez describes Beckett as an absurdist, in
the strict sense that Camus intended, and
attributes the "bleak meticulousness" of
Beckett's writing to his depression and
personal distaste for art. Alvarez examines
the language, style and content of the
stories, novels, plays, radio pieces, and
short prose texts.

6   ANDERSON, IRMGARD ZEYSS. "Beckett's 'Taber-
     nacle' in <u>Fin de partie</u>." <u>Romance   Notes</u> 14,
     no. 3 (Spring):417-20.
         Compares the dramatic setting for <u>Endgame</u>
     with a Jewish temple, identifying Beckett's
     two-fold purpose: "In one sense, the fact
     that misery such as that of the characters in
     <u>Fin de partie</u> exists in these surroundings
     may suggest the emptiness of religious
     institutions. At the same time, one is
     reminded of the fact that, throughout
     history, the house of God has served as a
     refuge, and that concurrently, it is in the
     divine dwelling place itself in which man is
     closer to God than anywhere else ..."

7   BAILEY, PAUL. "Chuffeying." <u>New Statesman</u>, 27
     July, pp. 124-25.
         Compares a Dickens character called
     Chuffey to Beckett's characters. Bailey very
     briefly reviews <u>First Love</u>, which he finds
     superior to Beckett's other works due to its
     clarity and humor.

8   BARBER, JOHN. "Why Mr. Beckett Came to Town".
     <u>Daily Telegraph</u> (London), 19 Feb., p. 11.
         Discusses Beckett's personal interest in
     the production of his plays, in particular
     his current production of <u>Not I</u> at the Royal
     Court Theatre.

9   *BATES, MERETE. "<u>Happy Days</u>." <u>Guardian</u>,
     8 Aug.
         Source: <u>French XX Bibliography</u>, no. 26
     (1974); unverified.

9a   BELLINGHAM, SUSAN, ANNE DENNISON, and JACQUELINE
     TUCKER, eds. <u>The Samuel Beckett Collection
     in McMaster University Library</u>. Hamilton,
     Ontario: University Library Press at
     McMaster University, 101 pp. (unpaginated).
         The collection has been categorized under
     five headings: original work in monograph
     form, original work first appearing in
     serials, translation by Beckett of work by
     others, critical works devoted entirely to
     Beckett, and critical work appearing in
     serials. Each entry includes the McMaster
     University library call number and those
     works that appear in the Federman and
     Fletcher bibliography are given the "F & F"
     reference within the entry.

10   BERMEL, ALBERT. "Hero and Heroine as Topo-
     graphical Features: <u>Krapp's Last Tape</u> (1958)
     and <u>Happy Days</u> (1961) by Samuel Beckett." In
     <u>Contradictory Characters: An Interpretation
     of the Modern Theater</u>. New York: E.P.
     Dutton, pp. 159-84 and passim.
         Describes two of Beckett's characters,
     Krapp (<u>Krapp's Last Tape</u>) and Winnie (<u>Happy
     Days</u>), as they relive moments from the past
     in order to escape the monotony and isolation
     of the present. Both characters are im-
     prisoned, Winnie in a mound of dirt, and
     Krapp in a circle of light, although "these
     characters do not need locks and jailers to
     keep them in place".

11   *BEZERRA, TERESA MARIA F. <u>Etude de trois
     oeuvres littéraires</u>. Fortaleza, Brazil, 78
     pp.

12   BOISDEFFRE, PIERRE DE. "Samuel Beckett ou la
     parlerie de la mort." In <u>Les Ecrivains de la
     Nuit ou la littérature change de signe</u>.
     Paris: Plon, pp. 283-93.
         Describes Beckett's characters, their
     existence outside of time, their words, their
     silence, their death.

13 BRIDEL, YVES. "Sur le temps et l'espace dans le
    théâtre de Samuel Beckett: <u>En attendant</u>
    <u>Godot</u> -- <u>Oh les beaux jours</u>." <u>Etudes de</u>
    <u>Lettres</u> 6, no. 2 (Apr.-June):59-73.
        In <u>Waiting for Godot</u> and <u>Happy Days</u> time
    and space are depicted as neutral, dis-
    oriented, and empty. In this respect they
    are representative of Beckett's dramatic
    works.

14 BRODERICK, JOHN. "Be an Instant Expert on
    Beckett." <u>Critic</u> 31, no. 4 (Mar.-Apr.):58-
    63.
        Offers general information on Beckett's
    major plays and novels, quotations of key
    passages, the influence of Dante, and
    criticism from a Catholic perspective.

15 BUSI, FREDERICK. "The Advents of Godot."
    <u>Religion in Life</u> 42, no. 2 (Summer):168-78.
        Explores a religious interpretation of
    <u>Waiting for Godot</u> which portrays Pozzo as
    Godot, "a horrific image of God."

16 CELATI, GIANNI. "Beckett, l'interpolation et le
    gag." Translated by Michel Plaisance.
    <u>Poétique</u> 14:225-34.
        Points out that Beckett introduced many
    new techniques in his first French works
    (<u>Premier Amour</u>, <u>Nouvelles</u> and <u>Molloy</u>) which
    stem from sources that were traditionally
    considered extra-literary, including cabaret,
    music-hall, and slapstick comedy.

17 CHADDAH, R.P. "Samuel Beckett." <u>Thought</u>
    (Delhi) 25, no. 43 (27 Oct.):18-20.
        Dicusses Beckett's career, the major
    themes of his novels, the continuity of theme
    in his works, and then briefly analyzes his
    major novels: <u>More Pricks than Kicks</u>, <u>Watt</u>,
    the trilogy and <u>How It Is</u>.

18 CLURMAN, HAROLD. "Theatre." <u>Nation</u> 216 (26
    Feb.):283-84.

Reviews <u>Endgame</u>, stressing the tragic and comic elements of the play.

19 COETZEE, J.M. "Samuel Beckett and the Temptations of Style." <u>Theoria</u> 41:45-50.
    Describes Beckett's latest fiction as having no content, only shape. Coetzee feels Beckett's fiction presents "two opposing impulses which permit a fiction of net zero: the impulse toward conjuration, the impulse toward silence."

20 _____. "Samuel Beckett's 'Lessness': An Exercise in Decomposition." <u>Computers and the Humanities</u> 7, no. 4 (Mar.):195-98.
    Takes a mathematical approach to "Lessness," studying the relations and repetitions of words, phrases, and sentences in the text. Coetzee again concludes (see 1973.19) that the two halves of the fiction cancel each other: "The subject of 'Lessness' is the plight of consciousness in a void, compelled to reflect on itself, capable of doing so only by splitting itself and recombining the fragments ... This endless enterprise of splitting and recombining is language, and it offers ... but the solace of the game, the killing of time."

21 COHN, RUBY. <u>Back to Beckett</u>. Princeton, N.J.: Princeton University Press, 274 pp.
    Expresses her desire "to get back to Beckett, to the works, which penetrate the width and depth of human experience." Cohn concentrates on the "unique verbal melody" of Beckett's words and what she believes to be Beckett's achievements turning her back on what she feels may be Beckett's own view of his writing as a failure. Through her analysis of Beckett's poetry, prose, and drama, she demonstrates Beckett's central obsession, man's mortality, and shows how "each of Beckett's genres examines the anatomy of that genre ..." and "delineates the human situation."

22   _____. "Grace Notes on Beckett's Environments."
        In Break Out! In Search of New Theatrical
        Environments. Edited by John Schevill.
        Chicago: Swallow Press, pp. 124-33.
             Examines the implications of the stage
        "environment" created in three of Beckett's
        plays: Waiting for Godot, Endgame, and Happy
        Days.

23   *COMBS, EUGENE. "The Shape of Chaos: An
        Interpretation of the Art of Samuel Beckett."
        United States Quarterly Review, (Spring), pp.
        235-42.

24   CORNWELL, ETHEL F. "Samuel Beckett: The Flight
        from Self." PMLA 88, no. 1 (Jan.):41-51.
             Points out a progressive flight from self-
        identity and a shift in tone from humor to
        desperation in Beckett's fiction. The
        protagonist gradually retreats from the
        physical world to the inner world of con-
        sciousness, the various stages of this
        evolution are illustrated by Murphy, Three
        Novels, Stories and Texts for Nothing, and
        How It Is. See 1977.23.

25   *DAVIES, RUSSELL. "Shades of Grey." Observer,
        16 Dec., p. 23.
             Source: French XX Bibliography, no. 26
        (1974); unverified.

26   DOBREZ, LIVIO. "Samuel Beckett's Irreducible."
        Southern Review: An Australian Journal of
        Literary Studies 6, no. 3 (Sept.):205-22.
             Studies the significance of the gradual
        reduction of subject matter in Beckett's
        works and the artist's obscure task of
        "speaking in such a way that nothing is
        expressed and that what is expressed is
        nothing."

27   *DUCKWORTH, COLIN. "All the Little Time, All
        the Little Strength: Samuel Beckett at 67."
        New Zealand Listener 73, no. 1,757:10-11.

28 DUKORE, BERNARD F. "Krapp's Last Tape as
    Tragicomedy." Modern Drama 15, no. 4
    (Mar.):351-54.
        Notes that Krapp's Last Tape combines
    visual and verbal comic techniques with a
    traditional tragic pattern. Reprinted:
    1980.25.

29 EGEBAK, NIELS. L'Ecriture de Samuel Beckett:
    Contribution à l'analyse sémiotique de textes
    littéraires contemporains. Copenhagen:
    Akademisk Forlag, 124 pp.
        Undertakes a semiotic study of the
    contemporary novel, in particular the works
    of Samuel Beckett: Murphy, the trilogy, and
    the short prose texts ending with Têtes-
    mortes. Egebak examines the trend in modern
    literature in which the "récit" is absorbed
    by the current discourse of the writer in the
    act of writing. He describes the "récit" and
    "discours" individually and then their
    interaction. Followed by a general biblio-
    graphy.

30 ESSLIN, MARTIN. "Not I/Krapp's Last Tape."
    Plays & Players 20, no. 6 (Mar.):39-40.
        Points out differences in the New York and
    London performances of Not I and describes
    the visual imagery and recurring themes of
    the play: the problem of the self, the
    nature of human personality and conscious-
    ness, old age, guilt, and scenes from
    everyday life. Esslin also briefly reviews
    the production of Krapp's Last Tape at the
    Royal Court Theatre.

31 FEDERMAN, RAYMOND. "Life in the Cylinder."
    Fiction International, no. 1 (Fall), pp. 113-
    117.
        Reviews The Lost Ones, in which Beckett
    for the first time confronts us with "an
    entire tribe of strange, voiceless, anony-
    mous, living creatures." A metaphor for
    humanity and the creative process, the

external reality.

32   FERRIMAN, ANNABEL. "Television Helps Students
      Visualize Beckett Plays." Times Higher
      Education Supplement (London), 30 Nov., p. 6.
      Due to the problems of teaching play-
      wrights such as Beckett whose works rely on
      visual effect or music for their impact, the
      British Universities Film Council has set up
      a group of audio-visual experts and teachers
      to explore the use of visual media in the
      teaching of drama.

33   FISCHER, ERNST. "Beckett's Endgame." In
      Existentialist Philosophy. Edited by James
      Gould and Willis H. Truitt. Encino, Calif.
      and Belmont, Calif.: Dickenson Publishing
      Co., pp. 296-302.
      Describes Endgame from the point of view
      of the struggle between master and servant:
      "... Who is going to checkmate whom? Or will
      it be just stalemate or a draw? Hamm cannot
      live without Clov. Can Clov live without
      Hamm?"

34   FRIEDMAN, MELVIN J. "Review-Essay: Samuel
      Beckett and His Critics Enter the 1970's."
      Studies in the Novel 5, no. 3 (Fall):383-99.
      Summarizes the recent criticism of
      Beckett's works: general studies, special-
      ized studies, books devoted in part to
      Beckett, and collections of essays.

35   *GIDAL, PETER. "Beckett and Art." Books and
      Bookmen 8, no. 3, Issue no. 87 (June):32-36.
      Source: French XX Bibliography, no. 26
      (1974); unverified.

36   GODARD, COLETTE. "En attendant Godot (en
      Bourgogne)." Monde, 1 Feb., p. 27.
      Reviews Waiting for Godot at the Théâtre
      de Bourgogne: director Michel Humbert
      proposes numerous new interpretations for
      Godot and demonstrates the possible rapports
      between the characters.

37   GREGORY, HORACE. "The Dying Gladiators of
     Samuel Beckett." In <u>Spirit of Time and
     Place</u>. New York: W.W. Norton & Co., pp.
     256-64.
          Reprint of 1956.17, 1961.32.

38   HAYMAN, RONALD. <u>Samuel Beckett</u>. London:
     Heinemann, 80 pp.
          As part of a series on contemporary
     playwrights, this critical study presents a
     general introduction to Beckett's plays
     (<u>Waiting for Godot</u>, <u>Endgame</u>, <u>All That Fall</u>,
     <u>Krapp's Last Tape</u>, <u>Embers</u>, <u>Happy Days</u>, <u>Words
     and Music</u>, <u>Cascando</u>, <u>Play</u>, <u>Eh, Joe</u>, and <u>Film</u>)
     and describes the evolution of "an individual
     style and an extraordinary individual
     theatrical vocabulary for translating
     [Beckett's] vision into concrete stage
     terms."

39   "In Brief." <u>New Republic</u> 168, no. 4 (27
     Jan.):29-30.
          Finds <u>The Lost Ones</u> remarkable because it
     excludes so much yet still remains readable:
     "it seems just an extension of Beckett's
     attempt to purify literature of irrelevan-
     cies. By his standard, a work becomes more
     successful as it says less about personali-
     ties, more about moods and relationships."

40   JOHNSON, DANIELLE C. "La Cruauté dans l'oeuvre
     de Samuel Beckett." <u>Présence Francophone</u>,
     no. 7 (Autumn), pp. 40-53.
          Compares three elements in the avant-garde
     dramas of Beckett, Ionesco, and Pinter:
     cruelty, violence, and suffering. Examples
     of Beckett's theatre are taken from <u>Endgame</u>
     and <u>Waiting for Godot</u>.

41   KANTRA, ROBERT A. "Beckett's Little Voices of
     Conscience." <u>Journal of Popular Culture</u> 6,
     no. 4 (Spring):731-39.
          Proposes that Beckett's plays may be as

simple as they seem on the surface: "that
is, the form of miming, song and dance, the
vehicle for the simplest forms of satire in
Vaudeville, burlesque, revue, or the 'more
naive and sentimental art of the music-
hall.'"

42   KENNER, HUGH. A Reader's Guide to Samuel
      Beckett. New York: Farrar, Straus and
      Giroux; London: Thames and Hudson, 208 pp.
        Presents a textual analysis of the poems,
      plays, novels, and prose pieces: Waiting for
      Godot, early poems and stories, Murphy, Watt,
      Mercier and Camier, the trilogy, Stories and
      Texts for Nothing, Endgame, Krapp's Last
      Tape, How It Is, Happy Days, Play, radio and
      television productions, Film, Come and Go,
      The Lost Ones, "Enough," "Imagination Dead
      Imagine," "Ping," and "Lessness."

43   *KILLINGER, JOHN. The Fragile Presence.
      Transcendance in Modern Literature. Phila-
      delphia: Fortress Press.

44   "Kindred Spirits." Sunday Times (London), 14
      Jan., p. 28.
        Reviews the production of Not I at the
      Royal Court Theatre. Billie Whitelaw's
      experiences and impressions of the play are
      described: "Not I is a 15 minute monologue
      in which an elderly woman recounts her
      disastrous life story, but because she's
      unable to accept the weight of its misery,
      repeatedly pretends that it's all happened to
      someone else."

45   KINGSTON, JEREMY. "Theatre." Punch 264 (24
      Jan.):124.
        Reviews Not I and Krapp's Last Tape in
      which Beckett conveys the experience of the
      mind desperate to express itself, to communi-
      cate its sensations even though its attempts
      may be partial, misleading or contradictory.

46   KNAPP, BETTINA.   "Interview with Roger Blin."
      Studies in Twentieth Century, nos. 11-12
      (Spring/Fall), pp. 1-20.
            Reprinted: 1975.64.

47   KNAPP, ROBERT S.   "Samuel Beckett's Allegory of
      the Uncreating Word."   Mosaic 6, no. 2
      (Winter):71-83.
            Points out that Beckett's fiction displays
      many characteristics of allegory: 1) the
      metaphysical and almost religious air in
      which the characters move, 2) biblical
      allusions, 3) a sense of layeredness -- the
      narrators appear to be acting out someone
      else's story, and 4) the endlessness of
      Beckett's repetitions.

48   KOCH, STEPHEN.   "The Manhattan Project."   World
      2, no. 12 (5 June):71-72.
            Reviews the Manhattan Project's production
      of Endgame directed by Andre Gregory. The
      new production portrays the "power" of
      Beckett's drama, yet feels the company's
      "environmental" set and the "obsessive"
      character of the American actors portraying
      Hamm and Clov who have transformed "Beckett's
      resonantly mute Irish despair and immobili-
      ty."

49   McHUGH, ROGER.   "Counterparts: Sean O'Casey and
      Samuel Beckett."   Moderna Språk 67, no.
      3:217-22.
            Analyzes the different formations,
      temperaments and language of the two authors
      in the hopes of demonstrating how "they
      reveal together something about the nature of
      dramatic literature and of its theatrical
      function."

50   No entry.

51   MAYER, HANS.   "Brecht, Beckett et un chien."
      Arc, no. 55, pp. 9-15.
            Analyzes Brecht's (Drums in the Night, Act
      IV) and Beckett's (Waiting for Godot, Act II)

use of the popular children's rhyme of the
dog in the kitchen. Beckett plays with a
"dramaturgy of identification" using this
circular refrain of the dog in an ironic
fashion, while Brecht utilizes the refrain to
demonstrate an aspect of the dramatic theory
of alienation effect. Mayer also discusses
Brecht's revised edition of <u>Waiting for
Godot</u>, theorizing that it is possible Brecht
rediscovered the refrain while studying
Beckett's play.

52   MEARES, RUSSELL. "Beckett, Sarraute and the
      Perceptual Experience of Schizophrenia."
      <u>Psychiatry</u> 26:61-69.
          Believes the works of Beckett and Sarraute
      include descriptions of emotional and
      perceptual states which may be successive
      stages in the development of schizophrenia.
      Meares offers a general discussion of their
      works, focusing on specific issues: anxiety,
      the search for silence, the domination by
      stimuli, change of meaning, emotional
      disconnection, hallucination, thought
      disorder, and catatonia.

53   MOOD, JOHN J. "Samuel Beckett's Impasse-
      Lessness." <u>Ball State University Forum</u> 14,
      no. 4 (Autumn):74-80.
          Discusses the "impasse" Beckett ex-
      perienced after having completed the trilogy
      as a "paradigm of the human situation in our
      time" and briefly describes the situation in
      "Lessness" as an example of Beckett's work
      after the impasse.

54   MOROT-SIR, EDWARD. "Pascal Versus Wittgenstein
      with Samuel Beckett as the Anti-Witness."
      <u>Romance Notes</u> 15, no. 2 (Winter):201-16.
          Analyzes Pascal's philosophy of language
      as a response to Wittgenstein and Beckett.

55   MURCH, ANNE C. "Tirer l'échelle? <u>Le Dépeupleur</u>
      de Samuel Beckett." <u>French Studies</u> 27, no. 4
      (Oct.):429-40.

Examines Beckett's <u>Lost Ones</u> as a logical
model of a game, which portrays the functioning of human society as it proceeds towards
the "unthinkable end."

56   NIGHTINGALE, BENEDICT. "Mouthpiece." <u>New
     Statesman</u> 85 (26 Jan.):135-36.
         Reviews <u>Not I</u> and <u>Krapp's Last Tape</u> at the
     Royal Court Theatre. Of the two plays he
     finds that <u>Not I</u> is the most moving and can
     be distinguished from most of Beckett's other
     work, as it is more individualized and
     straight forward in its implications.
     Reprinted: 1979.22.74.

57   OAKES, PHILIP and LESLIE GARNER, eds. "Coming
     On: Kindred Spirits." <u>Sunday Times</u> (Lon-
     don), 14 Jan., p. 28.
         Describes rehearsals of <u>Not I</u> and examines
     Billie Whitelaw's emotional response to the
     play.

58   PARK, ERIC. "John J. Mood and the Personal
     System -- A Further Note on Samuel Beckett's
     <u>Watt</u>." <u>PMLA</u> 88, no. 3 (May):529-30.
         In a letter to the editor, corrects John
     Mood's analysis of the "deliberate" errors in
     Samuel Beckett's <u>Watt</u>. See 1971.69.

59   REITER, SEYMOUR. "Submerged Structure in
     Beckett's <u>Waiting for Godot</u>." In <u>World
     Theater. The Structure and Meaning of Drama</u>.
     New York: Horizon Press, pp. 214-28.
         Demonstrates how meaning comes through
     the rhythmic movement of words and images,
     the rhythmic repetitions of words, and the
     patterned use of trivia in <u>Waiting for Godot</u>.

60   "The Residual Beckett." <u>Times Literary Supple-
     ment</u> (London), 12 Oct., pp. 1217-18.
         Examines the "failure" of some of
     Beckett's recently published pieces: <u>The
     Lost Ones</u>, <u>Breath and Other Shorts</u>, <u>Not I</u>,
     <u>First Love</u>. Some of the pieces are attempts
     to break new ground while others seem

somewhat repetitive: "The 'Residua' ...
creates images of states rather than processes, and that is why they cannot be proceeded
with, lead nowhere, and depend on the earlier
fictional process for intelligibility."

61 RICKS, CHRISTOPHER. "The Genius of Beckett."
    Sunday Times (London), 15 July, p. 39.
        Reviews First Love and Not I. Ricks
    comments on Beckett's translation of First
    Love from French to English, and then focuses
    on the mouth's self-deception and self-
    incrimination in Not I.

62 SCHLOSSBERG, EDWIN. Einstein and Beckett: A
    Record of an Imaginary Conversation with
    Albert Einstein and Samuel Beckett. New
    York: Links, 125 pp.
        Underlines the crucial relationship of
    observer and observed as this "imaginary
    conversation between one of the world's
    greatest thinkers and one of its most
    perceptive writers helps define not just the
    world we live in but also the way we live in
    it and can live in it." Followed by a
    selected bibliography.

63 SCHULTZ, HANS-JOACHIM. This Hell of Stories: A
    Hegelian Approach to the Novels of Samuel
    Beckett. The Hague: Mouton, 117 pp.
        This comparison of the works of Beckett
    and Hegel serves a dual purpose: to clarify
    the "absurdism" of Beckett's novels and to
    show it is like the Hegelian dialectic in
    that it is not a pure negativity. Schultz
    applies this criterion to various forms of
    the Beckett paradox, the absurdity of the
    self, of time, of art, of life and death.
    Comparisons are also made to Descartes and
    James Joyce.

64 SILVER, SALLY THRUN. "Satire in Beckett: A
    Study of Molloy, Malone Dies, and The
    Unnamable." Essays in French Literature 10
    (Nov.):82-99.

Believes Beckett follows Ronald Paulson's general definition of the satirist. Silver demonstrates how Beckett uses traditional satiric techniques to destroy social order, good manners, love, and philosophical systems.

65 SINGH, RAM SEWAK. "Samuel Beckett." In <u>Absurd Drama 1945-1965</u>. Delhi: Hariyana Prakashan, pp. 27-57.

Analyzes Beckett's works for the stage and radio: <u>Waiting for Godot</u> (static condition, time, irony, meaningless wait, suicide, cruelty of couple), <u>Endgame</u> (wait for death, comparison with <u>Hamlet</u>, world as womb, allegory of Beckett-Joyce relationship, fundamental questions of human existence), <u>All That Fall</u> (miniature of every man's journey from birth to death), <u>Embers</u> (sense of alienation), <u>Krapp's Last Tape</u> (feeling of loneliness), and <u>Happy Days</u> (man's will to live in face of death).

66 SORELL, WALTER. "Gorky and Beckett: Bitterness and Despair." <u>Cresset</u> 36, no. 3 (Jan.):23-25.

Whereas Gorky believed God is man's invention, "Beckett is preoccupied with interpreting God's silence in an existential manner ..." Beckett interprets this silence by creating "moral landscapes." Sorell briefly describes <u>Happy Days</u>, <u>Krapp's Last Tape</u>, <u>Act Without Words</u> and <u>Not I</u>.

67 STERNLICHT, SANFORD. "Samuel Beckett." In <u>British Winners of the Nobel Literary Prize</u>. Edited by W.E. Kidd. Norman, Okla.: University of Oklahoma Press, pp. 237-65.

Describes the awarding of the Nobel Prize by the Swedish Academy and reviews Beckett's major literary achievements, his dramas, novels, and poetry, briefly outlining the characters, themes, and situations portrayed in order to explain his impact and impor- tance: "No other living writer has better

expressed the existential loneliness of
contemporary Western man, the absurdity of
the illusions by which he drags himself
through his daily life, the depth of the
silent suffering everywhere, and the ul-
timately pitiful and pitiless truth of the
human condition."

68   TARRAB, GILBERT. "Samuel Beckett ou le langage
      en miettes." In Le Théâtre du nouveau
      langage. Vol. 1. Essai sur le drame de la
      parole. Montreal: Cercle du livre de
      France, pp. 207-301.
          Examines Beckett's theatrical works from
      the point of view of his creation of a new
      language for the theater: the failure of
      words to communicate, the lack of punctua-
      tion, the dislocation of time and space, the
      resolution of the plot, the use of gestures,
      the language of objects, and the use of
      lights. Tarrab comments on Beckett's
      contemporaries Arthur Adamov, Jean Tardieu,
      Jean Genet, and Antonin Artaud, and demon-
      strates the appearance of Artaud's ideas in
      Beckett's plays.

69   TOSCAN, RICHARD. "MacGowran on Beckett."
      Theatre Quarterly 3, no. 11 (July-Sept.):15-
      22.
          Portrays MacGowran's working relationship
      with Beckett in this interview: his affinity
      for Beckett's work, Beckett as a director,
      MacGowran's development of the role of
      Vladimir, the problems presented by Endgame,
      the compulsions of everyday life, the
      utilization of the television, the influence
      of Chaplin and Keaton, Beckett as an optimist
      and realist, and the problems of translation.

70   *WARD, NICOLE. "For Samuel Beckett: Notes
      Towards Silence." Delta (Spring), pp. 32-33.

71   WEIGHTMAN, JOHN. "Spool, Stool, Drool."
      Encounter 40, no. 4 (Apr.):37-38.
          Reviews Krapp's Last Tape and Not I

performed at the Royal Court Theatre by
Albert Finney and Billie Whitelaw.

72   ZILLIACUS, CLAS. "Samuel Beckett and His
       'Whoroscope.'" Moderna Språk 67, no. 1:4-6.
       Presents the circumstances under which
     Beckett wrote 'Whoroscope', the subject of
     the poem, two critics' reactions to it and
     Beckett's attitude toward it.

                         1973-1974

1   ROSE, GILBERT J. "On the Shores of Self:
       Samuel Beckett's Molloy -- Irredentism and
       the Creative Impulse." Psychoanalytic Review
       60, no. 4 (Winter):587-604.
       Believes Beckett's art (specifically
     Molloy) provides the opportunity to ex-
     perience the primary union of mother and
     child and the rebirth of early forms of self
     and world.

                           1974

1   ATLAS, JAMES. "The Prose of Samuel Beckett:
       Notes from the Terminal Ward." Poetry
       Nation, no. 2, pp. 106-17.
       Discusses the continuing spareness of
     Beckett's writing, the solitude and the motif
     of illness. Beckett's fiction is compared to
     that of Joyce, Proust, Flaubert, and Baude-
     laire. Reprinted: 1975.6.

2   ANDERSON, IRMGARD ZEYSS. "Samuel Beckett's Oh
       les beaux jours in the Light of the Bible."
       Cimarron Review, no. 26 (Jan.), pp. 39-41.
       Views Winnie's behavior as the essence of
     an ideal Christian relationship in marriage.
     He also suggests that the play may use the
     metaphor of marriage to symbolize the
     relationship between God and man.

3   BLACKSTOCK, MARY L.   "Jean-Paul Sartre and
     Samuel Beckett."   Language Quarterly 12, nos.
     3-4:44-50.
          Compares three themes in Beckett's Waiting
     for Godot and Sartre's The Flies: man's
     search for identity, his function in society,
     and the "penetration of the very fabric which
     constitutes that society."   While both
     writers view the human condition as irration-
     al and express man's despair at the discovery
     of a meaningless universe, there are basic
     differences in the presentation of their
     dramas: Sartre uses the conventional devices
     of representational drama, Beckett, on the
     other hand, uses structural devices of
     presentational drama to express his philo-
     sophy.

4   BLOCK, HASKELL M.   "Mallarmé and the Material-
     ization of the Abstract in the Modern Drama."
     In Aux sources de la vérité du théâtre
     moderne.   Edited by James B. Sanders.   Paris:
     Minard, pp. 41-51.
          Compares the role of the abstract in
     Mallarmé's theory of drama with the works of
     Ghelderode, Genet and Beckett: "... each of
     these playwrights has had to confront the
     same opposition that Mallarmé faced, between
     theater as spectacle and theater appealing to
     the mind or inward eye, and all of them have
     been concerned, both in their dramatic theory
     and in their plays, with the materialization
     of the abstract."

5   *BLYE, ROBERT.   "Some Versions of Pastoral."
     Guardian, 3 Oct., p. 10.

6   BOOTH, WAYNE C.   "Infinite Instabilities,"   In A
     Rhetoric of Irony.   Chicago and London:
     University of Chicago Press, pp. 253-77.
          Deals with the ambiguities of Beckett's
     kind of irony: "Instead of self-pity, the
     works convey a positively bouncy verve, a
     joyfully rich inventiveness that is an

inseparable part of the ironic reconstruc-
tions we are invited to make." Booth refers
to Albee, Socrates and Plato.

7   BOULAIS, VERONIQUE. "Samuel Beckett: Une
     écriture en mal de je." <u>Poétique</u> 17:144-32.
          Beginning with <u>Molloy</u>, Beckett has chosen
     to use the first person as the subject of his
     narratives. Boulais remarks that it was at
     this time that Beckett began to write the
     things that he "felt."

8   BRATER, ENOCH. "Beckett, Ionesco, and the
     Tradition of Tragicomedy." <u>College Litera-
     ture</u> 1, no. 2 (Spring):113-27.
          Believes Beckett has used comedy to
     express the incoherence and disorder in the
     world around him: "Humor could be anarchic,
     disruptive, and threatening. It fulfilled no
     expectation and respected no taboo; it could
     achieve its effects in turmoil, riot, and
     shock." Similarily the dislocation of
     language could be expressed through humour,
     since laughter is based on incongruities. In
     order to demonstrate the theoretical basis
     for Beckett's works, Brater considers the
     ideas of Antonin Artaud presented in <u>The
     Theater and its Double</u> and the concepts of
     Eugène Ionesco revealed in his <u>Fragments of a
     Journal</u> and <u>Notes and Counter Notes</u>.

9   _____. "The Empty Can: Samuel Beckett and Andy
     Warhol." <u>Journal of Modern Literature</u> 3, no.
     5 (July):1255-64.
          Compares Beckett and Warhol, showing that
     their resemblance stems from their deemphasis
     of the artist and the work of art in order to
     force the reader or spectator to confront
     himself through the artistic catalyst they
     have provided.

10   _____. "The 'I' in Beckett's <u>Not I</u>." <u>Twentieth
     Century Literature</u> 20, no. 3 (July):189-200.
          Considers the situation of the protagonist
     in <u>Not I</u>: the character's inability to

clearly remember past events, the disin-
heritance of the first-person singular, the
dissolution of self, the parallel between the
disconnected psychological state and Jungian
theory, and the mouth as an image of fragmentation and destruction. See 1981.1.

11   _____. "Noah, Not I, and Beckett's 'Incompre-
hensibly Sublime'" Comparative Drama 8, no.
3 (Fall):254-63.
        Traces possible biblical references to the
history of Noah in Beckett's Endgame and Not
I.

12   BRUNS, GERALD L. "The Storyteller and the
Problem of Language in Samuel Beckett's
Fiction." In Modern Poetry and the Idea of
Language. A Critical and Historical Study.
New Haven: Yale University Press, pp. 164-
85.
        Studies the problem of the function of
language, as a central theme in Beckett's
novels: "It derives from the opposition
between the pensum to speak and the impossibility of speech imposed by the dissocia-
tion of words and things, and even more from
the increasing inability of these story-
tellers to establish among words relationships of a kind that will generate deter-
minate discourse."

13   BUSI, FREDERICK. "Creative Self-Deception in
the Drama of Samuel Beckett." Research
Studies 42:153-60.
        Uses the question of Godot's function in
Waiting for Godot to examine the concept of
self-deception. In this context Busi views
Gogo and Didi as examples of schizophrenic
personality and compares Didi's final
disavowal of Gogo's intuition to Sartre's
description of "mauvaise foi" in L'Etre et le
néant.

14   _____. "Naming Day in No-Man's-Land: Samuel
Beckett's Use of Names in Waiting for Godot."

Boston University Journal 22, no. 1:20-29.
Attempts to demonstrate that "the multiple
meanings of character names indeed reinforce
Beckett's esthetics of deliberate equivocal-
ness and ambiguity. And far from detracting
from the central theme of waiting, these
titles may actually shed light upon the
ultimate object of the tramps' vigil." Busi
believes that the four main characters of the
play are different aspects of a dismembered
personality, and as such, are open to
numerous interpretations which would further
illustrate the ambiguity of Beckett's work.

15 _____. "Waiting for Godot: A Modern Don
Quixote?" Hispania 57, no. 4 (Dec.):876-
85.
Presents the similarities and differences
of character, theme, detail, myth and purpose
in Cervantes' Don Quixote and Beckett's
Waiting for Godot.

16 CLURMAN, HAROLD. "Edward Albee. The Zoo Story
and Beckett's Krapp's Last Tape." In The
Divine Pastime. New York: Macmillan, pp.
107-9.
Examines the plays as studies in loneliness.

17 _____. "Samuel Beckett." In The Divine
Pastime. New York: Macmillan, pp. 63-65.
Reviews Waiting for Godot. Clurman feels
that although despair and disenchantment are
at the heart of the play, Beckett offers a
vaudeville show on the surface, not unlike
the traditional commedia dell'arte.

18 _____. "Samuel Beckett. Happy Days." In The
Divine Pastime. New York: Macmillan, pp.
119-24.
Describes the "lives" of the characters in
Happy Days and the irony and repressed
tenderness expressed by Beckett.

Briefly reviews Jack MacGowran's one-man
show consisting of excerpts from Beckett's
novels, plays, prose pieces and poems.

19   COLLINS, P.H. "Proust, Time and Beckett's Happy
      Days." French Review 47, no. 6 (Spring):105-
      19.
           Believes Beckett could be writing a
      "dramatized commentary on Proust's work" in
      Happy Days. Collins compares Winnie to
      Proust's Tante Léonie, analyzing the use of
      the Proustian themes of time, habit and
      memory, and discussing the essential dif-
      ferences between the two works.

20   CORDERO, ANNE D. "Waiting, an Ambivalent Mood,
      in Beckett and Ionesco." Studies in the
      Twentieth Century, no. 13 (Spring), pp. 51-
      63.
           Feels that both authors convey "waiting"
      as an ambivalent notion to express the
      futility and senselessness of man's exis-
      tence. Beckett (Waiting for Godot) and
      Ionesco (La Soif et la faim) portray the
      tragic image of modern man: the irrelevance
      of time and place, the impossibility of
      happiness and man's absurd hope.

21   CURRIE, ROBERT. "Beckett's Transcendental
      Nihilism." In Genius. An Ideology in
      Literature. New York: Schochen; London:
      Chatto and Windus, pp. 171-93.
           Points out the ambiguity of Beckett's
      aesthetic theories when applied to his own
      works. Currie examines four topics fundamen-
      tal to a study of the balance of form and
      content in Beckett's writings: the world of
      habit, the failure of knowledge, existence
      and non-existence, nihilism and non-expres-
      sion.

22   DOBREZ, LIVIO. "Beckett and Heidegger:
      Existence, Being and Nothingness." Southern
      Review: An Australian Journal of Literary
      Studies 7, no. 2 (July):140-53.

Compares Heidegger's philosophy to the
world of Beckett: existence as being in the
world, the concept of existential "angst,"
existence and being, and being and nothingness.

23 _____. Beckett, Sartre and Camus: The Darkness
and the Light." <u>Southern Review: An
Australian Journal of Literary Studies</u> 7, no.
1 (Feb.):51-63.
Compares and contrasts the works and
philosophies of Sartre and Camus. Dobrez
comments on: the "en soi" and the "pour
soi," existential freedom vs. Beckettian
freedom, nausea, the absurd, and human
relations.

24 ESSLIN, MARTIN. "Worth the 'Wait.'" <u>Books and
Bookmen</u> 19, no. 9 (June):91-92.
Reviews <u>Texts for Nothing</u>, discussing some
of the recurring themes from Beckett's works
that appear in these short prose texts: the
exploration of the nature of the Self, the
quest for the loss of the Self, Beckett's
ability to laugh at the hopelessness of the
human condition, the beauty of the language,
and the power of the images.

25 ESTESS, TED L. "The Inenarrable Contraption:
Reflections on the Metaphor of Story."
<u>Journal of the American Academy of Religion</u>
42:415-34.
Examines the fate of the Metaphor of Story
in Beckett's fiction, demonstrating how
Beckett's writing exhibits a movement from an
active to a contemplative stance toward the
desire for stories. Estess goes on to
analyze Beckett's art from several different
perspectives: 1) admitting chaos into art,
2) fidelity to finitude and a fascination for
the infinite, 3) descent into the private
world of self, and 4) inaction.

26 GILMAN, RICHARD. "Beckett." <u>Partisan Review</u>
41, no. 1:56-76.

Comments on <u>Waiting for Godot</u>, <u>Endgame</u>,
<u>Happy Days</u>, and <u>Play</u>. Gilman feels that
Beckett's dramas exemplify Camus' definition
of the absurd and that Beckett is obsessed
with man's need to justify his existence:
"The theater in Beckett's hands has abandoned
events, direct clashes, inquiries, represen-
tations. What remains is the theatrical
impulse itself ... the painful necessity to
remain visible."

27   GRAVER, LAWRENCE. "Guides to the Ruins."
     <u>Partisan Review</u> 41, no. 4:622-25.
          Reviews A. Alvarez's <u>Samuel Beckett</u>, Hugh
     Kenner's <u>A Reader's Guide to Samuel Beckett</u>,
     and Samuel Beckett's <u>The Lost Ones</u>. Graver
     describes <u>The Lost Ones</u> as a miniature of
     Beckett's earlier works: "Beckett's Hell has
     always been here and now: a place of precise
     geography, obscure origins, and uncertain
     purpose, inhabited by creatures who seek,
     suffer, fail to find, and cannot stop
     seeking." Reprinted: 1979.22.72.

28   HAYWARD, SUSAN. "Le Rôle du monologue intérieur
     dans les romans de Samuel Beckett." <u>Language
     & Style</u> 7, no. 3 (Summer):181-91.
          Explores Beckett's use of interior
     monologue in his novels. Hayward distin-
     guishes four stages in the evolution of
     Beckett's prose: 1) in <u>Murphy</u> and <u>Watt</u>
     Beckett describes the thoughts of his
     characters; 2) in the <u>Stories</u> and the trilogy
     Beckett evokes the anguish of his characters
     confronted with the impossibility of express-
     ing themselves; 3) in <u>How It Is</u> Beckett
     destroys logical syntax; 4) in <u>Têtes-mortes</u>
     interior monologue is abandoned.

29   HUBERT, RENEE RIESE. "Microtexts: An Aspect of
     the Work of Beckett, Robbe-Grillet and
     Nathalie Sarraute." <u>International Fiction
     Review</u> 1, no. 1:9-16.
          Examines a sampling of the short texts of
     Beckett (<u>Texts for Nothing</u>), Robbe-Grillet

(Instantanés), and Sarraute (Tropismes) in
order to establish a relationship between the
three writers: "in their universe, explora-
tions focus on the ordinary, ... time
sequences disintegrate, ... words regain
their autonomy, ... the void and discon-
tinuity emerge again and again."

30 ISER, WOLFGANG. "Subjectivity as the Autogenous
Cancellation of Its Own Manifestations.
Samuel Beckett: Molloy, Malone Dies, The
Unnamable." In The Implied Reader. Patterns
of Communication in Prose Fiction from Bunyan
to Beckett. Baltimore: John Hopkins
University Press, pp. 164-78.
Studies the theme of subjectivity in the
trilogy: the formulation of the narrators'
observations, the conditions that bring them
out, the tendency to retract or modify
statements made throughout the narrative, the
functioning of consciousness and self-
representation, and the reader's contemplation of his own ideas.

31 _____. "When Is the End not the End? The Idea
of Fiction in Beckett." In The Implied
Reader. Patterns of Communication in Prose
Fiction from Bunyan to Beckett. Baltimore:
John Hopkins University Press, pp. 257-73.
Analyzes the variations on the "end theme"
in Beckett's novels. Iser points out that
the image of the end is a paradox which gives
rise to the creation of fictions. Thus, the
negativeness of Beckett's texts is due to the
fact that they do not satisfy our human needs
-- when we think we have found something to
satisfy our needs, we realize that what we
have found is only a fiction.

32 JACQUART, EMMANUEL C. Le Théâtre de dérision:
Beckett, Ionesco, Adamov. Paris: Gallimard,
313 pp.
After an introductory presentation of the
dramatists and the Théâtre de Dérision,
Jacquart classifies the three authors in the

"tradition" of the avant-garde theater and analyzes their work, presenting themes, structural elements, theatrical forms, rhetorical structures, and structures of communication characteristic of the Théâtre de Dérision. The conclusion situates the writers in the modern theater.

33   JONES, LOUISA. "Narrative Salvation in <u>Waiting for Godot.</u>" <u>Modern Drama</u> 17, no. 2 (June):179-88.
      Establishes Beckett's inconclusiveness and ambivalence about narrative, focusing on the parable of the thieves at Calvary as told by Vladimir to Estragon in <u>Waiting for Godot</u>.

34   *LINDBLAD, ISHRAT. "Towards Understanding 'Pozzo.'" <u>Tidskrift för Litteraturvelenskap</u> 3:279-85.

35   LOWENKRON, DAVID HENRY. "A Case for 'The Tragicall Historie of Hamm.'" <u>Arizona Quarterly</u> 30, no. 1 (Spring):217-28.
      Interprets the role of Hamm in <u>Endgame</u>, arguing that Hamm is indeed a tragic hero.

36   MAYER, HANS. "Brecht's <u>Drums</u>, a Dog, and Beckett's <u>Godot.</u>" In <u>Essays on Brecht. Theater and Politics</u>. Edited by Siegfried Mews and Herbert Knust. Chapel Hill: University of North Carolina Press, pp. 71-78.
      Compares Brecht's and Beckett's use of the story about "A dog (who) came in the kitchen/ and stole a crust of bread," noting differences in their use of the symbolical dog: "Whereas Beckett ironically employed the roundelay about the dog, the cook, and the tomb to serve his dramaturgy of empathy, Brecht felt it to be an especially good example for demonstrating the dramatics and dramaturgy of 'Verfremdung.'"

37   MAYOUX, JEAN-JACQUES. <u>Samuel Beckett</u>. Harlow, England: Longmans Group, Ltd., 1974. 48 pp.

Traces Beckett's literary development from his early poems to his final short prose texts.

38   MAYS, JAMES. "'Pons Asinorum': Form and Value in Beckett's Writing, with Some Comments on Kafka and de Sade." Irish University Review 4, no. 2 (Autumn):268-82.
Evaluates Beckett's "commitment as a writer to the opposition of content and form" and compares his works to those of Kafka and de Sade. Whereas Kafka tended to keep the inexplicable outside of the form, Beckett expressed negation within the form. In de Sade's The 120 Days of Sodom "irreconcilable" content is set against "exact and incongruous" form, as in the works of Beckett.

39   MERCIER, VIVIAN. "Unity of Inaction: Beckett and Racine." Nation 219, no. 5 (31 Aug.):149-51.
Believes Racine's arguments in his prefaces for Bérénice and Britannicus provide a strong defense for Beckett's dramaturgy. Mercier studies Beckett's "neo-classicism," comparing his works with Racine's Bérénice and Andromaque. Reprinted in part: 1977.65.

40   MIRSKY, MARK JAY. "Distilling the Human Pickle." Washington Post Book World, 25 Aug., pp. 1-2.
Reviews First Love and Other Stories, describing his three favorite texts, First Love, "Enough" and "Imagination Dead Imagine." Mirsky points out that Beckett's creatures "... speak not out of despair or exhaustion ... but such awful simplicity, such unsentimental directness, that one sees the dilemma of an existence rooted only in the animal certainties of the present ..."

41   *NYE, ROBERT. "Bikes in Heaven, Cars In Hell." Guardian, 18 Apr., p. 16.

42   OATES, JOYCE CAROL. "Anarchy and Order in

Beckett's Trilogy." In <u>New Heaven, New
Earth: The Visionary Experience in Litera-
ture</u>. New York: Vanguard Press, Inc., pp.
83-95.

Discusses the motif of the creative
consciousness in Beckett's trilogy, Beckett's
use of literalism, and the resemblance of
Beckett's world to that described by David
Hume in his <u>Treatise on Human Nature</u> and his
<u>Inquiry Concerning Human Understanding</u>.

43   ONIMUS, JEAN. "Les Formes de l'insolite dans le
      théâtre de Samuel Beckett." In <u>L'Onirisme et
      l'insolite dans le théâtre français contem-
      porain</u>. Edited by Paul Vernois. Paris:
      Editions Kleincksieck, pp. 119-34.

      Calls attention to the passage from the
      usual to the unusual in Beckett's works,
      denoting a different vision of the world and
      a unique method of perceiving people and
      things. Ominus emphasizes that this point of
      view in Beckett's fiction serves to make one
      aware of the "void" at the core of being, the
      "experience of the extreme," and the inco-
      herence of the human condition.

44   PARKIN, ANDREW. "Monologue into Monodrama:
      Aspects of Samuel Beckett's Plays." <u>Eire-
      Ireland</u> 9, no. 4:32-41.

      Demonstrates how monologue is essential to
      the structure of Beckett's plays: "Beckett
      makes increasing use of the monologue until
      it becomes the whole play, in a reduction so
      austere, that it takes us to the very limits
      of drama and theatre. As the negation of
      dialogue, it becomes another potent form of
      antitheatre."

45   PEARCE, RICHARD. "Enter the Frame." <u>Tri-
      Quarterly</u> 30 (Spring):71-82.

      Traces the development from fiction to
      surfiction, showing that as the narrator
      relinquishes his detached stance and his
      distance from his subject, the resulting
      picture loses its clarity and the medium

takes on an independence of its own. Samuel
Beckett's trilogy completes the transition
from fiction to surfiction and evokes a
"vital and creative sense of personality,
even though all the sources of personality --
the narrator's view and the narrator's voice
-- are denied."

46 PRINCE, GERALD. "Didi, Gogo et le Vaucluse."
    Romance Notes 15, no. 3 (Spring):407-9.
        Shows how the atmosphere of the Vaucluse,
    contrasted with the characters' present
    situation in Waiting for Godot, reinforces
    Beckett's vision of the difficulty of life,
    of being a man.

47 RABINOVITZ, RUBIN. "Style and Obscurity in
    Samuel Beckett's Early Fiction." Modern
    Fiction Studies 20, no. 3 (Autumn):399-406.
        Discusses Beckett's innovations in the
    novel form, brought about by his refusal to
    utilize traditional prose techniques.

48 REID, ALEC. "Samuel Beckett and the Failed Form
    -- An Introduction to Waiting for Godot."
    Forum 11, no. 3 (Winter):54-58.
        Feels Waiting for Godot represents mimetic
    art in its "failed form"; it portrays the
    ignorance and impotence that prevent us from
    "being."

49 RICKS, CHRISTOPHER. "Hide and Seek." Sunday
    Times (London), 13 Oct., p. 36.
        Reviews the recent English translation of
    Mercier and Camier, commenting on the
    "Irishness" of Beckett's translation. Ricks
    feels that Beckett has cut a great deal,
    giving much of the work a new tone.
    Reprinted: 1979.22.68.

50 RODWAY, ALLAN. "There's a Hole in Your Beckett:
    The Inflation of Minimalism." Encounter 42,
    no. 2 (Feb.):49-53.
        Contends that Beckett's work is overrated,
    his popularity "inflated": "... his plays

are medieval in their assumption that the end
of life is the whole life, that if there is
no purpose or reason beyond life there cannot
be any purposes or reasons with it -- false
conclusions, both of them."

51 SHENKER, ISRAEL. "Samuel Beckett," In Words
    and Their Masters. New York: Doubleday and
    Co., pp. 196-99.
       Quotes Beckett on his life and work.

52 SKERL, JENNIE. "Fritz Mauthner's 'Critique of
    Language' in Samuel Beckett's Watt."
    Contemporary Literature 15, no. 4
    (Autumn):474-87.
       Shows that Fritz Mauthner's 'Critique of
    language' provides the meaning for Watt's
    quest, while the theories of Ludwig Wit-
    tgenstein and logical positivism are of
    lesser importance than previously supposed.

53 SMITH, FREDERICK N. "The Epistemology of
    Fictional Failure: Swift's Tale of a Tub and
    Beckett's Watt." Texas Studies in Literature
    and Language 15, no. 4 (Winter):649-72.
       Argues that Swift's influence on Beckett
    was most critical during the composition of
    Watt, a turning point in the evolution of
    Beckett's fiction: "A Tale of a Tub showed
    him how to use a fractured literary structure
    and style in order to question the effects of
    literary form, the relationship between form
    and experience, and beyond -- the very
    possibility of human knowledge."

54 SMITH, STEPHANIE POFAHL. "Between Pozzo and
    Godot: Existence as Dilemma." French Review
    47, no. 5 (Apr.):889-903.
       Examines the dilemma of uncertainty in
    Waiting for Godot represented by a passage
    from St. Augustine referring to the two
    thieves. Smith extends the question of
    Christian salvation to include all of human
    existence. She analyzes the roles of the

characters, their attitudes, and the symbolism of Godot.

55   SOBOSAN, JEFFREY G. "Time and Absurdity in
      Samuel Beckett." Thought 49, no. 192
      (Mar.):187-95.
          Evaluates Beckett's attempts to solve the
      "riddle" of the individual man's insigni-
      ficance and mortality. Sobosan believes the
      most serious problem confronted in Beckett's
      work is that of escaping time: "For Beckett,
      the Néant within is the microcosmic self and
      it is striving toward the Nothing of the
      Void. The Self which exists (or non-exists)
      in nothingness ... is that which Beckett sees
      as the goal with which to equate the in-
      dividual's identity." Beckett's notion of
      the void is contrasted with traditional
      religious beliefs.

56   *SPRAGGINS, MARY. "Beckett's Molloy as Detec-
      tive Novel." Essays in Literature 2, no.
      2:11-33.
          Source: Annual Bibliography of English
      Language and Literature, 1974;unverified.

57   *STEVENS, IRMA NED. "Beckett's Texts for
      Nothing: An Inversion of Young's Night
      Thoughts." Studies in Short Fiction 11, no.
      2 (Spring):131-39.
          Examines the influence of the eighteenth-
      century school of graveyard writing on
      Beckett's Texts for Nothing. Stevens notes
      that Beckett alludes to the title of Edward
      Young's poem Night Thoughts in Text VIII.
      However, similar images and themes in these
      works lead toward opposing visions: Young's
      narrator views death in anticipation of an
      afterlife, while Beckett's characters seek
      the oblivion of death for its own sake.

58   SZANTO, GEORGE H. "Samuel Beckett: Dramatic
      Possibilities." Massachusetts Review 15, no.
      4 (Autumn):735-61.
          Discusses three modes of critique that

pertain to Beckett's work: 1) the search for
meaning, 2) the search for form, 3) dramatic
art in an Age of Technological Retention.
Szanto emphasizes the third mode of critique,
pointing out that Beckett's plays contribute
to the audience's desire for possible change.

59   *VIGNAL, PHILIPPE de. "Théâtre: Un soir tard
      d'ici quelque temps." Art Vivant, no. 51
      (July-Aug./Sept.), p. 31.

60   WICKER, BRIAN. "Samuel Beckett and the Death of
      the God-Narrator." Journal of Narrative
      Technique 4, no. 1 (Jan.):62-74.
      Documents the evolution in narrative form,
      language, meaning, time, and the narrator's
      representation of his setting in Beckett's
      prose works form Murphy to The Lost Ones.

61   ZILLIACUS, CLAS. "Scoring Twice: Pinget's La
      Manivelle and Beckett's The Old Tune."
      Moderna Språk 68, no. 1:1-10.
      Notes that when Beckett translates works
      by other writers he usually stays closer to
      the original than he does in renditions of
      his own works -- with one exception, The Old
      Tune, Beckett's "Dublinese" version of
      Pinget's play, La Manivelle. Zilliacus
      studies the two versions of the play, noting
      that Beckett has preserved the "meaning,
      mood, and feeling" of the play.

62   ZINMAN, TOBY SILVERMAN. "Readers' Queries:
      Measurements in Beckett's The Lost Ones."
      Notes and Queries 219, no. 10 (Oct.):377.
      Briefly questions the discrepancy in the
      dimensions of the cylinder of The Lost Ones
      in the French and English versions.

1975

1   ABBOTT, H. PORTER. "A Poetics of Radical
      Displacement: Samuel Beckett's Coming Up to
      Seventy." Texas Studies in Literature and

<u>Language</u> 17, no. 1 (Spring):219-38.
Uses the theory of radical displacement to
distinguish the works up through "From an
Abandoned Work" (1957) from the works that
follow. Abbott defines radical displacement
as "a literary strategy that ostensibly
denies expectations generated by a particular
form." Despite the fact that Beckett uses
radical displacement in his earlier works, he
utilizes a more direct treatment that is
missing in the more recent works, such as <u>How</u>
<u>It Is</u>, in which radical displacement "has
become a mode of structural containment."
Special emphasis is placed on <u>How It Is</u>, <u>Not</u>
<u>I</u>, <u>The Lost Ones</u>, "Imagination Dead Imagine,"
and "Enough."

2   _____. "King Laugh: Beckett's Early Fiction."
In <u>Samuel Beckett: A Collection of Criti-</u>
<u>cism</u>. Edited by Ruby Cohn. New York:
McGraw-Hill, pp. 51-62.
Studies Beckett's early fiction: <u>More</u>
<u>Pricks than Kicks</u>, <u>Murphy</u>, and <u>Watt</u>. Abbott
comments on their differences, tone, humor,
setting, and characters.

3   ALTER, JEAN. "Vers la mathématexte au théâtre:
en codant Godot." In <u>Sémiologie de la</u>
<u>représentation: Théâtre, télévision, bande</u>
<u>dessinée</u>. Edited by André Helbo. Paris:
Presses Universitaires de France, pp. 42-60.
Analyzes the fundamental structure of
<u>Waiting for Godot</u> by examining the external
and internal rapports between the two
dramatic unities of the play Vladimir/
Estragon and Pozzo/Lucky and the changes that
take place through time.

4   *ANDRADE, BEATRIX. "Madeleine Renaud retrouve
Beckett." <u>Express</u>, 31 Mar.-6 Apr., p. 32.

5   ASMUS, WALTER D. "Beckett Directs Godot."
<u>Theatre Quarterly</u> 5, no. 19 (Sept.-Nov.):19-
26.
Beckett's assistant for the production
describes the dramatist at work as a director

at the Schiller Theater in Berlin, recording
Beckett's explanations, interpretations, and
dialogues with the actors.

6   ATLAS, JAMES. "The Prose of Samuel Beckett:
    Notes from the Terminal Ward." In Two
    Decades of Irish Writing. A Critical Survey.
    Edited by Douglas Dunn. Chester Springs,
    Pa.: Dufour Editions, pp. 186-96.
         Considers the "spareness and economy" of
    Beckett's most recent works and the influence
    of Joyce, Proust, Baudelaire and Ireland on
    Beckett's work. Reprint of 1974.1.

7   AUSTER, PAUL. "From Cakes to Stones. Mercier
    and Camier [...]." Commentary 60, no. 1
    (July):93-95.
         Reviews Mercier and Camier, examining the
    rhythm and style of the text, the movement
    and conversations of the characters.

8   AVIGAL, SHOSHANA. "Beckett's Play: The
    Circular Line of Existence." Modern Drama
    18, no. 3 (Sept.):251-58.
         Studies the deceptive spatial grouping of
    the three characters, the spot light, and the
    audience in Beckett's Play.

9   BAIR, DEIDRE. "While Waiting for Godot." New
    York Times Book Review, 9 Mar., p. 19.
         Claims that Mercier and Camier reflects a
    time of depression and indecision in
    Beckett's life culminating with his final
    break and move to Paris in 1937. Bair feels
    this work marks the first step toward
    Beckett's mature fiction and is in many ways
    a precursor of Waiting for Godot.

10 *"Beckett au Conservatoire ..." Figaro, 22-23
    Feb., p. 21.
         Source: French XX Bibliography, no. 28
    (1976);unverified.

11 BILLINGTON, MICHAEL.   "Greenwich Theatre:
    Krapp's Last Tape." Guardian, 4 Dec., p. 10.

Reviews Max Wall's superb performance as
Krapp, emphasizing his comic sense, his
visual appropriateness for the role, and his
ability to portray the 69-year-old Krapp and
his youthful counterpart on tape.

12   BISHOP, TOM. "Camus and Beckett: Variations on
     an Absurd Landscape." Proceedings of the
     Comparative Literature Symposium (Texas Tech.
     Univ.) 8:53-69.
          Compares and contrasts the climactic
     oppositions in the works of Camus and
     Beckett, with special emphasis on Endgame,
     Happy Days, Waiting for Godot, How It Is, The
     Lost Ones, Ping, Krapp's Last Tape, First
     Love and Molloy.

13   BOYLE, KAY. "All Mankind Is Us." In Samuel
     Beckett: A Collection of Criticism. Edited
     by Ruby Cohn. New York: McGraw-Hill, pp.
     15-19.
          Describes meeting Beckett in 1930 and
     their discussion of sanity and insanity and
     her initial interpretation of Waiting for
     Godot as an evaluation of the French plight
     during World War II.

14   *BRADBY, D[AVID][H.] "Structures, dérision et
     théâtre ouvert." Français au Nigeria 10, no.
     3:16-22.

15   BRATER, ENOCH. "The 'Absurd' Actor in the
     Theater of Samuel Beckett." Educational
     Theater Journal 27, no. 2 (May):197-207.
          Explores the absurd figure in Beckett's
     theater. Brater feels that Beckett's
     characters are confronted with a level of
     absurdity that goes beyond the philosophical
     absurdity Camus described in The Myth of
     Sisyphus: "Within his familiar medium, now
     made unfamiliar to him, the actor must
     undergo physically on stage (not only
     emotionally) the same spirit of painful
     dislocation the man in the audience takes a
     lifetime to travel."

16   _____. "Brecht's Alienated Actor in Beckett's
        Theater." <u>Comparative Drama</u> 9, no. 3
        (Fall):195-205.
              Compares and contrasts the dramatic
        techniques of Beckett and Brecht. Whereas
        both authors base their works on intellectual
        or philosophical images, their presentation
        of their ideas on stage vary greatly:
        Brecht's theater is expansive, while
        Beckett's theater is reductive.

17   _____. "Dada, Surrealism, and the Genesis of
        <u>Not I</u>." <u>Modern Drama</u> 18, no. 1 (Mar.):49-
        59.
              Discusses the genesis of the play <u>Not I</u>,
        comparing it to Tristan Tzara's <u>The Gas
        Heart</u>, and Salvador Dali's film "un chien
        andalou."

18   _____. "Not Going Places." <u>New Republic</u> 172,
        no. 10 (8 Mar.):25-26.
              Believes the publication of <u>Mercier and
        Camier</u> provides the missing link in Beckett's
        literary creation. Brater describes the
        novel as a journey in words, a series of
        sudden encounters dictated by the laws of
        chance.

19   _____. "The Thinking Eye in Beckett's <u>Film</u>."
        <u>Modern Language Quarterly</u> 36, no. 2
        (June):166-76.
              Acknowledges that <u>Film</u> recapitulates in
        cinematic terms many of Beckett's literary or
        dramatic preoccupations.

20   BUSI, FREDERICK. "Joycean Echoes in <u>Waiting for
        Godot</u>." <u>Research Studies</u> 43:71-87.
              Demonstrates Joyce's influence on the
        writing of <u>Waiting for Godot</u>: "Joyce and
        Beckett strive to produce the effect of a
        unity of opposites by means of a sophisti-
        cated dramatic handling of circumlocutions
        primarily through comedy and parody, and only
        secondarily through philosophy."

21 CHALKER, JOHN. "The Satiric Shape of <u>Watt</u>." In
   <u>Beckett the Shape Changer.</u> Edited by
   Katharine Worth. London and Boston:
   Routledge and Kegan Paul, pp. 21-37.
   Considers some of the ways the satiric
   form is established in <u>Watt</u> and the effects
   of that form on the reader's relationship to
   the narrator and his story, with comparisons
   to the works of Sterne, Swift, and Sartre.
   See 1975.102.

22 COCKERHAM, HARRY. "Bilingual Playwright." In
   <u>Beckett the Shape Changer</u>. Edited by
   Katharine Worth. London and Boston:
   Routledge and Kegan Paul, pp. 141-57.
   Discusses several questions raised by
   Beckett's bilingualism: whether the transla-
   tions are to be regarded as works of art,
   Beckett's French style, differences between
   the French and English versions of the plays,
   and why Beckett chose to write in French.
   See 1975.102.

23 COHN, RUBY. "<u>Godot</u> par Beckett à Berlin."
   <u>Travail Théâtral</u> 20 (Summer):124-28.
   Describes the Schiller Theater's production of <u>Waiting for Godot</u>, directed by
   Beckett. Beckett's preparations, altera-
   tions, technical difficulties, and the
   symmetry of the text are presented.

24 _____, ed. "Inexhaustible Beckett: An Introduction." In <u>Samuel Beckett: A Collection
   of Criticism</u>. New York: McGraw-Hill,
   pp. 1-13.
   Summarizes the themes, situations, and
   characters of Beckett's prose and dramatic
   works through <u>How It Is</u> as an introduction to
   this collection of criticism. Cohn includes
   a chronology of Beckett's life and work (pp.
   vii-xvi) and a selected bibliography of books
   in English (pp. 137-38).

25 COOK, BRUCE. "Their One-Night Stands Serve
   Those Who Only Wait." <u>National Observer</u>, 22

Feb., p. 32.
Reviews an unusual production of Waiting
for Godot performed at prisons in Florida by
Bacchus Productions. The experience of
seeing a play in a prison, the reaction of
the audience, the use of southern dialect,
the effect of the fast pace of the production, and Pozzo's role being played by a
woman are examined.

26   COPELAND, HANNAH CASE. Art and the Artist in
      the Works of Samuel Beckett. Paris: Mouton
      and Co., 229 pp.
      Comments on the role of the artist and the
      dual significance of art as both creative act
      and created object. Copeland points out that
      Beckett feels it is the function of art to
      eliminate extraneous detail in order to
      reveal the truth: "the miserable emptiness
      and the utter futility of the human condi-
      tion."

27   COVENEY, MICHAEL. "Greenwich Theatre. Krapp's
      Last Tape." Financial Times, 4 Dec., p. 3.
      Describes Max Wall's outstanding perfor-
      mance in Krapp's Last Tape, directed by
      Patrick Magee.

28   *"Culture ... Les Grands Prix Nationaux." Monde
      [des Livres], 19 Dec., p. 14.

29   *CUSHMAN, ROBERT. "From Frayn to Beckett."
      Observer, 16 Mar., p. 29.

30   DIAMOND, ELIN. "'What? ... Who? ... No! ...
      She': The Fictionalizers in Beckett's
      Plays." In Samuel Beckett: A Collection of
      Criticism. Edited by Ruby Cohn. New York:
      McGraw-Hill, pp. 111-19.
      Studies three of Beckett's protagonists as
      they fictionalize their withdrawal from the
      reality of the present, Hamm in Endgame,
      Winnie in Happy Days, and Mouth in Not I:
      "For all three storytellers, the fictions are
      an attempt to supply what is lacking in their

actual existence: for Hamm, the ability to
end; for Winnie, the ability to act and
effect action, for the Mouth, the ability to
ojectify experience. The fictions are heroic
attempts, but they are, finally, failures.

31   *DICKIE, JAMES. "<u>Waiting for Godot</u>." <u>Isis</u>,
      6 Feb., p. 21.

32   DODSWORTH, MARTIN. "<u>Film</u> and the Religion of
      Art." In <u>Beckett the Shape Changer</u>. Edited
      by Katharine Worth. London and Boston:
      Routledge and Kegan Paul, pp. 163-82.
          Evaluates the "failure" of <u>Film</u>: the
      problems with the scenario, the realization
      by Schneider, and the quality of Beckett's
      work, with comparisons to John Cage's
      "Lecture on Nothing" and Beckett's <u>Eh Joe</u>.
      Dodsworth also shows <u>Film</u>'s affinities with
      oriental religion, Sartre's philosophy, and
      Proust's <u>Remembrance of Things Past</u>. See
      1975.102.

33   DOLAN, T.P. "A Note on "-ot" in <u>Godot</u>."
      <u>Language Quarterly</u> 14, nos. 1-2 (Fall-
      Winter):44.
          Suggests that the suffix -ot may be a
      modification of "wot" (ME-knows) which would
      indicate that "godot" means "God knows."
      Thus the play "tells us that the human mind
      can never hope to find out what is going to
      happen, because this is a piece of informa-
      tion which God always keeps to himself."

34   ELIOPULOS, JAMES. <u>Samuel Beckett's Dramatic</u>
      <u>Language</u>. The Hague and Paris: Mouton, pp.
      131.
          This concise description of Beckett's
      dramatic style is developed through three
      phases: 1) an examination of the rhetorical
      poetic elements (author, purpose, audience
      and occasion, method, medium, and subject
      matter); 2) a portrait of Beckett's literary
      development followed by an interpretation of
      the modern theatre movement; and 3) an

analysis of Beckett's dramatic language from
a structural approach. In conclusion these
stylistic qualities are assessed as they
impose upon dramatic situation, ideas, and
characters. A select bibliography is
included.

35   ELSOM, JOHN. "Clowning with Beckett."
     Listener, 11 Dec., p. 801.
          Praises Max Wall's performance in Krapp's
     Last Tape. Elsom feels that Wall has two
     qualities that enable him to succeed in this
     role: he has the skills of a good clown, and
     he shares Beckett's compassion for the human
     condition and can convey it to us. Reprinted:
     1980.28.

36   _____. "Filing Sand." Listener, 20 Mar., pp.
     390-91.
          Reviews Happy Days at the Old Vic,
     pointing out the visual and emotional aspects
     of the play: "it represents the slow
     sensation, not just of growing old, but of
     becoming gently buried by habits and
     memories."

37   ERICKSON, JOHN D. "Alienation in Samuel
     Beckett: The Protagonist as Eiron."
     Perspectives on Contemporary Literature 1,
     no. 2 (Nov.):62-63.
          Feels that Beckett's protagonist resembles
     the "eiron" or "ironical man" Aristotle
     describes in Book Four of the Nicomachean
     Ethics. Erickson examines the transfor-
     mation of the Beckettian protagonist from an
     apparently tragic figure to a nearly comic
     one in Murphy.

38   ESSLIN, MARTIN. "Alienation in Brecht, Beckett,
     and Pinter." Perspectives on Contemporary
     Literature 1, no. 1 (May):3-21. Beckett:
     pp. 18-19.
          Claims that Brecht exemplifies the Marxist
     meaning of alienation, Pinter demonstrates a
     fear of an unspecified alienation, and

Beckett provides "the supreme example of alienation."

39   _____. "Samuel Beckett and the Art of Broad-
        casting." Encounter 45, no. 3 (Sept.):38-46.
            Gives a detailed account of Beckett's work
        for broadcasting, his four plays for radio
        and their eventual production on the BBC's
        Third Programme, the broadcast of a number of
        Beckett's stage works, and his television
        play Eh Joe. Reprinted: 1980.29.

40   FINNEY, BRIAN. "'Assumption' to 'Lessness':
        Beckett's Shorter Fiction." In Beckett the
        Shape Changer. Edited by Katharine Worth.
        London and Boston: Routledge and Kegan Paul,
        pp. 63-83.
            Demonstrates the consistency of Beckett's
        works through an examination of: "Assump-
        tion," More Pricks than Kicks, First Love,
        "The Expelled," The End," "The Calmative,"
        Texts for Nothing, "Imagination Dead
        Imagine," "Enough," The Lost Ones, "Ping,"
        and "Lessness." Provides a selective
        bibliography of Beckett's shorter fiction.
        See 1975.102.

41   FLETCHER, JOHN. "Beckett as Poet." In Samuel
        Beckett: A Collection of Criticism. Edited
        by Ruby Cohn. New York: McGraw-Hill, pp.
        41-50.
            Reprinted: 1976.51.

42   GEBHARDT, RICHARD C. "Technique of Alienation
        in Molloy." Perspectives on Contemporary
        Literature 1, no. 2 (Nov.):74-84.
            Defines Beckett's techniques of alienation
        in Molloy: 1) the offensiveness of the
        characters, 2) the use of a misleading
        structure, 3) the employment of a disoriented
        time-frame, 4) the intrusion of self-
        conscious creating artists between the reader
        and the narrative, 5) the lack of credi-
        bility.

43   GLICKSBERG, CHARLES I.   "Samuel Beckett: The
     Cosmic Nihilist."   In The Literature of
     Nihilism.   Lewisburg, Pa.:   Bucknell Univer-
     sity Press; London: Associated Press, pp.
     234-45.
         Describes Beckett as a metaphysical
     novelist and the literary nihilist "par
     excellence":   "Dedicated to the elaboration
     of the single theme of failure, he reveals
     the pointlessness of life, the insignificance
     of man vis-à-vis the universe, and the
     importance of art."   Using Watt as an example
     Glicksberg demonstrates Beckett's attempt to
     portray the experience of Nothingness, the
     absolute of despair, the absurdity of
     existence, man's alienation from reality, the
     breakdown of communication and the collapse
     of the religious absolute.

44   GRAY, PAUL.   "Preparing for Godot."   Time 105
     (24 Mar.):78-79.
         Notes that Mercier and Camier differs from
     the works Beckett has published since,
     because it retains many elements of tradi-
     tional fiction: plot, ambulatory characters,
     and "'glimmers' of recognizable settings."

45   HARDY, BARBARA.   "The Dubious Consolations in
     Beckett's Fiction: Art, Love, and Nature."
     In Beckett the Shape Changer.   Edited by
     Katharine Worth.   London and Boston:
     Routledge and Kegan Paul, pp. 107-38.
         Examines the themes of art, love and
     nature as sources of meaning and pleasure in
     Beckett's fiction, with references to Sterne,
     Swift, Keats, Coleridge, and Stevens.   See
     1975.102.

46   HASSAN, IHAB.   "Joyce-Beckett: A Scenario in 8
     Scenes and a Voice."   In Paracriticisms:
     Seven Speculations of the Times.   Urbana:
     University of Illinois Press, pp. 63-73.
         Reprint of 1970.58, 1972.36.

47   _____. "Joyce, Beckett, and the Postmodern
        Imagination." TriQuarterly 34 (Fall):179-
        200.
            Contrasts the "two antithetical ways of
        the imagination" represented by Joyce and
        Beckett: "One, in high arrogance, invents
        language anew, and makes over the universe in
        parts of speech. The other, in deep humil-
        ity, restores to words their primal empti-
        ness, and mimes his solitary way into the
        dark." Hassan distinguishes modernism from
        postmodernism, makes a hypothetical distinc-
        tion within postmodernism, between its closed
        (pessimistic) and its open (optimistic)
        tendencies, and then questions the authority
        or popularity of Beckett's fiction.

48   HAYWARD, SUSAN. "Two Anti-Novels: Molloy and
        Jacques le fataliste." In Studies in
        Eighteenth Century French Literature. Edited
        by J.H. Fox, M.H. Waddicor,and D.A. Watts.
        Exeter: University of Exeter Press, pp. 97-
        107.
            Takes issue with the manner in which
        Beckett and Denis Diderot question the role
        of language and the novel, revealing their
        thoughts on the nature of language and its
        limitations, the use of a voyage as an
        obvious literary artiface, the questioning of
        the verity of the novel, the attempt to get
        closer to the inexpressible element in man,
        the obsession with objects, and the use of
        faltering language and circular structure to
        create a simultaneity of past, present and
        future.

49   _____. "The Use of Refrain in Beckett's Plays."
        Language and Style 8, no. 4 (Fall):284-92.
            Emphasizing the value of poetic language,
        focuses on the stylistic elements in
        Beckett's plays: "Beckett is trying to
        create a new awareness of language, to give
        it a more exact value through the use of
        basic sounds and simple rhythms, and one key
        device ... is the refrain."

50   HEISTEIN, JOZEF. "Le Roman de Beckett et les
      extrèmes du naturalism." Romanica Wratis-
      laviensia 10, no. 264:129-41.
           Traces the evolution of the art of
      narration in the trilogy, analyzing the
      Beckettian universe and the characters.
      Heistein compares Beckett's technique of the
      novel to that of naturalism. He demonstrates
      how Beckett alters the naturalist's vision to
      suit his own ends: instead of describing a
      concrete reality submitted to scientific
      observation, he presents a precarious reality
      or the contrary of reality.

51   HOBSON, HAROLD. "Private Lives." Sunday Times
      (London), 14 Dec., p. 33.
           Describes Patrick Magee's "Beckett
      Evening" in which he gave readings from
      Molloy, Malone Dies, "From an Abandoned
      Work," First Love and More Pricks Than Kicks.
      Hobson feels that Magee's voice is well
      suited to Beckett's prose and capable of
      great comic effects.

52   HOKENSON, JAN. "Three Novels in Large Black
      Pauses." In Samuel Beckett: A Collection of
      Criticism. Edited by Ruby Cohn. New York:
      McGraw-Hill, pp. 73-84.
           Analyzes the bleak world of dissolution
      portrayed in the trilogy: "After world,
      body, and even language dissolve, there
      remains being, undefined and unnamed but
      manifestly present in anguished rhythms,
      bitter comic tones, and sheer unending will
      to be."

53   *HOLMES, JANE. "Waiting for Godot." Cherwell
      151, no. 3 (5 Feb.):6.

54   ISAAC, DAN. "Beckett directs Godot in West
      Berlin." New York Times, 8 June, sec. 2, pp.
      1, 5.
           Criticizes Beckett's production of Godot
      at the Schiller Theater. Isaac feels that
      the "older Beckett-as-director does not

understand the younger Beckett-as-play-
wright," specifically citing the changes in
the scene which includes Lucky's speech.

55   ISER, WOLFGANG. "The Pattern of Negativity in
      Beckett's Prose." <u>Georgia Review</u> 29, no. 3
      (Fall):706-19.
           Utilizes Sartre's definition of negativity
      as "a concrete negativity that retains for
      itself that which it rejects, and is com-
      pletely colored by it." Iser believes that
      Beckett's continual use of negated statements
      in the trilogy becomes a method of communica-
      tion, "a structure of bringing forth -- at
      least potentially -- infinite possibilities."

56   JANVIER, LUDOVIC. "Place of Narration/Narration
      of Place." In <u>Samuel Beckett: A Collection
      of Criticism</u>. Edited by Ruby Cohn. New
      York: McGraw-Hill, pp. 96-110.
           Establishes two related kinds of place in
      Beckett's fiction: 1) the "place of narra-
      tion" -- where the actual telling takes
      place, and 2) the "narration of place" --
      where the landscapes, characters and
      activities are situated. Beckett's prose
      works are divided into five categories: A)
      <u>More Pricks than Kicks</u>, <u>Murphy</u>, <u>Watt</u>, <u>Mercier
      and Camier</u> (extratextual location, witness as
      narrator, etc.), B) <u>Stories</u> (extratextual
      location, first person narrator), C) <u>Molloy</u>,
      <u>Malone Dies</u>, <u>The Unnamable</u>, <u>Texts for Nothing</u>
      (intratextual location, first person nar-
      rator), D-1) "From an Abandoned Work," <u>How
      It Is</u>, "Enough" (extratextual location, first
      person narrator), D-2) "Imagination Dead
      Imagine," <u>The Lost Ones</u>, "Ping," "Lessness"
      (extratextual location, nonparticipating
      narrator). Janvier provides a table to
      follow the story and the system of designa-
      tion of place.

57   *JOHNSON, PATRICIA J. <u>A Gallery of Mirrors:
      Mask and Reality in Contemporary French
      Theater</u>. Parma: CEM, pp. 85-98.

58   *JULIET, CHARLES.   "Rencontre avec Bram Van
       Velde: Propose recueillis par Charles
       Juliet." Exit, nos. 6-7 (Winter), pp. 47-52.

59   KANTERS, ROBERT.   "Beckett: Ce que dit la
       bouche d'ombre." Express, 21-27 Apr., p. 16.
         Reviews the production of Not I at the
       Théâtre d'Orsay with Madeleine Renaud.
       Kanters feels that it is the image of the
       human condition that is presented -- all
       projects and memories are in vain, there is
       no more solitude since there is no one, no
       more despair since hope is inconceivable.

60   KELLMAN, STEVEN G.   "Beckett's Fatal Dual."
       Romance Notes 16, no. 2 (Winter):268-73.
         Points out the emphasis on dualities in
       the trilogy, with references to Descartes and
       Proust.

61   KENNEDY, ANDREW K.   "Beckett." In Six
       Dramatists in Search of a Language. Studies
       in Dramatic Language. London: Cambridge
       University Press, pp. 130-64.
         Defines Beckett's language as basically
       private: "words germinate in the skull of
       the speaker, at an inestimable distance from
       things and other persons, motive and argu-
       ment, local time and place." Kennedy
       discusses several aspects of the theoretical
       and practical concerns of Beckett's dramatic
       language: the deterioration of language,
       "dead" language, language games, parody,
       tediousness, memory, rhythmic and tonal
       effects, and dialogue vs. monologue.

62   KENNER, HUGH.   "Shades of Syntax." In Samuel
       Beckett: A Collection of Criticism. Edited
       by Ruby Cohn. New York: McGraw-Hill, pp.
       21-31.
         Focuses on Beckett's interest in the shape
       of sentences, as opposed to Joyce in whose
       works syntax provides a neutral background
       for the words it produces: "The business of
       a Beckett narrator is to order what he is

narrating. That means, to frame sentences,
to assert that tidy control. With each novel
his plight has grown more difficult. The
narrator of Murphy ... played facile games
... By contrast the narrator of How It Is
attacks this kind of problem head on, and
attacks no other."

63   KLEIN, THEODORE M. "Classical Myth and Sym-
      bolism in Camus and Beckett." Proceedings of
      the Comparative Literature Symposium (Texas
      Tech. University) 8:187-200.
         Traces the concept of the persona back to
      the ancient Greeks, especially Aeschylus, and
      then explores the fate of the persona in the
      works of Camus and Beckett.

64   KNAPP, BETTINA. "Roger Blin." In Off-Stage
      Voices. Interviews with Modern French
      Dramatists. Edited by Alba Amoia. Troy, New
      York: Whitston Publishing Co., pp. 21-40.
         Points out the major differences between
      theatre of Beckett and Genet and the dif-
      ferences in their directing techniques. Blin
      contrasts the way Beckett, Genet, and Ionesco
      depict the anxieties of our day and the
      possibilities for their theatre in the
      future. Reprint of 1973.46.

65   KRANCE, CHARLES. "Alienation and Form in
      Beckett's How It Is." Perspectives on
      Contemporary Literature 1, no. 2 (Nov.):85-
      103.
         Emphasizes Beckett's alienation of the
      creative impulse from the object of its
      creation. The alienation of the narrative
      consciousness performs a dual function: 1)
      it limits the realm of experience to the act
      of narrating, 2) it creates a metaphoric
      relationship between what is speaking and
      what is spoken.

66   _____. "L'Ouvre-boîte et la conscience narra-
      tive dans Comment c'est." Saggi 14:483-517.
         Examines the narrative voice in How It Is

from the point of view of the narrator's possessions, his "voyage," the system in which he operates, the doubling of the narrator's voice, his need of communication, his forward progression, allusions to a fourth part, and the significance of the can opener.

67   KROLL, JACK. "Far from Broadway." Newsweek 85, no. 14 (7 Apr.):80-82.
      Reviews Play, Come and Go, and The Lost Ones. Kroll finds David Warrilow's single-handed performance of Beckett's non-dramatic prose piece The Lost Ones the most "original and magical of all Beckett productions."

68   *LERRANT, JEAN-JACQUES. "En attendant Godot à Lyon." Figaro, 14 Mar., p. 29.
      Source: French XX Bibliography, no. 29 (1977);unverified.

69   LEVY, ERIC P. "The Metaphsyics of Ignorance: Time and Personal Identity in How It Is." Renascence 28, no. 1 (Autumn):27-38.
      Passes through four stages of inquiry in order to discern the interpretive principle of How It Is: 1) the origin and structure of allegory in the book, 2) the consistency of time, 3) the dissolution of personal identity, and 4) the impossibility of interpersonal relationships.

70   McMILLAN, DOUGALD. "Samuel Beckett." In "Transition." The History of a Literary Era. 1927-1938. London: Calder and Boyars, 303 pp.
      Acknowledges Beckett's contributions to Transition, his critical and philosophical statements which reflect his attitudes toward life and literature, his contribution to the formation of the aesthetic principles of the magazine, and his relationship to James Joyce, Hart Crane, and Eugene Jolas.

71   _____. "Samuel Beckett and the Visual Arts:
        The Embarrassment of Allegory." In Samuel
        Beckett: A Collection of Criticism. Edited
        by Ruby Cohn. New York: McGraw-Hill, pp.
        121-35.
            Notes Beckett's knowledge of art, his
        involvement with artists, his collaborative
        efforts with artists, his critical statements
        in his essays on painting, and the influence
        of the visual arts in his fiction ("A Dream
        of Fair to Middling Women," More Pricks than
        Kicks, Murphy, Watt, trilogy, How It Is,
        "Still", and Beckett's poetry).

72   MODRZEWSKA-WEGLINSKA, RENATA. "La Structure
        temporelle des pièces de théâtre de Samuel
        Beckett." Romanica Wratislaviensia 11, no.
        265:81-90.
            Utilizes I. Slavinska's methods of
        analysis for the classical theater to examine
        contemporary theatrical works and uses the
        notion of epistemological time to establish
        the semantic level of Beckett's plays, that
        is the manner in which the characters
        understand and experience time. The cyclical
        structure of Beckett's plays creates an
        impression of an infinite duration of action
        or of a mechanism that is impossible to stop.

73   MURPHY, VINCENT J. "Being and Perception:
        Beckett's Film." Modern Drama 18, no. 1
        (Mar.):43-48.
            Develops Beckett's personalized use of the
        dictum "Esse est percipi" as a structural
        principal for his work: "the relationship
        which is established between the artist and
        his characters in the Proustian aesthetic
        parallels that between the eye and the object
        in Film."

74   NIGHTINGALE, BENEDICT. "Highbrowbeaten." New
        Statesman 89 (21 Mar.):393-94.
            Briefly reviews Happy Days, disagreeing
        with the opinion that it is Beckett's most
        optimistic play: "The point, hardly a subtle

or understated one is that 'happy' people are those who are too oafish or dishonest to recognize the true nature of the world."

75 *NOURRY, PHILLIPPE. "L'Emploi du temps: Le Deuxième Degré." Figaro, 26-27 Apr., p. 21.

76 O'CONNOR, GARRY. "Dislocated Consciousness." In French Theatre Today. London: Pitman Publishing, pp. 51-55.
    Evaluates the human and artistic power of Beckett's fiction: "All Beckett has written is the result of meticulous and conscious choice; never, possibly, has there been a writer who has been so self-conscious, so careful, so unprepared to give anything away, or to let himself go. His work is as much a process of self-concealment as of self-revelation.

77 *OJO, S. ADE. "La Conception beckettienne du héros: L'Anti-héros." Français au Nigeria 10, no. 3:3-15.

78 PAOLUCCI, ANNE. "Waiting for Godot. By Samuel Beckett." Educational Theatre Journal 27, no. 1 (Mar.):118-19.
    Reviews Andrew Traister's production of Waiting for Godot at the 1974 Oregon Shakespearean Festival. Paolucci cites "orchestration" as the secret of Traister's success.

79 PARK, ERIC. "Fundamental Sounds: Music in Samuel Beckett's Murphy and Watt." Modern Fiction Studies 21, no. 2 (Summer):157-71.
    Proposes that Beckett is a "verbal or literary, musician" and examines Beckett's uses of music (in songs, as the substance of metaphor, as an aid to characterization or plot development, or in the arrangement of patterns of language) in the two early novels Murphy and Watt.

80 PEAKE, CHARLES. "The Labours of Poetical Excavation." In Beckett the Shape Changer.

Edited by Katharine Worth. London and
Boston: Routledge and Kegan Paul, pp. 41-59.
    Explores Beckett's attempt "to dig down to
the ideal core of the human creature and ...
[demonstrates] that to fail in attempting the
impossible might, at the same time, be to
succeed in creating genuinely original works
of art which could illuminate through the
process of their vain search, what it is to
be a man." See 1975.102.

81   PEARCE, RICHARD. "Enter the Frame." In
     Surfiction. Fiction Now ... and Tomorrow.
     Edited by Raymond Federman. Chicago:
     Swallow Press, pp. 47-57.
         Outlines the changes in approach that take
     place "... as the narrator relinquishes his
     detached stance and reduces his distance from
     the subject, he can no longer enclose the
     subject within his frame. The medium instead
     of being suppressed, asserts itself as an
     independent and vital part of the subject."
     Pearce feels that Beckett's trilogy completes
     the transition from fiction to surfiction,
     because the narrator's view and his voice are
     called into question, while the medium itself
     dominates the narrator, the characters, and
     the story.

82   REID, ALEX. "From Beginning to Date: Some
     Thoughts on the Plays of Samuel Beckett." In
     Samuel Beckett; A Collection of Criticism.
     Edited by Ruby Cohn. New York: McGraw-
     Hill, pp. 63-72.
         Discusses the circumstances surrounding
     the writing, production, and impact of
     Beckett's dramatic works: Waiting for Godot,
     Endgame, Krapp's Last Tape, Happy Days, Come
     and Go, Breath, Play, and Not I.

83   ROSE, MARILYN GADDIS. "Bilingual Insight:
     Language as Deception in Beckett and Julien
     Green." In Actes du VI<u>e</u> Congrès de l'As-
     sociation Internationale de Littérature
     Comparée/Proceedings of the 6th Congress of

the <u>International Comparative Literature
Association</u>. Edited by M. Cadot, D.H.
Malone, M. Szabolcsi, and M.V. Dimic.
Stuttgart: Erich Bieber, pp. 785-88.
   Looks at the authors' bilingualism,
examining Green's <u>Le Voyageur sur la terre</u>
and Beckett's <u>Malone meurt</u>, both of which
deal with characters who record their
experiences. Rose shows how both authors
transform their works into demonstrations of
language as a barrier to communication.

84   *RUS, MARTYN. "Samuel Beckett: <u>Premier Amour</u>
     /deuxième amour." <u>Rapports-Het Franse Boek</u>
     45, no. 1 (Mar.):1-7.

85   SAGE, VICTOR. "Innovation and Continuity in <u>How
     It Is</u>." In <u>Beckett the Shape Changer</u>.
     Edited by Katharine Worth. London and
     Boston: Routledge and Kegan Paul, pp. 87-
     103.
        In order to analyze the role of innova-
     tions in <u>How It Is</u>, feels that "it is
     necessary to examine the nature of our
     expectations and the role they play in those
     responses." See 1975.102.

86   SCHNEIDER, ALAN. "'Any Way You Like Alan':
     Working With Beckett." <u>Theatre Quarterly</u> 5,
     no. 19 (Sept.- Nov.):27-38.
        Describes his working relationship with
     Beckett over the years, his strict adherence
     to Beckett's texts, the difficulties he has
     experienced in producing the plays, and
     anecdotes from specific productions and
     conversations with Beckett.

87   SCHWARTZ, PAUL J. "Life and Death in the Mud:
     A Study of Beckett's <u>Comment c'est</u>."
     <u>International Fiction Review</u> 2, no. 1
     (Jan.):43-48.
        Analyzes the "adventure" of the narrator
     of <u>How It Is</u>, hypothesizing his death at the
     end of the novel: "Reason entertains him,
     keeps him from perceiving accurately his own

misery, keeps him alive, until the voice
defying logic ... dictates the creature's
death. As he dies, he annihilates along with
himself his false formulations, and nothing
remains in his wake."

88   SHARRATT, BERNARD. "Samuel Beckett: Language
     and Being There." Anglo-Irish Studies 1:1-
     35.
        Compares Beckett's skillful manipulation
     of language as an expression of the uncon-
     scious to various artists, linguists,
     psychologists and philosophers: the Dada-
     ists, Freud, Lacan, Heidegger, Descartes,
     Wittgenstein, Pascal, and T.S. Eliot, citing
     examples from "Whoroscope," Murphy, Watt,
     the trilogy, and Beckett's theater in
     general.

89   SOLOMON, PHILIP. Life After Birth: Imagery in
     Samuel Beckett's Trilogy. University,
     Mississippi: Romance Monographs Inc., 155
     pp.
        Aims to "'elucidate' each of the novels
     and the trilogy as a whole through a study of
     imagery." Five categories of images are
     considered: space, movement, softness,
     light, and animals. These images have been
     selected because of their frequency in the
     texts and because "it is through them that
     the three dimensions of the trilogy --
     existential, epistemological, aesthetic --
     are crystallized." Followed by a select
     bibliography.

90   *SPURLING, HILARY. "Son of Sherlock Holmes."
     Observer, 7 Dec., p. 29.

91   STEIN, WILLIAM BYSSHE. "Beckett's 'Whoro-
     scope': Turdy Ooscopy." ELH 42, no. 1
     (Spring):125-55.
        Discusses "Whoroscope" in detail, its
     meaning and language: Beckett "succeeds in
     transforming nonsense into a chilling
     revelation of sense -- the dreadful awareness

of the gulf that separates word and thing,
expression and reference, thought and
reality."

92   SUTCLIFF, H.L.   "Maeterlinck;'s <u>Les Aveugles</u> and
     Beckett's <u>En Attendant Godot</u>."   <u>Essays in
     French Literature</u> 12 (Nov.):1-21.
          Offers a detailed comparison of the
     playwrights, pointing out the similarities in
     the two works in which they are closest, and
     highlights the Symbolist roots of the avant-
     garde theatre.

93   SUTHER, JUDITH D.   "<u>Godot</u> Surpassed -- Eduardo
     Manet's <u>Holocaustum ou le Borgne</u>."   <u>Research
     Studies</u> 43, no. 1 (Mar.):45-51.
          Proposes that Beckett's play, though
     original at the time of its composition, has
     been surpassed by a more recent drama,
     Eduardo Manet's <u>Holocaustum ou le Borgne</u>.
     Suther contrasts the plays: the theme of the
     human condition in <u>Godot</u> is opposed to that
     of human nature in <u>Le Borgne</u>; the characters
     are opaque in <u>Godot</u> and distinct personality
     sketches in <u>Le Borgne</u>; the tone of <u>Godot</u> is
     "inert," while <u>Le Borgne</u> is full of life and
     action.

94   *TAGLIFERRI, ALDO.   "Mimésis et illusionisme: A
     propos de Joyce et Beckett."   In <u>Psycho-
     analyse et sémiotique</u>.   Edited by Armando
     Verdiglione.   Paris: 10/18 (Union Générale
     d'Editions), pp. 267-79.

95   _____.   "Transition trouvée et subversion de
     l'image chez Beckett."   <u>Tel Quel</u> 64 (Winter):
     81-90.
          Examines "images-concepts" in <u>The Un-
     namable</u>: unnamability, spherical forms, and
     the basic oppositions of light/darkness/,
     silence/speech, and stasis/movement.

96   TAKAHASHI, YASUNARI.   "Fool's Progress."   In
     <u>Samuel Beckett: A Collection of Criticism</u>.
     Edited by Ruby Cohn.   New York: McGraw-Hill,

pp. 33-40.
Analyzes the evolution of the Beckettian fool from More Pricks than Kicks through Not I, pointing out Beckett's achievement in reviving the tradition of the fool and his pronouncement of an end of the cycle: "Beckett's fool is an eschatological fool who appeared at the end of the fool tradition, a 'homo ludens' at the end of the tether, enacting his own death ..."

97 UNTERECKER, JOHN. "Fiction at the Edge of Poetry: Durrell, Beckett, Green." In Forms of Modern British Fiction. Edited by Alan Warren Friedman. Austin: University of Texas Press, pp. 165-99.
Demonstrates ways in which these three novelists parallel other novelists and poets, particularly James Joyce, James Wright, Wallace Stevens, and John Keats. Unterecker examines reality in modern fiction which he feels focuses on the present moment, much as a snapshot or film. Examples are taken from Henry Green's Pack My Bag and Loving, from Lawrence Durrell's Tunc and Nunquam and from Beckett's How It Is.

98 UPDIKE, JOHN. "Small Cheer for the Old Sod." New Yorker 51 (1 Sept.):62-66. Beckett: pp. 62-65.
Describes the journey of Mercier and Camier. Updike believes the novel has a pivotal place in Beckett's canon as the first prose work to be originally written in French: "... it seems to be the first motion of that remarkable postwar exertion whereby Beckett, casting off his native tongue and perhaps thereby moving out from under the shadow of his mentor Joyce, transformed himself ... from a slothful dilettante into a master ..."

99 WARDLE, IRVING. "A too Practiced Clown. Krapp's Last Tape/In Memory of Carmen Miranda Greenwich." Times (London), 4 Dec., p. 13.

Reviews Greenwich's production of <u>Krapp's Last Tape</u>, focusing on the articulation, movements and comic effects of Krapp (played by Max Wall).

100   WEBB, EUGENE. "The Ambiguities of Secularization: Modern Transformations of the Kingdom in Nietzsche, Ibsen, Beckett, and Stevens." In <u>The Dark Dove: The Sacred and Secular in Modern Literature</u>. Seattle, Wa.: University of Washington Press, pp. 34-87. Beckett: pp. 63-76.

Comments on the effects of the secularization of religious visions in the works of Nietzsche, Ibsen, Beckett and Stevens. Some of Beckett's works concentrate on the elements of the desacralized vision while others explore possible avenues of exit from it. <u>Waiting for Godot</u> emphasizes an analysis of the vision, while <u>Endgame</u> considers the possibility that beyond the limited horizon of traditional concepts there may be more to life than man supposed. In <u>Cascando</u> one of Beckett's characters seeks clarity of vision by telling a story about the quest for it and at the end of the play seems almost about to arrive at it. "As Beckett's characters draw closer, whether voluntarily or involuntarily, to the true vision, they have to leave behind every traditional concept of order or authority. This means, naturally, that all traditional imagery of the sacred, along with any analogues to it, such as Mr. Godot, must be deflated, and the characters vision thoroughly secularized."

101   WICKER, BRIAN. "Beckett and the Death of the God-Narrator." In <u>The Story-Shaped World. Fiction and Metaphysics: Some Variations on a Theme</u>. Notre Dame, Ind.: University of Notre Dame Press, pp. 169-83.

Demonstrates that the progressive disappearance of a sane and rational narrator leads to a deterioration of the fictional world into chaos. Wicker draws examples from the novels and plays from <u>Murphy</u> to <u>The Lost Ones</u>, "Ping", and "Lessness".

102 WORTH, KATHARINE, ed. "Introduction." In <u>Beckett the Shape Changer</u>. London and Boston: Routledge and Kegan Paul, pp. 3-18.
Introduces the focal point of the collection of essays, the transformation process: "How Beckett renews and reshapes himself from one form, language, genre, medium to another; how the characters take us into the pains, terrors, and jokes of the reshaping, ... how the illusion draws its strength from being exposed, handled, turned round for us to see how it is done, until finally there is no way of distinguishing how it is done from how it is." The chief concern of the critics is to register the form, tone, and mood of Beckett's prose and dramatic writings. This series of essays originated as a symposium on Beckett organized by Katharine Worth for the University of London Extramural Department. See 1975.21, 1975.22, 1975.32, 1975.40, 1975.45, 1975.80, 1975.85, 1975.103.

103 _____. "The Space and the Sound in Beckett's Theatre." In <u>Beckett the Shape Changer</u>. London and Boston: Routledge and Kegan Paul, pp. 185-218.
Considers the physicality of Beckett's dramatic technique, his handling of space and light in the stage plays, and sound in the radio plays. See 1975.102.

104 ZEIFMAN, HERSH. "Religious Imagery in the Plays of Samuel Beckett." In <u>Samuel Beckett: A Collection of Criticism</u>. New York: McGraw-Hill, pp. 85-94.
Examines religious imagery in Beckett's plays as a pattern which embodies the basic themes of Beckett's work: suffering, death, guilt, judgement, and salvation. Zeifman notes that Biblical imagery provides an ironic counterpoint to Christian

interpretation: "For the thrust of Beckett's religious reference suggests that man is the victim of a heartless metaphysical ruse, trapped in the midst of an alien and hostile world, his life a protracted and painful crucifixion without hope of transcendence."

105   ZILLIACUS, CLAS. Beckett and Broadcasting: A Study of the Works of Samuel Beckett for and in Radio and Television. Abo: Abo Akademi, 223 pp.
        Describes the progress of works for radio and television from initial conception to première on the air and then evaluates their radiogenic or videogenic qualities. Zilliacus also discusses the transposition of certain works to another media, for example radio works being expressed in visual language. Followed by an extensive bibliography.

1976

1   ADMUSSEN, RICHARD. "Samuel Beckett's Unpublished Writing." Journal of Beckett Studies, no. 1 (Winter), pp. 66-74.
        Identifies Beckett's unpublished manuscripts, providing the location (if known), date, number of pages, and content.

2   *AHUJA, CHAMAN. "Beckett's Theater of the Seventies." Panjab University Research Bulletin -- Arts, (Oct.), pp. 75-82.

3   *ARIKHA, AVIGDOR. Samuel Beckett by Avigdor Arikha; A Tribute to Samuel Beckett on His 70th Birthday [Exhibition at the] Victoria and Albert Museum, Feb.-May 1976. 10 p.

4   BAIR, DEIRDRE. "La Vision, enfin." In Samuel Beckett. Edited by Tom Bishop and Raymond Federman. Paris: Editions de l'Herne, pp. 114-19.
        Describes Beckett's writing and publications of the forties. See 1976.11.

5   BARGE, LAURA. "The Empty Heaven of Samuel
     Beckett." Cithara 15, no. 2 (May):3-19.
        Notes an "irreconcilable" religious
     paradox in Beckett's works: his simultaneous
     "rejection of any concept of God coupled with
     his obsession with the God-idea."

6   *BARNES, CLIVE. "Theater. Beckett in Washing-
     ton." New York Times 126, 11 Dec.:15.
        Source: French XX Bibliography, no. 30.
     (1978);unverified.

7   BERENGO, ADRIANO. "Samuel Beckett: 'The Mania
     for Symmetry.'" Gradiva 1, no. 1 (Sum-
     mer):21-37.
        Gives an account of the interdisciplinary
     seminar on the concept of "symmetry"
     sponsored by the Italian commission of UNESCO
     in collaboration with the Giorgio Cini
     foundation. This article deals with
     symmetrical dimension in Beckett's work,
     specifically Molloy's elaborate operation in
     sucking stones.

8   BERNAL, OLGA. "Le Glissement hors du language."
     In Samuel Beckett. Edited by Tom Bishop and
     Raymond Federman. Paris: Editions de
     l'Herne, pp. 219-25.
        Believes Watt provides the true beginning
     for the Beckettian novel, since it is Watt
     that produces a rupture in language: "the
     world is divided in two, man and things on
     one side, and words on the other." See
     1976.11

9   BILLINGTON, MICHAEL. "Waiting for Godot."
     Manchester Guardian Weekly, 2 May, p. 22.
        Reviews Beckett's production of Waiting
     for Godot at the Royal Court Theatre (from
     the Schiller Theatre, Berlin). Billington
     points out that although Beckett highlights
     the comic physical contrast between Gogo and
     Didi, he makes the play "a portrayal of a
     consistently bleak world in which the hope of
     salvation seems equally remote for all."

10   BISHOP, TOM. "Le Pénultième monologue." In
      Samuel Beckett. Edited by Tom Bishop and
      Raymond Federman. Paris: Editions de
      l'Herne, pp. 242-45.
         Briefly analyzes Not I. See 1976.11.

11   BISHOP, TOM and RAYMOND FEDERMAN, eds. Samuel
      Beckett. Paris: Editions de l'Herne, 366 p.
         This series of texts and articles devoted
      to Beckett represents various approaches to
      Beckett's works: extracts, quotations,
      translations, critical articles, influence
      studies, tributes and reminiscences.
      Followed by a chronology and select bibliog-
      raphy. See 1976.4, 1976.8, 1976.10, 1976.12,
      1976.13, 1976.19, 1976.25, 1976.33, 1976.49,
      1976.52, 1976.54, 1976.69, 1976.70, 1976.71,
      1976.72, 1976.77, 1976.82, 1976.85, 1976.90,
      1976.93, 1976.99, 1976.113, 1976.115,
      1976.118, 1976.131, 1976.133, 1976.135,
      1976.143, 1976.148.

12   BLIN, ROGER and TOM BISHOP. "Dialogue." In
      Samuel Beckett. Edited by Tom Bishop and
      Raymond Federman. Paris: Editions de
      l'Herne, pp. 141-46.
         In an interview with Roger Blin, describes
      his productions of Beckett's works, Waiting
      for Godot, Endgame, Krapp's Last Tape, and
      Happy Days, and his discussions with Beckett
      regarding the plays. See 1976.11.

13   BREE, GERMAINE. "Les Abstracteurs de quintes-
      sence de Beckett." In Samuel Beckett.
      Edited by Tom Bishop and Raymond Federman.
      Paris: Editions de l'Herne, pp. 318-25.
         Reprint of 1963.10; see 1976.11.

14   BREUER, HORST. "Disintegration of Time in
      Macbeth's Soliloquy 'Tomorrow and tomorrow,
      and tomorrow.'" Modern Language Review 71,
      no. 2 (Apr.):256-71.
         Uses Beckett's conception of time to help
      determine Macbeth's final situation and state
      of mind.

15   BREUER, ROLF. "The Solution as Problem:
      Beckett's <u>Waiting for Godot</u>." <u>Modern Drama</u>
      19, no. 3 (Sept.):225-36.
          Interprets the structure of <u>Godot</u> in view
      of its possible religious implications and
      its resemblance to theories developed by
      Bertrand Russell, Alfred Tarski, and Ludwig
      Wittgenstein. The problem of "waiting" is
      studied in detail.

16   BRIENZA, SUSAN AND ENOCH BRATER. "Chance and
      Choice in Beckett's 'Lessness.'" <u>Journal of
      English Literary History</u> 43, no. 2 (Summer):
      244-58.
          In their study of the grammar, structure,
      and images of "Lessness," the authors show
      how Beckett has redefined the way language
      communicates.

17   BROOK, PETER. "Dire oui à la boue." In <u>Samuel
      Beckett</u>. Edited by Tom Bishop and Raymond
      Federman. Paris: Editions de l'Herne, pp.
      232-35.
          Defends the "positive" aspects of
      Beckett's <u>Endgame</u> -- Beckett affords the
      spectators no moments of relief. The
      audience faces the play in much the same way
      an individual experiences the situations he
      lives. See 1976.11.

18   BURGHARDT, LORI HALL. "The Bawds of Euphony:
      Images of Women in Beckett's Early Poems."
      In <u>Samuel Beckett: The Art of Rhetoric</u>.
      Edited by Edouard Morot-Sir, Howard Harper,
      and Dougald McMillan III. Chapel Hill:
      Department of Romance Languages, University
      of North Carolina, pp. 151-56.
          Feels that the images of women represented
      in Beckett's early poems are vital to an
      understanding of his mature works: "These
      women provide the careful reader with nascent
      images, they reflect Beckett's evolving
      philosophical concerns, and they undergo a
      parallel diminuation of aim and representa-
      tion through concentration and distillation

that is so apparent in his plays and novels."
See 1976.107.

19   CALDER, JOHN. "La Concentration de Samuel
        Beckett." In <u>Samuel Beckett</u>. Edited by Tom
        Bishop and Raymond Federman. Paris:
        Editions de l'Herne, pp. 162-65.
           Believes Beckett's extraordinary power of
        concentration gives that something special to
        his works. Examples are taken from <u>Happy
        Days</u>, <u>Murphy</u>, "The Vulture," and "Imagination
        Dead Imagine." See 1976.11.

20   _____. "The Royal Court Theatre, London:
        Beckett's 70th Birthday Season." <u>Journal of
        Beckett Studies</u>, no. 1 (Winter), pp. 105-8.
           Criticizes the 1976 production of <u>Endgame</u>
        at the Royal Court Theatre, in which "much of
        the poetry, the tension, the emotion, was
        lost ..." Calder summarizes some of the past
        performances of the play, summarizing the
        situation of the characters, their relation-
        ship to each other, and Beckett's use of
        theology.

21   _____. "'Souffle' de Samuel Beckett." <u>Cahiers
        Renaud-Barrault</u> 93:5-7.
           Reprint of A51.

22   CHABERT, PIERRE. "Beckett as Director." <u>Gambit</u>
        7, no. 28:41-63.
           Describes his personal experiences working
        with Beckett and his production of <u>Krapp's
        Last Tape</u>. Chabert describes the staging of
        Krapp's ritual of recording and listening; a
        musical analogy of the text, the voice, and
        the movement on stage; and the fundamental
        problem of how to make theatrically possible
        a play based on listening. Reprinted:
        1980.14.

23   _____. "Samuel Beckett metteur en scène ou
        répéter <u>La Dernière Bande</u> avec l'auteur."
        <u>Revue d'Esthétique</u>, nos. 2-3, pp. 224-48.
           Relates his personal experiences during

Beckett's direction of <u>Krapp's Last Tape</u> and
examines Beckett's method of producing his
own texts.

24   CIORAN, E.M. "Encounter with Beckett."
      Translated from French by Raymond Federman
      and Jean Sommermeyer. <u>Partisan Review</u> 43,
      no. 2:280-85.
          Records his memories, his conception of
      Beckett's personality, Beckett's relationship
      to his characters, and common traits between
      Beckett and Wittgenstein. Reprinted:
      1979.22.75; see 1976.25.

25   _____. "Quelques Rencontres." In <u>Samuel
      Beckett</u>. Edited by Tom Bishop and Raymond
      Federman. Paris: Editions de l'Herne, pp.
      101-5.
          See 1976.24, 1976.11.

26   CISMARU, ALFRED and THEODORE KLEIN. "The
      Concept of Suicide in Camus and Beckett."
      <u>Renascence</u> 28, no. 2 (Winter):105-10.
          Points out that the concept of suicide
      reveals an unsuspected rapport between Camus
      and Beckett. Whereas both Camus and Beckett
      reject suicide, Camus' rejection represents
      an affirmation of life, while in Beckett the
      distinction between life and death becomes
      blurred thereby invalidating suicide.

27   *COE, RICHARD L. "Arena: Three More by
      Beckett." <u>Washington Post</u>, 18 Sept., p. B2.
          Source: <u>French XX Bibliography</u>, no. 29
      (1977);unverified.

28   *_____. "The Stark Imagery of Samuel Beckett."
      <u>Washington Post</u>, 10 Dec, p. D6.
          Source: <u>French XX Bibliography</u>, no. 30
      (1978);unverified.

29   *_____. "Still <u>Waiting for Godot</u> at Arena
      Stage." <u>Washington Post</u>, 25 Mar., p. C12.
          Source: <u>French XX Bibliography</u>, no. 29
      (1977);unverified.

30   COHN, RUBY. "Beckett's German <u>Godot</u>." <u>Journal of Beckett Studies</u>, no. 1 (Winter), pp. 41-49.
      Examines Beckett's approach to his German productions, in particular his direction of <u>Waiting for Godot</u> at West Berlin's Schiller Theater.

31   _____. "Shakespearean Embers in Beckett." In <u>Modern Shakespeare Offshoots</u>. Princeton, N.J.: Princeton University Press, pp. 375-88.
      Remarks Shakespearean "reminiscences" in Beckett's plays <u>Waiting for Godot</u>, <u>Endgame</u>, <u>Embers</u>, and <u>Happy Days</u>.

32   _____. "Warming Up for My Last Soliloquy." In <u>Samuel Beckett: The Art of Rhetoric</u>. Edited by Edouard Morot-Sir, Howard Harper, and Dougald McMillan III. Chapel Hill: Department of Romance Languages, University of North Carolina, pp. 105-18.
      Discusses the progression of Beckett's drama "toward a last soliloquy, as though the ideal play would be all soliloquy." Dramatic soliloquy and stage situation are examined as they are used in <u>Waiting for Godot</u>, <u>Endgame</u>, and <u>Not I</u>. See 1976.107; reprinted in part: 1977.21.

33   _____. "<u>Watt</u> à la lumière du <u>Château</u>." In <u>Samuel Beckett</u>. Edited by Tom Bishop and Raymond Federman. Paris: Editions de l'Herne, pp. 306-17.
      Reprint of 1961.16; see 1976.11.

34   COPELAND, HANNAH CASE. "The Couples in <u>Comment c'est</u>." In <u>Samuel Beckett: The Art of Rhetoric</u>. Edited by Edouard Morot-Sir, Howard Harper, and Dougald McMillan III. Chapel Hill: Department of Romance Languages, University of North Carolina, pp. 237-47.
      Reveals Beckett's two primary concerns in <u>How It Is</u> demonstrating how Beckett uses the

image of couples to portray the human
condition, and how couples illustrate the
dilemma of the artist. See 1976.107.

35   *CUSHMAN, ROBERT. "First Impressions."
     Observer, 14 Mar., p. 28.

36   _____. "In a Hellish Half-Light." Observer,
     23 May, p. 30.
        Reviews a triple bill of Beckett plays at
     the Royal Court Theatre, Play, That Time, and
     Footfalls: "Common to all three plays are
     the compulsive vomitings of the human voice
     and brain, and the hypnotic effect of thin
     white light." While he praises the perfor-
     mance of Play and Footfalls, Cushman finds
     That Time to be a disappointing rerun of
     Krapp's Last Tape "without the props."
     Reprinted: 1979.22.77.

37   DAVIES, MICHAEL. "Michael Davies' Notebook: Le
     Grand Sam Plays It Again." Observer, 2 May,
     p. 36.
        Describes the Beckett season at the Royal
     Court Theatre, with special reference to
     Billie Whitelaw's performance in Footfalls,
     directed by Beckett. Davies centers most of
     his comments on Beckett's personality,
     appearance and a few biographical notes.

38   DIETRICH, RICHARD F. "Beckett's Goad: From
     Stage to Film." Literature/Film Quarterly 4,
     no. 1 (Winter):83-89.
        Discusses the implicit differences between
     the play Act Without Words II and the film
     version of the play, "The Goad," directed by
     Paul Joyce. He believes that transposing the
     play from one medium to another has changed
     its meaning: "the stage play suggests that
     the condition of A and B is eternal and
     internal" while "the film play implies that
     the plague of impotence and futility that
     renders our existence pointless is a tem-
     porary, largely man-made thing."

39   EHRHARD, PETER. <u>Anatomie de Samuel Beckett</u>.
      Basel: Birkhaüser, 272 p.
      Focuses on an itinerary of physical
      degeneration in Beckett's fiction and
      outlines the significance and various aspects
      of the body and it organs. Followed by a
      bibliography of Beckett's works.

40   EISELE, THOMAS D. "The Apocalypse of Beckett's
      <u>Endgame</u>." <u>Cross Currents</u> 26, no. 1
      (Spring):11-32.
      Investigates the religious aspect of
      <u>Endgame</u> through two "facts" about the play:
      1) Clov is Christ and Hamm is man, and 2) the
      end of the game corresponds to the end of
      Christianity.

41   ELOVAARA, RAILI. <u>The Problem of Identity in
      Samuel Beckett's Prose: An Approach from
      Philosophies of Existence</u>. Helsinki:
      Suomalainen Tiedeakatemia, 301 p.
      Presents the problem of identity in Samuel
      Beckett's prose published up to the end of
      1975. Elovaara approaches the Beckett
      protagonist as a literary illustration of the
      theme of alienation as it is expressed by the
      philosophies of existence. The author takes
      into consideration the writings of Kierke-
      gaard, Nietzsche, Jaspers, Heidegger, Sartre,
      and Camus.

42   ELSOM, JOHN. "Godot's Arrival." <u>Listener</u> 95
      (29 Apr.):545.
      Reviews the Schiller Theatre's "model"
      production of <u>Waiting for Godot</u> (directed by
      Beckett in German) at the Royal Court
      Theatre. Elsom praises the visual quality of
      this production, examines Beckett's theatri-
      cal debt to music-hall, and relates his
      experiences seeing the play in German: not
      understanding German, encourages the viewer
      to "listen to the rhythmic balance of the
      phrases, and to see how they relate to the
      movements, without trying to follow the
      verbal sense as well."

43   _____. "Scraps and Scoops." <u>Listener</u> 95 (27
        May), p. 681.
            Reviews three productions at the Royal
        Court Theatre: <u>Play</u>, <u>That Time</u>, and <u>Foot-</u>
        <u>falls</u>, the latter two world premieres. Elsom
        emphasizes the precise timing and rhythms of
        <u>Play</u>, the memories in <u>That Time</u>, and the
        visual imagery and the guilts and memories
        revealed in <u>Footfalls</u>. Reprinted:
        1979.22.43.

44   ESSLIN, MARTIN. "A Theatre of Stasis --
        Beckett's Late Plays." <u>Gambit</u> 7, no. 28.
        Reprinted: 1980.29

45   _____. "<u>Godot</u>, the Authorized Version."
        <u>Journal of Beckett Studies</u>, no. 1 (Winter),
        pp. 98-100.
            Praises the Schiller Theatre's German
        production of <u>Waiting for Godot</u> at the Royal
        Court Theatre. This production stresses
        broad comic effects, in particular Beckett's
        indebtedness to the silent camera, the
        circus, and the music hall.

46   _____. "Voices, Patterns, Voices: Samuel
        Beckett's Later Plays." <u>Gambit</u> 7, no. 28:93-
        99.
            Demonstrates how Beckett has progressively
        reduced the physical movement of his charac-
        ters in the "monodrames" <u>Not I</u>, <u>That Time</u>,
        and <u>Footfalls</u>. The action of these plays has
        been condensed and intensified by focusing
        the viewer's attention on a part of the body:
        the mouth, eyes, or feet of the character.
        Reprinted: 1976.47.

47   _____. "Voix, schéma, voix." <u>Cahiers Renaud-</u>
        <u>Barrault</u> 93:9-22.
            Reprint of 1976.46.

48   FAHRENBACH, HANNELORE, and JOHN FLETCHER. "The
        'Voice of Silence': Reason, Imagination and
        Creative Sterility in <u>Texts for Nothing</u>."

Journal of Beckett Studies, no. 1
(Winter):30-36.
Demonstrates the disintegration of the
composite portrait of the rational man/crea-
tive poet in the Texts for Nothing.

49   FEDERMAN, RAYMOND. "Le Paradoxe du menteur."
     In Samuel Beckett. Edited by Tom Bishop and
     Raymond Federman.   Paris: Editions de
     l'Herne, pp. 183-92.
          Underlines the flagrant contradictions,
     forgetfulness, and/or ambivalence of
     Beckett's narrators. Examples are taken from
     the trilogy and Texts for Nothing. See
     1976.11.

50   _____. "Samuel Beckett: The Liar's Paradox."
     In Samuel Beckett: The Art of Rhetoric.
     Edited by Edouard Morot-Sir, Howard Harper,
     and Dougald McMillan III. Chapel Hill:
     Department of Romance Languages, University
     of North Carolina, pp. 119-41.
          Illustrates the cancellation of art in
     Beckett's prose works: "The world of Samuel
     Beckett is full of such paradoxes -- delibe-
     rate contradictions which negate every
     possibility of movement, knowledge, under-
     standing, and coherence on the part of the
     creatures that inhabit that world. Yet, the
     more these creatures are immobilized,
     dehumanized, the more they find themselves
     locked into fictional and verbal impasses,
     the more freedom they seem to gain to
     extricate themselves." Reprinted from
     1970.38; see 1976.107

51   FLETCHER, JOHN. "Beckett as Poet: A Second
     Look." Caliban: Annales Publiées par
     l'Université de Toulouse, n.s. 12:125-36.
          Updates his study of Beckett's poetry
     which was included in Martin Esslin's
     "Twentieth Century Views" series. Fletcher
     evaluates what he considers to be "the
     essential Beckett verse," from Echo's Bones
     and Other Precipitates (1935) to Trois poèmes
     (1948). Reprint of 1975.41.

52   _____. "Ecrivain bilingue." In <u>Samuel Beckett</u>.
        Edited by Tom Bishop and Raymond Federman.
        Paris: Editions de l'Herne, pp. 212-18.
            In order to discover some of Beckett's
        reasons for writing in French, Fletcher
        examines his works from the period of
        transition between 1942-1946. See 1976.11

53   _____. "Literature and the Problem of Evil,
        II." <u>Theology</u> 79, no. 672 (Nov.):337-43.
            Believes evil in Beckett's work is a
        metaphysical question rather than a moral
        problem: man's birth is a sin for which he
        is punished his entire life by a "malevolent
        force above God himself." One of Beckett's
        characters, Mr. Rooney in <u>All That Fall</u>,
        attempts to "'pay fate back' for life and for
        the arbitrary nature of the punishment
        represented by existence itself."

54   FRANKEL, MARGHERITA S. "Beckett et Proust: le
        triomphe de la parole." In <u>Samuel Beckett</u>.
        Edited by Tom Bishop and Raymond Federman.
        Paris: Editions de l'Herne, pp. 281-94.
            Discusses Proust's influence on Beckett's
        prose fiction -- sees Beckett as a continua-
        tion of Proust thirty years later. See
        1976.11.

55   FRIEDMAN, MELVIN J. "Introductory Notes to
        Beckett's Poetry." In <u>Samuel Beckett: The
        Art of Rhetoric</u>. Edited by Edouard Morot-
        Sir, Howard Harper, and Dougald McMillan III.
        Chapel Hill: Department of Romance
        Languages, University of North Carolina, pp.
        143-49.
            Likens the literary beginnings of Beckett
        to those of Joyce and Faulkner, who turned to
        poetry before they wrote fiction. Friedman
        briefly reviews several critics' remarks
        about Beckett's poetry, especially Lawrence
        Harvey in his <u>Samuel Beckett Poet and Critic</u>.
        See 1976.107.

56   GILBERT, STEPHEN W.   "Krapp's Last Tape.
     Greenwich."   Plays and Players 23, no. 5
     (Feb.):31-32.
          Offers a detailed description of Max
     Wall's brilliant performance in Krapp's Last
     Tape and then refutes Milton Shulman's review
     of the play in the Evening Standard.

57   GONTARSKI, STANLEY.   "Birth Astride a Grave:
     Samuel Beckett's Act Without Words, I."
     Journal of Beckett Studies, no. 1
     (Winter):37-40.
          Argues that "Act Without Words, I" is not
     obvious or banal, but rather Beckett's most
     concrete portrayal of the birth of existen-
     tial man.

58   GUSSOW, MEL.   "Beckett Continues to Refine His
     Vision."   New York Times, 26 Dec., pp. 22D,
     28D.
          Reviews That Time and Footfalls at the
     Kreeger Theater in Washington: "The plays --
     strange, hypnotic, and exquisite -- are
     organically linked with Beckett's other
     works.   The man in That Time is an older
     Krapp, except in this case the tape recorder
     is in his mind ... The woman in Footfalls is
     a sister both to Winnie ... in Happy Days,
     and to the woman in Not I.   All are trapped
     in a reflexive routine, a holding pattern."

59   _____.   "Exploring Beckett at Public Theater."
     New York Times, 5 Nov., p. 3C.
          Describes a rehearsal of the Mabou Mines
     theater company's production of Cascando at
     Joseph Papp's Public Theater.

60   _____.   "Stage: Beckett's Creative Cascando."
     New York Times, 13 Apr., p. 27.
          Describes the Mabou Mines theater com-
     pany's dramatization of Beckett's radio play
     Cascando, inventing a visual environment to
     match the subject: "seven actors are sitting
     silently around a long table ... each is

obsessively and endlessly involved in a
specific artistic task."

61   HAMILTON, ALICE and KENNETH HAMILTON.
      <u>Condemned to Life: The World of Samuel
      Beckett</u>. Grand Rapids, Michigan: Wm. B.
      Eerdmans Publ. Co., 232 pp.
         Deal with the misery of the human condi-
      tion as "not merely the most obvious theme in
      Beckett but ... also the best clue to
      interpreting his works." Human suffering is
      described in terms of the scope and limita-
      tions of the human consciousness, the failure
      and subsequent ridicule of religion, and the
      chaos of existence. Laughter seems to be the
      only bearable reaction to the pathetic human
      condition as it is presented in the earlier
      works. In the later works, words are all
      that can be salvaged from the "mess." It is
      through Beckett's experimentation with form
      and his efforts to fuse form and content in
      an artistically satisfying way that the
      Hamiltons feel Beckett has made the most
      significant contribution to modern fiction.

62   _____. "The Guffaw of the Abderite: Samuel
      Beckett's Use of Democritus." <u>Mosaic</u> 9, no.
      2 (Winter):1-14.
         Feel that one of Beckett's sources has
      been neglected -- his use of the life and
      thought of Democritus of Abdera, the near-
      contemporary of Socrates: "He draws from
      Democritus that which accords with his
      artist's vision, and here Democritus gives
      him confirmation of his own conviction that
      man faces the Nothing." The following works
      are examined: <u>More Pricks than Kicks</u>,
      <u>Murphy</u>, <u>Echo's Bones</u>, "The Calmative," <u>All
      That Fall</u>, <u>Molloy</u>, <u>Waiting for Godot</u>, <u>The
      Unnamable</u>, and <u>How It Is</u>.

63   HARPER, HOWARD. "<u>How It Is</u>." In <u>Samuel
      Beckett: The Art of Rhetoric</u>. Edited by
      Edouard Morot-Sir, Howard Harper and Dougald
      McMillan III. Chapel Hill: Department of

Romance Languages, University of North
Carolina, pp. 249-70.
    Examines the thematic and formal struc-
tures of How It Is, Beckett's struggle to
"recapture his previous work within an even
more powerful gravitational field."   See
1976.107.

64   HASSELBACK, HANS-PETER.   "Samuel Beckett's
      Endgame: A Structural Analysis."   Modern
      Drama 19, no. 1 (Mar.):25-34.
          Presents Beckett's fusion of form and
      content in Endgame.   Hasselback defines
      Beckett's two-part dramatic structure,
      exemplified by 1) the thematic elements of
      "ending" and "playing," and 2) two modes of
      dramatic tension, the conflict between Hamm
      and Clov, and the characters' inner con-
      flicts.

65   HAYMAN, RONALD.   "Beckett's Godot."   New Review
      3, no. 26 (May):66-67.
          Discusses Beckett's German language
      production of Waiting for Godot at the
      Schiller Theater: the problems of the actors
      and director, the source of the energy and
      comedy in the play, theatrical effects, the
      best moments of the production and Beckett's
      directorial innovations.

66   HESLA, DAVID.   "Being, Thinking, Telling, and
      Loving: The Couple in Beckett's Fiction."
      In Samuel Beckett: The Art of Rhetoric.
      Edited by Edouard Morot-Sir, Howard Harper,
      and Dougald McMillan III.   Chapel Hill:
      Department of Romance Languages, University
      of North Carolina, pp. 11-23.
          Studies the concept of the couple in
      Beckett's prose, the numerous possible
      couples formed in Murphy, in Molloy, and
      finally the "ultimate" couple in Beckett's
      fiction, the one formed by "the impersonal
      consciousness of the unnamable one who is
      speaking the words and the impersonal

consciousness of the unnamable one who is
reading them." See 1976.107.

67   HOBSON, HAROLD. "Men Without God." <u>Sunday</u>
      <u>Times</u> (London), 9 May, p. 38.
          Reviews Beckett's <u>Endgame</u> and Peter
      Shaffer's <u>Equis</u>. Hobson feels both dramas
      answer the question of what shall become of
      mankind when it no longer believes in God.

68   HUBERT, MARIE-CLAUDE. "Primauté du corps dans
      le théâtre de Samuel Beckett." <u>Travaux de</u>
      <u>Linguistique et de Littérature Publiés par le</u>
      <u>Centre de Philologie et de Littératures</u>
      <u>Romanes de l'Université de Strasbourg</u> 14, no.
      2:259-72.
          Stresses the closeness of the Beckettian
      couple, the inability or fear of separation,
      caused in most cases by the physical needs of
      the characters.

69   HUBERT, RENEE RIESE. "A la trace de 'Bing.'"
      In <u>Samuel Beckett</u>. Edited by Tom Bishop and
      Raymond Federman. Paris: Editions de
      l'Herne, pp. 253-58.
          Analyzes "Bing": "Bing" represents the
      last scene where verbal coherence replaces
      plot, where the word replaces the actor, and
      where "bing" starts in motion the vain
      attempt at monologue. See 1976.11

70   IONESCO, EUGENE. "A propos de Beckett." In
      <u>Samuel Beckett</u>. Edited by Tom Bishop and
      Raymond Federman. Paris: Editions de
      l'Herne, pp. 149-51.
          Notes that although the problem of
      existence, that of the metaphysical condition
      of man, may not be able to be solved, at
      least the expression of the problem helps man
      to better understand himself and his situa-
      tion. See 1976.11.

71   JANVIER, LUDOVIC. "Au travail avec Beckett."
      In <u>Samuel Beckett</u>. Edited by Tom Bishop and
      Raymond Federman. Paris: Editions de

l'Herne, pp. 137-40.
   Briefly discusses the translation of <u>Watt</u>
into French. See 1976.11.

72   _____. "Lieu dire." In <u>Samuel Beckett</u>. Edited
by Tom Bishop and Raymond Federman. Paris:
Editions de l'Herne, pp. 193-205.
   Juxtaposes two aspects of place in
Beckett's novels and short prose texts, the
location of the narrator and the narration of
place described by the narrator. See
1976.11.

73   KELLMAN, STEVEN G. "The Self-Begetting Novel."
<u>Western Humanities Review</u> 30, no. 2
(Spring):119-28.
   Proposes to define a sub-genre of the
Modern French, British, and American novel
which projects the illusion of art creating
itself. Beckett's trilogy is described as
representing the thematic limit of the self-
begetting novel.

74   *KELLY, KEVIN. "A Joyful 'Evening with
Beckett.'" <u>Boston Globe</u>, 9 Jan., p. 30.

75   KENNEDY, SIGHLE. "Spirals of Need: Irish
Prototypes in Samuel Beckett's Fiction." In
<u>Yeats, Joyce, and Beckett: New Light on
Three Modern Irish Writers</u>. Edited by
Kathleen McGrory and John Unterecker.
Lewisburg, Pa.: Bucknell University Press,
pp. 153-66.
   Defines Beckett's Irishness as that
element which constitutes in a work of art,
its "condensing spiral of need." Irish
references are studied in three of Beckett's
novels, <u>Watt</u>, <u>Malone Dies</u>, and <u>The Unnamable</u>.

76   KNOWLSON, JAMES. "Beckett and John Millington
Synge." <u>Gambit</u> 7, no. 28:65-81.
   Reprinted: 1976.77

77   _____. "Beckett et John Millington Synge."
<u>Cahiers Renaud-Barrault</u> 93:23-51.

In order to analyze Beckett's debt to
Synge, compares and contrasts the dramatic
writings of the two authors from the point of
view of characterization, atmosphere,
language, poetic techniques, and thematic
material. Reprint of 1976.76.

78   _____. "La Dernière bande at the Greenwood
Theatre." Journal of Beckett Studies, no. 1
(Winter), pp. 103-4.
Reviews the production of the French
version of Krapp's Last Tape by the French
theatrical organization, Prothéa. Knowlson
summarizes a few of the changes made to the
published text and examines Pierre Chabert's
performance as Krapp.

79   _____. "Good Heavens." Cahiers Renaud-
Barrault 93:52-59.
Contrasts an earlier version of Come and
Go, entitled "Good Heavens," with the final
draft of the play to demonstrate how Beckett
has condensed and universalized his vision.
Reprinted: 1976.80.

80   _____. "Good Heavens." Gambit 7, no. 28:101-
105.
Reprint of 1976.79

81   _____. "Krapp's Last Tape: The Evolution of a
Play, 1958-1975." Journal of Beckett
Studies, no. 1 (Winter), pp. 50-65.
Studies the evolution of Krapp's Last Tape
from its first production in London in 1958
to the 1975 Paris version.

82   KRISTEVA, JULIA. "Le Père, l'amour, l'exil."
In Samuel Beckett. Edited by Tom Bishop and
Raymond Federman. Paris: Editions de
l'Herne, pp. 246-52.
Remarks the "sacred" aspects of First Love
and Not I: the death of the father, the
arrival of the child, and the mouth of a
woman alone facing God. See 1976.11.

83   KROLL, JERI L. "Beckett and Grock: Kings of
     Clowns." Notes on Contemporary Literature
     6, no. 1:7-14.
        Discusses Beckett's allusions to a
     European performer, Grock, in Dream of Fair
     to Middling Women and More Pricks Than Kicks
     and Beckett's manipulation of clown routines
     in his later novels and plays.

84   LAHR, JOHN. "Beckett at Seventy." Plays and
     Players 23, no. 10 (July):10-12.
        The Royal Court Theatre's productions in
     honor of Beckett's seventieth birthday, which
     "chronicle the retreat of the body from play
     and the triumph of the disembodied world,"
     are each briefly reviewed: Waiting for
     Godot, Endgame, Play, That Time, Not I, and
     Footfalls.

85   LAMONT, ROSETTE. "Krapp, un anti-Proust." In
     Samuel Beckett. Edited by Tom Bishop and
     Raymond Federman. Paris: Editions de
     l'Herne, pp. 295-305.
        Highlights three of Beckett's writings
     that deal with time: "Whoroscope," "Proust,"
     and Krapps's Last Tape. See 1976.11.

86   LANGBAUM, ROBERT. "Beckett: The Self at Zero."
     Georgia Review 30, no. 4 (Winter):884-905.
        Believes Beckett's plays "intensify the
     atmosphere of early Eliot -- the atmosphere
     of the walking dead." Langbaum analyzes the
     limited extension of time, space and identity
     in the dramatic works.

87   LEE, ROBIN. "The Fictional Topography of Samuel
     Beckett." In The Modern English Novel: the
     Reader, the Writer and the Work. Edited by
     Gabriel Josipovici. New York: Barnes and
     Noble, pp. 206-24.
        Studies the mechanics of the creation of
     fictional space and the breakdown of forward
     narrative movement in Beckett's novels Watt,
     Murphy, Molloy, Malone Dies and The Unnamable
     and the short prose text "Lessness." The

term "fictional topography" is used to mean
the concept of space and the fictiveness of
place. The kinds of loci are also identified: the anecdotal (stories told by the
narrator) and the verbal (exhaustive accounts
of logical possibilities).

88   LEISURE, MARYSE J. "Murphy, or the Beginning of
      an Esthetic of Monstrosity." In Samuel
      Beckett: The Art of Rhetoric. Edited by
      Edouard Morot-Sir, Howard Harper, and Dougald
      McMillan III. Chapel Hill: Department of
      Romance Languages, University of North
      Carolina, pp. 189-200.
          Describes the abnormalities of the
      characters and objects in Beckett's Murphy
      according to specific medical classifica-
      tions: anatomical anomalies, physiological
      deformities, psychological monstrosities, and
      objects. See 1976.107.

89   LE MARINEL, JACQUES. "Le Thème du clochard dans
      En attendant Godot et dans Le Gardien."
      Revue d'Histoire du Théâtre 28, no. 3 (July-
      Sept.):266-73.
          Feels Beckett and Pinter have created the
      same type of character in their plays, the
      clown. Beckett's Vladimir and Estragon in
      Waiting for Godot and Pinter's Davies in Le
      Gardien have many traits in common: their
      physical and moral traits, their loss of the
      protective structures of society, their
      desire to seek security through a refuge or
      material comfort, and their inability to
      establish true human relationships.

90   LEVENTHAL, A.J. "Les Années trente." In Samuel
      Beckett. Edited by Tom Bishop and Raymond
      Federman. Paris: Editions de l'Herne, pp.
      109-13.
          Presents memories of Beckett from the
      thirties. See 1976.11.

91   LEVY, ERIC P. "Existence Searching Essence:
      The Plight of the Unnamable." Mosaic 10, no.

1 (Fall):103-13.
   States that in <u>The Unnamable</u> "the collapse
of essence is virtually complete; the voice
is a mere existence crying out that it
exists." Levy analyzes the character's
isolation, his attempt to mask his lack of
essence and his search for an essence to
define himself.

92 LINDBLAD, ISHRAT, "<u>Waiting for Godot</u>: Transla-
    tion or Revision?" <u>Studia Neophilologica: A
    Journal of Germanic and Romance Languages and
    Literature</u> 48:269-81.
       Analyzes variations in the French text of
    <u>Waiting for Godot</u> and the English translation
    of the play and concludes the English version
    of <u>Godot</u> is a "bleaker" play.

93 LINDON, JEROME. "Première rencontre." In
    <u>Samuel Beckett</u>. Edited by Tom Bishop and
    Raymond Federman. Paris: Editions de
    l'Herne, pp. 95-96.
       The editor of the Editions de Minuit
    describes his first contact with Beckett and
    the trilogy. See 1976.11.

94 McCRARY, JUDITH D. and RONALD G. McCRARY. "Why
    Wait for Godot?" <u>Southern Quarterly</u> 14, no.
    2 (Jan.):109-15.
       Studying the audience reaction to <u>Waiting
    for Godot</u>, demonstrates how Beckett forces
    the spectator to become an integral part of
    the play: "Beckett supplied the theme,
    waiting, and each spectator must wait, in his
    own way and on his own terms." The study
    analyzes various reactions to the play's
    premier performance and illustrates the
    effectiveness of the play in its lack of
    conventional dramatic structure by the play's
    performance at San Quentin Penitentiary in
    1957.

95 MacGOWRAN, JACK. "MacGowran on Beckett:
    Interview by Richard Toscan." <u>Theatre
    Quarterly</u> 3, no. 11 (July-Sept.):15-22.

MacGowran discusses his relationship with
Beckett, and Beckett as Director, then
comments on <u>Godot</u>, <u>Endgame</u>, <u>Happy Days</u>, <u>Act
Without Words II</u>, <u>Eh Joe</u>, the influence of
Chaplin and Keaton on Beckett, Beckett as
optimist and realist, and the problems of
translation.

96   McGRORY, KATHLEEN. "The Beckett Landscape." In
      <u>Yeats, Joyce and Beckett: New Light on Three
      Modern Irish Writers</u>. Edited by Kathleen
      McGrory and John Unterecker. Lewisburg, Pa.:
      Bucknell University Press, pp. 137-46.
          Presents photographs of the area in and
      around Dublin.

97   McGRORY, KATHLEEN and JOHN UNTERECKER, eds.
      "Interview with Jack MacGowran." In <u>Yeats,
      Joyce, Beckett: New Light on Three Modern
      Irish Writers</u>. Lewisburg, Pa.: Bucknell
      University Press, pp. 172-82.
          Provides an edited transcript of a public
      interview with Jack MacGowran at Western
      Connecticut State College, Danbury, Conn. on
      April 20, 1971. The authors deal with
      misconceptions about Beckett's works,
      Beckett's directing, his Irish background and
      the decay of his novelistic style.

98   McMILLAN III, DOUGALD. "<u>Echo's Bones</u>: Starting
      Points for Beckett." In <u>Samuel Beckett: The
      Art of Rhetoric</u>. Edited by Edouard Morot-
      Sir, Howard Harper, and Dougald McMillan III.
      Chapel Hill: Department of Romance Lan-
      guages, University of North Carolina, pp.
      165-87.
          Suggests <u>Echo's Bones</u> as a starting point
      for studying the coherence of Beckett's works
      as a whole since "In that first book of
      poems, we have the primary presentation of
      material that persists in transmuted form as
      an important element throughout Beckett's
      later works." See 1976.107.

99   MAGNAN, JEAN-MARIE. "Les Chaînes et Relais du
      néant." In <u>Samuel Beckett</u>. Edited by Tom
      Bishop and Raymond Federman. Paris:
      Editions de l'Herne, pp. 259-65.
           Demonstrates how Beckett's last two
      "novels," <u>The Unnamable</u> and <u>How It Is</u>, show
      the "temple of self" in ruins. See 1976.11.

100   MARKER, FREDERICK J. "Beckett Criticism in
      <u>Modern Drama</u>: A Checklist." <u>Modern Drama</u>
      19, no. 3 (Sept.):261-63.
           Surveys, in the chronological order of
      their appearance, the major contributions to
      Beckett scholarship that have appeared in
      <u>Modern Drama</u> since 1958.

101   MARTIN, GEORGE. "Friendship -- Basic Theme of
      <u>Bouvard et Pécuchet</u> and <u>En Attendant Godot</u>."
      <u>Language Quarterly</u> 14, nos. 3-4 (Spring-
      Summer):43-46.
           Feels that Flaubert's novel and Beckett's
      <u>Godot</u> are founded on the classic concept of
      friendship as exemplified by Platonic
      tradition. Discusses the couples' self-
      esteem and arrogance toward the outside
      world, their compassion for the downtrodden,
      the principal functions of the partners, and
      the differences between the couples.

102   MAURIAC, CLAUDE. "L'Espace sans ici ou ailleurs
      de Samuel Beckett." <u>Figaro Littéraire</u>, 3
      July, p. 14.
           Reviews <u>For Yet to End Again</u> and <u>Fizzles</u>,
      describing the vague images and characters.

103   MERCIER, VIVIAN. "Ireland/The World: Beckett's
      Irishness." In <u>Yeats, Joyce, and Beckett:
      New Light on Three Modern Irish Writers</u>.
      Edited by Kathleen McGrory and John Un-
      terecker. Lewisburg, Pa.: Bucknell Univer-
      sity Press, pp. 147-52.
           Discusses the relevance of Beckett's Irish
      background to his career as a writer and
      concludes: "Beckett's universality, in the
      last analysis, does not depend on impatria-

tion or expatriation, on Irishness, French-
ness, or cosmopolitanism: it depends on the
paradox of a unique self that has found its
bedrock in our common human predicament."
Reprinted and revised: 1977.65

104   MITCHELL, BREON. "Art in Microcosm: The
       Manuscript Stages of Beckett's Come and Go."
       Modern Drama 19, no. 3 (Sept.):245-60.
          Evaluates the literary, artistic, and
       mythological allusions in Come and Go, and
       then demonstrates how the balance and
       symmetry of the action and structure of the
       play is developed through the numerous stages
       of composition. The commentary is followed
       by an appendix listing all known manuscript
       stages of Come and Go and Va et vient, as
       well as all appearances of the original
       versions of the text.

105   MOORJANI, ANGELA B. "A Mythic Reading of
       Molloy." In Samuel Beckett: The Art of
       Rhetoric. Edited by Edouard Morot-Sir,
       Howard Harper, and Dougald McMillan III.
       Chapel Hill: Department of Romance Lan-
       guages, University of North Carolina, pp.
       225-35.
          Analyzes the narrative structure, and
       mythic content of Molloy, identifying three
       separate narrators, the narrator of the
       Preamble, Molloy, and Moran. See 1976.107.

106   MOROT-SIR, EDOUARD. "Samuel Beckett and
       Cartesian Emblems." In Samuel Beckett: The
       Art of Rhetoric. Edited by Edouard Morot-
       Sir, Howard Harper, and Dougald McMillan III.
       Chapel Hill: Department of Romance Lan-
       guages, University of North Carolina, pp. 25-
       104.
          Clarifies the history of Beckett
       criticism, commenting on philosophical
       interpretations based on Descartes and
       Cartesians, or the Existentialists. A new
       study of Beckett's poem, "Whoroscope" is
       introduced and the evolution of the Cartesian

images in Beckett's works from "Whoroscope"
to the most recent prose pieces is studied.
In an analysis of light in Beckett's works,
Morot-Sir makes note of some of the most
important Manichaean themes as they offer
similarities to Beckett's images, and then
assesses Beckett's language and his
originality. See 1976.107.

107   MOROT-SIR, EDOUARD, HOWARD HARPER, and DOUGALD
       MCMILLAN III, eds. <u>Samuel Beckett: The Art
       of Rhetoric</u>. Chapel Hill: Department of
       Romance Languages, University of North
       Carolina, 289 pp.
            Presents a collection of essays written
       for the symposium, "Samuel Beckett: The Art
       of Rhetoric," held at the University of North
       Carolina at Chapel Hill, April 4-6, 1974.
       The participants were interested in Beckett
       "as a man who has experienced the limits of
       language, has put words on trial, forced them
       to confess their failure, and refused to
       exonerate them through any illusory triumph."
       The essays have been grouped in four parts,
       representing different perspectives:
       Beckett's philosophy, Beckett's Rhetoric,
       Beckett's Poetry, and Beckett's Novels. See
       1976.18, 1976.32, 1976.34, 1976.50, 1976.55,
       1976.63, 1976.66, 1976.88, 1976.98, 1976.105,
       1976.123, 1976.134, 1976.139, 1976.145.

108   MURPHY, VINCENT J. "La Peinture de l'empêche-
       ment: Samuel Beckett's <u>Watt</u>." <u>Criticism</u> 18,
       no. 4 (Fall):353-66.
            After discussing the relationship of
       Beckett's writing to the visual arts,
       examines <u>Watt</u> from the point of view of a few
       of Beckett's critical writings. Murphy
       believes Beckett demonstrates the resistance
       of an object to representation "not only in
       terms of the impermeability of the object
       itself, but also in terms of the limitations
       of the subject," which Beckett refers to as
       "l'empêchement-objet" and "l'empêchement-
       oeil."

109   NELSON, ROBERT J. "Three orders in <u>En attendant</u> <u>Godot</u> and <u>Fin de partie</u>: A Pascalian Interpretation of Beckett." <u>French Forum</u> 1, no. 1 (Jan.):79-85.
     Analyzes the characters in <u>Waiting for</u> <u>Godot</u> and <u>Endgame</u> as they reflect the Pascalian orders of the mind, body, and charity.

110   NIGHTINGALE, BENEDICT. "Brain Cells." <u>New</u> <u>Statesman</u> 91 (28 May):723.
     Briefly reviews <u>Not I</u>, <u>That Time</u>, and <u>Footfalls</u> and mentions a revival of <u>Play</u> at the Royal Court Theatre. Nightingale describes the situations, the characters, and the possible meanings of Beckett's most recent creations: "Late Beckett writes with a grim beauty, using sharp, concentrated and resonant images of deprivation and anguish to draw attention to the human waste we see all around us, if usually in less extreme form. What worries me isn't his insistence on this waste, but his apparent belief that there's no point doing anything about it ..."
Reprinted: 1979.22.79.

111   _____. "Horse Sense." <u>New Statesman</u> 91 (30 Apr.):583.
     Briefly reviews the Schiller Theatre's performance of <u>Waiting for Godot</u> at the Royal Court Theatre, pointing out the grim setting, the discipline of the production, the balletic effects, and the fine characterization of the tramps.

112   NUDD, ROSEMARY, S.P. "The Perception of Other as Burden in the Trilogy of Samuel Beckett." <u>New Laurel Review</u> 6, no. 2:45-51.
     Explores the theme of the perception of others in the trilogy, viewing this agonizing responsibility as a burden for the perceiver: "... Moran, Molloy, Malone, and the Unnamable condemn themselves to a frustrating destiny seeking a self which can find fulfillment

only in some relation to another, while
perceiving the other as burden."

113   OSTROVSKY, ERIKA. "Le Silence de Babel." In
       Samuel Beckett. Edited by Tom Bishop and
       Raymond Federman. Paris: Editions de
       l'Herne, pp. 206-11.
            Out of the movement of Beckett's works
       towards silence the question of Beckett's
       bilingualism arises: "the confusion, the
       obsessive repetition of linguistic varia-
       tions, form the emblem of the limitation of
       human possibilities and translate the
       desperate limits of our condition." See
       1976.11.

114   PETER, JOHN. "Beckett's Bleak Progress."
       Sunday Times (London), 14 Nov., p. 40.
            Briefly reviews For to End Yet Again,
       comparing Beckett's prose pieces to one of
       Salvador Dali's works, "A Vision of Suspended
       Apocalypsis."

115   "La Pièce avant tout." In Samuel Beckett.
       Edited by Tom Bishop and Raymond Federman.
       Paris: Editions de l'Herne, pp. 229-31.
            Translation of a portion of the review
       appearing in the San Quentin Prison newspaper
       following the San Francisco Drama Workshop's
       presentation of Waiting for Godot at the
       prison in 1957. See 1976.11.

116   PILLING, JOHN. "Beckett's Proust." Journal of
       Beckett Studies, no. 1 (Winter), pp. 8-29.
            Studies the genesis of the Proust mono-
       graph and some of the problems related to it,
       in light of Beckett's marginal notes in his
       copy of A la recherche du temps perdu which
       is now part of the Reading University Beckett
       Archive.

117   _____. Samuel Beckett. London and Boston:
       Routledge and Kegan Paul, 224 pp.
            Gives a thorough account of Beckett's work
       to date (critical writing, prose, drama, and

poetry) based on Beckett's personal, intellectual, cultural, and literary background:
"He offers us a salutary reminder of the
genuine difficulty of being alive, but he is
a writer who can provide for others the
consolation he consistently refused himself."
A select bibliography is included.

118 PINGET, ROBERT. "Lettre." In Samuel Beckett.
Edited by Tom Bishop and Raymond Federman.
Paris: Editions de l'Herne, pp. 160-61.
Very briefly describes Beckett's dedica-
tion and generosity. See 1976.11.

119 POPKIN, HENRY. "Theatre." Nation 222, no. 25
(26 June):797-98.
Reviews Beckett's production of Waiting
for Godot at the Schiller Theater in West
Berlin. Popkin finds that Beckett has made
the action and the characters more human and
more symmetrical.

120 POUNTNEY, ROSEMARY. "Happy Days at the National
Theatre." Journal of Beckett Studies, no. 1
(Winter), pp. 100-103.
Compares the 1975 and 1976 productions of
Happy Days directed by Peter Hall, with Peggy
Ashcroft as Winnie.

121 _____. "On Acting Mouth in Not I." Journal
of Beckett Studies, no. 1 (Winter), pp. 81-85.
Reviews the Samuel Beckett Theatre
Company's production of Not I performed in
honor of the playwright's seventieth birthday.

122 _____. "Samuel Beckett's Interest in Form:
Structural Patterning in Play." Modern Drama
19, no. 3 (Sept.):237-44.
References her study of structure in Play
to the possible influences of the patterning
and purgatorial concepts in the works of
Dante, Joyce, Vico, and Yeats.

123   RABINOVITZ, RUBIN. "The Addenda to Samuel
        Beckett's <u>Watt</u>." In <u>Samuel Beckett: The Art
        of Rhetoric</u>. Edited by Edouard Morot-Sir,
        Howard Harper, and Dougald McMillan III.
        Chapel Hill: Department of Romance Lan-
        guages, University of North Carolina, pp.
        211-23.
            Considers the enigmatic quality of the
        addenda as it applies to the events in the
        rest of the novel. See 1976.107.

124   _____. "The Deterioration of Outside Reality in
        Samuel Beckett's Fiction." In <u>Yeats, Joyce,
        and Beckett: New Light on Three Modern Irish
        Writers</u>. Edited by Kathleen McGrory and John
        Unterecker. Lewisburg, Pa.: Bucknell
        University Press, pp. 167-71.
            Contrasts the vagueness of time and space
        in <u>Watt</u> with Beckett's earlier works.

125   RADIN, VICTORIA. "Abject Krapp." <u>Observer</u>, 14
        Mar., p. 29.
            Compares two productions of <u>Krapp's Last
        Tape</u>: Patrick Magee's at the Greenwich
        Theater and Beckett's own direction of the
        French language version at the Greenwood.
        <u>Krapp's Last Tape</u> is briefly contrasted with
        Robert Pinget's <u>L'Hypothèse</u>.

126   REID, ALEC. "Test Flight: Beckett's <u>More
        Pricks than Kicks</u>." In <u>The Irish Short
        Story</u>. Edited by Patrick Rafroidi and
        Terence Brown. Atlantic Highlands, N.J.:
        Humanities Press, pp. 227-35.
            Characterizes Beckett's first attempt at
        writing prose as the work of a young artist
        who delighted in parody and his own linguis-
        tic powers.

127   RICKS, CHRISTOPHER. "The Hermit of Art."
        <u>Sunday Times</u> (London), 12 Sept., p. 36.
            Describes the simplicity, clarity of
        language and Beckett's use of imagination in
        <u>Ill Seen Ill Said</u>.

128 ROJTMAN, BETTY. <u>Forme et signification dans le</u>
    <u>théâtre de Beckett</u>. Paris: A.G. Nizet, 245
    pp.
    Analyzes Beckett's theater from the point
    of view of the structuralists Ferdinand de
    Saussure, Roman Jakobson, and Roland Barthes,
    among others. She develops two distinct
    types of rapports in Beckett's drama,
    vertical and horizontal "tensions." These
    tensions serve a unique purpose, to camou-
    flage the real nature of the performance,
    that of escaping the condition of immobility.
    Thus the problem of traditional theater is
    reversed in Beckett's plays: the idea of
    dénouement does not exist, the end is
    forgotten in deference to the progress on
    which it depends. The text is followed by a
    select bibliography.

129 ROSEN, STEVEN. <u>Samuel Beckett and the Pessimis-</u>
    <u>tic Tradition</u>. New Brunswick, N.J.: Rutgers
    University Press, 252 pp.
    Provides a two-fold approach to Beckett's
    writing: 1) the function of meaning in
    Beckett's aesthetic (obscurity as essential
    to art, absence of consoling explanations,
    pessimism, skepticism, comic effect of
    generalizations, Beckett sages as comic
    figures), and 2) Beckett's thought in <u>Proust</u>
    (nihilism, spite, misanthropy, pessimism in
    Proust and Shopenhauer, relativism, time and
    habit). Comparisons are made with the
    writings and ideas of numerous authors:
    Shopenhauer, Joyce, Proust, Boethius,
    Kierkegaard, Dostoevsky, Céline, Camus,
    Sartre, Nietzsche, Socrates, Pythagoras,
    Democritus, Zeno, Empedocles, Heraclitus,
    Gorgias, Diogenes, Pascal, Thomas à Kempis,
    St. Augustine, Rousseau, Breton, Gide,
    Leibniz, Berkeley, Baudelaire, Descartes, and
    Bergson. A general bibliography is included.

130 SAINT-MARTIN, FERNANDE. <u>Samuel Beckett et</u>
    <u>l'univers de la fiction</u>. Montréal: Les
    Presses de l'Université de Montréal, 265 pp.

Discusses the relation of personal experience to language, the linearity of discourse, the associative rapport of words, and the impossibility of expressing reality through fiction. Saint-Martin depicts the tension created in Beckett's prose by the figurative or realistic "prétexte" of the fiction and the obvious subjectivity of the speaker.

131   SASTRE, ALFONSO. "Avant-garde et réalité." In _Samuel Beckett_. Edited by Tom Bishop and Raymond Federman. Paris: Editions de l'Herne, pp. 236-41.
      Examines diverse elements which make up _Waiting for Godot_: the profound reality, the music-hall tradition, tragi-comedy, an epitaph, a drama of "the anguish of being," and a "metaphysique" of boredom. See 1976.11.

132   SAVORY, JEROLD. J. "Samuel Beckett's _Waiting for Godot_ (Lucky's Speech)." _Explicator_ 35, no. 1 (Fall): 9-10.
      Notes that Lucky's speech may be a summary of _The Book of Job_, representing the inability of the Old Testament God to save Estragon and Vladimir.

133   SCHNEIDER, ALAN. "'Comme il vous plaira,' travailler avec Samuel Beckett." In _Samuel Beckett_. Edited by Tom Bishop and Raymond Federman. Paris: Editions de l'Herne, pp. 123-36.
      Discusses his presentations of Beckett's plays, his adherence to Beckett's texts and ideas, and his interactions with Beckett. See 1976.11.

134   _____. "Working With Beckett." In _Samuel Beckett: The Art of Rhetoric_. Edited by Edouard Morot-Sir, Howard Harper, and Dougald McMillan III. Chapel Hill: Department of Romance Languages, University of North Carolina, pp. 271-89.

Describes memories and impressions of
Beckett, his plays, and their productions.
See 1976.107.

135 SEAVER, RICHARD. "Beckett vient à l'Olympia
Press." In _Samuel Beckett_. Edited by Tom
Bishop and Raymond Federman. Paris:
Editions de l'Herne, pp. 97-100.
Author of one of the first general
introductions to Beckett's works, describes
his first encounter with Beckett, the
trilogy, and the publication of _Watt_. See
1952.3, 1976.11.

136 *SHERZER, DINA. "Saying is Inventing: Gnomic
Expressions in Molloy." In _Speech Play:
Research and Resources for Studying Linguis-
tic Creativity_. Edited by Barbara
Kirshenblatt-Gimblett. Philadelphia:
University of Pennsylvania Press, pp. 163-71.

137 _____. _Structure de la trilogie de Beckett:
"Molloy", "Malone meurt," "L'Innommable."_
The Hague: Mouton, 100 pp.
In this analysis of the formal structure
of each of the novels of the trilogy, Sherzer
studies the internal structure of the flow of
words, the role of the narrator's interven-
tions, the narrator's irregular style, the
discovery of a "new type" of language, and
the textual disorganization of the novels.
Followed by a selected bibliography.

138 SMITH, FREDERICK N. "Beckett and the Seven-
teenth Century 'Port Royal Logic.'" _Journal
of Modern Literature_ 5, no. 1 (Feb.):99-108.
Believes Beckett was influenced not only
by Descartes but also by the Jansenist
Antoine Artaud. Smith demonstrates how _Watt_
is a parody of Artaud's _The Port-Royal Logic_.

139 SMITH, STEPHANI POFAHL. "From Poetics to Anti-
Poetics." In _Samuel Beckett: The Art of
Rhetoric_. Edited by Edouard Morot-Sir,

Howard Harper, and Dougald McMillan III.
Chapel Hill: Department of Romance Languages, University of North Carolina, pp.
157-63.
 Points out a fundamental change in
Beckett's esthetics: in his early career his
view of art was poetic, while in his mature
works his emphasis is on dilemma, or an anti-
poetic stance. See 1976.107.

140   SPURLING, HILARY. "Voice of Two Masters."
      Observer, 9 May, p. 25.

141   SPURLING, JOHN. "Beckett at the Court."
      Spectator 236 (5 June):25.
       Reviews Play, That Time, and Footfalls at
      the Royal Court Theatre, remarking that
      Beckett's theatrical "method depends precise-
      ly on administering tragedy and comedy in
      equal doses."

142   STEMPEL, DANIEL. "History Electrified into
      Anagogy: A Reading of Waiting for Godot."
      Contemporary Literature 17, no. 2 (Spring):
      263-78.
       Reconstructs the allegorical, historical,
      moral, and anagogical levels of meaning in
      Waiting for Godot.

143   STRAUSS, WALTER A. "Le Belacqua de Dante et les
      clochards de Beckett." In Samuel Beckett.
      Edited by Tom Bishop and Raymond Federman.
      Paris: Editions de l'Herne, pp. 269-80.
       Adds a postface (10 years later) in order
      to view Beckett's works from more of a
      perspective: the process of total disin-
      tegration, and the precarious, but ever-
      present human elements of Beckett's fiction.
      Reprinted from 1959.43; see 1976.11.

144   TELLERMAN, ESTHER. "Beckett: Dire l'innom-
      mable." Action Poétique 66 (June):129-143.
       Analyzes The Unnamable: the narrator,
      subject matter, disintegration of language,
      and metaphor of the spiral.

145 TRITT, WILLIAM. "Statistics on Proper Names in
     <u>Murphy</u>." In <u>Samuel Beckett: The Art of</u>
     <u>Rhetoric</u>. Edited by Edouard Morot-Sir,
     Howard Harper, and Dougald McMillan III.
     Chapel Hill: Department of Romance Lan-
     guages, University of North Carolina, pp.
     201-10.
          Arranges the proper names referred to in
     <u>Murphy</u> in 10 categories: literature,
     painting and sculpture, biblical references,
     mythological characters, philosophers,
     miscellaneous, historical references,
     psychologists, and physical and biological
     scientists. See 1976.107.

146 WASSERMAN, JERRY. "Watt's World of Words."
     <u>Bucknell Review</u> 22, no. 2 (Fall):123-38.
          While "most critics see Watt's verbal
     constructions as logical attempts to isolate
     and understand phenomena," on the contrary,
     Wasserman argues that Watt's alienation is so
     great that he attempts to create an auto-
     nomous verbal universe to contain his
     experiences.

146a WARDLE, IRVING. "People in a Timeless Limbo:
     <u>Play</u> and Other Plays." <u>Times</u> (London), 21
     May, p. 13.
          Reviews the Royal Court Theatre's produc-
     tions of <u>That Time</u> and <u>Footfalls</u>, contrasting
     the recent dramatic pieces with <u>Play</u>:
     "Beckett's energy goes not into exploring
     alternatives possibilities for creatures who
     have reached their destinations, but in
     discovering new forms in which they can more
     eloquently voice their despair." Both plays
     present the theme of obsessive memory and
     visually portray the total blackness of the
     void which surrounds the characters.
     Reprinted: 1979.22.76.

147 WEBB, EUGENE. "Pozzo in Bloomsbury: A Possible
     Allusion in Beckett's <u>Waiting for Godot</u>."
     <u>Journal of Modern Literature</u> 5, no. 2
     (Apr.):326-31.

Studies the significance of the name Pozzo
in Waiting for Godot, linking the character
to John Maynard Keynes: "Lord Keynes was far
more than an ordinary man of wealth; as an
economist, he was also a theorist of wealth,
and as a member of the Bloomsbury group, he
was in addition a champion of a particular
conception of civilization."

148   WELLERSHOFF, DIETER. "Toujours moins, presque
      rien, essai sur Beckett." In Samuel Beckett.
      Edited by Tom Bishop and Raymond Federman.
      Paris: Editions de l'Herne, pp. 169-82.
         Describes the vicious circle in Beckett's
      works created by the narrator's wish to
      finish his discourse and his inability to end
      his narration. Examples are taken from the
      trilogy and Texts for Nothing. See 1976.11.

149   WILCHER, ROBERT. "'What's It meant to mean?'
      An Approach to Beckett's Theater." Critical
      Quarterly 18, no. 2 (Summer):9-37.
         Explores the implications of the statement
      "form is content, content is form," the
      inappropriateness of an allegorical approach
      to the plays, and the impact of the plays in
      performance.

150   WORTH, KATHARINE. "Audio-visual Beckett."
      Journal of Beckett Studies, no. 1 (Winter):
      85-88.
         Describes the production of the television
      play Eh Joe and the radio plays Words and
      Music and Embers for the University of
      London's Department of Extra-Mural Studies.

151   _____. "Beckett's Fine Shades: Play, That
      Time, and Footfalls." Journal of Beckett
      Studies, no. 1 (Winter), pp. 75-80.
         Reviews the performances at the Royal
      Court Theatre in May 1976 in honor of
      Beckett's seventieth birthday.

152   ZEIFMAN, HERSH. "Being and Non-Being: Samuel
      Beckett's Not I." Modern Drama 19, no. 1

(Mar.):35-46.
Notes that in <u>Not I</u> Beckett creates
another disembodied character struggling to
attain salvation and free herself from the
suffering she is experiencing: "The action
of <u>Not I</u> is a metaphor of the search for a
non-existant salvation not simply on the
metaphysical level, but on the artistic, as
well.

1977

1   ABBOTT, H. PORTER. "A Grammar for Being Else-
     where." <u>Journal of Modern Literature</u> 6
     (Feb.):39-96.
          Believes that the writing of <u>Waiting for
     Godot</u> had a profound effect on <u>The Unnamable</u>.
     Abbott points out that Beckett used the same
     type of short phrasal units that he perfected
     in <u>Godot</u> as a structural base for the
     following prose.

2   ADAMS, ROBERT MARTIN. "Samuel Beckett." In
     <u>After Joyce: Studies in the Fiction after
     Ulysses</u>. New York: Oxford University Press,
     pp. 90-113.
          Describes Joyce's influence on Beckett,
     concentrating on Beckett's connections and
     contracts with Joyce, the differences and
     similarities of their backgrounds and
     literary styles, Beckett's liberation from
     Joyce, Beckett's approach to the sacred, his
     attitude toward the absurd, and his fascina-
     tion with the concepts of ending and finality.

3   ALVAREZ, A. "Shudders of the Mind." <u>Observer</u>,
     5 June, p. 29.
          Reviews <u>Collected Poems in English and
     French</u> and <u>Ends and Odds</u>. Alvarez distin-
     guishes these two periods in Beckett's
     literary career, noting that the poetic
     clarity of Beckett's later work, especially
     his dramatic prose, express his true genius,
     while his early poetry is marked by mannerism
     and pedantry.

4   ASMUS, WALTER. "Rehearsal Notes for the German
     Première of Beckett's That Time and Footfalls
     at the Schiller Theater Werkstatt, Berlin."
     Journal of Beckett Studies, no. 2 (Summer),
     pp. 82-95.
          Records remarks and observations which
     relate to the difficulties encountered in
     this production of That Time and Footfalls.

5   *AUSTER, PAUL. "Ending without End." Saturday
     Review 4, no. 15 (20 Apr.):20-23.
          Source: French XX Bibliography, no. 30
     (1978); unverified.

6   *BAIR, DEIRDRE. "'No-Man's-Land, Hellespont or
     Vacuum': Samuel Beckett's Irishness." Crane
     Bag 1, no. 2:14.

7   BARGE, LAURA. "The Beckett Hero." PMLA 92, no.
     5 (Oct.):1007-8.
          Defends her article "'Coloured Images' in
     the 'Black Dark,'" restating her premise that
     the Beckett hero represents a search for, not
     a fleeing from the essence of self.

8   _____. "'Colored Images' in the 'Black Dark':
     Samuel Beckett's Later Fiction." PMLA 92,
     no. 2 (Mar.):273-84.
          Focuses on several issues as they relate
     to Beckett's recent fiction: person, place,
     movement, consciousness, light, and nature.
     See 1977.23.

9   _____. "Life and Death in Beckett's Four
     Stories." South Atlantic Quarterly 76, no. 3
     (Summer):332-47.
          Believes the Nouvelles (Stories) and First
     Love mark a transition in Beckett's canon:
     Beckett shifts from the third person to first
     person, the hero concentrates on the
     microcosm and a quest for the "essence of
     human experience," the hero is in exile and
     is abused by the elements that make up his
     world, and his mind and body are deteriorat-
     ing. Barge concentrates on the concept of

mortality in the stories: death defined,
death as metaphor, death as continuation of
life, and death in the fiction that follows.

10   BERNAL, OLGA. "Samuel Beckett: l'écrivain et
le savoir." Journal of Beckett Studies, no.
2 (Summer), pp. 59-62.
        Presents Beckett's exclusion of knowledge
and order in his fictional world.

11   BERNHEIMER, CHARLES. "Grammacentricity and
Modernism." Mosaic 11, no. 1 (Fall):103-16.
Beckett: pp. 112-15.
        Comments on Joyce, Kafka, and Beckett as
the leading figures in the modernist tradition deriving from Flaubert. Bernheimer
believes Beckett has gone the farthest to
combine the literary methods of Flaubert,
Joyce, and Kafka, since he makes the inex-
pressiveness of language the very subject of
his work.

12   BERTAGNOLLI, LESLIE. "Mario Dessy's Attesa: A
Futurist Analogue of Beckett's Waiting for
Godot." Notes on Contemporary Literature 7,
no. 5:4.
        Points out the similarities between Mario
Dessy's Attesa and Beckett's Godot: the
titles, the basic action, the analogy between
life and the act of waiting, and the language.

13   BILLINGTON, MICHAEL. "Beckett." Guardian,
19 Apr., p. 10.
        Reviews the BBC production of two Beckett
premiers Ghost Trio and "... but the clouds
..." as well as a film of the Royal Court's
Not I. Billington describes the beauty of
the images, Beckett's minimalism and the
successes and failures of the televised
performances.

14   BRATER, ENOCH. "Books Considered." New
Republic 176, no. 16 (5 Mar.):31-32.
        Considers Beckett's exploration of minute

forms in <u>Ends and Odds</u> and <u>Fizzles</u>. Brater notes that Beckett's work is condensed, sharpened, and highly stylized: "For each is a tiny constellation of inventiveness and suggestiveness in which an unassimilated feeling, a sensation or a mood is the frail remnant of some human experience gone but not forgotten."

15 _____. "Fragment and Beckett's Form in <u>That Time</u> and <u>Footfalls</u>." <u>Journal of Beckett Studies</u>, no. 2 (Summer), pp. 70-81.
Examines the possibilities of fragmentation in Beckett's recent small-scale dramas.

16 _____. "Still/Beckett: The Essential and Incidental." <u>Journal of Modern Literature</u> 6, no. 1 (Feb.):1-16.
Describes the highlights of the activities in honor of Beckett's seventieth birthday, the production of his new plays <u>That Time</u> and <u>Footfalls</u>, and the publication of his newest texts, <u>Fizzles</u> and <u>Ends and Odds</u>. The text "Still," "Beckett's verbal equivalent of solitude," is analyzed in detail from the point of view of language, characterization, action, and narration. As an introduction to this special issue devoted to Beckett, Brater demonstrates how Beckett continues to involve his readers in his work in the present as it "continues to affect his readers as a constant becoming, a timeless, endless, boundless, rendezvous with a text which is only as limited as process itself."

17 BRIENZA, SUSAN D. "<u>The Lost Ones</u>: The Reader as Searcher." <u>Journal of Modern Literature</u> 6, no. 1 (Feb.):148-68.
Provides a comprehensive study of the styles and themes of the <u>The Lost Ones</u>. The characters, their activities and emotions are discussed and special emphasis is placed on the narrator's visual descriptions and language.

18   BUSI, FREDERICK. "Lucky, Luke and Samuel
     Beckett." Research Studies 45:100-104.
          Identifies the origin of Lucky's name,
     emphasizing the relationship of this
     character's name to Saint Luke.

19   CALDER, JOHN. "'The Lively Arts': Three Plays
     by Samuel Beckett on BBC 2, 17 Apr. 1977."
     Journal of Beckett Studies, no. 2 (Summer),
     pp. 117-21.
          Previews three plays written for
     television: Not I (adapted from the stage),
     Ghost Trio, and ... but the clouds ... The
     characters, themes and visual field are
     examined.

20   COE, RICHARD. "The Barest Essentials." Times
     Literary Supplement (London), 15 July,
     p. 873.
          Reviews Collected Poems in English and
     French and the collector's edition of the
     "Drunken Boat" translation, making the point
     that in Beckett's development as a poet there
     has been "a prolonged conflict, not so much
     between ideas and language, as between
     experience (facts) and language." Reprinted:
     1979.22.83.

21   COHN, RUBY. "Outward Bound Soliloquies."
     Journal of Modern Literature 6, no. 1
     (Feb.):17-38.
          Points out that Beckett's plays tend
     toward soliloquy: the characters reveal
     their inner lives in order to create a more
     intense relationship with the audience.
     Reprinted in part from 1976.32.

22   CORMIER, ROMONA and JANIS L. POLLISTER. Waiting
     for Death: The Philosophical Significance of
     "En attendant Godot." University, Ala.:
     University of Alabama Press, 155 pp.
          This study evaluates the existing
     criticism of Waiting for Godot, and analyzes
     Beckett's "world view" as it is exposed in
     the play, an approach that "concentrates upon

the tedium and absurdity that envelop life."
Each chapter deals with a different aspect of
the play: characters, memory and identity,
time and place, communication, waiting for
death, tragedy or comedy, philosophy and
literature. The text is followed by a select
bibliography.

23   CORNWELL, ETHEL. "The Beckett Hero." PMLA 92,
     no. 5 (Oct.):1006-7.
          In a letter to the editor refutes the
     position of Laura Barge in her article
     "'Coloured Images' in the 'Black Dark':
     Samuel Beckett's Later Fiction" in which she
     suggests that the Beckett hero retreats
     inward to discover the "true self" (see
     1977.8). Cornwell believes the Beckett hero
     seeks the self in order to escape it (see
     1973.24).

24   CUNNINGHAM, VALENTINE. "Travelling Hopelessly."
     Times Literary Supplement (London), 15 Apr.,
     p. 450.
          Makes the point that although the Four
     Novellas have all been published previously,
     it is important that they should now become
     available together in order to clarify the
     order of Beckett's early post-war work.
     Cunningham finds that the heroes of these
     nouvellas are making "the typical journey
     through the Beckettian middle -- of life and
     of fiction," and they are beginning to
     reflect more on their narratives -- Beckett's
     interests now "tend more towards the art of
     fiction itself than towards telling stories
     just for themselves."

25   DAVIS, ROBIN J. "Beckett Bibliography after
     Federman and Fletcher." Journal of Beckett
     Studies, no. 2 (Summer), pp. 63-69.
          Introduces difficulties to be encountered
     by bibliographers of Samuel Beckett, in
     particular those involved in compilation and
     those involved in the recording and publish-
     ing of the information.

26   DEARLOVE, J.E.   "'Last Images':   Samuel
     Beckett's Residual Fiction."   Journal of
     Modern Literature 6, no. 1 (Feb.):104-26.
        Notes that Beckett's prose pieces "Im-
     agination Dead Imagine," "Ping," and "Less-
     ness" strive for a more objective pose than
     his previous works.   In her analysis of this
     "objective pose," Dearlove examines the
     essential situations, minimal language, and
     "self-disintegrating" form of the texts:
     "Instead of a scintillating, print-oriented,
     and traditional art, Beckett offers, first,
     the spoken narration of an impotent narrator
     struggling with language and then impersonal
     and abstract images expressed in simple yet
     elliptic words and phrases."

27   ESSLIN, MARTIN.   "Beckett's Rough for Radio."
     Journal of Modern Literature 6 (Feb.):95-103.
        Feels that the Rough for Radio is "con-
     cerned with aspects of artistic creation,
     with voices and streams of music emanating
     from more or less mysterious sources, and the
     dependence of the principal characters on
     these and their more or less successful
     attempts at achieving some sort of control
     over them."   Reprinted: 1980.29.

28   ESTESS, TED L.   "Dimensions of Play in the
     Literature of Samuel Beckett."   Arizona
     Quarterly 33, no. 1 (Spring):5-25.
        Believes that playing "is the principal
     strategy by which Beckett's people establish
     existential meaning, however ephemeral and
     truncated, in a time when all inherited
     paradigms of meaning have dissolved into
     nothingness."   Estess examines several
     important dimensions of play in Beckett's
     fictional world: 1) diversionary, 2)
     temporal, 3) psychosocial, 4) ontological,
     and 5) linguistic or aesthetic.

29   FITCH, BRIAN.   Dimensions, structures, et
     textualité dans la trilogie romanesque de

Beckett. Paris: Lettres Modernes Minard,
205 pp.
Focuses his attention on three aspects of
Beckett's trilogy: dimensions, structures,
and textuality. The section on dimensions
analyzes the mental "space," or representation and expression. Under the heading
structures, Fitch discusses several topics:
the breakdown of syntax, time and space, the
hypothetical nature of the stories and
personages, the experience of the reader, and
the impossible situation of the author.
Finally, textuality includes formal, seman-
tic, and phonetic associations, syntactical
symmetry, linking of sentences, rhyme,
alliteration, etc. A select bibliography is
included.

30   GATES, DAVID. "Scraps from Beckett's Workshop."
      Virginia Quarterly Review 53, no. 4
      (Autumn):776-84.
      Considers the style and content of
      Beckett's latest works Fizzles and Ends and
      Odds. Gates feels that these works are for
      the most part minor, and serve to expand our
      sense of the beckettien "milieu."

31   GLASS, PEYTON III. "Beckett: Axial Man."
      Educational Theatre Journal 29 (Oct.):362-73.
      Examines the emptiness and isolation of
      Beckett's theatre: "Confidence gives way to
      confusion, despair, acquiescence, or simply,
      random activity. Beating against the walls
      of the cage ceases, and measuring the
      perimeter of the cell begins." Glass focuses
      on the spatial aspects of Act Without Words I
      and II and Waiting for Godot.

32   GONTARSKI, S.E. Beckett's "Happy Days": A
      Manuscript Study. Columbus, Ohio: Publica-
      tions Committee, Ohio State University
      Libraries, 86 pp.
      Focusing on form and process, proposes to
      reconstruct Beckett's composition of Happy
      Days, and then to use that information to

further our understanding of the play.
Gontarski feels that this subject is particularly valuable because of Beckett's own
analytical interest in the creative process.
The themes, style, comic devices and literary
allusions are discussed in detail. Followed
by a select bibliography.

33   _____. "Crapp's First Tapes: Beckett's
Manuscript Revisions of Krapp's Last Tape."
Journal of Modern Literature 6 (Feb.):61-68.
Evaluates seven preliminary stages (four
typescripts and three partial holograph
versions) of Krapp's Last Tape in order to
show how "Beckett exploited the technical and
dramatic potential of the tapes, amplified
and universalized Krapp's conflict, and
orchestrated the tone of the play from the
singular pathos of stage one to the final
patho-comedic ensemble."

34   GUSSOW, MEL. "Stage: Wait no Longer for the
Definitive Godot." New York Times, 31 Mar.,
p. 19C.
Reviews the West Berlin Schiller Theater's
production of Waiting for Godot at the
Brooklyn Academy of Music. As director of
the play Beckett accentuates the contrast and
symbiosis of Didi and Gogo, the visual aspect
of the play, and the human comedy as well as
tragedy.

35   _____. "Theater: Endgame in a Desert." New
York Times, 29 Mar., p. 36.
Sees Endgame as the "vision after the
apocalypse," or what happens after Waiting
for Godot. Gussow criticizes the setting and
pace of this production by Alan Schneider at
the Roundabout Stage Two.

36   HAMBURGER, MICHAEL. "The Poetry of Samuel
Beckett." PN Review 5, no. 1:15-16.
In a review of Collected Poems in English
and French, discusses several aspects of
Beckett's poetry: reduction, bilingualism,

abstraction, hermeticism, and critical
response.

37   HAMILTON, ALICE and KENNETH HAMILTON. "The
     Process of Imaginative Creation in Samuel
     Beckett's How It Is." Mosaic 10, no. 4
     (Summer):1-12.
          Presents "the artist's obligation to
     express" as a central theme in How It Is:
     "... How It Is is not only a work about the
     suffering through which the artist comes to
     experience his creative powers. The book
     also describes the special suffering of the
     artist that is caused by his artistic
     vocation, namely, loneliness."

38   HAYMAN, DAVID. "Some Writers in the Wake of the
     Wake." TriQuarterly 38 (Winter):3-38.
     Beckett: pp. 12-17.
          Traces the influence of Joyce's Wake on
     Twentieth-Century writers, Beckett, Burgess
     and Christine Brooke-Rose among others.
     Hayman believes that Beckett's later work is
     more "post-Wake" than his first works: "Like
     the Wake, Beckett's later narratives and
     plays deal exclusively with lowest common-
     denominator human situations, emblems for the
     human condition in, through, and beyond
     history."

39   HILL, LESLIE. "Fiction, Myth, and Identity in
     Samuel Beckett's Novel Trilogy." Forum for
     Modern Language Studies 13, no. 3 (July):230-
     39.
          Identifies the novels of the trilogy as "a
     negation of their fictions and as a progres-
     sive elimination of their impulsion to
     narrate." The ambiguity and heterogeneity of
     the adventure of writing is also considered.

40   HOBSON, HAROLD. "Samuel Beckett: Giant Under
     the Microscope." Sunday Times (London), 8
     May, p. 41.
          Points out the importance of Beckett's
     achievement, recognized in 1938 by Denis

Healey and later praised by the contributors to The Journal of Beckett Studies. Hobson briefly comments on Beckett's Collected Poems in English and French.

41 HUBERT, MARIE-CLAUDE. "Primauté du corps dans le théâtre de Samuel Beckett." In Travaux de linguistique publié par le Centre de Philologie et de Littératures Romanes de l'Université de Strasbourg. Strasbourg: Etudes Littéraires, pp. 259-72.
    Emphasizes the profound attachment demonstrated by the Beckettian couple. Whether or not the characters can support each other, they are inseparable. When the couple is separated (Play, Eh Joe, Krapp's Last Tape), time stops for the characters.

42 HVISTENDAHL, MARION. "Samuel Beckett -- From Bitches to Beautification." Cresset 40, nos. 9/10 (Sept.-Oct.):15-18.
    Individually describes Beckett's female dramatic figures, pointing out that Beckett's women are less anti-life than his men, provide a more positive approach to love, and are frequently less inactive than their male counterparts.

43 "In Memoriam: George Reavey (1907-1976)." Journal of Beckett Studies, no. 2 (Summer), pp. 1-8.
    Tributes to George Reavey, including an introductory tribute by Beckett and a selection of Reavey's poems chosen by Beckett.

44 JACQUART, EMMANUEL C. "Sémantique et sémiotique chez Beckett." Bonnes Feuilles 6, no. 2 (Spring):9-22.
    Proposes to define the author's intentions in Endgame by: 1) examining the author's point of view, 2) discovering the obscurities and allusions, and 3) reading the text exactly as it is.

45 JONES, CHRISTOPHER J. "Bergman's <u>Persona</u> and
    the Artistic Dilemma of the Modern Narra-
    tive." <u>Literature/Film Quarterly</u> 5, no. 1
    (Winter):75-88. Beckett: pp. 85-86.
        Believes that in his novel <u>Molloy</u>, Beckett
    works with aesthetic problems similar to
    those of Bergman's <u>Persona</u>: the two artists
    are preoccupied with the "aesthetic impasse"
    -- "the artist's sense of failure at the task
    of shaping a story from the incoherent and
    indeterminate material which the modern world
    provides."

46 JONES, DOROTHY F. "Beckett's 'Colloque Sen-
    timental.'" <u>French Review</u> 50, no. 3
    (Feb.):460-66.
        Demonstrates that Beckett's play <u>Happy
    Days</u> like Verlaine's poem "Colloque Sentimen-
    tal" focuses on the problematical relation-
    ship of two lovers. Quotations are taken
    from the French version of Beckett's play.

47 KARATSON, ANDRE. "Le 'Grotesque' dans la prose
    du XXe siècle (Kafka, Gombrowicz, Beckett)."
    <u>Revue de Littérature Comparée</u> 51, no. 2
    (Apr.-June):169-78.
        Defines "grotesque," compares examples
    taken from the works of Kafka, Gombrowicz and
    Beckett, and surveys the importance of the
    grotesque style in modern literature.

48 KENNEDY, SIGHLE. "'The Simple Games That Time
    Plays with Space -- ' An Introduction to
    Samuel Beckett's Manuscripts of <u>Watt</u>."
    <u>Centerpoint</u> 2, no. 3:55-61.
        Outlines his full-length study of the
    manuscripts of <u>Watt</u>, pointing out Beckett's
    vision of art as it evolved from his initial
    essay on <u>Finnegans Wake</u> to his writing of
    <u>Watt</u>. Kennedy compares Beckett's views to
    those of Schopenhauer, and indicates the
    influence of Aristotle's ten basic categories
    on the creation <u>Watt</u>.

49   *KERMODE, FRANK. "Beckett Aboard Rimbaud's
      Boat." <u>Daily Telegraph</u> (London), 12 May, p.
      11.
          Source: <u>British Humanities Index</u>, 1977;
      unverified.

50   KERN, EDITH. "Beckett as 'Homo Ludens.'"
      <u>Journal of Modern Literature</u> 6 (Feb.):47-60.
          Explores the ludic quality of Beckett's
      <u>Waiting for Godot</u>, with special emphasis on
      Lucky's tirade in the first act. Kern relies
      heavily on the finding of the critics V.A.
      Kolve and Robert Garapon.

51   KILROY, THOMAS. "Two Playwrights: Yeats and
      Beckett." In <u>Myth and Reality in Irish
      Literature</u>. Edited by Joseph Ronsley.
      Waterloo, Ont: Wilfred Laurier University
      Press, pp. 183-95.
          Studies the effect of theatricalism upon
      plays of Beckett and Yeats when those plays
      are considered as literature.

52   KNOWLSON, JAMES. "George Reavey and Samuel
      Beckett's Early Writing: Interview with
      George Reavey by James Knowlson." <u>Journal of
      Beckett Studies</u>, no. 2 (Summer), pp. 9-14.
          Discusses Reavey's acquaintance with
      Beckett and the publication of Beckett's
      works.

53   KOPSCHITZ, M.H. "See What is Happening Here:
      Variants in the Text of 'Ping.'" <u>Library</u> 32,
      no. 1 (Mar.):57-60.
          Analyzes the differences between the
      English text of "Ping," in <u>No's Knife</u> and
      that of the first English version of "Ping"
      printed in <u>Encounter</u>, (Feb. 1967).

54   KRIEGER, ELLIOT. "Samuel Beckett's <u>Texts for
      Nothing</u>: Explication and Exposition."
      <u>Modern Language Notes</u> 92, no. 5 (Dec.):987-
      1000.
          Categorizes the four basic oppositions in
      <u>Texts for Nothing</u> which determines the form

and content of the work: 1) reader/text, 2)
narrator/body or text/character, 3) narrator/
mind or text/plot and 4) day/night or black/
white, printed word/blank page, lamplight/
closed book.

55   KRIEGSMAN, ALAN M. "Variations on Godot."
      Washington Post, 25 Feb., p. 87.
           Reviews a variation of Waiting for Godot
      entitled "Thunder and Sweet Wine" performed
      by the Earth Onion Women's Theater, in which
      all of the actors are women and Lucky and
      Pozzo have been replaced by Blanche and
      Stella from A Streetcar Named Desire.

56   KROLL, JERI L. "The Surd as Inadmissible
      Evidence: The Case of Attorney-General v.
      Henry McCabe." Journal of Beckett Studies,
      no. 2 (Summer), pp. 47-58.
           Discusses the actual case of Henry McCabe
      who was tried and hung for murder in 1926.

57   LANGBAUM, ROBERT. "Beckett: Zero Identity."
      In The Mysteries of Identity: A Theme in
      Modern Literature. New York: Oxford
      University Press, pp. 120-44.
           Portrays Beckett's unindividuated charac-
      ters, the waste land without landmarks or
      direction in which they find themselves, and
      the slow and irregular movement of time they
      experience. References are made to Descar-
      tes, Wordsworth, Locke, Eliot, Proust, Yeats,
      Lawrence.

58   *LIVINGSTON, PAISLEY and TOBIN SIEBERS.
      "Glancing Blows: Towards a Panoptical
      Discipline." Oxford Literary Review 2, no.
      3:28-34.

59   LODGE, DAVID. "Postmodernist Fiction." In The
      Modes of Modern Writing. Metaphor, Metonymy
      and the Typology of Modern Literature.
      Ithaca, N.Y.: Cornell University Press, pp.
      220-245.
           Attempts a profile of postmodernist

fiction, utilizing examples from Beckett's
More Pricks Than Kicks, Murphy, Watt and the
trilogy to demonstrate specific characteristics in postmodernist fiction: uncertainty,
contradiction, permutation, and discon-
tinuity.

60   LOUZOUN, MYRIAM. "Fin de partie de Samuel
     Beckett. Effacement du monde et dynamisme
     formel." In Les Voies de la création
     théâtrale, V. Edited by Denis Bablet and
     Jean Jacquot. Paris: Editions du Centre
     National de la Recherche Scientifique, pp.
     377-445.
          Offers a detailed analysis of Endgame:
     the form of the works, the creation of space,
     the characters (physical traits, mobility,
     needs, desires), communication between the
     characters, and language (paradigms, rhythm,
     "vocal interpretation of Hamm's story),
     followed by a brief conversation" with Roger
     Blin.

61   MAHON, DEREK. "The Existential Lyric." New
     Statesman 93 (25 Mar.):403-4.
          Reviews Beckett's Collected Poems in
     English and French, discussing his transla-
     tion and the maturation of his verse in
     French.

62   MARTIN, GEORGE. "'Pozzo and Lucky': A Key to
     Godot." American Benedictine Review 28, no.
     4 (Dec.):397-412.
          Feels that Pozzo and Lucky provide an
     insight into every character in Waiting for
     Godot as well as into the art, temperament
     and philosophy of Beckett. Martin compares
     and contrasts specific aspects of the
     characters, inseparability, pride, restless
     movement, the role of the boy (as angel-
     annunciator or angel-guardian), and Lucky's
     speech (the central motif of the speech --
     partnership).

63   MAYS, J.C.C. "Mythologized Presences: <u>Murphy</u>
     in Its Time." In <u>Myth and Reality in Irish</u>
     <u>Literature</u>. Edited by Joseph Ronsley.
     Waterloo, Ont.: Wilfrid Laurier University
     Press, pp. 197-218.
         Examines the nature of Beckett's allusions
     to specific individuals and the two plots (on
     the circumference and at the center) in
     <u>Murphy</u>.

64   MENDELSON, EDWARD. "<u>The Caucasian Chalk Circle</u>
     and <u>Endgame</u>." In <u>Homer to Brecht. The</u>
     <u>European Epic and Dramatic Traditions</u>.
     Edited by Michael Seidel and Edward Mendel-
     son. New Haven: Yale University Press, pp.
     336-52.
         Believes modernism is characterized by the
     attention paid to the observer rather than to
     observed fact as in realism. The emphasis on
     this aspect of perception can take different
     forms, in some cases it is the author's
     intent to change the observer as in the
     political purposes of Brecht's plays, in
     other cases the purpose is limited to an
     observation of the observing self as in
     Beckett's work.

65   MERCIER, VIVIAN. <u>Beckett/Beckett</u>. New York:
     Oxford University Press, 254 pp.
         Outlines a dialectical approach to
     Beckett's works, focusing on the following
     oppositions: Ireland/The World, Gentleman/
     Tramp, Classicism/Absurdism, Painting/Music,
     Eye/Ear, Artist/Philosopher, Woman/Man. An
     earlier version of Chapter 2 was published,
     in 1976.103, and parts of Chapter 4 represent
     a revised version of 1974.39.

66   MOORE, JOHN REES. "The Exhilarating Mr.
     Beckett." <u>Shenandoah</u> 28, no. 3 (Spring):74-
     96.
         Studies the characters, situations,
     symbols and ambiguities of the Beckettian
     universe in three of Beckett's plays, <u>Waiting</u>
     <u>for Godot</u>, <u>Endgame</u>, and <u>Happy Days</u>.

67   MOORJANI, ANGELA B. "Narrative Game Strategies
      in Beckett's <u>Watt</u>." <u>Esprit Créateur</u> 17, no.
      3 (Fall):235-44.
          Attempts a non-linear reading of <u>Watt</u> to
      account for the novel's multiple narrative
      levels, and finds that the horizontal and
      vertical discontinuities, and the mirror and
      echo games relate to the other discontinu-
      ities of the novel.

68   NORTHAM, JOHN. "Waiting for Prospero." In
      <u>English Drama: Forms and Development. Essays</u>
      <u>in Honor of Muriel Clara Bradbrook</u>. Edited
      by Marie Axton and Raymond Williams.
      Cambridge: Cambridge University Press, pp.
      186-202.
          Utilizes an analysis of the masque from
      <u>The Tempest</u> as a point of reference for a
      comparison with three modern plays: <u>Rosmer-</u>
      <u>sholm</u>, <u>Ghost Sonata</u>, and <u>Waiting for Godot</u>.

69   OJO, SAMUEL ADEOYA. "L'Universalité et la
      permanence du message beckettien: Conception
      supranationale de la littérature." <u>Neo-</u>
      <u>helicon</u> 5, no. 2:195-215.
          Explores the universality of Beckett's
      message, the expansion of his personal
      horizons (national, religious, and linguis-
      tic), the anonymity of his characters, the
      neutrality of their environments, and the
      timelessness of their situations.

70   PALMER, HELEN H. ed. <u>European Drama Criticism:</u>
      <u>1900-1975</u>. Folkestone, Kent: William Dawson,
      pp. 40-46.
          Offers a bibliography of critical books
      and articles on Beckett's major plays.

71   PERLMUTTER, RUTH. "Beckett's <u>Film</u> and Beckett
      and <u>Film</u>." <u>Journal of Modern Literature</u> 6,
      no. 1 (Feb.):83-94.
          Points out Beckett's objectives in <u>Film</u>:
      he portrays the "inescapability of self-
      perception," the paradox of presence and

absence, and the question of self-definition
in art and life.

72   PILLING, JOHN. "Beckett After Still." Romance
     Notes 18, no. 2 (Winter):280-87.
       Discusses the effect of "Beckett's
     continuing mediation on the nature of
     imagination," in his most recent prose: "As
     the Story Was Told Me," "Pour Bram," and "For
     to End Yet Again".

73   _____. "Fizzles: For to end yet again and
     other fizzles by Samuel Beckett." Journal of
     Beckett Studies, no. 2 (Summer), pp. 96-100.
       Claims that with the publication of Ends
     and Odds it is now possible to understand
     Beckett's writing over the last twenty years.

74   POWLICK, LEONARD. "Temporality in Pinter's The
     Dwarfs." Modern Drama 20, no. 1 (Mar.):67-
     75.
       Notes the stylistic and thematic influence
     of Beckett's Watt on Pinter's The Dwarfs.

75   RABINOVITZ, RUBIN. "Time, Space, and Verisimil-
     itude in Samuel Beckett's Fiction." Journal
     of Beckett Studies, no. 2 (Summer), pp. 40-
     46.
       Establishes Beckett's readjustment of
     space-time reality: in his fictional works,
     the time-space world follows the world of the
     imagination.

75a RATCLIFFE, MICHAEL. "Kinship with Godot."
     Times (London), 18 Apr., p. 6.
       Reviews the world premiere of two tele-
     vision plays, Ghost Trio and ... but the
     clouds ..., and the television performance of
     Not I: "There is no doubt that the reduc-
     tionist scale and austerity of Beckett's late
     work is effective on the small screen,
     although the dynamics are pitched so low that
     if the plays were any longer you might well
     drop off." Reprinted: 1979.22.82.

76   REID, ALEC. "Beckett, the Camera, and Jack
      MacGowran," In <u>Myth and Reality in Irish
      Literature</u>. Edited by Joseph Ronsley.
      Waterloo, Ont.: Wilfrid Laurier University
      Press, pp. 219-25.
           Studies the role of inanimate objects in
      Beckett's works, with special emphasis placed
      on the use of the camera in <u>The Goad</u>, <u>Film</u>,
      <u>Eh Joe</u> and <u>From Beginning to End</u>, and
      Beckett's close relationship with Jack
      MacGowran.

77   ROJTMAN, BETTY. "Un retour à l'origine: Etude
      structurale de <u>Tous ceux qui tombent</u>."
      <u>Romance Notes</u> 18, no. 1 (Fall):11-17.
           Highlights the mounting dramatic intensity
      in <u>All That Fall</u>, analyzing Mrs. Rooney's
      departure for the station to pick up her
      husband and their return to her initial
      starting point.

78   SACHNER, MARK J. "The Artist as Fiction: An
      Aesthetics of Failure in Samuel Beckett's
      Trilogy." <u>Midwest Quarterly</u> 18, no. 2
      (Winter):144-55.
           Believes the new status of art as seen by
      Harold Rosenberg in his work <u>The De-defini-
      tion of Art</u> is epitomized in literature by
      the works of Samuel Beckett: "Beckett's
      novels put the concern of art beyond its
      visible object, beyond even 'the fiction of
      the artist' in the act of manipulating that
      object, and deep into the artistic conscious-
      ness as it perceives itself in action."

79   SAGE, VICTOR. "Dickens and Beckett: Two Uses
      of Materialism." <u>Journal of Beckett Studies</u>,
      no. 2 (Summer):15-39.
           Shows that Beckett and Dickens are both
      concerned with materialism, although they
      demonstrate a concept that neither Bergson
      nor Huizinga take into account: "the idea
      ... of a system which can get older without
      using up time."

80   SCHNEIDER, ALAN. "I Hope to be Going on With
      Sam Beckett -- and He With Me." New York
      Times, 18 Dec., p. 5D.
          Comments on his working relationship with
      Beckett over the years and the importance of
      form and music to Beckett's plays: "...
      content inevitably comes from form itself.
      Meaning rests in his sounds and images. It
      is precisely from the ambiguities and
      unexpected juxtapositions that the dramatic
      tension arises."

81   SCHNEIDER, JOSEPH LEONDAR. "Beckett's Waiting
      for Godot." Explicator 35, no. 4 (Summer):9-
      10.
          Equates Godot with Sidhe, minor Irish
      deities famous in Irish folklore, described
      by Yeats in The Celtic Twilight and The Wind
      Among the Reeds.

82   SEGRE, ELISABETH BERGMAN. "Style and Structure
      in Beckett's 'Ping': That Something Itself."
      Journal of Modern Literature 6, no. 1
      (Feb.):127-47.
          In order to trace the variations and the
      constants of the repetitions in "Ping,"
      studies four aspects of the word-groups which
      range from a single word to 16 words: 1)
      individual words and their semantic value, 2)
      words in limited contexts and their connota-
      tive poles, 3) the syntactic, formal, and
      semantic variants within each word-group
      series, and 4) the phonetic patterning which
      plays a strong structural role.

83   *SLATTERY, E.M. "The Theatre of the Absurd,
      with Special Reference to Samuel Beckett's
      Waiting for Godot." Communiqué 3, no. 1:82-
      100.

84   SMITH, CECIL. "Waiting for Godot." Los Angeles
      Times T.V. Times, 26 June - 2 July, p. 4.
          Reviews the Los Angeles Theater's tele-
      vision production of Waiting for Godot with
      Dana Elcar, Donald Moffat, Ralph Waite and

Bruce French. Although the play was restaged
in the desert to approximate Beckett's
nothingness, Smith feels that the "play is
played not for its metaphysical metaphor,
whatever Beckett's intention, but for itself
-- a mad Vaudeville concocted of clowns and
claptrap ..."

85   SPARLING, RUSSEL. "The Anti-Transcendental
      Function of Pozzo and Lucky in Beckett's
      <u>Waiting for Godot</u>." <u>Notes on Contemporary
      Literature</u> 7, no. 5 (Dec.):2.
          Describes the three phases in a "great
      undeceiving" in which Vladimir and Estragon's
      image of humanity is shattered: 1) in the
      first phase Estragon and Vladimir mistake
      Pozzo for Godot; 2) in the second phase Pozzo
      is a parody of Godot; 3) in the third phase
      Pozzo is blind, suffering and helpless.

86   SUTCLIFFE, TOM. "Opera." <u>Guardian</u>, 17 July,
      p. 10.
          Briefly describes a musical production of
      "Neither" at the Rome Opera.

87   TATHAM, CAMPBELL. "<u>Watt</u>-Knots Enhance Endo-
      genous Entropy." <u>Boundary</u> 5, no. 2
      (Winter):351-62.
          Imitates stylistic elements of several of
      Beckett's texts, refers to numerous critical
      works on Beckett, and demonstrates the
      extension of the concept of entropy to
      cybernetics.

88   THOMAS, LLOYD SPENCER. "Krapp: Beckett's Aged
      Narcissus." <u>CEA Critic</u> 39, no. 2:9-11.
          Depicts Krapp as an aged Narcissus
      drowning in drink and dreams.

89   *THOMAS, MICHAEL. "Towards an Understanding of
      Samuel Beckett." <u>Oxford Literary Journal</u>,
      no. 2 (Autumn), pp. 30-31.

90   USHER, SHAUN. "Beckett's Off-Break Had Me
      Stumped!" <u>Daily Mail</u> (London), 18 Apr.

Reviews the television premiere of <u>Ghost
Trio</u> and <u>... but the clouds ...</u> and an
approved film version of <u>Not I</u>: "Martin
Esslin ... made the most helpful contribution. He advised audiences not to try to
make sense of the plays as stories, but treat
them as music, surrender to them in the same
way, and hope to take away images and
emotions."

91   Van PETTEN, CAROL. "Modulations of Monologue in
     Beckett's <u>Comment c'est</u>." <u>Symposium</u> 31, no.
     3 (Fall):243-55.
          Studies the modulations of the narrator's
     monologue in <u>How It Is</u>: the variations of
     style, tone, rhythm, pace and arrangement,
     patterns and repetitions of word groups.

92   WARDLE, IRVING. "Breathing life into Beckett."
     <u>Times</u> (London), 20 Sept., p. 10.
          Points out that Peter Hall's production of
     <u>Happy Days</u> becomes more of a two-character
     play than a monologue.

93   WHITAKER, THOMAS R. <u>Fields of Play in Modern
     Drama</u>. Princeton, N.J.: Princeton Univer-
     sity Press, pp. 17-24.
          Attempts to reinterpret modern drama in
     terms of the power of all drama to lead us
     toward participation: "We always participate
     through two mutually inclusive modes. When
     we act, we present ourselves to witnesses.
     When we witness, we attend to actors. But
     every actor is also an implicit witness,
     every witness an implicit actor." In this
     context, Whitaker discusses the difficulty of
     identifying oneself with the vision of life
     presented in <u>Happy Days</u>.

94   WINKLER, ELIZABETH HALE. "The Clown and the
     Absurd: Samuel Beckett." In <u>The Clown in
     Modern Anglo-Irish Drama</u>. Bern: Herbert
     Lang, pp. 205-52.
          Details Beckett's use of clowns and
     clowning techniques in <u>Waiting for Godot</u> and

the subsequent reduction of clowning antics
in the works which follow: Endgame, Krapp's
Last Tape, Happy Days, Acts Without Words I
and II, and Film.

95   WINSTON, MATTHEW. "Watt's First Footnote."
      Journal of Modern Literature 6 (Feb.):69-82.
         States that the first footnote in Watt
      deserves close attention because it "signals
      us to modify our expectations about the kind
      of book we are reading, it introduces the
      controlling presence of a narrator, and it
      begins a reflection ... on what it means to
      'say' something, anything, in a work of
      fiction."

96   ZEIFMAN, HERSH. "The Alterable Whey of Words:
      The Texts of Waiting for Godot." Educational
      Theatre Journal 29, no. 1 (Mar.):77-84.
         Compares two differing texts of Waiting
      for Godot: the first American edition (Grove
      Press, 1954) and the first British edition
      (Faber & Faber, 1956).

1977-1978

1   ROMANO, JOHN. "Beckett Without Angst."
      American Scholar 47, no. 1 (Winter):95-102.
         Evaluates how readers are affected by
      Beckett's work through two approaches: one
      through his comic effects and the other
      through his early critical essays. Rather
      than conferring pain his works have the
      opposite effect, that of a reprieve or a stay
      of execution.

1978

1   ACHESON, JAMES. "Beckett, Proust, and Schopen-
      hauer." Contemporary Literature 19, no. 2
      (Spring):165-79.
         Feels Beckett's Proust demonstrates that
      Remembrance of Things Past is an original

adaptation of Schopenhauer's theory of music
to the writing of fiction, which no critic
had noticed before. Acheson discusses
Schopenhauer's influence on Beckett and
Proust.

2   BAIR, DEIRDRE. <u>Samuel Beckett: A Biography</u>.
     New York: Harcourt Brace Jovanovich, 736 pp.
          Describes Beckett's life, and comments on
     his writing, relationships and friends. Bair
     intended "to concentrate on the life of
     Samuel Beckett's mind, to find out as much as
     she could about the circumstances that led to
     the writing of each work, to place these
     works within the framework of his daily
     life." Her sources of information include
     written criticism, personal interviews,
     correspondence, telephone conversations, and
     conversations with Beckett himself. Many
     critics quote the biography as a source,
     others vehemently oppose it. See 1980.29.6,
     1981.102, 1982.19, 1984.72, 1984.79.

3   BARRY, A. DAVID. "Beckett: L'Entropie du
     langage et de l'homme." <u>French Review</u> 51,
     no. 6 (May):853-63.
          Proposes a theory of language which is
     evident in Beckett's drama and demonstrates
     an entropic progression of man and language:
     man and his language are gradually reduced to
     nothingness. Examples are taken from <u>Waiting
     for Godot</u>, <u>Endgame</u>, <u>Krapp's Last Tape</u>, <u>Happy
     Days</u>, and <u>Play</u>.

4   *BENSON, MARY. "Blin on Beckett." <u>Theater</u> 10,
     no. 1:90-93.

5   _____. "Roger Blin and Beckett." <u>London
     Magazine</u> 18, no. 7 (Oct.):52-57.
          Interviews Roger Blin questioning him
     about his first productions of <u>Godot</u> and
     <u>Endgame</u>, as well as his new production of
     <u>Godot</u> at the Comédie Française. Blin also
     comments on directing and acting in Beckett's
     plays.

6   BISHOP, TOM. "The Loneliest Monologue:
     Beckett's Theater in the Seventies." October,
     no. 6 (Fall), pp. 31-45.
          Examines the isolation and helplessness of
     the Beckettian personae of the seventies.
     The plays display a greater sense of abstrac-
     tion (fragmentation of narrative, deper-
     sonalization of character) and a forced
     focusing of our attention on minimal visual
     matter.

7   BORIE, MONIQUE. "'... aussi dénué d'histoire
     que le premier jour': Notes sur Beckett."
     Travail Théâtral, no. 32-33 (July-Dec.), pp.
     33-41.
          Discusses the inability of the Beckettian
     narrator to construct the unities of time and
     space or to create a whole story.

8   BRATER, ENOCH. "A Footnote to Footfalls:
     Footsteps of Infinity on Beckett's Narrow
     Space." Comparative Drama 12, no. 1
     (Spring):35-41.
          Explores Beckett's challenge to his
     audience's power of perception in Footfalls.
     The figure eight traced by May becomes the
     symbol for infinity when it is turned on its
     side: "As members of the audience we become
     obsessed with the materialization of
     Beckett's precise illusion, its menace, and
     its progressive validation."

9   _____. "Collected Poems in English and French
     by Samuel Beckett." New Republic 178, no. 7
     (18 Feb.):33-35.
          Emphasizing Beckett's lyricism in his
     prose and drama, reviews his poems as they
     correspond to the phases of his literary
     career.

10   BRONSEN, DAVID. "Consuming Struggle vs. Killing
     Time: Preludes to Dying in the Dramas of
     Ibsen and Beckett." In Aging and the
     Elderly. Humanistic Perspectives in Geron-
     tology. Edited by Stuart F. Spiker, Kathleen

M. Woodward and David D. Van Tassel.
Atlantic Highlands, N.J.: Humanities Press,
pp. 261-81.
    Compares the portrayal of the aged in
Ibsen's three late plays The Master Builder,
John Gabriel Bockman, and When We Dead Awaken
with all of Beckett's dramas: "The characters in these works by Ibsen and those of
Beckett are caught up in the absorbing
preoccupation of how to cope with life while
posing insistent questions that imply they
have never found peace."

11   CAMPBELL, SUEELLEN. "Krapp's Last Tape and
      Critical Theory." Comparative Drama 12, no.
      3 (Fall):187-99.
          Discusses thematic and structural paral-
      lels to several major issues addressed by
      twentieth century critical theory: "the
      nature of genres, the characteristics of
      literary and non-literary language, the
      importance of history in interpretation, and
      the role of readers and critics as creators
      of a work's meaning through interpretation
      and evaluation."

12   CAVE, RICHARD. "Two Views of Purgatory:
      Beckett and Yeats at the Edinburgh Festival,
      1977." Journal of Beckett Studies, no. 3
      (Summer), pp. 121-27.
          Discusses the staging of Beckett's Embers
      and Yeat's Purgatory at the Edinburgh
      Festival. Beckett's radio play was presented
      in mime to a recording of the text. Cave
      criticizes the visual realization of the play
      which "made the experience seem utterly
      unnatural and remote ..."

13   COHN, RUBY. "Earlier Endgames." Modern Drama
      21, no. 2 (June):109-19.
          Analyzes two early versions of Endgame in
      two acts, one located at the Ohio State
      University library, and the other in the
      Beckett collection of Reading University.

14   CONNORS, PATRICIA. "Samuel Beckett's 'Whoro-
      scope' as a Dramatic Monologue." <u>Ball State
      University Forum</u> 19, no. 2 (Spring):26-32.
           Evaluates the form of "Whoroscope," noting
      that the poem juxtaposes a pole for intel-
      ligibility and a pole for unintelligibility:
      "Beckett's poem, operating as a dialogue of
      the knowable and the impenetrable, illus-
      trates a movement in the genre untypical of
      the twentieth century, tending away from the
      interior monologue and the novel toward the
      drama ..."

15   CORR, PAUL J. "Beckett's 'Still.'" <u>Explicator</u>
      37, no. 1 (Fall):41.
           Briefly reviews "Still": affirming
      immobility in the face of movement, "Still"
      emphasizes the disparity between fiction and
      reality.

16   *CORVIN, MICHEL. "Analyse stylistique d'un
      texte de Beckett." <u>Organon</u> 78:67-88.

17   COURNOT, MICHEL. "<u>En attendant Godot</u> à Avig-
      non." <u>Monde</u>, 19 July, p. 13.
           Due to either his poor choice of actors or
      his misunderstanding of Beckett's <u>Waiting for
      Godot</u>, Cournot believes the Czech Otomar
      Krejca has failed to present Beckett's play
      in its true dimensions.

18   *DAVIS, R.J. "Beckett as Translator." <u>Long
      Room</u>, nos. 16-17 (Spring-Autumn), pp. 29-34.

19   DEARLOVE, JUDITH. "The Voice and its Words:
      How It Is in Beckett's Canon." <u>Journal of
      Beckett Studies</u>, no. 3 (Summer), pp. 56-75.
           Defines a tripartite division of Beckett's
      canon: the works written before <u>How It Is</u>
      are "concerned with the problems of a
      mind/body dualism"; <u>How It Is</u> marks a
      turning point in Beckett's literary career
      and focuses on the "identification of the
      self with the voice and an acceptance, if not
      celebration, of the life of the imagination";

and the pieces written after <u>How It Is</u> "turn
from an emphasis upon the mind's limitations
to consideration of its imaginative construc-
tions." Dearlove discusses the shift in
Beckett's framework and the conceptual and
structural changes that occur in <u>How It Is</u>
and the works that follow.

20   ESSLIN, MARTIN. "Beckett at the Open Space."
      <u>Plays and Players</u> 26, no. 3 (Dec.):20-21.
          Reviews the San Quentin Drama Workshop's
      productions of <u>Krapp's Last Tape</u> and <u>Endgame</u>
      in West Berlin, describing Beckett's help
      with directing and advice, and the actors'
      total dedication to Beckett's conception.

21   FLETCHER, BERYL S., JOHN FLETCHER, BARRY SMITH,
      AND WALTER BACHEM. <u>A Student's Guide to the</u>
      <u>Plays of Samuel Beckett</u>. London and Boston:
      Faber and Faber, 222 pp.
          Offers a general introduction to Beckett's
      drama: a select bibliography, a biographical
      table, an introduction to modernism, a
      discussion of the Theater of the Absurd and
      the problems of interpretation, and a
      commentary dedicated to each of Beckett's
      plays.

22   FLETCHER, JOHN. "Beckett and the Medium: Rough
      for Radio?" <u>Caliban</u> 15, no. 14, fasc. 1:2-
      18.
          Discusses the history of Beckett's
      association with the B.B.C., the sonic decor,
      the structure and themes of the radio plays.
      Fletcher feels that Beckett's writing is
      "rough for radio" in the sense of being
      "tentative and exploratory" as well as
      sometimes "stretching the medium beyond its
      capabilities." Reprinted: 1978.23.

23   _____. "Beckett and the Medium: Rough for
      Radio?" In <u>Papers of the Radio Literature</u>
      <u>Conference, 1977</u>. Edited by Peter Lewis.
      Durham: Dept.of English, University of

Durham, pp. 157- 73.
Reprint of 1978.22.

24   FLETCHER, JOHN and JOHN SPURLING. Beckett: A
      Study of His Plays. London: Methuen, 152
      pp.
          Analyzes Beckett's major plays individual-
      ly (Eleuthéria, Waiting for Godot, Endgame,
      All That Fall, Krapp's Last Tape, Embers, Eh
      Joe, Words and Music, Cascando, Happy Days,
      Play, Acts Without Words, Film, Come and Go,
      Breath) and comments on their performance and
      the audience response.

25   FREADMAN, ANNE et al. "Ce petit peuple de
      chercheurs ..." Australian Journal of French
      Studies 15, no. 2 (Jan.-Apr.):79-100.
          Presents a report of an honours seminar
      held in the French Dept. at the University of
      Sydney in which the project of textual
      analysis of The Lost Ones is divided into
      three sections: 1) syntagmatic segmentation
      into the macro-structures of the text; 2)
      temporal structures, as a product of the
      textual progressions as well as of the
      "thematics" of time; 3) the text and al-
      legory.

26   FRYE, NORTHROP. "The Nightmare Life in Death."
      In Northrup Frye on Culture and Literature.
      Chicago: University of Chicago Press, pp.
      219-29.
          Reprint of 1960.22, 1970.47.

27   *HARGREAVES, ANNA. "A Computer-Aided Study of
      Beckett's Plays and Translations." Revue,
      no. 1, pp. 25-43.

28   HENKELS, ROBERT M. "Novel Quarters for an Odd
      Couple: Apollo and Dionysus in Beckett's
      Watt and Pinget's The Inquisitory." Studies
      in Twentieth Century Literature 2 (Spring):
      141-57.
          Examines Watt and The Inquisitory in light

of two questions regarding the new novel:
"From what uncharted recesses of the mind and
spirit does art emerge? And can a work of
art engage the reader in the creative process
directly instead of describing it from the
outside?" Henkels calls attention to the
struggle between reason and unreason on the
treatment of time, space, and plot in these
novels.

29   IEHL, DOMINIQUE. "Grotesque et signification
      dans le théâtre de Beckett et de Dürrenmatt."
      <u>Caliban</u> 15, no. 14, fasc. 1:19-33.
           Defines "grotesque" as a style in the
      theater in which meaning and language are
      reduced but not destroyed. Iehl compares the
      works of Beckett and Dürrenmatt to
      demonstrate Beckett's influence on European
      theater.

30   *ISER, WOLFGANG. <u>The Act of Reading. A Theory</u>
      <u>of Aesthetic Response</u>. Baltimore and London:
      The John Hopkins University Press, 239 pp.

31   JACQUART, EMMANUEL. "Un singulier pluriel ou
      les pièges de la signification chez Beckett."
      In <u>Ethique et esthétique dans la littérature</u>
      <u>française du XXe siècle</u>. Edited by Maurice
      Cagnon. Saratoga, Calif.: Anna Libre, pp.
      191-99.
           Discusses Beckett's aesthetic of ambiguity
      and indecisiveness. The Beckettian text
      poses two types of difficulties. The first
      consists in decoding the text, the "message",
      the second in being able to interpret what
      the text says or finding the meaning the
      author gives the "message."

32   KAUFFMANN, STANLEY. "Border Country." <u>New</u>
      <u>Republic</u> 178 (14 Jan.):22-25.
           Describes three of Beckett's plays being
      produced at the Manhattan Theater Club in New
      York, <u>Play</u>, <u>That Time</u>, and <u>Footfalls</u>.
      Kauffman believes that the central feature of
      a Beckett play is the "image," next in

importance is the sound of the voices, and
then "All else follows from and through those
considerations."

33   *KENNEDY, SIGHLE.   "'The Famine and Feasting of
     the Ages': Samuel Beckett's Occult Endnotes
     to <u>Krapp's Last Tape</u>." <u>Centerpoint</u> 3, no.
     1:83-92.

34   KLINE, MICHAEL B. "<u>Waiting for Godot</u> as
     Entropic Myth." <u>Michigan Academician</u> 10, no.
     4 (Spring):393-402.
          Believes <u>Waiting for Godot</u> is set against
     the myth of the Passion, yet denied the
     promise of redemption. Kline remarks that
     Beckett refuses to allow the myth of the
     Passion to resolve the contradictions of the
     play, thus producing a tragicomical view of a
     modern world grown remote from the efficacy
     of myth.

35   KNOWLSON, JAMES. "Extracts from an Unscripted
     Interview with Billie Whitelaw." <u>Journal of
     Beckett Studies</u>, no. 3 (Summer), pp. 85-90.
          In her discussion of her performances of
     <u>Play</u>, <u>Not I</u>, and <u>Footfalls</u>, Billie Whitelaw
     emphasizes the difficulties of the parts, the
     technical problems she encountered, her
     feelings about the plays, and the experience
     of working with Beckett.

36   KRANCE, CHARLES. "Montaigne's Last Krapp." <u>New
     York Literary Forum</u> 2:45-67.
          Compares Montaigne's examination of his
     self-portraits made at ten year intervals
     with Krapp listening to the voice of his past
     selves on his tape recorder.

37   KROLL, JERI L. "Belacqua as Artist and Lover:
     'What a Misfortune.'" <u>Journal of Beckett
     Studies</u>, no. 3 (Summer), pp. 10-39.
          Undertakes an analysis of Belacqua ("Dream
     of Fair to Middling Women," <u>More Pricks than
     Kicks</u>) and his relationship with women. Kroll
     studies Beckett's treatment of women in his

early fiction (with special emphasis on his
story "What a Misfortune") and the reasons
for Belacqua's "romantic miscarriages."

38   LEE, VERA G.   "Beckett on Proust." <u>Romanic</u>
     <u>Review</u> 69, nos. 1-2 (Jan.-Mar.):196-206.
     Examines the interpretive aspect of
     Beckett's <u>Proust</u> as a confrontation of two
     literary minds that converge in Schopen-
     hauer's philosophy, and demonstrates how
     problems of language and style intensify a
     fundamental dissimilarity between the two
     writers.

39   *LEVY, ERIC.   "The Beckettian Narrator in Six
     Stories and <u>Nouvelles</u>." <u>Canadian Journal of</u>
     <u>Irish Studies</u> 4, no. 1:26-36.

40   _____.   "Voice of Species: The Narrator and
     Beckettian Man in Three Novels." <u>ELH</u> 45, no.
     2 (Summer):343-58.
     Demonstrates the unique situation of the
     protagonist in the trilogy. There is but one
     speaker in the three novels and this narrator
     is transformed into the stories he tells. In
     order to do this each novel draws support
     from an established literary form: <u>Molloy</u>
     utilizes the epic and memoir, <u>Malone Dies</u>
     relies on the death bed confession, and <u>The</u>
     <u>Unnamable</u> emphasizes philosophical discourse.
     Beckettian man is not "Everyman": "his voice
     is no longer the private wail of one man in
     pain, but that of humanity, the human
     species."

41   LITTLE, J.P.   "Form and the Void. Beckett's <u>Fin</u>
     <u>de partie</u> and Ionesco's <u>Les Chaises</u>." <u>French</u>
     <u>Studies</u> 32, no. 1 (Jan.):46-54.
     Compares <u>Endgame</u> with <u>The Chairs</u>, em-
     phasizing the stage settings, the basic
     themes, the goals of the characters, the way
     the authors have translated their visions
     directly into dramatic terms.

42   MERCIER, VIVIAN.   "Samuel Beckett, Bible
       Reader."   Commonweal 105, no. 9 (28
       Apr.):266-68.
           Stresses Beckett's familiarity with the
       King James Version of the Bible, the Anglican
       Book of Common Prayer, and the Irish Church
       Hymnal.   Mercier relates common experiences
       as a boarder at Portora Royal School, and
       points out religious references in Beckett's
       writing.

43   MERIVALE, PATRICIA.   "Endgame and the Dialogue
       of King and Fool in the Monarchical Meta-
       drama."   Modern Drama 21, no. 2 (June):121-
       36.
           Remarks that the King of tragedy and the
       Fool of comedy are brought together in a
       closed setting, in order to reflect the
       absurdist theme of playing theatrical games
       while waiting for death.

44   MIGNON, PAUL-LOUIS.   "Samuel Beckett ou la
       représentation du néant."   In Panorama du
       théâtre au XXe siècle.   Paris: Gallimard,
       pp. 160-65.
           Briefly outlines the essential elements of
       Beckett's plays: the characters, their
       surroundings, their actions, the uncertainty
       and absurdity of life.

45   MOONEY, MICHAEL E.   "Molloy, Part I: Beckett's
       'Discourse on Method.'"   Journal of Beckett
       Studies, no. 3 (Summer), pp. 40-55.
           Considers the question of Beckett's "anti-
       Cartesianism" as it applies to Molloy, Part
       I.   Molloy is seen as a "transformation of
       the Discourse as a philosophic myth" or as a
       "disturbingly humorous inversion of the
       Discourse."

46   MOUNIN, GEORGES.   "La 'Mise en question' du
       langage dans la littérature actuelle."   In La
       Littérature et ses technocraties.   Paris:
       Casterman, pp. 133-41.
           Discusses the unusual use of language in

Waiting for Godot, with special emphasis on
Lucky's speech.

47   OMESCO, ION.   La Métamorphose de la tragédie.
     Paris: Presses Universaires de France, pp.
     55-58, 123-27, 142-49, 188-97, 202-18, 225-
     38, and passim.
          Comments on many of Beckett's dramas
     throughout his discussion of the form and
     evolution of tragedy (character, action,
     plot, discourse): Act Without Words,I,
     Embers, Krapp's Last Tape, Waiting for Godot,
     Endgame, and Happy Days.

48   PILLING, JOHN. "Beckett in Manhattan." Journal
     of Beckett Studies, no. 3 (Summer), pp. 127-
     28.
          Evaluates Alan Schneider's production of
     Play, That Time, and Footfalls at the
     Manhattan Theatre Club. In this small
     theatre the plays created an oppressive
     atmosphere. While Footfalls was "electric,"
     Play seemed much too slow.

49   _____. "The Significance of Beckett's 'Still.'"
     Essays in Criticism 28, no. 2 (Apr.):143-54.
          Analyzes "Still," "Sounds" and "Still 3,"
     three texts which resemble each other in
     their aim of re-establishing tranquility.

50   POSTLEWAIT, THOMAS. "Self-Performing Voices:
     Mind, Memory and Time in Beckett's Drama."
     Twentieth Century Literature 24, no. 4
     (Winter):473-91.
          Examines Beckett's preoccupation with the
     solitary voice, perception, the act of
     consciousness, temporal discontinuity, and
     spatial separation.

51   REID, ALEC. "From Beginning to Date: Some
     Thoughts on the Plays of Samuel Beckett."
     Threshold, no. 29 (Autumn), pp. 57-70.
          Comments on the basic dramatic situations
     of Waiting for Godot, Endgame, Acts Without
     Words, Krapp's Last Tape, All That Fall,

Happy Days, *Play*, and <u>Not I</u>. The novelty of Beckett's plays lies in their ability to relate to individual spectators who understand the plays on their own terms and from their own experiences.

52   ROJTMAN, BETTY.   "Une structure de récurrence: <u>La Dernière Bande</u>." <u>Hebrew University Studies in Literature</u> 6, no. 2 (Autumn):294-320.

Utilizing <u>Krapp's Last Tape</u> as an example, demonstrates how the dramatic structure and theatrical principles Beckett employs in his plays makes the hope of "ending" an impossible quest, a vicious circle in which the character's futile situation will be repeated indefinitely.

53   ROLLINS, RONALD. G.   "Old Men and Memories: Yeats and Beckett." <u>Eire-Ireland: A Journal of Irish Studies</u> 13, no. 3 (Fall):106-19.

Compares William Butler Yeats' <u>Purgatory</u> to Beckett's <u>Krapp's Last Tape</u>. Both old men reexperience some joyful and painful but similar experiences from their past: "... their days of youthful vigor when the world was alive with color, movement, and hope; their different involvements in the deaths of their fathers; their ambivalent reactions to the decline and deaths of their mothers ... and the inexorable erosion of their early dreams and ambitions that were replaced by despair and cynical, obscene jesting with the passage of the years."

54   SCHWARTZ, ALFRED.   "Condemned to Exist."   In <u>From Büchner to Beckett. Dramatic Theory and the Modes of Tragic Drama</u>. Ohio University Press: Athens, Ohio, pp. 334-56.

Offers a critical study of the modes of tragic drama on the modern stage in which Beckett's theater reflects the demise of tragedy: "The death of tragedy is due not to despair, but more precisely to the degradation of the human actor, leading to

indifference before the spectacle of man made
into a thing."

55   SHERZER, DINA. "De-construction in Waiting for
      Godot." In The Reversible World. Symbolic
      Inversion in Art and Society. Edited by
      Barbara Babcock. Ithaca: Cornell University
      Press, pp. 129-46.
      Discusses the different ways Beckett
      manipulates rules of language and speech,
      making use of the components of the speech
      event described by Jakobson (1960) and
      elaborated by Hymes (1972): "(1) ... the
      communication established between characters
      in particular contexts, (2) the manipulation
      of the rules of semantic association, (3) the
      use of different registers of language, (4)
      the use of semantic paradigms and synonyms,
      (5) the use of common expressions and
      clichés, (6) the exploitation of the dif-
      ferent meanings of a single word, and (7) the
      use of sounds and the sequences of sounds."

56   _____. "Dialogic Incongruities in the Theater
      of the Absurd." Semiotica 22, no. 3/4:269-85.
      Considers the following problems in the
      plays of Beckett, Diaz, Ionesco, and Pinter:
      organization of dialogues, face-to-face
      interactions, and interplay between com-
      ponents of dialogues.

57   S[IMON], A[LFRED]. "Godot et la subversion."
      Esprit n.s. II, 5, no. 17 (May):180-81.
      Compares certain aspects of Roger Blin's
      1953 production of Waiting for Godot with his
      1978 staging of the play: the roles of the
      actors, the staging, and the audience's
      acceptance of the play.

58   *SIMPSON, EKUNDAYO. Samuel Beckett, traducteur
      de lui-même: Aspects de bilinguisme lit-
      téraire. Québec: Centre International de
      Recheche sur le Bilinguisme, 212 pp.

59   STATES, BERT O. <u>The Shape of Paradox: An Essay
      on "Waiting for Godot."</u> Berkeley: Univer-
      sity of California Press, 120 pp.
          Examines St. Augustine's paradox of the
      two thieves as a model for the structural
      dialectic of <u>Waiting for Godot</u>. States
      analyzes the play from the point of view of
      the images, themes, time, place, plot, and
      characters with references to Shakespeare,
      Kafka, Kierkegaard, Ibsen, and Chekhov:
      "Beckett's fondness for the 'shape' of the
      parable of the two thieves suggests ... the
      undefinable power that is released when two
      clear and opposed statements are brought into
      perfect symmetry. You do not simply have
      damnation and/or salvation but a portable
      model of the world's capacity to conster-
      nate."

60   STOTT, CATHERINE. "Waiting for <u>Molloy</u>." <u>Sunday
      Telegraph</u> (London), 22 Oct.
          Presents an interview with Billie Whitelaw
      in which she describes her acting in
      Beckett's plays and her current role in Simon
      Gray's <u>Molloy</u>.

61   SUBRAHMANIAN, K. "<u>The Unnamable</u> -- An Indian
      Interpretation." <u>Literary Criterion</u> 13, no.
      1:62-64.
          Points out the similarities between the
      Unnamable's desire to go beyond the world of
      name and form and the Indian goddesses
      Lalita, who is "beyond name and form" and
      Kali, the goddess of destruction.

62   SZANTO, GEORGE H. "Samuel Beckett and Dramatic
      Possibilities in an Age of Technological
      Retention." In <u>Theater & Propaganda</u>. Austin
      and London: University of Texas Press, pp.
      145-77.
          Evaluates Beckett's dramatic works from
      the following points of view: 1) the search
      for meaning, 2) the search for form -- the
      basic form of the failed quest, and 3)
      dramatic art in an age of technological

retention (describes the sequence from
cultural revolution to communicational
revolution to political revolution --
Beckett's plays are regarded as part of the
communicational revolution).

63   *TOYAMA, JEAN YAMASAKI. "Self, Voice and
     Language in Molloy." Degré Second: Studies
     in French Literature, no. 2 (June), pp. 191-
     213.

64   VAIS, MICHEL. "Samuel Beckett." In L'Ecrivain
     scénique. Montreal: Les Presses de
     l'Université du Québec, pp. 91-106.
        Describes Beckett's stage directions:
     props, scenery, music, costumes, make-up, and
     lighting.

65   WATTS, CEDRIC. "The Ambushes of Beckett's
     Waiting for Godot (A Lecture in a Series on
     Tragedy)." Kwartalnik Neofilologiczny 25,
     no. 2:187-200.
        Analyzes Waiting for Godot as an absurdist
     drama, as a parody of traditional drama:
     "... the comedy depends for much of its force
     on our sense that tragic archetypes are being
     inverted or reflected in a diminishing
     distorting mirror; and the serious undercur-
     rent of the humor lies in the suggestion that
     secular man, in his lonely selfhood, has not
     aggrandized but diminished himself."

66   WORTH, KATHARINE. "Beckett." In The Irish
     Drama of Europe from Yeats to Beckett.
     Atlantic Highlands, N.J.: Humanities Press
     Inc., pp. 241-65.
        Finds Beckett to be the heir of Yeats and
     Irish/French drama. Worth examines Beckett's
     affinities with his predecessors Maeterlinck,
     Synge, O'Casey, and Yeats.

67   ZATLIN, LINDA GERTNER. "La Tragédie de la
     vieillesse chez Ionesco et Beckett." In
     Ethique et esthétique dans la littérature
     française du XXe siècle. Edited by Maurice

Cagnon. Saratoga, CA.: Anma Libri, pp. 201-
14.
    Concentrates on the depiction of aging in
the dramatic works of Ionesco and Beckett.
Beckett's characters demonstrate mental and
physical decay, loss of memory and verbal
adeptness, as well as the physical well-being
that would make them productive, useful human
beings. Their isolation and the boring
routine of their days makes them view their
situation with despair and welcome death as a
relief. Zatlin comments on Waiting for
Godot, All That Fall, Endgame, Krapp's Last
Tape, and Eh Joe.

1979

1   ACHESON, JAMES. "Murphy's Metaphysics."
      Journal of Beckett Studies, no. 5 (Autumn),
      pp. 9-23.
          Claims that since the omniscient narrator
      of Murphy limits himself to a subjective
      description of his character's mind, it is
      because Beckett's "larger purpose is to
      demonstrate satirically that it is impossible
      to draw absolutely certain conclusions about
      metaphysical issues." Acheson points out
      Beckett's use of the philosophers Leibniz,
      Schopenhauer, and Geulincx in his satiric
      attack.

2   ADMUSSEN, RICHARD. The Samuel Beckett Manu-
      scripts: A Study. Boston: G.K. Hall & Co.,
      148 pp.
          Documents the nature and location of
      Beckett's unpublished works. Admussen
      describes the manuscripts of the published
      and unpublished works, as well as other
      unpublished material that is of interest to
      the Beckett Scholar. He provides the
      following information for each entry: title
      (if any), first line of the text, number of
      pages, writing instrument, type of paper,
      number of sheets, description of contents,

date and place of composition (if indicated),
amount of revisions, marginalia, remarks and
location of the manuscript. Additional
information provided in the appendices
includes: a chronological list of those
works by Beckett for which firm dates of
composition have been established from
manuscript notations, a description of a
manuscript notebook sold at auction which is
currently unavailable to the public, and six
autograph drafts of "Bing."

3   *BALDWIN, HELENE L. "The Theme of the Pilgrim
      in the Works of Samuel Beckett." Christian
      Scholar's Review 8:217-28.

4   BINNS, RONALD. "Beckett, Lowry and the Anti-
      Novel." In The Contemporary English Novel.
      Edited by Malcolm Bradbury and David Palmer.
      London: Arnold, pp. 88-111.
         Sees Beckett and Lowry as the links
      between the modernism of 1920's and the
      fiction of the late 1950's and 1960's. Binns
      follows their careers, comparing and con-
      trasting their lives and their works: "Lowry
      and Beckett are indeed different kinds of
      modern writers: one romantically assertive,
      the other infinitely recessive ... In their
      best works we see the comic virtues of the
      anti-novel; in their lesser works and in the
      zigzags of their careers we also see some of
      its limitations."

5   BOSWORTH, DAVID. "The Literature of Awe."
      Antioch Review 37, no. 1 (Winter):4-26.
      Beckett: pp. 17-22.
         Discusses the works of Kurt Vonnegut and
      Beckett as examples of literature of despair.
      Bosworth feels that the characters of
      Beckett's trilogy are portrayed in a state of
      ignorance, impotence and loneliness and for
      this reason imply their incompetence as
      narrators.

6   BRENNAN, ANTHONY S. "Winnie's Golden Treasury:
     The Use of Quotations in Happy Days."
     Arizona Quarterly 35, no. 3 (Autumn):205-27.
        Examines the poems and plays from which
     Winnie quotes in order to point out the
     parallels and contrasts to her situation.
     The quotations Winnie uses are all concerned
     with death or despair, yet she glosses over
     these emotional passages "as though they were
     jingles on the back of a package of corn-
     flakes."

7   BUNING, M. "Lessness Magnified." In From
     Caxton to Beckett. Edited by Jacques B.H.
     Alblas and Richard Todd. Amsterdam:
     Editions Rodopi, pp. 101-21.
        Describes and interprets "Lessness" based
     on the recorded version done by Martin Esslin
     for the BBC in 1971, pointing out the
     interaction and interdependence between the
     six voices and the thematic statements.

8   COHN, RUBY. "Words Working Overtime: Endgame
     and No Man's Land." Yearbook of English
     Studies 9:188-203.
        Focuses on the use of repetition (re-
     frains, simple doublets, echo doublets,
     "pounders") in Endgame and Pinter's No Man's
     Land.

9   "Cortot and Godot." Listener, 11 Jan., p. 47.
        Quotes John Calder and Rick Cluchey on
     Beckett's musicianship, from his conception
     of his works in terms of music to his
     knowledge of the tonal properties of the
     actor.

10   COUSINEAU, THOMAS. "Watt: Language as Inter-
     diction and Consolation." Journal of Beckett
     Studies, no. 4 (Spring), pp. 1-13.
        Concentrates "on the illusory nature of
     consciousness and on the loss of an original,
     unrepressed subjectivity" which he believes
     are the central issues in Watt. To aid in
     the development of these motifs, he draws on

two concepts: Jacques Lacan's "stade du miroir," which treats the three moments in the development of infantile consciousness and Paul Ricoeur's dialectic of destruction and renewal.

11   CROSSETTE, BARBARA.   "Off Broadway Offers Yeats and Beckett."   New York Times, 12 Oct., pp.1C, 6C.
       Reviews the adaptation of Mercier and Camier for the stage by the Mabou Mines Company, describing the characters' journey and the elaborate sets which engross the audience in a "world of fiction" typical of the "feeling one has when one steps into a good book ..."

12   CULIK, HUGH.   "Mindful of the Body: Medical Allusions in Beckett's Murphy."   Eire-Ireland 14, no. 1 (Spring):84-101.
       Points out that the medical imagery in Murphy gives direct expression to the mind-body duality, connects characters who otherwise seem unrelated, and provides irony.

13   CUNNINGHAM, VALENTINE.   "Foetality."   New Statesman 97 (1 June):796-97.
       Briefly reviews All Strange Away, commenting on the circular textuality of the prose: "Emmo and Emma imagine and write each other as Beckett imagines and writes them."

14   DAVIS, ROBIN J., ed.   Samuel Beckett: Checklist and Index of His Published Work, 1967-1976. Sterling, Scotland: Library, University of Sterling, 71 pp.
       Compiles a chronological bibliography of Beckett's works published from 1967 to 1976 inclusive.

15   DIETRICH, R.F.   "God, Godot, and Pozzo."   Notes on Contemporary Literature 9, no. 4:9-10.
       Briefly examines the relationship between God, Godot, and Pozzo: "... 'God' is what we

want, 'Godot' is what we would settle for
..., and 'Pozzo' is what we get ..."

16   ELTON, LEWIS. "On a Possible Source of En
     attendant Godot." Quinquereme 2, no. 2
     (July):198-203.
          Examines Marcel Jouhandeau's Véronicaeana
     as a possible source for Waiting for Godot,
     considering three possible effects: similar-
     ities in the characters portrayed, similari-
     ties in style and form, and direct or almost
     direct quotation.

17   FISCHER, EILEEN. "The Discourse of the Other in
     Not I: A Confluence of Beckett and Lacan."
     Theater 10, no. 3 (Summer):101-3.
          Compares the verbal structure of Not I to
     the communication between a patient and
     analyst, and then relates Beckett's drama to
     works by Jacques Lacan (Ecrits, The Language
     of Self: The Function of Language in Psycho-
     analysis).

18   *FLIEGER, JERRY ALINE. "The 'Infinite Enter-
     tainment': Modernity and the Comic Mode in
     French Literature." Structuralist Review 1,
     no. 3 (Summer):3-13.

19   FRANK, ELLEN EVE. Literary Architecture. Essays
     toward a Tradition: Walter Pater, Gerard
     Manley Hopkins, Marcel Proust, Henry James.
     Berkeley, Los Angeles, London: University of
     California Press, pp. 236-38, 301-3, and
     passim.
          Focuses on the relationship between
     architecture and literature. Frank believes
     Beckett's works establish the parallel
     between mind and architecture, specifically
     in the description of Murphy's mind and the
     Unnamable's definition of himself.

20   GAVARD-PERRET, J.P. "Pas suivie de Quatre
     Esquisses, Poèmes, Cette Fois (That Time) par
     Samuel Beckett." Esprit, n.s., 3, no. 2
     (Feb.):140-41.

Reviews Beckett's recent texts, pointing
out the incomprehensible presence of the
human being in time, and the representation
of reality through its absence or a negative
or contradictory portrayal.

21   GLUCK, BARBARA REICH. Joyce and Beckett:
      Friendship and Fiction. Lewisburg, Pa.:
      Bucknell University Press, 225 pp.
           Calls attention to the importance of
      Joyce's influence on Beckett. Following a
      preliminary chapter on the personal friend-
      ship of Beckett and Joyce, she analyzes three
      distinct periods in Beckett's literary
      career: 1) Beckett's earliest short stories
      and poems deliberately emulate Joyce's style;
      2) the first novels Murphy, Watt, and Mercier
      and Camier represent a transitional stage, at
      which time Beckett began to develop his own
      stylistic techniques; 3) finally, the trilogy
      and the dramatic works signal Beckett's
      discovery of a new identity which had to be
      resolved within the Joycean framework he
      utilized. Two short appendexes are included:
      "Beckett and Irish Literature" and "Joyce and
      the Jews."

22   GRAVER, LAWRENCE AND RAYMOND FEDERMAN, eds.
      Samuel Beckett: The Critical Heritage.
      London, Henley and Boston: Routledge & Kegan
      Paul, 372 pp.
           Chronologically records the critical
      responses to Beckett's fiction, Beckett's
      reputation and achievements. Eighty-three
      articles, interviews and reviews are re-
      printed, representative of each of Beckett's
      works. Titles of the articles are not
      included, nor do the editors indicate if a
      passage is an excerpt. The text is followed
      by a select bibliography.

           1. "Proust by Samuel Beckett," p. 39.
               Reprint of 1931.4.

2. Dobrée, Bonamy. "Symbolism To-day,"
       p. 40.
          Reprint of 1931.1.

3. F[lint], F.S. "<u>Proust</u> by Samuel
       Beckett," pp. 40-41.
          Reprint of 1931.2

4. Muir, Edwin. "New Short Stories,"
       pp. 42-43.
          Reprint of 1934.3.

5. "<u>More Pricks than Kicks</u>," pp. 43-44.
          Reprint of 1934.2.

6. "<u>Murphy</u>. By Samuel Beckett,"
       pp. 45-46.
          Reprint of 1938.1.

7. Thomas, Dylan. "Recent Novels,"
       pp. 46-48.
          Reprint of 1938.4.

8. O'Brien, Kate. "Fiction," pp. 48-49.
          Reprint of 1938.2.

9. Nadeau, Maurice. "En avant vers nulle
       part," pp. 50-54.
          Reprint of 1951.8.

10. Bataille, Georges. "Le Silence de
       Molloy," pp. 55-64.
          Reprint of 1951.2.

11. Pouillon, Jean. "<u>Molloy</u>," pp. 64-67.
          Reprint of 1951.12.

12. Pingaud, Bernard. "Le Roman. Samuel
       Beckett: <u>Molloy</u>," pp. 67-70.
          Reprint of 1951.11.

13. Mercier, Vivian. "Godot, Molloy et
       Cie.," pp. 70-73.
          Reprint of A226.

14. Toynbee, Philip. <u>Observer</u>, 18 Dec.
    1955, p. 11. Graver, pp. 73-76.
    Feels that <u>Molloy</u>, is "unen-
    durably boring" to read and that
    Beckett "fails as a serious
    novelist because he has involved
    himself in a false emotional
    simplification."

15. Nadeau, Maurice. "<u>Malone meurt</u> par
    Samuel Beckett," pp. 77-78.
    Reprint of 1952.1.

16. Seaver, Richard. "Samuel Beckett: An
1952   Introduction," pp. 79-88.
    Reprint of 1952.3.

17. Zegel, Sylvain. "Au Théâtre de
    Babylone: <u>En attendant Godot</u> de
    Samuel Beckett," pp. 88-89.
    Reprint of 1953.18.

18. Lemarchand, Jacques. "<u>En attendant
    Godot</u> de Samuel Beckett, au Théâtre
    de Babylone," pp. 89-92.
    Reprint of 1953.11.

19. Anouilh, Jean. "Godot ou le sketch
    des <u>Pensées</u> de Pascal traité par
    les Fratellini," p. 92.
    Reprint of 1953.1.

20. Hobson, Harold. "Godot and After,"
    pp. 93-95.
    Reprint of A150.

21. Tynan, Kenneth. "New Writing," pp.
    95-97.
    Reprint of 1955.9.

22. Fraser, G.S. "They Also Serve," pp.
    97-104.
    Reprint of 1956.13.

23.   Bentley, Eric. "The Talent of Samuel
      Beckett," pp. 104-11.
         Reprint of 1956.5.

24.   B., C. San Quentin News, 28 Nov.
      1957, pp. 1, 3. Graver,
      pp. 111-13.
         Reviews Waiting for Godot,
      summarizing the action of the play
      and empathizing with the situation
      of the characters: "It was an
      expression, symbolic in order to
      avoid all personal error, by an
      author who expected each member of
      his audience to draw his own
      conclusions, make his own errors.
      It asked nothing in point, it
      forced no dramatized moral on the
      viewer, it held out no specific
      hope."

25.   Marcabru, Pierre. Arts-Spectacles,
      10-16 May 1961, p. 14. Graver, pp.
      113-15.
         Reviews Roger Blin's production
      of Waiting for Godot at its Théâtre
      de France eight years after its
      presentation at the Théâtre de
      Babylone. Marcabru examines the
      impact the play now has, noting
      that the exacting symmetry and
      structure of the play are too
      obvious: "Eight years ago all this
      was not as perceptible. Construc-
      tion was effaced by surprise.
      Surprise is dead, what remains is a
      somewhat too methodical arrange-
      ment. We are surrounded by curt,
      dry, yet cajoling speeches ... only
      the stomach is affected. And this
      is the great power of Waiting for
      Godot: nausea rises, malaise
      remains."

26. Blanchot, Maurice. "Où maintenant?
    Qui maintenant?" pp. 116-21.
        Reprint of 1953.3.

27. Seaver, Richard. <u>Nimbus</u> (Autumn
    1953), pp. 61-62. Graver, pp. 122-
    24.
        Reviews <u>Watt</u>, focusing on Watt's
    acceptance, inertness, and lack of
    rapport with the other characters
    in the novel.

28. Hartley, Anthony. "Samuel Beckett,"
    pp. 125-29.
        Reprint of 1953.9.

29. Jean, Raymond. "Ancien et nouveau
    Beckett: Un personnage nommé
    Watt," pp. 129-31.
        Reprint of 1969.58.

30. Pingaud, Bernard. "'Dire, c'est
    inventer,'" pp. 132-36.
        Reprint of 1969.84.

31. Lalou, Renée. "Le Livre de la
    semaine: <u>Nouvelles et textes pour
    rien</u>," pp. 137-39.
        Reprint of 1955.4a.

32. Bonnefoi, Genevieve. "<u>Textes pour
    rien</u>?" pp. 139-45.
        Reprint of 1956.7.

33. Shenker, Israel. "Moody Man of
    Letters," pp. 146-49.
        Reprint of 1956.34.

34. "The Train Stops," pp. 150-53.
        Reprint of 1957.45.

35. Davie, Donald. "Kinds of Comedy,"
    pp. 153-60.
        Reprint of 1958.9.

36. Hobson, Harold. "Samuel Beckett's New
     Play," pp. 161-64.
          Reprint of 1957.12.

37. Tynan, Kenneth. "Theatre -- A
     Philosophy of Despair,"
     pp. 164-66.
          Reprint of 1957.46.

38. Bernard, Marc. "Fin de partie,"
     pp. 166-68.
          Reprint of 1957.2a.

39. Lemarchand, Jacques. "Fin de partie
     de Samuel Beckett, au Studio des
     Champs-Elysées," pp. 168-171.
          Reprint of 1957.23.

40. Atkinson, Brooks. "The Theatre:
     Beckett's Endgame," pp. 171-72.
          Reprint of 1958.1a.

41. Schneider, Alan. "Waiting for
     Beckett: A Personal Chronicle,"
     pp. 173-88.
          Reprint of 1958.30.

42. Tynan, Kenneth. Observer, 2 Nov.
     1958, p. 19. Graver, pp. 189-92.
          Parodies Beckett's plays in his
     review of Krapp's Last Tape and
     Endgame at the Royal Court Theatre.

43. Brustein, Robert. "Krapp and a little
     Claptrap," pp. 192-93.
          Reprint of 1960.2.

44. Pritchett, V.S. "An Irish Oblomov,"
     pp. 194-98.
          Reprint of 1960.44.

45. Kermode, Frank. "Beckett, Snow, and
     Pure Poverty," pp. 198-205.
          Reprint of 1960.35.

46. Frye, Northrup. "The Nightmare Life
    in Death," pp. 206-14.
       Reprint of 1960.22.

47. Aubarède, Gabriel d'. "En attendant
    ... Beckett," pp. 215-17.
       Reprint of 1961.3.

48. Driver, Tom F. "Beckett by the
    Madeleine," pp. 217-23.
       Reprint of 1961.18.

49. Nadeau, Maurice. "Comment c'est par
    Samuel Beckett," pp. 224-29.
       Reprint of 1961.49.

50. Federman, Raymond. "Comment c'est,"
    pp. 229-31.
       Reprint of A95.

51. Mayoux, J.J. "Comment c'est,"
    pp. 231-35.
       Reprint of 1961.44.

52. Kenner, Hugh. "Voices in the Night,"
    pp. 236-52.
       Reprint of 1961.41.

53. Times Literary Supplement (London), 21
    May 1964, p. 429. Graver, pp.
    252-54.
       Believes How It Is demonstrates
    the collapse of all structures:
    "... both the structure and the
    collapse are formal representa-
    tions of man's vain compulsion to
    impose an order and a signifi-
    cance on his experience."

54. Updike, John. "How How It Is Was,"
    pp. 254-57.
       Reprint of 1964.99.

55.   Brustein, Robert. "An Evening of
      Déjà-Vu,'" pp. 258-61.
            Reprint of 1961.11.

56.   Dennis, Nigel. "No View from the
      Toolshed," pp. 261-66.
            Reprint of A74.

57.   Simon, Alfred. "Le Degré zéro du
      tragique," pp. 266-71.
            Reprint of 1963.72.

58.   Davie, Donald. "Nightingales,
      Anangke," p. 272.
            Reprint of A71.

59.   Brustein, Robert. "Mid-Season
      Gleanings," pp. 273-74.
            Reprint of 1964.12a.

60.   Federman, Raymond. "Film,"
      pp. 275-83.
            Reprint of 1966-1967.1

61.   "The Essential Q," pp. 284-85.
            Reprint of B185.

62.   Ricks, Christopher. <u>Listener</u>, 3 Aug.
      1967, pp. 148-49. Graver,
      pp. 286-91.
            Reviews <u>No's Knife</u>, <u>Come and Go</u>,
      <u>Eh Joe</u>, John Fletcher's <u>Samuel
      Beckett's Art</u>, and John Calder's
      <u>Beckett at Sixty</u>, commenting on
      Beckett's "pitiless depleting of
      language and situation," and the
      recent flood of Beckett Criticism.

63.   Lodge, David. "Some Ping Understood,"
      pp. 291-301.
            Reprint of 1968.41.

64a. "Samuel Beckett Wins Nobel Prize,"
p. 302.
Reprint of 1969.99a.

64b. "Samuel Beckett Goes Into Hiding,"
p. 303.
Reprint of 1969.98.

65. Marissel, Andre. "Beckett, Prix Nobel
de Littérature: L'Eternelle
désintégration," pp. 303-6.
Reprint of 1969.66.

66. Piatier, Jacqueline. "Beckett en ses
vertes années," pp. 307-8.
Reprint of A250.

67. Alvarez, A. Observer, 6 Oct. 1974,
p. 30. Graver, pp. 308-10.
Discusses the importance of
Mercier and Camier as a predecessor
of Waiting for Godot.

68. Ricks, Christopher. "Hide and Seek,"
pp. 311-12.
Reprint of 1974.49.

69. Fabre-Luce, Anne. "Rites
crépusculaires," pp. 313-15.
Reprint of 1971.29.

70. Bosquet, Alain. Combat, 29 March
1971, p. 10. Graver, pp. 316-21.
Reviews Mercier and Camier,
First Love, and The Lost Ones,
presenting the themes of solitude,
absurdity, and nothingness as they
appear in these works, ending with
a vision of the space age in The
Lost Ones: "Here Beckett is no
longer attacking man, but the very
myth of man propelling himself out
of his natal habitat. Or rather,
he makes of the astronaut and the
cosmonaut the symbols of our

enslavement: to weight and
weightlessness, to the infinitely
great and the infinitely small, to
paralyzing introspection and to
self-transcendence."

71. "Can't Stop Climbing," pp. 321-23.
        Reprint of 1972.9.

72. Graver, Lawrence. "Guides to the
        Ruins," pp. 323-27.
        Reprint of 1974.27.

73. Oliver, Edith. "Off Broadway.
        Beckett Back to Back," pp. 328-29.
        Reprint of 1972.56a.

74. Nightingale, Benedict. "Mouthpiece,"
        pp. 329-33.
        Reprint of 1973.56.

75. Cioran, E.M. "Encounter with
        Beckett," pp. 334-39.
        Reprint of 1976.24.

76. Wardle, Irving. "People in a
        Timeless Limbo: Play and Other
        Plays," pp. 340-42.
        Reprint of 1976.146a.

77. Cushman, Robert, "In a Hellish Half-
        Light," pp. 342-44.
        Reprint of 1976.36.

78. Elsom, John. "Scraps and Scoops,"
        pp. 344-46.
        Reprint of 1976.43.

79. Nightingale, Benedict. "Brain Cells,"
        pp. 346-48.
        Reprint of 1976.110.

80. Cunningham, Valentine. New Statesman,
        29 Oct. 1976, p. 607. Graver,
        pp. 349-50.

Reviews <u>For to End Yet Again</u>,
finding hope in the limited motion
of the characters, and narrators,
this "Postponing of apocalypse."

81. Alvarez, A. "Literary Chamber Music,"
pp. 350-51.
Reprint of All.

82. Ratcliffe, Michael. "Kinship with
Godot," pp. 352-53.
Reprint of 1977.75a.

83. Coe, Richard. "The Barest Essentials," pp. 354-58.
Reprint of 1977.20.

23 GUERS-MARTYNUK, SIMONE. "L'Alchimie du théâtre
de Beckett dans <u>Fin de partie</u>." <u>Chimères</u> 12,
no. 2:16-24.
Analyzes <u>Endgame</u> as an example of "Théâtre
Alchimique" as described by Antonin Artaud in
his <u>Théâtre et son double</u>. Guers-Martynuk
examines the unities of time, place and
action and the symbols presented in the play.

24 *GURY, J. "Chronique des fureteurs et curieux.
704. Samuel Beckett et la résistance
française." <u>Cahiers de l'Iroise</u> 26, n.s.,
no. 1 (Jan.-Mar.).

25 GUSSOW, MEL. "Drama: Beckett Novel Adapted."
<u>New York Times</u>, 26 Oct., p. 3C.
Reviews Frederick Neumann's adaptation of
<u>Mercier and Camier</u> for the stage, describing
the difficulty of the adaptation, the stage,
the use of David Warrilow as an omniscient
storyteller, and the "Irishness" of the
actors' portrayals.

26 _____. "Irene Worth Finds Beckett Uplifting."
<u>New York Times</u>, 1 June, p. 10C.
Records a conversation with Irene Worth
and director Andrei Serban before the first
performance of <u>Happy Days</u> at the New York

Shakespeare Festival Public Theater in which they speak of their admiration for Beckett and his play and Ms. Worth's interpretation of the role.

27 HAMMOND, B.S. "Beckett and Pinter: Towards a Grammar of the Absurd." <u>Journal of Beckett Studies</u>, no. 4 (Spring), pp. 35-42.
    Contrasts the way Beckett (<u>Endgame</u>) and Pinter (<u>The Birthday Party</u>) ushered in a new era for dramatic dialogue: Pinter's "stripped-down idiom" is mimetic of spontaneous discourse, while Beckett liberated himself from an over-dependence on ordinary language.

28 HAYMAN, RONALD. "Godot and After" and "Beckett and Before." In <u>Theatre and Anti-Theatre. New Movements Since Beckett</u>. New York: Oxford University Press, pp. 1-16, 17-47.
    Describes the originality of Beckett's theater, and analyzes the evolution of his dramas, play by play, from <u>Waiting for Godot</u> through <u>Not I</u>. In order to better understand how he wrote <u>Waiting for Godot</u>, Hayman looks at Beckett's earlier development in the context of minimalism, reductionism and the other negative tendencies of anti-art.

29 HERBERT, HUGH. "Billie up to her Neck in Beckett." <u>Guardian</u>, 30 May, p. 12.
    Billie Whitelaw describes her experiences working with Beckett as a director. She feels Beckett is precise, but sensitive: "he does not direct, he conducts, as though it were music."

30 HENDERSON, ROBERT. "Laying Bare the Text and Score." <u>Daily Telegraph</u> (London), 21 Apr., p. 11.
    Emphasizes Beckett's interest in modern music, in particular his affinity with the composers Bartok and Webern. Henderson describes those elements in 20th century music that might assist Beckett in his own

writing: the simplicity of many contemporary
scores, the search for new forms, the
willingness to confront failure, and the use
of silence.

31   HENKELS, ROBERT M., Jr. Robert Pinget. The
     Novel as Quest. University, Ala.: Univer-
     sity of Alabama Press, pp. 212-18.
          Juxtaposes Pinget and Beckett in order to
     assess Pinget's place among the new novelists
     and to disprove the idea that Pinget is
     Beckett's disciple.

32   IEHL, DONIMIQUE. "L'Indéterminé chez Kafka et
     Beckett." In Mélanges offerts à M. le
     professeur André Monchoux. Toulouse:
     Université de Toulouse-Le Mirail, pp. 229-45.
          Compares the fiction of Beckett and Kafka,
     pointing out that Beckett begins where Kafka
     left off -- the two dimensions of Beckett's
     work, parody and play, appear as two limits
     in Kafka's world.

33   KERR, WALTER. "Quietus." In Journey to the
     Center of the Theater. New York: Alfred A
     Knopf, pp. 190-93.
          Contrasts Bert Lahr's performance in the
     Broadway production of Waiting for Godot with
     that of Paul Price in Alan Schneider's off-
     Broadway production in 1971. He feels that
     Lahr "completed things," in the play whereas
     Waiting for Godot should be a play of
     incompletion, "of stirrings aborted and
     satisfactions withheld."

34   KEYSSAR, HELENE. "Theatre Games, Language Games
     and Endgame." Theatre Journal 31, no. 2
     (May):221-38.
          Describes her rehearsal experiences in
     directing Endgame at Amherst College in 1975,
     noting the importance of the activity of the
     words, the allusions, the ambiguities, the
     language games, the humor, the setting, and
     the differences between their productions in
     French and in English.

35 KNOWLSON, JAMES AND JOHN PILLING. <u>Frescoes of
    the Skull: The Later Prose and Drama of
    Samuel Beckett</u>. London: J. Calder, 292 pp.
        Claiming "no attempt at uniformity of
    style or method," the authors of this text
    provide individual studies of Beckett's first
    attempts at prose and drama ("Dream of Fair
    to Middling Women" and "Eleuthéria"), his
    post-trilogy prose, and drama after <u>Endgame</u>.
    The last three chapters are devoted to
    specific topics of interest: the critical
    writing of Beckett, and Beckett's admiration
    for the plays of John Millington Synge and
    for Heinrich von Kleist's essay "On the
    Marionette Theater." A select bibliography
    is included.

36 KNOWLSON, JAMES. "<u>Happy Days</u> directed by Samuel
    Beckett, Royal Court Theatre, London, June
    1979." <u>Journal of Beckett Studies</u>, no. 5
    (Autumn), pp. 141-43.
        Reviews Beckett's first production in
    English of <u>Happy Days</u>, pointing out the minor
    changes in the text, the innovations, the
    alternation of tone, and Billie Whitelaw's
    strengths as an actress.

37 _____. "Review: <u>Pas</u> and <u>Pas moi</u> at the Théâtre
    d'Orsay, Paris, 11 Apr. 1978." <u>Journal of
    Beckett Studies</u>, no. 4 (Spring), pp. 72-73.
        Reviews the 1978 Paris production of
    <u>Footfalls</u> and <u>Not I</u>, emphasizing the visual
    and auditory aspects of the plays.

38 KROLL, JACK. "Beckett by Two." <u>Newsweek</u> 93, no.
    25 (18 June):89.
        Compares and contracts two performances of
    <u>Happy Days</u>, Beckett's production at London's
    Royal Court Theatre with Billy Whitelaw and
    Andrei Serban's staging at Joseph Papp's
    Public Theater with Irene Worth, commenting
    on Beckett's satire of the "romantic idea of
    the eternal female" and his caricature of the
    relationship between Winnie and Willie.

39 LAWLEY, PAUL. "Symbolic Structure and Creative
    Obligation in <u>Endgame</u>." <u>Journal of Beckett
    Studies</u>, no. 5 (Autumn), pp. 45-68.
        Discusses the symbolic organization,
    visual imagery, and function of language in
    the play: "... <u>Endgame</u> works by indirection:
    image, symbol, narrative, gesture and echo
    all converge patiently on a centre which is,
    like Hamm himself, unstable, indefinable,
    perhaps even non-existent."

40 LEVY, ERIC P. "Looking for Beckett's Lost
    Ones." <u>Mosaic</u> 12, no. 3 (Spring):163-70.
        Recognizes that the fundamental problem of
    the narrator of <u>The Lost Ones</u> is his aware-
    ness of having already dealt with the same
    predicament. Levy demonstrates how the text
    refers back to earlier works for both the
    details of the story and its narrative
    approach.

41 MODRZEWSKA, RENATA. "La Communication verbale
    dans les pièces de théâtre de Samuel
    Beckett." <u>Romanica Wratislaviensia</u> 14, no.
    416:81-99.
        Analyzes verbal communication beginning
    with the study of Beckettian metalanguage and
    then adapts Jakobson's model for the elements
    of communication to Beckett's plays: 1) the
    organization of reality and its role in the
    act of communication, 2) the temperament of
    the speakers, 3) the relations between the
    characters implied by their verbal interac-
    tion, 4) the content of the messages, and 5)
    the character of the information contained in
    the messages. Finally, Modrzewska considers
    the functions of the verbal exchanges.

42 *_____. "Le Jeu dans le théâtre de
    Samuel Beckett." In <u>Le Drame d'avant-garde
    et le théâtre</u>. Edited by Jósef Heistein.
    Warsaw: Panstwowe Wydawnictwo Naukowe, pp.
    69-83.

43   MURPHY, PETER. "'All Strnge Away' by Samuel
         Beckett." <u>Journal of Beckett Studies</u>, no. 5
         (Autumn), pp. 99-113.
             Views "All Strange Away" as the missing-
         link vital to an appraisal of Beckett's
         subsequent works. This text establishes the
         basic issues and a context, "a set of
         'signifieds,' to which the 'signs' of the
         later works ... are also drawn in the attempt
         to reveal the truth and meaning of the
         creative act."

44   _____. "The Nature and Art of Love in
         'Enough.'" <u>Journal of Beckett Studies</u>, no. 4
         (Spring), pp. 14-34.
             Believes 'Enough' is a pastoral in which
         the contradictions of inner life are tem-
         porarily resolved in the rite of art. The
         pastoral myth is examined through three
         topics: nature, art, and love. The essen-
         tial myth governing the depiction of the
         creative act is that of Orpheus.

45   OLIVER, EDITH. "Winnie by Worth." <u>New Yorker</u>
         55, no. 18 (18 June):92-93.
             Reviews Andrei Serban's production of
         <u>Happy Days</u>. Although Irene Worth does an
         excellent job, as Winnie, the performance
         "seems deficient in feeling and misses the
         underlying rhythm of this beautiful play."

46   RABINOVITZ, RUBIN. "<u>Molloy</u> and the Archetypal
         Traveller." <u>Journal of Beckett Studies</u>, no.
         5 (Autumn), pp. 25-44.
             Notes that Beckett has drawn on a number
         of works for the allusions to voyages in
         <u>Molloy</u>: <u>The Odyssey</u>, <u>The Aeneid</u>, <u>The Bible</u>,
         Dante's <u>Divine Comedy</u>, St. Augustine's
         <u>Confessions</u>, Bunyan's <u>Pilgrim's Progress</u>,
         Kierkegaard's <u>Fear and Trembling</u>, Goethe's
         <u>Faust</u>. These allusions as well as details
         from Beckett's own life provide different
         dimmensions to the travel theme: "Beckett's
         technique is to build up successive layers of
         mythic themes, a sense of archetypal

significance is introduced when similar
elements in a number of myths coalesce."

47 RABKIN, ERIC S. "The Mythic Coherence of
    <u>Molloy</u>." <u>South Carolina Review</u> 12, no. 1
    (Fall):12-20.
        Examines <u>Molloy</u> as a unified work enriched
    by the Oedipus myth.

48 "Return of a Native." <u>Guardian</u>, 23 Aug.
        Summarizes Jessica Tandy's acting career,
    and records a few of her impressions of
    Beckett. Tandy has acted in Beckett's <u>Not I</u>
    and <u>Happy Days</u>.

49 ROBINSON, MICHAEL. "From Purgatory to Inferno:
    Beckett and Dante Revisited." <u>Journal of
    Beckett Studies</u>, no. 5 (Autumn):69-82.
        While Dante's vision provides a context
    for many of the characters and situations in
    Beckett's fiction, Dante's systems differ
    dramatically from that of Beckett: "Through
    his enormous presumption to know God's
    judgement, Dante's vision of the after life
    is concrete ... But in Beckett's world,
    meaning is withheld and the characters can
    only speculate on infernal punishment or
    purgatorial progress.

50 SCHLUETER, JUNE. "Beckett's Didi and Gogo, Hamm
    and Clov." In <u>Metafictional Characters in
    Modern Drama</u>. New York: Columbia University
    Press, pp. 53-69.
        Demonstrates the duality of Beckett's
    characters in <u>Waiting for Godot</u> and <u>Endgame</u>,
    through their use of language, which is
    interpreted on both the philosophical and
    aesthetic levels.

51 SEGRE, CESARE. "The Function of Language in
    Samuel Beckett's <u>Acte sans paroles</u>." In
    <u>Structures and Time. Narration, Poetry,
    Models</u>. Translated by John Meddemmen.
    Chicago and London: University of Chicago
    Press, pp. 225-44.

Considers the status of language (spoken
vs. written) in <u>Act Without Words</u>: on the
stage there are no words yet the printed
directions for the production of the play do
constitute an idependent literary text.
Segre studies the text of the play in order
to determine "whether, by its very constitu-
tion, it can contain a stock of meanings and
sense which, on the first hypothesis, will be
of assistance in producing the work on stage,
and, on the second, will reveal or define
semiotic values."

52   SHERZER, DINA. "Beckett's <u>Endgame</u> or What Talk
      Can Do." <u>Modern Drama</u> 22, no. 3 (Sept.):291-
      303.
         Observes how the characters talk, how they
      speak to each other, and the effects and
      results that speech produces. The characters
      use language and speech to show how the text
      has the power to "claw": "the text claws
      through its message of man's predicament in
      the world, it claws through the characters'
      sinister game, it claws at language and
      through language by its constant unsettling
      and unnerving disruptions."

53   STEFAN, JUDE. "L'Expression en poésie."
      <u>Nouvelle Revue Française</u>, no. 312 (1 Jan.),
      pp. 75-80.
         Reviews Beckett's <u>Poems</u>, finds this work
      must be taken as seriously as Beckett's other
      fiction, since they represent the same
      tonality and pessimistic vision.

54   TENENBAUM, ELIZABETH BRODY. "Beckett's Pozzo
      and Lucky: The Alternative to <u>Waiting for
      Godot</u>." <u>Studies in the Humanities</u> 7, no.
      2:27-33.
         Interprets the roles of Pozzo and Lucky in
      <u>Waiting for Godot</u> taking into account basic
      critical approaches to the characters.
      Tenenbaum identifies the characters as
      representatives of two complementary forces:
      the political and economic order (Pozzo) and

the intellectual and aesthetic forces
(Lucky). Portraying man as a social being,
Pozzo and Lucky serve as foils for Vladimir
and Estragon who represent man in a state of
independence from all social values.

55   Van TASSEL, DANIEL E. "Rise and Fall in
     Beckett's All That Fall." Eire-Ireland 14,
     no. 4 (Winter):83-90.
        Believes the structure of All That Fall
     reverses the direction of movement in the
     Biblical passage from which the play derives
     its title -- the characters are lifted up
     only so that they may decline and fall.

56   *VERCKO, RADOJKA. "Time, Place and Existence in
     the plays of Samuel Beckett." Acta Neophilo-
     logica 12:29-38.

57   WHITAKER, THOMAS R. "Playing Hell." Yearbook
     of English Studies 9:167-87. Beckett: pp.
     174-77.
        Imagines a descent through several circles
     of hell by studying the "theatrical hills" of
     four plays: Sartre's No Exit, Beckett's
     Play, Genet's Screens and Pinter's No Man's
     Land.

58   WILCHER, ROBERT. "The Museum of Tragedy:
     Endgame and Rosencrantz and Guildenstern are
     Dead." Journal of Beckett Studies, no. 4
     (Spring), pp. 43-54.
        Analyzes Endgame and Rosencrantz and
     Guildenstern are Dead in the context of
     Hamlet and the tradition of tragic art in
     general: "Beckett by adopting the pure form
     of meaning derived from a shared world-view,
     has contrived to offer the modern audience an
     experience of tragedy emptied of explicit
     tragic significance.

59   WILSON, ROBERT N. "Samuel Beckett. The Social
     Psychology of Emptiness." In The Writer as
     Social Seer. Chapel Hill: University of
     North Carolina Press, pp. 134-44.

Looks at the characters and environment
portrayed in Waiting for Godot and Endgame,
focusing on several themes: deprivation,
hostility, anarchy, enervation, sexlessness,
hopelessness, and meaninglessness.

1979-1980

1   *HOLZBERG, RUTH. "Beckett et Le Clézio: La
     Chaîne Sado-Masochiste et le monologue du
     scripteur." Modern Language Studies 10, no.
     1 (Winter):60-68.

1980

1   ACHESON, JAMES. "Chess with the Audience:
     Samuel Beckett's Endgame." Critical Quarter-
     ly 22, no. 2 (Summer):33-45.
          Suggests that the game imagery in Endgame
     refers to the confrontation between the
     characters on stage and the audience, "check-
     mate occurs when we recognize that the play
     is deliberately designed to resist even the
     most ingenious of explanations." Acheson
     examines different interpretations of the
     play -- naturalistic, symbolic or allegorical
     and expressionistic.

2   BARBER, JOHN. "Max Wall's Study in Tough
     Loneliness." In Theatre Workbook I: Samuel
     Beckett, "Krapp's Last Tape." Edited by
     James Knowlson. London: Brutus Books,
     p. 119.
          Briefly describes Max Wall's restraint of
     the clownish side of Krapp and the extraordi-
     nary contrast between his youthful recorded
     voice and his aged counterpart. See 1980.60.

3   BEHAR, HENRI. "Le Théâtre d'aujourd'hui sous le
     signe de Jarry." In Jarry dramaturge. Paris:
     Librarie A.-G. Nizet, pp. 197-242.

Examines Jarry's influence on contemporary
dramatists (especially Beckett and Ionesco).
Behar feels that Beckett's dramas exhibit
many innovations or characteristics found in
works by Jarry: disruption of logical
sequence, ambiguity of the artistic message,
theatrical effect, conception of time and
space, singular character (personnage
solitaire) correspondence of "geste" and
"parole," circus games, unity of contraries,
humor, cruelty, essential truth, and affirmation of the original nature of man.

4   BEN-ZVI, LINDA. "Samuel Beckett, Fritz Mauth-
       ner, and the Limits of Language." PMLA 95,
       no. 2 (Mar.):183-200.
         Outlines Fritz Mauthner's background and
       Beckett's response to Mauthner's Beiträge zu
       einer Kritik der Sprache ("Contributions
       toward a Critique of Language"). Ben-Zvi
       studies the possible influence this work had
       on Beckett's use of language, in particular
       their shared recognition of the limits of
       language.

5   BOVE, PAUL A. "The Image of the Creator in
       Beckett's Postmodern Writing." Philosophy
       and Literature 4, no. 1 (Spring):47-65.
         Discusses Beckett's presentation of the
       creative possibilities of anxiety in his
       essay on Proust, and illustrates the dramati-
       zation of anxiety in the Moran section of
       Molloy. References are made to Kierkegoard
       and Heidegger.

6   BRATER, ENOCH. "Why Beckett's 'Enough' is More
       or Less Enough." Contemporary Literature 21,
       no. 2 (Spring):252-66.
         Points out the complexity of the short
       prose text, "Enough": its multiple levels of
       meaning, romantic allusions, numerical
       irregularities, and ambiguous sexual images.
       "Enough" is contrasted with "Imagination Dead
       Imagine" and Mercier and Camier.

7 BRIENZA, SUSAN AND PEGGY A. KNAPP. "Imagination
   Lost and Found: Beckett's Fiction and Frye's
   Anatomy." <u>Modern Language Notes</u> 95, no. 4
   (May):980-94.
        Inspect Beckett's recent fictions and use
   them to test Frye's hypothesis of fictional
   modes. Frye's theory of a transitional stage
   between irony and a renewal of myth is used
   to analyze "Imagination Dead Imagine,"
   "Ping," and <u>The Lost Ones</u>.

8 BUSI FREDERICK. <u>The Transformation of Godot</u>.
   Lexington: University Press of Kentucky,
   143 p.
        Studies the significance of onomastic
   techniques in <u>Waiting for Godot</u>, tracing the
   etymological derivations of the names of the
   characters and examining the associated
   dramatic themes. Busi considers "Beckett's
   affinities with Cervantes and the indebted-
   ness of both authors to the tradition of the
   commedia dell'arte, and the figure of
   Harlequin, with special emphasis on the
   notion of interchangeable character roles."
   The chapters that follow contain detailed
   discussions of Beckett's use of the play-
   within-a-play as a dramatic device, his debt
   to James Joyce, and the significance and
   ramifications of those religious and psychological themes which bear upon the development of the self.

9 *BUTLER, IAN CHRISTOPHER. <u>After the Wake: An
   Essay on the Contemporary Avant-Garde</u>.
   Oxford: Oxford University Press, 200 p.

10 *BUTLIN, RON. "Alone in Company." <u>New Edinburgh Review</u>, no. 51 (Autumn), pp. 35-36.

11 CALDER, JOHN. Letter to the Editor. <u>Listener</u>,
   10 Jan., p. 51.
        Defends Beckett as "the author who has
   most excited the academic world over the last
   30 years."

12   CAMPBELL, R.J. "On Saying the Unsayable."
      Critical Quarterly 22, no. 3 (Autumn):69-77.
      Beckett: pp. 72-74.
           Notes that both Antonin Artaud and Beckett
      found language to be inadequate to express
      certain things "which lie beyond expression
      but which are, none the less, conveyed in
      their work." Campbell also presents this
      idea from the point of view of the writings
      of Ludwig Wittgenstein.

13   CHABERT, PIERRE. "Beckett at the Homes of
      Molière, Vilar ... and Some Youngsters or a
      Time for Revivals." Gambit 9, no. 35:55-61.
           Discusses the coincidence and the irony of
      two revivals of Waiting for Godot in settings
      as prestigious as they are diverse: the
      Comédie Française and the Palais des Papes in
      Avignon.

14   _____. "Samuel Beckett as Director." In
      Theatre Workbook I: Samuel Beckett, "Krapp's
      Last Tape." Edited by James Knowlson.
      London: Brutus Books, pp. 85-107.
           Describes his experience working with
      Beckett when he was directing La Dernière
      Bande. Chambert shows how Beckett envisages
      the realization of his texts on stage,
      commenting on 1) the ritual of listening and
      recording, 2) his work on the text and the
      voice, 3) action, the body and space, 4)
      musicality and rhythm of the text. Reprint
      of 1976.22; see 1980.60.

15   CHAILLET, NED. "With Samuel Beckett in the
      Rehearsal Room." Times (London), 28 July,
      p. 11.
           Calls attention to the experiences of Rick
      Cluchey and the San Quentin Drama Workshop
      working with Beckett and performing his
      plays.

16   *CLUCHEY, RICK. "My Years with Beckett." New
      Edinburgh Review, no. 51 (Autumn), pp. 18-21.
      Reprinted: 1980.17, 1980.22.

17   _____. "My Years with Beckett." In <u>Theatre
         Workbook I: Samuel Beckett, "Krapp's Last
         Tape</u>." Edited by James Knowlson. London:
         Brutus Books, pp. 120-23.
              Comments on his initial experiences acting
         in Beckett's dramas, the interest Beckett's
         plays held for prison audiences and his
         friendship with Beckett. Reprint of 1980.16;
         see 1980.60.

18   CLUCHEY, RICK AND MICHAEL HAERDTER. "<u>Krapp's
         Last Tape</u>: Production Report." In <u>Theatre
         Workbook I: Samuel Beckett, "Krapp's Last
         Tape</u>." Edited by James Knowlson. London:
         Brutus Books, pp. 124-41.
              Offers a detailed account of the produc-
         tion of <u>Krapp's Last Tape</u> in collaboration
         with Beckett in Berlin, discussing the
         identity of Krapp, the production of the
         tape,the stage set, costumes, the principles
         of light and dark, and excerpts from the
         rehearsal diary. See 1980.60.

19   CLURMAN, HAROLD. "Theatre." <u>Nation</u> 230 (16
         Feb.):187-88.
              Discusses four productions of <u>Endgame</u> that
         he has seen, emphasizing the dreariness of
         the play and contrasting Beckett with Pinter.

20   COHN, RUBY. <u>Just Play: Beckett's Theater</u>.
         Princeton, N.J.: Princeton University Press,
         313 p.
              Examines Beckett's twenty-one complete
         plays and their performances. Cohn discusses
         three abandoned or revised plays, "Human
         Wishes," "Eleuthéria," and <u>Endgame</u>, and then
         devotes her attention to Beckett "Theatri-
         cians" and Beckett's directing, drawing on
         her own impressions and recollections.

21   CONDE, GERARD. "Théâtre musical à Avignon:
         L'Austérité fertile de Beckett." <u>Monde</u>, 23
         July, pp. 1, 13.
              Describes Heinz Hollinger's musical
         productions of <u>Come and Go</u> and <u>Not I</u> at the

Chapelle des Pénitents Blancs d'Avignon. The
instrumentation, the adaptation of the texts,
the use of different languages and the
changes in the sets and the number of actors
are discussed.

22   De SOLLAR, JOHN P. "Sound and Sense in Samuel
      Beckett's Drama and Fiction." Irish Studies
      1:133-52.
            Examines selected passages from a recorded
      reading of Malone Dies, The Unnamable and
      Endgame given by Jack MacGowran under
      Beckett's supervision in order "to see why
      and how [Beckett's] prose increases in its
      eloquence and depth of expression as the
      verbal means are systematically reduced."

23   *DUCKWORTH, COLIN. "Beckett's Early Background:
      A New Zealand Biographical Appendix." New
      Zealand Journal of French Studies 1, no. 2
      (Oct.):59-67.

24   *DUDKIEWICZ, JADWIGA. "The Problem of Time in
      Samuel Beckett's Waiting for Godot." Acta
      Universitatis Lodziensis 66:99-117.
            Source: French XX Bibliography, no. 34
      (1982); unverified.

25   DUKORE, BERNARD F. "Krapp's Last Tape as
      Tragicomedy." In Theatre Workbook I: Samuel
      Beckett, Krapp's Last Tape." Edited by James
      Knowlson. London: Brutus Books, pp. 146-50.
            Reprint of 1973.28; see 1980.60.

26   DYSON, J. PETER. "Waiting for Godot and The
      Mikado: The Game of Time." Language Notes
      18, no. 1 (Sept.):46-48.
            Points out the resemblance of a scene from
      Waiting for Godot and one from Gilbert and
      Sullivan's operetta The Mikado in which irony
      and somberness are juxtaposed in order to
      emphasize the meaninglessness of time.

27   ELAM, KEIR. The Semantics of Theater and Drama.
      London: Methuen, pp. 145-48.

Uses a passage from <u>Endgame</u> as an example
of an analysis of "discourse" based on the
work of Alessandro Serpieri in which a number
of micro-sequences indicating the characters'
change of semiotic axis within the macro-
sequence are distinguished.

28   ELSOM, JOHN. "Clowning with Beckett." In
      <u>Theatre Workbook I: Samuel Beckett, "Krapp's
      Last Tape."</u>   Edited by James Knowlson.
      London: Brutus Books, pp. 115-17.
           Reprint of 1975.35; see 1980.60.

29   ESSLIN, MARTIN. <u>Mediations: Essays on Brecht,
      Beckett, and the Media</u>. Baton Rouge:
      Louisiana State University Press, 248 p.
           Presents articles on a variety of topics
      reflecting Esslin's role as a "mediator"
      between the cultural areas of the various
      national spheres of the West.

           1.   "Beckett and His Interpreters," pp.
                75-92.
                     Reprint of 1965.23.

           2.   "Beckett's Novels," pp. 93-110.
                     Reprint of 1962.26.

           3.   "Beckett's Poems -- Some Random
                Notes," pp. 111-16.
                     Reprint of 1967.7.

           4.   "A Theater of Stasis -- Beckett's Late
                Plays," pp. 117-24.
                     Demonstrates how Beckett's later
                plays condense and concentrate
                elements that have always been
                present; the stasis in these plays
                provides "maximal intensification
                of the tensions that make conven-
                tional plays dramatic." Reprint of
                1976.44

> 5. "Samuel Beckett and the Art of
>   Broadcasting," pp. 125-54.
>   Reprint of 1975.39 and incor-
>   porates 1977.27.
>
> 6. "The Unnamable Pursued by the
>   Unspeakable," pp. 155-67.
>   Reviews Deirdre Bair's Beckett
>   biography.

30   FEHLMANN, GUY. "Aspects de la dualité chez
     Beckett." Gaeliana 2:23-32.
         Explores the question of duality in
     Beckett's work: the couple, symmetry, visual
     and auditive relations, the notion of
     original sin, and Beckett's bilingualism.

31   FLETCHER, JOHN. Novel and Reader. London:
     Boston: Marion Boyars, pp. 110-20.
         Examines Molloy as a detective novel and
     then as a modern transposition of the Ulysses
     legend. The relationship of the narrators
     Molloy and Moran with the images of the
     mother-figure and father-figure is presented
     and compared to the situation of the hero in
     Leopold von Sacher-Masoch's novel Venus in
     Furs.

32   FLIEGER, JERRY ALINE. "Blanchot and Beckett:
     En attendant Godot as 'Discontinuous' Play."
     French Forum 5, no. 2 (May):156-67.
         Blanchot's concept of the "discontinuous"
     theater of Brecht in which the spectator
     maintains his distance from the surface
     action of the play is applied to Beckett's
     Waiting for Godot. In this context the humor
     of clowns is used as an important structuring
     device to maintain the separation between the
     audience and actors.

33   FRANK, LEAH D. "Joseph Chaikin Stages Beckett's
     'Comedy About Suffering.'" New York Times,
     13 Jan., sec. 2, pp. 5, 23.
         Reviews the production of Endgame at the
     Manhattan Theatre Club. The director, Joseph

Chaikin, stresses the "humor" of the play:
"... the amazing thing about Beckett is how
he takes you to depths of agony and then
turns it into an immense joke with burlesque
turns and routines that are almost vaudevil-
lian."

34   FREE, WILLIAM J. "Beckett's Plays and the
      Photographic Vision." Georgia Review 34, no.
      4 (Winter):801-12.
         Distinguishes the passive nature of
      photographic images from the active nature of
      the narrative process, and points out
      Beckett's achievement of a pictorial quality
      in his plays and the methods he uses to
      minimize the possibility of narrative
      understanding.

35   FREESE, WOLFGANG; ANGELA B. MOORJANI. "The
      Esoteric and the Trivia: Chess and Go in the
      Novels of Beckett and Kawabata." Perspec-
      tives on Contemporary Literature 6:37-48.
         Analyzes the significance of these two
      games in Murphy and Yasunari Kawabata's The
      Master of Go: "In these novels, startling
      shifts from expected game strategies parallel
      the collapse of a philosophical and social
      order. The subtle structural features of
      each game, annotated in the texts, echoed in
      the plots, set up tensions between the
      trivial and the esoteric aspects of this
      dissolution and generate at times a drastic
      humor announcing the defeat of an old order."

36   FRIEDBERG-DOBRY, LOIS. "Four Saints in Two
      Acts: A Note on the Saints Macarius and the
      Canonization of Gogo and Didi." Journal of
      Beckett Studies, no. 6 (Autumn), pp. 117-19.
         Compares St. Marcarius the Elder and St.
      Marcarius the Younger to two of Beckett's
      couples, Mercier and Camier, and Gogo and
      Didi.

37   FRIEDMAN, MELVIN J. "Samuel Beckett." In A
      Critical Bibliography of French Literature.

Vol. 6, Part 3. Edited by Douglas W. Alden
and Richard A. Brooks. Syracuse University
Press, pp. 1865-86.
Presents a representative selection of
critical writings about Beckett. The entries
are briefly annotated and organized according
to subject matter: bibliography, general
studies, the novel, individual novels and
nouvelles, drama (in general), Waiting for
Godot, other plays, poetry, cinema, influences and comparisons, philosophical influences. Reviews are listed for the critical
books on Beckett.

38   GONTARSKI, S.E. "Beckett's Voice Crying in the
Wilderness, from 'Kilcool' to Not I." Papers
of the Biographical Society of America 74,
no. 1 (Jan.-Mar.):27-47.
Studies the complex details of the
composition of Not I. Gontarski considers
possible sources for the play and the phases
of composition of the manuscript "Kilcool"
and the manuscripts and typescripts of Not I,
and images and memories of Ireland.

39   _____. "The Making of Krapp's Last Tape."
In Theatre Workbook I: Samuel Beckett,
"Krapp's Last Tape." Edited by James
Knowlson. London: Brutus Books, pp. 14-23.
Examines patterns of revision in the seven
stages of composition of Krapp's Last Tape.
The image of the old man listening to tape
recordings remained constant through the
seven versions, while the pattern and shape,
the tone and tempo, the possibilities of the
tape recorder, and Krapp's fundamental
conflict were developed through revision.
See 1980.60.

40   _____. "'Making Yourself All Up Again': The
Composition of Samuel Beckett's That Time."
Modern Drama 23, no. 2 (June):112-20.
Believes the composition of That Time
demonstrates three major phases in Beckett's
creative process: 1) the early drafts of the

memories are recorded in near final form,
suggesting close connections between Beckett
and the Surrealists, 2) the play's dramatic
tension changes, and 3) Beckett's major
creative struggle is with shape.

41   GUSSOW, MEL.   "The Stage: Chaikin Directs
     Beckett's Endgame." New York Times, 14 Jan.,
     p. 12C.
          Feels that Endgame lacks the playfulness
     of Godot and in contrast seems inanimate.
     Gussow introduces the references to The
     Tempest comparing Hamm to Prospero and Clov
     to Caliban.

42   HARRINGTON, JOHN P.   "'That Red Branch Bum was
     the Camel's Back': Beckett's Use of Yeats in
     Murphy." Eire-Ireland 15, no. 3 (Fall):
     86-96.
          Points out that Murphy mocks Yeats' use of
     resolution of contraries: the themes of
     self-conflict and disorder are developed in
     Murphy through references to Yeat's work.

43   HAYMAN, RONALD.   "Beckett's German Production:
     Das letzte Band, Schiller-Theater Werkstatt,
     Berlin, October, 1969." In Theatre Workbook
     I: Samuel Beckett, "Krapp's Last Tape."
     Edited by James Knowlson. London: Brutus
     Books, pp. 67-70.
          Interviews Martin Held (Krapp) focusing on
     Beckett's method of directing the role of
     Krapp, and comparisons with Beckett's other
     figures. See 1980.60.

44   HEBERT, HUGH.   "Brief Encounter with a Stage
     Irishman." Guardian, 17 May, p. 11.
          Describes his "friendly chat" with Beckett
     at the San Quentin Drama Workshop's rehearsal
     of Endgame in London, discussing Beckett's
     present work and his recent productions.
     Reprinted: 1980.45.

45   _____.   "Brief Encounter with a Stage Irishman."
     Manchester Guardian Weekly 122, no. 23

(1 June):19.
Reprint of 1980.44.

46   HENKLE, ROGER B.   "Beckett and the Comedy of
      Bourgeois Experience." <u>Thalia: Studies in
      Literary Humor</u> 3, no. 1 (Spring-Summer):35-
      38.
           Shows how Beckett dispels the tensions
      inherent in the act of reading, the reader's
      need to maintain "the temporal, causative,
      sequential orientation that grips us to the
      narrative, and to the anxieties of inter-
      pretation." In <u>Molloy</u> and <u>Malone Dies</u>, when
      the narrator parodies the human experiences
      he recounts, breaks off the narrative,
      becomes vague or denies its very existence --
      the tension dissolves.

47   HENNING, SYLVIE DEBEVEC.   "Narrative and Textual
      Doubles in the Works of Samuel Beckett."
      <u>Sub-Stance</u> 29:97-104.
           Makes observations based on the confronta-
      tion between man and his doubles and between
      a text and its doubles in <u>Krapp's Last Tape</u>
      and <u>Film</u>: whereas man fails to recover his
      double in both works, Beckett's texts are
      doubles and lead to a renewed artistic vigor.

48   *HOLZBERG, RUTH.   "Le Solipsisme beckettien: Du
      clair obscur existentiel à la lumière
      aveuglante de la conscience."   In <u>Bulletin
      1980-81. Société des Professeurs Français en
      Amérique</u>. New York: Société des Professeurs
      Français en Amérique.

49   HONORE, LIONEL P.   "Metaphysical Anguish and
      Futility in <u>Molloy</u>."   <u>Kentucky Romance
      Quarterly</u> 27, no. 4:435-44.
           Discusses metaphysical anguish and
      futility in <u>Molloy</u>: the futility of the
      characters' actions coupled with the obses-
      sive need to "go on," the opposition between
      the decay of the material body and the
      increased inner awareness of the characters,

self-mockery, self-hatred, and the duality
between life and death.

50   JONES, ANTHONY. "The French Murphy: From 'Rare
      Bird' to 'Cancre'." <u>Journal of Beckett
      Studies</u>, no. 6 (Autumn), pp. 37-50.
           Comments on textual variants in the
      English and French versions of <u>Murphy</u>. Jones
      discovers that the narrator's attitude toward
      Murphy in the French text has become more
      distant and less sympathetic.

51   *KALAGA, W. "Metanarrator and his Delegates:
      The Evolution of Narrative Strategy in the
      Novels of Samuel Beckett." <u>Literature</u>
      (Vilnius) 22, no. 3:61-81.

52   KELLMAN, STEVEN G. "Beckett's Trilogy." In <u>The
      Self-Begetting Novel</u>. New York: Columbia
      University Press, pp. 129-43.
           Views the novels of the trilogy as self-
      conscious extensions of the French tradition,
      stressing 1) the characters fascination with
      death or the urge to escape from the self,
      and their "mania for symmetry" and 2) the
      falsehood of fiction.

53   KELLY, KATHERINE. "The Orphic Mouth in <u>Not I</u>."
      <u>Journal of Beckett Studies</u>, no. 6 (Autumn),
      pp. 73-80.
           Compares the mouth in <u>Not I</u> to Ovid's
      version of the myth of Orpheus, focusing on
      the written text of the play as the reader
      experiences it, with occasional references to
      the stage production.

54   *KENNEDY, SIGHLE. "Samuel Beckett's Language:
      'Danger: Explosive Materials.'" <u>Centerpoint</u>
      4, no. 2, issue 13 (Fall):135-37.

55   KERN, EDITH. "Beckett's Multi-Lingual Exis-
      tence." <u>Centerpoint</u> 4, no. 2, issue 13
      (Fall):133-35.
           Beckett calls to our attention the poetic
      effects Joyce achieved through his approach

to language which reflected the thinking of
Giambattista Vico and utilized the insertion
of foreign language phrases, literary
translation or allusion in the text.

56 KNOWLSON, JAMES, ed. "American Première:
Provincetown Playhouse, New York, January,
1960." In Theatre Workbook I: Samuel
Beckett, "Krapp's Last Tape." London:
Brutus Books, pp. 52-64.
Interviews Alan Schneider (Director) and
Donald David (Krapp), commenting on the
difficulty of producing Krapp's Last Tape,
the director's aims, Krapp's relationship
with the objects on stage, Schneider's
interpretation of Beckett's play, and Krapp's
costume and movements. See 1980.60.

57 _____, ed. "French Première: La Dernière
Bande. Théâtre Récamier, Paris, March,
1960." In Theatre Workbook I: Samuel
Beckett, "Krapp's Last Tape." London:
Brutus Books, pp. 65-66.
Interviews Roger Blin (Director), briefly
mentioning the selection of R.J. Chauffard
for the role of Krapp, his costume and use of
props. See 1980.60.

58 _____, ed. "Greenwich Theatre, London, December, 1975." In Theatre Workbook I: Samuel
Beckett, "Krapp's Last Tape." London:
Brutus Books, pp. 108-15.
Interviews Max Wall (Krapp) emphasizing
the potential difficulties of the role, the
advantage of working with Patrick Magee as
the director, the way Wall's music-hall
background helped him in acting, his deliberate restraint and his introduction of a lack
of resignation and a bitter irony to the
part. See 1980.60.

59 _____, ed. "Notes on the Text." In Theatre
Workbook I: Samuel Beckett, "Krapp's Last
Tape." London: Brutus Books, pp. 24-40.
Comments on expressions and phrases in the

British and American editions of the play,
changes in the text, production changes in
the set, costume, lighting, props, and stage
business. See 1980.60.

60   _____, ed. Theatre Workbook I: Samuel Beckett,
        "Krapp's Last Tape."   London: Brutus Books,
        176 pp.
            Includes reviews of the play in perfor-
        mance, as well as critical material on the
        genesis and interpretation of the play and a
        bibliography of articles and monographs. See
        1980.2, 1980.14, 1980.17, 1980.18, 1980.25,
        1980.28, 1980.31, 1980.43, 1980.56, 1980.57,
        1980.58, 1980.59, 1980.61, 1980.62, 1980.66,
        1980.85, 1980.91, 1980.104, 1980.111,
        1980.112, 1980.114.

61   _____, ed. "Two Paris Productions by Beckett:
        Théâtre Récamier, May, 1970 and Théâtre
        d'Orsay, April, 1975." In Theatre Workbook
        I: Samuel Beckett, "Krapp's Last Tape."
        London: Brutus Books, pp. 80-85.
            Interviews Jean Martin (Krapp) discussing
        with him his interpretation of the role and
        the use of stage props in the play. See
        1980.60

62   _____, ed. "World Première: Royal Court
        Theatre, London, October, 1958." In Theatre
        Workbook I: Samuel Beckett, "Krapp's Last
        Tape." London: Brutus Books, pp. 42-47.
            Interviews the actor, Patrick Magee, and
        the director, Donald McWhinnie, commenting on
        Magee's costume and movements in the play,
        the development of the play, the choice of
        Magee, and the set of the first production.
        See 1980.60.

63   *KRISTEVA, JULIA. "The Father, Love, and
        Banishment." In Desire in Language: A
        Semiotic Approach to Literature and Art.
        Edited by Leon S. Roudiez. Translated by
        Thomas Gora, Alice Jardine, and Leon S.
        Roudiez. Oxford: Blackwell, pp. 148-58.

64   LAASS, HENNER. "Exploration of the Non-Feasi-
         ble: Syntactic Ambiguity in Some Poems of
         Samuel Beckett." In <u>Poetic Knowledge:
         Circumference and Centre.</u> Papers from the
         <u>Wuppertal Symposium 1978</u>. Edited by Roland
         Hagenbüchle and Joseph T. Swann. Bonn:
         Bouvier, pp. 100-13.
              Analyzes four poems from the 1961 edition
         of Beckett's <u>Poems in English</u> grouped
         together under the heading "Quatre Poems."
         These poems reflect the author's artistic
         preoccupations in his later fiction and drama
         -- the experience of the fundamental inade-
         quacy of language -- or the gap between the
         individual mind and the phenomena of the
         outer world.

65   LA BARDONNIE, MATHILDE. "<u>Endgame</u>, de Samuel
         Beckett: Quatre Acteurs américains."
         <u>Monde</u>, 22 Feb., pp. 1, 22.
              Reviews Joseph Chaikin's production of
         <u>Endgame</u> at the Centre Américain, acknowledg-
         ing Chaikin's portrayal of the humor of the
         play.

66   LAMONT, ROSETTE. "Krapp: Anti-Proust." In
         <u>Theatre Workbook I: Samuel Beckett, "Krapp's
         Last Tape."</u> Edited by James Knowlson.
         London: Brutus Books, pp. 158-73.
              Interprets <u>Krapp's Last Tape</u> as a parody
         of Proust's <u>Remembrance of Things Past</u>. See
         1980.60.

67   *_____. "Samuel Beckett's Multi-Lingual Exis-
         tence: Temptations of the Logos." <u>Center-
         point</u> 4, no. 2, issue 13 (Fall):132-47.

68   LARTICHAUX, JEAN YVES. "Au commencement la
         voix." <u>Quinzaine Littéraire</u>, no. 322 (1-15
         Apr.), pp. 5-6.
              Enumerates variations in the text of
         <u>Company</u>, and remarks how the story of the
         narrator's life gradually emerges through the
         creation of the text.

69   LAWLEY, PAUL. "Embers: An Interpretation."
      Journal of Beckett Studies, no. 6 (Autumn),
      pp. 9-36.
          Attempts to locate the "real centre" of
      Embers and to show how it succeeds. Com-
      parisons with Tennyson and Freud are intro-
      duced

70   LEIGH, JAMES. "Another Beckett: An Analysis of
      Residua." In The Analysis of Literary Texts.
      Current Trends in Methodology. Edited by
      Randolph D. Pope. Ypsilanti, Mich.:
      Bilingual Press, pp. 314-30.
          Studies several aspects of the three texts
      that make up Residua ("Enough," "Imagination
      Dead Imagine," and "Ping"), pointing out the
      links between the texts, the deviations, the
      verb tenses, the relationship between
      narration and discourse (textual present),
      the function of "ping" as punctuation, etc.

71   *LEONARD, J. New York Times, 22 Dec., 16C.
          Source: Index to Book Reviews in Humani-
      ties, 1980;unverified.

72   LE SIDANER, JEAN-MARIE. "Entendre dans le
      noir." Magazine Littéraire, no. 164 (Sept.),
      pp. 54-55.
          Highlights the flow of thoughts and images
      in Beckett's short work Company.

73   LEVIN, BERNARD. "Fiction 1: The Bare Horizon
      of Samuel Beckett." Sunday Times (London),
      29 June, p. 42.
          Offers his interpretation of Company,
      "which is that [Beckett] has now inspected
      the human condition from every possible
      angle, and come finally to the conclusion
      that it is irremediably absurd." Levin
      addresses the questions of the narrator's
      aloneness, his memories, and the cessation of
      the voice.

74   LEVY, ERIC P. Beckett and the Voice of Species:
      A Study of the Prose Fiction. Totowa, N.J.:

Barnes & Noble; Dublin: Gill and Macmillan
Ltd., 145 pp.
   Believes Beckett's fictions respond to the
need to structure experience and redefine the
poles of self and world in the twentieth
century. Levy undertakes an explanation of
the self-conscious introspection of the
Beckettian narrator and Beckett's portrayal
of the vacancy of human experience in his
novels: "To this end he develops his
remarkable narrator who becomes a universal
human voice, the voice of species, seeking in
the void the certainties of subject and
object that once made human experience
intelligible." A select bibliography is
included.

75   *LIBERA, ANTONI. "Beckett: Five Questions."
     Centerpoint 4, no. 2, issue 13 (Fall):146-47.

76   _____. "Structure and Pattern in That Time."
     Translated by Aniela Korzeniowska. Journal
     of Beckett Studies, no. 6 (Autumn), pp. 81-
     89.
        Analyzes the three voices, their stories
     and images, their methods of presentation,
     the rhythm of their relationships with each
     other, and the structure of the play.

77   *LYONS, W.H. "Backtracking Beckett." In
     Literature and Society: Studies in Nine-
     teenth and Twentieth Century French Litera-
     ture. Presented to R.J. North. Birmingham:
     Goodman for University of Birmingham, pp.
     214-20.

78   MAYOUX, J.-J. "Comment se tenir compagnie?"
     Critique, (Nov.), pp. 1105-7.
        Examines the multiple identity of the
     narrator in Company and the question of time
     (the factual present and the unverifiable
     past).

79   *MEGGED, MATTI. "Exile into Silence in
      Beckett's First French Writings." <u>Center-
      point</u> 4, no. 2, issue 13 (Fall):138-40.

80   MENZIES, JANET. "Beckett's Bicycles." <u>Journal
      of Beckett Studies</u>, no. 6 (Autumn),
      pp. 97-105.
           Explores the bicycle motif in Beckett's
      works. Menzies feels it is the most powerful
      motif by which Beckett communicates the
      struggle between the desire for motion and
      the desire for stasis: "the bicycle is
      integral to Beckett's work; its appearance,
      possession and disappearance coincide with
      and reflect changes in the physical status of
      characters and even in the tone of the
      narrative."

81   MORRISON, KRISTIN. "Defeated Sexuality in the
      Plays and Novels of Samuel Beckett."
      <u>Comparative Drama</u> 14, no. 1 (Spring):18-34.
           Analyzes the elusive sexual references in
      Beckett's plays showing them to be "sig-
      nificant metaphors for the misery of human
      life itself."

82   NEILL, MARY. "Trees, Tombs, and Tape-Recorders:
      The Emblematic Tradition and the Theatre of
      Samuel Beckett." <u>English Studies in Canada</u>
      6, no. 3:307-22.
           Finds that Beckett's stage settings
      incorporate the emblematic tradition of
      medieval and Renaissance drama as well as the
      images of modern theatrical innovation.
      Neill points out two techniques related to
      Emblematic staging which Glynne Wickham
      stresses: 1) the major scenic emblems which
      were in use as visual images from medieval
      pageantry to the Stuart era and 2) the
      conventional use of the theater itself as a
      metaphor for human experience.

83   *NIKOLAEVSKLAYA, A. "My Art is Just a Cry."
      <u>Foreign Literature</u> 12:237-40.

84   *NORRISH, P.J. "Elements of Christianity in
       French Post-Christian Drama: A Comparison
       between <u>Le Maître de Santiago</u> and <u>En atten-</u>
       <u>dant Godot</u>." <u>New Zealand Journal of French</u>
       <u>Studies</u> 1, no. 1 (May):50-74.

85   OBERG, ARTHUR K. "<u>Krapp's Last Tape</u> and the
       Proustian Vision." In <u>Theatre Workbook I:</u>
       <u>Samuel Beckett, "Krapp's Last Tape.</u>" Edited
       by James Knowlson. London: Brutus Books,
       pp. 151-57.
            Reprint of 1966.57; see 1980.60.

86   O'HARA, J.D. "A Writer at the Mercy of Memory."
       <u>New York Times Book Review</u>, 2 Nov., p. 7.
            Claims <u>Company</u> is a fictional autobio-
       graphy, a report on a "life from the inside."
       O'Hara remarks that the voice has been split
       into three parts: the voice of memory, the
       unwilling rememberer, and the unhappy
       perceiver.

87   *PIATIER, JACQUELINE. "T'en souvient-il? --
       <u>Compagnie</u> de Samuel Beckett; <u>Geneviève</u>, de
       Jean Renoir." <u>Monde [hebdomadaire]</u>, 7-13
       Feb., p. 12.

88   *POIROT-DELPECH, BERTRAND. "<u>Compagnie</u>, de
       Samuel Beckett; <u>Geneviève</u>, de Jean Renoir:
       T'en souvient-il?" <u>Monde [des Livres]</u>, 8
       Feb., pp. 17, 19.

89   POSNOCK, ROSS. "Beckett, Valéry and <u>Watt</u>."
       <u>Journal of Beckett Studies</u>, no. 6 (Autumn),
       pp. 51-62.
            Compares Beckett and Valéry through their
       critiques of the novel as a genre.

90   PRINZ, JESSICA. "Foirades/Fizzles/Beckett/
       Johns." <u>Contemporary Literature</u> 21, no. 3
       (Summer):480-510.
            Details the collaboration of Beckett and
       Jasper Johns for an edition of <u>Fizzles</u>,
       pointing out their independence in the
       project, their styles and techniques, and the

similarities in artistic sensibilities and
strategies. Reproductions of many of Jasper
Johns' works are included.

91   "Production Plan of Krapp's Last Tape by Samuel
      Beckett." In Theatre Workbook I: Samuel
      Beckett, "Krapp's Last Tape." Edited by
      James Knowlson. London: Brutus Books, pp.
      141-44.
          Presents a copy of notes written by
      Beckett in Stuttgart in 1977. See 1980.60.

92   QUINSAT, GILLES. "Samuel Beckett: Compagnie."
      Nouvelle Revue Française, no. 328 (1 May),
      pp. 101-5.
          Analyzes the roles of the two voices in
      Company.

93   *[RICKS, CHRISTOPHER]. "Christopher Ricks on
      Samuel Beckett: A Talk to the Literary
      Society (ed. by David Winzar)." Oxford
      Literary Journal, no. 4, pp. 2-3.

94   ROBINSON, FRED MILLER. "Samuel Beckett: Watt."
      In The Comedy of Language. Studies in Modern
      Comic Literature. Amherst: The University
      of Massachusetts Press, pp. 127-74.
          Discusses Beckett's characteristic
      paradoxes (light vs. darkness, outer vs.
      inner world, individual vs. universal voice,
      etc.) as a background for his examination of
      the comedy of the central images and ideas in
      Watt.

95   ROSE, MARGARET. "A Critical Analysis of the
      Non-Verbal Effects in Beckett's Dramatic
      Works." ACME 33, no. 3 (Sept.-Dec.):509-21.
          Evaluates Beckett's concept of reality,
      the role of language, the simplification of
      his dramatic style and his use of alternative
      forms of expression (such as mime, the use of
      rhythm and music, props, lighting and
      movement, and sound effects).

96   SENART, PHILIPPE. "La Revue théâtrale."
     Nouvelle Revue des Deux Mondes, no. 12
     (Dec.), pp. 695-704. Beckett: pp. 697-98.
         In his review of Endgame at the Comédie-
     Française, points out that Beckett's theater
     represents the last avatar of expiring
     humanity.

97   SHERZER, DINA. "Didi, Gogo, Pozzo, Lucky:
     Linguistes déconstructeurs." Etudes
     Littéraires 13, no. 3 (Dec.):539-58.
         Demonstrates Beckett's manipulative use of
     language in Waiting for Godot, focusing on
     discourse, verbal interactions, syntax,
     semantics, and sounds or sequence of sounds.
     Reprinted: 1980.98.

98   _____. "Didi, Gogo, Pozzo, Lucky: linguistes
     déconstructeurs." In Théâtre et théâtralité.
     Québec: Les Presses de l'Université Laval,
     pp. 539-58.
         Reprint of 1980.97.

99   SIMON, JOHN. "Murder at the Manhattan." New
     York 13, no. 4 (28 Jan.):58.
         Criticizes the staging of Endgame at the
     Manhattan Theater: "A production in which
     the play's most moving moment ... can fall
     utterly, unmovingly flat is worse than no
     production at all."

100 SMITH, MARILYN J. "Condemned to Survival: The
     Comic Unsuccessful Suicide." Comparative
     Literature Studies 17, no. 1 (Mar.):26-32.
     Beckett: p. 30.
         Analyzes six examples of unsuccessful
     suicides from literary works, among them that
     of Vladimir and Estragon in Beckett's Waiting
     for Godot: "Growing frustrations, bitter-
     ness, disappointments, and in some cases
     boredom, bring the characters to the brink of
     self destruction, but for lack of true
     commitment or control, they fail. We as
     viewers of their failures respond in a
     humorous manner because the authors either

make it clear that their characters are not
capable of success or that the attempt is
merely a ploy to bring about their desired
change."

101   SOLOMON, PHILIP H. "Purgatory Unpurged: Time,
       Space, and Language in 'Lessness.'" Journal
       of Beckett Studies, no. 6 (Autumn), pp. 63-
       72.
            Elucidates two aspects of "Lessness": the
       thematics of the purgatorial situation it
       depicts, and the "lyricism" of its pur-
       gatorial language.

102   SZOGYI, ALEX. "Beckett in Tandem." Centerpoint
       4, no. 2, issue 13 (Fall):143-46.
            Suggests that Beckett deserves to be read
       in a bilingual edition, "in tandem." Szogyi
       indicates some of the differences and
       innuendoes of Beckett's French and English
       versions of his works, pointing out that many
       times Beckett "found a new way to express
       what he already expressed so well.

103   TAYLOR, THOMAS J. "That Again: A Motif
       Approach to the Beckett Canon." Journal of
       Beckett Studies, no. 6 (Autumn), pp. 107-16.
            Comments on the frequent recurrence of
       recognizable elements throughout Beckett's
       canon, and presents an initial attempt to
       index Beckettian motifs in "From an Abandoned
       Work."

104   Transcription of Samuel Beckett's manuscript
       "Magee Monologue." In Theatre Workbook I:
       Samuel Beckett, Krapp's Last Tape." Edited
       by James Knowlson. London: Brutus Books,
       pp. 14-15.
            See 1980.60

105   TREGLOWN, JEREMY. "Fables from the Dark."
       Times Literary Supplement (London), 27 June,
       p. 726.
            Reviews Company: "The fiction exists on
       the brink of non-existence, and through

proposition and counter-proposition constantly threatens to cancel itself out. Yet this
minimalism and self-contradiction make it
both a touching metaphor for human life and a
vehicle through which the largest and
strongest emotions about birth, childhood,
love, old age and impending death un-
equivocally make themselves felt."

106   VALENCY, MAURICE. "Beckett." In The End of the
      World. An Introduction to Contemporary
      Drama. New York: Oxford University Press,
      pp. 388-418.
         Believes Beckett represents a very
      advanced stage of 19th century symbolism,
      "the point at which the symbol symbolizes
      only itself, and poetry ceases to convey
      anything." Valency suggests that Waiting for
      Godot belongs to the stage of symbolism, he
      feels Godot is a metaphor even if Beckett
      refuses "to assume responsibility for its
      significance." Endgame, Krapp's Last Tape,
      All That Fall, and Happy Days, are also
      briefly analyzed.

107   Van WERT, WILLIAM F. "'To Be Is To Be Per-
      ceived': Time and Point of View in Samuel
      Beckett's Film." Literature/Film Quarterly
      8, no. 2 (Apr.):133-40.
         Considers Beckett's creation of a tension
      between perceiving and perceived and his
      solution of the technical problems caused by
      this double vision in Film: "The solution
      was to set up rigidly opposing points of view
      in the level of remove of perception, the
      degree of focus in perception, and the
      succession in terms of time for perception."

108   VAUGHAN, M.F. "Beckett's Naming of Godot."
      Studia Neophilologica 52, no. 1:119-22.
         Examines the use of diminuatives in
      Waiting for Godot, such as God-ot and Tod-og
      (Godot backwards), and analyzes the sig-
      nificance of God and death in the play.

109   VOS, MELVIN. "The Drama of Performing: The
       Locus of Beckett's Theatre." In <u>Great
       Pendulum of Becoming: Images in Modern
       Drama</u>. Grand Rapids: Christian University
       Press, pp. 93-109.
          Evaluates the use of dramatic elements in
       <u>Waiting for Godot</u>, noting the significance of
       the metaphor of the stage as world in
       Beckett's drama.

110   WADE DAVID. "All By Yourself in Beckett
       Country." <u>Times Saturday Review</u> (London), 19
       July, p. 11.
          Reviews the Radio 3 Reading of <u>Company</u> by
       Patrick Magee: "The combination of Beckett's
       prose and Magee's voice has now become
       something of a radio tradition. The voice
       must be one of the most individual and
       recognizable with its hollow, gritty, lilting
       qualities. It is hypnotic almost ... it is
       an advocate for the words it delivers and the
       ideas and the images they contain.

111   WALKER, ROY. "Love, Chess and Death." In
       <u>Theatre Workbook I: Samuel Beckett, "Krapp's
       Last Tape."</u> Edited by James Knowlson.
       London: Brutus Books, pp. 48-51.
          Reprint of 1958.37; see 1980.60.

112   WARDLE, IRVING. "Review of <u>Krapp's Last Tape</u>."
       In <u>Theatre Workbook I: Samuel Beckett,
       "Krapp's Last Tape."</u> Edited by James
       Knowlson. London: Brutus Books, pp. 117-18.
          Characterizes Krapp's role as a "literary
       case of anal fixation" and the casting of Max
       Wall in the part as an obvious choice with
       some drawbacks. See 1980.60.

113   ZILLIACUS, CLAS. "Review: Beckett Versus
       Brecht in Helsinki, 1979." <u>Journal of
       Beckett Studies</u>, no. 6 (Autumn), pp. 129-33.
          Examines Bertolt Brecht's attraction to
       <u>Waiting for Godot</u>, his plans to restage or
       rewrite the play, the interdependent

positions the two dramatists occupy, and the
light they shed on each other.

114   _____. "Suggestions for T.V. Krapp by
Samuel Beckett." In Theatre Workbook I:
Samuel Beckett, "Krapp's Last Tape." Edited
by James Knowlson. London: Brutus Books,
pp. 70-79.
         Presents a three-page typescript "Sugges-
tions for T.V. Krapp" written by Beckett and
comments on Beckett's attitude to the problem
of a television production and the changes
made necessary by the medium. See 1980.60.

1980-1984

1   *ACHOLONU, C.O. "A Touch of the Absurd:
Soyinka and Beckett." African Literature
Today 14:12-18.

1981

1   ACHESON, JAMES. "Madness and Mysticism in
Beckett's Not I." AUMLA 55 (May):91-101.
         Points out two flaws in Enoch Brater's
interpretation of Not I: first, his article
was based on a commentary and thus does not
mention passages in Jung which suggest
different interpretive possibilities; and
second, Brater wrote his article prior to the
translation of Not I into French. Acheson
feels that the French translation utilizes a
greater concentration of religious language,
introducing the possibility that the play may
be concerned with a mystical experience. See
1974.10.

2   ACKERLEY, C.J. "'In the Beginning was the Pun':
Samuel Beckett's Murphy." AUMLA 55 (May):15-
22.
         Links Murphy's Cartesian anguish to the
conception of the pun.

3   ALBRIGHT, DANIEL. "Beckett." In <u>Representation</u>
      <u>and the Imagination: Beckett, Kafka,</u>
      <u>Nabokov, and Schoenberg</u>. Chicago and London:
      University of Chicago Press, pp. 150-208.
          Suggests that in Beckett's major novels
      their is no such thing as an image. Albright
      examines the aesthetic governing Beckett's
      depiction of images: the few vestiges of
      images in his early works, his denunciation
      of self-expression in the "Three Dialogues,"
      Beckett's "realism" (the realism of fundamen-
      tal sounds, imagination, and artistic
      representation), Beckett's use of a language
      that has attained the dignity of being --
      that refers to nothing beyond itself, the
      story (or autobiography) of the self, the
      creation of fictions, and the characters'
      metamorphoses of identity.

4   ARTHUR, KATERYNA. "<u>Murphy</u>, "Gerontion" and
      Dante." <u>AUMLA</u> 55 (May):54-67.
          Shows how the references to Dante's
      <u>Commedia</u> and Dante's cosmology contribute to
      our understanding of <u>Murphy</u> and T.S. Eliot's
      "Gerontion." Arthur notes that both writers
      are interested in creating characters and
      worlds which lack the structure of <u>Commedia</u>,
      however the writers differ in their inter-
      pretation of states of human isolation.

5   BALDWIN, HELENE L. <u>Samuel Beckett's Real</u>
      <u>Silence</u>. University Park: Pennsylvania
      State University Press, 170 pp.
          Outlines the "rubric of mysticism and
      metaphysical quest" in two periods of
      Beckett's career: 1) the middle period
      (1946-1956), including <u>Watt</u>, <u>Waiting for</u>
      <u>Godot</u> and the trilogy which "are basically
      mystical and concerned with theological
      concepts, and are full of religious al-
      lusion," and 2) the later period (1966 to
      present) including <u>The Lost Ones</u> and <u>Not I</u> in
      which there appears to be a return to the
      mood of the middle period. Followed by a
      select bibliography.

6   BERLIN, NORMAND. "Boundary Situation: <u>King
     Lear</u> and <u>Waiting for Godot</u>." In <u>The Secret
     Cause. A Discussion of Tragedy</u>. Amherst:
     University of Massachusetts Press, pp. 87-
     107.
          Through a comparison of <u>King Lear</u> and
     <u>Waiting for Godot</u>, attempts to find Shakes-
     peare in Beckett and to investigate the
     common ground of tragedy on which they meet,
     "in man's ability to go on in the face of
     darkness and uncertainty, even when to go on
     means to sit on the ground and wait."

7   *BISHOP, TOM. "Dire, se dire, rien dire." <u>Art
     Press</u>, no. 51 (Sept.), pp. 4-6.

8   BLACKMAN, MAURICE. "Acting Without Words:
     Artaud and Beckett and Theatrical Language."
     <u>AUMLA</u> 55 (May):68-76.
          Explores Beckett and Antonin Artaud's
     parallel attitudes towards language, par-
     ticularly stage language. Blackman believes
     Beckett realizes Artaud's fantasy:
     "Beckett's various theatrical compositions
     illustrate a discourse beyond words alone
     which impinges directly on the imagination so
     as to communicate complex metaphysical ideas
     directly through the senses and the emotions
     and bypass the discursive logic of the
     intellect."

9   BLIN, ROGER. "Trente-trois ans après." <u>Nouvel
     Observateur</u>, 26 Sept.-2 Oct., p. 100.
          Offers a description of a few technical
     problems involved in the production of
     <u>Waiting for Godot</u>.

10   BORIE, MONIQUE. "Beckett ou l'unité perdue et
     les paradigmes dégradés." <u>Mythe et théâtre
     aujourd'hui: une quete impossible? ...
     Beckett, Genet, Grotowski, le Living Théâtre</u>.
     Paris: Nizet, pp. 27-67.
          Observes the loss of the sense of the
     human condition and the obsessive search and
     the impossible recovery of mythic temporality

in Beckett's theater, focusing on: the loss
of communication with the divine, degradation
of the mythic scenario of death and resurrec-
tion, the rupture of relations between
succeeding generations, failure of memory,
and the degradation and nostalgy of mythic
time.

11   *BOURNIQUEL, CAMILLE. "L'Image de toute
      création." Monde [des Livres], 16 Oct.,
      pp. 15, 22.

12   BRATER, ENOCH. "Company by Samuel Beckett."
      New Republic 184, no. 13 (28 Mar.):39-40.
           Remarks that since it is impossible to
      verify the characters and images portrayed in
      Company, language itself is to be relied on.

13   _____. "Privilege, Perspective, and Point of
      View in Watt." College Literature 8, no. 3
      (Fall):209-26.
           Details Beckett's manipulation of point of
      view in the four narrations of Watt, focusing
      on the problems of narrative sequence,
      identifiable perspective, the effect of
      incoherence and discontinuity, and the
      relation of chronological time to the four
      parts.

14   BROWNE, JOSEPH. "The 'Crritic' and Samuel
      Beckett: A Bibliographic Essay." College
      Literature 8, no. 3 (Fall):292-309.
           Evaluates the major critical response to
      Beckett up to 1968 and the most useful and
      thorough critical materials from that date to
      1981, dividing the bibliography into four
      parts: general, prose fiction, theater, and
      miscellaneous (poetry, criticism, radio,
      television, film).

15   BURGIN, RICHARD. "Company." Parabola 6, no. 4
      (Oct.):116-18.
           Reviews Company, indicating Beckett's
      return to themes used in previous works:
      time, memory, identity, the multiplicity of

narrative voices, the deterioration or displacement of self-awareness, and references to the real world.

16 *CALDER, JOHN. "Spirit Level." Guardian, 20 May, p. 10.

17 CANTOR, JAY. "Twenty-two (Broken) Notes on Samuel Beckett." In The Space Between. Literature and Politics. Baltimore and London: John Hopkins University Press, pp. 105-23.
Utilizes themes from Beckett's works to present his own experiences and reflections.

18 CARR, JAY. "Bare Bones: As Lady Slips Her Moorings, Beckett Sounds a Hopeful Note." Detroit News, 19 Apr., 1-6E.
Reviews the production of Rockaby in Buffalo, N.Y., explaining the significance of the "tenderly elegiac note" in Beckett's Rockaby, that sets it apart from his other plays: "She seems a child wanting a familiar and beloved bedtime story not to end. It is as if she is fighting sleep -- but not desperately, not altogether."

19 CARRABINO, VICTOR. "Beckett and Hegel: The Dialectic of Lordship and Bondage." Neophilologus 65, no. 1 (Jan.):32-41.
Examines Hegel's dialectic of the Master/slave relationship which he developed in Pheonomenology of Mind, as it pertains to Beckett's plays Waiting for Godot and Endgame.

20 CHRISTENSEN, INGER. "Samuel Beckett's Trilogy: Circling Disintegration." In The Meaning of Metafiction, A Critical Study of Selected Novels by Sterne, Nabokov, Barth, and Beckett. Bergen: Universitetsforlaget, pp. 97-150.
Deals with the three novels of the trilogy separately, analyzing the narrator's conception of his own situation and how this

influences the narrative and the narrator's relationship to the reader. Lastly, he compares the presentation of the narrative in the three parts of the trilogy, pointing out the importance of the circle both in connection with the thematic aspect of the novels and as a narrative device.

21 CLAVEL, ANDRE. "Beckett: Une littérature 'top-secret.'" Nouvelles Littéraires 59 (23-30 Apr.):49.
    Believes Beckett's most recent works, Company and Ill Seen Ill Said represent a return to the style of the early novels, the voice is simply more fragile.

22 CLUCHEY, RICK. "Mes Années avec Beckett." Translated by Jacqueline Barbé. Art Press, no. 51 (Sept.), p. 12.
    Reprint of 1980.16, 1980.17.

23 COHN, RUBY. "La Femme 'fatale' chez Beckett." Translated by Marie-Claire Pasquier. Cahiers Renaud-Barrault 102:93-107.
    Analyzes Beckett's female characters and his references to women in general in his plays, "Human Wishes," Come and Go, Endgame, All That Fall, Happy Days, Eh Joe, Not I, Footfalls, and Rockaby.

24 COURNOT, MICHEL. "Beckett: Sans feu ni lieu." Monde, 17 Sept., p. 17.
    Describes Beckett's characters as allegorical figures, categorized as either clowns or under-privileged workers.

25 CREPU, MICHEL. "L'Automne avec Beckett." Esprit, n.s., 5, no. 12 (Dec.):145-47.
    Reviews the presentations at the Beckett Festival organized by the Centre d'Etude de Civilisation Française de l'Université de New York at the Pompidou Center (Paris): Symposiums, productions of Krapp's Last Tape, Happy Days, Rockaby, Ohio Impromptu, Ill Seen Ill Said, First Love, and film versions of

Film, All That Fall, Acts Without Words, Play, and ... but the clouds ...

26 _____. "Samuel Beckett: Mal vu mal dit."
Esprit, n.s., 5, no. 9 (Sept.):148-49.
Reviews Ill Seen Ill Said, emphasizing the
bodily movements of the character and the
"failure" of language, "... to say everything, to say nothing ..."

27 *DiPIERRO, JOHN C. Structures in Beckett's
"Watt." York, South Carolina: French
Literature Publications Co., 116 pp.

28 DORAN, EVA. "Au Seuil de Beckett: Quelques
notes sur 'Dante ... Bruno. Vico ...
Joyce.'" Stanford French Review 5, no. 1
(Spring):121-27.
Summarizes and comments on the content of
Beckett's article, "Dante ... Bruno. Vico
... Joyce," pointing out essential themes
common to Beckett's art.

29 DUNCAN, JOSEPH E. "Godot Comes: Rosencrantz
and Guildenstern Are Dead." Ariel 12, no. 4
(Oct.):57-70.
Demonstrates similarities and differences
between Waiting for Godot and Tom Stoppard's
Rosencrantz and Guildenstern Are Dead.
Duncan feels that Stoppard's characters
resemble Didi and Gogo, although they are in
a completely different situation: Didi and
Gogo experience waiting, while Rosencrantz
and Guildenstern feel caught up by an
incomprehensible and inescapable force. He
points out that the structures of the two
plays differ as well: Waiting for Godot is
circular and repetitive, while Rosencrantz
and Guildenstern Are Dead is basically
linear.

30 ELSOM, JOHN. "Lone Stars." Listener, 5 Mar.,
pp. 325-26.
Reviews the latest production of Waiting
for Godot in London performed by a visiting

troup from the Baxter Theater in South
Africa: "The myth has been given a particular context, most unlike Beckett and yet
most effective. It has become more of a
parable than a myth, teaching, rather than
unlocking, about the situation of the Blacks
in South Africa."

31   FARRALL, STEPHANIE. "Talking about What Happens
      Off ... Fabulation in <u>Waiting for Godot</u>."
      <u>AUMLA</u> 55 (May):77-90.
         Claims that Beckett breaks with the
      traditional treatment of fabulation in order
      to emphasize the situation on stage. Farrall
      points out that Beckett creates an impression
      of uncertainty through the following devices:
      questions, vague references, emphasis on poor
      memory, pauses and statements which undercut
      something just affirmed, and structural
      devices of repetition and variation.

32   FINLAY, MARIKE. "<u>Foirades</u> de Beckett: Métony-
      mie à la lettre/ Métaphore à l'oeuvre/
      Embrayage du discours dualiste." In <u>Au jour
      le siècle, I: Ecrivains de la modernité:
      Roussel, Blanchot, Bataille, Beckett, Simon</u>.
      Edited by Brian Fitch. Paris: Minard, pp.
      65-88.
         Analyzes the structural elements in
      <u>Fizzles</u>: the paradoxical style of the work,
      this work as a miniature sample of Beckett's
      style, Beckett as a dualist, the problem of
      dualism as it fits into Beckett's discourse,
      the dual character of the vocabulary (mind/
      body), the categories of space and time,
      intentional word play, the shifting between
      code and message, the instability of the
      message, and his attempt to go beyond a fixed
      discourse. Reprinted: 1981.33.

33   _____. "<u>Foirades</u> de Beckett: Métonymie à la
      lettre, métaphore à l'oeuvre, embrayage du
      discours dualiste." <u>Revue des Lettres
      Modernes</u>, nos. 605-610, pp. 65-88.
         Proposes to show how the problem of

dualism fits into Beckett's monologue in
Fizzles, and how the interweaving of perspectives is achieved (metaphysics, logic,
poetry). Finlay examines vocabulary, word
groups, grammar, and verbal categories.
Reprint of 1981.32.

34   FLETCHER, JOHN. "'A Place in the Series':
      Beckett's Literary Development." _College
      Literature_ 8, no. 3 (Fall):271-82.
          Outlines the three major phases of
      Beckett's literary development: 1) a
      preoccupation with the "real" world (up to
      the outbreak of WW II), 2) a concentration on
      the world of the mind (in the nineteen-
      forties), and 3) an exploration of the world
      of language (from 1950 to the present).

35   _____. "Reading Beckett with Iris Murdoch's
      Eyes." _AUMLA_, 55 (May):7-14.
          Considers the function of comic heroes and
      comic narrative in the works of Iris Murdoch,
      Samuel Beckett, and Raymond Queneau.

36   GAVIN, WILLIAM J. "En attendant la mort:
      Plato's Socrates, Tolstoy's Ivan Ilych, and
      Beckett's _Waiting for Godot_." _Soundings: An
      Interdisciplinary Journal_ 64, no. 2 (Summer):
      217-32.
          Argues that viewing Plato's and Tolstoy's
      portraits as acceptance portraits of death is
      oversimplistic, Beckett's _Waiting for Godot_
      is an attempt to resolve the issue of the
      acceptance/denial of death: "Beckett shows
      us the impossibility of awaiting death and
      Plato shows us the same thing by demonstrat-
      ing the necessity of selecting a specific
      anticipated death ... both authors inten-
      tionally leave us with an ironic feeling,
      because both manage to disclose indirectly
      that attending to, or preparing for, death is
      both necessary and impossible."

37   GENTY, CHRISTIAN. _Histoire du Théâtre National
      de l'Odéon. (Journal de Bord). 1782-1982._

Paris: Librairie Fischbacher, 320 pp.
Lists performances of Beckett's works at
the Odeon Theater.

38   GODARD, COLETTE. "Actualité de Samuel Beckett:
Café Amérique, Come and Go, et Le
Dépeupleur." Monde, 10 Oct., p. 28.
Reviews Come and Go and The Lost Ones,
describing the basic situations portrayed.

39   _____. "Beckett et David Warrilow au Festival
d'Automne. Welcome to Godot." Monde, 6
Oct., p. 19.
In an interview David Warrilow comments on
his performances of Beckett's Piece of
Monologue, Ohio Impromptu, and Rockaby and
his need to concentrate on the spoken word
and the rythm, deemphasizing the meaning of
the words.

40   _____. "Dis Joe, Piece of Monologue au Centre
Pompidou: La Lumière de Beckett." Monde, 24
Oct., p. 25.
Describes the character portrayed by David
Warrilow in Eh Joe and Piece of Monologue as
an individual separated from himself yet
confronting himself.

41   GOLDEN, SEAN. "Familiars in a Ruinstrewn Land:
Endgame as Political Allegory." Contemporary
Literature 22, no. 4 (Fall):425-55.
After a preliminary study of style and
language, examines the works of Joyce and
Beckett (especially Endgame). Since the
problem of the contemporary writer is
complicated by form as well as content,
Golden questions how "the proletarian, or
colonial, or feminist writer [can] create art
without using the forms and conventions
handed down by bourgeois, imperial, or
patriarchal systems without thereby per-
petuating the hegemony and ideology of those
systems?"

42   *GONTARSKI, STANLEY. "La Voix pleurant dans le
         désert." <u>Art Press</u>, no. 51 (Sept.),
         pp. 13-15.

43   HALE, JANE ALISON. "Beckett's Theater as
         Grisaille." <u>Stanford French Review</u> 5, no. 2
         (Fall):189-97.
            Demonstrates the use of gray as the
         predominant tone in Beckett's theater:
         identifying Beckett's use of images and the
         implications of his portrayal of a gray world
         compared to the tradition and symbolism of
         medieval grisaille.

44   HARRINGTON, JOHN P. "The Irish Landscape in
         Samuel Beckett's <u>Watt</u>." <u>Journal of Narrative
         Technique</u> 11, no. 1 (Winter):1-11.
            Believes that <u>Watt</u> represents a sig-
         nificant innovation in Beckett's work through
         its use of obscure environments and narrative
         discontinuities. Harrington notes that the
         literary, cultural, and geographical dimen-
         sions of <u>Watt</u>'s Irish landscape are an
         important aspect of the novel and help to
         explain the formation of Beckett's original
         style in the trilogy.

45   HENNING, SYLVIE DEBEVEC, "Samuel Beckett's <u>Film</u>
         and <u>La Dernière Bande</u>: Intratextual and
         Intertextual Doubles." <u>Symposium</u> 35, no. 2
         (Summer):131-53.
            Investigates the confrontation between man
         and his doubles, between a text and its
         doubles in <u>Film</u> and <u>Krapp's Last Tape</u>: "In
         both works, the protagonist is trying to
         achieve an integral, totalized personality,
         either by eliminating the disturbing supple-
         ments, or by integrating them. The failure
         of both tactics points to problems in the
         traditional logic of identity and dif-
         ference."

46   *HIGGINS, AIDAN. "Meeting Mr. Beckett." <u>New
         Edinburgh Review</u> 56:12-15.

47   HUTCHINGS, WILLIAM. "'The Unintelligible Terms
      of an Incomprehensible Damnation': Samuel
      Beckett's The Unnamable, Sheol, and St.
      Erkenwald." Twentieth Century Literature 27,
      no. 2 (Summer):97-112.
         Compares The Unnamable with the biblical
      references to the land in Sheol and the
      medieval legend of St. Erkenwald.

48   IONESCO, EUGENE. "Les Trois Coups de théâtre de
      la rentrée: Des Agonisants si tranquilles."
      Nouvel Observateur, 26 Sept.-2 Oct., pp.
      98-100.
         Describes the Beckettian character,
      Beckett's gift for expressing the inexpres-
      sible, and the role of literature, specifi-
      cally his own work, in Beckett's life.

49   ISER, WOLFGANG. "The Art of Failure: The
      Stifled Laugh in Beckett's Theater."
      Bucknell Review. Theories of Reading,
      Looking, and Listening. Edited by Harry R.
      Garvin. Lewisburg, Pa.: Bucknell University
      Press, pp. 139-89.
         Observes that Beckett's plays include a
      comic element which induces a "self-frustrat-
      ing" laughter in the spectator: "Even if one
      cannot say with certainty that the individual
      spectator is shocked at his own laughter,
      what is clear is that the laughter has lost
      its contagious nature. It cannot set off a
      chain reaction in Beckett's theater; it is
      the stifled laugh of the individual, and not
      the liberating communal laugh by means of
      which members of an audience confirm one
      another's reactions." Iser examines the
      nature of comedy and laughter in general and
      the comic structures of Waiting for Godot and
      Endgame.

50   ISSACHAROFF, MICHAEL. "Space and Reference in
      Drama." Poetics Today 2, no. 3 (Spring):211-
      24.
         Utilizes the works of Beckett as examples
      of two extremes in his study of dramatic

space: examples of totally mimetic theater
and of almost totally diegetic theater.

51   JACOBS, RICHARD. "From Nought Anew: Samuel
         Beckett's Company." Agenda 18, no. 4
         (Winter-Spring):181-85.
              Analyzes Company, commenting on the fact
         that the narrator's fictive past appears to
         be Beckett's own in many instances.

52   _____. "The Lyricism of Beckett's Plays."
         Agenda 18, no. 4 (Winter-Spring):105-111.
              Points out the importance of the rhythmic
         patterns in Beckett's plays: "It is an
         inviolable paradox wished on Beckett's
         characters that, however persistently doomed
         their attempts to invent novelistic or
         dramatic (a priori prosaic) structures for
         their lives, their utterances still achieve
         lyrical (elevated, free-floating) status."

53   KAELIN, EUGENE F. The Unhappy Consciousness:
         The Poetic Plight of Samuel Beckett.
         Dordrecht and Boston: D. Reidel Publishing
         Co., 325 pp.
              Views Beckett as a "philosophical" writer;
         pointing out that "Beckett uses the struc-
         tures of a philosophical idea merely as
         a convenience, a device, to lend its related-
         ness to the field of experimental depth
         significations ..." Kaelin analyzes
         Beckett's creative works from the point of
         view of phenomenological structuralism and
         attempts to demonstrate the degree to which
         the philosophical structures of Beckett's
         works have changed. The author refers to the
         philosophical works of Hegel, Heidegger,
         Sartre and Merleau-Ponty.

54   KENNEDY, ANDREW K. "Endgame and the End of (a)
         Tragedy." In Papers from the First Nordic
         Conference for English Studies, Oslo (17-19
         September, 1980). Oslo: Inst. of Eng.
         Studies, University of Oslo, pp. 95-108.
              Examines the relation between Endgame and

tragedy and tragicomedy, especially in its vision and in the structure of its ending. Kennedy also presents some questions raised by the concept of "modern tragedy."

55 KNAPP, BETTINA L. "Samuel Beckett: Compagnie." French Review 55, no. 1 (Oct.):152-53.
    Reviews Company, "Beckett's mystical and scientific quest into the nature of Being, the Nought, and Non-Being," analyzing the voice of its reminiscences.

56 _____. "Samuel Beckett. Mal vu mal dit." French Review 55, no. 2 (Dec.):300-301.
    Reviews Ill Seen Ill Said, evaluating the contrasting colors black/white, space, and time as they are experienced by the female protagonist.

57 KROLL, JERI L. "'I Create Therefore I Am': The Artist's Mind in Samuel Beckett's Fiction." AUMLA 55 (May):36-53.
    Studies the mind of the artist, focusing on Beckett's first heroes, Belacqua Shuah and Murphy whom Kroll feels "set out the issues most clearly."

58 LARTICHAUX, JEAN-YVES. "La Solitude des hauts sommets." Quinzaine Littéraire, no. 348 (16-31 May), p. 5.
    Briefly reviews Ill Seen, Ill Said describing the images, the importance of light, and the succinctness and purity of Beckett's prose.

59 *LEE, G. FARRELL. "Grotesque and the Demonism of Silence: Beckett's Endgame." Notre Dame English Journal of Religion in Literature 14, no. 1 (Winter):59-70.

60 LEROUX, MONIQUE. "Beckett célébré." Quinzaine Littéraire, no. 358 (1-15 Nov.), pp. 28-29.
    Describes several performances of Beckett's plays, the directors' desires to

follow the author's intentions, and the
dramatization of Beckett's prose.

61   LITTLE, J.P. Beckett: "En attendant Godot" and
      "Fin de partie."   London: Grant and Cutler,
      83 pp.
          Analyzes Waiting for Godot and Endgame
      with special emphasis on the impact of the
      plays, the importance of "play," Beckett's
      preoccupation with form and language, the
      theme of time, and the tragic and comic
      elements in these plays.

62   *LUPU, MICHAEL. "Conversation avec Alan
      Schneider." Translated by Martine Bourdeau.
      Art Press, no. 51 (Sept.), p. 11.

63   McMILLAN, DOUGALD and MARTHA FEHSENFELD. "De La
      Dernière Bande à Pas: Structure dramatique
      et controle technique." Translated by Marie-
      Claire Pasquier. Cahiers Renaud-Barrault
      102:113-28.
          Notes Beckett's gradual mastery of
      dramatic technique and his creation of a play
      (Footfalls) in which all of the elements --
      lighting, sound, movement and text are well
      integrated.

64   *MASIH, I.K. Plays of Samuel Beckett. Atlantic
      Highlands, N.J.: Humanities Press, 127 pp.

65   MITGANG, HERBERT. "Beckett in Paris." New York
      Times Book Review, 25 Jan., p. 35.
          Describes a casual meeting with Beckett in
      a café, offering general remarks on Beckett's
      bilingualism, his wartime experiences, and
      the integrity of his work.

66   *MODRZEWSKA, RENATA. "Les Virtualités de
      réception dans la dramaturgie de Samuel
      Beckett." Romanica Wratislaviensia 16:59-82.

67   MUNDHENK, MICHAEL. "Samuel Beckett: The
      Dialectics of Hope and Despair." College
      Literature 8, no. 3 (Fall):227-48.

Emphasizes the importance of recognizing
the dialectics of both despair and hope in
Beckett's works. Mundhenk calls attention to
Beckett's despair as it is revealed in his
awareness of contemporary forms of alienation: alienation of artistic means, alienation from artistic product, alienation of
self and alienation from fellow men. Yet the
author believes Beckett goes on to reveal the
inhumanity of alienation, and through his
self-negating writing, reveals a "faint
hope": "His self-conscious investigation
into the impossibility and obligation of the
act of writing is the core of his work:
making of failure a success ..."

68   NIGHTINGALE, BENEDICT. "In the Snakepit." New
     Statesman 101 (27 Feb.):25-26.
          Reviews the Baxter Theatre of Capetown's
     production of Waiting for Godot, in which two
     blacks were cast as the two tramps, and the
     setting became South Africa. Although
     Nightingale feels that limiting the play's
     meaning to an allegory about apartheid
     distorts it, he does point out the outcome of
     such a production.

69   O'HARA, J.D. "Where There's a Will There's a
     Way Out: Beckett and Schopenhauer." College
     Literature 8, no. 3 (Fall):249-70.
          Studies Beckett's commitment to philo-
     sophy, in particular his predilection for
     Schopenhauer. O'Hara claims The Unnamable
     best represents Beckett's literary use of
     Schopenhauer's ideas: the duality of will
     and intellect, the primacy of the individual
     consciousness, the possibility of escaping
     one's self, the verbal nature of existence,
     and the entrapment of the individual in time.

70   PAINE, SYLVIA. "Beckett, Nabokov, Nin, Motives
     and Modernism. Port Washington, N.Y.:
     Kennikat Press, pp. 12-47.
          Focuses on the unresolvable tension
     between the sensuous and the transcendent in

Beckett's works, especially his late collection <u>Fizzles</u>. Paine points out that each of
the short prose texts offers a halfhearted
attempt to deal with the rift between mind
and body but ends up unable to explain it.

71 PASQUIER, MARIE-CLAIRE. "A Propos de <u>Oh les
    beaux jours</u>." <u>Cahiers Renaud-Barrault</u> 101
    (Mar.):89-92.
        Comments on <u>Happy Days</u>, the confrontation
    of the visible (light) and the audible
    (Winnie's voice) and the similarity of
    Winnie's loss of body and culture -- her
    forgetfulness of the "classics," etc.

72 _____. "<u>Pas moi</u>, <u>Pas</u>." <u>Cahiers Renaud-Barrault</u>
    102:108-12.
        Beckett's recent drama (<u>Not I</u>, <u>Footfalls</u>)
    is characterized by the fragmentation of
    language deprived of body, memory and hearing
    and sustained solely by the will to speak
    which must be obeyed.

73 PEGNATO, LISA J. "Breathing in a Different
    Zone: Joseph Chaikin." <u>TDR: The Drama
    Review</u> 25, no. 3:7-18.
        Describes Chaikin's career and gives some
    insight into his work as an actor-director
    through his approach to Beckett's material,
    his acting in <u>Texts</u> (a staged adaption of
    Beckett's prose works <u>Texts for Nothing</u> and
    <u>How It Is</u>), and his appearance in and
    direction of <u>Endgame</u>.

74 *PERLOFF, MARJORIE. "'The Space of a Door':
    Beckett and the Poetry of Absence." In <u>The
    Poetics of Indeterminacy: Rimbaud to Cage</u>.
    Princeton, N.J.: Princeton University Press,
    pp. 200-47.

75 POPKIN, HENRY. "Beckett at 75." <u>Listener</u> 105
    (30 Apr.):590.
        Reviews two plays commissioned to cele-
    brate Beckett's 75th birthday, <u>Rockaby</u> which
    premiered at the State University of New York

at Buffalo, and <u>Ohio Impromptu</u> which pre-
miered in Columbus, Ohio. Popkin points out
similarities between <u>Rockaby</u> and <u>Footfalls</u>
(in both plays the daughter is more forlorn
and isolated than the mother). <u>Ohio Im-
promptu</u> presents another image of isolation,
in this play however Popkin feels the
characters and the bitter situation of the
broken romance which is read from the book
appear to be trapped in a time warp.

76   PROBYN, CLIVE T. "Waiting for the Word: Samuel
      Beckett and Wole Soyinka." <u>Ariel: A Review
      of International English Literature</u> 12, no. 3
      (July):35-48.
           Establishes similarities between the
      Nigerian dramatist Wole Soyinka's play <u>The
      Road</u> and Beckett's <u>Waiting for Godot</u> and
      <u>Endgame</u>: the absurdity of waiting, the
      search for meaning in a meaningless world,
      the unknowable past and future, characters
      locked in their private worlds, etc.

77   RENNER, CHARLOTTE. "The Self-Multiplying
      Narrators of <u>Molloy</u>, <u>Malone Dies</u> and <u>The
      Unnamable</u>." <u>Journal of Narrative Technique</u>
      11, no. 1 (Winter, 1981):12-32.
           Examines the trilogy as a continuous
      fiction narrated by more than one voice,
      comparing Beckett's work to James Hogg's
      <u>Private Memoirs and Confessions of a Jus-
      tified Sinner</u>, Brontë's <u>Wuthering Heights</u>,
      Dickens' <u>Bleak House</u> and Faulkner's <u>Absalom,
      Absalom!</u> Incorporating Beckett's view of
      fiction and language, Renner analyzes the
      narrators of the trilogy, their self-image,
      invented fictions, attempts to silence the
      false voices through them.

78   RIGGS, LARRY W. "Esthetic Judgement and the
      Comedy of Culture in Molière, Flaubert, and
      Beckett." <u>French Review</u> 54, no. 5
      (Apr.):680-89. Beckett: pp. 688-89.
           Briefly discusses Beckett's plays and
      novels: "All three of the writers considered

here appear to use comedy to reject a
language of fixed meanings and to enforce a
constant ironic perception of the rift
between language and experience." Riggs
notes that they emphasize form rather than
content.

79   ROBINSON, FRED MILLER. "'An Art of Superior
      Tramps': Beckett and Giacometti." Centen-
      nial Review 25, no. 4 (Fall):331-44.
           Concentrates on "Beckett's and Giacometti's
      walking figures in order to understand, in
      some depth, the peculiar space in which these
      characters exist, and the phenomenology of
      our perceiving them in this space."
      Robinson compares their works and discusses
      their friendship and artistic sympathy.

80   ROLIN-JANZITI, JEANNE. "Le Système générateur
      dans Molloy de Samuel Beckett." Lingua e
      Stile 16, no. 2 (Apr.-June):255-70.
           Studies the function of the preliminary
      pages of Molloy (the situation of Molloy and
      the account of A and B) in the macro-struc-
      ture of the novel and attempts to pinpoint
      the elements that link Molloy to the twenti-
      eth century movement of experimentation.

81   ST.-PIERRE, PAUL. "Comment c'est de Beckett:
      Production et déception du sens." In Au Jour
      le siècle, I: Ecrivains de la modernité:
      Roussel, Blanchot, Bataille, Beckett, Simon.
      Edited by Brian Fitch. Paris: Minard, pp.
      89-113.
           Contrasts modern texts with traditional
      ones pointing out that the modern text does
      not have a "signifié," but rather refers back
      to itself seen in the act of referring. Four
      elements which generally establish meaning
      are analyzed in reference to Comment c'est to
      show how they introduce play ("jeu") into the
      modern text: quotation, repetition, contrast
      between spoken word and writing, and the
      status of "je" (the subject "I"). Reprinted:
      1981.82

82   _____. "Comment c'est de Beckett: Production
      et déception du sens." Revue des Lettres
      Modernes, nos. 605-610, pp. 89-113.
      Reprint of 1981.81.

83   *SCARPETTA, GUY. "Samuel Beckett: Négatif
      singulier." Art Press, no. 51 (Sept.),
      pp. 7-9.

84   SCHIRMER, GREGORY A. "The Irish Connection:
      Ambiguity of Language in All That Fall."
      College Literature 8, no. 3 (Fall):283-91.
         Evaluates the two kinds of language used
      in All That Fall -- the bleak side of the
      play is expressed through the inherent
      deceptiveness of language, while the voice of
      Mrs. Rooney, her humor, and creativity
      represent the only voice of emotion in the
      lifeless environment of the play. References
      are made to Synge and O'Casey.

85   SIMS, ROBERT L. "Company. By Samuel Beckett."
      South Atlantic Review 46, no. 3 (Sept.):84-
      86.
         Briefly reviews Company, considering the
      work as an autobiographical statement which
      contains many of Beckett's familiar themes
      and reinforces the idea that a writer really
      only writes one work.

86   SMITH, FREDERIK N. "An Error in Beckett's How
      It Is." Papers of the Bibliographical
      Society of America 75, no. 3:353.
         Points out the erroneous appearance of the
      word "subtrophical" instead of "subtropial"
      on page 42 of the Grove Press edition of How
      It Is.

87   *SMITH, STEPHANI P. "Beckett's Absent Children:
      A Reading of Fin de partie." Nigerian
      Journal of French Studies 1 (Nov.):49-60.

88   STUART, MALCOLM. "Notes on Place and Place
      Names in Murphy." RANAM: Recherches
      Anglaises et Américaines, no. 14, pp. 227-35.

Believes the occasional use of place names in Murphy combine to create a sense of "spirit of place" despite the fact that the use of setting and local color in the novel is minimized. Stuart examines specific references to place names underlining their association with the characters and their integration into a network of verbal motifs.

89   STYAN, J.L. "Theatre of the Absurd: Beckett and Pinter." In Modern Drama in Theory and Practice. Vol. 2. Symbolism, Surrealism, and the Absurd. Cambridge: Cambridge University Press, pp. 124-37. Beckett: pp. 124-34.

Makes the observation that playwrights of the Theater of the Absurd adopted stylistic methods to hold the attention of the audience, "almost universally, the methods adopted were those of farce, and laughter was found to be the most successful device in disarming a wary audience." Styan points out that Beckett's early plays utilized the techniques of mime, music hall, circus, and commedia dell'arte. The first production of Waiting for Godot at the Théâtre de Babylone (directed by Roger Blin) is described, as well as the response to the play, its American première in Miami, and Beckett's supervision or direction of future productions. Styan briefly reviews Endgame and then makes general observations about the evolution of Beckett's dramatic art after Endgame.

90   SUSINI, CHRISTIAN. "Murphomania: Murphy et sa catharsis." RANAM: Recherches Anglaises et Américaines, no. 14, pp. 213-25.

Examines the story of Murphy and his catharsis taken in the etymological sense of the process of transformation or regeneration of an individual.

91   *SUTCLIFFE, H.U. "Beckett and Maeterlinck."
      <u>Essays in French Literature</u>, no. 18 (Nov.),
      pp. 10-21.

92   TAKAHASHI, YASUNARI. "Qu'est-ce qui arrive?
      Beckett et le Nô: Comparaisons Struc-
      turales." Translated by Corinne Fournier.
      <u>Cahiers Renaud-Barrault</u> 102:73-84.
           Points out the similarities between
      Beckett's plays (<u>Waiting for Godot</u>, <u>Krapp's
      Last Tape</u>, <u>Not I</u>, <u>That Time</u>, <u>Eh Joe</u>, <u>Ohio
      Impromptu</u>) and the Noh Theater, and states
      that Beckett never imitated the Noh or was
      directly influenced by it.

93   TETSUO, KISHI. "Des voix de nulle part:
      Langage et espace dans le théâtre de Beckett
      et le Nô." <u>Cahiers Renaud-Barrault</u> 102:85-
      92.
           By its utilization of language and space,
      feels the Noh theater is unrealistic and non-
      representational. Tetsuo finds the same
      quality of abstraction in Beckett's plays,
      especially the most recent plays, <u>Not I</u>, <u>That
      Time</u>, <u>Footfalls</u>, and <u>A Piece of Monologue</u>.

94   *TOYAMA, JEAN YAMASAKI. "Voice, Self and
      Language in <u>L'Innommable</u>." <u>Degré Second:
      Studies in French Literature</u>, no. 5 (July),
      pp. 93-113.

95   *WARRILOW, DAVID. "<u>A Piece of Monologue</u>:
      Interview avec Guy Scarpetta." <u>Art Press</u>,
      no. 51 (Sept.), pp. 10-11.

96   WOOD, MICHAEL. "Comedy of Ignorance." <u>New York
      Review of Books</u> 28, no. 7 (30 Apr.):49-52.
           Reviews <u>Rockaby and Other Short Pieces</u> and
      <u>Company</u> in addition to three critical texts
      devoted to Beckett. Wood emphasizes images
      conjured up by memories, imagination, the
      "spatialization of the unseeable mind."

97   _____. "Samuel Beckett: <u>Company</u>." <u>New York
      Review of Books</u> 28, no. 7 (30 Apr.):49-52.

Title as listed by <u>French XX Bibliography</u>. Article is same as 1981.96.

98   _____. "Samuel Beckett: <u>Rockaby</u> and Other Short Pieces." <u>New York Review of Books</u> 28, no. 7 (30 Apr.):49-52.
          Title as listed by <u>French XX Bibliography</u>. Article is same as 1981.96.

99   WORTH, KATHARINE. "Beckett and the Radio Medium." In <u>British Radio Drama</u>. Edited by J. Drakakis. Cambridge: Cambridge University Press, pp. 191-217.
          Analyzes the plays Beckett wrote specifically for radio: <u>All That Fall</u>, <u>Embers</u>, <u>Words and Music</u>, <u>Cascando</u>, and <u>Rough for Radio</u> from the point of view of Beckett's innovations and achievements in the use of the radio medium. She also discusses Beckett's handling of blindness, his treatment of pauses and silences, his use of music as a character in its own right, his avoidance of montage, his introduction of elements of self-consciousness, and his evolution of "a subtle and often humorous technique for conveying the strange human ability to draw sounds out of thin air and build them up into a world without the aid of sight." In her discussion of <u>Embers</u>, <u>Words and Music</u>, and <u>Cascando</u>, Worth draws from her experiences in producing the plays for the University of London Audio-Visual Centre.

100   ZURBRUGG, NICHOLAS. "Beyond Beckett: Reckless Writing and the Concept of the Avant-garde within Post-Modern Literature." <u>Yearbook of Comparative and General Literature</u>, no. 30, pp. 37-56.
          Distinguishes between 1) modernist and post-modernist creativity and 2) "mainstream" experimental creativity and avant-garde experimental creativity. Zurbrugg examines the creativity of Beckett's fictions and the extent to which Beckett's art is characteristic of the contemporary avant garde.

101   _____. "From 'Gleam' to 'Gloom' -- The Volte
        Face Between the Criticism and Fiction of
        Samuel Beckett." AUMLA 55 (May):23-35.
            Demonstrates the dichotomy separating two
        phases of Beckett's writing, his early
        criticism and subsequent fiction. Zurbrugg
        feels that Beckett's early criticism advo-
        cates literary ideals which are later
        transgressed.

102   *_____. "Samuel Beckett, Deirdre Bair, Company,
        and the Art of Bad Bibliography." In Reading
        Life History: Griffith Papers on Biography.
        Edited by James Walter. Nathan, Queensland:
        Griffith University, Institute for Modern
        Biography, pp. 1-9.

1981-1982

1   POWER, MARY. "Samuel Beckett's 'Fingal' and the
        Irish Tradition." Journal of Modern Litera-
        ture 9, no. 1:151-56.
            Demonstrates Beckett's use of Irish
        sources in "Fingal," the second story in More
        Pricks Than Kicks, suggesting the influence
        of Joyce, Swift, and Wilde.

2   ROQUIN, CLAUDE. "La Très Peu Sainte Trinité de
        Samuel Beckett." Bulletin 1981-1982:
        Société des Professeurs Français en Amerique,
        pp. 51-61.
            Highlights the interdependance of the two
        parts of Molloy, the possible transformation
        of Moran into Molloy, the similarities of the
        characters and their backgrounds.

1982

1   ABBOTT, H. PORTER. "The Harpooned Notebook:
        Malone Dies and the Conventions of Interca-
        lated Narrative." In Samuel Beckett,
        Humanistic Perspectives. Edited by Morris
        Beja. Columbus: Ohio State University

Press, pp. 71-79.
Demonstrates how <u>Malone Dies</u> carries on a
traditional mode of the novel: the non-
retrospective narrative, focusing on three
conventions, or topoi, the threatened
manuscript, the merging of the times of
narrative and narration, and the blank entry.
See 1982.12.

2   ADORNO, THEODOR W. "Trying to Understand
     <u>Endgame</u>." <u>New German Critique</u>, no. 26
     (Spring/Summer), pp. 119-50.
         Studies <u>Endgame</u> from numerous perspec-
     tives: existentialism, history, charac-
     terization, time, space, localization,
     Beckettian situations, dissociation, humor,
     form, disintegration of language, and major
     themes.

3   ANDONIAN, CATHLEEN CULOTTA. "Conceptions of
     Inner Landscapes: The Beckettian Narrator in
     the Sixties and Seventies." <u>Symposium</u> 36,
     no. 1 (Spring):3-13.
         Analyzes the conceptual abilities of the
     narrators in Beckett's recent works through a
     study of the rapport between author-narrator
     and fiction. The narrator's perception of
     the characters and environments depicted
     correspond to Tzvetan Todorov's classifi-
     cations of narration presented in his article
     "Les Catégories du récit littéraire."

4   ANDREW, NIGEL. "The Last Modernist." <u>Times</u>
     (London), 26 August, p. 6.
         Reviews <u>Ill Seen Ill Said</u> describing the
     images and characters portrayed. Andrew
     finds a new resurgence in Beckett's style and
     imagination.

5   APPLEYARD, BRYAN. "At the Edge of Existence."
     <u>Times</u> (London), 9 Dec., p. 9.
         Offers a general introduction to Beckett's
     work as a background for his latest play
     <u>Rockaby</u>.

6   ASLAN, ODETTE. "En attendant Godot de Samuel
     Beckett." In Les Voies de la création
     théâtrale, 10: Krejca-Brook. Edited by
     Denis Bablet. Paris: Editions du Centre
     National de la Recherche Scientifique, pp.
     187-238.
         Presents a very precise, detailed account
     of the 1980 Paris production of Waiting for
     Godot, directed by Otomar Krejca: setting,
     actors, costumes, stage directions, and the
     actors' movements, expressions, and intona-
     tions documented by numerous drawings and
     photos.

7   *ASQUITH, ROSALIND. "Beckett and Billie."
     Observer, 12 Dec., p. 29.

8   ASTIER, PIERRE. "Beckett's Ohio Impromptu: A
     View from the Isle of Swans." Modern Drama
     25, no. 3 (Sept.):331-41.
         Discusses the origin of the play, its
     relationship to "Quad" and an abandoned piece
     of monologue, and the significance of place
     names in the work.

9   *BAIR, DEIRDRE. "'Back the Way He Came ... or
     in Some Quite Different Direction': Company
     in the Canon of Samuel Beckett's Writing."
     Pennsylvania English: Essays in Film and the
     Humanities 9, no. 1 (Fall):12-19.

10   BEAUSANG, MICHEL. "L'Exil de Samuel Beckett:
     La Terre et le texte." Critique 38, nos.
     421-422 (June-July):561-75.
         Points out that in his fiction Beckett has
     minimized the influence of his native
     homeland, his Protestant upbringing and
     physical reality, in order to explore the
     effects of the reduction of body and of
     language on the text.

11   BEER, ANN. "Beckett in Oxford: The San Quentin
     Drama Workshop Krapp's Last Tape and End-
     game." Journal of Beckett Studies, no. 8
     (Autumn), pp. 141-47.

Mentions the changes Beckett made in
Krapp's Last Tape and Endgame, and the
performances of the actors.

12   BEJA, MORRIS, ed. Samuel Beckett, Humanistic
Perspectives. Columbus: Ohio State University Press, 227 pp.
Presents a collection of essays suggesting
the multiplicity of perspectives and approaches offered at the symposium, "Samuel
Beckett: Humanistic Perspectives," sponsored at Ohio State University in May, 1981.
A reproduction of Beckett's manuscript for
Ohio Impromptu as well as three typescript
versions are included in an appendix. See
1982.1, 1982.16, 1982.25, 1982.26, 1982.38,
1982.47, 1982.62, 1982.63, 1982.68, 1982.79,
1982.94, 1982.101, 1982.106, 1982.110,
1982.112.

13   BEN-ZVI, LINDA. "The Schismatic Self in 'A
Piece of Monologue'" Journal of Beckett
Studies, no. 7 (Spring), pp. 7-17.
Considers the theme of the fragmented self
in Beckett's writing and the innovations
found in "A Piece of Monologue" (time, the
outer void, the images of birth and death,
and the form of the play).

14   *BILLINGTON, MICHAEL. "Two New Plays. Radio
Three Magazine 1, no. 1 (Oct.):20-21.

15   BOVE, PAUL A. "Beckett's Dreadful Postmodern:
The Deconstruction of Form in Molloy." In
De-Structing the Novel: Essays in Applied
Postmodern Hermeneutics. Troy, N.Y.:
Whitston Publishing Co., pp. 185-221.
Part of a larger comparative study of
Soren Kierkegaard and Beckett, offers an
analysis of the second part of Molloy "as an
example of fictional destruction and of its
edifying -- or 'affective' -- use of dread to
drive its readers out of the comforting
illusion of aesthetic distance."

16   BRATER, ENOCH. "The <u>Company</u> Beckett Keeps: The
      Shape of Memory and One Fablist's Decay of
      Lying." In <u>Samuel Beckett, Humanistic
      Perspectives</u>. Edited by Morris Beja.
      Columbus: Ohio State University Press, pp.
      157-71.
          Demonstrates how <u>Company</u> "draws on the
      allusive texture of Beckett's formidable
      literary past and ... how he now transforms
      it into something we may not have seen in
      precisely these same terms before." See
      1982.12.

17   _____. "Light, Sound, Movement and Action in
      Beckett's <u>Rockaby</u>." <u>Modern Drama</u> 25, no. 3
      (Sept.):342-48.
          Because <u>Rockaby</u> restricts its subject
      matter and directs our attention to the
      formal elements of the play as performance,
      light, sound, movement and action must take
      place within a limited stage space in which a
      single condensed image is represented.

18   BRIENZA, SUSAN. "'Imagination Dead Imagine': The
      Microcosm of the Mind." <u>Journal of Beckett
      Studies</u>, no. 8 (Autumn), pp. 59-74.
          Feels that the style of "Imagination Dead
      Imagine" marks a new direction for Beckett.
      Brienza feels that for the first time,
      Beckett achieves a style that imitates a
      descent into the imagination: "Beckett
      filled the empty space created by the
      omission of the real world and the death of
      the imagination with mere words, and his
      stylistic problem in this piece was to use
      language that would conjure up something and
      yet create nothing at the same time."

19   BRINK, ANDREW. "Samuel Beckett's <u>Endgame</u> and
      Schizoid Ego." <u>Sphinx</u> 4, no. 2, issue 14:87-
      100.
          Considers <u>Endgame</u> in light of 1) Deirdre
      Bair's (See 1978.2) information about
      Beckett's psychoanalytic treatment with Dr.
      W.R. Brion at the Tavistock Clinic in London,

2) a series of papers on schizophrenia
published by Dr. Brion, and 3) the Fairbairn-
Guntrip formulation of the theory of schizoid
states: "Endgame's context is the psycho-
dynamic study of family life, of child-
parent interaction as it leads to the
splitting off and internalization of ego
constituents in the maturational process ...
The conflict was fully revealed to Beckett in
psychotherapeutic treatment, but only after a
long period of assimilation could it be
simplified to the degree it is in the play."

20   BRUCK, JAN. "Beckett, Benjamin and the Modern
     Crisis in Communication." New German
     Critique, no. 26 (Spring-Summer), pp. 159-71.
        Moving toward a sociological perspective,
     compares Walter Benjamin's theory of literary
     production in his Illuminations essays with
     Waiting for Godot and the novels of the
     trilogy: "But whereas in Beckett's work the
     breakdown of society and the crisis in
     communication and aesthetic representation
     take the form of a total negation, ...
     Benjamin, from the vantage point of his
     materialistic philosophy, regards the crisis
     as a necessary stage in the historical
     development from capitalist to proletarian
     society."

21   BRUGIERE, BERNARD. "Murphy de Samuel Beckett:
     Ironie et parodie dans un récit de quête."
     Etudes Anglaises 35, no. 1 (Jan.-Mar.):39-
     56.
        Studies Murphy's quest -- the characters
     who surround him, the recurrent cycle of
     creation and destruction, and the anti-hero
     as an ironic figure through whom we recog-
     nize, in a parodic, degraded form, previous
     literary styles.

22   CASTILLO, DEBRA A. "Beckett's Metaphorical
     Towns." Modern Fiction Studies 28, no. 2
     (Summer):189-200.
        Discusses Beckett's depiction of the city:

characteristics, concept of a city as a
labyrinth or microcosm of a larger system,
ordering of time and space, characters'
alienation from culture, ideals, organization
of society, etc.

23   CAVE, RICHARD. "Film, Directed By David Clark
      and Starring Max Wall. British Film In-
      stitute, 1979." Journal of Beckett Studies,
      no. 7 (Spring), pp. 134-38.
          Examines Clark's version of Film, discuss-
      ing the relationship of O and E, and the
      significance of technical changes introduced,
      such as the addition of color and sound.

24   CHABERT, PIERRE. "The Body in Beckett's
      Theater." Journal of Beckett Studies, no. 8
      (Autumn), pp. 23-28.
          Believes Beckett approaches the body in
      his theater just as he utilizes any other raw
      material "which may be modified, sculpted,
      shaped and distorted for the stage." It
      undergoes metamorphoses to explore the
      relationships between the body and movement,
      space, objects, light, and words.

25   COE, RICHARD N. "Beckett's English." In Samuel
      Beckett, Humanistic Perspectives. Edited by
      Morris Beja. Columbus: Ohio State Univer-
      sity Press, pp. 36-57.
          Evaluates Beckett's use of English: his
      translations of his own work and that of
      others, and his early works written in
      English, commenting on a duality and a
      contradiction in his writing, "a tug-of-war
      between poetry and non-poetry, between
      'style' and 'nonstyle.'" See 1982.12.

26   COHN, RUBY. "Beckett's Theater Resonance." In
      Samuel Beckett, Humanistic Perspectives.
      Edited by Morris Beja. Columbus: Ohio State
      University Press, pp. 3-15.
          Examines Beckett's theater resonance:
      sets, props, shapes, numbers, costumes,

symbols, and structures, with an addendum on
Ohio Impromptu. See 1982.12.

27 CONLEY, TOM. "Crutches." Chicago Review 33,
    no. 2:84-92.
        Analyzes the significance of the titles of
    Beckett's works in English and French:
    "Beckett's titles neither explicate nor
    obfuscate. They neither announce nor
    summarize ... One thing for sure: the titles
    function when they are scripted as an
    extension -- not as a deferment or a summa-
    tion -- of the text, and when they are read,
    as Beckett forces us to read them, between
    and across at least two languages."

28 CONNOR, STEVEN. "Beckett's Animals." Journal
    of Beckett Studies, no. 8 (Autumn), pp. 29-
    44.
        Finds that animals are usually subjects of
    interest in their own right: animals are
    used for the sake of a joke; animals provoke
    a sense of mystery and uncertainty; animals
    are victims of cruelty; birds often represent
    spiritual and artistic yearning; animals
    remain impersonal, will-less and objective,
    and animals provide the narratives with
    moments of calm. References are made to
    Schopenhauer, Descartes, and Malebranche.

29 CRAIG, GEORGE. "The Voice of Childhood and
    Great Age." Times Literary Supplement
    (London), 27 Aug., p. 921.
        Reviews Ill Seen Ill Said, considering
    three elements present in all Beckett's work:
    1) a particular conception of age, 2) the
    field of the words "I" and/or "self" and 3)
    the question of language (translation in
    particular).

30 CRONIN, ANTHONY. "Samuel Beckett: Murphy
    Becomes Unnamable." In A Heritage Now.
    Irish Literature in the English Language.
    Dingle Co. Kerry, Ireland: Brandon Book
    Publishers, pp. 169-84.

Looks at the common characteristics of
Beckett's people, especially Murphy, Molloy,
Malone and the Unnamable: "Taken together
they may be said to compose a sort of
archetypal Beckett man, the most extreme of
all the anti-heroes and the one from whom all
vestiges of the heroic or even the likeable
have been most thoroughly eliminated."
Cronin sums up the final condition of the
Beckettian character at the end of the
trilogy -- the inability to act coupled with
the compulsion to create.

31   *CUDDY, LOIS A. "Beckett's 'Dead Voices' in
      Waiting for Godot: New Inhabitants of
      Dante's Inferno." Modern Langauge Studies
      12, no. 2 (Spring):48-61.

32   CULIK, HUGH. "Entropic Order: Beckett's
      Mercier and Camier." Eire-Ireland 17, no. 1
      (Spring):91-106.
          Illustrates Beckett's use of disintegra-
      tive processes within an ordered framework in
      his first French novel, Mercier and Camier.
      Although Beckett uses the basic formula of
      the journey or quest motif in his novel, he
      downplays plot, character, setting, and
      motivation.

33   _____. "Samuel Beckett's Molloy: Transfor-
      mation and Loss." American Imago: A
      Psychoanalytic Journal for Culture, Science
      and the Arts 39, no. 1 (Spring):21-29.
          Utilizes Anton Ehrenzweig's work, The
      Hidden Order of Art, to help define the
      relationship between the imagery of Molloy
      and the novel's three quests: "Molloy for
      his mother, Moran for Molloy, and the novel
      itself for a language that minimizes the
      losses of transforming the primary process
      vision into creative art."

34   *CUSHMAN, KEITH. "Molloy: Beckett's 'Nourish-
      ing and Economical Irish Stew.'" University
      of Dayton Review 15, no. 3 (Spring):75-82.

35   DAVIES, RUSSELL. "The Modest Magic of Samuel
       Beckett's Interpreter." Sunday Times
       (London), 19 Dec., p. 40.
         Describes the roles Billie Whitelaw has
       played in Beckett's dramas Rockaby, Happy
       Days and Not I.

36   DEARLOVE, J.E. Accommodating the Chaos: Samuel
       Beckett's Nonrelational Art. Durham, N.C.:
       Duke University Press, 175 pp.
         Defines Beckett's interest in a nonrela-
       tional art through his early critical pieces
       and interviews, and then proceeds to explore
       the strategies and forms Beckett adopts in
       his efforts to create a nonrelational art.

37   _____. "Composing in the Face of Chaos: Paul
       Hindemith and Samuel Beckett." Mosaic 15,
       no. 3 (Sept.):43-53.
         Compares and contrasts the attitudes and
       works of Beckett with those of the composer
       Paul Hindemith. Although Beckett's world is
       one of "fallen open endlessness" and Hin-
       demith's is one of "hermetically sealed
       spheres," their demands, techniques, and
       attitudes resemble one another.

38   _____. "'Syntax Upended in Opposite Corners':
       Alterations in Beckett's Linguistic
       Theories." In Samuel Beckett, Humanistic
       Perspectives. Edited by Morris Beja.
       Columbus: Ohio State University Press, pp.
       122-28.
         Traces the evolution of Beckett's linguis-
       tic attitudes: "... Beckett moves from a
       celebration of syntax at the expense of
       semantic content, through both identification
       and later dissociation of the two, to a
       period of reconciliation in which he accepts
       the solace of form as being itself an
       adequate semantic comment." See 1982.12.

39   DOHERTY, FRANCIS. "Krapp's Last Tape: The
       Artistry of the Last." Irish University
       Review 12, no. 2 (Autumn):191-204.

Compares and contrasts <u>Krapp's Last Tape</u>
with the work of Shelley and Samuel Johnson
from the point of view of "the nature of the
work of art, the nature of the self, and the
nature of endings."

40   EADE, J.C. "The Seventh Scarf: A Note on
     <u>Murphy</u>." <u>Journal of Beckett Studies</u>, no. 7
     (Spring), pp. 115-17.
          Examines the details of Murphy's horo-
     scope, which Eade discovers has neither an
     actual nor a rational astrological base.

41   FEHSENFELD, MARTHA. "Beckett's Late Works: An
     Appraisal." <u>Modern Drama</u> 25, no. 3 (Sept.):
     355-62.
          Points out Beckett's originality and
     continuing evolutionary development in his
     late works written from 1977 to 1981:
     <u>Company</u>, <u>Rockaby</u>, <u>Ohio Impromptu</u>, <u>Ghost Trio</u>,
     <u>...but the clouds...</u>, and <u>Quad</u>.

42   FITCH, BRIAN. "<u>L'Innommable</u> and the Hermeneutic
     Paradigm." <u>Chicago Review</u> 33, no. 2:100-
     106.
          Calls attention to the experience of
     reading, the reader's expectations, and
     regression in Beckett's prose, situating
     Beckett's texts at the point before language
     becomes literature. Fitch shows how the
     status of language and the problem of
     identity are put in question in <u>The Un-
     namable</u>.

43   FLEISSNER, ROBERT F. "Godotology, Revisited:
     The Hidden Anagram for Gott/Tod." <u>Germanic
     Notes</u> 13, no. 3:35-37.
          Reviews past explanations for the name
     Godot and then proposes that Godot is
     Nietzschean in origin, a nameplay on
     Zarathustra's "Gott ist tot."

44   GANS, ERIC. "Beckett and the Problem of Modern
     Culture," <u>Sub-Stance</u> 35:3-15.
          Presents Beckett's esthetic of failure,

using <u>Waiting for Godot</u> as an example, and
then situates it in a historical view of
culture.

45   *GENET, JACQUELINE. "Formes et chaos dans le
       <u>Murphy</u> de Beckett." <u>Gaeliana</u>, no. 4, pp.
       181-200.

46   GILULA, DWORA. "Estragon is not a Historian,
       but Vladimir is." <u>Hebrew University Studies
       in Literature</u> 10:138-61.
           Proposes a non-religious interpretation of
       the Parable of the Two Thieves in <u>Waiting for
       Godot</u>, emphasizing that what Vladimir is
       really concerned with is the verifying of the
       historical truth. Gilula contrasts Vladimir
       and Estragon's comprehension of the situa-
       tion, their memories of the past, and their
       outlook for the future.

47   GONTARSKI, S.E. "<u>Film</u> and Formal Integrity."
       In <u>Samuel Beckett, Humanistic Perspectives</u>.
       Edited by Morris Beja. Columbus: Ohio State
       University Press, pp. 129-36.
           Remarks differences in the two holograph
       versions of <u>Film</u>, pointing out Beckett's
       concern for balance, realistic detail,
       motivation for O's behavior, the use of
       sound, and the thematic use of medium. See
       1982.12.

48   *_____. "Samuel Beckett, James Joyce's
       'Illstarred Punster.'" In <u>The Seventh of
       Joyce</u>. Edited by Bernard Benstock.
       Bloomington: Indiana University Press, pp.
       29-36.

49   _____. "The World Première of <u>Ohio Impromptu</u>,
       Directed by Alan Schneider at Columbus,
       Ohio." <u>Journal of Beckett Studies</u>, no. 8
       (Autumn), pp. 133-36.
           Outlines the two movements of the play, a
       past emotional liaison and a present solution
       to the turmoil. The difference between the
       reading and the stage action provides the

drama: "Beckett is certainly meditating ...
on the play within the occasion, the artist
speaking to his critics."

50   GUREWITCH, MORTON.   "Beckett and the Comedy of
     Decomposition." <u>Chicago Review</u> 33, no. 2:93-
     99.
          Notes Beckett's use of grotesque comedy in
     the trilogy, relating Freud's analysis of
     comedy and Ruby Cohn's comments on the
     metaphysical implications of comedy. See
     1962.21.

51   HANSFORD, JAMES. "'Imagination Dead Imagine':
     The Imagination and Its Context." <u>Journal of
     Beckett Studies</u>, no. 7 (Spring), pp. 49-70.
          Traces the discovery of the created image
     in "Imagination Dead Imagine," analyzing the
     role of memory, perception, time, space, and
     narrative consciousness.

52   _____. "Seeing and Saying in 'As the Story Was
     Told.'" <u>Journal of Beckett Studies</u>, no. 8
     (Autumn), pp. 75-93.
          Offers a close textual study of Beckett's
     "As the Story Was Told," which was submitted
     on request as a contribution to a memorial
     volume for Günther Eich (<u>Günter Eich zum
     Gedachtnis</u>. Frankfort: Suhrkamp Verlag,
     1975, pp. 10-13). Hansford demonstrates
     "that the text is concerned with the nature
     of creative activity, with the relationship
     between story-telling and truth-seeking and
     between 'Imagination' and 'Fancy' ..."

53   HARRINGTON, JOHN P. "Pynchon, Beckett, and
     Entropy: Uses of Metaphor." <u>Missouri Review</u>
     5, no. 3 (Summer):129-38.
          Although entropy is used in a similar
     fashion in Pynchon's story "Entropy" and
     Beckett's novel <u>Murphy</u>, their later fiction
     displays a gradual divergence in their use of
     this metaphor: "Rather than privilege,
     remoteness, and finality, ... Beckett's

metaphor implies uniformity, presence, and process."

54   HAYMAN, DAVID. "Joyce/Beckett/Joyce." Journal of Beckett Studies, no. 7 (Spring), pp. 101-7.
        Proposes a comparison of the works of Joyce and Beckett, examining two unexplored shared traits: the use of a complex voice and of self-generating texts. Reprinted: 1982.55.

55   _____. "Joyce/Beckett/Joyce." In The Seventh of Joyce. Edited by Bernard Benstock. Bloomington: Indiana University Press; Brighton: Harvester, pp. 37-43.
        Reprint of 1982.54.

56   HENNING, SYLVIE D. "Film: A Dialogue between Beckett and Berkeley." Journal of Beckett Studies, no. 7 (Spring), pp. 89-99.
        Believes that Film is an attempt to work through the logic of George Berkeley's main thesis in Principles of Human Knowledge in order to point out the weak spot in his work: "E and O remain apart, even in the moment of self-perceivedness, because for Beckett, all perception requires two ... Hence there can never be full unity of the self, nor any perfect self-identity -- not, at least that we would ever be aware of."

57   HENRY, PARRISH DICE. "Got It at Last, My Legend: Homage to Samuel Beckett." Georgia Review 36, no. 2 (Summer):429-34.
        Reviews Company, noting references to Beckett's previous works (Film, Godot, Happy Days, Endgame, The Unnamable, More Pricks than Kicks), and the movie Limelight (with Buster Keaton and Charlie Chaplin).

58   HOBSON, HAROLD. "Chances of Salvation." Times Literary Supplement (London), 17 Dec., p. 1392.
        Reviews Alan Schneider's production of

Rockaby with Billie Whitelaw at the Cottesloe
Theatre and the preceding reading of the
short story "Enough."

59   *HOFFMAN, ANNE GOLUMB.   "First Love First Hate:
      On Reading Beckett's Fiction." Recovering
      Literature, no. 10, pp. 43-55.

60   JACQUART, EMMANUEL. "Les Mots sous les maux."
      Travaux de Linguistique et Littérature 20,
      no. 2:167-77.
          Studies Beckettian comedy in Endgame from
      the point of view of "play" theory, and
      categorizes different types of comedy: 1)
      flirting with sacrilege and taboo, 2) farce
      and puns, and 3) nonsense.

61   *JONGH, NICHOLAS de. "Cottesloe: Rockaby."
      Guardian, 11 Dec., p. 6.

62   KERN, EDITH. "Beckett Modernity and Medieval
      Affinities." In Samuel Beckett, Humanistic
      Perspectives. Edited by Morris Beja.
      Columbus: Ohio State University Press, pp.
      26-35.
          Notes that Beckett's use of alogical
      circularity in Waiting for Godot resembles
      the Medieval notion of the insignificance of
      the individual: "The focus is rather on
      mankind and its unchanging structures and
      needs within the universe. The individual is
      but the transitory and ephemeral link in
      Nature's unending chain of birth, life, and
      death." See 1982.12.

63   KNOWLSON, JAMES. "Beckett's 'Bits of Pipe.'"
      In Samuel Beckett, Humanistic Perspectives.
      Edited by Morris Beja. Columbus: Ohio State
      University Press, pp. 16-25.
          Studies the quotations that are found in
      the English and French versions of Happy
      Days, "stressing how much this creation of a
      multiplicity of voices, levels, tones, and
      registers demands by way of active involve-
      ment on the part of the spectator. By a

technique that clearly owes far more to
suggestion and ambiguity than it does to
reference, the spectator is able to move
freely between these different levels,
questioning, judging, and often supplying
what is hinted at rather than stated." See
1982.12.

64   KOLENDA, KONSTANTIN. "Meanings Exhausted:
      Beckett's Waiting for Godot." In Philosophy
      in Literature, Metaphysical Darkness and
      Ethical Light. Totowa, N.J.: Barnes &
      Noble, pp. 147-63.
          Interprets Waiting for Godot, discussing:
      non-action, the setting, the theme of
      waiting, distractions or entertainment,
      Lucky's speech, the relationship of Vladimir
      and Estragon, the parody of Western values,
      and the pessimistic vs. positive elements in
      the play. Kolenda emphasizes that the
      "Spiritual immobility" of Vladimir and
      Estragon is balanced by the companionship,
      mutual trust and support -- their "intensely
      felt shared predicament can result in an
      occasional ability to transcend it."

65   KOWZAN, TADEUSZ. "Signe zéro de la parole."
      Degrés 10, no. 31 (Summer):a1-a16.
          Examines four dramatic works from the
      period 1954-1972, in which words are not used
      to present the drama: Albert Camus' La Vie
      d'artiste, Beckett's Act Without Words II,
      Peter Handke's Das Mundel will Vormund sein,
      and Fraz Xaver Kroetz's Wunschkonzert. Each
      work is analyzed from two perspectives: 1)
      the problem of "signe zéro de la parole" from
      the point of view of the presentation, and 2)
      the written text as a series of linguistic
      signs or as a literary product.

66   KRANCE, CHARLES. "Beckett and the Literature of
      Ruin. Introduction." Chicago Review 33, no.
      2:79-83.
          Introduces three texts in this issue of
      Chicago Review which were originally pre-

sented at the Ohio Symposium in a seminar
entitled "Beckett and the Literature of
Ruin." Krance makes the point that Beckett
is one of three major writers of the twentieth century. Unlike the other two "corner-
stones", Joyce and Proust, Beckett makes the
concept of limitation the subject of his
writing.

67   LEVY, ERIC P. "Company: The Mirror of
      Beckettian Mimesis." Journal of Beckett
      Studies, no. 8 (Autumn), pp. 95-104.
          Through a step by step examination of the
      prose text Company, reveals how Beckett
      chooses to portray human experience as an act
      of imagination, a self-referential closed
      system in his works.

68   LIBERA, ANTONI. "The Lost Ones: A Myth of
      Human History and Destiny." In Samuel
      Beckett, Humanistic Perspectives. Edited by
      Morris Beja. Columbus: Ohio State Univer-
      sity Press, pp. 145-56.
          Analyzes the two realities presented in
      The Lost Ones, one objective and one subjec-
      tive. Libera characterizes the life in the
      cylinder as it is seen and understood by the
      observer and then attempts to determine the
      meaning of this world. See 1982.12.

69   McCARTHY, JANE. "A Week of Samuel Beckett."
      Sunday Times Magazine (London), 12 Dec.,
      p. 7.
          Comments on the Beckett season for BBC2,
      describing Quad and Billie Whitelaw's
      emotional response to Not I and Happy Days.

70   MARTINOIR, FRANCINE de. "Quelques éclats de
      voix." Quinzaine Littéraire, no. 379 (1-15
      Oct.), p. 13.
          Briefly reviews Catastrophe et autres
      dramaticules, pointing out that in each drama
      certain words, rhythms or sonorities are
      repeated. In each a consciousness attempts

to go beyond itself, to reach the "exterior"
and in each case it is doomed to failure.

71   *MAYOUX, JEAN-JACQUES. "Beckett en quête de
     lui-même." Gaeliana, no. 4, pp. 139-55.

72   MAYS, J.C.C. "Beckett in Dublin: The San
     Quentin Drama Workshop, Krapp's Last Tape and
     Endgame." Journal of Beckett Studies, no. 8
     (Autumn), pp. 136-40.
        Points out the strengths and weaknesses of
     the San Quentin Workshop's performance of
     Krapp's Last Tape and Endgame, the modifica-
     tions introduced by Beckett, and the audience
     response.

73   *_____. "Undertaking Murphy and the Question of
     Apmonia." Gaeliana, no. 4, pp. 159-78.

74   MEGGED, MATTI. "Beckett and Giacometti."
     Partisan Review 49, no. 3:400-406.
        Compares the cases in which Beckett and
     Giacometti discussed their art, found that
     their tone and philosophy were different, yet
     their feeling of failure and the need to
     continue creating were mutual. Megged
     presents other similarities between these
     artists: 1) they both ceased to believe in
     the possibility of representing reality by
     means of art, 2) they concentrated on the
     image of the human head as the part of the
     body that alludes to the imaginary world
     created by the artist, 3) their figures live
     in an imaginary space created by the artist,
     and 4) they negate the material existence of
     their subjects who are present through their
     silence and their absence.

75   MILLER, JANE. "Writing in a Second Language."
     Raritan 2, no. 1 (Summer):115-32. Beckett:
     pp. 125-28.
        Compares Beckett to two other bilingual
     writers, Joseph Conrad and Vladimir Nabokov.

76   *MONTAUT, ANNIE. "Narration, récit et
      désémiotisation dans <u>Le Dépeupleur</u> de Samuel
      Beckett." <u>Dalhousie French Studies</u> 4
      (Oct.):98-112.

77   MOONEY, MICHAEL E. "Presocratic Scepticism:
      Samuel Beckett's <u>Murphy</u> Reconsidered." <u>ELH</u>
      49, no. 1 (Spring):214-34.
            Feels that Beckett's fiction, beginning
      with <u>Murphy</u>, can be better understood by
      reference to the pre-Socratic philosopher
      Democritus of Abdera and to the scepticism of
      Sextus Empiricus than by reference to
      Cartesianism. Mooney traces Beckett's
      manipulation of imagery in <u>Murphy</u> and then
      interprets the images in terms of two pre-
      Socratic philosophies: the atomism of
      Democritus and Leucippus, and the episte-
      mology of Anaxagora.

78   MOORJANI, ANGELA B. <u>Abysmal Games in the Novels</u>
      <u>of Samuel Beckett</u>. Chapel Hill: University
      of North Carolina Press, 166 pp.
            Analyzes how Beckett's novels undermine
      textual linearity and the myths of self-
      transparency by turning words into toys and
      writing into abysmal play. The first part of
      the study concentrates on narrative redupli-
      cation, on the repetition of mirror and echo
      games, while the second part focuses on
      thematic mise en abyme.

79   MORRISON, KRISTIN. "Neglected Biblical Al-
      lusions in Beckett's Plays: 'Mother Pegg'
      Once More." In <u>Samuel Beckett, Humanistic</u>
      <u>Perspectives</u>. Edited by Morris Beja.
      Columbus: Ohio State University Press, pp.
      91-98.
            Comments on Beckett's use of biblical
      allusion and relates the Mother Pegg passage
      from <u>Endgame</u> to the <u>New Testament</u> parable
      about the wise and foolish virgins. See
      1982.12.

80   _____.   "The Rip Word in A Piece of Monologue."
        Modern Drama 25, no. 3 (Sept.): 349-54.
            Discusses the verbal play around the
        phrase "Waiting on the rip word" from A Piece
        of Monologue.

81   MURPHY, PETER J.   "Narrative Strategies in
        Samuel Beckett's 'From An Abandoned Work.'"
        English Studies in Canada 8, no. 4
        (Dec.):465-82.
            Explores the question of fictional
        identity in "From an Abandoned Work,"
        relating this text to Beckett's other prose
        and poetry: "From as early on as 'Alba' and
        Dream, (from fair to...) the colour 'white'
        has offered a way of blanking out the
        relationship between self and world, author
        and character, 'From an Abandoned Work' is
        more than a well organized and skillfully
        rendered series of dream images. It is a
        warning and a prophecy. A major conflict in
        the works after How It Is is between the
        hunger for 'whiteness,' ....and the hunger
        for words that will validate being."

82   _____.   "The Nature of Allegory in The Lost
        Ones, or the Quincunx Realistically Con-
        sidered." Journal of Beckett Studies, no. 7
        (Spring), pp. 71-88.
            Believes The Lost Ones rewrites the
        hermetic tradition in which the world was
        regarded as a book to show that "the book is
        its own world, the cylinder is a world unto
        itself." In order to demonstrate that The
        Lost Ones can be seen as a reinterpretation
        of the hermetic tradition compares Beckett's
        work with The Garden of Cyrus by Sir Thomas
        Browne.

83   *NINANE de MARTINOIR, FRANCINE.   "Etude de
        texte, Samuel Beckett, L'Innommable." Ecole
        des Lettres, 1 May, pp. 25-32.

84   *NYE, ROBERT.   "A Breakthrough for Beckett."
        Guardian, 16 Sept., p. 8.

85   O'DONOGHUE, BERNARD. "Irish Humor and Verbal
      Logic." Critical Quarterly 24, no. 1
      (Spring):33-40.
          Points out three recurrent stylistic
      techniques in Beckett's writing that are
      common in Irish literature: 1) the minute
      observation of detail in objects, 2) extreme
      and often unhelpful specificity, and 3) a
      love of pedantic scholarship. O'Donoghue
      believes Beckett has also inherited two other
      traditions: 1) the system of irony -- the
      framework and operations of Aristotelian
      logic, and 2) the essence of the Irish joke.
      References are made to Flann O'Brien, Swift,
      James Stephens, Sterne, and Joyce among
      others.

86   O'HARA, J.D. "Jung and the Narratives of
      Molloy." Journal of Beckett Studies, no. 7
      (Spring), pp. 19-47.
          Interprets the psychological nature of the
      archetypical journeys in Molloy as the
      acting-out of Jungian myths.

87   *OTTAWAY, ROBERT. "Say it Again, Sam. Again."
      Radio Times, 11-17 Dec., p. 21.

88   PASTORELLO, FELIE. "La Réception par la
      presse." In Les Voies de la création
      théâtrale, 10. Edited by Denis Bablet.
      Paris: Centre Nationale de la Recherche
      Scientifique, pp. 239-50.
          Records the press statements referring to
      Dtoma Krejca's production of Waiting for
      Godot, pointing out Krejca's emphasis on the
      "human" dimension of the play and the
      antithetical character of the two couples
      Vladimir/Estragon and Pozzo/Lucky, as well as
      the aesthetic effects of the scene.

89   PEARCE, RICHARD. "From Joyce to Beckett: The
      Tale That Wags the Telling." Journal of
      Beckett Studies, no. 7 (Spring), pp. 109-14.
          Traces the self-generating elements of
      Beckett's texts to Ulysses where "Joyce's

language liberated itself from the consciousness of his characters and even the narrator
to become an autonomous physical presence
..." Reprinted: 1982.90.

90   _____. "From Joyce to Beckett: The Tale That
Was the Telling." The Seventh of Joyce.
Edited by Bernard Benstock. Bloomington:
Indiana University Press; Brighton. Har-
vester, pp. 44-49.
Reprint of 1982.89.

91   PERLOFF, MARJORIE. "Between Verse and Prose:
Beckett and the New Poetry." Critical
Inquiry 9, no. 2 (Dec.):415-33.
Evaluates the form of Beckett's short text
Ill Seen Ill Said, examining the subject, the
voices, discourse patterns, thematic develop-
ment, and associative rhythm with references
to John Ashbery, Robert Creeley, Barbara
Einzig, Kathleen Fraser, Michael Davidson,
and Guy Davenport. Perloff feels that
Beckett's free prose is really very close to
free verse.

92   "Photographic Record of Beckett Productions."
Journal of Beckett Studies, no. 7 (Spring),
pp. 119-25.
Presents photographs of the Baxter Theatre
Company's production of Waiting for Godot at
the Old Vic on February 18, 1981.

93   PILLING, JOHN. "Company by Samuel Beckett."
Journal of Beckett Studies, no. 7 (Spring),
pp. 127-31.
Offers a critical analysis of the text of
Company, the character's relationships with
mother and father, the light/dark and "now"/
"then" confrontations, and Beckett's self-
plagiarism.

94   RABINOVITZ, RUBIN. "Unreliable Narrative in
Murphy." In Samuel Beckett, Humanistic
Perspectives. Edited by Morris Beja.
Columbus: Ohio State University Press,

pp. 58-70.
Studies the use of errors and inconsistencies in Murphy. See 1982.12.

95 RAFROIDI, PATRICK. "Pas de Shamrocks pour Sam Beckett? La Dimension irlandaise de Murphy." Etudes Irlandaises 7 (Dec.):71-81.
Points out Beckett's love-hate relationship with his native land, his use of sarcasm and parody in Murphy, and similarities he shared with Joyce.

96 READ, DAVID. "Artistic Theory in the Work of Samuel Beckett." Journal of Beckett Studies, no. 8 (Autumn), pp. 7-22.
Defines the artist's world as a microcosm of creation devised by his will but presented through the personality of his creature. The artist conveys his image of being to the artisan who determines its nature through his choice of language. Between this being and the language used to depict it there is an absence of relation: "Beckett's form is moving toward the infinity of pi, toward the 'literature of the un-word.'"

97 ROSE, MARILYN GADDIS. "Decadence and Modernism: Defining by Default." Modernistic Studies: Literature and Culture 1920-1940 4:195-206.
Works towards a definition of the French oriented decadence of 1870-1914 by eliminating Joyce and Beckett from its ranks: both Joyce and Beckett wrote poems that were within the English literary tradition.

98 ROTHENBERG, JOHN. "A Form of Tension in Beckett's Fiction." Degré Second: Studies in French Literature 6 (July):157-76.
Focuses on a form of tension in Beckett's fiction, the awareness that fiction, and language itself, are inadequate vehicles of expression.

99 SILVERMAN, HUGH J. "Beckett, Philosophy, and the Self." In The Philosophical Reflection

of Man in Literature. Selected Papers From
Several Conferences Held by the International
Society for Phenomenology and Literature in
Cambridge, Mass. Edited by Anna-Theresa
Tymieniecka. Dordrecht, Holland and Boston:
Reidel, pp. 153-60.
    Proposes to show how language establishes
the presence of self in the trilogy.

100   SIMON, RICHARD KELLER. "Dialectical Laughter:
      A Study of Endgame." Modern Drama 25, no. 4
      (Dec.):505-13.
          Believes Endgame is "a study of and
      participation in the meaning of laughter."
      Simon studies the interaction of the laughter
      present in the text and the audience's
      laughter, Beckett's use of comic devices, and
      the storyteller-listener relationship between
      Hamm and the other characters in the play.

101   SMITH, FREDERIK N. "Fiction as Composing
      Process: How It is." In Samuel Beckett,
      Humanistic Perspectives. Edited by Morris
      Beja. Columbus: Ohio State University
      Press, pp. 107-21.
          Comments on the allusions in How It Is
      that represent the various stages of the
      writing process, the dilemma between the
      chaos of the artist's inspiration and the
      need to give form to that inspiration, and
      Beckett's efforts to prevent How It Is from
      giving the appearance of a conventionally
      printed text. See 1982.12.

102   TAKAHASHI, YASUNARI. "Qu'est-ce qui arrive?
      Some Structural Comparisons of Beckett's
      Plays and Noh." In Samuel Beckett, Humanis-
      tic Perspectives. Edited by Morris Beja.
      Columbus: Ohio State University Press, pp.
      99-106.
          Describes the origin and structure of Noh
      and compares some of the structural peculi-
      arities of Beckett's plays to the Japanese
      dramatic form: "In both Zeami's and
      Beckett's theater, nothing happens

(everything has already happened), but
someone does come out of an unknown 'sacred'
country that Beckett in one of his latest
plays, <u>Ohio Impromptu</u>, calls the 'profounds
of mind ...' Beckett under a malediction
undreamed of by Zeami, has had to delve down
into the depths of modern self-consciousness
where it threatens to turn into solipsism,
autism, and schizophrenia ..." See 1982.12.

103   _____. "The Theater of the Mind: Samuel Beckett
and the Noh." <u>Encounter</u> 58, no. 4 (Apr.):66-
73.
Defines Noh drama, illustrates the
distinction between Western drama and Noh
drama, and compares Beckett's theater to the
Noh. Many of Beckett's plays resemble the
second part of Noh: "... the voice as Shite
[protagonist] arriving out of an alien time-
space dimension versus the character as Waki
[secondary character] listening to that
voice, without any possibility of dialogue
between them."

104   TAUBMAN, ROBERT. "Beckett's Buttonhook."
<u>London Review of Books</u> 4, no. 19 (21 Oct.-3
Nov.):16-17.
Reviews <u>Ill Seen Ill Said</u>, presenting the
familiar Beckett themes: isolation, absence
of hope, approach of death, and the modernist
manner that uses metaphor and symbolism to
half-suggest a meaning. Taubman points out
similarities between Beckett's work and
Wordsworth's "Lucy" poems.

105   TAYLOR, THOMAS. "<u>Footfalls</u> and <u>Not I</u>: The La
Mama Production of 1980." <u>Journal of Beckett
Studies</u>, no. 7 (Spring), pp. 132-34.
Discusses the reduced effectiveness of
this production in which the director
disregarded many of Beckett's very specific
stage directions.

106   THIHER, ALLEN. "Wittgenstein, Heidegger, the
Unnamable and Some Thoughts on the Status of

Voice in Fiction." In <u>Samuel Beckett,</u>
<u>Humanistic Perspectives</u>. Edited by Morris
Beja. Columbus: Ohio State University
Press, pp. 80-90.
   Suggests some homologies between issues
raised in Samuel Beckett's <u>The Unnamable</u> and
theoretical positions found primarily in the
work of Wittgenstein and Heidegger, with
allusions to the structuralist views of
language derived from the work of Ferdinand
de Saussure. See 1982.12.

107 TOYAMA, JEAN YAMASAKI. "Beckett Trilogy:
       Problematics of the Origin, Problem of
       Language." <u>Degré Second: Studies in French</u>
       <u>Literature</u> 6 (July):135-55.
          Discusses the trilogy from the point of
       view of a search for origins: "Throughout
       the trilogy there is a steady erosion of all
       possible origins -- self, voice, God, artist
       -- accomplished through a demonstration of
       the nature of language which is repetition, a
       deformation rather than a representation."
       Some of the myths of origination are ex-
       amined: birth, artistic creation, mother-
       hood, and the origin of beginning.

108 VELISSARIOU, ASPASIA. "Language in <u>Waiting for</u>
       <u>Godot</u>." <u>Journal of Beckett Studies</u>, no. 8
       (Autumn), pp. 45-57.
          Believes <u>Waiting for Godot</u> inaugurates the
       project which undermines Beckett's subsequent
       drama: to present the search for self and
       meaning in terms of a dramatic language which
       derives its power from its own self-question-
       ing and its "obligation to express."

109 WERLICH, EGON. "'Go and See Is He Hurt': On
       the Meaning of 'Godot' in Beckett's <u>Waiting</u>
       <u>for Godot</u>." In <u>Festschrift für Karl</u>
       <u>Schneider</u>. Edited by Ernst Dick and Kurt
       Jankowsky. Amsterdam/Philadelphia: John
       Benjamins Publishing Co., pp. 561-72.
          Analyzes <u>Godot</u> from the point of view of
       two key verbs in the play "go" and "do"

(Go-do-t), comparing Vladimir and Estragon's
situation to the Biblical parable of the Good
Samaritan: "The spectator realizes that for
Vladimir and Estragon Godot is a mere
surrogate of vaguely associated selfish ideas
of hope and salvation who will one day come
and do something good for them ... In Waiting
for Godot the spectator witnesses how two
people drain all sense from their lives by
losing sight of the demands of the situation
before them."

110   ZEIFMAN, HERSH. "Come and Go: A Criticule."
       In Samuel Beckett, Humanistic Perspectives.
       Edited by Morris Beja. Columbus: Ohio State
       University Press, pp. 137-44.
           Presents a brief textual analysis of Come
       and Go. See 1982.12.

111   ZOPES, JACK. "Beckett in Germany/Germany in
       Beckett." New German Critique, no. 26
       (Spring-Summer), pp. 151-58.
           Examines Beckett's influence on postwar
       German theater: 1) Beckett's personal
       involvement with Germany, 2) the production
       of his plays, 3) his influence on German
       playwrights, and 4) tendencies of scholarly
       investigation, in particular the significance
       of Theodore Adorno's essay "Trying to
       Understand Endgame." See 1982.2.

112   ZURBRUGG, NICHOLAS. "Beckett, Proust, and
       Burroughs and the Perils of 'Image Warfare.'"
       In Samuel Beckett, Humanistic Perspectives.
       Edited by Morris Beja. Columbus: Ohio State
       University Press, pp. 172-87.
           Compares Beckett's, Proust's, and
       Burrough's use of image, finding that critics
       have mistakenly tried to interpret Beckett by
       comparing instead of contrasting Proust and
       Beckett. See 1982.12.

1982-1983

1   LYONS, CHARLES R.   "Perceiving Rockaby -- As a
    Text, as a Text by Samuel Beckett, as a Text
    for Performance." Comparative Drama 16, no.
    4 (Winter):297-311.
       Considers the illusion and authenticity of
    dramatic character in Beckett's plays and
    novels and then focuses on the techniques
    used in the plays from Not I onwards. In the
    later plays Beckett's characters appear to be
    confined in the text, rather than in an
    enclosed space, they become the represen-
    tation of the compulsive repetition of words
    that have less and less significance for
    them.

1983

1   ACHESON, JAMES. "The Act of Failure: Samuel
    Beckett's Molloy." Southern Humanities
    Review 17, no. 1 (Winter):1-18.
       Evaluates "the art of failure" in
    Beckett's writing, analyzing Beckett's
    comments on the subject in the Duthuit
    dialogues, and then interpreting Molloy and
    Moran's failure to describe their states of
    mind, referring to Proust and Jung.

2   ANDREW, NIGEL. "Meremost Minimum." Listener
    110 (11 Aug.):26.
       Feels that Worstward Ho predictably
    follows Beckett's previous work: skeletal
    cast, pared down language, desperate attempts
    to get started, carry on, and end.

3   *ANZIEU, DIDIER. "Un soi disjoint, une voix
    liante: l'écriture narrative de Samuel
    Beckett." Nouvelle revue de Psychanalyse,
    no. 28 (Autumn).

4   *L'Autre dans la sensibilité anglo-saxonne.
    Reims: Presses Universitaires de Reims.

5   BAIR, DEIDRE. "Concealing and Revealing: The
     Biographer's Work." Quadrant 127, nos. 1-2
     (Jan.-Feb.):13-18.
          Outlines her approach to biography (in
     reference to her Beckett biography and her
     current project, a biography of Simone de
     Beauvoir) and describes her interviews with
     the two authors.

6   *BALDWIN, H.L. "Memories, Echoes and Trinities
     in Beckett's Company." Christianity &
     Literature 32, no. 2 (Winter):37-43.

7   BOURAOUI, HEDI. "Beckettology." In The
     Critical Strategy. Downsview, Ontario: C.W.
     Press, pp. 99-112.
          Parodies Beckett's fictional world and his
     prose style.

8   *BRADBROOK, MURIEL CLARA. "En attendant Godot."
     In Aspects of Dramatic Form in the English
     and Irish Renaissance. Brighton, Sussex:
     Harvester Press; Totowa, N.J.: Barnes and
     Noble Books, pp. 173-86.
          Reprint of 1972.5.

9   BRATER, ENOCH. "Mis-takes, Mathematical and
     Otherwise, in The Lost Ones." Modern Fiction
     Studies 29, no. 1 (Spring):93-109.
          Offers a critical study of The Lost Ones,
     describing in detail his mathematical and
     linguistic errors which contrast sharply with
     the stability of the visual image: "Although
     words and numbers suffer chronic instability,
     Beckett's picture creates a new center for
     sound, idea, and color. The Lost Ones is
     more a scenario than short story, for Beckett
     has designed this work for the eye more than
     for the mind."

10   *BURGESS, ANTHONY. "Bubbles from the Eternal
     Mud." Observer, 30 Oct., p. 33.

11   BURKMAN, KATHERINE H.   "Hirst as Godot: Pinter
      in Beckett's Land."   Arizona Quarterly 39,
      no. 1 (Spring):5-14.
          Compares Waiting for Godot with Pinter's
      No Man's Land. Burkman feels that Pinter may
      have been unconsciously influenced by Waiting
      for Godot, since the play has become such a
      potent image in our times, and "there is no
      doubt that Pinter shed some new light on the
      enigma of Godot."

12   CHABERT, PIERRE.   "Samuel Beckett: Lieu
      physique, théâtre du corps."   Cahiers Renaud-
      Barrault 106:80-98.
          Provides a slightly revised edition of an
      article read at the Beckett Symposium at Ohio
      State University in May 1981 ("The Use of the
      Body in Beckett's Theatre"). Chabert
      describes the manipulation of the body in
      Beckett's theater: the fragmentation of
      visibility, the hiding and subsequent
      unveiling of the body, immobility, the
      reduction of actor and scene to the spoken
      word, the concentration on the voice pro-
      jected in space, and the dramatization of a
      specific part of the body.

13   COUSINEAU, THOMAS J.   "Molloy and the Paternal
      Metaphor."   Modern Fiction Studies 29, no. 1
      (Spring):81-91.
          Utilizes Jacques Lacan's interpretation
      of the stages in the child's passage through
      the Oedipal configuration to analyze the two
      parts of Molloy and the differences in the
      two characters and their goals: "... the
      desire for protection in Molloy is related to
      two distinct parental figures, the mother for
      Molloy and the father for Moran ... Molloy's
      mother and Youdi occupy the maternal and
      paternal poles of the Oedipal triangle, and
      Molloy and Moran represent the third term
      seen from two different perspectives. They
      both attempt to anchor themselves within the
      triangle, and to assure their stability

within the world, by aligning themselves with a specific parental figure."

14 CULIK, HUGH. "The Place of Watt in Beckett's Development." Modern Fiction Studies 29, no. 1 (Spring):57-71.

Uses Eugene Jolas' manifesto "Poetry is Vertical" (signed by Beckett) and Gottfried Benn's article "The Structure of the Personality" as a starting point for an analysis of the nature of language in Watt (the language of the nervous system/the language of the body).

15 DIS, CLAUDE. "Samuel Beckett: Catastrophe." Nouvelle Revue Française, no. 260 (1 Jan.), pp. 107-8.

In Catastrophe, recognizes the same emptiness, immobility, solitude and whiteness of Beckett's other late prose works.

16 DOBREZ, L.A.C. "To End Yet Again: Samuel Beckett's Recent Work." In Transformations in Modern European Drama. Edited by Ian Donaldson. Atlantic Highlands, N.J.: Humanities Press; London: Macmillan, pp. 130-46.

Focuses on the element of "unknowing" in Beckett's work, with particular reference to That Time and Not I.

17 _____. "Samuel Beckett and the Impossibility of Literary Criticism." Southern Review: Literary and Interdisciplinary 16, no. 1 (Mar.):74-85.

Juxtaposes Company and Three Dialogues, and postulates a variety of interpretive approaches to Company as an "act" or a "Text for Nothing" which resists the objectification of traditional literary criticism.

18 DORSEY, JOHN T. "Images of the Absurd Life: Betsyaku's Ido and Beckett's En attendant Godot." Comparative Literature Studies 20, no. 1 (Spring):24-33.

Compares the dramatic situations in
Betsuyaku Minoru's Ido and Waiting for Godot
from numerous perspectives: the type of
situation portrayed in the plays can be
described as an impasse or a dramatic image
of the absurdity of modern life; the characters know what they are doing (moving and
waiting) but are unsure about why they are
doing it and about how they should proceed;
their goals are vague; the characters in both
plays have made an irrational commitment, and
the end if not the goal of their actions is
probably death.

19   DUCKWORTH, COLIN. "Beckett's Educations
      sentimentales: From Premier Amour to La
      Dernière Bande and Ohio Impromptu."
      Australian Journal of French Studies 20, no.
      1 (Jan.-Apr.):61-70.
          Examines the inability of Beckett's
      characters to experience romantic love in
      First Love, Krapp's Last Tape, and Ohio
      Impromptu with reference to Sartre's La
      Nausée and Flaubert's L'Education sentimen-
      tale. Duckworth points out that woman has
      been reduced to her basic sexual function,
      and has been rejected for two reasons: 1)
      she provides a distraction, and 2) the
      Beckettian character fears being taken over
      or possessed by the Other.

20   ESSLIN, MARTIN. "Visions of Absence: Beckett's
      Footfalls, Ghost Trio and ... but the clouds
      ..." In Transformations in Modern European
      Drama. Edited by Ian Donaldson. Atlantic
      Highlands, N.J.: Humanities Press; London:
      Macmillan, pp. 119-29.
          Points out that all three of these plays
      are concerned with the themes of death and
      the loss of loved ones and concentrate on the
      image of poetic metaphor rather than the
      intellectual content of the text.

21   FITZ-SIMON, CHRISTOPHER. "Conservatives and
      Shape-Changers/After 1950." The Irish

<u>Theatre</u>. London: Thames and Hudson, pp.
184-201.
Considers the 1953 Paris production of
<u>Waiting for Godot</u> the most significant event
in "Irish" theatre, which changed the course
of Western theatre. Fitz-Simon describes
Beckett's career, the major imagery of each
play, and briefly compares Beckett's work to
the symbolist theater.

22   FOSTER, DENNIS A. "All Here is Sin: The
        Obligation in <u>The Unnamable</u>." <u>Boundary 2: A</u>
        <u>Journal of Postmodern Literature</u> 12, no. 1
        (Fall):81-100.
        Describes the consequences of Beckett's
unsettling use of the first person narrator
in <u>The Unnamable</u>: the reader's identification with the authorial being, Beckett's
rejection of authorial power, his embracing
of "impotence," the denial of an objective
world to be narrated, the compulsion to
continue, and the pursuit of perfection.

23   FRIEDMAN, MELVIN J. "George Moore and Samuel
        Beckett: Cross Currents and Correspon-
        dences." In <u>George Moore in Perspective</u>.
        Edited by Janet Egleson Dunleavy. Totowa,
        N.J.: Barnes & Noble Books, pp. 117-31.
        These two Irishmen, whose careers touched
briefly (though indirectly), are compared and
contrasted from several points of view:
their views of art and literature, their
opinions of Joyce and Proust, their criticism
and fiction, their chosen geographical
terrain (France, Germany, England), their
"celibate characters, and the lighter side of
their fiction."

24   GONTARSKI, S.E. "The Anatomy of Beckett's <u>Eh</u>
        <u>Joe</u>." <u>Modern Drama</u> 26, no. 4 (Dec.):425-34.
        Analyzes the textual history of <u>Eh Joe</u>,
emphasizing the importance of the earliest
drafts in revealing Beckett's fundamental
creative decisions. Gontarski feels that the
early manuscripts offer evidence that Beckett

worked on form and content separately: "Only
after the monologue was essentially recorded
did Beckett turn his attention to camera
moves, or the way in which he would break up
his monologues ... and then to both setting
and opening mime."

25   _____.   "The Intent of Undoing in Samuel
       Beckett's Art."   Modern Fiction Studies 29,
       no. 1 (Spring):5-23.
          Emphasizes the existence of predictable
       patterns in Beckett's artistic creation --
       Beckett's revisions of his works tend toward
       simplicity and abstraction, an undoing or a
       devolution: "This process often entails the
       conscious destruction of logical relations,
       the fracturing of consistent narrative, the
       abandonment of linear argument, and the
       substitution of more abstract patterns of
       numbers, music and so forth to shape a work."

26   _____.   "Text and Pre-Texts of Samuel Beckett's
       Footfalls."   Papers of the Bibliographical
       Society of America 77, no. 2:191-95.
          Reveals inconsistencies in four versions
       of Beckett's Footfalls: Footfalls (Faber,
       1976), Beckett's annotated copy, Ends and
       Odds (Grove, 1976) and Ends and Odds (Faber,
       1977).

27   GROVES, DAVID.   "Beckett's Molloy."   Explicator
       41, no. 3 (Spring):53-54.
          In a brief discussion of Molloy, points
       out that "Beckett conveys a solipsistic sense
       that human consciousness is inherently self-
       referring, subjective, and incapable of
       ultimate truth," reinforcing this impression
       of solipsism with Moran's reference to "the
       Obidil" (libido backwards).

28   GUERIN, JEANYVES.   "L'Automne avec Beckett."
       Nouvelle Revue Française, no. 371 (Dec.), pp.
       95-99.
          Reviews three "dramaticules" produced by
       Pierre Chabert: Rockaby, Ohio Impromptu, and

Catastrophe. Guérin gives an account of the
characters, their situations, the general
character of the plays, and the performance
of the actors.

29   GUSSOW, MEL. "Beckett Distills His Vision."
      New York Times, Sunday 31 July, p. 3.
          Reviews three plays at the Harold Clurman
      Theatre directed by Alan Schneider: Ohio
      Impromptu, Catastrophe, and What Where.
      Gussow compares Ohio Impromptu with Krapp's
      Last Tape -- the reader replays a story with
      stops and starts and finally arrives at the
      end. Catastrophe is interpreted as "a
      politically prescient black comedy about
      man's enslavement by the state," while he
      feels What Where appears to be another
      assault on totalitarianism, contrary to Alan
      Schneider's view of the play as the depiction
      of "the impossibility of defining the nature
      of existence."

30   *HAMBROSE, J. Best Sellers 43 (Oct.):261.

31   HAYMAN, RONALD. "Radio Meets Theatre."
      Listener 109 (9 June):32.
          Emphasizes the importance of the radio
      medium for theater. Hayman claims that radio
      has made the theater more modern, and has
      trained an audience to listen.

32   HILL, LESLIE. "The Name, the Body, The Un-
      namable." Oxford Literary Review 6, no.
      1:52-67.
          Discusses the implications of the scenes
      of bodily violence at the end of Malone Dies,
      Malone's slipping into the silence of self
      and the Unnamable's lack of identity: "In
      The Unnamable the trilogy loses its focus as
      the attempt to locate a fictional persona for
      the writing and as an investigation of its
      fantastic genealogy to transform itself into
      a perpetual questioning of that heterogeneous
      point of encounter between langauge and body

which is the site of its narrator's absent
name."

33   HOGAN, ROBERT. "Trying to Like Beckett." In
     "Since O'Casey" and Other Essays on Irish
     Drama." Totowa, N.J.: Barnes and Noble
     Books, pp. 113-18.
        Summarizes Beckett's career, and what he
     considers to be the greatest influences on
     Beckett as a writer -- Joyce, Ireland and
     illness. He feels that Beckett's attempt to
     mold form to content is his most daring and
     least successful innovation: "As Beckett's
     world-view is of an intolerable existence
     which it is not worthwhile terminating, the
     appropriate Beckettian form is necessarily a
     worthless one, an anti-form. Such a form
     evokes neither emotion nor amusement, it
     passes the time at worst tediously and at
     best tolerably."

34   JACQUART, EMMANUEL. "Le Duo-Duel Beckett-
     Nietzsche." Travaux de Linguistique et de
     Littérature 21, no. 2:57-77.
        Examines the possibility of a Nietzschean
     influence on Beckett -- a "duo-duel" -- an
     artistic "exercise" in which Beckett used
     some of Nietzsche's themes as a sounding
     board. Jacquart compares and contrasts
     themes found in Nietzsche's works with those
     in Endgame.

35   *KANTERS, ROBERT. "Beckett: Le Verbe est
     mort." Express, 7 Oct., p. 30.

36   KENNER, HUGH. "Ever Onward. Worstward Ho. By
     Samuel Beckett." New York Times Book Review,
     18 Dec., pp. 9, 22.
        Reviews Worstward Ho, briefly commenting
     on the situation of the two characters, the
     punctuation and language used, and Beckett's
     central metaphor of "the writer, trying to
     conceive something, get it down; also trying
     out patterns of elegance."

37   KRANCE, CHARLES. "Odd Fizzles: Beckett and the
      Heavenly Sciences." Bucknell Review 27, no.
      2:96-107.
          Comments on parallels and similarities
      between the processes involved in Beckett's
      recent writings and the recent theories in
      astronomy and astrophysics (black holes,
      white dwarfs, "equals-but-opposites" prin-
      ciple of astrophysics, "big bang" theory of
      creation).

38   LA BARDONNIE, MATHILDE. "Beckett au Rond-
      Point: Silences." Monde, 21 Sept., p. 20.
          Reviews Pierre Chabert's production of
      Rockaby, Ohio Impromptu and Catastrophe which
      La Bardonnie feels fortuitously represents a
      logical sequence: introduction, exposition,
      recapitulation.

39   LAWLEY, PAUL. "Counterpoint, Absence and the
      Medium in Beckett's Not I." Modern Drama 26,
      no. 4 (Dec.):407-14.
          Analyzes Not I in order to demonstrate the
      principal that "less is more" in Beckett's
      drama. Lawley contrasts the visual image on
      stage with the text: "It is the Mouth as an
      'emblem of absence' of which, ultimately, the
      stage-text counterpoint makes us so acutely
      aware. What enables Beckett to renovate
      clichés involving the body, by bringing
      particular textual details up against a
      single stage image, is the absence of the
      body from that image."

40   _____. "Samuel Beckett's 'Art and Craft': A
      Reading of Enough." Modern Fiction Studies
      29, no. 1 (Spring):25-41.
          Examines Beckett's attitude toward
      creativity with reference to an article by
      Peter Murphy, "The Nature and Art of Love in
      'Enough'" (See 1979.44). Lawly analyzes
      "Enough," considering: the connection
      between birth and artistic creativity in
      Beckett's novels and plays; the pregnant male
      as symbol of the latency, necessity and

impossibility of creation; the paradoxical
absence of a well-defined source for the
narrative voice; the alienation of language;
and the heightened awareness of metaphor.

41   LEVENSON, JILL L. "Hamlet andante/Hamlet
     allegro: Tom Stoppard's Two Versions."
     Shakespeare Survey 36:21-28.
         Considers Tom Stoppard's debt to Beckett:
     direct quotations, dislocation of time,
     minimalized scene, address to audience, play
     within a play, and shifting from a less
     poetic to a more poetic idiom to indicate
     another kind of change.

42   LORSCH, SUSAN E. Where Nature Ends. Literary
     Responses to the Designification of Land-
     scape. Rutherford, Madison, Teaneck, N.J.:
     Fairleigh Dickinson University Press; London
     and Toronto: Associated University Presses,
     pp. 158-60.
         Uses illustrations from Watt and Molloy to
     demonstrate the narrator's subjectivity in
     his presentation of the details of landscape.

43   LYONS, CHARLES R. Samuel Beckett. New York:
     Grove Press, 207 pp.
         Presents a brief biography, a general
     introduction to Beckett's works and a
     detailed analysis of the theatrical images of
     character, space, and time in his most
     significant plays, radio dramas, television
     scripts, and film: Waiting for Godot,
     Endgame, All That Fall, Krapp's Last Tape,
     Embers, Happy Days, Words and Music, Cascan-
     do, Play, Film, Eh Joe, Not I, That Time,
     Footfalls, A Piece of Monologue, Rockaby, and
     Ohio Impromptu.

44   MILLER, JUDITH G. "The Theatrics of Triangular
     Trysts, or Variations on a Form: Labiche,
     Vitrac, Beckett." Modern Drama 26, no. 4
     (Dec.):447-54.
         Evaluates triangular farces by Labiche,
     Vitrac (Entrée Libre), and Beckett (Play).

Miller points out that Vitrac and Beckett
borrow the format of the love triangle to
satirize what the structure represents:
"Beckett has craftily enticed his public to
participate in the facile divertissement of
the eternal triangle, only to transform the
figure into a derisive metaphor for the Holy
Trinity. Sexuality and civilization give way
to metaphysics."

45 MITCHELL, BREON. "A Beckett Bibliography: New
Works 1976-1982." Modern Fiction Studies 29,
no. 1 (Spring):131-52.
Provides an updated bibliography of
primary texts in French and English since
1976, including sixty-six new or newly
translated texts. The works are arranged
chronologically, with all known appearances
of each text indicated. This bibliography
continues those of Raymond Federman and John
Fletcher, and Robin J. Davis. See 1970.39,
1979.14.

46 MORRISON, KRISTIN. Canters and Chronicles: The
Use of Narrative in the Plays of Samuel
Beckett and Harold Pinter. Chicago:
University of Chicago Press, 235 pp.
Discusses the presentation of narratives
as a modern psychological equivalent of the
soliloquy in the plays of Beckett and Pinter:
"Now the telling of a story allows characters
that quintessentially 'modern,' Freudian
opportunity to reveal deep and difficult
thoughts and feelings while at the same time
concealing them as fiction or at least
distancing them as narration." Most of
Beckett's plays are discussed in detail: All
That Fall, Embers, Endgame, Krapp's Last
Tape, Ohio Impromptu, A Piece of Monologue,
Play, Waiting for Godot, and Words and Music.

47 MOUTOTE, DANIEL. "Prise en compte du lecteur
dans le 'nouveau roman.'" Journal de
Psychologie Normale et Pathologique 80, nos.

1-2 (Jan.-June):117-31. Beckett: pp. 124-
30.
Considers the psychology of the novel with
respect to the problem of its reception in
four works: Butor's La Modification,
Sarraute's Les Fruits d'or, Robbe-Gillet's La
Jalousie, and Beckett's How It Is. Moutote
points out that the reader of How It Is must
read, invent, and "rewrite" the work at the
same time -- due to the lack of punctuation
the work must be "rewritten" in the reader's
mind to "exist" as a literary statement.

48   MURCH, ANNE C. "Considérations sur proxémique
      dans le théâtre de Samuel Beckett." Aus-
      tralian Journal of French Studies 20, no. 3
      (Sept.-Dec.):307-39.
         Interprets the "relations proxémiques" in
      Beckett's dramatic texts. Murch applies E.T.
      Hall's term "proxémie" (man's use of space as
      a cultural product) and his description of
      three levels of spacial experience:
      (architectural space, scenic space, and
      interpersonal space) to Beckett's dramatic
      works: Waiting for Godot, Endgame, Krapp's
      Last Tape, Happy Days, Play, Come and Go, Not
      I, Footfalls, That Time, Solo, Rockaby, and
      Ohio Impromptu.

49   *NEUMANN, GUI. "Diderot précurseur de Beckett:
      La Modernité dans Jacques le fataliste." New
      Zealand Journal of French Studies 4, no. 1
      (May):43-58.

50   PASQUIER, MARIE-CLAIRE. "Blanc, gris, noir,
      gris, blanc." Cahiers Renaud-Barrault
      106:61-79.
         Studies the use of words in Beckett's
      fiction: the differences between the early
      works and the recent works, the "reality" of
      words, the invalidation or annulment of
      words, the choice of words, the lack of a
      better medium, bilingualism, the influence of
      Joyce in the early works, and the absence of
      color and detail in the later works.

51   PEARCE, RICHARD. "Samuel Beckett's <u>Watt</u> and his
      Trilogy." In <u>The Novel in Motion. An
      Approach to Modern Fiction</u>. Columbus: Ohio
      State University Press, pp. 48-55.
          Establishes Beckett's debt to Joyce -- his
      realization of the creative power of language
      in <u>Watt</u> and the trilogy, and his discovery of
      "its full autonomy as a capricious, threaten-
      ing, and literally self-denying force."

52   RABINOWITZ, RUBIN. <u>Fizzles</u> and Samuel Beckett's
      Earlier Fiction." <u>Contemporary Literature</u>
      24, no. 3 (Fall):307-21.
          Links <u>Fizzles</u> to Beckett's earlier
      fiction, pointing out that the allusions,
      sentence structure and punctuation of the
      first four texts ressemble those of Beckett's
      earlier works, while the second half of
      <u>Fizzles</u> resembles more closely the works
      published after 1965.

53   READ, DAVID. "Beckett's Search for Unseeable
      and Unmakeable: <u>Company</u> and <u>Ill Seen Ill
      Said</u>." <u>Modern Fiction Studies</u> 29, no. 1
      (Spring):111-25.
          Calls attention to the fact that <u>Company</u>
      and <u>Ill Seen Ill Said</u> begin at the moment
      when Beckett faced disintegration in <u>The
      Unnamable</u>: "But to the new fiction Beckett
      brings his experience of working in dramatic
      form. The one in the dark is spared the
      unbearable task of narration. He and the
      reader are alike witnesses to and addressees
      of the twin voices of self-perception and
      reason." Read compares Beckett's techniques
      in these prose pieces to those he attributes
      to Beckett's friend Avigdor Arikha -- the
      ambiguity of the relation between the eye and
      external reality, the expression of entropy,
      the realization that the real is indistin-
      guishable from the imagined (confusion
      between eye and mind) and the process of
      disintegration.

54   *"La Rentrée théâtrale sous le signe du star
       system." Quotidien de Paris, 6 Sept., pp.
       32-33.

55   *RIGGS, LARRY W. "Slouching Toward Conscious-
       ness: Destruction of the Spectator Role in
       En attendant Godot and Fin de partie." Degré
       Second: Studies in French Literature, no. 7
       (July), pp. 57-79.

56   ROSEN, CAROL. "Endgame." In Plays of Impasse.
       Contemporary Drama Set in Confining Institu-
       tions. Princeton, N.J.: Princeton Univer-
       sity Press, pp. 268-76.
           Views Endgame as an abstracted version of
       the contemporary play of impasse in which
       illness, old age, and death are portrayed in
       an oppressive, enclosing set.

57   SCRUTON, ROGER. "Minimal Beckett." Encounter
       55 (Mar.):48-50.
           Briefly analyzes the plays in which
       Beckett's characters, who have become both
       the subject and object of attention, contrive
       to vanish from the scene: Krapp's Last Tape,
       Rockaby, Not I, and Catastrophe.

58   SIMON, ALFRED. Beckett. Paris: Pierre
       Belfond, 293 pp.
           Examines in detail: 1) Beckett's literary
       career (the beginnings, bilingualism, his
       theatrical successes, his directors, "ab-
       sence" in his theater, silence, characteris-
       tics of Beckett's people, humor, absurdity,
       powerlessness, religion, time, death, the new
       novel, language), 2) a chronology of
       Beckett's life, and 3) an analysis of each of
       Beckett's works that have been written or
       translated into French. Reprinted in part:
       1983.59.

59   _____. "Rencontre." Esprit, no. 2
       (Feb.), pp. 3-7.
           Reprinted from 1983.58.

60   SIMON, R. THOMAS. "'Faint, though by No Means
        Invisible': A Commentary on Beckett's
        <u>Footfalls</u>." <u>Modern Drama</u> 26, no. 4
        (Dec.):435-46.
            Focuses on the intense movement of the
        character in <u>Footfalls</u>, the sound of her
        footsteps, and the centrality of the problem
        of dialogue which conveys Beckett's feelings
        about the burdens of language and conscious-
        ness, the image of a failed relationship, and
        the theme of thwarted birth.

61   SMITH, FREDERICK N. "Beckett's Verbal
        Slapstick." <u>Modern Fiction Studies</u> 29, no. 1
        (Spring):43-55.
            Finds that linguistic humor in Beckett's
        English novels is demonstrated through the
        juxtaposition of different "lexical fields,"
        pointing out "the extreme subtlety with which
        Beckett interweaves his learned, colloquial,
        and poetic dictions into a style poised
        uneasily between high seriousness and
        bufoonery."

62   *SMITH, ROCH C. "Homo Mensura: Beckett's Clown
        of Illusion in the Trilogy." <u>West Virginia
        University Philological Papers</u>, no. 29, pp.
        70-75.

63   _____. "Naming the M/inotaur [sic]: Beckett's
        Trilogy and the Failure of Narrative."
        <u>Modern Fiction Studies</u> 29, no. 1 (Spring):73-
        80.
            Elaborates on Richard Macksey's view of
        the dissolution of character in the trilogy
        as an "imprisonment of the self within the
        labyrinth": "For it is part of the nar-
        rator's dilemma throughout the trilogy that
        he is at once the hunter and the hunted, the
        weaver of the labyrinth and the beast it
        encloses ... he cannot find a means of
        escape, and all attempts to do so entangle
        him further in his verbal prison. The enemy
        is within, so the narrator must be both
        executioner and victim."

64   WATSON, G.J. "Beckett and Pinter: Empty
      Spaces and Closed Rooms." In Drama: An
      Introduction. New York: St. Martin's Press,
      pp. 171-97. Beckett: pp. 171-85.
         Defines Beckett's contribution to the
      Theatre of the Absurd through two charac-
      teristics of his drama: 1) his tendency to
      destroy the dramatic illusion ("reminding the
      audience that it is an audience in a
      theatre") and 2) the sense of the futility of
      life it portrays. Watson analyzes Waiting
      for Godot through a series of short exposés
      on different topics: the lack of a realisti-
      cally depicted social background, the absence
      of action, Christian imagery, "man's help-
      lessness in his delusion that some power
      outside himself exists that will give meaning
      to his life" (Pozzo), waiting as an empty and
      sterile "activity," habit and the void
      (Proust), circularity, "passing the time in
      the dark," dialogue, music hall, and
      Beckett's humanism.

65   WORTHEN, WILLIAM B. "Beckett's Actor." Modern
      Drama 26, no. 4 (Dec.):415-24.
         Studies the dialectic between text and
      body in Play, Not I, and Endgame, pointing
      out 1) the effect of the actor's bodily
      stress and discomfort, and 2) the distinction
      between physical presence and verbal absence.

66   WRIGHT, IAIN. "'What Matter Who's Speaking?'
      Beckett, the Authorial Subject and Contem-
      porary Critical Theory." Southern Review:
      Literary and Interdisciplinary 16, no. 1
      (Mar.):5-30.
         Opposes poststructuralist interpretations
      of Beckett's works on the grounds that
      although Beckett's texts deconstruct all
      their authorial subjects and the possibility
      of being an author, Beckett the author is
      persistently present. Through a discussion
      of the trilogy, Wright demonstrates that
      Beckett's work cannot be read as an open
      text.

67   *YORK, R.A. "Presuppositions and Speech Acts in
      Beckett's Fin de partie." Proceedings of the
      Royal Irish Academy 83, no. 8:239-50.

68   ZINMAN, TONY. "Harmony Lost in The Lost Ones."
      American Notes and Queries 21, nos. 5-6
      (Jan.-Feb.):77-78.
           Briefly compares the notions of harmonious
      spatial relationships in the English and
      French versions of The Lost Ones, demonstrat-
      ing that in the French version the height of
      the cylinder is equal to the distance across
      it: "Existence of the abode is so barren,
      the vision of the work is so deadened, that
      mere matching of dimensions may be thought of
      as harmony."

                    1983-1984

1   *WEST, PAUL. "Deciphering a Beckett Fiction on
      His Birthday." Parnassus: Poetry in Review
      11, no. 2 (Fall/Winter 1983 & Spring/Summer
      1984):319-22.

                      1984

1   AVILA, WANDA. "The Poem within the Play in
      Beckett's Embers." Language and Style 17,
      no. 3 (Summer):193-205.
           Examines the language of Embers in terms
      of Jan Mukarovsky's theory of foregrounding
      and of Geoffrey N. Leech's rhetorical and
      linguistic analysis of the possible types of
      foregrounding in order to demonstrate how the
      poem focuses the meaning of the play and to
      substantiate Roger Blin's assertion that
      Embers is Beckett's most admirable work.

2   BARGE, LAURA. "Beckett's Skull/Cliff in 'La
      Falaise.'" Romance Notes 25, no. 2
      (Winter):109-20.
           Interprets "La Falaise," originally
      written as a "témoignage" for a Bram van

Velde exhibition in 1975, a descriptive
comment which focuses on a search for human
elements in the scene. Barge gives an
account of Beckett's art of failure, the
limitations of language, the Beckettian
vision of Christ and Beckett's use of the
Manichean mythology.

3   BARNES, BEN. "Aspects of Directing Beckett."
    Irish University Review 14, no. 1
    (Spring):69-87.
        Highlights Beckett's "brilliant" manipula-
    tion of the medium, and then analyzes
    Estragon's relation to the landscape, people,
    and objects he encounters. Barnes briefly
    discusses the challenges for the actor in
    Beckett's later stage works.

4   *BEAUSANG, MICHEL. "Watt: Logique, démence,
    aphasie." In Beckett avant Beckett: Essais
    sur le jeune Beckett (1930-1945). Edited by
    Jean-Michel Rabaté. Paris: Presses de
    l'Ecole Normale Supérieure, pp. 153-72.

5   BEN-ZVI, LINDA. "Fritz Mauthner for Company."
    Journal of Beckett Studies, no. 9, pp. 65-88.
        Compares the theme of verifiability in
    Company with its presentation in "Dream of
    Fair to Middling Women," in order to trace
    the influence of Fritz Mauthner's Beiträge zu
    einer Kritik der Sprache on Beckett's
    fiction.

6   BENSON, MICHAEL. "Moving Bodies in Hardy and
    Beckett." Essays in Criticism 34, no. 3
    (July):229-43. Beckett: pp. 236-39.
        Feels that Hardy's method of presenting
    individuals who are not altogether in control
    of their limbs is echoed in Watt, the
    trilogy, and "The Expelled." Benson
    demonstrates how Beckett uses movement in two
    ways: he examines in minute detail the move-
    ments of his characters, or he withdraws

their means of propulsion.

7   BERMAN, DAVID. "Beckett and Berkeley." Irish
       University Review 14, no. 1 (Spring):42-45.
           Examines Beckett's explicit references to
       Berkeley, then comments on possible indirect
       allusions.

8   *BILLINGTON, MICHAEL. "Edinburgh: Beckett."
       Guardian, 15 Aug., p. 7.

9   BROWN, JOHN RUSSEL. "Mr. Beckett's Shake-
       speare." In Shakespeare's Wide and Universal
       Stage. Edited by C.B. Cox and D.J. Palmer.
       Manchester, England: Manchester University
       Press, pp. 1-17.
           Contrasts the new dramatists and
       Shakespearean critics using Waiting for Godot
       as an example. Brown presents the symbols
       and characters of the play pointing out that
       the symbols in Beckett's drama do not reveal
       the play's unity -- [which] depends on the
       progressive revelation of the innermost
       natures of the four major characters through
       the apparently inconsequential repetitions
       and dialogue and stage-business." This
       method of analyzing a play is applied to
       Richard III and Measure for Measure.

10   *BRUN, BERNARD. "Sur le Proust de Beckett." In
       Beckett avant Beckett: Essais sur le jeune
       Beckett (1930-1945). Edited by Jean-Michel
       Rabaté. Paris: Presses de l'Ecole Normale
       Supérieure, pp. 79-91.

11   BUTLER, LANCE St. JOHN. Samuel Beckett and the
       Meaning of Being. A Study in Ontological
       Parable. London: Macmillan Press; New
       York: St. Martins Press, 222 pp.
           Undertakes a philosophical reading of
       Beckett's work, using three philosophical
       analogues for Beckett: Heidegger's Being and
       Time, Sartre's Being and Nothingness, and
       Hegel's Phenomenology of Mind. Butler deals
       with the philosophers, their worlds, their

languages and their methods, in each case,
showing how a particular view fitted into a
Beckettian pattern. He suggests that
Beckett's works are ontological parables as
is demonstrated by the self-destructive
nature of his fiction.

12   BUTTNER, GOTTFRIED. Samuel Beckett's "Watt."
      Translated by Joseph P. Dolan. Philadelphia:
      University of Pennsylvania Press, 188 pp.
          Presents the genesis of the novel, reviews
      the critical studies of Beckett's work,
      summarizes the events of the novel with
      respect to its gnosiological content ("inner
      substance"), analyzes the meaning of the
      compositional elements, and presents a
      discussion of the underlying gnosiological
      aspect of Watt as revealed by a close reading
      of the text.

13   *CHAMBON, BERTRAND du. "Analyse avec paroles."
      Prépublications 90 (Oct.):12-14.

14   CORFARIU, MANUELA and DANIELLA ROVENTAFRUMUSANI.
      "Absurd Dialogue and Speech Acts: Beckett's
      En attendant Godot." Poetics 13, no. 1-2
      (Apr.):119-33.
          Analyzes absurd dialogue in Waiting for
      Godot, by means of an abductive procedure:
      textual syntagmaticts (rule formulation),
      textual application, validation and inter-
      pretation.

15   COUSINEAU, THOMAS J. "Descartes, Lacan, and
      Murphy." College Literature 11, no. 3
      (Fall):223-32.
          Applies Lacan's theories to Murphy's
      tripartite analysis of his mind and demon-
      strates Beckett's use of irony to question
      the validity of the Cartesian mind-body
      dualism.

16   CUNNINGHAM, VALENTINE. "A Master's More of

Less." Times Literary Supplement (London),
10 Feb., pp. 135-36.
    Reviews Worstward Ho, Disjecta (Ruby Cohn,
ed.), and A Samuel Beckett Reader (John
Calder, ed.), outlining Ruby Cohn and John
Calder's approaches to Beckett's work.
Cunningham questions whether Worstward Ho
represents the beginning of a new late phase
in Beckett's career or whether it represents
a continuation of the type of prose Beckett
wrote in Ill Seen Ill Said.

17   *DANINO, EMILE. "Un Patin pensant."
      Prépublications 90 (Oct.):15-19.

18   DAVIS, ROBIN. Work in Progress on Samuel
      Beckett: 1984. Stirling, Scotland:
      University of Stirling, unpaginated.
          Lists the replies he received from a
      circular sent to colleagues in British and
      Irish Universities. Davis classified the
      responses into the following categories --
      productions, books, contributions to books,
      theses, and journal articles, with an index
      of names.

19   DEANE, SEAMUS. "Joyce and Beckett." Irish
      University Review 14, no. 1 (Spring):57-68.
          Explores Beckett and Joyce's common
      backgrounds ("exile, experimentation, heroic
      dedication and Dublin") and the differences
      between their writing styles.

20   DOLAN, T.P. "Samuel Beckett's Dramatic Use of
      Hiberno-English." Irish University Review
      14, no. 1 (Spring):46-56.
          Analyzes Beckett's use of Hiberno-English
      (the way the Irish speak English) in All That
      Fall and his English translation of Robert
      Piaget's La Manivelle (The Old Time).

21   FITCH, BRIAN T. "La Problématique de l'étude de
      l'oeuvre bilingue de Beckett." Symposium 38,
      no. 2 (Summer):91-112.
          Believes that Beckett's fiction poses

problems of methodology since Beckett is
bilingual. Fitch feels that each text should
be analyzed as a separate entity, considering
the first "version" (whether in French or
English) and the second "version," and then
studying the rapports between the two
versions. The initial paragraph of The
Unnamable is examined phrase by phrase in
order to illustrate this method of analysis.

22 *GAUTIER, JEAN-JACQUES. "Un grand acteur exalte
le texte: Compagnie de Samuel Beckett."
Figaro Magazine, no. 272. (8-14 Dec.), p. 43.

23 *GENET, JACQUELINE. "Beckett et l'écriture des
autres (Murphy)." In Beckett avant Beckett:
Essais sur le jeune Beckett (1930-1945).
Edited by Jean-Michel Rabaté. Paris:
Presses de l'Ecole Normale Supérieure, pp.
121-33.

24 GONTARSKI, S.E. "Review: Quad I & II:
Beckett's Sinister Mime(s)." Journal of
Beckett Studies, no. 9, pp. 137-38.
Reviews the mimes filmed for German
television and presented Oct. 8, 1981,
describing the symmetrical movements of the
actors and differences between the two works.

25 GUSSOW, MEL. "A Lavish Beckett Portfolio
Revives a Family Tradition." New York Times
Book Review, 15 Apr., p. 27.
Describes the new Overbook Press edition
of The Lost Ones with fantastical illus-
trations by Charles Klabunde.

26 *HANSEN, KIRSTEN LUND. "Savior (-) vivre ou
paroles sans acte?" Prépublications 90
(Oct.):29-36.

27 HIGGINS, AIDAN. "Foundering in Reality: Godot,
Papa, Hamlet and Three Bashes at Festshrift."
Irish University Review 14, no. 1 (Spring):
93-101.
Analyzes the interval of waiting in Godot

and considers how the character of this
interval would change if the play were to end
with the arrival of Godot. Higgins briefly
discusses the tone and characters of the most
recent prose pieces.

28   HILL, LESLIE. "Reading Beckett's Remainders."
      French Studies 38, no. 2 (Apr.):173-87.
           Summarizes two alternate views of
      Beckett's late prose works: 1) as an
      exercise in negation in order to express the
      void, or 2) as the condensed essence of
      Beckett's vision. Hill feels that these
      texts should be scrutinized as a "singular
      corpus of text." The texts of the last 15
      years are examined from the point of view of
      literary definition, narrational authority,
      and their own homogeneity as narrative
      structures.

29   HOMAN, SIDNEY. Beckett's Theaters: Interpreta-
      tions for Performance. Lewisburg, Pa.:
      Bucknell University Press; London:
      Associated University Presses, 256 pp.
           Offers a detailed study of each of
      Beckett's dramatic works in English that
      exists in repertory, focusing on the action,
      the basic unities, the major themes and
      images, the characters and their relation-
      ships, the role of the audience, the inner
      world vs. the external world, the issues of
      art and the role of the playwright, the
      visual and verbal dimensions of his theater,
      and the various media Beckett utilized.

30   JENKINS, ALAN. "Exactions of the Theatre."
      Times Literary Supplement (London), 7 Sept.,
      p. 997.
           Reviews Ohio Impromptu, What Where, and
      Catastrophe directed by Alan Schneider,
      describing the situation portrayed in each
      play.

31   _____. "The Power to Claw: On Samuel Beckett."
      Encounter 63, no. 2 (July-Aug.):51-55.

Reviews <u>Disjecta</u>: "Each piece, each
sentence almost, is akin to an act of
aggression; for all the marvelous lucidity of
the writing and the bracing sharpness of
response, the reviews are not really in the
business of elucidation ... this criticism
conveys a rebarbative, throwaway brilliance,
impassioned and impatient, above all a kind
of challenge ..."

32   JOHNSON, TONI O'BRIEN. "<u>The Well of the Saints</u>
      and <u>Waiting for Godot</u>: Stylistic Variations
      on a Tradition." In <u>The Irish Writer and the
      City</u>. Edited by Maurice Harmon. Gerrards
      Cross, Buckinghamshire: Colin Smythe;
      Totowa, N.J.: Barnes & Noble, pp. 90-102.
         Compares John Synge's <u>The Well of the
      Saints</u> with <u>Waiting for Godot</u>: the use of a
      roadside setting, tramps, blindness and
      interdependence (the combination of which
      originates in the French medieval drama), as
      well as the use of langauge and contradic-
      tion, and references to the body.

33   *KALB, JONATHON. "Theater in New York. Acting
      Beckett: Two Versions of <u>Ohio Impromptu</u>."
      <u>Theater</u> 15, no. 5 (Summer/Fall):48-53.

34   *LAKE, CARLTON, Linda Eichhorn, and Sally Leach.
      <u>No Symbols Where None Intended: A Catalogue
      of Books, Manuscripts and Other Material
      Related to Samuel Beckett in the Collections
      of the Humanities Research Center</u>. Austin:
      Humanities Research Center, University of
      Texas at Austin, 185 pp.

35   LAWLEY, PAUL. "Beckett's Dramatic Counterpoint:
      A Reading of <u>Play</u>." <u>Journal of Beckett
      Studies</u>, no. 9, pp. 25-41.
         Feels that "the further structure and
      stage-picture press towards abstraction the
      more surely do they endow the text with a
      capacity for a strange life of its own ... a
      counterpoint-life." In <u>Play</u>, Lawley reveals
      two types of "counterpoint": 1) the inter-

weaving of three independent voices, each
unaware of the other two, and 2) the relationship between text and stage-picture. The
creation of counterpoint and the effects are
discussed.

36 *LECERCLE, ANN. "La Redoutable Symétrie de
    l'oeuf pourri ou une poétique de la suture."
    In <u>Beckett avant Beckett: Essais sur le
    jeune Beckett (1930-1945)</u>. Edited by Jean-
    Michel Rabaté. Paris: Presses de l'Ecole
    Normale Supérieure, pp. 47-78.

37 LEES, HEATH. "<u>Watt</u>: Music, Tuning and
    Tonality." <u>Journal of Beckett Studies</u>, no.
    9, pp. 5-24.
        Exposes the importance of musical themes
    to <u>Watt</u>, examining specific musical referen-
    ces in the narration and the imagery of
    tuning and untuning with its parallel to
    existence of the ladder.

38 *LEVY, SHIMON. "Notions of Audience in
    Beckett's Plays." <u>Assaph: Studies in the
    Arts</u> 1, no. 1, sec. C:71-81.

39 *LIBERA, ANTONI. "Samuel Beckett's <u>Catastro-
    phe</u>." <u>Quadrant</u> 28, nos. 1-2 (Jan.-Feb.):106-
    9.

40 LITTLE, ROGER. "Beckett's Mentor: Rudmose-
    Brown: Sketch for a Portrait." <u>Irish
    University Review</u> 14, no. 1 (Spring):34-41.
        Describes Thomas Rudmose-Brown, Professor
    of Romance Languages at Trinity College from
    1909 to 1942: his ideals, prejudices,
    interest in contemporary French writers, and
    appeal to students.

41 *McMILLAN, JOYCE. "Edinburgh: Beckett Double
    Bill." <u>Guardian</u>, 23 Aug., p. 10.

42 MAHON, DEREK. "A Noise Like Wings: Beckett's
    Poetry." <u>Irish University Review</u> 14, no. 1
    (Spring):88-92.

                    Considers Beckett "a minor and idiosyn-
               cratic poet." Mahon proposes a list of 14
               poems which he feels are Beckett's best
               poems, and then briefly comments on "Dieppe,"
               "Saint-Lô," and Beckett's best "poetry," an
               excerpt from Waiting for Godot.

43   *MAROWITZ, CHARLES. "End Game Played too
      Well." Guardian, 23 Nov., p. 11.

44   *MAYS, J.C.C. "Bibliographie du jeune Beckett."
      In Beckett avant Beckett: Essais sur le
      jeune Beckett (1930-1945). Edited by Jean-
      Michel Rabaté. Paris: Presses de l'Ecole
      Normale Supérieure, pp. 187-94.

45   *_____. "Les Racines irlandaises du jeune
      Beckett." In Beckett avant Beckett: Essais
      sur le jeune Beckett (1930-1945). Edited by
      Jean-Michel Rabaté. Paris: Presses de
      l'Ecole Normale Supérieure, pp. 11-26.

46   _____. "Young Beckett's Irish Poets." Irish
      University Review 14, no. 1 (Spring):18-33.
               Takes issue with Beckett's alienation from
      his roots and the influence of Ireland and
      Irish writers on his writing: "His revulsion
      against [being Irish] must be understood in
      relation to the demands and pressures of the
      situation in which he found himself -- that
      is, the Ireland of the nineteen-thirties ...
      Beckett's Irishness displays itself in his
      detachment from literary forms and langauge,
      in the streak of cruelty and violence that
      runs through his writing along with the
      humour and elegance."

47   MOROT-SIR, EDOUARD. "Grammatical Insincerity
      and Samuel Beckett's Non-Expressionism:
      Space, Subjectivity, and Time in The Un-
      namable." In Writing in a Modern Temper.
      Essays on French Literature and Thought in
      Honor of Henri Peyre. Edited by Mary Ann
      Caws. Saratoga, Calif.: Anma Libri & Co.,
      pp. 224-39.

Qualifies Beckett's texts as non-expressionist, "... a trying fight against the traditional rhetoric ornaments; ... [and], against the universal functions of linguistic referentiality, which are description, naming, ... and narration." An examination of the "non-expressionist values of Beckett's aesthetic of reference" follows the order suggested at the beginning of The Unnamable: "Where now? Who now? When now?"

48   MURCH, ANNE C. "Quoting from Godot: Trends in Contemporary Theatre." Journal of Beckett Studies, no. 9, pp. 113-29.
     Demonstrates how the characters and images from Waiting for Godot have become "living images" with which twentieth century man can identify. Murch feels the characters can be used as models, they have become "a cross between archetypes and stereotypes, inviting identification over a wide spectrum of existential situations." The success of the play at the San Quentin penitentiary, the Australian production of the play in Melbourne, and the National Theatre of Strasbourg's production of Ils allaient obscurs sous la nuit solitaire, a play inspired by Waiting for Godot are discussed.

49   *MURPHY, CAROL J. "Vite motus!' Mum is the Word in Beckett's Compagnie." Degré Second: Studies in French Literature, no. 8 (July), pp. 27-34.

50   MURPHY, PETER. "Orpheus Returning: The Nature of Myth in Samuel Beckett's 'Still' Trilogy." International Fiction Review 11, no. 2 (Summer):109-12.
     Proposes that Beckett's later works demonstrate a movement towards a regeneration of the Orpheus myth, "with an emphasis upon its first stage in which the archetypal artist once again directs his words towards the world." Murphy examines the reappearance

of the Orpheus myth in "Still," "Sounds," and "Still 3."

51 MURRAY, CHRISTOPHER. "Beckett Productions in Ireland: A Survey." Irish University Review 14, no. 1 (Spring):103-25.
      Presents a history of professional productions of Beckett's plays in Ireland through 1983.

52 NOGUCHI, REI. "Style and Strategy in Endgame." Journal of Beckett Studies, no. 9, pp. 101-11.
      Questions why Hamm and Clov speak the way they do in Endgame, focusing on the essential conversational situation, their hierarchical relationship, Clov's attempts to oust Hamm from his solicitor position, and Clov's strategy of accommodation.

53 NYKROG, PETER. "In the Ruins of the Past: Reading Samuel Beckett Intertextually." Comparative Literature 36, no. 4 (Fall):289-311.
      Feels it's time to take a fresh look at Beckett's early plays: Waiting for Godot, Endgame, and Krapp's Last Tape. (Act Without Words, I is considered briefly as a transitional play). Nykrog does not agree with the critics who state that Beckett's plays are devoid of plot, character and meaningful dialogue, "on the contrary, the early plays by Beckett not only deal with something, they have an articulate and identifiable scope." Hidden relationships from text to text are examined as they help identify and give added meaning to this "trilogy" of plays.

54 *OJO, S. ADE. "La Crise du christianisme dans l'oeuvre de Samuel Barclay Beckett." Neohelicon 11, no. 1:361-80.

55 OXENHANDLER, NEAL. "Seeing and Believing in Dante and Beckett." In Writing in a Modern Temper. Essays on French Literature and

Thought in Honor of Henri Peyre. Edited by
Mary Ann Caws. Saratoga, Calif: Anma Libri
& Co., pp. 214-23.
    Believes Beckett's work is situated at the
juncture point of the modern and the postmodern. Beckett remains a formalist to whom
continuity is essential. Examining the
Dante/Beckett relationship, Oxenhandler
compares The Commedia with More Pricks than
Kicks and How It is. In More Pricks than
Kicks "Dante's account of suffering and
horror is used ironically by Beckett to
underscore his vision of modern life." How
It Is introduces an environment similar to
the Inferno.

56   *PASQUIER, MARIE-CLAIRE. "La Rose et le homard:
      Vie et mort de Belqcqua Shuah." In Beckett
      avant Beckett: Essais sur le jeune Beckett
      (1930-1945). Edited by Jean-Michel Rabaté.
      Paris: Presses de l'Ecole Normale Supér-
      ieure, pp. 27-45.

57   "Photographic Record of Recent Beckett Produc-
      tions." Journal of Beckett Studies, no. 9,
      pp. 130-35.
          Reproduces photos of the Paris production
      of Rockaby, Ohio Impromptu, and Catastrophe
      directed by Pierre Chabert at the Théâtre du
      Rond-Point, and the New York production of
      Ohio Impromptu, Catastrophe, and What Where
      directed by Alan Schneider at the Harold
      Clurman Theater.

58   PHILLIPS, K.J. "Beckett's Molloy and The
      Odyssey." International Fiction Review 11,
      no. 1 (Winter):19-24.
          Believes Molloy is a parody of The
      Odyssey: both works are divided into two
      parts, both emphasize parents and children,
      both novels present quests, both protagonists
      make a descent to an "underworld," both
      protagonists' wanderings alternate between
      peaceable and hostile forces, etc. The major
      difference between the two works is the

outcome of the quests: Odysseus returns to
his kingdom, while Molloy and Moran's fate is
uncertain.

59   *PIETTE, ALAIN. "Theater in Brussels. Beckett
      after the Deluge." Theater 15, no. 5
      (Summer/Fall):54-56.

60   PILLING, JOHN. "Review: 'Lessness' at the
      Oxford Playhouse, 17-20 February 1982,
      performed by the Rohan Theatre Group,
      Director and Designer Lucy Baily." Journal
      of Beckett Studies, no. 9, pp. 138-41.
         Describes Lucy Baily's innovations in
      producing "Lessness" for the stage, and
      compares the effectiveness of the prose text,
      the radio version, and the stage production.

61   *RABATE, ETIENNE. "Watt à l'ombre de Plume.
      L'Ecriture du désoeuvrement." In Beckett
      avant Beckett: Essais sur le jeune Beckett
      (1930-1945). Edited by Jean-Michel Rabaté.
      Paris: Presses de l'Ecole Normale Supér-
      ieure, pp. 135-51.

62   RABINOVITZ, RUBIN. The Development of Samuel
      Beckett's Fiction. Urbana: University of
      Illinois Press, 241 pp.
         Discusses new techniques that Beckett
      developed early in his career as a novelist,
      in the period before he began to write in
      French: the aesthetics of silence, the
      importance of inner reality, obscured deeper
      meaning, obsession with death, psychiatry,
      uses of repetition, unreliable narrative, and
      philosophy (Descartes, Schopenhauer).

63   *RASKIN, RICHARD. "On Beckett's Acte sans
      paroles and Games People Play." Prépublica-
      tions 90 (Oct.):44-50.

64   RONGIERAS, E. "La Tragi-comédie beckettienne."
      Revue d'Histoire du Théâtre 36, no. 1 (Jan.-
      Mar.):27-29.

Demonstrates that the absence of transcendency determines the tragic and comic
elements in Beckett's plays, founding the
basis for the tragic conflict (not being able
to live in the absence of an absolute and
knowing one is condemned to live thus), the
absurdity of this contradiction, and the
ambiguity of time.

65   *SALEM, DANIEL. "L'Attente de Samuel Beckett."
      ULULA: Graduate Studies in Romance Languages
      1:57-62.

66   *SCHWAB, GABRIELE. "On the Dialectic of Closing
      and Opening in Samuel Beckett's End-game
      [sic]." Translated by D. L. Selden. In
      Concepts of Closure. Edited by David F.
      Hult. New Haven, Conn.: Yale University
      Press, pp. 191-202.
           Reprinted: 1984.67.

67   *_____. "On the Dialectic of Closing and
      Opening in Samuel Beckett's Endgame." Yale
      French Studies, no. 64, pp. 191-202.
           Source: MLA International Bibliography,
      1984; unverified. Reprint of 1984.66.

68   SINTUREL, YVES. "Beckett: Fin de partie. Le
      Point final du début à la fin." In Le Point
      final: Actes du Colloque International de
      Clermont-Ferrand, n.s., no. 20. Edited by
      Alain Montandon. Clermont-Ferrand: Associa-
      tion des Publications de la Faculté des
      Lettres et Sciences Humaines, pp. 169-82.
           Documents several aspects of Beckett's
      obsession with "ending" in Endgame: 1) the
      first word of the play is "fini", placing us
      in an impasse, a "situation limite" from the
      very beginning, 2) the constant repetition of
      different forms of the verb finir (to end),
      3) the wait for the end, 4) spatial represen-
      tations, 5) figures of time, 6) the charac-
      ters, 7) Hamm's recounting of a story acts as
      a mirror reflecting numerous images ("mettre

en abîme"), and 8) the curtain falls before the end, stopping the action of the play.

69   *TOPIA, ANDRE. "Murphy on Beckett Baroque." In Beckett avant Beckett: Essais sur le jeune Beckett (1930-1945). Edited by Jean-Michel Rabaté. Paris: Presses de l'Ecole Normale Supérieure, pp. 93-119.

70   TOYAMA, JEAN YAMASAKI. "Malone, the Unoriginal Centre." Journal of Beckett Studies, no. 9, pp. 89-99.
     Compares and contrasts the narrators of Molloy and Malone Dies, examining their roles in the narratives, the fictions they create, their goals and failures, the creator/ creature paradox, the inner and outer selves, and Christ imagery.

71   VIRNOT, DELPHINE. "Film de Samuel Beckett." Esprit, no. 89 (May), pp. 175-76.
     Reinterprets the movements of the camera, identified with the eye of the audience, and the actor (Buster Keaton) in Film, declaring that a man who refuses to be seen, and has but one eye -- refuses to recognize self-awareness, or the reciprocity of consciousness.

72   WAKELING, PATRICK. "Looking at Beckett -- The Man and the Writer." Irish University Review 14, no. 1 (Spring):5-17.
     Considers Beckett as a "schizoid" writer, discussing details from Beckett's life and works, quoting frequently from Deirdre Bair's Beckett biography. See 1978.2.

73   WATERS, MAUREEN, "Samuel Beckett's Murphy." In The Comic Irishman. Albany: State University of New York Press, pp. 110-22.
     Analyzes Murphy from the point of view of the individual characters (Murphy, Celia, Cooper, Willougby Kelly), philosophical references (Newton, Descartes, Menippean Satire, Geulinx), the influence of other

writers (Dante, Joyce, Synge, Swift), comic
style, and the portrayal of Irish life.

74 *WEIGHTMAN, JOHN. "Absurdist Drama and
     Religion." In <u>Drama and the Actor</u>. Edited
     by James Redmond. Cambridge, Mass.:
     Cambridge University Press, 303 pp.

75 *WORTH, KATHARINE. "Yeats and Beckett."
     <u>Gaéliana</u> 6:203-13.

76 ZURBRUGG, NICHOLAS. "Beckett, Proust, and
     'Dream of Fair to Middling Women.'" <u>Journal
     of Beckett Studies</u>, no. 9, pp. 43-64.
          Believes "Dream of Fair to Middling Women"
     illustrates the basic differences between
     Beckett and Proust's responses to the limits
     of language and perception. Contrasting the
     themes, images, characters, and experiences
     portrayed in the two works, Zurbrugg demon-
     strates that "'Dream' is fundamental to an
     understanding of Beckett's vision, ...
     because, as a predominately anti-Proustian
     novel, it continually illustrates its
     obsession with the evasion of self-knowledge
     ..."

Appendix A

A List of Brief Articles, Reviews,
and Parts of Books Devoted to
Beckett or His Works*

1   "A Trifle from Beckett." _Times_ (London), 24
    Jan. 1966, p. 4. (_Act Without Word II_, _Come
    and Go_, _All That Fall_)

2   AARON, JULES. "_Krapp's Last Tape_, _Not I_, _Happy
    Days_, _Act Without Words I_ [....]." _Educa-
    tional Theatre Journal_ 25, no. 1 (Mar.
    1973):102-4.

3   ABEL, LIONEL. "The Theater and the Absurd." In
    Metatheater: A New View of Dramatic Form.
    New York: Hill and Wang, pp. 140-46.
    (_Endgame_)

4   ABIRACHED, ROBERT. "Carnet de théâtre." _Etudes_
    310 (July-Sept. 1961):131-34. Beckett: pp.
    132-33. (_Waiting for Godot_)

5   _____. "Le Roman moderne en France." _Français
    dans le monde_ 4, no. 29 (Dec. 1964):6-9.

6   ACKROYD, PETER. "Baubles, Bangles, Pearl
    Beads." _Spectator_, 29 Mar. 1974, pp. 393-
    94. (_Texts for Nothing_)

7   ADMUSSEN, RICHARD. "A New Dimension in Beckett
    Studies: The Manuscripts." _Proceedings:
    Pacific Northwest Conference on Foreign
    Languages_. Edited by Walter C. Kraft.

---

*References to entries in Appendix A will include
the number of the entry preceded by the letter A.

Corvalles: Oregon State University, 1973, pp. 178-81. (Manuscripts for <u>Play</u> and <u>The Lost One</u>)

8   ALBERES, R[ENE]-M[ARILL]. "Le Culte de l'Onirique." <u>Nouvelles Littéraires</u>, 18 Mar. 1971, p. 5. (<u>The Lost Ones</u>)

9   _____. <u>Littérature: Horizon 2000</u>. Paris: Editions Albin Michel, 1974, pp. 69-75. (<u>Molloy</u>)

10   ALTER, ANDRE. "<u>En attendant Godot</u> n'était pas une impasse. Beckett le prouve dans sa seconde pièce." <u>Figaro Littéraire</u>, 12 Jan. 1957, pp. 1-4. (<u>Endgame</u>, <u>Waiting for Godot</u>)

11   ALVAREZ, A. "Literary Chamber Music." <u>Observer</u> 19 Dec. 1976, p. 22. Reprinted: 1979.22.81. (<u>For to End Yet Again</u>)

12   AMORY, MARK. "Humbug." <u>Spectator</u> 246 (20 June 1981):26-28. (<u>Waiting for Godot</u>)

13   AUBERY, PIERRE. "Surréalisme et littérature actuelle." <u>Kentucky Romance Quarterly</u> 14, no. 1 (1967):33-42. (Surrealism)

14   BAQUE, FRANÇOISE. "L'Eternel retour: Samuel Beckett." In <u>Le Nouveau roman</u>. Paris: Bordas, 1972, pp. 97-100. (Time)

15   BANN, STEPHEN. "Tensions of Authorship." <u>Cambridge Review</u> 85 (13 June 1964):524. (<u>How It Is</u>)

16   BARR, DONALD. "One Man's Universe." <u>New York Times Book Review</u>, 21 June 1959, pp. 4, 26. (<u>Watt</u>)

17   BARRAULT, JEAN-LOUIS. "<u>Oh les beaux jours</u>." <u>Avant-Scène</u>, no. 313 (15 June 1964), p. 9. (<u>Happy Days</u>)

18 _____. "La Petite Salle." In <u>Souvenirs pour demain</u>. Paris: Editions du Seuil, 1972, pp. 323-24. (Blin, <u>Happy Days</u>)

19 BEAUFORT, JOHN. "So-So Days Off Broadway: The Bitter and the Comic." <u>Christian Science Monitor</u>, 18 June 1979, p. 15. (<u>Happy Days</u>)

20 "Beckett Play for B.B.C." <u>Times</u> (London), 1 Nov., p. 8. (<u>Words and Music</u>)

21 "Beckett (Samuel). <u>Mercier et Camier</u>. Roman." <u>Bulletin Critique du Livre Français</u> 298 (Nov. 1970):1074.

22 "Beckett (Samuel). <u>Premier Amour</u>." <u>Bulletin Critique du Livre Français</u> 298 (Nov. 1970):1074. (<u>First Love</u>)

23 B[ELMONT], G[EORGES]. "Les Hommes les idées les faits." <u>Arts Loisirs</u>, no. 76 (8-14 Mar. 1967), pp. 16-17. (<u>Film</u>, <u>Play</u>)

24 _____. "Lettre de Londres: Avec <u>Fin de partie</u> Beckett a atteint la perfection classique." <u>Arts-Spectacles</u> 614 (10-16 Apr. 1957):1-2. (<u>Endgame</u>, <u>Waiting for Godot</u>)

25 BENTLEY, ERIC. <u>The Life of Drama</u>. New York: Atheneum, 1965, pp. 99-101, 348-51. (<u>Waiting for Godot</u>, despair)

26 BERGONZI, BERNARD. "Early Beckett." <u>Guardian</u>, 9 Feb. 1962, p. 7. (<u>Poems in English</u>)

27 "Bibliography Bulletin for 1981: Samuel Beckett." <u>Irish University Review</u> 12, no. 2 (Autumn, 1982):211-212.

28 BILLINGTON, MICHAEL. "<u>Oh, les beaux jours</u>: Oxford Playhouse." <u>Times</u> (London), 15 Mar. 1971, p. 10. (<u>Happy Days</u>)

29 _____. "<u>Waiting for Godot</u>." <u>Guardian</u>, 11 June 1981, p. 9.

30   BINCHY, MAEVE. "A 'Messiah' Comes to Rehear-
      sal." Observer, 18 May 1980, p. 5.
      (Endgame)

31   BIRMINGHAM, WILLIAM. "The Unnamable." Cross
      Currents 9, no. 1 (Winter 1959):74. (The
      Unnamable)

32   BISHOP, TOM. "Samuel Beckett: Working Multi-
      Lingually." Centerpoint 4, no. 2, issue 13
      (Fall 1980):140-42. (Self-translations)

33   BLOCKER, H. GENE and WILLIAM HANNAFORD. "Samuel
      Beckett." In Introduction to Philosophy.
      New York, Cincinnati, Toronto, London,
      Melbourne: D. Van Nostrand Co., 1974, pp.
      265-66. (Meaninglessness, time)

34   BONNEFOY, CLAUDE. Conversations with Eugène
      Ionesco. Translated by Jan Dawson. London:
      Faber and Faber, 1970, 184 pp. (Beckett's
      style)

35   BOSQUET, ALAIN. "L'Univers déliquescent de
      Samuel Beckett." In Injustice. Paris:
      Editions de la Table Ronde/La Table Ronde de
      Combat, 1969, pp. 105-12. (Murphy, trilogy)

36   BOURGEADE, PIERRE. "Beckett -- Chausettes-
      gabardine." Nouvelle Revue Française, no.
      307 (1 Aug. 1978), pp. 103-5.

37   BRATER, ENOCH. "Brief Review: Company by
      Samuel Beckett." New Republic 184, no. 13
      (28 Mar. 1981):39-40.

38   BREE, GERMAINE and MARGARET GUITON. "An End and
      Some Beginnings." In The French Novel from
      Gide to Camus. New York: Harcourt, Brace &
      World, 1962, pp. 234-41. (New Novel)

39   BREE, GERMAINE and ALEXANDER Y. KROFF. Twen-
      tieth Century French Drama. New York:
      Macmillan, 1969, pp. 521-23, and passim.
      (Endgame)

40   BRENNER, JACQUES. "L'Avant-garde au théâtre
      s'est reformée." <u>Arts-Spectacles</u> 414 (5-11
      June 1953):3.

41   BRIGGS, RAY. "Samuel Beckett's World in
      Waiting: I.   The Life of an Enigmatic New
      Idol of the Avant-Garde of Two Continents."
      <u>Saturday Review of Literature</u> 40 (8 June
      1957):14.

42   BROWN, JOHN RUSSELL. <u>Theatre Language: A Study
      of Arden, Osborne, Pinter and Wesher</u>. New
      York: Taplinger Pub. Co., 1972. (Beckett's
      influence on English dramatists)

43   BRUCE, GEORGE. "Christmas Tree Waits for
      Godot." <u>Sunday Times</u> (London), 24 Dec. 1967,
      p. 45.

44   BRUEZIERE, MAURICE. "Samuel Beckett." In
      <u>Histoire descriptive de la littérature
      contemporaine</u>. Paris: Berger-Levrault,
      1975, pp. 399-410. (<u>The Lost Ones</u>)

45   BRUSTEIN, ROBERT S. <u>The Theatre of Revolt, An
      Approach to the Modern Drama</u>. Little, Brown
      and Co.: Boston, 1962, pp. 28-32. (Existen-
      tial drama)

46   BRYDEN, RONALD. "Theatre: Godot for Children."
      <u>Observer</u>, 22 Mar. 1970, p. 32. (<u>Waiting for
      Godot</u>)

47   BURGESS, ANTHONY. "Enduring Saturday." In
      <u>Urgent Copy Literary Studies</u>. London:
      Jonathan Cape, 1968, pp. 85-87. (Absurd,
      <u>Waiting for Godot</u>)

48   C., M. "<u>La Dernière Bande</u> de Samuel Beckett:
      La Fraîcheur du gâtisme." <u>Monde</u>, 28 Sept.
      1983, p. 22. (<u>Krapp's Last Tape</u>)

49   CAIN, ALEX MATHESON. "Far Lower than the
      Angels." <u>Tablet</u> 216 (10 Nov. 1962):1082-83.
      (<u>Happy Days</u>)

546

50   CALDER, JOHN. "Beckett's <u>Play</u>." [Letter to]
     <u>Times Literary Supplement</u> (London), 23 Apr.
     1964, p. 343. (<u>Play</u>)

51   _____. "Samuel Beckett's New Play." <u>Gambit</u> 4,
     no. 16 (1969):6-7. ("Breath")

52   CHAMPIGNY, ROBERT. "Interprétation de <u>En</u>
     <u>Attendant Godot</u>." <u>PMLA</u> 75, no. 3 (June
     1960):329-31. (<u>Waiting for Godot</u>)

53   CHARBONNIER, G[EORGES]. "Notes de livres:
     romans. Samuel Beckett: <u>Molloy</u>." <u>Nef</u> 8,
     nos. 77/78 (June-July 1951):250-51.

54   CLURMAN, HAROLD. "Samuel Beckett." In <u>Lies</u>
     <u>Like Truth: Theatre Reviews and Essays</u>. New
     York: Macmillan, 1958, pp. 220-25. (<u>Waiting</u>
     <u>for Godot</u>, <u>Endgame</u>)

55   _____. "Theatre." <u>Nation</u> 211 (7 December
     1970):605-6. (Jack MacGowran)

56   _____. "<u>The Zoo Story</u> and Beckett's <u>Krapp's</u>
     <u>Last Tape</u>, 1960." In <u>The Naked Image</u>
     <u>Observations on the Modern Theatre</u>. New
     York: Macmillan, 1966, pp. 13-15. (Loneli-
     ness)

57   COHN, RUBY. "Acting for Beckett." <u>Modern Drama</u>
     9, no. 3 (Dec. 1966):237.

58   _____. "<u>Beckett Anthology</u> by Samuel Beckett."
     <u>Educational Theatre Journal</u> 24, no. 2 (May
     1972):198-99. (Jack MacGowran)

59   _____. "Beckett for Comparists: A Review Essay
     of Books Published in the Last Two Years."
     <u>Comparative Literature Studies</u> 3, no. 4
     (1966):451-57.

60   COHN, RUBY and LILLY PARKER, eds. <u>Monologues de</u>
     <u>Minuit</u>. New York: Macmillan Co., 1965, pp.
     12-14, 118-20. (<u>Krapp's Last Tape</u>, <u>Texts for</u>
     <u>Nothing</u>)

61 "Company by Samuel Beckett." New Yorker, 9 Feb.
    1981, p. 118.

62 CONNOLLY, CYRIL. "Facing the true horror."
    Sunday Times (London), 16 July 1967, p. 43.
    (No's Knife, Come and Go)

63 COOKE, JUDY. "On All Fours." New Statesman 100
    (18 July 1980):22. (Company)

64 COOKE, RICHARD P. "Beckett and Pinter." Wall
    Street Journal, 7 Jan. 1964, p. 18. (Play)

65 _____. "Beckett Downtown." Wall Street
    Journal, 15 Sept. 1965, p. 16. (Happy Days)

66 COONEY, SEAMUS. "Beckett's Murphy." Explicator
    25, no. 1 (Sept. 1966), Item 3.

67 CORR, PAUL J. "Beckett's 'Still'." Explicator
    37, no. 1 (Fall, 1978), p. 41.

68 CORRIGAN, ROBERT W. "The Image of Man in
    Contemporary Theatre." Forum 3 (Summer
    1959):46-55. Beckett: pp. 52-53. (Waiting
    for Godot)

69 CROZIER, MARY. "Not So Much a Revolution."
    Tablet 219 (6 Mar. 1965):271. (Jack Mac-
    Gowran, Beginning to End)

70 CURTISS, THOMAS QUINN. "Beckett: He Never
    Complains, Never Explains." New York Times,
    27 Feb. 1966, Sec. 2, p. 13. (Film version
    of Play)

71 DAVIE, DONALD. "Nightingales, Anangke." New
    Statesman 63 (5 January 1962):20-21.
    Reprinted: 1979.22.58. (Poems in English)

72 DAVIS, ROBIN. "Radio and Samuel Beckett."
    Prompt, no. 5 (1964), pp. 46-50. (All That
    Fall, Embers, Words and Music, Cascando)

73 DEMING, BARBARA. "John Osborne's War Against the Philistines." <u>Hudson Review</u> 11, no. 3 (Autumn 1958):411-19. (<u>Endgame</u>)

74 DENNIS, NIGEL. "No View from the Toolshed." <u>Encounter</u> 20, no. 1 (Jan. 1963):37-39. Reprinted: 1979.22.56. (<u>Happy Days</u>)

75 DENT, ALAN. "Films That Belong to History." <u>Illustrated London News</u>, 4 Dec. 1965, p. 40. (<u>Film</u>)

76 DODSWORTH, MARTIN. "Last Things." <u>English</u> 26, no. 124 (Spring 1977):82-89. (<u>Ends and Odds</u>, <u>That Time</u>, <u>Footfalls</u>, <u>For to End Yet Again</u>)

77 DORT, BERNARD. "<u>En attendant Godot</u>, pièce de Samuel Beckett." <u>Temps Modernes</u> 8 (May 1953):1842-45. (<u>Waiting for Godot</u>)

78 DUBOIS, JACQUES. <u>L'Institution de la littérature: Introduction à une sociologie</u>. Paris: Nathan, 1978, pp. 174-81. (<u>Waiting for Godot</u>)

79 DUFFY, PATRICIA. [Letter to] <u>Tribune</u> (London), 25 Jan., p. 11. (<u>All That Fall</u>)

80 DUMUR, GUY. "Du côté de l'horreur." <u>Nouvel Observateur</u>, 21-27 Apr. 1975, pp. 85-66. (<u>Not I</u>, <u>Krapp's Last Tape</u>)

81 _____. "Le Sourcier du néant." <u>Nouvel Observateur</u>, 16-22 Feb. 1970, p. 47. (<u>Happy Days</u>)

82 DUNOYER, JEAN-MARIE. "Au Théâtre Oblique: Un Samuel Beckett bilingue." <u>Mondes des Arts et des Spectacles</u>, 6-12 June 1974, p. 11. (<u>Play</u>, <u>Krapp's Last Tape</u>, <u>Breath</u>)

83 DURANT, JACK D. "<u>How It Is</u> by Samuel Beckett." <u>Studies in Short Fiction</u> 2, no. 3 (Spring 1965), 299-301.

84   DUTOURD, JEAN. Le Paradoxe du critique suivi de
      Sept Saisons: Impressions de théâtre.
      Paris: Flammarion, 1972, Beckett passim.
      (Krapp's Last Tape, Acts Without Words,
      Waiting for Godot, Endgame, Happy Days)

85   DUVIGNAUD, JEAN and JEAN LAGOUTTE.   "Beckett:
      ça est là ..." In Le Théâtre contemporain:
      Culture et contre-culture. Paris: Librairie
      Larousse, 1974, pp. 59-66.

86   EAGLETON, TERRY. "Translation and Transfor-
      mation." Stand 19, no. 3 (1977):72-77.
      Beckett: pp. 75-76. (Collected Poems in
      English and French)

87   EDER, RICHARD. "Two Short Beckett Plays are
      'Chamber Music.'" New York Times, 19 Dec.
      1977, p. 44. (That Time, Footfalls)

88   ELLMANN, RICHARD. James Joyce. New York:
      Oxford University Press, 1959, Beckett
      passim. (Friendship with Joyce)

89   ELSEN, CLAUDE. "Une épopée du non-sens." Table
      Ronde, no. 42 (June 1951), pp. 135-39.
      (Absurdity in Kafka, Greene and Beckett)

90   ERNST, FISCHER. "Beckett's Endgame." In
      Existentialist Philosophy. Edited by James
      A. Gould and Willis H. Truitt. Encino,
      Calif. and Belmon, Calif.: Dickenson
      Publishing Co., Inc. 1973, pp. 296-302.

91   ESSLIN, MARTIN. "Doing the Little Soldier."
      New Statesman 80 (4 Sept. 1970):276-77.
      (More Pricks than Kicks)

92   "Etre ou ne pas être." Figaro, 24 Oct. 1969, p.
      15. (Waiting for Godot)

93   EVANS, GARETH LLOYD. "Waiting for Godot at
      Nottingham." Guardian, 27 Jan. 1971, p. 8.

Appendix A

550

94   F., L.B.   "All That Fall by Samuel Beckett Has a
      Concert Reading."   New York Times, 8 Oct.
      1957, p. 41.

95   FEDERMAN, RAYMOND.   "Comment c'est."   French
      Review 34, no. 5 (May 1961):594-95.
      Reprinted: 1979.22.50. (How It Is)

96   FEHSENFELD, MARTHA.   "Fiction, Samuel Beckett.
      Compagnie."   World Literature Today 55
      (Spring 1981):268.   (Company)

97   FENTON, JAMES.   "The Clown and the Circus."
      Sunday Times (London), 14 June 1981, p. 39.
      (Waiting for Godot)

98   FENVES, PETER.   "Samuel Beckett's Company."
      Chicago Review 33, no. 1 (1982):104-6.

99   FERRIS, PAUL.   "Radio Notes."   Observer, 28 June
      1959, p. 18.   (Embers)

100 FERTIG, HOWARD.   "Waiting for Godot."   In The
      Village Voice Reader: A Mixed Bag from the
      Greenwich Village Newspaper.   Edited by
      Daniel Wolf and Edwin Fancher.   Garden City,
      N.Y.: Doubleday, 1962.   Reprinted by Grove
      Press, New York, 1963, pp. 67-69.

101 FIELDING, DAPHNE.   Emerald and Nancy. Lady
      Cunard and her Daughters.   London: Eyre and
      Spottiswoode, 1968, p. 194.   ("Whoroscope")

102 FINNEY, BRIAN H.   "Beckett's 'Lessness.'"
      [Letter to] New Statesman 79 (22 May 1970):
      7-35.

103 FITCH, NOEL RILEY.   Sylvia Beach and the Lost
      Generation. A History of Literary Paris in
      the Twenties and Thirties.   New York and
      London: W.W. Norton & Co., 1983, pp. 277-
      78.   (Joyce)

104   FLANNER, JANET. <u>Paris Journal. Vol. II (1965–
       1971).</u> Edited by William Shawn. New York:
       Atheneum, 1971, pp. 338-39, 380-81. (Nobel
       Prize, "Whoroscope," Jack MacGowran)

105   FLETCHER, JOHN. "Conclusion: Towards a New
       Concept of Theatre: Adamov, Beckett and
       Arrabal." In <u>Forces in Modern French Drama:
       Studies in Variations on the Permitted Lie.</u>
       Frederick Ungar Publishing Co.: New York,
       1972, pp. 188-210. Beckett: pp. 198-205.

106   _____. <u>New Directions in Literature. Critical
       Approaches to a Contemporary Phenomenon.</u>
       London: Calder and Boyars, 1968, pp. 91-95.

107   _____. "<u>To End Yet Again.</u>" <u>Times Higher
       Education Supplement</u> (London), 1 July 1977,
       p. 18. (<u>Ends and Odds</u>, <u>Collected Poems in
       English and French</u>)

108   "Foreign Origins: Expatriate Writers in Paris."
       <u>Times Literary Supplement</u> (London), 27 May
       1955, p. x.

109   FOUCHET, MAX-POL. "Une chronique de la décom-
       position." In <u>Les Appels</u>. Paris: Mercure
       de France, 1967, pp. 107-10. (<u>Molloy</u>)

110   FOWLIE, WALLACE. <u>Climate of Violence: The
       French Literary Tradition from Baudelaire to
       the Present</u>. New York: Macmillan, 1967, pp.
       220-24, 256-59. (Solitude, inner self)

111   _____. "Fallen Out of the World." <u>New York
       Herald Tribune Book Week</u>, 23 Nov. 1958, p. 4.
       (<u>The Unnamable</u>)

112   FRASER, G.S. <u>The Modern Writer and His World:
       Continuity and Innovation in Twentieth-
       Century English Literature</u>. New York:
       Frederick A. Praeger Publishers, 1965, pp.
       61-64. First published in Great Britain by
       Derek Verschoyle, 1953. (<u>Waiting for Godot</u>)

113 FRIEDMAN, MELVIN J. "A Note on Leibniz and
     Samuel Beckett." Romance Notes 4, no. 2
     (Spring 1963):93-96. (Couples)

114 "From Ashcans, a Nobel Prize." Life 67, no. 19
     (7 Nov. 1969):93-94.

115 FULTON, ROBIN. "Endlessness." Guardian, 29
     June 1972, p. 14. (The Lost Ones, Dante)

116 GARDNER, LLEW. "Mummy, Why Do I Keep Running in
     Circles?" Tribune (London), 7 Nov. 1958, p.
     11. (Endgame, Krapp's Last Tape)

117 GASCOIGNE, BAMBER. "From the Head." Spectator
     209 (27 July 1962):115. (Act Without Words
     II)

118 _____. Twentieth Century Drama. London:
     Hutchinson University Library, 1962, pp. 184-
     88. (Waiting for Godot)

119 GASSNER, JOHN. "Broadway in Review." Educa-
     tional Theatre Journal 10 (May 1958),
     pp. 122-31. Beckett: p. 131. (Endgame)

120 GAUTIER, JEAN-JACQUES. "Au Théâtre de l'Odéon.
     Oh! Les Beaux Jours de Samuel Beckett." In
     Théâtre d'aujourd'hui. Dix ans de critique
     dramatique et des entretiens avec M. Abadi
     sur le Théâtre et la critique. Paris:
     Julliard, 1972, pp. 141-43. (Happy Days)

121 _____. "3 Mai 1957. Studio des Champs-Elysées.
     Fin de partie de Samuel Beckett." In Deux
     Fauteuils d'orchestre pour Jean-Jacques
     Gautier and J. Sennep. Paris: Flammarion,
     1962, pp. 195-96. (Endgame)

122 GENET. "Letter from Paris." New Yorker 40 (22
     Feb. 1964):98-110. Beckett: pp. 102-4.
     (Happy Days)

123 _____. "Letter from Paris." <u>New Yorker</u> 38 (4 Mar. 1961):95-100. Beckett: p. 100. (<u>How It Is</u>)

124 GILL, BRENDAN. "The Theatre." <u>New Yorker</u> 55 (7 Jan. 1980):57. ("A Piece of Monologue," <u>Film</u>)

125 _____. "The Theatre." <u>New Yorker</u> 55 (21 Jan. 1980):96. (<u>Endgame</u>)

126 GILLIATT, PENELOPE. "Beckett." In <u>Unholy Fools: Wits, Comics, Disturbers of the Peace: Film and Theatre</u>. New York: Viking Press, 1973, pp. 20-23. (<u>Waiting for Godot</u>)

127 GLENAVY, LADY BEATRICE. <u>Today We Will Only Gossip</u>. London: Constable,1964, 206 pp. (Biographical, <u>Endgame</u>)

128 GLICKSBERG, CHARLES. "Forms of Madness in Literature." <u>Arizona Quarterly</u> 17 (Spring 1961):42-53. (Creative use of madness, Freud)

129 GODARD, COLETTE. "Beckett par David Warrilow, à Saint-Denis: Le Sourire et le néant." <u>Monde</u>, 18 Mar. 1983, p. 21. (<u>That Time</u>, <u>Solo</u>)

130 "Godot has arrived." <u>Times</u> (London), 24 Oct. 1969, p. 11. (Nobel Prize)

131 GOODHEART, EUGENE. "Literature as a Game." <u>TriQuarterly</u> 52 (Fall 1981):134-49. Beckett: pp. 137-39. (<u>Endgame</u>, <u>Waiting for Godot</u>, trilogy)

132 GOTH, MAJA. <u>Franz Kafka et les lettres fran-çaises (1928-1955)</u>. Paris: Librairie José Corti, 1956, pp. 120-22.

133 G[REACEN], R[OBERT]. "Contemplation." <u>Tribune</u> (London), 4 Sept. 1970, p. 15. (<u>More Pricks than Kicks</u>)

554

134   GRENIER, JEAN.   "Samuel Beckett, un monument
      singulier."   <u>Arts-Spectacles</u> 418 (3-9 July
      1953):5-6.   (<u>The Unnamable</u>, schizophrenia)

135   GRESSET, MICHEL.   "<u>Comédie</u>."   <u>Mercure de France</u>
      351 (July-Aug. 1964):546-47.   (<u>Play</u>)

136   GRIFFEN, LLOYD W.   "Beckett, Samuel, <u>How It Is</u>.
      <u>Poems in English</u>."   <u>Library Journal</u> 89 (1 May
      1964):1964.

137   [GRINDEA, MIRON].   "Involved with Music."   <u>Adam:</u>
      <u>International Review</u> 35, nos. 337-339
      (1970):2-4.

138   GUEZ, GILBERT.   "<u>Lettre Morte</u> et <u>La Dernière</u>
      <u>Bande</u>."   <u>Paris-Théâtre</u> 13, no. 160 (1960):39-
      41.   (<u>Krapp's Last Tape</u>)

139   GUTHKE, KARL S.   "A Stage for the Anti-Hero:
      Metaphysical Farce in the Modern Theatre."
      <u>Studies in the Literary Imagination</u> 9, no. 1
      (Spring 1976):119-37.   Beckett: pp. 126-31.
      (<u>Waiting for Godot</u>, <u>Act without Words</u>,
      metaphysical farce)

140   HAMILTON, ALEX.   "Beckett at 70."   <u>Listener</u>, 22
      Apr. 1976, p. 511.   (<u>Embers</u>, "Rough for
      Radio," Jack MacGowran's program of Beckett's
      Poems)

141   HARRIS, ROBERT R.   "Beckett, Samuel. <u>The</u>
      <u>Collected Works</u>. <u>More Pricks Than Kicks</u>."
      <u>Library Journal</u> 95 (15 Dec. 1970):4278.
      (<u>More Pricks Than Kicks</u>, Irish style)

142   HARRIS, WENDELL V.   "Style and the Twentieth-
      Century Novel."   <u>Western Humanities Review</u>
      18, no. 2 (Spring 1964):127-40.   Beckett:
      pp. 139-40.

143   HARRISON, KENNETH.   "Mr. Beckett Finds Himself."
      <u>Books and Bookmen</u> 3, no. 7 (Apr., 1958):21.
      (<u>Watt</u>, <u>Malone Dies</u>, Joyce)

144   HASSETT, JOSEPH M. "Godel, Hofstadter,
       Beckett." College Literature 8, no. 3 (Fall
       1981):311-12. (Trilogy)

145   HAYMAN, DAVID. "Double-Distancing. An At-
       tribute of the 'Post-Modern' Avant-Garde."
       Novel 12, no. 1 (Fall 1978):33-47. Beckett:
       pp. 39-41. (Play, Not I)

146   HEDBERG, JOHANNES. "Some Thoughts on Three
       Poems by Samuel Beckett." Moderna Språk 68
       (1974):11-18. ("The Vulture," "Cascando,"
       "Saint-Lô")

147   HEINEGG, PETER. "Collected Poems in English and
       French." America 138 (14 Jan. 1978):27.

148   HOBSON, HAROLD. "Blinded by Lights." Sunday
       Times (London), 7 Feb. 1971, p. 25. (End-
       game)

149   _____. "Godot and After." In Encore: The
       Sunday Times Book. Edited by Leonard
       Russell. London: Michael Joseph, 1963, pp.
       315-18. Reprint of 150A. (Humor and waiting
       for the future in Godot)

150   _____. "Godot and After." Sunday Times
       (London), 7-14 Aug. 1955, p.11. Reprinted:
       1979.22.20.

151   _____. "Theatre." Sunday Times (London), 7
       Feb. 1971. (Endgame)

152   _____. "Theatre." Sunday Times (London), 11
       Feb. 1973. (Not I)

153   _____. "With a Frightened Lustre." Sunday
       Times (London), 17 Jan. 1965, p. 43.
       (Waiting for Godot)

154   HOLLOWAY, DAVID. "Welcome Award: International
       Writer." Daily Telegraph (London), 24 Oct.
       1969, p. 15.

556

155   HOLLOWAY, RONALD. "Beckett in Berlin."
       Financial Times, 4 Dec. 1973, p. 3. (Schil-
       ler Theater)

156   HOROVITZ, MICHAEL. "Images Forever Fixed."
       Spectator 252 (31 Mar. 1984):25. (Collected
       Shorter Plays)

157   HOWES, VICTOR. "Beckett's Ceaseless Search."
       Christian Science Monitor, 13 Dec. 1972, p.
       15. (The Lost Ones)

158   HUGHES, CATHERINE. "Beckett at 70." America
       134 (10 Apr. 1976):316-17. (Waiting for
       Godot, Endgame, Happy Days, Play, Not I)

159   HUNTER, JIM. "In the Cylinder." Listener, 22
       June 1972, p. 879. (The Lost Ones)

160   HUTCHINSON, MARY. "All the Livelong Way." (In
       French) Adam: International Review 337-339
       (1970):73-74. (Molloy, The Unnamable)

161   INGHAM, PATRICIA. "The Renaissance of Hell."
       Listener 62 (3 Sept. 1959):349-51. (Sartre,
       Anouilh, Cocteau, Tennessee Williams)

162   INNES, CHRISTOPHER. Holy Theatre. Ritual and
       the Avant Garde. Cambridge: Cambridge
       University Press, 1981, pp. 209-14. (Bibli-
       cal echoes, ritualisation, "play," expres-
       sionist monodrama)

163   "It's This Way? How It Is by Samuel Beckett."
       Newsweek 63, no. 8 (24 Feb. 1964):93. (How
       It Is, comedy)

164   ITZIN, CATHERINE. "Beckett's Happy Burial
       Alive." Tribune (London), 28 Mar. 1975,
       p. 7. (Happy Days)

165   _____. "Different Kinds of Deaths and Exits."
       Tribune (London), 2 Feb. 1973, pp. 6-7.
       (Krapp's Last Tape, Not I)

166   JEAN, RAYMOND. "Ancien et nouveau Beckett: Sur
       Watt." In <u>Pratique de la littérature</u>.
       <u>Roman/Poésie</u>. Paris: Editions du Seuil,
       1978, pp. 79-81. (<u>Watt</u>)

167   JENKINS, ALAN. "Voices in the Dark." <u>Times
       Literary Supplement</u> (London), 26 Sept. 1980,
       p. 1063. (<u>Company</u>)

168   JOHNSON, B.S. "Exploration." <u>Spectator</u>, 26
       June 1964, p. 858. (<u>How It Is</u>, <u>Cascando</u>)

169   JONGE, ALEX de. "Oxford Playhouse. <u>Oh! les
       beaux jours</u>." <u>Financial Times</u>, 16 Mar. 1971,
       p. 3. (<u>Happy Days</u>)

170   JONGH, NICOLAS de. "Krapp's Last Tape at the
       Aldwych." <u>Manchester Guardian</u>, 30 Apr. 1970,
       p. 10. (Pessimism)

171   JORDAN, JOHN. "The Irish Theatre -- Retrospect
       and Premonition." In <u>Contemporary Theatre</u>.
       Edited by John Russell Brown and Bernard
       Harris. London: Edward Arnold, 1962, pp.
       165-83. Beckett: 181-82. (<u>Waiting for
       Godot</u>)

172   JOUFFROY, ALAIN. "Une clé pour Beckett."
       <u>Express</u>, 6-12 Dec. 1965, p. 127.

173   No entry.

174   KANTERS, ROBERT. "Samuel Beckett." In <u>L'Air
       des lettres ou tableau raisonnable des
       lettres françaises d'aujourd'hui</u>. Paris:
       Bernard Grasset, 1973, pp. 215-18. (<u>Endgame</u>)

175   KARPF, ANNE. "Radio. Sad Sense." <u>Listener</u> 108
       (4 Nov. 1982):29. (<u>Ill Seen Ill Said</u>)

176   KEARNS, PATRICIA. "An Irish Playwright in
       France: The Development of Samuel Beckett as
       a Dramatist." In <u>France-Ireland Literary
       Relations</u>. Edited by G. Fehlmann, P.

Rafoidi, et. al. Paris: Editions Univer-
sitaires, 1974, pp. 249-57. (Waiting for
Godot, Endgame, Krapp's Last Tape, Happy
Days)

177   KENNEBECK, EDWIN. "The Moment of Cosmic Ennui."
       Commonweal 61, no. 13 (31 Dec. 1954):365-66.
       (Waiting for Godot)

178   KENNEDY, ALAN. Meaning and Signs in Fiction.
       New York: St. Martin's Press, 1979, pp. 131-
       33. (Language)

179   KENNER, HUGH. "The Absurdity of Fiction."
       Griffin 8 (Nov. 1959):13-16. (Trilogy, act
       of writing, identity)

180   KERMODE, FRANK. "Waiting on Beckett." Daily
       Telegraph (London), 24 Apr. 1976, p. 9.
       (Humor)

181   KERN, EDITH. The Absolute Comic. New York:
       Columbia University Press, 1980. (Waiting
       for Godot, Watt)

182   KILROY, THOMAS. "Stink of Artifice." Times
       Literary Supplement (London), 13 Dec. 1974,
       p. 1405. (Mercier and Camier)

183   KING, PETER R. "Beckett and the Sixth Form."
       Use of English 21, no. 3 (Spring 1970):234-
       37, 240. (Endgame)

184   KITCHIN, LAWRENCE. "The Cage and the Scream."
       Listener 69 (24 Jan. 1963):157-59. (Prison,
       Endgame, Happy Days)

185   _____. "Samuel Beckett's Play." Listener 71
       (30 Apr., 1964):718-19. (Play)

186   KNAPP, ROGER. "An Interview with Roger Blin."
       Tulane Drama Review 7, no. 3 (Spring 1963):1-
       11-25. Beckett: pp. 122-24. (Genet)

187 KNIGHT, G. WILSON. "The Kitchen Sink: On
     Recent Developments in Drama." <u>Encounter</u> 21,
     no. 6 (Dec. 1963):48-54. (<u>Waiting for Godot</u>)

188 KNOWLSON, JAMES. "<u>La Derniére Bande</u> at the
     Greenwood Theatre." <u>Journal of Beckett
     Studies</u>, no. 1 (Winter 1976), pp. 103-4.
     (<u>Krapp's Last Tape</u>)

189 KOSTELANETZ, RICHARD. "The Old Frontier."
     <u>Partisan Review</u> 49, no. 1 (1982):156-58.
     (<u>Company</u>)

190 KROLL, JACK. "Theater: Down to the Mouth."
     <u>Newsweek</u> 80, no. 23 (4 Dec. 1972):70.
     (<u>Krapp's Last Tape</u>, <u>Happy Days</u>, <u>Act Without
     Words I</u>, <u>Not I</u>, Alan Schneider)

191 LA BARDONNIE, MATHILDE. "Actualité de Samuel
     Beckett: <u>La Dernière Bande</u>." <u>Monde</u>, 10 Oct.
     1981, p. 28. (Rick Cluchey, <u>Krapp's Last
     Tape</u>)

192 "<u>Lahr</u> in Middle of Riddle." <u>Life</u> 40, no. 19 (7
     May 1956):155-58. (<u>Waiting for Godot</u>)

193 LAMBERT, J.W. "Faces of Humanity." <u>Sunday
     Times</u> (London), 21 Jan. 1973, p. 29. (<u>Not I</u>,
     <u>Krapp's Last Tape</u>)

194 _____. "Plays in Performance." <u>Drama</u> 68
     (Spring 1963):20-27. (<u>Happy Days</u>)

195 _____. "Splendour and Severity." <u>Sunday Times</u>
     (London), 12 July 1964, p. 25. (<u>Endgame</u>)

196 "Late Night Show from Beckett - New Arts
     Theatre: End of the Day." <u>Times</u> (London),
     18 Oct. 1962, p. 18. (Jack MacGowran)

197 LEMARCHARD, JACQUES. "<u>En Attendant Godot</u> de
     Samuel Beckett au Théâtre Hébertot." <u>Figaro
     Littértaire</u>, 30 June 1956, p. 12. (<u>Waiting
     for Godot</u>)

560

198 _____. "Le Theatre: Estival 64, au Pavillon de Marsan." <u>Figaro Littéraire</u>, 2-8 July 1964, p. 24. (<u>Play</u>)

199 LE SAGE, LAURENT. "Samuel Beckett." In <u>The French New Novel. An Introduction and a Sampler</u>. University Park: Pennsylvania State University Press, 1962, pp. 46-57. (<u>Molloy</u>, <u>Malone Dies</u>)

200 LEYBURN, ELLEN DOUGLASS. "Comedy and Tragedy Transposed." <u>Yale Review</u> 53, no. 4 (June 1964):553-62. (Ionesco)

201 "Life in the Mud." <u>Times Literary Supplement</u> (London), 7 Apr. 1961, p. 213. (<u>How It Is</u>)

202 LLOYD-EVANS, GARETH. "<u>Happy Days</u>." <u>Guardian</u>, 29 Jan. 1981, p. 9. (<u>Happy Days</u>)

203 LUCCIONI, GENNIE. "<u>La Dernière Bande</u>, suivi de <u>Cendres</u>." <u>Esprit</u> 28 (May 1960):913-15. (<u>Krapp's Last Tape</u>, <u>Embers</u>)

204 _____. "Samuel Beckett: <u>Comment c'est</u>." <u>Esprit</u> 29, no. 294 (Apr. 1961):710-13. (<u>How It Is</u>)

205 McAULEY, GAY. "Samuel Beckett's <u>Come and Go</u>." <u>Educational Theatre Journal</u> 18, no. 4 (Dec. 1966):439-42.

206 MacNIECE, LOUIS. "Godot on TV." <u>New Statesman</u> 62 (7 July 1961):27-28. (Cinemagraphic techniques)

207 _____. <u>Varieties of Parable</u>. London: Cambridge University Press, 1965, pp. 140-46 (<u>Malone Dies</u>)

208 No entry.

209 MACRON, MICHELE. "<u>Oh les beaux jours</u> de Samuel Beckett." <u>Signes du Temps</u> 3 (Dec. 1963):46. (<u>Happy Days</u>)

210 MADDOCKS, MELVIN. "Black Irish Fairy Tales."
     <u>Christian Science Monitor</u>, 27 July 1967, p.
     7. (<u>Stories and Texts for Nothing</u>)

211 MADELAINE, R.E.R. "Happy-Though-Married Hardy."
     <u>Notes and Queries</u> 227, no. 4 (Aug. 1982), pp.
     348-49. (<u>All That Fall</u>, Rev. Edward John
     Hardy's <u>How to be Happy Though Married</u>)

212 MAGNAN, JEAN-MARIE. "Samuel Beckett ou les
     chaines et relais du néant." <u>Cahiers du Sud</u>
     50, no. 371 (Apr.-May 1963):73-76. (<u>How It
     Is</u>, narrator's refusal to tell stories)

213 MANNERS, MARYA. "A Seat in the Stalls."
     <u>Reporter</u> 13 (20 Oct. 1955):42-43. (<u>Waiting
     for Godot</u>)

214 MARCABRU, PIERRE. "Décomposition des êtres et
     du language." <u>Arts-Spectacles</u> 618 (8-14 May
     1957):2. (<u>Endgame</u>, <u>Act Without Words</u>)

215 _____. "<u>En Attendant Godot</u> au Théâtre Héber-
     tot." <u>Arts-Spectacles</u> 573 (20-26 June
     1956):3. (<u>Waiting for Godot</u>)

216 MARCUS, FRANK. "Writ Small." <u>Sunday Telegraph</u>
     (London), 23 May 1976, p. 18. (<u>Play</u>, <u>That
     Time</u>, <u>Footfalls</u>)

217 MARKS, JONATHAN. "MacGowran's Beckett/Beckett's
     MacGowran." <u>Yale/Theatre</u> 3, no. 2 (1971):84-
     89. (Jack MacGowran)

218 MARTIN, MARCEL. "Le Point de la semaine."
     <u>Lettres Françaises</u>, 23 Feb.-1 Mar. 1967, p.
     26. (<u>Film</u>, film version of <u>Play</u>)

219 MAURIAC, CLAUDE. "Le Cinéma: Samuel Beckett à
     la Pagode." <u>Figaro Littéraire</u>, 23 Feb. 1967,
     p. 14. (Buster Keaton, <u>Film</u>, <u>Play</u>)

220 MAUROC, DANIEL. "The New French Literary Avant
     Garde." <u>Points</u> 17 (Autumn 1953):44-51.

562

Beckett: pp. 47-48. (Psychological time, man animalized, deteriorated consciousness)

221 _____. "Watt." Table Ronde, no. 70 (Oct. 1953), pp. 155-56. (Watt)

222 MAYERSBERG, PAUL. "The Shared Dream." Listener 68 (27 Sept. 1962):473-75. (Stream-of-consciousness technique, cinema)

223 MAYOUX, J.-J. "Actualité de Samuel Beckett: La Quête du mal dire." Monde, 10 Oct. 1981, p. 28. (Company, Ill Seen Ill Said)

224 _____. "'From an Abandoned Work' ... Krapp's Last Tape." Etudes Anglaises 12, no. 2 (Apr.-June 1959):181-82.

225 MAYS, JAMES. "Samuel Beckett, Company." Irish University Review 11, no. 1 (Spring 1981):124-25.

226 MERCIER, VIVIAN. "Godot, Molloy et Cie." New Statesman and Nation 50 (3 Dec. 1955):754. Reprinted: 1979.22.13. (Problem of "self-hood")

227 MICHEL, MARCELLE. "May-B à Créteil: Beckett revu par Maguy Marin." Monde, 13 Jan 1982, p. 16. (Dance)

228 MIGNON, PAUL-LOUIS. "Samuel Beckett." Avant-Scéne 313 (15 June 1964):8. (Major stages in Beckett's literary career)

229 MILSTEIN, DIANA. "Samuel Beckett: An Exhibition. University of Reading Library." New Theatre Magazine, Samuel Beckett Special Issue 11, no. 3 (1971):26-27.

230 MONNIER, ADRIENNE. "Un Nouveau Dedalus." Arts-Spectacles 418 (3-9 July 1953):5. ("Anna Livia Plurabelle")

231   MORGAN, EDWIN. "Neither Here nor There." <u>Times</u>
      <u>Literary Supplement</u> (London), 21 Jan. 1977,
      p. 49. ("For to End Yet Again")

232   MOROT-SIR, EDOUARD. "L'Idéalisme philosophique
      et les techniques littéraires au vingtième
      siècle." In <u>Symbolism and Modern Literature</u>
      <u>Studies in Honor of Wallace Fowlie</u>. Edited
      by Marcel Tetel. Durham, N.C.: Duke
      University Press, 1978, pp. 44-62. (Referen-
      ces to philosophers)

233   _____. "Samuel Beckett. <u>Pour finir encore et</u>
      <u>autres foirades</u>." <u>French Review</u> 51, no. 1
      (Oct. 1977):131-32. ("For to End Yet Again")

234   MOURGUE, GERARD. <u>Dieu dans la littérature</u>
      <u>d'aujourd'hui</u>. Paris: France-Empire, 1961,
      p. 236. (<u>Waiting for Godot</u>, messiah)

235   MURRAY, JOHN J. "Beckett, Samuel. <u>The Lost</u>
      <u>Ones</u>." <u>Best Sellers</u> 32 (1 Jan. 1973):449-50.
      (Measurements, routes of escape, characters)

236   NADEAU, MAURICE. "La Dernière Tentative de
      Samuel Beckett." <u>Lettres Nouvelles</u> 1, no. 7
      (Sept. 1953):860-64. (<u>The Unnamable</u>)

237   NEILL, EDWARD. "<u>Fizzles</u>." <u>PN Review</u> 10, vol.
      6, no. 2 (1979):61-62.

238   "The Nether World of No." <u>Time</u> 90, no. 2 (14
      July 1967):90. (<u>Stories and Texts for</u>
      <u>Nothing</u>)

239   "New Beckett Work." <u>Times</u> (London), 8 Jan.
      1959, p. 5. (<u>The Unnamable</u>)

240   NIGHTINGALE, BENEDICT. "Bog Godot." <u>New</u>
      <u>Statesman</u> 81 (29 Jan. 1971):157. (<u>Waiting</u>
      <u>for Godot</u>, sardonic humor)

241   NORES, DOMINIQUE. "<u>Fin de partie</u> de Samuel
      Beckett." <u>Lettres Nouvelles</u>, Sept.-Oct.
      1968, pp. 160-61. (<u>Endgame</u>)

564

242   O'HARA, J.D.   "It's All Over But the Waiting."
      <u>Chicago Tribune Book World</u>, 22 June 1969, p.
      4.   (<u>Cascando and Other Short Pieces</u>)

243   _____.   "Small Works, Large in Meaning: <u>First
      Love and Other Shorts</u>."   <u>New York Times Book
      Review</u>, 15 Sept. 1974, p. 46.   (Beckett's
      increasingly disciplined style, <u>First Love</u>,
      <u>Not I</u>)

244   OLIVER, EDITH.   "Public Pleasures."   <u>New Yorker</u>
      53, no. 46 (2 Jan. 1978):47-50.   Beckett:
      pp. 49-50.   (<u>Play</u>, <u>That Time</u>, <u>Footfalls</u>)

245   ONIMUS, JEAN.   "L'Homme égaré: Notes sur le
      sentiment d'égarement dans la littérature
      actuelle."   <u>Etudes</u> 283 (Oct.-Dec. 1954):320-
      29.   (<u>Molloy</u>)

246   ORMEROD, BEVERLY.   "Beckett's <u>Waiting for
      Godot</u>."   <u>Explicator</u> 32, no. 9 (May 1974):Item
      70.   (Implications of bare tree)

247   PACKARD, WILLIAM.   "Absurdist Plays Disrupt
      Comfortable Certainties."   <u>Wall Street
      Journal</u>, 15 Sept. 1966, p. 16.   (<u>Waiting for
      Godot</u>, Theater of Absurd)

248   PEYRE, HENRI.   "Samuel Beckett."   In <u>Contem-
      porary French Literature. A Critical Anthol-
      ogy</u>.   New York, Evanston, London: Harper and
      Row, 1964, pp. 316-36.   (Summarizes <u>Waiting
      for Godot</u>, <u>Endgame</u> in French)

249   PHELPS, GILBERT.   "Radio: Man and Boy."
      <u>Listener</u>, 13 Sept. 1973, p. 354.   (<u>The Lost
      Ones</u>, Medieval theology)

250   PIATIER, JACQUELINE.   "Beckett en ses vertes
      années."   <u>Monde [des Livres]</u>, 13 June 1970,
      p. 1.   Reprinted: 1979.22.66.   (<u>Mercier and
      Camier</u>, <u>First Love</u>)

251   _____.   "Un halètement dans la boue: <u>Comment
      c'est</u> de Samuel Beckett."   <u>Monde</u>, 11 Feb.

1961, p. 9. (<u>How It Is</u>, journey, inner consciousness)

252 PINETTE, G. "Samuel Beckett. <u>Tous ceux qui tombent</u>." <u>Books Abroad</u> 32, no. 4 (Autumn 1958):384. (<u>All That Fall</u>, Kafka)

253 PINGAUD, BERNARD. "<u>Molloy</u>." <u>Esprit</u> 19, no. 182 (Sept. 1951):423-25.

254 POIROT-DELPECH, BERTRAND. "<u>Fin de partie</u> de Samuel Beckett." <u>Monde</u>, 21 Apr. 1972, p. 27. (<u>Endgame</u>)

255 POTTER, DENIS. "Taking the Mickey." <u>Sunday Times</u> (London), 24 Apr. 1977, p. 38. (Television production, <u>Not I</u>)

256 POULET, ROBERT. "Faits nouveaux de l'après-deux-guerres." <u>Ecrits de Paris</u>, Feb. 1969, pp. 94-100. Beckett: pp. 98-100. (Trilogy, <u>Waiting for Godot</u>, <u>Endgame</u>)

257 _____. "Samuel Beckett." In <u>La Lanterne Magique</u>. Paris: Nouvelles Editions Debresse, 1956, pp. 236-42. (<u>Molloy</u>, <u>Malone Dies</u>, <u>Waiting for Godot</u>)

258 POWLICK, LEONARD. "Beckett's <u>Waiting for Godot</u>." <u>Explicator</u> 37, no. 1 (Fall 1978):10-11.

259 PRIEUR, JEROME. "Samuel Beckett et Alan Schneider: <u>Film</u>." In <u>Nuits Blanches. Essai sur le cinéma</u>. Paris: Gallimard, 1980, pp. 220-22. (Image of fleeing figure)

260 "Prince of Darkness." <u>Times Literary Supplement</u> (London), 17 June 1960, p. 381. (Trilogy)

261 PRITCHETT, V.S. "An Irish Oblomov." <u>New Statesman</u> 59 (2 Apr. 1960):489. (Trilogy)

566

262 _____. "Saints and Rogues." <u>Listener</u> 68 (6 Dec. 1962):957-59. (Literary language vs. vernacular in modern novel)

263 PUMPHREY, ARTHUR. "Arthur Pumphrey at the Theatre." <u>Theatre Arts</u> 45, no. 11 (Nov. 1961):57-58. (<u>Happy Days</u>)

264 QUIN, ANN. "<u>How It Is</u> by Samuel Beckett." <u>Aylesford Review</u> 6, no. 3 (Summer-Autumn 1964):190-92.

265 R., M.H. "<u>Happy Days</u>: A Play in Two Acts, by Samuel Beckett." <u>Dubliner</u>, no. 5 (Sept.-Oct. 1962), pp. 56-61.

266 RADIN, VICTORIA. "Beckett." <u>Observer</u>, 14 Dec. 1975, p. 22. (Patrick Magee reading Beckett)

267 RAINOIRD, MANUEL. "<u>En Attendant Godot</u>." <u>Monde Nouveau/Paru</u> 11, no. 103 (Aug.-Sept. 1956):115-17. (<u>Waiting for Godot</u>)

268 RATCLIFFE, MICHAEL. "Flesh and Bone." <u>Sunday Times</u> (London), 3 Jan. 1965, p. 19. (<u>Waiting for Godot</u>)

269 [RENAUD, MADELEINE, EUGENE IONESCO, JEAN ANOUILH, ALAN SIMPSON, MARCEL ACHARD.] "Quelques réactions." <u>Figaro</u>, 24 Oct. 1969, p. 15. (Nobel Prize)

270 RICHARDSON, JACK. "Shakespeare and Beckett." <u>Commentary</u> 51, no. 4 (Apr. 1971):76-78. (<u>Waiting for Godot</u>)

271 RICKS, CHRISTOPHER. "The End of Time." <u>Sunday Times</u> (London), 2 July 1972, p. 40. (<u>The Lost Ones</u>)

272 ROBLES, M. "Cain -- an Unfortunate." <u>Modern Languages</u> 50, no. 2 (June 1969):57-59. (Biblical allusions, Unamuno, Baudelaire, Steinbeck)

273 ROBSON, JEREMY. "Poet of the Theatre." Tribune
     (London), 26 Jan. 1962, p. 11. (Poems in
     English)

274 ROTHSCHILD, VICTORIA. "And How the Fable Too."
     PN Review 18, vol. 7, no. 4 (1980):58.
     (Company)

275 ROTONDARO, FRED. "Beckett, Samuel. Stories and
     Texts for Nothing." Best Sellers 27 (1 Aug.
     1967):166.

276 ROUBINE, JEAN-JACQUES. "Samuel Beckett: En
     Attendant Godot (Théâtre Récamier)."
     Nouvelle Revue Française 18, no. 210 (1 June
     1970):941-42. (Waiting for Godot)

277 S., P.H. "The Times Diary: Beckett Scraps."
     Times (London), 25 Oct. 1969, p. 6.
     (Manuscripts)

278 S[AINER], A[RTHUR]. "Theatre: Embers."
     Village Voice, 7 Mar. 1963, p. 12.

279 SALACROU, ARMAND. "Ce n'est pas un accident
     mais une réussite." Arts-Spectacles 400 (27
     Feb.-5 Mar. 1953):1. (Waiting for Godot)

280 "Samuel Beckett Wins Nobel Literature Prize."
     Publishers' Weekly 196, no. 18 (3 Nov.
     1969):29-30.

281 "Samuel Beckett Wins Nobel Prize." Times
     (London), 24 Oct. 1969, p. 1.

282 "Samuel Beckett's: Comment c'est." Recent
     French Books: A Quarterly Choice 2 (1961):8-
     9. (How It Is)

283 SANDIER, GILLES. "Le Vrai mistère de Godot."
     Arts et Loisirs, 22 (23 Feb.-1 Mar. 1966), p.
     18. (Waiting for Godot)

568

284   SANDOR, IVAN. "Shakespeare, Dürrenmatt, Beckett and Havel." New Hungarian Quarterly 7, no. 22 (Summer 1966):187-90. (Waiting for Godot)

285   SCHNEIDER, MARCEL. "Ionesco-Beckett." In La Littérature fantastique en France. Paris: Librairie Arthème Fayard, 1964, pp. 399-402. (Waiting for Godot)

286   SEAVER, RICHARD. "Samuel Beckett." Nimbus 2, no. 2 (Autumn 1953):61-62. (Watt)

287   SENART, PHILIPPE. "Samuel Beckett." In Chemins critiques d'Abellio à Sartre. Paris: Plon, 1966, pp. 29-32. (Significance of voice in Beckett's novels)

288   SHANK, THEODORE J., ed. A Digest of 500 Plays. New York: Crowell-Collier Press; London: Collier-Macmillan, 1963, pp. 201-3. (Waiting for Godot, Endgame, Happy Days)

289   SHORTER, ERIC. "Richness of Beckett's Godot." Daily Telegraph (London), 27 Jan. 1971, p. 10. (Waiting for Godot)

290   SHOUT, JOHN D. "Andrei Serban Directs Irene Worth in Happy Days." Journal of Beckett Studies, no. 5 (Autumn 1979), pp. 144-45.

291   SIMON, JOHN. "A Theater Chronicle." Hudson Review 14, no. 4 (Winter 1961-62):586-92. Beckett: p. 589. (Happy Days)

292   _____. "Black Despair, Blackened Humor." New York 6, no. 8 (19 Feb. 1973):74. (Endgame)

293   _____. "Up To Here with Serban." New York 12, no. 26 (25 June 1979):71-72. (Happy Days)

294   "Slow Motion." Times Literary Supplement (London), 25 Apr. 1958, p. 225. (Endgame)

295   [SMITH, MICHAEL, and MERVYN WALL]. "Michael Smith Asks Mervyn Wall Some Questions About

the Thirties." <u>Lace Curtain</u>, no. 4 (Summer
1971), pp. 77-86. (Biographical, Beckett's
comments on suicide)

296   SMITH, R.D. "Back to the Text." In <u>Contem-
porary Theatre</u>. Edited by John Russell Brown
and Bernard Harris. London: Edward Arnold,
1962, pp. 117-38. Beckett: pp. 127-36.
(<u>Waiting for Godot</u>, communication)

297   "Stamping on Mr. Beckett's Verbal Treadmill."
<u>Times</u> (London), 8 Apr. 1964, p. 10. (<u>Play</u>)

298   STEFAN, JUDE. "Samuel Beckett: <u>Mal vu mal
dit</u>." <u>Nouvelle Revue Française</u>, no. 344 (1
Sept. 1981), pp. 126-27. (<u>Ill Seen Ill Said</u>)

299   STYAN, J.L. "The Published Play After 1956.
II." <u>British Book News</u>, no. 301 (Sept.
1965), pp. 601-5.

300   "Talk of the Town: Beckett." <u>New Yorker</u> 40 (8
Aug. 1964):22-23. (<u>Film</u>)

301   TALLMER, JERRY. "Beckett's <u>Endgame</u>." In <u>The
Village Voice Reader: A Mixed Bag from the
Greenwich Village Newspaper</u>. Edited by
Daniel Wolf and Edwin Fancher. Garden City,
N.Y.: Doubleday, 1962. Reprinted by Grove
Press, New York, 1963, pp. 180-82.

302   _____. "<u>Godot</u> on Broadway." In <u>The Village
Voice Reader: A Mixed Bag from the Greenwich
Village Newspaper</u>. Edited by Daniel Wolf and
Edwin Fancher. Garden City, N.Y.: Double-
day, 1962. Reprinted by Grove Press, New
York, 1963, pp. 69-72. (<u>Waiting for Godot</u>)

303   _____. "Theatre: <u>All That Fall</u>." <u>Village
Voice</u>, 1 Jan. 1958, p. 11. (Mrs. Rooney's
journey)

304   _____. "Theatre: Four by Beckett." <u>Village
Voice</u>, 23 Dec. 1959, p. 7. (<u>Act Without
Words I & II</u>, <u>Embers</u>, <u>All That Fall</u>)

570

305 TAYLOR, JOHN RUSSELL. "Critic on the Hearth."
     Listener 70 (21 Nov. 1963):854-55. (Krapp's
     Last Tape)

306 _____. "Oh! Les Beaux Jours." Plays and
     Players 12, no. 9 (June 1965):42. (Happy
     Days, bilingualism)

307 TEMKINE, RAYMONDE. "Genet, Beckett, Arrabal."
     Europe 53, no. 557 (Sept. 1975):199-201.
     (Krapp's Last Tape)

308 THOORENS, LEON. "Le Labyrinthe." Revue
     Générale Belge, no. 10 (Dec. 1968), pp. 145-
     50. (Television adaptation of All That Fall)

309 TOOR, DAVID. "Beckett's Waiting for Godot."
     Explicator 29, no. 1 (Sept. 1970):Item 1.
     (Theological implications of boy)

310 TOUCHARD, PIERRE AIMEE. "Un théâtre nouveau."
     Avant-Scène Fémina-Théâtre 156 (1957):1-2.
     (Ionesco, Endgame)

311 TREGLOWN, JEREMY. "Fables from the Dark."
     Times Literary Supplement (London), 27 June
     1980, p. 726. (Company, memories)

312 TREWIN, J.C. "Waiting and Waiting." Il-
     lustrated London News, 1 Oct. 1955, p. 582.
     (Waiting for Godot)

313 _____. "The World of the Theatre: Busts, Urns,
     etc." Illustrated London News, 18 Apr. 1964,
     p. 620. (Play)

314 TYNAN, KENNETH. "Waiting for Godot." In
     Curtains. Selections from the Criticism and
     Related Writings. New York: Atheneum, p.
     272. (Bert Lahr)

315 ULIBARRI, SABINE R. "Mexican Anthology." New
     Mexico Quarterly 29, no. 3 (Autmun 1959):355-
     56. (Translations)

316   Van ITALLIE, JEAN-CLAUDE. "Alan Schneider." In
      Behind the Scenes: Theater and Film Inter-
      views from the Transatlantic Review. Edited
      by Joseph F. McCrindle. New York: Holt,
      Rinehart and Winston, 1971, pp. 279-92.
      (Form of Happy Days, content of Endgame)

317   VEDRES, NICOLE. "En Attendant Beckett."
      Mercure de France 330 (May 1957):134-36.
      (Endgame)

318   VERDOT, GUY. "Beckett continue d'attendre
      Godot." Figaro Littéraire, 12 Mar. 1960, p.
      3. (Krapp's Last Tape, biographical)

319   VICTOR, E. "Theatre." Tablet 227 (3 Feb.
      1973):110-11. (Krapp's Last Tape, Not I)

320   WALKER, ROY. "In the Rut." Listener 58 (19
      Dec. 1957):1047-48. (Molloy, "From an
      Abandoned Work")

321   _____ . "Samuel Beckett's Double Bill: Love,
      Chess and Death." Twentieth Century 164, no.
      982 (Dec. 1958):533-44.

322   WALL, STEPHEN. "Samuel Beckett." In History of
      Literature in the English Language, Vol. 7.
      The Twentieth Century. London: Barrie &
      Jenkins, 1970, pp. 224-28. (Themes in
      Beckett's novels: senility, human distress,
      isolation, unreliability of information)

323   "Watch Out, Buster, You're Being Watched." Life
      57, no. 7 (14 Aug. 1964):85-88. (Film)

324   WEST, PAUL. "Deciphering a Beckett Fiction on
      His Birthday." Parnassus 11, no. 2 (Fall-
      Winter, 1983 and Spring-Summer 1984):319-22.
      (Texts for Nothing)

325   _____ . "Hell or Heaven? Hell and Heaven?"
      Washington Post Book World 7, no. 52 (24 Dec.
      1972):5. (The Lost Ones)

326 WHEALE, NIGEL. "The Picture of Nobody." <u>Poetry</u>
      <u>Review</u>, Jan. 1979, pp. 56-57. (<u>Collected</u>
      <u>Poems in French and English</u>)

327 WILLIAMS, RAYMOND. <u>Modern Tragedy</u>. Stanford,
      Calif.: Stanford University Press; London:
      Chatto & Windus, 1966, pp. 153-55. (Polar
      opposition of characters in <u>Waiting for</u>
      <u>Godot</u>)

328 "Work Gave Theatre New Language." <u>Times</u>
      (London), 13 Dec. 1964, p. 4. (<u>Waiting for</u>
      <u>Godot</u>)

329 WORSLEY, T.C. "Cactus Land." <u>New Statesman and</u>
      <u>Nation</u> 50 (13 Aug. 1955):184-88. (<u>Waiting</u>
      <u>for Godot</u>, Comedy)

330 YOUNG, B.A. "Nottingham Playhouse. <u>Waiting for</u>
      <u>Godot</u>." <u>Financial Times</u>, 28 Jan. 1971, p. 3.

331 ZERAFFA, MICHEL. "Reprises importantes."
      <u>Europe</u> 39, nos. 387-88 (July-Aug. 1961):351-
      52. (<u>Waiting for Godot</u>, décor by Giacometti
      accentuates "solitude of theatrical space")

332 ZIMMER, CHRISTIAN. "Les Larmes de l'homme."
      <u>Temps Modernes</u> 22, no. 251 (Apr. 1967):1894-
      1902. Beckett: 1897-99. (<u>Film</u>, <u>Play</u>)

333 ZINNES, HARRIET. "<u>Molloy</u>." <u>Books Abroad</u> 31,
      no. 1 (Winter, 1957):30-31. (<u>Molloy</u>, Kafka)

334 _____. "<u>Murphy</u>." <u>Books Abroad</u> 32, no. 2.
      (Spring 1958):132.

Appendix B

A List of Articles and Books
that Briefly Mention Beckett or His Works,
or Provide Very General Information
about the Author*

1   "A First Glance at New Books." <u>Everyman</u>, 26
Mar. 1931, p. 270.

2   "A ne pas manquer cette semaine." <u>Nouvel
Observateur</u>, 9-15 Feb. 1970, p. 5.

3   "A partir du 28 février Ionesco, Beckett et
Pinget aux lundis du Théâtre de France."
<u>Monde</u>, 20 Jan. 1966, p. 12.

4   ABIRACHED, ROBERT. "Carnet de théâtre." <u>Etudes</u>
35 (Apr.-May-June 1960):404-7.

5   _____. <u>La Crise du personnage dans le théâtre
moderne</u>. Paris: Bernard Grasset, 1978, 506
pp.

6   _____. "Samuel Beckett." In <u>Ecrivains
d'aujourd'hui,1940-1960: Dictionnaire an-
thologique et critique</u>. Edited by Bernard
Pingaud. Paris: Grasset, 1960, pp. 93-98.

7   _____. "Sur le roman moderne en France."
<u>Français dans le Monde</u> 29 (Dec. 1964):6-9.

8   ADAMS, P. Review of <u>Mercier and Camier</u>.
<u>Atlantic Monthly</u> 235 (May 1975):104.

*References to entries in Appendix B will include
the number of the entry preceded by the letter B

574

9   ALBERES, R.-M. Métamorphoses du roman. Paris: Albin-Michel, 1966, pp. 140-41.

10 ALLAN, ELKAN. "Krapp Changes His Tape." Sunday Times (London), 26 Nov. 1972, p. 52.

11 ALLEN, BRUCE. "Samuel Beckett. Mercier and Camier." Library Journal 100 (15 May 1975):1007.

12 ALTER, ROBERT. Partial Magic: The Novel as a Self-Conscious Genre. Berkeley: University of California Press, 1975, 248 pp.

13 AMORY, MARK. "Women Alone." Spectator 249 (18-25 Dec. 1982):48-49.

14 ANSORGE, PETER. "World Theatre Season: What You Need to Know." Plays and Players 15, no. 8 (May 1968):52-55.

15 ANZIEU, DIDIER. Le Corps de l'oeuvre: Essais psychanalytiques sur le travail créateur. Paris: Editions Gallimard, 1981, 377 pp.

16 APPEL, ALFRED, Jr. "Conversations with Nabokov." Novel 4, no. 3 (Spring 1971):209-22.

17 ARCHWAY. "Spotlight on Rome. A Beckett Not Canonised." New Christian, no. 108 (13 Nov. 1969), p. 8.

18 ASHMORE, JEROME. "Interdisciplinary Roots of the Theater of the Absurd." Modern Drama 14, no. 1 (May 1971):72-83.

19 ASLAN, ODETTE. L'Acteur au XXe siècle. Paris: Editions Seghers, 1974, 398 pp.

20 ASTRE, G. ALBERT. "Notes." Critique 19 (Nov. 1963):1020-21.

21 No entry.

22 AULETTA, ROBERT. "Hello Columbus: A Playwright
    Explores Wonder and Terror." New Catholic
    World 218 (Jan.-Feb. 1975):23-27.

23 "Avant-Garde Plays on French Official Stage."
    Times (London), 19 Mar. 1966, p. 15.

24 "Avec Samuel Beckett: La Quête du mal dire."
    Monde, 10 Oct. 1981, p. 1.

25 AVRECH, MIRA. "A Friend Recalls Affectionately
    a Shy Nobel Prize Playwright Named Samuel
    Beckett." People Weekly, 13 Apr. 1981, pp.
    75, 79-80.

26 B., J.R. "Short Notices." Critical Quarterly
    22, no. 3 (Autumn 1980):93.

27 BABY, YVONNE. "Au Festival du court métrage de
    Tours: Conformisme des documentaires et
    actualité du Temps de Locuste." Monde,
    1 Feb. 1967, p. 18.

28 BALAKIAN, ANNA. "Relativism in the Arts, and
    the Road to the Absolute." In Relativism in
    the Arts. Edited by Betty Jean Craige.
    Athens: University of Georgia Press, 1983,
    pp. 75-98.

29 BALTA, PAUL. "En bref. Etranger: Théâtre
    français en Algérie." Monde [des Arts et des
    Spectacles], 20 June 1974, p. 22.

30 BANVILLE, JOHN. "Out of the Abyss." Irish
    University Review 14, no. 1 (Spring 1984):
    102.

31 BARBER, JOHN. "Double Study of Scared Souls."
    Daily Telegraph (London), 30 Jan. 1975, p.
    13.

32 _____. "Max Wall's Study in Tough Loneliness."
    Daily Telegraph (London), 4 Dec. 1975, p. 15.

33   _____. "World Theatre: Beckett's Grim Plays of Disillusion." <u>Daily Telegraph</u> (London), 30 Apr. 1971, p. 14.

34   BARBOUR, THOMAS. "Beckett and Ionesco." <u>Hudson Review</u> 11, no. 2 (Summer 1958):271-77.

35   BARISSE, RITA. "Books and Bookmen Abroad: Paris." <u>Books and Bookmen</u> 1 (Dec. 1955):56.

36   BARJON, LOUIS. "Une littérature de 'décomposition'?" <u>Etudes</u> 311 (Oct. 1961):45-60.

37   BARRAULT, JEAN-LOUIS. "Notre 'petite salle.'" <u>Cahiers Renaud-Barrault</u> 44 (Oct. 1963):3-5.

38   _____. "Un théâtre-laboratoire." <u>Nouvel Observateur</u>, no. 274 (9-15 Feb. 1970), p. 42.

39   BARTHES, ROLAND. "Le Théâtre français d'avant-garde." <u>Français dans le Monde</u>, no. 2 (June-July 1961), pp. 10-15.

40   BASTIAENEN, ETIENNE. "Où va le théâtre? 1. Le Théâtre occidental: Eclatement ou renaissance?" <u>Revue Nouvelle</u> 75, no. 2 (Feb. 1982):179-88.

41   BATEMAN, MICHAEL. "Waiting for Beckett." <u>Sunday Times</u> (London), 16 Nov. 1969.

42   BAXENDALL, LEE. "The Revolutionary Moment." <u>Drama Review</u> 13, no. 2 (Winter 1968):92-107.

43   BAXTER, K.M. <u>Speak What We Feel: A Christian Look at the Contemporary Theatre</u>. London: SCM Press, 1964, pp. 80-83.

44   BEAUFORT, JOHN. "New York, Off Broadway." <u>International Theatre Annual</u>, no. 5 (1961), pp. 68-83.

45   "Beckett Film Causes an Uproar at Festival." <u>Times</u> (London), 3 Sept. 1966, p. 6.

46 "Beckett/Fugard Double Bill." _Times_ (London), 23 Jan. 1975, p. 8.

47 "Beckett on Proust." _Times Literary Supplement_ (London), 30 Dec. 1965, p. 1208.

48 "Beckett, Samuel: _Ends and odds: Eight New Dramatic Pieces_." _Choice_ 14, no. 4 (Apr. 1977):196.

49 "Beckett-sur-scène." _Nouvel Observateur_, no. 881 (26 Sept.- 2 Oct. 1981), p. 100.

50 "Beckett's Challenge to Irish Actor." _Times_ (London), 26 Nov. 1965, p. 15.

51 "Beginning to End." _Radio Times_, 3 Aug. 1967, p. 23.

52 BEIGBEDER, MARC. "Le Théâtre à l'âge métaphysique." _Age Nouveau_ 9, no. 85 (Jan. 1954):30-41.

53 _____. _Le Théâtre en France depuis la libération_. Paris: Bordas, 1959, pp. 142-44 and _passim_.

54 BENEDETTI, ROBERT. "Metanaturalism: The Metaphorical Use of Environment in the Modern Theatre." _Chicago Review_ 17, nos. 2-3 (1964):24-32.

55 BENNETT, KENNETH C. "The Affective Aspect of Comedy." _Genre_ 14, no. 2 (Summer 1981):191-205.

56 BENTLEY, ERIC. _The Theatre of Commitment and Other Essays on Drama in Our Society_. London: Methuen & Co. Ltd., 1968, 241 pp.

57 BERGONZI, BERNARD. "Character and Liberalism." _New Blackfriars_ 50, no. 594 (Nov. 1969):745-53.

58   _____. The Situation of the Novel. London:
       Macmillan, 1970, 226 pp.

59   BERMAN, AUDRY. "Off Stage." Village Voice, 19
       Apr. 1973, p. 77.

60   BILLINGTON, MICHAEL. "Krapp/Not I at the Royal
       Court." Guardian, 17 Jan. 1973, p. 8.

61   BLANCHOT, MAURICE. "A Rose is a Rose ..."
       Nouvelle Revue Française 11 (July 1963):86-
       93.

62   _____. L'Espace littéraire. Paris: Gallimard,
       1955, 295 pp.

63   BLAU, HERBERT. "The Popular, the Absurd, and
       the Entente Cordiale." Tulane Drama Review
       5, no. 3 (Mar. 1961):119-51.

64   _____. "Precipitations of Theater: Words,
       Presence, Time Out of Mind." In Psychology
       and Literature: Some Contemporary Direc-
       tions. Baltimore, Md.: John Hopkins
       University Press, 1980, pp. 127-45.

65   BLEIKASTEN, ANDRE. "Faulkner et le nouveau
       roman." Langues Modernes 60, no. 4 (July-
       Aug. 1966):54-64.

66   BLOCH-MICHEL, J. "Nouveau roman et culture des
       masses." Preuves 121 (Mar. 1961):17-28.

67   _____. Le Présent de l'indicatif, essai sur le
       nouveau roman. Paris: Gallimard, 1963, 142
       pp.

68   BOISDEFFRE, PIERRE de. "L'Anti-Théâtre total:
       Samuel Beckett ou la mort de l'homme." In
       Une histoire vivante de la littérature
       d'aujourd'hui, 1938-1958. Paris: Le Livre
       Contemporain, 1958, pp. 678-80.

69 _____. Les Ecrivains français d'aujourd'hui.
Paris: Presses Universitaires de France,
1967, 127 pp.

70 _____. Où va le roman?" Table Ronde 164 (Sept.
1961):15-27.

71 _____. "Samuel Beckett." In Dictionnaire de
littérature contemporaine. Paris: Editions
Universitaires, 1962, pp. 180-86.

72 _____. "Samuel Beckett ou l'au-delà." In Une
histoire vivante de la littérature
d'aujourd'hui, 1938-1958. Paris: Le Livre
Contemporain, 1958, pp. 299-300.

73 _____. "Un nouveau roman français." Etudes 301
(Apr. 1959):70-79.

74 BONDY, FRANÇOIS. "France: The New Puritans."
Censorship, no. 1 (Autumn 1964), pp. 7-9.

75 BONNEFOI, GENEVIEVE. "Livres-jouets pour
adultes." Nouvel Observateur, 8-14 Feb.
1967, p. 43.

76 [BONNEFOY, CLAUDE]. "Samuel Beckett." In
Dictionnaire de littérature française
contemporaine. Edited by Claude Bonnefoy,
Tony Cartano, and Daniel Oster. Paris:
Jean-Pierre Delange, 1977, pp. 40-44.

77 BOOTH, WAYNE C. Critical Understanding. The
Powers and Limits of Pluralism. Chicago and
London: University of Chicago Press, 1979,
408 pp.

78 BOUCHE, CLAUDE. "La Théorie littéraire
matéraliste en France (1965-1975)." Revue
des Langues Vivantes 43, no. 1 (1977):3-22.

79 BOULTON, MARJORIE. The Anatomy of the Novel.
London and Boston: Routledge & Kegan Paul,
1975, 199 pp.

80   BOURGEADE, PIERRE. "Quinze jours: Mai
     revient." <u>Quinzaine Littéraire</u>, no. 27 (1-15
     May 1967), p. 28.

81   BOURQUE, JOSEPH H. "Theatre of the Absurd: A
     New Approach to Audience Reaction." <u>Research
     Studies</u> 36, no. 4 (Dec. 1968):311-24.

82   BRAY, BERNARD. "La Notion de structure dans le
     nouveau roman." In <u>La Notion de structure</u>.
     Edited by Samuel Dresden, Levi Geshiere, and
     Bernard Bray. La Haye: Van Goor Zonen,
     1961, pp. 51-68.

83   BRECHON, R. "Le Confort intellectuel."
     <u>Français dans le Monde</u> 17 (June 1963):6-7.

84   BREE, GERMAINE. <u>The Contemporary French Novel,
     1950-1960</u>. New York: Cultural Services of
     the French Embassy, 1960, 6 pp.

85   _____. <u>French Theater Today, 1950-60</u>. New
     York: Cultural Services of the French
     Embassy, 1959, 7 pp.

86   "Briefing: Vanishing Trick." <u>Observer</u>, 3 July
     1966, p. 18.

87   BRENNER, JACQUES. <u>Journal de la vie littéraire
     (1964-1966)</u>. Vol. 2. Paris: René Julliard,
     1966, 307 pp.

88   BRINCOURT, ANDRE. <u>Les Ecrivains du XXe siècle.
     Un Musée imaginaire de la littérature
     mondiale</u>. Paris: Editions Retz, 1979, pp.
     92-96.

89   BROADBENT, JOHN BARLAY. "Allegory of the
     Windvane." <u>Spectator</u> 208 (6 Apr. 1962):453-
     54.

90   BROCKETT, OSCAR G. <u>The Theatre: An Introduc-
     tion</u> New York: Holt, Rinehard and Winston,
     1969, 607 pp.

91   BROMBERT, VICTOR. The Romantic Prison. The
      French Tradition. Princeton, N.J.:   Prince-
      ton University Press, 1978, 241 pp.

92   BROOKE-ROSE, CHRISTINE. "Dynamic Gradients."
      London Magazine 4, no. 12 (Mar. 1965):89-96.

93   BROWN, JOHN RUSSELL. "Dialogue in Pinter and
      Others." Critical Quarterly 7 (Autumn
      1965):225-43.

94   BRUSTEIN, ROBERT. "On Theater." New Republic
      168, no. 7 (17 Feb. 1973):20.

95   BRYDEN, RONALD. "Theatre: Vintage '58."
      Cambridge Review 76 (15 Jan. 1955):257.

96   BUCHET, EDMOND. Les Auteurs de ma vie ou ma vie
      d'éditeur. Paris: Buchet-Chastel, 1969, 354
      pp.

97   BULL, PETER. "Waiting for God knows What."
      Plays and Players 3, no. 8 (May 1956):7.

98   BURGESS, ANTHONY. "Master Beckett." Spectator
      219 (21 July 1967):79.

99   "Busy Theater Life in Warsaw." Times (London),
      12 Aug. 1963, p. 12.

100   C., G. "La Rentrée au théâtre: II. --
      Spectacles d'une durée limitée et salles à
      vocation populaire." Monde, 2 Sept. 1970, p.
      15.

101   CAIN, ALEX MATHESON. "Exploring Old Avenues."
      Tablet, 25 July 1964, p. 838.

102   CAMBON, GLAUCO. "Immediacies and Distances."
      Poetry 95 (Mar. 1960):379-81.

103   CAMP, ANDRE. "L'Actualité théâtrale." Avant-
      Scène, no. 492 (1 Apr. 1972), pp. 38-39.

104   CARTER, THOMAS H. "Molloy." Shenandoah 7, no.
          3 (Summer 1956):53-54.

105   CATTAUI, GEORGES. "Proust et les lettres anglo-
          américaines." Table Ronde 192 (Jan.
          1964):36-47.

106   CAUTE, DAVID. The Illusion. An Essay on
          Politics, Theatre and the Novel. London:
          Panther Books Limited, 1972, 267 pp.

107   CAVAN, ROMILLY. "Drama." Books and Bookmen 17,
          no. 8 (May 1972):76-78.

108   "Chahut pour une comédie." Monde, 30 Aug. 1966,
          p. 10.

109   CHALON, JEAN. "Les Débuts obscurs d'écrivains
          célèbres." Figaro Littéraire, 11 Mar. 1972,
          pp. 13-14.

110   _____. "Lettres: Cette Semaine ... Revolution
          dans le livre? Du livre-objet ..." Figaro
          Littéraire, 31 July-6 Aug. 1967, p. 16.

111   CHAMBERS, ROSS. "French Wheezes." Nation
          (Sydney), no. 113 (23 Feb. 1963), p. 18.

112   CHAMPIGNY, ROBERT. Le Genre romanesque, essai.
          Monte Carlo: Regain, 1963, 189 pp.

113   CHAPSAL, MADELEINE. "Le Jeune Roman." Express,
          12 Jan. 1961, p. 31.

114   CHARAIRE, GEORGES. "Realism and the Crisis of
          Reason." New Hungarian Quarterly 6, no. 20
          (Winter 1965):92-98.

115   CHESHIRE, DAVID. "The First Season at Stoke-on-
          Trent." Prompt, no. 3 (1963), p. 33.

116   CHIARI, JOSEPH. The Aesthetics of Modernism.
          London: Vision Press, 1970, pp. 120-21.

117   _____. The Contemporary French Theatre -- The
       Flight from Naturalism. London: Rockliff,
       1958, p. 226.

118   CLEVERDON, DOUGLAS. "Radio Features and Drama
       at the BBC." Times Literary Supplement
       (London), 26 Feb. 1970, pp. 229-30.

119   CLOUARD, HENRI and R. LEGGEWIE. French Writers
       of Today. New York: Oxford University
       Press, 1965, 364 pp.

120   CLURMAN, HAROLD. "The Idea of the Theater: A
       Conversation with Digby R. Diehl." Transat-
       lantic Review 16 (Summer 1964):17-24.

121   _____. "Theatre." Nation 184 (22 June 1957):
       554-56.

122   _____. "Theatre." Nation 212, no. 18 (3 May
       1971):570-72.

123   COHN, DORRIT C. Transparent Minds. Narrative
       Modes for Presenting Consciousness in
       Fiction. Princeton, N.J.: Princeton
       University Press, 1978, 331 pp.

124   COHN, ROBERT GREER. The Writer's Way in France.
       Philadelphia: University of Pennsylvania
       Press; London: Oxford University Press,
       1960, 447 pp.

125   COHN, RUBY. "European Theatre, Spring 1966, a
       Sampling." Drama Survey 5, no. 3 (Winter
       1966-67):286-92.

126   _____. "The World of Harold Pinter." Tulane
       Drama Review 6, no. 3 (Mar. 1962):55-68.

127   COLEBY, J. "Plays in Print: Ends and Odds by
       Samuel Beckett." Drama / The Quarterly
       Theatre Review, no. 125 (Summer 1977), pp.
       75-77.

584

128   _____. "Plays in Print: <u>Footfalls</u>." <u>Drama /
The Quarterly Theatre Review</u>, no. 123 (Winter
1976), p. 70.

129   _____. "Plays in Print: <u>Happy Days/Oh les
beaux jours</u> by Samuel Beckett." <u>Drama / The
Quarterly Theatre Review</u>, no. 129 (Summer
1978), pp. 84-86.

130   COLLINS, R.G. "Divagations on the novel as
Experiment." <u>Mosaic</u> 4, no. 3 (Spring
1971):1-11.

131   COLMANT, G. "La Recherche de l'absolu." <u>Revue
Nouvelle</u> 36, no. 9 (15 Sept. 1962):235-39.

132   "Comment - <u>Waiting for Godot</u>." <u>Meanjin</u> 15, no.
2 (Winter 1956):132.

133   CONCHON, GEORGES. "Lettres aux radicaux de la
littérature non figurative." <u>Figaro Lit-
téraire</u>, 20-26 Apr. 1970, pp. 14-15.

134   COOKE, RICHARD P. "The Theatre." <u>Wall Street
Journal</u>, 26 Mar. 1964, p. 14.

135   COPPAY, FRANK L. "Mini-max Discourse." <u>Sub-
Stance</u>, no. 26 (1980), pp. 19-26.

136   CORRIGAN, BEATRICE. "Pirandello and the Theatre
of the Absurd." <u>Cesare Barbieri Courier</u> 8
(Spring 1966):3-6.

137   COURNOT, MICHEL. "... Et à la Cartoucherie de
Vincennes: <u>Textes pour rien</u> par J.-C. Fall."
<u>Monde</u>, 8 Oct. 1981, p. 25.

138   COVENEY, MICHAEL. "Royal court: <u>Not I /
Statements</u>." <u>Financial Times</u>, 30 Jan. 1975,
p. 3.

139   COX, C.B. and A.E. DYSON, eds. <u>The Twentieth
Century Mind. History, Ideas, and Literature
in Britain. III. 1945-65.</u> London, Oxford,

and New York: Oxford University Press, 1972, pp. 428-34.

140 COX, JAMES T., MARGARET PUTNAM, and MARVIN WILLIAMS. "Textual Studies in the Novel: A Selected Checklist, 1950-74." <u>Studies in the Novel</u> 7, no. 3 (Fall 1975):470.

141 CRAIG, H.A.L. "Poetry in the Theater." <u>New Statesman</u> 60 (12 Nov. 1960):734-36.

142 "<u>Les Créatures</u> et <u>Comédie</u> au Festival de Venise." <u>Monde</u>, 9 July 1966, p. 10.

143 CRICKILLON, JACQUES. "Tradition et subversion en littérature." <u>Marginales</u> 25, no. 8 (Dec. 1970):1-14.

144 CRINKLAW, DON. "Tests to Pass." <u>National Review</u> 25, no. 3 (19 Jan. 1973):101-2.

145 CRUTTWELL, PATRICK. "Fiction Chronicle." <u>Hudson Review</u> 17, no. 2 (Summer 1964):303-11.

146 CUNNINGHAM, VALENTINE. "Money Talks." <u>New Statesman</u> 88 (18 Oct. 1974):546.

147 CURLEY, DOROTHY. "Beckett, Samuel. <u>Stories and Texts for Nothing</u>." <u>Library Journal</u> 92 (July 1967):2600.

148 CURTIS, JEAN-LOUIS. <u>Un miroir le long du chemin: Journal (1950-1958)</u>. Paris: Julliard, 1969, 283 pp.

149 CUSHMAN, KEITH. "Beckett, Samuel. <u>The Lost Ones</u>." <u>Library Journal</u> 98 (1 Jan. 1973):84.

150 D., J.-M. "En bref. Recherche: <u>Comédie</u> de Samuel Beckett à la Biennale." <u>Monde</u>, 3 Oct. 1973, p. 23.

151 DAMIENS, CLAUDE. "Regards sur le 'theatre nouveau': Beckett, Ionesco, Genet, Duras,

Adamov." Paris-Théâtre, no. 173 (1961), pp. 12-13.

152   DAVIS, ROBERT GORHAM. "Rimbaud and Stravrogen in the Havard Yard." New York Times Book Review, 28 June 1970, pp. 2, 38.

153   DAWSON, HELEN. "Drama: The Enigmatic Nobel Prizewinner." Socialist Commentary, Dec. 1969, pp. 36-37.

154   DELEUZE, GILLES, and FELIX GUATTARI. Capitalisme et schizophrénie: L'Anti-Oedipe. Paris: Editions de Minuit, 1972, 470 pp.

155   D[ETREZ], C[ONRAD]. "Sous le signe de Beckett." Magazine Littéraire, no. 165 (Oct. 1980), pp. 70-71.

156   DHINGRA, BALDOON. "Leaves from a Paris Diary." Aryan Path 28, no. 5 (May 1957):284-85.

157   DHOMME, S. "Des auteurs à l'avant-garde du théâtre." Cahiers Renaud-Barrault 3, no. 13 (Oct. 1955):112-18.

158   DOMENACH, JEAN-MARIE. "Résurrection de la tragédie." Esprit 338 (May 1965):995-1015.

159   DONOGHUE, DENIS. "How It Was." New Statesman, 25 Mar. 1966, p. 428.

160   _____. The Ordinary Universe: Soundings in Modern Literature. London: Faber and Faber, 1968, 320 pp.

161   DRIVER, TOM F. "Search for Conflict." Nation 194 (21 Apr. 1962), pp. 350-54.

162   "Dublin Honorary Degres." Times (London), 26 Feb. 1959, p. 12.

163   DUCKWORTH, COLIN. "Introduction." AUMLA 55 (May 1981):5-6.

164 DUMUR, GUY. "Des bouffons sagaces." <u>Nouvel</u>
     <u>Observateur</u>, no. 500 (10-16 June 1974), p. 77.

165 _____. "Les Métamorphoses du théâtre d'avant-
     garde (à propos de cinq reprises récentes)."
     <u>Théâtre Populaire</u>, no. 42 (2nd trim. 1961),
     pp. 100-106.

166 _____. "Le Nouveau Roman." <u>France-Observateur</u>,
     9 Mar. 1961, pp. 15-17.

167 DUQUESNE, JACQUES. <u>Dieu pour l'homme</u>
     <u>d'aujourd'hui</u>. Paris: Grasset, 1970, 308 pp.

168 _____. "Dieu revient." <u>Express</u>, 30 Mar.-5 Apr.
     1970, pp. 30-33.

169 DUSSANE, BEATRIX. "<u>La Dernière Bande</u>." <u>Mercure</u>
     <u>de France</u> 339 (June 1960):317-19.

170 DUVIGNAUD, JEAN. "Au delà du langage." <u>Théâtre</u>
     <u>de France</u> 4 (1954):64.

171 _____. <u>The Sociology of Art</u>. Trans. by Timothy
     Wilson. London: Paladin, 1967, 159 pp.

172 _____. <u>Le Théâtre, et après</u>. Paris: Casterman,
     1971, 148 pp.

173 EASTMAN, RICHARD M. "The Open Parable:
     Demonstration and Definition." <u>College</u>
     <u>English</u> 22, no. 1 (Oct. 1960):15-18.

174 "Ecrivains." <u>Quinzaine Littéraire</u>, no. 19 (1-15
     Jan. 1967), p. 15.

175 "Edition." <u>Express</u>, 11-17 May 1970, p. 63.

176 "<u>Eh, Joe</u>: Plans." <u>Times</u> (London), 26 Nov. 1965,
     p. 15.

177 ELSOM, JOHN. "A Thread over Ruins." <u>Listener</u>, 1
     Apr. 1976, pp. 415-16.

588

178 _____. "Beckett Country." <u>Listener</u> 105 (25 June 1981):825-26.

179 _____. "Recantation." <u>Listener</u> 104 (21 Aug. 1980):252-53.

180 _____. "Samuel Beckett, Max Wall and Me." <u>Contemporary Review</u> 242 (May 1983):261-65.

181 _____. "Side by Side-Step." <u>Listener</u>, 13 May 1976, p. 67.

182 "English and French." <u>Times Literary Supplement</u> (London), 27 May 1960, p. 337.

183 ENNIS, JULIAN. "Waiting for Godot [poem]." <u>Anglo-Welsh Review</u> 15, no. 36 (Summer 1966):55.

184 ERVAL, FRANÇOIS. "Le Prix B. B." <u>Express</u> 11, May 1961, pp. 33-34.

185 "The Essential Q." <u>Times Literary Supplement</u> (London), 30 June 1966, p. 570. Reprinted: 1979.22.61.

186 ESSLIN, MARTIN. <u>An Anatomy of Drama</u>. New York: Hill and Wang, 1977, 125 pp.

187 _____. "The Mind as a Stage." <u>Theatre Quarterly</u> 1, no. 3 (July-Sept 1971):5-11.

188 _____. <u>The People Wound: The Plays of Harold Pinter</u>. London, 1970, 280 pp.

189 _____. "Pinter and the Absurd." <u>Twentieth Century</u> 169 (Feb. 1961):176-85.

190 _____. "The Theater of the Absurd." <u>Tulane Drama Review</u> 4 (May 1960):3-15. Reprint: <u>Essays in the Modern Drama</u>. Edited by Morris Freedman. Boston: D.C. Heath, 1964, pp. 320-34.

191 EWART, GAVIN. "Play by Samuel Beckett." London
     Magazine 4, no. 2 (May 1964):95-96.

192 F., S. "Beckett au Festival de Royan." Quin-
     zaine Littéraire, no. 93 (16-30 Apr. 1970), p.
     27.

193 "FANTASIO." "Ce Mois qui court." Revue Générale
     Belge 89 (Mar. 1953):994-1000.

194 FAUCHEREAU, SERGE. Philippe Soupault: Vingt
     mille et un jours: Entretiens avec Serge
     Fauchereau. Paris: Pierre Belfond, 1980, 286
     pp.

195 FEDERMAN, RAYMOND. "A Writer's Forum on Moral
     Fiction." Fiction International, no. 12
     (1980), pp. 10-11.

196 FENTON, JAMES. "The Comic Side of a Search for
     Death." Sunday Times (London), 3 Aug. 1980,
     p. 38.

197 FIESCHI, JEAN-ANDRE, and ANDRE TECHINE. "Venise
     65: Commentaires." Cahiers du Cinéma, no.
     171 (Oct. 1965), pp. 47-53.

198 "Film of Waiting for Godot." Times (London), 4
     Sept. 1962, p. 7.

199 FITCH, BRIAN. "Bardamu dans sa nuit à lui."
     Bulletin des Jeunes Romanistes 8 (Dec.
     1963):31-36.

200 No entry.

201 FLOWER, DEAN. "Fiction Chronicle." Hudson
     Review 30, no. 2 (Summer 1977):299-312.

202 FORD, BORIS, ed. The Modern Age. Baltimore,
     Md.: Penguin, 1963, 559 pp.

203 "Forty-eight Playwrights in Apartheid Protest."
     Times (London), 26 June 1963, p. 12D.

590

204   FOWLER, ROGER. <u>Linguistics and the Novel</u>.
       London: Methuen and Co. Ltd., 1977.

205   FOWLIE, WALLACE. <u>French Literature: Its History
       and Its Meaning</u>. Englewood Cliffs, N.J.:
       Prentice-Hall, Inc., 1973, 369 pp.

206   _____. "The French Novel: Quests and Ques-
       tions." In <u>The Languages of Criticism and the
       Sciences of Man: The Structuralist Controver-
       sy</u>. Edited by Richard Macksey and Eugenio
       Donato. Baltimore, Md.: John Hopkins
       University Press, pp. 39-68.

207   "French Plays in London." <u>Times</u> (London), 4 Feb.
       1976, p. 9.

208   FRIEDMAN, MELVIN J. "Book Reviews." <u>Wisconsin
       Studies in Contemporary Literature</u> 3, no. 3
       (Fall 1962):100-106.

209   _____. "John Hawkes and Flannery O'Connor. The
       French Background." <u>Boston University Journal</u>
       21, no. 3 (Fall 1973):34-44.

210   _____. "The Neglect of Time: France's Novel of
       the Fifties." <u>Books Abroad</u> 36 (Spring
       1962):125-30.

211   G., P.-A. "Théâtre d'hier et d'aujourd'hui."
       <u>Nouvelles Littéraires</u>, 29 Oct. 1970, p. 13.

212   GALEY, MATTHIEU. "Vingt ans après ou les
       survivants du nouveau roman." <u>Express</u>, 4 Apr.
       1981, pp. 26-27.

213   GASSNER, JOHN and EDWARD QUINN, eds. <u>The
       Reader's Encyclopedia of World Drama</u>. New
       York, 1969, p. 56.

214   GAUDY, RENE. <u>Arthur Adamov</u>. Paris: Stock,
       1971.

215   GELB, P. "Strictly Controversial: Most
      Playwrights are Fascists." <u>Tulane Drama
      Review</u> 3, no. 1 (Oct. 1958):58-60.

216   GELLERT, R. "Catch 62." <u>New Statesman</u> 65 (4
      Jan. 1963):24-25.

217   GERARD, MARTIN. "Is Your Novel Really Neces-
      sary?" <u>X: A Quarterly Review</u> 1, no. 1 (Nov.
      1959):46-52.

218   GERHART, MARY. "The 'New' Literature and
      Contemporary Religious Consciousness."
      <u>Anglican Theological Review</u> 62, no. 1 (Jan.
      1980):42-63.

219   GIBNEY, FRANK. "The 'Nothing' Plays and How They
      Have Grown on Us." <u>Horizon</u> 1, no. 2 (Nov.
      1958):62-65.

220   GIBSON, ROBERT. "Letter from Paris." <u>London
      Magazine</u> 1, no. 3 (Apr. 1954):56-61.

221   GIELGRID, VAL. <u>Years in a Mirror</u>. London, 1965.

222   GILBERT, STUART, ed. <u>Letters of James Joyce</u>.
      London: Faber, 1957, 437 pp.

223   GILLOT, JACKY. "Festival Talk." <u>Listener</u>, 28
      Aug. 1980, p. 283.

224   GILMAN, RICHARD. "Out Goes Absurdism -- in Comes
      the New Naturalism." <u>New York Times</u>, 19 Mar.
      1978, p. 6.

225   GIRARD, GILLES, REAL OUELLET, and CLAUDE RIGAULT.
      <u>L'Univers du théâtre</u>. Paris: Presses
      Universitaires de France, 1978, 230 pp.

226   GIRARD, MARCEL. <u>Guide illustré de la littérature
      française moderne de 1918 à nos jours</u>. Paris:
      Pierre Seghers, 1949, 350 pp.

227   GIRARD, R. "Où va le roman?" <u>French Review</u> 30
      (Jan. 1957):201-6.

228   GIRODIAS, MAURICE.   "Confessions of a Bootleg-
        ger's Son."   <u>Censorship</u>, no. 3 (Summer 1965),
        pp. 2-16.

229   GLAVIN, ANTHONY.   "<u>Eh Joe and Other Writings</u> by
        Samuel Beckett."   <u>Dublin Magazine</u> 6, nos. 3 &
        4 (Autumn/Winter 1967):91-92.

230   GLEN-DOEPEL, WILLIAM.   "Dead Centre."   <u>Tablet</u> 224
        (9 May 1970):456.

231   GODARD, COLETTE.   "Beckett au Festival d'automne
        ... <u>Premier Amour</u>, par Christian Colin."
        <u>Monde</u>, 8 Oct. 1981, p. 25.

232   _____.   "Beckett-Barbeau au Lucernaire."   <u>Monde</u>,
        11 Apr. 1975, p. 27.

233   _____.   "'Ils allaient obscurs sous la nuit
        solitaire; d'après Samuel Beckett."   <u>Monde</u>, 9
        Nov. 1979, p. 30.

234   _____.   "Une grande saison de théâtre à Milan:
        <u>Les Bas-Fonds</u>, vus par Giorgio Strehler."
        <u>Monde</u>, 10 Dec. 1970, p. 17.

235   "Godot, Go Home."   In <u>The Village Voice Reader:
        A Mixed Bag from the Greenwich Village
        Newspaper</u>.   Edited by Daniel Wolf and Edwin
        Fancher.   Garden City, N.Y.:   Doubleday, 1962,
        p. 84.

236   GOODHEART, EUGENE.   <u>The Cult of the Ego.   The
        Self in Modern Literature</u>.   Chicago and
        London: University of Chicago Press, 1968,
        225 pp.

237   GOODLAD, J.S.R.   <u>A Sociology of Popular Drama</u>.
        London, 1971, 240 pp.

238   GORDON, GILES.   "Stopped People Shouldn't Start."
        <u>Books and Bookmen</u> 2, no. 4 (Jan. 1966):48-52.

239   GORELICK, MORDECAI.   "An Epic Theatre Catechism."
        <u>Tulane Drama Review</u> 4, no. 1 (Sept. 1959):90-
        95.

240   GORMAN, HERBERT SHERMAN. <u>James Joyce, A Defini-
      tive Biography</u>. London: John Lane, 1941, 354
      pp.

241   GOTTESMAN, RONALD and SCOTT BENNETT, eds. <u>Art
      and Error: Modern Textual Editing</u>. London:
      Methuen & Co. Ltd., 1970, 317 pp.

242   GOUHIER, HENRI. "Le Théâtre." <u>Table Ronde</u> 159
      (Mar. 1961):179.

243   _____. "Le Théâtre." <u>Table Ronde</u> 163 (July-
      Aug. 1961):145-49.

244   _____. "Le Théâtre." <u>Table Ronde</u> 164 (Sept.
      1961):151.

245   GRAY, WALLACE. "The Uses of Incongruity."
      <u>Educational Theater Journal</u> 15, no. 4 (Dec.
      1963):343-47.

246   GRIGSON, GEOFFREY, ed. <u>The Concise Encyclopedia
      of Modern World Literature</u>. London: Hutchin-
      son; New York: Hawthorn Books, 1963, 512 pp.

247   GRUBER, WILLIAM E. "The Wild Men of Comedy:
      Transformations in the Comic Hero from
      Aristophanes to Pirandello." <u>Genre</u> 14, no. 2
      (Summer 1981):207-27.

248   GUGGENHEIM, PEGGY. "Confessions of Peggy
      Guggenheim." <u>Guardian</u>, 29 Dec. 1979, p. 7.

249   GUITON, MARGARET and GERMAINE BREE. <u>An Age of
      Fiction</u>. New Brunswick, N.J.: Rutgers
      University Press, 1957, p. 237.

250   GUTHKE, KARL. <u>Modern Tragicomedy: An Investiga-
      tion into the Nature of the Genre</u>. New York:
      Random House, 1966, 204 pp.

251   H., N. "Caviare to the General." <u>Dublin
      Magazine</u> 2 (July-Sept. 1934):84-85.

594

252 HAFLEY, JAMES. "The Human Image in Contemporary Art." Kerygma 3 (Summer 1963):25-34.

253 HAMILTON, IAIN. "Nonfiction." Illustrated London News 251 (5 Aug. 1967):28-29.

254 HANDMAN, WYNN. "'Let These New Plays Happen to You.'" New York Times, 20 Mar. 1977, pp. 28-35.

255 HANOTEAU, GUILLAUME. "Beckett un Prix Nobel irlandais qui écrit son oeuvre en français." Paris-Match, 1 Nov. 1969, pp. 28-29.

256 Hassan, Ihab and Sally Hassan, eds. Innovation/Renovation. New Perspectives on the Humanities. Madison: University of Wisconsin Press, 1983, 373 pp.

257 HAYMAN, DAVID. "The Unnamable." Texas Quarterly 1, no. 2 (Spring 1958):127-28.

258 HAYTER, AUGY. "Beckett Old and New." Plays and Players 13, no. 9 (June 1966):69.

259 HEILMAN, ROBERT BECHTOLD. Tragedy and Melodrama. Versions of Experience. Seattle and London: University of Washington Press, 1968, 326 pp.

260 HENDERSON, ROBIN A. "Beckett Country." Spectator 199 (4 Oct. 1957):434.

261 HEPBURN, NEIL. "Company Limited." Listener, 31 July 1980, p. 155.

262 HEPPENSTALL, RAYNER. The Intellectual Part. London: Barrie and Rockliff, 1963.

263 HIGGINS, AIDAN. "Beckett in Berlin." Atlantis, no. 1 (Mar. 1970), pp. 53-54.

264 HINCHLIFFE, ARNOLD P. Modern Verse Drama. London: Methuen and Co. Ltd., 1977, 80 pp.

265   HIRSCH, FOSTER. "What Makes Drama Dramatic."
       Nation 219, no. 11 (12 Oct. 1974):346-47.

266   HOBSON, HAROLD. "Back to the Wall." Sunday
       Times (London), 7 Dec. 1975, p. 39.

267   HODGART, MATTHEW. "Nevertheless." Guardian, 21
       July 1967, p. 5.

268   HOFFMAN, FREDERICK J. "The Religious Crisis in
       Modern Literature." Comparative Literature
       Studies 3, no. 3 (1966):263-72.

269   HOFSTADTER, ALBERT. "The Tragicomic: Concern in
       Depth." Journal of Aesthetics and Art
       Criticism 24, no. 2 (Winter 1965):295-302.

270   HOMAN, SIDNEY. "When the Theater Turns to
       Itself." New Literary History 2 (1971):407-
       17.

271   [Honorary Degree]. Times (London), 3 July 1959,
       p. 9.

272   HOPE-WALLACE, PHILIP. "Beckett Plays at the
       Aldwych." Guardian, 30 Apr. 1971, p. 10.

273   _____. "Theatre." Time and Tide 39 (8 Nov.
       1958):1344-45.

274   HOPPER, STANLEY R. "Irony, the Pathos of the
       Middle." Crosscurrents 12, no. 1 (Winter
       1962):31-40.

275   HORN, JOHN. "Beckett and Ionesco: The Acting is
       Good." New York Herald Tribune, 19 Apr. 1966,
       p. 23.

276   HOWARD, MAUREEN, HUGH KUNE, and LEONARD MICHAELS.
       "Writers' Writers." New York Times Book
       Review, 4 Dec. 1977, pp. 3, 58, 62.

277   HOWARD, MICHAEL S. Jonathan Cape, Publisher:
       Herbert Jonathan Cape, G. Wren Howard (1921-
       1971). London: Jonathan Cape, 1971, p. 137.

278   HUBBS, CLAYTON A.   "Chekhov and the Contemporary
      Theatre."   Modern Drama 34, no. 3 (Sept.
      1981:357-66.

279   HUBERT, RENEE RIESE.   "Patterns in the Anti-
      Novel."   Forum 3, no. 11 (Fall 1962):11-15.

280   HUGHES, DANIEL J.   "Reality and the Hero: Lolita
      and Henderson and the Rain King."   Modern
      Fiction Studies 6, no. 4 (Winter 1960-
      1961):345-64.

281   "L'Humanité et ses lecteurs: Le Critique
      critiqué."   Monde, 29 Oct. 1971, p. 23.

282   HUNTER, G.K.   "English Drama 1900-1960."   In
      History of Literature in the English Language.
      Vol. 7:   The Twentieth Century.   Edited by
      Bernard Bergonzi.   London: Sphere Books
      Limited, 1970, pp. 310-35.

283   HURREN, KENNETH.   "Music Master."   Spectator, 15
      May 1976, p. 27-28.

284   _____.   "Return of the Native."   Spectator, 13
      Dec. 1975, p. 770.

285   HUTCHINSON, MARY.   "All That Fall."   Listener, 7
      Feb. 1957, p. 235.

286   HUTCHISON, ROBERT.   "Endpiece: John Arden at
      Home."   Tribune (London), 13 Sept. 1963, p.
      9.

287   IONESCO, E.   "There Is No Avant-Garde Theater."
      Evergreen Review 1, no. 4 (1957):101-5.

288   "The Irish Author, Samuel Beckett ..."   Guardian,
      27 Oct. 1969, p. 2.

289   ISOU, ISIDORE.   Les Pompiers du nouveau roman:
      Sarraute, Robbe-Grillet, Butor, Simenon,
      Beckett, Ionesco.   Paris: Centre de
      Creativité.   Editions Lettristes, 1977.

290   ISSACHAROFF, MICHAEL. "Texte théâtral et
       didascolecture." Modern Language Notes 96,
       no. 4 (May 1981):809-23.

291   JAMESON, STORM. Parthian Words. London:
       Collins & Harvill Press, 1970, pp. 75-76.

292   JARRETT-KERR, MARTIN, Father. The Secular
       Promise. Christian Presence Amid Contemporary
       Humanism. London: SCM Press, 1964, pp. 166-
       75.

293   JEAN, RAYMOND. "M. le coincé." Nouvel Obser-
       vateur, 13-19 Apr. 1966, p. 49.

294   JOHNSON, B.S. "Nothing from the Bargain Base-
       ment." New Statesman 74 (14 July 1967):54.

295   JOLAS, MARIA. "English and French." Times
       Literary Supplement (London), p. 369.

296   JONES, ADRIAN BROOKHOLDING. "Twice Told Tales."
       Tablet 219 (9 Jan. 1965):46-47.

297   JONES, MERVYN. "Top Marks to the Amateurs."
       Tribune (London), 13 Dec. 1963, p. 14.

298   JONGH, NICHOLAS de. "Happy Days at the Young
       Vic." Guardian, 3 June 1971, p. 10.

299   JOSIPOVICI, GABRIEL. "Linearity and Fragmenta-
       tion." Prospice 1 (Nov. 1973):53-58.

300   JOST, E.F. "How It Is by Samuel Beckett."
       America 110 (29 Feb. 1964):291.

301   JOST, FRANÇOIS. "Le Je à la recherche de son
       identité." Poétique, no. 24 (1975), pp. 479-
       87.

302   KANE, MICHAEL. "A Letter from Zurich." Lace
       Curtain, no. 2 (Spring 1970), pp. 42-44.

303   KANTERS, ROBERT. "L'Oeil écoute." Nef 24, n.s.,
       no. 29 (Jan.-Mar. 1967):81-86.

304   KARATSON, ANDRE. "Prespectives historiques sur
       le déracinement." In <u>Déracinement et littéra-
       ture</u>. Lille: Presses de l'Université de
       Lille, 1982, pp. 13-34.

305   KARL, FREDERICK R. "Pursuit of the Real."
       <u>Nation</u> 194, no. 16 (21 Apr. 1962):345-49.

306   KAUFFMANN, STANLEY. "On Theatre." <u>New Republic</u>
       169, no. 6 (11 Aug. 1973):20, 32-33.

307   _____. "On Theater." <u>New Republic</u> 164, no. 8
       (20 Feb. 1971):24, 35.

308   KAUFMAN, R.J. "On the Newness of the New Drama."
       <u>Tulane Drama Review</u> 6 (June 1962):94-106.

309   KAZIN, ALFRED. "The Literary Mind." <u>Nation</u> 201,
       no. 8 (20 Sept. 1965):203-6.

310   KEARNS, GEORGE. "Fiction Chronicle." <u>Hudson</u>
       <u>Review</u> 34, no. 2 (Summer 1981):299-313.

311   KEEN, SAM. <u>To a Dancing God</u>. London: Collins;
       New York: Harper & Row, 1970, 166 pp.

312   KELLMAN, BARNET. "Alan Schneider: The Direc-
       tor's Career." <u>Theatre Quarterly</u> 3, no. 11
       (July-Sept. 1973):23-27.

313   KENNER, HUGH. "Art in a Closed Field." <u>Virginia</u>
       <u>Quarterly Review</u> 38 (Summer 1962):597-613.

314   _____. "Twelve Days to Despair." <u>New York Times</u>
       <u>Book Review</u>, 28 Jan. 1968, pp. 4, 40.

315   KERMODE, FRANK. <u>The Sense of an Ending.</u>
       <u>Studies in the Theory of Fiction</u>. New York:
       Oxford University Press, 1967, 187 pp.

316   KERR, WALTER. <u>Tragedy and Comedy</u>. London,
       Sydney, and Toronto: Bodley Head; New York:
       Simon & Schuster, 1967, pp. 277-78, 321-23.

317 KILLAIN, LORD. "The Plight of the Theatre."
Tablet 224 (21 Mar. 1970):276-78.

318 KINGSTON, JEREMY. "Godot--Botherer." Punch 253
(2 Aug. 1967):182.

319 _____. "Novelist's Theatre." Books and Bookmen
12, no. 2 (Nov. 1966):83, 101.

320 KITCHEN, LAURENCE. "The Wide Stage: On Epic
Drama." Listener 69 (11 Apr. 1963):631-33.

321 KLEIN, MAVIS. "Margin of Error." Encounter 30,
no. 6 (June 1968):93.

322 KNAPP, BETTINA. "Interview with Jean-Louis
Barrault." Studies in Twentieth Century, nos.
11-12 (Spring/Fall 1973), pp. 21-26. Reprint:
Off-Stage Voices. Interviews with Modern
French Dramatists. Edited by Alba Amoia.
Troy, N.Y.: Whitston Publishing Co., 1975,
pp. 41-46.

323 _____. "The Parisian Theatrical Scene: 1963-
64." Books Abroad 38, no. 4 (Autumn
1964):371-73.

324 KOTT, JAN. "The Icon and the Absurd." Drama
Review 14, no. 1 (Fall 1969):17-24.

325 KRAUSE, DAVID. "The Victory of Comic Defeat."
In The Profane Book of Irish Comedy. Ithaca,
N.Y.: Cornell University Press, 1982, pp.
223-83. Beckett pp. 262-63 and passim.

326 KROLL, JACK. "Britain Onstage." Newsweek 87,
no. 12 (22 March 1976):74-78.

327 KUHN, REINHARD. The Demon of Noontide. Ennui in
Western Literature. Princeton, N.J.:
Princeton University Press, 1977, 395 pp.

328 KUSTOW, MICHAEL. "Halfway House." International
Theatre Annual, no. 5 (1961), pp. 244-54.

329   LAGROLET, JEAN. "La Vie littéraire: Nouveau
      réalism?" Nef 15, no. 13 (Jan. 1958):62-70.

330   LAING, RONALD DAVID. The Divided Self, a Study
      of Sanity and Madness. London: Tavistock
      Publications, 1960, 246 pp.

331   LALOU, RENEE. Le Roman français depuis 1900.
      Paris: Presses Universitaires de France,
      1960, 127 pp.

332   LARTHOMAS, PIERRE. Le Langage dramatique: Sa
      Nature et ses procédés. Paris: Librairie
      Armand Colin, 1972, 478 pp.

333   LAURENSON, DIANA and ALAN SWINGEWOOD. The
      Sociology of Literature. London: MacGibbon &
      Kee, 1971, 281 pp.

334   LAWS, FREDERICK. "Drama and Light Entertain-
      ment." Listener 73 (4 Mar. 1965):347.

335   LEAVIS, FRANK RAYMOND. "Joyce and the Revolution
      of the World." Scrutiny 2 (Sept. 1933):193-
      201.

336   LEBESQUE, MORVAN. "Le Théâtre aux enfers:
      Artaud, Beckett et quelques autres." Cahiers
      Renaud-Barrault 22-23 (May 1958):191-96.
      Reprint: Antonin Artaud et le théâtre de
      notre temps. Paris: René Julliard, 1958,
      p. 452.

337   LECLERC, GUY. Les Grandes Aventures du théâtre.
      Paris: Editeurs Français Réunis, 1965, 395
      pp.

338   LEE, RONALD J. "Irony and Religious Mystery in
      the Contemporary Theatre." Soundings 52, no.
      3 (Fall 1969):350-64.

339   LEECH, CLIFFORD. "When Writing Becomes Absurd."
      Colorado Quarterly 13 (Summer 1964):6-24.

340 LEES, F.N. "Samuel Beckett." Memoirs and
Proceedings of the Manchester Literary and
Philosophical Society 104 (1961-62):33-47.

341 LEMARCHAND, JACQUES. "L'Ecole de Paris ou dix
ans de théâtre." Avant-Scène, no. 375 (1 Mar.
1967), pp. 51-52.

342 _____. "Spectacle Beckett, Pinget, Ionesco:
l'Odéon." Figaro Littéraire, 17 Mar. 1966, p.
14.

343 LENNON, PETER. "La Vie parisienne." Guardian,
9 June 1966, p. 9.

344 LENOIR, JEAN-PIERRE. "Parisian Theatre on the
Brink." Tribune (London), 2 Nov. 1956, p. 8.

345 LEVI, ALBERT W. Literature, Philosophy and the
Imagination. Bloomington: Indiana University
Press, 1963, p. 186.

346 LEWIS, ALLAN. "The Fun and Games of Edward
Albee." Educational Theatre Journal 16, no. 1
(Mar. 1964):29-39.

347 LIOURE, MICHEL. Le Drame de Diderot à Ionesco.
Paris: Armand Colin, 1973, pp. 250-56.

348 LODGE, DAVID, ed. Twentieth Century Literary
Criticism. A Reader. London: Longman, 1972,
703 pp.

349 _____. Working with Structuralism. Essays and
Reviews of Nineteenth and Twentieth Century
Literature. Boston and London: Routledge &
Kegan Paul, 1981, 219 pp.

350 LONDON, MERRIE. "To Make a Short Beckett Piece."
Modern Drama 18, no. 1 (Mar. 1975):60.

351 LOTTMAN, HERBERT. "One of the Quiet Ones." New
York Times Book Review, 22 Mar. 1970, pp. 5,
28-29.

602

352   _____. "Where They Eat and Ate in Paris." New
        York Times Book Review (London), 21 June 1970,
        pp. 8-16.

353   LOY, J. ROBERT. "'Things' in Recent French
        Literature." PMLA 71, no. 1 (Mar. 1956):27-
        41.

354   [LUKACS, GEORG]. "Entretien: Lukacs -- revenir
        au concret." Quinzaine Littéraire, no. 17 (1-
        15 Dec. 1966), pp. 4-5.

355   _____. The Meaning of Contemporary Realism.
        London: Merlin Press, 1963, 137 pp.

356   LUTWACK, LEONARD. The Role of Place in Litera-
        ture. Syracuse, N.Y.: Syracuse University
        Press, 1984, pp. 41-42, 224-25, 243-44.

357   MacCABE, C. "Uneasiness in Culture." Cambridge
        Review 93, (2 June 1972):174-77.

358   McCALL, DOROTHY. The Theatre of Jean-Paul
        Sartre. New York and London: Columbia
        University Press, 1969, pp. 144-45.

359   McINERNY, JOHN M. "Beckett, Samuel. Mercier and
        Camier." Best Sellers 35 (June 1975):63.

360   MACKSEY, RICHARD. "The Artist in the Labyrinth:
        Design or Dasein." Modern Language Notes 77
        (May 1962):239-56.

361   MACKWORTH, CECILE. "French Writing Today. Les
        Coupables." Twentieth Century 161 (May
        1957):459-68.

362   MAGILL, FRANK N., ed. Cyclopedia of World
        Authors. New York: Harper, 1958, pp. 84-86.

363   MALLARD, WILLIAM. The Reflection of Theology in
        Literature. A Case Study in Theology and
        Culture. San Antonio, Texas: Trinity
        University Press, 1977, 271 pp.

364 MAMBRINO, JEAN. "Carnet de théâtre: Madame se meurt, Madame est morte." Etudes 332 (May 1970):728-29.

365 MANDEL, OSCAR. "Artists without Masters." Virginia Quarterly Review 39, no. 3 (Summer 1963):401-19.

366 MANNING, HUGO. "A Man to Remember." Adam 35, nos. 337-339 (1970):76-77.

367 MARCEL, GABRIEL. Théâtre et religion. Lyon: Vitte, 1959, 107 pp.

368 MARCORELLES, LOUIS. "Social Theatre in France and Great Britain: Between Brecht and Cinema." International Theatre Annual, no. 5 (1961), pp. 204-15.

369 MASSEY, IRVING. The Uncreating Word. Romanticism and the Object. Bloomington, Ind. and London: Indiana University Press, 1970, pp. 123-28.

370 MASSON, DANIELLE. Sisyphe ou l'illusion d'optique: Réflexions sur l'absurde. Vouillé: Diffusion de la Pensée Française, 1974, 111 pp.

371 MATTHEWS, J.H. The Inner Dream. Céline as Novelist. Syracuse, N.Y.: Syracuse University Press, 1978, 236 pp.

372 _____. "Nathalie Sarraute: An Approach to the Novel." Modern Fiction Studies 6 (Winter 1960-61):337-44.

373 MAURIAC, CLAUDE. "Robert Pinget, les oiseaux-mouches et les hannetons." Figaro Littériare, 8 Mar. 1975, p. 17.

374 _____. "Samuel Beckett est aussi un poète." Figaro, 3 Feb. 1960, p. 14.

375   [MAURIAC, FRANÇOIS].   Le Bloc-notes de François
       Mauriac."   Fiagro Littéraire, 3-9 Nov. 1969,
       pp. 6-7.

376   _____ .   Le Dernier Bloc-notes, 1968-1970.   Paris:
       Flammarion, 1970, 354 pp.

377   MELLOWN, ELGIN W.   "Beckett, Samuel Barclay
       (1906-   )."   In Descriptive Catalogue of the
       Bibliographies of 20th Century British
       Writers.   Troy, N.Y.:   Whitston Publishing
       Co., 1972, pp. 19-20.

378   MERCIER, VIVIAN.   "James Joyce and the French New
       Novel."   Tri-Quarterly, no. 8 (Winter 1967),
       pp. 205-19.

379   _____ .   "My Life in the New Novel."   Nation, 11
       Apr. 1966, pp. 434-36.

380   _____ .   The New Novel from Queneau to Pinget.
       New York: Ferrar, Straus and Giroux, 1971.

381   MERCURE, JEAN.   "Le Théâtre de la Ville: Un
       théâtre en accord avec son public."   Avant-
       Scène Théâtre, no. 624 (15 Feb. 1978), pp. 5-
       6.

382   MERRITT, JAMES D.   "Samuel Beckett: Poems in
       English."   Books Abroad 38, no. 2 (Spring
       1964):192.

383   MICHA, RENE.   "L'Homme indistinct."   Nouvelle
       Revue Française 10, no. 110 (Feb. 1962):306-
       12.

384   _____ .   "Le Nouveau Roman."   Arc 4 (Autumn
       1958):45-50.

385   _____ .   "Une nouvelle littérature allégorique."
       Nouvelle Revue Française 2, no. 16 (Apr.
       1954):696-706.

386   MICHEL, GEORGES. "Quel Public? Quelle Par-
       ticipation?" <u>Nef</u> 24, n.s., no. 29 (Jan.-Mar.
       1967):65-70.

387   MILLER, J. HILLIS. "The Anonymous Walkers."
       <u>Nation</u> 190, no. 17 (23 Apr. 1960):351-54.

388   MILLETT, KATE. "Portrait of a Woman Reading."
       <u>Chicago Tribune Book World</u> 4, no. 4 (22 Nov.
       1970):8.

389   MINOGUE, VALERIE. "Picasso and the Apple. The
       French New Novel." <u>Quadrant</u> 21, no. 8 (Aug.
       1977):68-72.

390   "Miscellany: Dropping Out." <u>Guardian</u>, 24 Oct.
       1969, p. 11.

391   MITCHELL, JULIAN. "Master Class." <u>New Statesman</u>
       89, (11 Apr. 1975):483-84.

392   MOLE, JACK. "After the Death of God." <u>Listener</u>
       77 (11 May 1967):614-16.

393   _____. "What to Do with the Body." <u>Listener</u> 70
       (5 Sept. 1963):339-40.

394   MOORE, JOHN. "Samuel Beckett's Drama." <u>South
       Central Bulletin</u> 33, no. 3 (Oct. 1973):120.

395   MORGAN, DAVID R. "And Now the Void: Twentieth-
       Century Man's Place in Modern Tragedy."
       <u>Contemporary Review</u> 234, no. 1361 (June
       1979):315-20.

396   MORLEY, SHERIDAN. "Theatre." <u>Punch</u> 270 (2 June
       1976):1012.

397   MORRISSETTE, BRUCE. "The New Novel in France."
       <u>Chicago Review</u> 15, no. 3 (Winter-Spring
       1962):1-19.

398   MROSOVSKY, KITTY. "The Empire of Who." <u>Times
       Educational Supplement</u> (London), 12 Mar. 1976,
       p. 20.

606

399   No entry.

400   MULLER, A.   "Techniques de l'avant-garde."
      Théâtre Populaire 18 (1 May 1956):21-29.

401   MUNTEANU, ROMUL.   "En marge d'une poétique de la
      farce tragique." Cahiers Roumains d'Etudes
      Littéraires, no. 1 (1980), pp. 29-45.

402   MURDOCH, IRIS.   "Against Dryness." Encounter 16
      (Jan. 1961):16-20. Beckett: p. 19.

403   MURPHY, H.   "Pass All Who Have Entered There."
      Dublin Magazine 10, no. 3 (Autumn/Winter 1973-
      1974):118.

404   MUSARRA-SCHRODER, ULLA. Le Roman-mémoires
      moderne. Pour une typologie du récit à la
      première personne. Précédé d'un modèle
      narratologique et d'une étude du roman-
      mémoires traditionnel de Daniel Defoe à
      Gottfried Keller. Amsterdam and Maarssen:
      APA-Holland University Press, 1981, 393 pp.

405   NAGY, PETER.   "The 'Anti-Theatre.'" New Hun-
      garian Quarterly 3, no. 5 (Jan.-Mar.
      1962):139-50.

406   "New Books and Reprints: Proust." Times
      Literary Supplement (London), 2 Apr. 1931, p.
      274.

407   NEWBY, HOWARD.   "Radio, Television and the Arts."
      Listener, 22 Jan. 1976, pp. 75-76.

408   "Le New York Times: 'L'Académie suédoise a fait
      preuve d'audace.'" Figaro, 25-26 Oct. 1969,
      p. 9.

409   NICOLAS, ALBERT.   "Note sur l'individu et la
      société dans les romans de Samuel Beckett."
      Annales de l'Université d'Abidjan 6D (1973):
      343-46.

410   NIGHTINGALE, BENEDICT. "Iron in the Soul." New
      Statesman 89 (7 Feb. 1975):184.

411   _____. "Through the Slips." New Statesman 90
      (12 Dec. 1975):764.

412   "Nobel Prize for Beckett." Financial Times, 24
      Oct. 1969, p. 3.

413   NOON, WILLIAM T. "God and Man in Twentieth-
      Century Fiction." Thought 37 (1962):35-56.

414   _____. "Modern Literature and the Sense of
      Time." Thought 33 (1958-1959):571-603.

415   NORES, DOMINIQUE. "Caen: Colloque sur le
      théâtre." Quinzaine Littéraire, no. 31 (1-15
      July 1967), p. 26.

416   _____. "Situation du jeune théâtre." Lettres
      Nouvelles 32 (Feb. 1963):213-224.

417   NYE, ROBERT. "Pick of the Paperbacks." Tribune
      (London), 6 Dec. 1963, p. 12.

418   O'CASEY, SEAN. "Not Waiting for Godot (1956)."
      In Blasts and Benedictions. London: Macmil-
      lan; New York: St. Martin's Press, 1967, pp.
      51-52. Reprint of 419B.

419   _____. "Not Waiting for Godot (1956)." Encore
      (Easter 1956). Reprinted: 418B.

420   O'CONNOR, JOHN J. "T.V.: Subtle Godot, Unset-
      tling Passport." New York Times, 29 June
      1977, p. 23C.

421   O'CONNOR PHILIP. "The Greatest Exponent of
      Nihilism." Adam: International Review 35,
      nos. 337-339 (1970):77-78.

422   O'FLAHERTY, KATHLEEN. The Novel in France, 1945-
      1965. A General Survey. Cork: Cork Univer-
      sity Press, 1973, 168 pp.

423 "Oh! les beaux jours dans les Maisons de la
     Culture." Monde, 1 Oct. 1966, p. 14.

424 OLIVER, WILLIAM. "Between Absurdity and the
     Playwright." Educational Theatre Journal 15
     (Oct. 1963):224-35.

425 OLIVIER, CLAUDE. "Le Tragique du défi." Lettres
     Françaises, 26 Apr.-2 May 1972, pp. 10-11.

426 _____. "La Vie encore là ..." Lettres Fran-
     çaises, 18-24 Feb. 1970, p. 18.

427 O'MEARA, JOHN J. Letter to the Editor. Times
     Literary Supplement (London), 6 Apr. 1956, p.
     207.

428 "On the Margin." X: A Quarterly Review 1 (Mar.
     1960):158-60.

429 "Our Examination." Times Literary Supplement
     (London), 12 Dec. 1936, p. 1037.

430 "Out of the Air: Hot Days and Underdogs."
     Listener, 30 July 1970.

431 OXENHANDLER, NEAL. "Toward the New Aesthetic."
     Contemporary Literature 11, no. 2 (Spring
     1970):169-91.

432 PALFRY, ISTVAN. "Modern English Drama Through
     Hungarian Eyes." Hungarian Studies in English
     5 (1971):137-49.

433 PARKER, GERALD D. "The Modern Theatre as
     Autonomous Vehicle." Modern Drama 16, nos. 3-
     4 (Dec. 1973):373-91.

434 PARIS, JEAN. "The Clock Struck 29." Reporter 15
     (4 Oct. 1956):39-40.

435 P[EARSON], K[ENNETH]. "Arts News: Beckett
     Play." Sunday Times (London), 7 Feb. 1971, p.
     23.

436 PEEL, MARIE. "Power and Pattern V. Morality. 1. Poetry and Drama." Books and Bookmen 18, no. 1 (Oct. 1972):38-42.

437 PELLEGRIN, JEAN. "Les Ineffables." Poétiques 37 (Feb. 1979):1-9.

438 PERRIN, MICHEL. "La Monnaie de la pièce ... de Samuel Beckett." Nouvelles Littéraires, 2 Mar. 1961, p. 2.

439 _____. "Voici le discours que Samuel Beckett ne prononcera pas à Stockholm." Figaro Littéraire, 15-21 Dec. 1969, p. 14.

440 PETER, JOHN. "A Sense of Drama and Discovery." Sunday Times (London), 13 Apr. 1975, p. 35.

441 _____. "Jack MacGowran on O'Casey and Beckett." Times (London), 18 Mar. 1967, p. 7.

442 PETERKIEWICZ, JERZY. The Other Side of Silence: The Poet at the Limits of Language. London and New York: Oxford University Press, 1970, pp. 74-75.

443 "Petites Nouvelles." Monde, 5 May 1970, p. 17.

444 PEVEL, HENRI. "Résonances mallarméennes du nouveau roman." Médiations 7 (Spring 1964): 95-113.

445 PEYRE, HENRI. The Contemporary French Novel. New York: Oxford University Press, 1955, pp. 307-8.

446 PICON, GAETAN. Panorama de la nouvelle littérature française. Paris: Gallimard, 1960, 678 pp.

447 PIEMME, JEAN-MARIE. "Propos sur le nouveau théâtre." Revue des Langues Vivantes 34, no. 5 (1968):514-18.

448   PINTER, HAROLD. "Pinter: Between the Lines."
       Sunday Times (London), 4 Mar. 1962, p. 25.

449   PIVOT, BERNARD. "L'Aigle franco-irlandais."
       Figaro Littéraire, 26 Jan. 1967, p. 2.
       (Photo)

450   "Playwright's name." Times (London), 17 Oct.
       1967, p. 9.

451   PLEYNET, MARCELIN. Spirito Peregrino: Chroniques
       du Journal Ordinaire 1979. Paris: Hachette,
       1981, 152 pp.

452   POIROT-DELPECH, BERTRAND. "Théâtre: L'Appel du
       silence." Nouvelle Revue Française, no. 229
       (Jan. 1972), pp. 100-103.

453   POPKIN, HENRY. "Williams, Osborne or Beckett?"
       New York Times Magazine, 13 Nov. 1960, pp. 32-
       33, 119-121. Reprint: Essays in the Modern
       Drama. Edited by Morris Freedman. Boston:
       D.C. Heath, 1964, pp. 235-42.

454   POULET, ROBERT. "Suite des faits-nouveaux."
       Ecrits de Paris, Mar. 1969, pp. 97-102.

455   _____ . "Suite et fin des faits-nouveaux."
       Ecrits de Paris, Apr. 1969, pp. 91-97.

456   PRAZ, MARIO. Mnemosyne. The Parallel Between
       Literature and the Visual Arts. Princeton,
       N.J.: Princeton University Press, 1970, 276
       pp.

457   PRENTKI, TIM. "Requiem for the Living." In
       Francis Warner: Poet and Dramatist. Knott-
       ing, Eng.: Sceptre; Atlantic Highlands, N.J.:
       Humanities Press, 1977, pp. 88-109.

458   "Prince of Darkness." Times Literary Supplement
       (London), 17 June 1960, p. 381.

459   PRITCHETT, V.S. "Mild and Bitter." New States-
       man, 23 May 1959, pp. 728-29.

460   "Programme Notes." Prompt, no. 2 (Spring 1963),
       pp. 35-37.

461   PRYCE-JONES, DAVID. "Classics and Commercials."
       Spectator 212 (17 Apr. 1964):516.

462   RADIN, VICTORIA. "Starvation Diet." New
       Statesman 108 (7 Sept. 1984):34.

463   RAWSON, CLAUDE J. Gulliver and the Gentle
       Reader. Boston: Routledge & Kegan Paul,
       1973, 200 pp.

464   RAZUM, HANNES. "Theater of the Absurd." World
       Theater 10, no. 4 (1961):37-43.

465   REDA, JACQUES. "N'attendons plus Godot."
       Marginales 11, nos. 50-51 (Dec. 1956):63-64.

466   REYNOLDS, GILLIAN. "Beckett's 'Lessness' on
       Radio 3." Guardian, 25 Feb. 1971, p. 10.

467   _____. "Liverpool Everyman: Waiting for Godot."
       Guardian, 26 Nov. 1970, p. 8.

468   RICARDOU, JEAN. Le Nouveau Roman. Paris:
       Editions du Seuil, 1973, 185 pp.

469   RICHARDSON, MAURICE. "TV Review." Observer, 10
       July 1966, p. 21.

470   RICKS, CHRISTOPHER. "Lies." Critical Inquiry 2,
       no. 1 (Autumn 1975):121-42.

471   ROBBE-GRILLET, ALAIN. "The Case for the New
       Novel." New Statesman 61 (17 Feb. 1961):261-
       64.

472   _____. "Nouveau Roman, homme nouveau." Revue de
       Paris 9 (Sept. 1961):115-121. Reprinted:
       Pour un nouveau roman. Paris: Editions de
       Minuit, 1963, pp. 143-53.

473   RODGER, IAN. "Zoos, Corals and Follies."
       Listener 61 (29 Jan. 1959):225-26.

474   RONSE, HENRI. "Littérature et silence."
      Synthèses, nos. 236-237 (Jan.-Feb. 1966), pp.
      41-48.

475   ROSENBAUM, JONATHAN. "My Favorite Films/Texts/
      Things." Film Comment 12, no. 6 (Nov.-Dec.
      1976):51-56.

476   ROSENBERG, MARVIN. "A Metaphor for Dramatic
      Form." Journal of Asthetics and Art Criticism
      17, no. 2 (Dec. 1958):174-80.

477   ROSS, M. "New Fiction." Listener 71 (23 Jan.
      1964):165.

478   ROSSET, CLEMENT. "La Nostalgie du présent."
      Nouvelle Revue Française, no. 333 (1 Oct.
      1980), pp. 100-103.

479   _____. "Propos d'outre-monde." Nouvelle Revue
      Française, no. 305 (1 June 1978), pp. 79-85;
      no. 306 (1 July 1978), pp. 89-95; no. 307 (1
      Aug. 1978), pp. 83-89; no. 308 (1 Sept. 1978),
      pp. 121-25.

480   ROSTAND, CLAUDE. "Le Théâtre de Bielefeld: Un
      monopéra." Figaro Littéraire, 15 July 1961,
      p. 12.

481   ROWE, KENNETH T. A Theatre in Your Head. New
      York: Funk and Wagnalls, 1960, pp. 242-43.

482   ROWELL, GEORGE. "A Theatre Institute?" New
      Theatre Magazine 11, no. 3 (1971):2.

483   ROY, CLAUDE. Défense de la littérature. Paris:
      Gallimard, 1968, 191 pp.

484   _____. "L'Utilité de ne pas tout comprendre."
      Nouvelle Revue Française 11, no. 124 (1 Apr.
      1963):703-9.

485   RYSTEN, FELIX S. A. False Prophets in the
      Fiction of Camus, Dostoevsky, Melville, and

Others. Coral Gables, Fla.: Miami University Press, 1972, 139 pp.

486   "Samuel Beckett, Prix Nobel de Littérature." Figaro, 24 Oct. 1969, pp. 1, 15.

487   SANDIER, GILLES. "Corneille architecte du songe." Arts et Loisirs 25 (16-22 Mar. 1966):17.

488   SARRAZAC, JEAN-PIERRE. L'Avenir du drame: Ecritures dramatiques contemporaines. Lausanne: Editions de l'Aire, 1981, 198 pp.

489   SARTRE, JEAN-PAUL. "Epic Theater and Dramatic Theater." In Sartre on Theater. Edited by Michael Contat and Michael Rybalka. New York: Pantheon, 1976, pp. 77-120. Beckett: pp. 99-100.

490   _____. "Myth and Reality in the Theatre." Gambit: An International Drama Bi-Monthly 3, no. 9 (1968):55-68.

491   SAUREL, RENEE. "En attendant un nouveau théâtre." Temps Modernes 17, no. 183 (July 1961):180-83.

492   SAVONA, JEANNETTE LAILLON. "Didascalies as Speech Art." Modern Drama 25, no. 1 (Mar. 1982):25-35.

493   SAY, A de. "Roussillon." Arc 1, no. 2 (Spring 1958):83.

494   SCHECHNER, RICHARD. "TDR Comment: Theater Criticism." Tulane Drama Review 9 (Spring 1965):13-24.

495   SCHNEIDER, PIERRE. "Play and Display." Listener 51 (28 Jan. 1954):174-76.

496   SCHOFER, PETER. ed. "Texte modèle (Acte sans paroles, I)." In Poèmes, pièces, prose.

Introduction à l'analyse des textes littéraires français. New York: Oxford University Press, 1973, p. 175.

497 SCOTT, BERNARD E. "The Press of Freedom:
Waiting for God." In The Village Reader: A
Mixed Bag from the Greenwich Village News-
paper. Edited by Daniel Wolf and Edwin
Fancher. Garden City, N.Y.: Doubleday, 1962.
Reprinted: New York: Grove Press, 1963, pp.
79-84.

498 SCOTT, NATHAN A. The Broken Center: Studies in
the Theological Horizon of Modern Literature.
New Haven and London: Yale University Press,
1966, 252 pp.

499 _____. Negative Capability: Studies in the New
Literature and Religious Situation. New
Haven: Yale University Press, 1969, 173 pp.

500 SEMMLER, CLEMENT. "Our Examination Round His
Factification ..." Meanjin 21, no. 4
(1962):519-21.

501 SENART, PHILIPPE. "La Fin de l'homme." Table
Ronde 182 (Mar. 1963):113-19.

502 _____. "La Revue théâtrale: De Jean Genet à
Samuel Beckett." Revue des Deux Mondes, no. 8
(Aug. 1975), pp. 450-53.

503 SEYMOUR-SMITH, MARTIN. "Who's Who in Twentieth
Century Literature? New York: McGraw-Hill,
1977, 414 pp.

504 SHARTAR, I. MARTIN. "Mallarmé to Beckett: The
Theatre of the Mind." South Atlantic Bulletin
31, no. 1 (Jan. 1966):4.

505 SHIRLEY, DON. "Godot." Washington Post, 29 June
1977, p. 8C.

506 SHORTER, ERIC. "Brooks and Others in Avignon."
Drama, no. 134 (Autumn 1979), pp. 33-40.

507   SIGAL, CLANCY. "Leave Yahooism to Your Enemies."
       Tribune (London), 23 Nov. 1962, p. 8.

508   SIMON, ALFRED. Dictionnaire du théâtre français
       contemporain. Paris: Larousse, 1970, pp.
       90-92.

509   _____. "Paris et la vocation populaire du
       théâtre." Esprit 29 (Dec. 1961):939-41.

510   _____. "Le théâtre est-il mortel?" Esprit 26
       (Jan. 1958):1-21. Beckett: p. 16.

511   SIMON, JOHN. "Subsidized Violence." New York 3,
       no. 50 (14 Dec. 1970), p. 68.

512   _____. "Le Tréteau de Paris." New York 3, no.
       20 (18 May 1970), p. 64.

513   SKELTON, ROBIN. "Jack Coughlin: Irish Por-
       traits." Malahat Review 22 (Apr. 1972):
       63-72.

514   SMITH, MICHAEL. "Considering a Poetic." Lace
       Curtain, no. 3 (Summer 1970), pp. 45-50.

515   SOLOTAROFF, THEODORE. "Silence, Exile, and
       Cunning." New American Review, no. 8 (Jan.
       1970), pp. 201-19.

516   SPANOS, WILLIAM V. "The Detective and the
       Boundary: Some Notes on the Postmodern
       Literary Imagination." Boundary 2 1, no. 1
       (Fall 1972):147-68.

517   SPENDER, STEPHEN. "With Lukacs in Budapest."
       Encounter 23 (Dec. 1964):53-57.

518   "Spotlight's Godot Always Ends in an Open Forum."
       Eastern Evening News, 6 Nov. 1969, p. 23.

519   SPURLING, HILARY. "Death Bed Scenes." Spec-
       tator, 28 Mar. 1970, pp. 420-21.

616

520   STAMBOLIAN, GEORGE and ELAINE MARKS, eds.
      Homosexualities and French Literature.
      Cultural Contexts / Critical Texts. Ithaca,
      N.Y. and London: Cornell University Press,
      1979, 387 pp.

521   STANFORD, DERECK. "An Elementary Demonstration."
      Books and Bookmen 16, no. 3 (Dec. 1970):31-2.

522   STANKIEWICZ, MARKETA GOETZ. "Slawomir, Mrozek:
      Two Forms of the Absurd." Contemporary
      Literature 12, no. 2 (Spring 1971):188-203.

523   STAROBINSKI, JEAN. "Note sur Rabelais et le
      langage." Tel Quel, no. 15 (Autumn 1963), pp.
      79-81.

524   STEINER, GEORGE. "The Future of the Book: I.
      Classic Culture and Post-Culture." Times
      Literary Supplement (London), 2 Oct. 1970, pp.
      1,121-1,123.

525   _____. Language and Silence. Harmondsworth,
      1969, 440 pp.

526   STERNBERG, JACQUES. "Le Moi littéraire."
      Magazine Littéraire, no. 42 (July 1970),
      p. 6.

527   STEWART, SUSAN. Nonsense. Aspects of Intertex-
      tuality in Folklore and Literature. Baltimore
      and London: John Hopkins University Press,
      1978, 228 pp.

528   STRATFORD, PHILIP. "Creativity and Commitment in
      Contemporary Theatre." Humanities Association
      of Canada Bulletin, 15, no. 2 (Autumn
      1964):35-39.

529   STRAUSS, WALTER A. Descent and Return. The
      Orphic Theme in Modern Literature. Cambridge,
      Mass.: Harvard University Press, 1971, 295
      pp.

530   STYAN, J.L.   The Dramatic Experience.   Cambridge,
       Mass.: Cambridge University Press, 1965, 154
       pp.

531   _____ .   The Elements of Drama.   Cambridge, Mass.:
       Cambridge University Press, 1960.

532   "The Sunday Times Guide to the Modern Movement in
       the Arts.   2.   Literature: Men who Changed
       the Nature of the 20th Century Writing."
       Sunday Times (London), 14 May 1967, pp. 54-55.

533   "The Sunday Times Guide to the Modern Movement in
       the Arts: 4. Theatre." Sunday Times (Lon-
       don), 28 May 1967, p. 25.

534   SURMELIAN, LEON.   Techniques of Fiction Writing:
       Measure and Madness.   Garden City, N.Y.:
       Doubleday & Co., Inc., 1968, 274 pp.

535   TADIE, JEAN-YVES.   Le Récit poétique.   Paris:
       Presses Universitaires de France, 1978, 206
       pp.

536   TARRAB, GILBERT.   Le Happening: Analyse pscho-
       sociologique.   Paris: Publication de la
       Société d'Histoire du Théâtre, 1968, 102 pp.

537   TAUBMAN, ROBERT.   "Forties Fable."   New States-
       man, 18 Feb. 1966, pp. 232-34.

538   TAYLOR, JOHN RUSSELL.   Anger and After: A Guide
       to the New British Drama.   Revised edition.
       London: Methuen & Co. Ltd., 1969, 391 pp.

539   TEMPLE, R. Z.   "The 'I' and the Eye: Reality in
       the Work of Virginia Wolf, Robbe-Grillet,
       Sarraurte and Beckett."   In Le Réel dans la
       littérature et dans la langue.   Actes du Xe
       Congrès de la Fédération Internationale des
       Langues et Littératures Modernes.   Strasbourg:
       29 Aug.-3 Sept. 1966.   Paris: Librairie C.
       Klincksieck, 1967, 324 pp.

618

540 TEYSSEDRE, BERNARD. "Réalisme critique et avant-garde." <u>Lettres Nouvelles</u>, no. 16 (July 1961), pp. 144-54.

541 THIEBAUT, MARCEL. "Le 'Nouveau roman.'" <u>Revue de Paris</u> 65 (Oct. 1958):140-55.

542 THOMPSON, WILLIAM I. "Freedom and Comedy." <u>Tulane Drama Review</u> 9, no. 3 (Spring 1965):216-30.

543 TINT, HERBERT. <u>France since 1918</u>. London: B.T. Batsford Ltd., 1970, pp. 192-94.

544 TOMLINSON, SANDRE W. "Frost's 'The Draft Horse.'" <u>Explicator</u> 42, no. 4 (Summer 1984):28-29.

545 TOUCHARD, PIERRE-AIME. "Qu'est-ce que le théâtre révolutionnaire?" <u>Quinzaine Littéraire</u>, no. 56 (1-15 Sept. 1968), pp. 24-25. Reprinted from: <u>Le Théâtre et l'angoisse des hommes</u>. Paris: Editions du Seuil, 1968, 221 pp.

546 _____. "Le Théâtre: Ce qu'il en reste." <u>Monde</u>, 20-21 Dec. 1970, p. 13.

547 _____. "La Vie théâtrale: A la recherche d'un langage." <u>Monde</u>, 4 Mar. 1970, p. 19.

548 "Tout oublier ..." <u>Nouvel Observateur</u>, no. 123 (22-29 Mar. 1967), p. 35.

549 TREWIN, J.C. "Barrault in London." <u>Illustrated London News</u>, 4 Oct. 1969, p. 27.

550 _____. "Drama and Light Entertainment." <u>Listener</u>, 21 July 1966, p. 103.

551 _____. "A Man Called Kean." <u>Illustrated London News</u> 258 (13 Feb. 1971):33.

552 _____. "Plays in Performance." <u>Drama</u>, no. 77 (Summer 1965), pp. 16-23.

553 _____. "Royal and Ancient." Illustrated London News 241 (17 Nov. 1962):804.

554 _____. "A Time to Laugh." Illustrated London News 261 (Sept. 1973):96.

555 _____. "Voices from the Void." Illustrated London News 264 (July 1976):59.

556 TRILLING, LIONEL. Sincerity and Authenticity. London: Oxford University Press, 1972, 188 pp.

557 TUBE, HENRY. "Things Happen to the Other One." Spectator 220 (29 Mar. 1968):406.

558 "Twelve Cheers for Joyce." Times Literary Supplement (London), 6 Apr. 1962, p. 234.

559 TYLER, PARKER. "Is Man a Clown? Is Fellini? And What's a Clown?" Evergreen Review 17, no. 96 (Spring 1973):98-122.

560 TYNAN, KENNETH. "Krapp's Last Tape and Endgame." In Curtains. Selections from the Criticism and Related Writings. New York: Atheneum, 1961, pp. 225-28.

561 UNTERECKER, JOHN. "Notes on Off-Broadway Theater." Evergreen Review 2, no. 8 (Spring 1959):152-63.

562 UPDIKE, JOHN. "Future of the Novel." Books and Bookmen 14, no. 7 (Apr. 1969):22-24.

563 _____. "Pinget." New Yorker 55, no. 31 (17 Sept. 1979):165-69.

564 USHER, ARLAND. "The Contemporary Thought of Ireland." Dublin Magazine 22, n.s., no. 3 (July-Sept. 1947):24-30.

565 VALDES, MARIO J. and OWEN J. MILLER, eds. Interpretation of Narrative. Toronto, Buffalo

and London: University of Toronto Press, 1978, 202 pp.

566   VALENCY, MAURICE. "Flight into Lunacy." <u>Theatre Arts</u> 44 (Aug. 1960):8-9, 68-69.

567   VEDRES, NICOLE. "La Baleine des Invalides." <u>Mercure de France</u> 341 (Apr. 1961):684-88.

568   VEST, QUENTIN. "Samuel Beckett. <u>Collected Poems in English and French</u>." <u>Library Journal</u> 103 (1 Jan. 1978):96.

569   VIATTE, AUGUSTE. "La Littérature dans l'impasse." <u>Revue de l'Université Laval</u> 15 (Nov. 1960):254-59.

570   _____. "Le 'Nouveau roman.'" <u>Revue de l'Université Laval</u> 16 (Oct. 1961):122-28.

571   _____. "Panorama des lettres françaises." <u>Revue de l'Université Laval</u> 18 (Dec. 1963):327-32.

572   VIGEE, CLAUDE. "Les Artistes de la faim." <u>Comparative Literature</u> 9, no. 2 (Spring 1957):97-117.

573   VIRMAUX, ALAIN. <u>Antonin Artaud et le théâtre</u>. Paris: Seghers, 1970, 351 pp.

574   WADE, DAVID. "Harold." <u>Listener</u> 76 (20 Oct. 1966):588.

575   WAELTI-WALTERS, J. "Autonomy and Metamorphosis." <u>Romantic Review</u> 73, no. 4 (Nov. 1982):505-14.

576   WAGER, WALTER, ed. <u>The Playwright Speaks</u>. London: Longmans, 1969, 230 pp.

577   WALKER, ROY. "Judge not ..." <u>Listener</u> 57 (9 May 1957):767-68.

578   WALTERS, RAYMOND. "Repeat Performance." <u>New York Times Book Review</u>, 6 July 1958, p. 10.

579   WARDLE, IRVING. Introduction. New English
       Dramatists 12: Radio Plays. Harmondsworth,
       1968, 190 pp.

580   _____. "Shame and Dignity." Times (London), 30
       Jan. 1975, p. 8.

581   WATSON, GEORGE. The Story of the Novel. London:
       Macmillan Press Ltd., 1979, 166 pp.

582   "Waves in a Teacup: French Novelists and Their
       Spheres." Times Literary Supplement (London),
       13 Oct. 1961, pp. 712-13.

583   WAYMARK, PETER. "World Theatre 71." Times
       (London), 2 Feb. 1971, p. 12.

584   WELLWARTH, GEORGE E. "Why Samuel Beckett Writes
       in French." Books Abroad 23 (Summer 1949):
       247-48.

585   WENTZ, JOHN C. "The Second MLA Conference on
       Modern Drama." Modern Drama 3 (Feb. 1961):
       335-38.

586   WEST, PAUL. The Modern Novel. London: Hutchin-
       son University Library, 1963. Vol. 1, pp.
       197-200.

587   WHITE, KENNETH, ed. Alogical Modern Drama.
       Amsterdam: Rodopi, 1982.

588   _____. "How Will the Human Species Change?" In
       Man's New Shapes: French Avant-Garde Drama's
       Metamorphoses. Washington, D.C.: University
       Press of America, Inc., 1979, pp. 46-60.

589   WIEHE, JANET. "Beckett, Samuel. Company."
       Library Journal 105 (15 Nov. 1980):2430.

590   WILDER, AMOS N. "Mortality and Contemporary
       Literature." Harvard Theological Review 58,
       no. 1 (Jan. 1965):1-20.

622

591   WILLIAMS, CLIFFORD. "Saints or Martyrs." Drama,
       no. 69 (Summer 1963), pp. 31-33.

592   WILLIAMS, RAYMOND. Drama in Performance.
       London: C.A. Watts & Co., 1968, 198 pp.

593   _____. "New English Drama." Twentieth Century
       170, no. 1011 (Autumn 1961):169-80.

594   WILMETH, DON B. "The Latest Decade of Theatre:
       Death or Deliverance?" Choice 8, no. 12 (Feb.
       1972):1557-62.

595   WILSHER, PETER. "Radio: Compulsive Subtlety."
       Sunday Times (London), 11 Oct. 1964, p. 44.

596   WILSON, COLIN. Beyond the Outsider: The
       Philosophy of the Future. London: Arthur
       Barker, 1965, 236 pp.

597   _____. Eagle and Earwig. Essays on Books and
       Writers. London: John Baker, 1965, 278 pp.

598   WILSON, R.J. "Who Likes Beckett?" Tribune
       (London), 20 Nov. 1962, p. 8.

599   WING, GEORGE W. "Octavio Paz: Anthology of
       Mexican Poetry." Books Abroad 33, no. 4
       (Autumn 1959):465.

600   WOLFSON, LOUIS. Le Schizo et les langues.
       Paris: Gallimard, 1970.

601   WORMS, JEANNINE. "Du roman." Cahiers des
       Saisons, no. 24 (Winter 1961), pp. 451-53.

602   _____. "Poésie et roman-compassion et beauté."
       Mercure de France, no. 1180 (Dec. 1961), pp.
       650-56.

603   WORSLEY, T.C. "Minority Culture." New Statesman
       and Nation 53 (26 Jan. 1957):97-98.

604   _____. "Puzzle Corner." New Statesman, 13 Apr.
       1957, pp. 473-74.

605   YOUNG, B.A. "8th World Theatre. Season 1971."
       Financial Times, 2 Feb. 1971, p. 3.

606   YOUNG, KENNETH. "Still Waiting for Beckett."
       Sunday Telegraph (London), 17 Sept. 1978, p.
       12.

607   ZEGEL, SYLVAIN. "Godot est arrivé sans se
       presser ..." Figaro Littéraire, 20 Oct. 1966,
       p. 12.

608   ZERAFFA, MICHAEL. Fictions. The Novel and
       Social Reality. New York: Penguin Books,
       1976. Translated from French: Roman et
       société. Paris: Presses Universitaires de
       France, 1971, 183 pp.

609   _____. "Le Théâtre -- Beckett, Schehadé,
       Shakespeare." Europe 35, no. 144 (Dec.
       1957):159-62.

610   ZYLA, WOLODYMYR T. "1975 Camus Symposium at
       Texas Tech." South Central Bulletin 35, no. 2
       (Summer 1975):41-42.

Appendix C

Location of Periodicals and Newspapers
in which Critical Works on Beckett
Have Appeared

Académie Royale de Langue et de Littérature Françaises
(Brussels)

Accent: A Quarterly of New Literature (Urbana, Ill.)

Acme: Annali della Facoltà di Lettere e Filosofia
(Milan)

Acta Neophilologica (Ljubljana, Yugoslavia)

Action (New York)

Action (Paris)

Action Poétique (Marseille)

Adam: International Review (London)

Africain Literature Today (New York)

Age Nouveau (Paris)

Agenda (London)

Ambit (London)

America (New York)

American Benedictine Review (Newark, N.J.)

American Book Collector (Arlington Heights, Ill.)

American Image: A Psychoanalytic Journal for Culture, Science, and the Arts (Brooklyn, N.Y.)

American Notes and Queries (New Haven, Conn.)

American Scholar (New York)

American Society of Legion of Honor Magazine (see Laurels)

Anglican Theological Review (Evanston, Ill.)

Anglo-Irish Studies (Chalfont St. Giles, England)

Anglo-Welsh Review (Pembroke Dock, Wales)

Annales de l'Université d'Abidjan (Abidjan, Ivory Coast)

Annals (Paris)

Antigonish Review (St. Francis Xavier University, Antigonish, Nova Scotia)

Antioch Review (Yellow Spring, Ohio)

Approach Magazine (Oxford, England)

Arc (Aix-en-Provence, France)

Ariel: A Review of International English Literature (University of Calgary, Calgary)

Arizona Quarterly: A Journal of Literature, History, Folklore (University of Arizona, Tucson)

Art Press (Paris) In French

Art Vivant (Paris)

Arts (See Arts-Spectacles)

Arts Loisirs (See Arts-Spectacles)

Arts et Loisirs (See Arts-Spectacles)

Arts-Spectacles (Paris)

Aryan Path (Bombay)

Aspects (Brussels)

Assaph: Studies in the Arts (Tel-Aviv University)

Atlantic Monthly (Boston, Mass.)

Atlantis (Dublin)

Atlas: The Magazine of the World Press (New York)

Audience (Cambridge, Mass.)

AUMLA: Journal of the Australasian Universities
   Language and Literature Association (Christchurch,
   New Zealand)

Australian Journal of French Studies (Monash
   University, Clayton, Victoria)

Avant-Scène (Paris)

Aylesford Review (Aylesford, Kent)

BBC Quarterly (London)

Ball State University Forum (Muncie, Ind.)

Baltimore Evening Sun (Baltimore, Md.)

Best Sellers (Scranton, Pa.)

Biblio (Paris)

Bonnes Feuilles (Penn State University, University
   Park, Pa.)

Book Collector (London)

Book Week (New York Herald Tribune, Washington Post,
   San Francisco Examiner; merged with Books Today
   (Chicago Tribune) to form Book World)

Book World   (Chicago)

Bookman   (London)

Books Abroad: An International Literary Quarterly
    (Norman, Okla.)

Books and Bookmen   (London)

Boundary 2: A Journal of Postmodern Literature
    (State University of New York at Binghamton,
    Binghamton, N.Y.)

British Book News: A Selection of Books Published in
    Britain   (London)

Bucknell Review   (Lewisburg, Pa.)

Bulletin Critique du Livre Français   (Paris)

Bulletin de l'Académie Royale de Langue et de Littéra-
    ture Françaises (See Académie Royale de Langue et
    de Littérature Françaises)

Bulletin de la Société des Professeurs Français en
    Amérique   (New York)

Bulletin des Jeunes Romanistes   (Strasbourg)

Cahiers de la Compagnie Madeleine Renaud - Jean Louis
    Barrault   (See Cahiers Renaud-Barrault)

Cahiers de l'Iroise   (Brest, France)

Cahiers des Quatre Saisons   (See Cahiers des Saisons)

Cahiers des Saisons   (Paris)

Cahiers du Chemin   (Paris)

Cahiers du Cinéma   (Paris)

Cahiers du Sud   (Marseille)

Cahiers du Théâtre   (Paris)

Cahiers Irlandais (Paris)

Cahiers Renaud-Barrault (Paris)

Cahiers Romains d'Etudes Littéraires (Bucarest)

Calcutta Review (University of Calcutta, Calcutta)

Calgary Herald (Calgary, AB)

Caliban: Annales Publiées par la Faculté des Lettres
    de Toulouse (Toulouse, France)

Cambridge Quarterly (Cambridge)

Cambridge Review (Cambridge)

Canadian Journal of Irish Studies (Canadian Associa-
    tion for Irish Studies, Vancouver, B.C.)

Canard Enchaîné (Paris)

Carleton Miscellany (Northfield, Minn.)

Carrefour (Paris)

Catholic World (See New Catholic World)

CEA Critic: An Official Journal of the College
    English Association (Texas A & M University,
    College Station, Tex.)

Censorship (London)

Centennial Review of Arts & Sciences (Michigan State
    University, East Lansing, Mich.)

Centerpoint: A Journal of Interdisciplinary Studies
    (New York)

Cesare Barbieri Courier (Trinity College, Hartford,
    Conn.)

Chelsea Review (New York)

<u>Cherwell</u>   (Oxford)

<u>Chicago Review</u>   (University of Chicago, Chicago)

<u>Chicago Tribune Book World</u>   (See <u>Book World</u>)

<u>Chimera</u>   (See <u>Westwind</u>)

<u>Chimères: A Journal of French and Italian Literature</u>
   (University of Kansas, Lawrence, Kans.)

<u>Choice</u>   (New York)

<u>Christian Century: A Journal of Religion</u>   (Chicago)

<u>Christian Science Monitor</u>   (Boston, Mass.)

<u>Christian Scholar</u>   (New York)

<u>Christian Scholar's Review</u>   (See <u>Soundings</u>)

<u>Christianity and Literature</u>   (Grand Rapids, Mich.)

<u>Christianity Today</u>   (Washington, D.C.)

<u>Cimarron Review</u>   (Stillwater, Okla.)

<u>Circuit</u>   (London)

<u>Cithara: Essays in the Judaeo-Christian Tradition</u>
   (St. Bonaventure, N.Y.)

<u>College English</u>   (University of Chicago, Chicago)

<u>College Literature</u>   (West Chester State College, West
   Chester, Pa.)

<u>Colloquium</u>   (New York, N.Y.)

<u>Colorado Quarterly</u>   (Boulder, Colo.)

<u>Columbia University Forum</u>   (New York)

<u>Combat</u>   (Paris)

Commentary   (New York)

Commonweal: A Weekly Review of Literature, the Arts,
   and Public Affairs   (New York)

Communiqué   (University of North Pietersburg)

Comparative Drama   (Kalamazoo, Mich.)

Comparative Literature   (University of Oregon, Eugene,
   Oreg.)

Comparative Literature Studies   (Formerly University
   of Maryland, College Park, Now University of
   Illinois, Urbana)

Computers and the Humanities   (Osprey, Fla.)

Confluent

Contemporary Literature   (University of Wisconsin,
   Madison, Wis.)

Contemporary Review   (London)

Costerus   (Amsterdam)

Courrier Dramatique de l'Ouest   (Rennes, France)

Crane Bag   (Dublin)

Cresset   (Valparaiso, Ind.)

Criterion   (London)

Critic   (London)

Critical Inquiry   (Chicago)

Critical Quarterly   (London)

Critical Review   (Melbourne; Sydney)

Critical Survey   (Hull, England)

<u>Criticism: A Quarterly for Literature and the Arts</u>
(Wayne State University, Detroit, Mich.)

<u>Critique</u> (Paris)

<u>Critique: Studies in Modern Fiction</u> (Minneapolis,
Minn.)

<u>Cross Currents</u> (New York)

<u>Culture: Revue Trimestrielle, Sciences Religieuses
et Sciences Profanes au Canada</u> (Quebec)

<u>Daedalus</u> (Cambridge, Mass.)

<u>Dalhousie French Studies</u> (Dalhousie University,
Halifax, Nova Scotia)

<u>Dalhousie Review</u> (Halifax, Nova Scotia)

<u>Degré Second: Studies in French Literature</u>
(Blacksburg, Va.)

<u>Degrés</u> (Brussels)

<u>Delos: A Journal on and of Translation</u> (National
Translation Center, Austin, Tex.)

<u>Delta</u> (Cambridge, England)

<u>Descant</u> (Texas Christian University, Fort Worth,
Tex.)

<u>Diacritics</u> (Cornell University, Ithaca, N.Y.)

<u>Diogenes: An International Review of Philosophy and
Humanistic Studies</u> (New York)

<u>Disque Vert</u> (Paris and Brussels)

<u>Drama at Calgary</u> (Calgary)

<u>Drama/The Quarterly of Theatre Review</u> (London)

<u>Drama Critique</u> (Lancaster, N.Y.)

Drama Review   (New York)

Drama Survey   (Minneapolis, Minn.)

Dublin Magazine   (Dublin)

Dubliner (See Dublin Magazine)

Economist   (London)

Ecrits de Paris: Revue des Questions Actuelles
   (Paris)

Educational Theater Journal   (Columbia, Mo.)

Eire-Ireland: A Journal of Irish Studies   (St. Paul,
   Minn.)

ELH: A Journal of English Literary History
   (Baltimore, Md.)

Elle   (Paris)

Encore: The Voice of Vital Theatre   (London)

Encounter   (London)

Encounters   (LaCrosse, Wis.)

English: The Magazine of the English Association
   (London)

English Studies: Essays and Studies by Members of the
   English Association   (Oxford, England)

English Studies   (Amsterdam)

English Studies in Africa   (Johannesburg)

English Studies in Canada   (University of Toronto
   Press, Downsview, Ont.)

Entretiens sur les Lettres et les Arts   (Rodez,
   France)

Esprit   (Paris)

Esprit Créateur   (Louisiana State University, Baton Rouge, La.)

Essays and Studies (See English Studies)

Essays in Criticism: A Quarterly of Literary Criticism   (Oxford, England)

Essays in French Literature   (University of Western Australia, Nedlands, Australia)

Etudes   (Paris)

Etudes Anglaises: Grande-Bretagne-Etats-Unis   (Paris)

Etudes de Lettres   (Lausanne, Switzerland)

Etudes Françaises   (University of Montreal Press, Montreal)

Etudes Irlandaises   (Villeneuve d'Ascq, France)

Etudes Littéraires   (Aix-en-Provence, France)

Europa Magazine   (London)

Europe   (Paris)

European   (London)

Evergreen Review   (New York)

Everyman   (Cleveland, Ohio)

Exit   (New York)

Explicator   (University of South Carolina, Columbia)

Express   (Paris)

Fiction International   (Canton, N.Y.)

Figaro   (Paris)

Figaro Littéraire   (Paris)

<u>Figaro Magazine</u> (Paris)

<u>Film Comment</u> (New York, N.Y.)

<u>Film Quarterly</u> (University of California, Berkeley, Calif.)

<u>Financial Times</u> (London)

<u>Florida Review</u> (Tallahassee, Fla.)

<u>Foreign Literature</u> (Moscow)

<u>Forum</u> (University of Houston, Houston, Tex.)

<u>Forum for Modern Language Studies</u> (St. Andrews, Scotland)

<u>Français dans le monde</u> (Paris)

<u>France-Asie</u> (Paris)

<u>France-Observateur</u> (Paris)

<u>French Forum</u> (Lexington, Ky.)

<u>French Review</u> (New York)

<u>French Studies</u> (Oxford, England)

<u>Fu Jen Studies</u> (Peking, China)

<u>Gambit</u> (Edinburgh)

<u>Gambit: International Theatre Review</u> (London)

<u>Genre</u> (University of Oklahoma, Norman, Okla.)

<u>Georgia Review</u> (University of Georgia, Athens, Ga.)

<u>Germanic Notes</u> (Lexington, Ky.)

<u>Gradiva</u> (State University of New York at Stony Brook, Stony Brook, N.Y.)

Granta (Cambridge)

Griffin (New York)

Guardian (London)

Hartford Studies in Literature (West Hartford, Conn.)

Harvard Theological Review (Cambridge, Mass.)

Hebrew University: Studies in Literature (Jerusalem)

Hermathena (Dublin and London)

Hibernia (Dublin)

Hispania: A Journal Devoted to the Interests of the
  Teaching of Spanish and Portuguese (University of
  Cincinnati, Cincinnati, Ohio)

Honest Ulsterman (Portrush, Co., Antrim, Ireland)

Horizon (London)

Hudson Review (New York)

Humanist (London)

Humanities Association of Canada Bulletin (University
  of Western Ontario, London, Ont.)

Hungarian Studies in English (L. Kossuth University,
  Debrecen)

ICA Bulletin (Institute of Contemporary Art Bulletin,
  Boston)

Icarus (Dublin)

Illustrated London News (London)

International Fiction Review (Fredericton, N.B.)

International Herald Tribune (Paris)

International Theatre Annual   (New York)

Iô   (Berkeley, Calif.)

Ireland: A Journal of Irish Studies   (St. Paul, Minn.)

Irish Digest   (Dublin)

Irish Studies   (Cambridge)

Irish Times   (Dublin, Ireland)

Irish University Review   (Shannon, Ireland)

Irish Writing: The Magazine of Contemporary Irish Literature Tales   (Cork, Ireland)

Isis   (Oxford)

James Joyce Quarterly   (University of Tulsa, Tulsa, Okla.)

Journal de Psychologie Normale et Pathologique (Paris)

Journal of Aesthetics and Art Criticism   (New York)

Journal of Analytical Psychology   (London)

Journal of Beckett Studies   (London and New York)

Journal of Bible and Religion   (See Journal of the American Academy of Religion)

Journal of English Literary History (See ELH)

Journal of General Education   (University of Chicago, Chicago)

Journal of Modern Literature   (Temple University, Philadelphia, Pa.)

Journal of Narrative Technique   (Eastern Michigan University Press, Ypsilanti, Mich.)

<u>Journal of Popular Culture</u> (Bowling Green, Ohio)

<u>Journal of Social Issues</u> (New York)

<u>Journal of the American Academy of Religion</u>
    (Chambersburg, Pa.)

<u>Journal of the Australasian Universities Language and
    Literature Association</u> (See AUMLA)

<u>Kentucky Romance Quarterly</u> (Lexington, Ky.)

<u>Kenyon Review</u> (Kenyon College, Gambier, Ohio)

<u>Kinesis</u> (Carbondale, Ill.)

<u>KOMOS: A Quarterly of Drama and Arts of the Theater</u>
    (Clayton, Australia)

<u>Kwartalnik Neofilogiczny</u> (Warsaw)

<u>Lace Curtain</u> (New Writers' Press, Dublin)

<u>Language and Style: An International Journal</u>
    (Southern Illinois University, Carbondale, Ill.)

<u>Language Notes</u>

<u>Language Quarterly</u> (University of Southern Florida,
    Tampa, Fla.)

<u>Langues Modernes</u> (Paris)

<u>Laurels. American Society of Legion of Honor Magazine</u>
    (New York)

<u>Left Wing</u> (Leeds, England)

<u>Lettres Françaises: Grand Hebdomadaire Littéraire,
    Artistique et Politique</u> (Paris)

<u>Lettres Nouvelles</u> (Paris)

<u>Lettres Romanes</u> (Université Catholique de Louvain,
    Louvain, Belgium)

Library: A Quarterly Review of Bibliography (London)

Library Journal (New York)

Life (Chicago)

Lingua e Stile (Bologna, Italy)

Linguistica Antverpiensia (Antwerp)

Listener (London)

Literary Criterion (Bombay)

Literature (Vilnius)

Literature and Ideology (Toronto)

Literature and Psychology (New York)

Literature/Film Quarterly (Salisbury State College, Salisbury, Md.)

Littératures: Annales publiées par la Faculté des Lettres et Sciences Humaines de Toulouse (Toulouse, France)

Long Room (Dublin)

Magazine Littéraire (Paris)

Malahat Review (Victoria, BC)

Manchester Guardian (Manchester, England)

Manchester Guardian Weekly (Manchester, England)

Manchester Literary and Philosophical Society: Memoirs and Proceedings (Manchester, England)

Manuscripts (Tyler, Tex.)

Marginales (Brussels)

Marxism Today (London)

Massachusetts Review: A Quarterly of Literature, the
    Arts and Public Affairs   (Amherst, Mass.)

Meanjin Quarterly: A Review of Arts and Letters in
    Australia. (University of Melbourne, Melbourne,
    Australia)

Médiations: Revue des Expressions Contemporaines
    (Paris)

Proceedings of the Manchester Literary and Philosophi-
    cal Society   (Manchester, England)

Mercure de France   (Paris)

Merkur   (Stuttgart, Germany)

Merlin: A Collection of Contemporary Writing   (Paris)

Meta: Journal des Traducteurs   (Montreal)

Michigan Academician: Papers of the Michigan Academy
    of Science, Arts, and Letters   (Ann Arbor, Mich.)

Midwest Quarterly: A Journal of Contemporary Thought
    (Kansas State College of Pittsburg, Pittsburg,
    Kans.)

Minerva's Kvartalsskrift
    (Konservative Studenterforening, Oslo)

Missouri Review   (Columbia, Mo.)

Modern Drama   (University of Kansas, Lawrence, Kans.)

Modern Fiction Studies   (Purdue University, Lafayette,
    Ind.)

Modern Language Forum   (Los Angeles, Calif.)

Modern Language Journal   (New York)

Modern Language Notes   (Baltimore, Md.)

Modern Language Quarterly   (Seattle, Wash.)

Modern Language Review   (Cambridge)

Modern Language Studies   (Oxford, England)

Modern Languages: A Review of Foreign Letters,
Science and the Arts   (London)

Modern Review   (New York)

Moderna Spräk   (Stockholm)

Modernist Studies: Literature and Culture, 1920-1940
   (Edmonton, Alberta)

Monde   (Paris)

Monde des Arts et des Spectacles   (Paris)

Monde [des Livres]   (Paris)

Monde Hebdomadaire   (Paris)

Monde Nouveau/Paru   (Paris)

Monks Pond   (Trappist, Ky.)

Mosaic: A Journal for the Comparative Study of
   Literature and Ideas   (Winnipeg, Canada)

Mundus Artium: A Journal of International Literature
   and the Arts   (Richardson, Tex.)

Nation   (New York)

Nation   (Sydney)

National Observer   (New York)

National Review   (New York)

Nef   (Paris)

Neohelicon   (Budapest)

Neophilolgus: An International Journal of Modern and
     Medieval Language and Literature   (Amsterdam)

Neuphilologische Mitteilungen   (Helsingfors)

New American Review   (New York)

New Blackfriars   (London)

New Catholic World   (New York)

New Chapter   (London)

New Christian (See New Man)

New Durham   (Durham University, Durham, England)

New Edinburgh Review   (Edinburgh University Student
     Publications Board, Edinburgh)

New English Weekly: A Review of Public Affairs,
     Literature and the Arts   (London)

New German Critique   (Milwaukee, Wis.)

New Hungarian Quarterly   (Budapest)

New Laurel Review
     (Pennington School, Pennington, N.J.)

New Leader   (New York)

New Left Review   (London)

New Literary History: A Journal of Theory and
     Interpretation   (Baltimore, Md.)

New Mexico Quarterly   (University of New Mexico,
     Albuquerque, N. Mex.)

New Republic: A Journal of Opinion   (New York)

New Republic: Journal of Politics and the Arts
     (New York)

New Review: An International Notebook for the Arts
    (Paris)

New Society: The Social Science Weekly   (London)

New Statesman   (London)

New Statesman and Nation   (London)

New Theatre Magazine   (Bristol, England)

New World Writing   (New York)

New Yorker   (New York)

New Zealand Journal of French Studies   (Palmerston,
    North N. Z.)

New Zealand Listener   (New Zealand Broadcasting
    Service, Wellington, N. Z.)

Newsweek   (New York)

Nieuw Vlaams Tijdschrift   (Antwerp)

Nimbus   (Bolivia)

Northwest Review   (University of Oregon, Eugene,
    Oregon)

Northwest Review   (Winnipeg, Canada)

Notes and Queries: For Readers and Writers, Collec-
    tors and Librarians   (Oxford University Press,
    London)

Notes on Contemporary Literature   (Carrollton, Ga.)

Notre Dame English Journal: A Journal of Religion in
    Literature   (Notre Dame, Ind.)

Nottingham French Studies   (Cambridge)

Nouvel Observateur   (Paris)

Nouvelle Revue des Deux Mondes   (Paris)

Nouvelle Revue Française   (Paris)

Nouvelles Littéraires: Lettres-Arts-Sciences-Spectacles   (Paris)

Novel: Forum on Fiction
    (Brown University, Providence, R.I.)

Observateur   (Paris)

Observer   (London)

October   (Cambridge, Mass.)

Organon: A Journal of the Arts and Sciences
    (Cheney, Wash.)

Oxford Literary Review   (Oxford, England)

Oxford Mail   (Oxford, England)

Oxford Times   (Oxford, England)

Papers of the Biographical Society of America
    (New York)

Papers on Language and Literature   (Southern Illinois
    University, Edwardsville, Ill.)

Parabola: The Magazine of Myth and Tradition
    (New York)

Paris - Match   (Paris)

Paris - Théâtre   (Paris)

Parnassus: Poetry in Review   (New York)

Partisan Review   (New York)

Peace News   (London, England)

People Weekly   (Chicago, Ill.)

Personalist   (University of Southern California, Los
   Angeles, Calif.)

Perspective   (Washington University, St. Louis, Mo.)

Perspective: A Quarterly of Literature and the Arts,
   (See Perspective: A Quarterly of Modern
   Literature)

Perspective: A Quarterly of Modern Literature   (St.
   Louis, Mo.)

Perspectives on Contemporary Literature   (Louisville,
   Ky.)

Philosophy and Literature   (University of Michigan -
   Dearborn, Dearborn, Mich.)

Plaisir de France   (Paris)

Plays and Players   (London)

Ploughshares: An Occasional of the Arts   (Cambridge,
   Mass.)

PMLA   (Publications of the Modern Language Association
   of America, New York)

PN Review   (Manchester, England)

Poetics   (The Hague)

Poetics Today   (Tel Aviv)

Poétique: Revue de Théorie et d'Analyse Littéraires
   (Paris)

Poetry: A Magazine of Verse   (Chicago)

Poetry Nation   (See PN Review)

Poetry Review   (London)

Points   (Paris)

<u>Prairie Schooner</u> (Lincoln, Nebr.)

<u>Prepublications</u> (Aarhus, Denmark)

<u>Présence Francophone</u> (Sherbrooke, Quebec)

<u>Preuves</u> (Paris)

<u>Proceedings of the Comparative Literature Symposium</u>
  (Texas Tech University)

<u>Proceedings of the Fourth Congress of the Interna-
  tional Comparative Literary Association</u>
  (The Hague)

<u>Proceedings of the Royal Irish Academy</u> (Dublin)

<u>Prompt</u> (London, England)

<u>Prospice</u> (Shirley, England)

<u>Psychiatry: Journal for the Study of Interpersonal
  Processes</u> (Washington, D.C.)

<u>Psychoanalytic Review</u> (New York)

<u>Publishers' Weekly</u> (Whitinsville, Mass.)

<u>Punch</u> (London)

<u>Quandrant: An Australian Quarterly Review</u> (Sydney,
  Australia)

<u>Quarterly Journal of Speech</u> (Baton Rouge, La.)

<u>Queen's Quarterly</u> (Kingston, Ont.)

<u>Quinquereme</u> (Bath, School of Modern Languages,
  University of Bath)

<u>Quinzaine Littéraire</u> (Paris)

<u>Quotidien de Paris</u> (Paris)

<u>Radio Times</u> (London)

Ramparts   (Menlo Park, Calif.)

Raritan: A Quarterly Review   (New Brunswick, N.J.)

Recent French Books   (New York and Paris)

Recherches Anglaises et Américaines   (Strasbourg,
    France)

Recovering Literature   (La Jolla, Calif.)

Réforme   (Paris)

Religion in Life: A Christian Quarterly of Opinion
    and Discussion   (New York)

Renascence: A Critical Journal of Letters   (Marquette
    University, Milwaukee, Wis.)

Reporter   (New York)

Research Studies   (Washington State University,
    Pullman, Wash.)

Review of Contemporary Fiction   (Elmwood Park, Ill.)

Revue   (Liège, Belgium)

Revue d'Esthétique   (Paris)

Revue d'Histoire du Théâtre   (Paris)

Revue de Littérature Comparée   (Paris)

Revue de l'Université de Bruxelles   (Brussels)

Revue de l'Université Laval   (Quebec)

Revue de Paris   (Paris)

Revue des Deux Mondes (See Nouvelle Revue des Deux
    Mondes)

Revue des Langues Vivantes   (Brussels)

<u>Revue des Lettres Modernes</u> (Paris)

<u>Revue des Sciences Humaines</u> (Lille, France)

<u>Revue Générale Belge</u> (Brussels)

<u>Revue Nouvelle</u> (Paris)

<u>Romance Notes</u> (Chapel Hill, N.C.)

<u>Romanic Review: A Quarterly Publication of the Department of Romance Languages in Columbia University</u> (Columbia University, New York)

<u>Romanica Wratislaviensia</u> (Wroclaw)

<u>Saggi e Ricerche di Letteratura Francese</u> (Milan)

<u>Samedi Soir</u> (Paris)

<u>Saturday Review/World</u> (See <u>World</u>)

<u>Saturday Review of Literature</u> (New York)

<u>Scandinavian Studies</u> (Menasha, Wis.)

<u>Scrutiny</u> (Cuttach, India)

<u>Semiotica</u> (The Hague, Mouton)

<u>Sewanee Review</u> (Sewanee, Tenn.)

<u>Shakespeare Survey</u> (Cambridge)

<u>Shenandoah: The Washington Lee University Review</u> (Lexington, Va.)

<u>Show</u> (New York)

<u>Shreveport Journal</u> (Shreveport, La.)

<u>Signes du Temps</u> (Paris)

<u>Sixty-One</u> (Leeds, England)

Socialist Commentary (London)

Socialist Leader (London)

Soundings: An Interdisciplinary Journal (Nashville, Tenn.)

South Atlantic Bulletin (University, Ala.)

South Atlantic Quarterly (Durham, N.C.)

South Carolina Review (Greenville, S.C.)

South Central Bulletin (New Orleans)

Southerly: A Review of Australian Literature (Sydney, Australia)

Southern Humanities Review (Auburn, Ala.)

Southern Quarterly (University of Southern Missippi, Hattiesburg, Miss.)

Southern Review (Baton Rouge, La.)

Southern Review: An Australian Journal of Literary Studies (University of Adelaide)

Southwest Review (Austin and Dallas, Tex.)

Spectacle du Monde (Paris)

Spectator: A Weekly Review of Politics, Literature, Theology, and Art (London)

Spectrum (Goleta, Calif.)

Sphinx: A Magazine of Literature and Society (University of Regina, Regina)

Stand (Newcastle Upon Tyne, England)

Stanford French Review (Saratoga, Calif.)

Studi Francesi (Torino, Italy)

650

Studia Neophilologica: A Journal of Germanic and
    Romance Languages and Literatures (Uppsala)

Studies in English and American Philology (Budapest)

Studies in Literature (Brooklyn College, Brooklyn
    N.Y.)

Studies in Religion: A Canadian Journal (University
    of Toronto Press, Toronto)

Studies in Short Fiction (Newberry, S. C.)

Studies in the Humanities (University of Colorado,
    Boulder, Colo.)

Studies in the Literary Imagination (Atlanta, Ga.)

Studies in the Novel (Denton, Tex.)

Studies in the Twentieth Century (Troy, N.Y.)

Studies in Twentieth Century Literature (Manhattan,
    Kans.)

Sub-Stance (Madison, Wis.)

Sunday Telegraph (London)

Symposium (Syracuse University, Syracuse, N.Y.)

Synthèses (Brussels)

Table Ronde (Paris)

Tablet: A Weekly Newspaper & Review (London)

TDR: The Drama Review See Drama Review

Tel Quel (Paris)

Témoignage Chrétien (Paris)

Temps Modernes (Paris)

Tendances: Cahiers de Documentation   (Paris)

Texas Quarterly   (Austin, Tex.)

Texas Studies in Literature and Language: A Journal of
    the Humanities   (Austin, Tex.)

Thalia: Studies in Literary Humor   (University of
    Ottawa, Ottawa)

Theater   (New Haven, Conn)   Continues Yale / Theatre

Theatre Annual   (New York)

Theatre Arts   (New York)

Théâtre d'Aujourd'hui   (Paris)

Théâtre de France   (Paris)

Theatre Journal   (Baltimore, Md.)

Théâtre Populaire   (Paris)

Theatre Quarterly   (London)

Theatre Research   (Florence, later London)

Theology Today   (Princeton, N.J.)

Theoria: A Journal of Studies in the Arts, Humanities
    and Social Sciences   (Natal, South Africa)

Thought   (Delhi)

Thought   (Fordham University, New York)

Threshold   (Belfast, Ireland)

Thyrse   (Brussels)

Tidskrift for Litteraturvelenskap   (Lund)

Time   (New York)

Time and Tide (London)

Tomorrow (Oxford, England)

Trace (London and Hollywood, Calif.)

Tracks (Coventry, England)

Transatlantic Review (London, Rome and New York)

Transition (Paris)

Travail Théâtral (Lausanne, Switzerland)

Travaux de Linguistique et de Littérature Publiés par
le Centre de Philologie et de Littératures Romanes
de l'Université de Strasbourg (Strasbourg, France)

Tri-Quarterly (Evanston, Ill.)

Tulane Drama Review See Drama Review

Twentieth Century (London)

Twentieth Century Literature: A Scholarly and
Critical Journal (Hempstead, N.Y.)

ULULA: Graduate Studies in Romance Languages
Unisa English Studies (Pretoria)

United States Quarterly Review

University of Dayton Review (Dayton, Ohio)

University of Kansas City Review (Kansas City, Mo.)

Use of English (Edinburgh, Scotland)

Victorian Poetry (Morgantown, W.Va.)

Village Voice (New York)

Virginia Quarterly Review (University of Virginia,
Charlottesville, Va.)

654

<u>Yearbook of Comparative and General Literature</u>
  (Indiana University, Bloomington, Ind.)

<u>Yearbook of English Studies</u> (Cambridge)

<u>Yeats Studies</u> (Dublin)

<u>Zagadnienia Rodzajow Literackid</u> (Lodz)

Author Index

Aaron, Jules, A2

Abbey, Edward, 1959.1

Abbott, H. Porter, 1970.1,
1973.1, 1975.1, 1975.2,
1977.1, 1982.1

Abel, Lionel, 1959.2,
1963.1, 1963.2, A3

Abirached, Robert, 1964.1,
1966.1, 1966.2, A4, A5,
B4, B5, B6, B7

Achard, Marcel, A269

Acheson, James, 1978.1,
1979.1, 1980.1, 1981.1,
1983.1

Acholonu, C.O., 1980-
1984.1

Ackerley, C.J., 1981.2

Ackroyd, Peter, A6

Adams, Georges, 1961.1

Adams, P., B8

Adams, Robert M., 1969.1,
1977.2

Adams, Val, 1966.3

Admussen, Richard, 1973.2,
1973.3, 1976.1, 1979.2,
A7

Adorno, Theodor W.,
1969.2, 1982.2

Ahuja, Chaman, 1976.2

Albérès, Renée M., 1962.1,
1970.2, A8, A9, B9

Alblas, Jacques, 1979.7

Albright, Daniel, 1981.3

Alden, Douglas, 1980.37

Allan, Elkan, B10

Allen, Bruce, B11

Alley, J.N., 1963.3

Allsop, Kenneth, 1958.1

Alpaugh, David, 1966.4,
1966.5, 1973.4

Alter, André, 1969.102,
1970.3, A10

Bergonzi, Bernard, 1968.5, 1970.65, A26, B57, B58, B282

Berlin, Normand, 1967.10, 1981.6

Berman, Audry, B59

Berman, David, 1984.7

Bermel, Albert, 1973.10

Bernal, Olga, 1968.6, 1968.7, 1969.12, 1976.8, 1977.10

Bernard, Marc, 1957.2a, 1966.10

Bernheimer, Charles, 1977.11

Bersani, Jacques, 1970.9

Bersani, Leo, 1966.11, 1970.10

Bertagnolli, Leslie, 1977.12

Besse, Jean, 1967.11

Bezerra, Teresa M., 1973.11

Bialos, Anne, 1961.6

Billington, Michael, 1975.11, 1976.9, 1977.13, 1982.14, 1984.8, A28, A29, B60

Binchy, Maeve, A30

Binns, Ronald, 1979.4

Birmingham, William, A31

Bishop, Morris, 1966.12

Bishop, Tom, 1969.13, 1975.12, 1976.10, 1976.11, 1976.12, 1978.6, 1981.7, A32

Blackman, Maurice, 1981.8

Blackstock, Mary L., 1974.3

Blakey, J., 1968.8

Blanchot, Maurice, 1953.3, 1959.5, 1959.6, 1964.6, 1969.14, B61, B62

Blanzat, Jean, 1951.3, 1961.7, 1963.7

Blau, Herbert, 1960.1, 1962.8, 1964.7, 1967.12, 1967.13, B63, B64

Bleikasten, André, B65

Blin, Roger, 1953.4, 1976.12, 1981.9

Bloch-Michel, J., B66, B67

Block, Haskell M., 1962.9, 1974.4

Blocker, H. Gene, A33

Bloomfield, Anthony, 1958.3

Bruns, Gerald L., 1969.16, 1970.14, 1971.9, 1974.12

Brustein, Robert S., 1960.2, 1961.11, 1964.12a, 1965.11, 1965.12, A45, B94

Bryden, Ronald, 1964.13, 1965.13, A46, B95

Bryer, J.R., 1964.14, 1970.15, 1972.7

Buchet, Edmond, B96

Bull, Peter, 1959.8, 1967.17, B97

Buning, M., 1979.7

Burgess, Anthony, 1966.17, 1983.10, A47, B98

Burghardt, Lori Hall, 1976.18

Burgin, Richard, 1981.15

Burkman, Katherine, 1983.11

Burns, Jim, 1971.11

Busi, Frederick, 1972.8, 1973.15, 1974.13, 1974.14, 1974.15, 1975.20, 1977.18, 1980.8

Butler, Harry L., 1962.13

Butler, Ian Christopher, 1980.9

Butler, Lance St. John, 1984.11

Butler, Michael, 1961.12

Butlin, Ron, 1980.10

Büttner, Gottfried, 1984.12

Cadot, Michel, 1975.83

C., G., B100

C., M., A48

Cagnon, Maurice, 1978.31, 1978.67

Cain, Alex M., 1964.15, A49, B101

Caine, Cindy S.A.M., 1970.16

Calder, John, 1967.18, 1970.17, 1976.19, 1976.20, 1976.21, 1977.19, 1980.11, 1981.16, A50, A51

Calder-Marshall, Arthur, 1934.1

Cambon, Glauco, B102

Camp, André, B103

Campbell, R.J., 1980.12

Campbell, SueEllen, 1978.11

Camproux, Charles, 1961.13

Davies, Russell, 1973.25,
1982.35

Davin, Dan, 1956.10

Davis, Robert G., B152

Davis, Robin J., 1971.10,
1972.7, 1977.25,
1978,18, 1979.14,
1984.18, A72

Davis, William V., 1971.21

Davison, Peter, 1965.20

Dawson, Helen, B153

Deane, Seamus, 1984.19

Dearlove, Judith E.,
1977.26, 1978.19,
1982.36, 1982.37,
1982.38

Deguy, Michel, 1966.27

Dejean, Jean-Luc, 1971.22

Deleuze, Gilles, B154

Delfosse, G., 1954.1

Delye, Huguette, 1960.10

Deming, Barbara, A73

Dennis, Nigel, 1963.18a,
1971.23, A74

Dennison, Anne, 1973.9a

Dent, Alan, A75

De Sollar, J.P.   1980.22

De Stefano, Sister Mary
V., 1964.23

Detrez, Conrad, B155

Dhingra, Baldoon, B156

Dhomme, S., B157

Diamond, Elin, 1975.30

Dick, Ernst S., 1982.109

Dickie, James, 1975.31

Dietrich, Richard F.,
1976.38, 1979.15

Dillon, John, 1960.11

Dimic, M.V., 1975.83

DiPierro, John C., 1981.27

Dis, Claude, 1983.15

Dobrée, Bonamy, 1931.1,
1956.11, 1958.10,
1967.30

Dobrez, L.A.C., 1983.16,
1983.17

Dobrez, Livio, 1973.26,
1974.22, 1974.23

Dodsworth, Martin,
1975.32, A76

Doherty, Francis, 1971.24,
1972.19, 1982.39

Dolan, T.P., 1975.33,
1984.20

Fitch, Brian T., 1961.25,
1977.29, 1981.32,
1981.81, 1982.42,
1984.21, B199

Fitch, Noel Riley, A103

Fitzgerald, T.M., 1960.17

Fitz-Simon, Christopher,
1983.21

Flanner, Janet, 1953.7,
1965.27, A104, A122

Fleissner, Robert F.,
1982.43

Fletcher, Beryl S.,
1978.21

Fletcher, D., 1962.27,
1963.25

Fletcher, John, 1961.26,
1961.27, 1962.28,
1963.26, 1964.30,
1964.31, 1965.28,
1965.29, 1965.30,
1965.31, 1965.32,
1965.33, 1965.34,
1965.35, 1966.31,
1966.32, 1966.33,
1967.41, 1967.42,
1969.41, 1970.40,
1970.41, 1970.42,
1972.26, 1975.41,
1976.48, 1976.51,
1976.52, 1976.53,
1978.21, 1978.22,
1978.23, 1978.24,
1980.31, 1981.34,
1981.35, A105, A106,
A107

Flieger, Jerry Aline,
1979.18, 1980.32

Flint, F.S., 1931.2

Flood, Ethelbert, 1961.28

Flower, Dean, B201

Ford, Boris, B202

Ford, Peter, 1965.36

Fortier, Paul, 1971.35

Foster, Dennis A., 1983.22

Fothergill, Robert,
1965.37

Fouchet, Max-Pol, 1951.5,
A109

Foucré, Michèle, 1970.43

Fournier, Edith, 1961.29,
1970.44

Fowler, Roger, B204

Fowlie, Wallace, 1959.16,
1960.18, 1970.45, A110,
A111, B205, B206

Fox, J.H., 1975.48

Francher, Edwin, 1962.5,
1962.7, 1962.54,
1962.65, 1962.74

Francis, Richard L.,
1965.38

Frank, Ellen Eve, 1979.19

Hubert, Renée-Riese,
1962.41, 1966.39,
1969.54, 1971.49.
1974.29, 1976.69, B279

Hudson, Derek, 1958.12

Hudson, Roger, 1964.52

Hughes, Catherine,
1962.42, 1962.43,
1970.64, A158

Hughes, D.A., 1967.56

Hughes, Daniel J., B280

Hughson, Kenneth, 1957.15

Hult, David F., 1984.66

Hunt, Albert, 1971.50

Hunter, G.K., 1970.65,
B282

Hunter, Jim, A159

Hurley, Paul J., 1965.48

Hurren, Kenneth, B283,
B284

Hutchings, William,
1981.47

Hutchinson, Mary, 1956.21,
A160, B285

Hutchison, Robert, B286

Hvistendahl, Marion,
1977.42

Iehl, Dominique, 1978.29,
1979.32

Ingham, Patricia, A161

Inglis, Brian, 1956.22

Inglis, Ruth, 1972.40

Innes, C.D., A162

Ionesco, Eugène, 1976.70,
1981.48, A269, B287

Isaac, Dan, 1975.54

Iser, Wolfgang, 1966.40,
1974.30, 1974.31,
1975.55, 1978.30,
1981.49

Issacharoff, Michael,
1981.50, B290

Isou, Isidore, B289

Itzin, Catherine, A164,
A165

Jacobs, Richard, 1981.51,
1981.52

Jacobsen, Josephine,
1963.37, 1964.53,
1965.49, 1967.79,
1968.35

Jacquart, Emmanuel C.,
1972.41, 1974.32,
1977.44, 1978.31,
1982.60, 1983.34

Jacquot, Jean, 1977.60

Le Vot, André, 1972.51

Levy, Alan, 1956.25,
1967.65

Levy, Eric P., 1975.69,
1976.91, 1978,39,
1978.40, 1979.40,
1980.74, 1982.67

Levy, Shimon, 1984.38

Lewis, Allan, 1962.52,
B346

Lewis, John, 1964.63

Lewis, Peter, 1978.23

Leyburn, Ellen D., A200

Libera, Antoni, 1980.75,
1980.76, 1982.68,
1984.39

Lindblad, Ishrat, 1974.34,
1976.92

Lindon, Jérome, 1976.93

Lioure, Michel, B347

Little, J.P., 1978.41,
1981.61

Little, Roger, 1984.40

Littlejohn, David, 1963.43

Livingston, Paisley N.,
1977.58

Lloyd-Evans, Gareth, A202

Lodge, David, 1968.41,

1971.63, 1977.59, B348,
B349

Logue, Christopher,
1957.27

Lombardi, Thomas W.,
1968.42

London, Merrie, B350

Lorich, Bruce, 1970.86

Lorsch, Susan E., 1983.42

Lottman, Herbert R., B351,
B352

Louzoun, Myriam, 1977.60

Lowenkron, David H.,
1974.35

Loy, J. Robert, B353

Luccioni, Gennie, 1960.37,
A203, A204

Luchs, Fred E., 1960.38

Lukács, Georg, B354, B355

Lumley, Frederick,
1956.26, 1967.66

Lupu, Michael, 1981.62

Lutwack, Leonard, B356

Lyons, Charles R.,
1964.64, 1967-1968.1,
1971-1972.1, 1982-
1983.1, 1983.43

Lyons, W.H., 1980.77

Manners, Marya, 1967.69, A213

Manning, Hugo, B366

Marcabru, Pierre, 1959.28, A214, A215

Marcel, Gabriel, 1957.30, 1964.66, B367

Marcorelles, Louis, B368

Marcus, Frank, 1969.65, A216

Marguet, Arthur, 1967.70

Marinello, Leone J., 1963.47

Marissel, André, 1963.48, 1963.49, 1963.50, 1964.67, 1969.66, 1969.67, 1970.88

Marker, Frederick, 1976.100

Marks, Jonathan, A217

Markus, Thomas B., 1963.51

Marowitz, Charles, 1962.55, 1963.52, 1964.68, 1965.9, 1984.43

Marrigan, Nick, 1966.49

Martel, François, 1972.53

Martin, George, 1976.101, 1977.62

Martin, Marcel, A218

Martinoir, Francine de, 1982.70, 1982.83

Masih, I.K., 1981.64

Massey, Irving, B369

Masson, Danielle, B370

Mather, Ian, 1969.68

Matthews, Honor, 1967.71, 1968.44

Matthews, J.H., 1964.33, B371, B372

Maulnier, Thierry, 1957.31, 1963.53

Mauriac, Claude, 1956.28, 1956.29, 1958.24, 1959.30, 1969.69, 1969.70, 1976.102, A219, B373, B374,

Mauriac, François, B375, B376

Mauroc, Daniel, A220, A221

Mayer, Hans, 1973.51, 1974.36

Mayersberg, Paul, A222

Mayoux, Jean-Jacques, 1957.32, 1959.31, 1960.39, 1961.44, 1965.55, 1966.50, 1966.51, 1967.73, 1967.74, 1971.65, 1972.54, 1974.37,

Read, Herbert, 1969.90

Rechtien, Brother John, S.M., 1964.82

Réda, Jacques, B465

Redmond, James, 1984.74

Reid, Alec, 1960.45, 1962.63, 1964.83, 1968.52, 1972.61, 1974.48, 1975.82, 1976.126, 1977.76, 1978.51, 1983.53

Reiter, Seymour, 1972.62, 1973.59

Renaud, Madeleine, 1966.62, A269

Renner, Charlotte, 1981.77

Rexroth, Kenneth, 1956.33, 1959.40, 1964.84

Reynolds, Gillian, B466, B467

Reynolds, Stanley, 1969.91

Rhodes, S.A., 1963.68

Ricardou, Jean, B468

Richardson, Jack, A270

Richardson, Maurice, B469

Rickels, Milton, 1962.64

Ricks, Christopher, 1964.85, 1964.86, 1966.63, 1972.63,

1973.61, 1974.49. 1976.127, 1980.93, A271, B470

Rigault, Claude, B225

Riggs, Larry W., 1981.78, 1983.55

Riva, Raymond T., 1970.108

Robb, Peter, 1970.109

Robbe-Grillet, Alain, 1953.14, 1963.69, 1965.63, 1965.64, 1967.89, B471, B472

Robinson, Andrew, 1967.90

Robinson, C.J. Bradbury, 1971.77

Robinson, Fred Miller, 1980.94, 1981.79

Robinson, Michael, 1970.110, 1979.49

Robinson, Robert, 1957.38

Robles, M., A272

Robson, Jeremy, A273

Rodger, Ian, 1959.41, B473

Rodway, Allan, 1974.50

Rojtman, Betty, 1976.128, 1977.77, 1978.52

Rolin-Janziti, Jeanne, 1981.80

Subject Index

1980.74, 1981.5,
1981.14, 1983.45,
1984.18, 1984.34,
1984.44, 1984.51, A27,
B377

Bicycle, motif, 1965.50,
1980.80

Bilingualism, 1959.29,
1960.34, 1961.15,
1961.36, 1965.15,
1967.6, 1967.42,
1968.56, 1969.55,
1970.75, 1971.94,
1972.24, 1972.35,
1972.50, 1972.54,
1972.74, 1973.61,
1973.69, 1974.49,
1974.61, 1975.22,
1975.83, 1976.52,
1976.71, 1976.92,
1976.95, 1976.113,
1977.36, 1977.61,
1978.18, 1978.58,
1979.34, 1980.30,
1980.50, 1980.55,
1980.67, 1980.102,
1982.10, 1982.25,
1982.29, 1982.75,
1983.50, 1983.58,
1983.68, 1984.20, A32,
A82, A306, A315, B584

Biographical Notes,
1946.1, 1953.4,
1953.17, 1956.34,
1957.3, 1957.17a,
1958.25, 1960.1,
1960.10, 1960.28,
1961.5, 1962.5,
1962.18, 1962.28,
1962.70, 1963.34,
1963.35, 1964.43,
1964.46, 1964.70,

1964.100, 1965.72,
1966.53, 1966.74, 1966-
1967.3, 1967.7,
1967.18, 1968.48,
1968.65, 1969.9,
1969.15, 1969.29,
1969.30, 1969.36,
1969.56, 1969.68,
1969.72, 1969.123,
1970.17, 1970.32,
1971.72, 1972.13,
1972.21, 1972.32,
1972.68, 1974.51,
1975.13, 1976.12,
1976.22, 1976.24,
1976.25, 1976.37,
1976.90, 1976.93,
1976.96, 1976.117,
1976.134, 1976.135,
1977.69, 1978.2,
1978.21, 1978.41,
1979.48, 1980.16,
1980.17, 1980.23,
1981.48, 1981.51,
1981.65, 1981.85,
1983.5, 1983.43,
1983.58, 1984.40,
1984.72, A127, A295,
A318, B25, B248

Birth (or regret of)
1970.21, 1982.13,
1982.107, 1983.40,
1983.60

Black Humor, 1957.13,
1970.77, A292

Blake, William, 1966.63,
1971.54

Blanchot, Maurice,
1967.103, 1970.14,
1980.32

1976.80, 1976.104,
1978.24, 1979.22.62,
1980.21, 1981.23,
1981.38, 1982.110,
1983.48, A1, A62, A205

Comedy, 1956.17, 1957.37,
1958.26, 1959.10,
1960.44, 1962.21,
1963.10, 1964.56,
1965.67, 1966.41,
1966.43, 1966.66,
1967.38, 1967.51,
1967.76, 1968.10,
1969.112, 1970.24,
1970.79, 1970.80,
1970.99, 1971.16,
1971.42, 1971.69,
1972.5, 1972.61,
1972.64, 1973.18,
1976.45, 1976.129,
1977.22, 1977-1978.1,
1978.65, 1979.18,
1980.46, 1980.94,
1981.35, 1981.49,
1981.78, 1982.50,
1982.60, 1982.100,
1984.73, A163, A329,
B55, B247, B316, B325,
B542

Commedia dell'arte,
1966.46, 1980.8

Communication, 1968.24,
1968.42, 1972.33,
1973.45, 1973.68,
1975.83, 1977.22,
1977.60, 1978.55,
1979.41, A296

Company, 1980.68, 1980.72,
1980.73, 1980.78,
1980.86, 1980.87,
1980.88, 1980.92,

1980.105, 1980.110,
1981.12, 1981.15,
1981.21, 1981.51,
1981.55, 1981.85,
1981.96, 1981.97,
1981.102, 1982.9,
1982.16, 1982.41,
1982.57, 1982.67,
1982.93, 1983.6,
1983.17, 1983.53,
1984.5, 1984.22,
1984.49, A37, A61, A63,
A96, A98, A167, A189,
A223, A225, A274, A311,
B261, B589

Computer-aided study,
1978.27

Conrad, Joseph, 1970.95,
1982.75

Correspondance, 1958.29,
1964.95

Couples, 1962.41, 1963.33,
1965.49, 1967.78,
1968.18, 1969.38,
1969.92, 1970.124,
1971.25, 1971.30,
1971.59, 1972.27,
1976.34, 1976.66,
1976.68, 1976.101,
1977.41, 1977.62,
1979.54, 1980.30,
1982.64, 1982.88,
1984.52, A113

Crane, Hart, 1975.70

Creation of fiction,
1953.3, 1958.20,
1959.23, 1964.48,
1965.55, 1966.11,
1970.53, 1971.48,

"Théâtre de dérision,"
1972.41, 1974.32

"Theatre of the Absurd,"
1961.17, 1963.23,
1963.24, 1967.79,
1968.2, 1971.68,
1972.56, 1973.59,
1977.83, 1978.21, A247

"Theatrum mundi," 1962.20,
1967.26, 1980.109

Thermodynamics, 1969.28

Thomas à Kempis, 1976.129

Time, 1960,10, 1961.62,
1962.71, 1963.14,
1964.53, 1964.74,
1966.64, 1967.60,
1967.94, 1967.107,
1968.7, 1968.10,
1968.62, 1969.2,
1969.93, 1970.13,
1970.18, 1970.101,
1971.31, 1971.42,
1971.84, 1971.95,
1972.4, 1972.25,
1972.72, 1973.12,
1973.13, 1973.68,
1974.19, 1974.20,
1974.55, 1974.60,
1975.69, 1975.72,
1976.14, 1976.85,
1976.86, 1976.124,
1976.129, 1977.22,
1977.29, 1977.75,
1978.1. 1978.28,
1978.50, 1978.59,
1979.20, 1979.23,
1979.56, 1980.24,
1980.26, 1980.78,
1980.101, 1980.107,
1981.10, 1981.13.

1981.15, 1981.32.
1981.56, 1981.61,
1982.2, 1982.13,
1982.51, 1983.58,
1984.47, 1984.64, A14,
A33, A220, B210, B414

Titles, 1982.27

Todorov, Tzvetan, 1982.3

Tolstoy, Count Leo,
1981.36

Tragedy, 1964.60, 1967.32,
1967.76, 1967.104,
1968.10, 1971.6,
1972.5, 1973.18,
1974.35, 1977.22,
1978.47, 1978.54,
1978.65, 1979.58,
1981.6, 1981.54, B259,
B316, B395

Tragicomedy, 1956.10,
1959.33, 1962.72,
1965.38, 1965.52,
1969.26, 1970.8,
1970.27, 1970.73,
1971.6, 1971.19,
1971.23, 1971.25,
1971.74, 1973.28,
1974.8, 1976.131,
1978.43, 1980.25,
1981.54, 1981.61,
1984.64, B250, B269

Transition, 1975.70

Translation, 1956.23,
1960.19

Trilogy, 1953.9, 1953.12,
1955.6, 1956.27,
1956.33, 1956.34,